Prentice Hall

LITERATURE

All-in-One
Workbook

Grade Eight

PEARSON

Upper Saddle River, New Jersey
Boston, Massachusetts
Chandler, Arizona
Glenview, Illinois

BQ Tunes Credits
Keith London, Defined Mind, Inc., Executive Producer
Mike Pandolfo, Wonderful, Producer
All songs mixed and mastered by Mike Pandolfo, Wonderful
Vlad Gutkovich, Wonderful, Assistant Engineer
Recorded November 2007 – February 2008 in SoHo, New York City, at Wonderful, 594 Broadway

PEARSON

ISBN-13: 978-0-13-366813-1
ISBN-10:   0-13-366813-4

8 9 10   13 12

CONTENTS

UNIT 5 Drama

Anne Frank and Me by Cherie Bennett

The Governess by Neil Simon

The Governess

"The Ninny" by Anton Chekhov

The Diary of Anne Frank, *Act I,* by Frances Goodrich and Albert Hackett

The Diary of Anne Frank, *Act I*

The Diary of Anne Frank, *Act II,* by Frances Goodrich and Albert Hackett

The Diary of Anne Frank, *Act II*

from Anne Frank: The Diary of a Young Girl by Anne Frank
from Anne Frank Remembered by Miep Gies

UNIT 6   Themes in Folk Literature

"Water Names" by Lan Samantha Chang

"Coyote Steals the Sun and Moon" Zuñi myth, retold by Richard Erdoes and Alfonso Ortiz

"Why the Waves Have Whitecaps" by Zora Neale Hurston

"Coyote Steals the Sun and Moon" and "Why the Waves Have Whitecaps"

"Brer Possum's Dilemma" by Jackie Torrence
"John Henry" Traditional

from **"The People, Yes"** by Carl Sandburg
"Chicoria" adapted by José Griego y Maestas, retold by Rudolfo A. Anaya

"Brer Possum's Dilemma," "John Henry," *from* **"The People, Yes," "Chicoria"**

"Davy Crockett's Dream" by Davy Crockett
"Paul Bunyan of the North Woods" by Carl Sandburg
"Invocation" from John Brown's Body by Stephen Vincent Benét

from **Out of the Dust** by Karen Hesse

"Ellis Island" by Joseph Bruchac

from **Out of the Dust** and **"Ellis Island"**

"Choice: A Tribute to Martin Luther King, Jr." by Alice Walker

"An Episode of War" by Stephen Crane

"Choice: A Tribute to Martin Luther King, Jr." and "An Episode of War"

from My Own True Name by Pat Mora
"Words to Sit in, Like Chairs" by Naomi Shihab Nye

Reading Fluency Practice and Assessment

Standardized Test Practice

Answer Sheets

Mission Impossible, performed by Hydra

I just finished lunch, stomach in knots /

Was it the food or the stress? /

See, I'm in school and next period's the big math test /

I studied hard but I'm feeling a little nervous /

I gotta get my lucky hat and hopefully it'll serve its purpose /

Last I remember, I left it in my locker that I share with my teammate Roger /

Me and him play soccer.

Open it up (oh no!) and my hat's not there / Just then I hear this kid Matt calling... /

Ay! Over here!

He says "I saw Roger a while ago, he said that he was going home sick /

But he had your hat, that's **evidence** he stole it!"

Now some people think Matt is a little bit mean /

And may be **biased** since Roger took his spot on the team /

He says "I can **prove** it! / remember you got it on your birthday? /

He said he wish he had one just like it in the worst way!"

I'm not really sure if I should believe what he said /

Is it true or just fantasy made up in his head /

He said "what's gonna convince you? Your friend is the worst! /

He just needed to hide the evidence, he didn't need to go to see the nurse /

Need to **investigate** it further just ask Julie or Derrick /

They were at your party too, they can **confirm** that he said it!

It's a whodunit / where is it? / what's the truth? /

Do I trust my instincts, my friends, or just the proof? /

Will I find out in time? It seems **illogical** /

I've got 5 minutes left, this is mission impossible.

Now Matt trying to **persuade** me Roger stole my hat is crazy /

But he **observed** him with my hat, so I don't know, maybe /

I need to find the facts quick so I can ace this test /

So I ask Julie her opinion and she said more or less...

"Yeah he said he wanted one like it, it is a really nice hat /

But do I think that he stole it? I'd have to **contradict** that /

Continued

I mean, he's your best friend I never see him without you /
So Matt's **theory** that he stole it in my **opinion** is **doubtful** /

It's a whodunit / where is it? / what's the truth? /
Do I trust my instincts, my friends, or just the proof? /
Will I find out in time? It seems illogical /
I've got two minutes, this is mission impossible.

I wish that he was here so I could ask if what they're saying is **factual** /
Doing well without my hat just doesn't seem practical /
Julie seemed **objective** since she had nothing to gain...
Just then I hear my math teacher calling my name...
I saw your friend in the nurse's office and he looked a little queasy /
Are you ready for this math test? This one's not going to be easy /
Oh, he asked me to give this, you dropped leaving lunch real fast /
and said he had a hunch you'd want it for just this class /
Something about it being lucky, but if you studied you won't need it /
Nevertheless here you go, class please be seated.

Song Title: **Mission Impossible**
Artist / Performed by Hydra
Vocals: Rodney "Blitz" Willie
Lyrics by Rodney "Blitz" Willie
Music composed by Keith "Wild Child" Middleton
Produced by Keith "Wild Child" Middleton
Technical Production: Mike Pandolfo, Wonderful
Executive Producer: Keith London, Defined Mind

Unit 1: Fiction and Nonfiction
Big Question Vocabulary—1

The Big Question: Is truth the same for everyone?

Thematic Vocabulary

doubtful: *adj.* not certain or not likely to happen; other forms: *doubtfully, doubt, undoubtedly*

evidence: *n.* facts, details, or statistics that prove something is true; other form: *evident*

factual: *adj.* true; based on facts; other form: *fact*

fantasy: *n.* an idea or a belief that is not based on facts; other form: *fantastic*

illogical: *adj.* not sensible or reasonable; other forms: *logic, logical*

Carol told this story to Simone, Anna, and Ramon: "Yesterday, the most amazing thing happened to me. I was walking in Elmwood Park when a large white bird landed on the path in front of me. It had a strange, golden glow around it. Suddenly, the bird turned to me and said, 'You will have good luck for the rest of your life.' Then it disappeared in a puff of smoke."

Each of Carol's friends had a different reaction to the story.

DIRECTIONS: *Use the word(s) given in parentheses to write what each friend said to Carol.*

(doubtful)

Simone

(fantasy, illogical)

Anna

Ramon **(evidence, factual)**

Unit 1: Fiction and Nonfiction
Big Question Vocabulary—2

The Big Question: Is truth the same for everyone?

Thematic Vocabulary

bias: *n.* a definite leaning toward a certain point of view, regardless of opposing facts

   v. to influence or change the opinions of someone; other forms: *biased, biasing*

confirm: *v.* to make firm or establish as true; other forms: *confirming, confirmed, confirmation*

contradict: *v.* to disagree with a point of view by stating that the opposite is true; other forms: *contradicting, contradicted, contradiction*

investigate: *v.* to focus on and search into an event or issue, in order to learn the truth; other forms: *investigating, investigated, investigation*

observation: *n.* a spoken or written comment about something that has been noticed; other forms: *observe, observing, observed*

A. DIRECTIONS: *Review the Thematic Vocabulary words and their definitions shown above. Then, write the Thematic Vocabulary word that best completes each group of related words.*

1. reaction, remark, description, _____

2. deny, dispute, challenge, _____

3. prejudice, injustice, preference, _____

4. prove, assert, verify, _____

5. explore, inquire, study, _____

B. DIRECTIONS: *Complete each sentence by filling in the blank with the correct Thematic Vocabulary word.*

1. Because I totally disagreed with his point of view, I felt forced to _____ him.

2. It's important to _____ each theory in order to gather facts that prove it to be true.

3. I'm sure that cats can be wonderful pets, but I must admit that I have a _____ toward dogs.

4. Before leaving for the airport, I'll call the airline to _____ that the plane will arrive at noon.

5. Sir Isaac Newton made his _____ about gravity after being hit on the head by an apple that fell from a tree.

Unit 1: Fiction and Nonfiction
Big Question Vocabulary—3

The Big Question: Is truth the same for everyone?

Thematic Vocabulary

objective: *adj.* relying on facts rather than personal opinions; other forms: *object, objectively*

opinion: *n.* a personal viewpoint or feeling that cannot be proved true; other forms: *opine, opinionated*

persuade: *v.* to influence the thoughts or actions of others; other forms: *persuading, persuaded, persuasion*

prove: *v.* to use facts to confirm that something is true; other forms: *proving, proved, proof*

theory: *n.* an idea that is supported by evidence but is not fully proved to be true; other forms: *theorize, theorizing, theorized, theories*

A. DIRECTIONS: *Answer each question.*

1. What might a scientist do to prove that a *theory* is true? _____
_____

2. What might you say to *persuade* a child to drink a glass of milk? _____
_____

3. Why is it important that a judge be *objective*? _____
_____

4. What is the difference between facts and *opinions*? _____
_____

5. What facts would you use to *prove* that vegetables come from plants? _____
_____

B. DIRECTIONS: *According to an old folk tale, the moon is made of green cheese. Write a paragraph in which you use facts to challenge that theory. Use as many Thematic Vocabulary words as you can.*

_____
_____
_____
_____

Name _____ Date _____

Unit 1: Fiction and Nonfiction
Applying the Big Question

 Is truth the same for everyone?

DIRECTIONS: *Complete the chart below to apply what you have learned about the ways that people see the truth. One row has been completed for you.*

Example	The "truth" about someone or something	Event	Effect	What I Learned
From Literature "A Retrieved Reformation"	Ben Price thinks that Jimmy V. is still a thief.	Jimmy uses his skills to save a girl's life.	Price decides that Jimmy really has changed his life.	The "truth" about a person can change.
From Literature				
From Science				
From Social Studies				
From Real Life				

Patricia C. McKissack
Listening and Viewing

Segment 1: Meet Patricia C. McKissack
- How does Patricia and Fred McKissack's writing collaboration allow them to write many more books than if they wrote independently? What do you think the benefits of writing with a coauthor might be?

_____

_____

_____

_____

Segment 2: Fiction and Nonfiction
- How does Patricia C. McKissack make her fictional stories "real"? Why do you think Patricia C. McKissack uses the phrase "ticktock" repeatedly in "The 11:59"?

_____

_____

_____

_____

Segment 3: The Writing Process
- How do Patricia and Fred McKissack divide the steps in the writing process? Which of these steps do you think is the most important and why?

_____

_____

_____

_____

Segment 4: The Rewards of Writing
- What advice does Patricia C. McKissack give students about how they should approach writing? In what ways do you agree with her?

_____

_____

_____

_____

Learning About Fiction and Nonfiction

Literature may be either **fiction** or **nonfiction.** The following chart compares and contrasts these two types of literature.

Characteristics	Fiction	Nonfiction
Overall Features	Fiction is prose that tells an imaginary story about people, animals, or other **characters.** Each character has particular **traits,** or qualities, that can affect the story. The story's sequence of events is its **plot,** which begins with a **conflict,** or problem, and ends with a **resolution,** or conclusion. The **setting** is the time and place when events in the story occur. The story's **theme** is its message about life.	Nonfiction is prose that deals only with real people, events, or ideas. Nonfiction works present facts or discuss ideas. Nonfiction works reflect the **author's style,** or use of language, including dialect, rhythm, and organization. The overall feeling of the writing is its **mood** or **atmosphere.**
Perspective	A story can be told from **first-person point of view,** the perspective of a character in the story; or from **third-person point of view,** the perspective of a narrator outside the story.	Nonfiction works are written from the perspective or **point of view** of the author, who is a real person.
Sample Forms	short stories, novellas, novels	speeches, editorials, articles, research papers, biographies
Author's Purpose	to entertain	to persuade, inform, or entertain

DIRECTIONS: *Read each item. Decide whether it is a work of fiction or nonfiction, and then write* fiction *or* nonfiction *on the line provided.*

_____ 1. a piece of literature that tells about a ten-foot-tall lumberjack

_____ 2. a piece of literature that presents facts about "man-eating" plants

_____ 3. a piece of literature that urges readers to collect and use rainwater

_____ 4. a piece of literature that tells about the childhood of a famous real-life artist

_____ 5. a piece of literature about a kangaroo who misplaces her pocket

"The 11:59" by Patricia C. McKissack
Model Selection: Fiction

Fiction is prose that tells a story about characters or events from the author's imagination. The **characters** in a work of fiction are the people or animals who take part in the story's action. Characters have **traits,** or characteristics, that can affect the story's events. In "The 11:59," for example, Lester is a spellbinding storyteller. Through his stories, the reader learns about events that will happen to Lester later on.

A story's series of events is its **plot.** A plot usually begins with a problem, or **conflict,** and ends with a conclusion, or **resolution.** The plot of "The 11:59" hinges on the conflict between Lester's story about a mysterious train and the reality of his physical condition.

DIRECTIONS: *Read this passage from "The 11:59," and answer the questions that follow.*

Suddenly [Lester] felt a sharp pain in his chest. At exactly the same moment he heard the mournful sound of a train whistle, which the wind seemed to carry from some faraway place. Ignoring his pain, Lester looked at the old station. He knew nothing was scheduled to come in or out till early morning. Nervously he lit a match to check the time. 11:59!

"No," he said into the darkness. "I'm not ready. I've got plenty of living yet."

Fear quickened his stop. Reaching his small apartment, he hurried up the steps. His heart pounded in his ear, and his left arm tingled. He had an idea, and there wasn't a moment to waste. But his own words haunted him. *Ain't no way to escape the final ride on the 11:59.*

"But I'm gon' try!" Lester spent the rest of the night plotting his escape from fate.

1. What is Lester's **conflict**? _____

   _____

2. What **character traits** is Lester shown to have in this passage? List two.

   _____

3. How do these **character traits** set the rest of the story in motion? _____

   _____

4. Tell what **resolution** ends Lester's conflict—and the story itself.

   _____

from **The Baker Heater League** by Patricia C. and Fredrick McKissack
Model Selection: Nonfiction

Nonfiction is prose in which authors present people, events, and ideas from real life. Nonfiction works can report facts and present ideas. They also might present the author's opinions.

A work of nonfiction can sometimes refer to fictional, or imaginary, ideas. For example, *The Baker Heater League* describes some of the legends surrounding famous railroad men. Many details in these legends are fictional. However, it is a *fact* that Pullman porters liked to tell and retell these fanciful legends.

When deciding what kinds of facts and details to include in a nonfiction work, an author thinks about his or her **purpose.**

- To **persuade** readers, an author may use forceful facts and opinions.
- To **entertain** readers, an author may include amusing or unusual facts and details.
- To **inform** readers, an author may use a wide range of facts about a single topic.

DIRECTIONS: *Read this passage from* The Baker Heater League, *and answer the questions that follow.*

The real John Henry, believed to be a newly freed slave from North Carolina, joined the West Virginia steel-driving team hired to dig out the Big Bend Tunnel for the C. & O. Railroad, circa 1870. Many stories detail the life and adventures of this two hundred-pound, six-foot man who was so strong he could drive steel with a hammer in each hand. John Henry's death occurred after competing with a steam drill, winning and then dying.

1. What **real-life person** does this passage describe? _____

   What did this person do for a living? _____

2. List two **facts** from the passage.

   Fact 1: _____

   _____

   Fact 2: _____

   _____

3. Why do the authors include both facts and legends in *The Baker Heater League*? (*Hint*: What **purposes** do the authors have for writing the article?) _____

   _____

   _____

"**Raymond's Run**" by Toni Cade Bambara
Writing About the Big Question
Is truth the same for everyone?

Big Question Vocabulary

bias	confirm	contradict	doubtful	evidence
factual	fantasy	illogical	investigate	objective
observation	opinion	persuade	prove	theory

A. *Use a word from the list above to complete each sentence.*

1. Just before a race, a runner sometimes has a _____ about winning effortlessly.

2. In a very close race, judges might be _____ about who had won.

3. If you make the _____ that someone runs every day, you might assume he or she is in training.

4. Diane's personal _____ about running is that it's more boring than golf, but I disagree.

B. *Follow the directions in responding to each of the items below. Answer in complete sentences.*

1. Describe two different times when the outcome of a contest was not obvious at first.

   _____

   _____

2. Write two sentences explaining how the truth about the outcome of one of these contests was discovered or decided upon. Use at least two of the Big Question vocabulary words.

   _____

   _____

   _____

C. *In "Raymond's Run," the narrator discovers that winning a race is not the most important thing in her life. Complete the sentence below. Then, write a short paragraph in which you elaborate on your statement and connect it to the Big Question.*

   A person's view of other family members depends on _____

   _____

   _____

   _____

   _____

"**Raymond's Run**" by Toni Cade Bambara
Reading: Make Predictions and Support Them

When you **make predictions** about a story, you make informed guesses about what will happen next based on story details and your own experience. You can **support your predictions** by finding clues in the story that hint at what will happen next.

As you read, try to **predict,** or make reasonable guesses, about what is going to happen. Keep track of your predictions and your support for them. Notice when the story includes details that could support predictions of more than one outcome. Some stories keep you guessing in order to hold your interest and build suspense.

These questions may help you predict what might happen next in a story:

- How would you describe the main character's personality?
- What is important to the main character?
- Does the main character think or speak about the future?
- Do other characters do or say things that hint at the future?

Have you had experiences with people, places, or events that remind you of the ones in the story?

DIRECTIONS: *The following chart lists details from "Raymond's Run." Use the questions above to make predictions based on those details as you read the story. Then, in the third column, write down what actually happens.*

Details From Story	Prediction	Actual Outcome (If Known)
1. Squeaky and Gretchen are good runners, and each girl is sure she is the one who will win the race.		
2. Mr. Pearson hints to Squeaky that she should let Gretchen win the race.		
3. Raymond climbs the fence to meet Squeaky after the race.		
4. After the race, Gretchen and Squeaky smile at each other.		

"Raymond's Run" by Toni Cade Bambara
Literary Analysis: Plot

Plot is the sequence of related events in a short story. As you read, identify the following parts of the story's plot:

- **Exposition:** the basic information about the characters and the situation
- **Conflict:** a struggle between two opposing forces in the story
- **Rising action:** the events in the story that increase the tension that readers feel
- **Climax:** the high point of the story, usually the point at which the eventual outcome is revealed
- **Falling action:** the events that follow the climax
- **Resolution:** the final outcome

A. DIRECTIONS: *The following six sentences describe the plot of "Raymond's Run," but they are out of order. Write a number on the line before each part to indicate the order in which the event takes place in the story. Then, write the name of the plot part that the event represents. The parts of the plot are* exposition, conflict, rising action, climax, falling action, *and* resolution.

___ 1. _____ Squeaky and Gretchen congratulate each other.

___ 2. _____ Squeaky looks after her older brother, and she anticipates a race.

___ 3. _____ Squeaky stands up for her brother and defends her reputation as the fastest runner in the neighborhood.

___ 4. _____ The race ends, and Raymond begins to climb the fence that separates him from the runners.

___ 5. _____ Squeaky meets a group of girls from the neighborhood while practicing for the race.

___ 6. _____ Squeaky realizes that Raymond could be a good runner and thinks about coaching him.

B. DIRECTIONS: *Look at the sentences you labeled "rising action" and "falling action." On the lines below, write two details that describe the rising action of "Raymond's Run" and two details that describe the falling action. The details might describe events, actions, a conversation, or a character's thoughts.*

Rising action:

1. _____

2. _____

Falling action:

1. _____

2. _____

"Raymond's Run" by Toni Cade Bambara
Vocabulary Builder

Word List

    prodigy   reputation   liable   pageant   periscope   gesture

A. DIRECTIONS: *Follow the instructions for writing a sentence using each Word List word. Be sure to make the meaning of the vocabulary word clear.*

    Example: Use *prodigy* in a sentence about a music student.

    Sentence: Soon the prodigy Kayla was playing the violin better than her teacher.

1. Use *prodigy* in a sentence about a child who solves math problems.

    _____

2. Use *reputation* in a sentence about the behavior of an animal.

    _____

3. Use *liable* in a sentence about a fast runner.

    _____

4. Use *pageant* in a sentence about a springtime event.

    _____

5. Use *periscope* in a sentence about a submarine.

    _____

6. Use *gesture* in a sentence about welcoming a new neighbor.

    _____

B. WORD STUDY: *The Greek root -scope- means "an instrument for seeing or observing." Revise each sentence so that the underlined word containing the root -scope- is used logically. Be sure not to change the underlined word.*

1. The astronomer used a *microscope* to study the moon.

    _____

2. Jessica looked through her *telescope* to study a strand of her own hair.

    _____

3. The pilot consulted the *stethoscope* to make sure the plane was level.

    _____

4. The doctor used a *gyroscope* to listen to the patient's breathing.

    _____

Name _____ Date _____

"A Retrieved Reformation" by O. Henry
Writing About the Big Question

 Is truth the same for everyone?

Big Question Vocabulary

bias	confirm	contradict	doubtful	evidence
factual	fantasy	illogical	investigate	objective
observation	opinion	persuade	prove	theory

A. *Use a word from the list above to complete each sentence.*

1. A warden might try to _____ a criminal to "live straight."

2. If a man is carrying a set of burglar's tools, that fact seems to _____ suspicions that the man is a burglar.

3. As detectives _____ the scene of a robbery, they might learn the truth about who the thief is.

4. The _____ and clues that point to the truth might include fingerprints.

B. *Follow the directions in responding to each of the items below. Answer in complete sentences.*

1. Suppose that your best friend has a challenging goal in mind. It might be doing well on a test, learning a new skill, planning a good party, or anything else. Write three statements of truth you would use to help your friend succeed.

   _____

   _____

   _____

2. Choose one of those statements, and explain why it would work. Use at least two of the Big Question vocabulary words.

   _____

   _____

C. *In "A Retrieved Reformation," a former thief tries to re-invent the truth about his life. Complete the sentence below. Then, write a short paragraph in which you explain how your statement connects to the Big Question.*

   In trying to start a different kind of life, a person needs to _____

   _____

   _____

   _____

Name _____   Date _____

"A Retrieved Reformation" by O. Henry
Reading: Make Predictions and Support Them

When you **make predictions** about a story, you make informed guesses about what will happen next based on story details and your own experience. You can **support your predictions** by finding clues in the story that hint at what will happen next.

As you read, **predict,** or make reasonable guesses about, what is going to happen. Keep track of your predictions and your support for them. Notice when the story includes details that could support predictions of more than one outcome. Some stories keep you guessing in order to hold your interest and build suspense.

These questions may help you predict what might happen next in a story:

- How would you describe the main character's personality?
- What is important to the main character?
- Does the main character think or speak about the future?
- Do other characters do or say things that hint at the future?
- Have you had experiences with people, places, or events that remind you of the ones in the story?

DIRECTIONS: *The following chart lists details from "A Retrieved Reformation." Use the questions above to make predictions based on those details as you read the story. Then, in the third column, write down what actually happens.*

Details From Story	Prediction	Actual Outcome (If Known)
1. Just out of prison, Jimmy looks "fondly" at his safe-cracking tools.		
2. Investigating a series of safecrackings, Ben Price recognizes them as Jimmy's work.		
3. In a new town, Jimmy makes eye contact with an attractive woman and "[becomes] another man."		
4. Jimmy works honestly for a year and is engaged to marry the woman. Ben Price arrives in town.		

Name _____ Date _____

"A Retrieved Reformation" by O. Henry
Literary Analysis: Plot

Plot is the sequence of related events in a short story. As you read, identify the following parts of the story's plot:

- **Exposition:** the basic information about the characters and the situation
- **Conflict:** a struggle between two opposing forces in the story
- **Rising action:** the events in the story that increase the tension that readers feel
- **Climax:** the high point of the story, usually the point at which the eventual outcome is revealed
- **Falling action:** the events that follow the climax
- **Resolution:** the final outcome

A. DIRECTIONS: *The following six sentences describe the plot of "A Retrieved Reformation," but they are out of order. Write a number on the line before each part to indicate the order in which the event takes place in the story. Then, write the name of the plot part that the event represents. The parts of the plot are* exposition, conflict, rising action, climax, falling action, *and* resolution.

___ 1. _____ Ben Price pretends he does not know Jimmy and walks away.

___ 2. _____ Jimmy looks "fondly" at his safecracking tools.

___ 3. _____ A prison warden encourages Jimmy to "live straight."

___ 4. _____ Agatha is accidentally locked in a safe.

___ 5. _____ Ben Price, a detective, pursues Jimmy; Jimmy falls in love.

___ 6. _____ Jimmy cracks the safe to free Agatha.

B. DIRECTIONS: *Look at the sentences you labeled "rising action" and "falling action." On the lines below, write two details that describe the rising action of "A Retrieved Reformation" and two details that describe the falling action. The details might include events, actions, a conversation, or a character's thoughts.*

Rising action:

1. _____

2. _____

Falling action:

1. _____

2. _____

Name _____ Date _____

"**A Retrieved Reformation**" by O. Henry
Vocabulary Builder

Word List

alibi   anguish   perceived   rehabilitate   retribution   unobtrusively

A. DIRECTIONS: *Write the Word List word that answers each question. Use each vocabulary word only once.*

1. The safecrackers slipped out of the bank without being noticed. How did the burglars move? _____

2. When Agatha is locked in the safe, her mother is extremely worried. What emotion is Agatha's mother feeling? _____

3. Ben Price is determined to see Jimmy Valentine punished for his crimes. What does Ben Price want? _____

4. The burglar tells the police he was somewhere else when the crime was committed. What is the burglar offering to the police? _____

5. After seeing how well Jimmy Valentine was dressed, the clerk became aware of his own lack of taste. You might say he _____ his own shortcomings.

6. Jimmy works in the prison shoe shop, learning a new trade. What is the prison system trying to do for him? _____

B. WORD STUDY: The Latin root -*trib*- means "to give in return; repay." Answer each of the following questions using one of these words containing -*trib*-: *attribute, tributary, contributory.*

1. When you are writing a research paper, why is it important to *attribute* a quotation to the person who said it or wrote it? _____

   _____

2. How does a *tributary* stream add to the volume of a river? _____

   _____

3. How might you have a *contributory* role in raising money for a good cause? _____

   _____

"**Raymond's Run**" by Toni Cade Bambara
"**A Retrieved Reformation**" by O. Henry

Integrated Language Skills: Grammar

Common and Proper Nouns

Nouns may be classified as common or proper. A **common noun** names any person, animal, place, thing, or idea. It is not capitalized unless it is the first word in a sentence.

The <u>girl</u> met another <u>girl</u> on a <u>street</u> and talked about a <u>race</u> they would run the next <u>day</u>.

A **proper noun** names a particular person, animal, place, thing, or idea. A proper noun is always capitalized.

<u>Squeaky</u> met <u>Gretchen</u> on <u>Broadway</u> and talked about the race they would run on <u>May Day</u>.

A. DIRECTIONS: *In the following paragraph, underline the common nouns once and the proper nouns twice.*

It was Sunday morning, the day of the Chicago Marathon. The weather was crisp and

clear, a perfect day for a long race. Sara had trained for six months. She ran long and short

distances every week to build up her endurance and strength. She ran along the lakefront

paths, on the paths in Lincoln Park Zoo, and along the streets of the city neighborhoods.

Sara felt anticipation, sure that she was ready for the race.

B. Writing Application: *Write sentences following the directions in each item. In your sentences, underline the common nouns once and the proper nouns twice.*

1. Use a proper noun in a question you might ask your teacher.

   _____

2. Use a common noun in a sentence about an activity you enjoy.

   _____

3. Use a proper noun in a sentence about your town or city.

   _____

4. Use a common noun in a question you might ask about a marathon race.

   _____

"Raymond's Run" by Toni Cade Bambara
"A Retrieved Reformation" by O. Henry

Integrated Language Skills: Support for Writing a New Ending

Plan a **new ending** to "Raymond's Run" in which Squeaky loses the race to Gretchen, or to "A Retrieved Reformation" in which Ben Price arrests Jimmy Valentine. Use the following chart to come up with narration and dialogue you can use for your ending. In the second column, write your ideas about the characters' thoughts, feelings, actions, or dialogue. Base your responses on the personality traits described in the first column. As you write your new ending, remember the experiences that the characters share. Look for places in the story that indicate each person's thoughts and feelings about the other.

Characters' Personality Traits	Thoughts That Characters Might Have, Actions They Might Take, Things They Might Say

In your new ending, remember to use the pronouns *he, she, him, her,* and *they* in reference to the characters; in your dialogue, match the characters' voice and personality.

"**Gentleman of Río en Medio**" by Juan A. A. Sedillo
Writing About the Big Question
Is truth the same for everyone?

Big Question Vocabulary

bias	confirm	contradict	doubtful	evidence
factual	fantasy	illogical	investigate	objective
observation	opinion	persuade	prove	theory

A. *Use a word from the list above to complete each sentence.*

1. To any sensible person, it would seem _____ for a man to turn down extra money for his property.

2. You would not usually have to try to _____ someone to accept more money.

3. To _____ someone's false claim of land ownership, the real owner would have to produce a deed to the land.

4. Neighbors generally have a high _____ of a person who is generous and kind.

B. *Follow the directions in responding to each of the items below. Answer in complete sentences.*

1. Suppose that a group of neighbors turns an empty, abandoned lot into a community vegetable garden. Then, someone presents evidence of ownership of the land. Write two sentences supporting your opinion of who you think should get the vegetables.

_____

_____

2. What fantasy do you have about a perfect children's park? Which parts of your fantasy could actually come true? Write two sentences to answer these questions, using at least two of the Big Question vocabulary words.

_____

_____

C. *In "Gentleman of Río an Medio," an old man becomes involved in a dispute over the value of property. Complete the sentence below. Then, write a short paragraph in which you connect your answer to the Big Question.*

A person selling a house may be biased about his or her property because

_____

_____

_____

"**Gentleman of Río en Medio**" by Juan A. A. Sedillo
Reading: Make Predictions and Read Ahead
to Confirm or Modify Them

When you **make predictions,** use details in what you read to make logical, informed guesses about what will happen later in a story. **Reading ahead to confirm or modify predictions** helps you remain focused on the connections between events.

As you read, look for details that suggest a certain outcome. Make a prediction about what will happen next. Then, read ahead to see if you were right. Use new details to confirm or modify your original predictions. Finally, make new predictions—and repeat the process. Here are some guidelines for making predictions as you read:

- Consider characters' traits, actions, and relationships to other characters.
- Consider the events that have already occurred.
- Consider the setting and the kinds of events likely to occur in that setting.
- Consider the message that the writer might want to convey.
- Take into account any knowledge you have about similar situations in real life or in books or movies that you are familiar with.

DIRECTIONS: *The following chart lists details from "Gentleman of Río en Medio." Use the questions above to make predictions based on those details as you read the story. Then, read ahead to confirm or modify your prediction. In the third column, note whether your prediction was correct, and write what actually happens.*

Details From Story	Prediction	Confirmation/Correction of Prediction
1. Don Anselmo is offered twice as much money for his land as had been agreed on.		
2. After the sale of the land, the children of the village continue to play in the orchard.		
3. Don Anselmo declares that he did not sell the trees in the orchard when he sold his land.		

"Gentleman of Río en Medio" by Juan A. A. Sedillo
Literary Analysis: Conflict

Conflict is the struggle between two opposing forces.

- In **external conflict,** a character struggles against another character, natural forces, or some aspect of society. In "Gentleman of Río en Medio," the unidentified Americans are in conflict with Don Anselmo as they try to negotiate the purchase of his property.
- **Internal conflict** is a struggle between competing feelings, beliefs, needs, or desires within a single character. For example, if a character faces a loss of some kind, he or she might struggle to maintain a sense of pride or dignity.
- In the **resolution,** problems are worked out to eliminate the conflict.

The following passages from "Gentleman of Río en Medio" tell something about the characters on each side of the story's external conflict. As you reread these passages, think about the internal conflicts with which the characters might be struggling.

> It took months of negotiation to come to an understanding with the old man. He was in no hurry. What he had the most of was time. He lived up in Río en Medio, where his people had been for hundreds of years. He tilled the same land they had tilled.

> "Don Anselmo, about the ranch you sold to these people. They are good people and want to be your friends and neighbors always. When you sold to them you signed a document, a deed, and in that deed you agreed to several things. One thing was that they were to have complete possession of the property. Now, Don Anselmo, it seems that every day the children of the village overrun the orchard and spend most of their time there."

DIRECTIONS: *Use the information in the preceding passages, along with your knowledge of the rest of the story, to answer these questions.*

1. What is the external conflict in "Gentleman of Río en Medio"?

   _____

   _____

   _____

2. With what internal conflict might Don Anselmo be struggling?

   _____

3. With what internal conflict might the Americans be struggling?

   _____

4. How are the conflicts resolved?

   _____

   _____

"Gentleman of Río en Medio" by Juan A. A. Sedillo
Vocabulary Builder

Word List

deed   descendants   negotiation   possession   preliminary   quaint

A. DIRECTIONS: *Answer each question with* yes *or* no. *Then, explain your answer.*

1. Does a *preliminary* event follow the main event?

   _____

2. Are you likely to know any of your *descendants*?

   _____

3. Can merely thinking about something be called a *deed*?

   _____

4. Does *negotiation* always lead to a favorable outcome?

   _____

5. If you have *possession* of something, have you given it away?

   _____

6. Would you call a magnificent modern palace a *quaint* home?

   _____

B. WORD STUDY: The Latin root -*limin*- means "threshold," the entrance or beginning point of something, such as a career or a house. Answer each of the following questions using one of these words containing -*limin*-: *subliminal, sublime,* and *eliminate.* Explain your answer.

1. If an advertiser uses *subliminal* advertising, are you consciously aware of it?

   _____

   _____

2. If you *eliminate* a food from your diet, do you continue to eat it?

   _____

   _____

3. Would you consider a *sublime* moment to be an ordinary moment?

   _____

   _____

"Cub Pilot on the Mississippi" by Mark Twain
Writing About the Big Question

Is truth the same for everyone?

Big Question Vocabulary

bias	confirm	contradict	doubtful	evidence
factual	fantasy	illogical	investigate	objective
observation	opinion	persuade	prove	theory

A. *Use a word from the list above to complete each sentence.*

1. Some bullies seem to have a _____ against people who dress in an unusual way.

2. Such an attitude is not based on anything _____, but rather on prejudice and mistrust.

3. Maya's _____ about unusual clothing is that it is interesting.

4. It is hard to have a fair and _____ attitude toward a person who is always scowling.

B. *Follow the directions in responding to each of the items below. Answer in complete sentences.*

1. List two truths that you can say about most bullies. Use at least two of the Big Question vocabulary words.

   _____

   _____

2. Describe an experience you or a friend once had with a bully, and tell how you handled it.

   _____

   _____

C. *In "Cub Pilot on the Mississippi," a young man endures the abuse of a bully but defends his brother against the same bully. Complete the sentence below. Then, write a short paragraph in which you connect your statement to the Big Question.*

Bullies are _____

_____

_____

_____

_____

_____

"Cub Pilot on the Mississippi" by Mark Twain
Reading: Make Predictions and Read Ahead
to Confirm or Modify Them

When you **make predictions,** use details in what you read to make logical, informed guesses about what will happen later in a story. **Reading ahead to confirm or modify predictions** helps you remain focused on the connections between events.

As you read, look for details that suggest a certain outcome. Make a prediction about what will happen next. Then, read ahead to see if you were right. Use new details to confirm or modify your original predictions. Finally, make new predictions—and repeat the process.

Here are some guidelines to consider for making predictions as you read:

- Consider characters' traits, actions, and relationships with other characters.
- Consider the events that have already occurred.
- Consider the setting and the kinds of events likely to occur in that setting.
- Consider the message that the writer might want to convey.
- Take into account any knowledge you have about similar situations in real life or in books or movies you are familiar with.

DIRECTIONS: *The following chart lists details from "Cub Pilot on the Mississippi." Use the questions above to make predictions based on those details as you read the story. Then, read ahead to confirm or modify your prediction. In the third column, note whether your prediction was correct, and write what actually happens.*

Details From Story	Prediction	Confirmation/Correction of Prediction
1. He was a middle-aged, long, slim, bony, smooth-shaven, horsefaced, ignorant, stingy, malicious, snarling, fault-hunting, mote magnifying tyrant.		
2. I often wanted to kill Brown, but . . . a cub had to take everything his boss gave, in the way of . . . comment and criticism; and we all believed that there was a . . . law making it a penitentiary offense to strike or threaten a pilot . . . on duty.		
3. The racket had brought everybody to the hurricane deck, and I trembled when I saw the old captain looking up from amid the crowd. I said to myself, "Now I *am* done for!"		

Name _____ Date _____

"Cub Pilot on the Mississippi" by Mark Twain
Literary Analysis: Conflict and Resolution

Conflict is the struggle between two opposing forces.

- In **external conflict,** a character struggles against another character, natural forces, or some aspect of society.
- **Internal conflict** is a struggle between competing feelings, beliefs, needs, or desires within a single character.

In the **resolution** of a story, problems are worked out in a way that eliminates the conflict.

The following passages from "Cub Pilot on the Mississippi" tell something about the characters' external conflicts and about one character's internal struggle. As you reread these passages, think about the conflicts with which the characters are struggling.

> He was a middle-aged, long, slim, bony, smooth-shaven, horsefaced, ignorant, stingy, malicious, snarling, fault-hunting, mote magnifying tyrant. I early got the habit of coming on watch with dread at my heart. No matter how good a time I might have been having with the off-watch below, and no matter how high my spirits might be when I started aloft, my soul became lead in my body the moment I approached the pilothouse.

> I often wanted to kill Brown, but this would not answer. A cub had to take everything his boss gave, in the way of vigorous comment and criticism; and we all believed that there was a United States law making it a penitentiary offense to strike or threaten a pilot who was on duty.

DIRECTIONS: *Use the information in the preceding passages, along with your knowledge of the rest of the story, to answer these questions.*

1. What is the external conflict in "Cub Pilot on the Mississippi"?

   _____

   _____

2. What is the internal conflict?

   _____

   _____

3. How are the conflicts resolved?

   _____

   _____

   _____

   _____

   _____

   _____

"Cub Pilot on the Mississippi" by Mark Twain
Vocabulary Builder

Word List

confronted   contemptuously   emancipated
judicious   malicious   pretext

A. DIRECTIONS: *Revise each sentence so that the italicized Word List word is used logically. Be sure to include the vocabulary word in your revised sentence.*

Example: When the rain clouds appeared, the baseball fans shouted with *delight*.

Revision: When the rain clouds disappeared, the baseball fans shouted with delight.

1. Because his motives were sound, Brown needed a *pretext* to find fault with Twain.
   _____

2. By attacking Brown, Twain showed that he was *judicious*.
   _____

3. Twain *confronted* Brown with a smile and a friendly handshake.
   _____

4. Everyone liked Brown because he was so *malicious*.
   _____

5. After he was *emancipated* from the tyranny of Brown, Twain felt like a slave.
   _____

6. By looking at Twain *contemptuously*, Brown showed his approval of him.
   _____

B. WORD STUDY: The Latin root *-judex-* means "judge." Answer the following questions using one of these words containing *-judex-*: *judgment, judicial, adjudicate*.

1. Why might your *judgment* about fashion and style be different from your mom's?
   _____
   _____

2. If a person commits a crime, how might he or she get involved in the *judicial* system?
   _____
   _____

3. To *adjudicate* a case fairly, what information must a judge have?
   _____
   _____

"**Gentleman of Río en Medio**" by Juan A. A. Sedillo
"**Cub Pilot on the Mississippi**" by Mark Twain

Integrated Language Skills: Grammar

Plural Nouns

A **plural noun** refers to more than one person, place, thing, or idea—for example, *girls, towns, books, beliefs.* The plurals of most nouns are formed by adding an *-s* to the end of the word. The plurals of certain nouns, however, are formed according to different rules. This chart shows some of the rules for forming plural nouns:

Rule	Examples
For words that end in *-x*, *-ch*, or *-sh*, add *-es*.	box, box**es**; church, church**es**; sash, sash**es**
For words that end in a consonant plus *-y*, change the *y* to *i* and add *-es*.	pony, pon**ies**; fly, fl**ies**
For some words that end in *-f* or *-fe*, change the *-f* or *-fe* to *-ves*.	calf, cal**ves**; knife, kni**ves**; *but* roof, roofs.
For some words, the plural form is a different word.	goose, g**ee**se; mouse, m**ice**; wom**an**, wom**en**

A. DIRECTIONS: *Underline each plural noun in the following sentences.*

1. Last year I took a trip west with several friends.
2. We stayed at a ranch where oxen grazed outside our window.
3. We hiked in the desert and found fossils of animal teeth.
4. I found time to read while sitting next to the river, near low bushes of sweet-smelling sage.
5. On our last night, we were lucky enough to see three shooting stars.

B. Writing Application: *Write a paragraph about a trip you have taken or would like to take. Use at least five plural nouns that are not formed by adding -s to the end of the word. Then, underline all the plural nouns in your paragraph.*

_____

_____

_____

_____

_____

_____

"Gentleman of Río en Medio" by Juan A. A. Sedillo
"Cub Pilot on the Mississippi" by Mark Twain

Integrated Language Skills: Support for Writing a Letter

When you write a **letter,** you have a particular audience—a person or group of people—in mind. In addition, you usually have a particular purpose. You might be describing a trip you are taking, telling what you are doing in school or with your friends, requesting a service, or thanking someone for a gift.

As you draft your letter, think about these points:

- the person to whom you are writing
- your purpose for writing

DIRECTIONS: *Use your answers to these questions in your letter to Don Anselmo.*

1. What does Don Anselmo care about most?_____

2. What gift has Don Anselmo given to the children? _____

3. What did the children probably enjoy about playing in the orchard?

   _____

4. How have the children benefited from Don Anselmo's solution to the conflict?

   _____

DIRECTIONS: *Use your answers to these questions in your letter to your friend about your steamboat experiences.*

1. What was your first impression of the steamboat? Did your first impression change? If so, how? What impression do you hold now?

   _____

   _____

2. What is the pilot like? How does he or she treat you? What are you learning?

   _____

   _____

3. What are the other crew members like? Do you interact with them?

   _____

   _____

4. Have you been ashore? What have you seen? What have you done?

   _____

   _____

"Old Ben" by Jesse Stuart
"Fox Hunt" by Lensey Namioka

Writing About the Big Question

Is truth the same for everyone?

Big Question Vocabulary

bias	confirm	contradict	doubtful	evidence
factual	fantasy	illogical	investigate	objective
observation	opinion	persuade	prove	theory

A. *Use a word or words from the list above to complete each sentence.*

1. Most people seem to have a _____ against snakes.

2. All the _____ seems to _____ that snakes are dangerous creatures.

3. The Chinese story about a fox who becomes a girl is clearly a

   _____.

4. It is completely _____ to believe that a girl could really be a fox.

B. *Follow the directions in responding to each of the items below. Answer in complete sentences.*

1. Describe two different times when you felt a special connection to a wild animal.

   _____

   _____

2. Write two sentences explaining your theory about why one of those special connections occurred. Use at least two of the Big Question vocabulary words.

   _____

   _____

C. *In these stories, each main character has a special connection to a wild animal. Complete the sentence below. Then, write a short paragraph in which you give an example to support your opinion.*

   Relationships between wild animals and people _____

   _____

   _____

   _____

   _____

   _____

   _____

"**Old Ben**" by Jesse Stuart
"**Fox Hunt**" by Lensey Namioka
Literary Analysis: Narrative Structure

Narrative structure is the form or pattern a story follows. In some stories, authors may break the straight timeline by using one or both of these two common devices:

- A **flashback** is a scene within a narrative that interrupts the sequence of events to relate events that occurred in the past. A flashback often reveals something important about a character.
- **Foreshadowing** is the use of clues hinting at events that are going to occur later in the plot of a narrative. Foreshadowing creates suspense by keeping readers guessing.

DIRECTIONS: *Read the passages from "Old Ben" and "Fox Hunt." Then, answer the questions.*

One morning in July when I was walking across a clover field to a sweet-apple tree, I almost stepped on him. There he lay coiled like heavy strands of black rope. He was a big bull blacksnake. We looked at each other a minute, and then I stuck the toe of my shoe up to his mouth. He drew his head back in a friendly way. He didn't want trouble. Had he shown the least fight, I would have soon finished him. My father had always told me there was only one good snake—a dead one.

1. Identify one detail that foreshadows the friendship between the narrator and the snake.

   _____

2. Identify one detail that hints at what will ultimately happen to Ben.

   _____

3. Which of the two details you identified helps the author create suspense? In what way? _____

   One night, while he was struggling to stay awake over his book, [Fujin] heard a soft voice behind him. "A fine, hardworking young man like you deserves to pass the examination."

   Fujin whirled around and saw a beautiful girl standing behind him. Somehow she had appeared without making any noise. She had huge, bewitching eyes that slanted sharply. Could he be dreaming?

   "Let me help you," continued the girl. "I can act as a tutor and coach you."

   "And that was how your ancestor, Liang Fujin, got the coaching he needed to pass the examinations," said Andy's mother.

4. Explain why this passage is a flashback. _____

   _____

5. What does this flashback reveal about Andy, his goals, or his motives? _____

   _____

6. Explain the element of foreshadowing in this passage. _____

   _____

"**Old Ben**" by Jesse Stuart
"**Fox Hunt**" by Lensey Namioka
Vocabulary Builder

Word List

affectionate   decadent   partition   scarce   studious   tantalized

A. DIRECTIONS: *For each numbered item, write a new sentence so that the underlined vocabulary word makes sense. Be sure not to change the vocabulary word.*

Example: When fresh tomatoes are <u>scarce</u>, we enjoy them at every meal.
Revised sentence: When fresh tomatoes are <u>scarce</u>, we use canned ones.

1. The <u>decadent</u> nobleman was honest and hard working.

_____

2. The <u>affectionate</u> little girl pinched her cousin.

_____

3. Carmen was <u>tantalized</u> by the beautiful bracelet she had received.

_____

4. With the help of a <u>partition</u>, the twins created one large room out of two smaller rooms.

_____

5. Mom has a hard time persuading my <u>studious</u> brother to do his homework.

_____

B. DIRECTIONS: *Circle the letter of the word or phrase that is most nearly the same in meaning to the word in CAPITAL LETTERS.*

1. PARTITION:
   A. divider   B. problem   C. conflict   D. request
2. STUDIOUS:
   A. comical   B. strict   C. nervous   D. bookish
3. DECADENT:
   A. everlasting   B. corrupt   C. generous   D. depressed
4. AFFECTIONATE:
   A. mean   B. rebellious   C. loving   D. clinging
5. SCARCE:
   A. abundant   B. fearful   C. not plentiful   D. not sharp
6. TANTALIZED:
   A. tricked   B. lied   C. teased   D. equaled

"**Old Ben**" by Jesse Stuart
"**Fox Hunt**" by Lensey Namioka

Integrated Language Skills: Support for Writing to Compare Narrative Structures

Before you draft your essay comparing and contrasting the narrative structures of these stories, complete the graphic organizers below. For each selection, list examples of foreshadowing and/or flashback that the author uses. Then, for each example, tell how it affects the reader or the story. For example, does the reader feel suspense? Does the example reveal something important about a character? Does it make you think differently about something or someone in the story?

"Old Ben"	
Examples of Foreshadowing	**Effect on Reader or Story**
1.	1.
2.	2.
Examples of Flashback	**Effect on Reader or Story**
1.	1.
2.	2.

"Fox Hunt"	
Examples of Foreshadowing	**Effect on Reader or Story**
1.	1.
2.	2.
Examples of Flashback	**Effect on Reader or Story**
1.	1.
2.	2.

Now, use your notes to write an essay comparing and contrasting the narrative structures of "Old Ben" and "Fox Hunt."

All-in-One Workbook

from **An American Childhood** by Annie Dillard

Writing About the Big Question

Is truth the same for everyone?

Big Question Vocabulary

bias	confirm	contradict	doubtful	evidence
factual	fantasy	illogical	investigate	objective
observation	opinion	persuade	prove	theory

A. *Use a word from the list above to complete each sentence.*

1. Some children have a _____ about monsters that can be disproved easily.

2. These children are so young that they still live in a _____ world sometimes.

3. In their minds, if the monster could find _____ of their existence, it would destroy them.

4. As they grow up, they finally realize the logical explanation of their _____ fears.

B. *Follow the directions in responding to each of the items below. Answer in complete sentences.*

1. Describe a childhood fantasy that used to frighten you. Use at least two of the Big Question vocabulary words.

_____

_____

2. Explain how you finally realized the truth and overcame your fear.

_____

_____

_____

C. *In* An American Childhood, *Annie Dillard's perception of the world around her is influenced by her youthful imagination. Complete the sentence below. Then, write a short paragraph in which you connect your answer to the Big Question.*

What is perceived as reality depends on _____

_____

_____

_____

_____

from **An American Childhood** by Annie Dillard

Reading: Recognize Details That Indicate the Author's Purpose

The **author's purpose** is his or her reason for writing. Learn to **recognize details that indicate the author's purpose.** The author's purpose and the types of details in the work affect the way you read the work. Look for these types of details:

- To *inform*, an author might use facts and technical language. Pause frequently to check your understanding, and take notes from material written to inform you.
- To *persuade*, an author might include reasons that lead readers to agree with an opinion. With this kind of writing, question the author's statements and check facts.
- To *entertain*, an author might provide details that amuse, intrigue, horrify, or fascinate readers. With such material, pay attention to sensory images.

Frequently, the author has both a general purpose and a specific purpose in mind. In the excerpt from *An American Childhood,* Dillard's *general* purpose is to entertain you by telling about an event in her childhood. Dillard provides details that entertain in a *particular* way by arousing curiosity and perhaps frightening you, as in the following sentences.

I lay alone and was almost asleep when the thing entered the room by flattening itself against the open door and sliding in. It was a transparent, luminous oblong.

A. DIRECTIONS: *Read each passage from* An American Childhood. *From the list, choose the item or items that best identify the author's specific purpose in that passage. Alternatively, you may describe the author's specific purpose in words of your own.*

to make readers curious   to frighten readers   to give readers a sense of relief

1. When I was five, growing up in Pittsburgh in 1950, I would not go to bed willingly because something came into my room.

   _____

2. I heard the rising roar it made when it died or left. I still couldn't breathe. I knew— it was the worst fact I knew, a very hard fact—that it could return again alive that same night.

   _____

3. What, precisely, came into the bedroom? A reflection from the car's oblong windshield. Why did it travel in two parts? The window sash split the light and cast a shadow.

   _____

B. DIRECTIONS: *Write one or two sentences in which you entertain readers with details that frighten them. You might tell about something you were afraid of as a young child.*

_____

_____

_____

All-in-One Workbook
36

Name _____ Date _____

from **An American Childhood** by Annie Dillard
Literary Analysis: Mood

Mood, or atmosphere, is the overall feeling that a literary work or passage creates for the reader. The mood of a work might be somber, joyful, sentimental, and so on. A variety of elements contributes to the mood of a work.

- Words, such as *whooping*, and images, such as "two joined parts, a head and a tail, like a Chinese dragon."
- Setting, such as "I could see the door whiten at its touch. . . ."
- Events, such as "When I needed someone most, I was afraid to stir. . . ."

A writer chooses words carefully in order to create a particular mood. As you read the following passage from *An American Childhood*, notice how the underlined words help create a mood of fear.

> Most often, restless, it came back. The light stripe slipped in the door, ran searching over Amy's wall, stopped, stretched lunatic at the first corner, raced wailing toward my wall, and vanished into the second corner with a cry.

A. DIRECTIONS: *Write the words in each passage from the selection that contribute to the mood of fear.*

1. Every night before it got to me it gave up. It hit my wall's corner and couldn't get past. It shrank completely into itself and vanished like a cobra down a hole.

   _____

2. Night after night I labored up the same long chain of reasoning, as night after night the thing burst into the room where I lay awake and Amy slept prettily and my loud heart thrashed and I froze.

   _____

3. It raced over the wall, lighting it blue wherever it ran; it bumped over Amy's maple headboard in a rush, paused, slithered elongate over the corner, shrank, flew my way, and vanished into itself with a wail.

   _____

B. DIRECTIONS: *Write one or two sentences using some of the words you underlined in the passages above and any others you think of. Your goal is to create a mood of fear. You might begin by recalling an unusual character or situation in a book or movie. Underline the words you use to help create the mood.*

_____

_____

_____

_____

Name _____ Date _____

from **An American Childhood** by Annie Dillard
Vocabulary Builder

Word List

ascent   conceivably   luminous   overwhelming   serene   willingly

A. DIRECTIONS: *Respond to each numbered item by writing a sentence that uses one word from the word list. Underline that word.*

1. Describe the numbers on a watch that you can read in a dark room.

   _____

   _____

2. Describe the mood you might feel at the end of a day when things went your way.

   _____

   _____

3. How do scientists express the likelihood that temperatures will go up throughout the world in the future?

   _____

4. Describe how you might feel as you climbed a steep hill.

   _____

   _____

5. Explain why a leader might prefer a volunteer over someone who is forced to participate in a project.

   _____

   _____

6. Tell about a time you found it almost impossible to control your emotions.

   _____

   _____

B. WORD STUDY The Latin root -*lum*- means "light." Explain your answers to the following questions, using one of these words containing -*lum*-: *luminous, luminary, illuminate.*

1. Would you be able to see a *luminous* object in the dark?

   _____

2. What might you use to *illuminate* a cabin that had no electricity?

   _____

3. Would a *luminary* in a certain field know a lot or a little about the subject?

   _____

"The Adventure of the Speckled Band" by Sir Arthur Conan Doyle
Writing About the Big Question
Is truth the same for everyone?

Big Question Vocabulary

bias	confirm	contradict	doubtful	evidence
factual	fantasy	illogical	investigate	objective
observation	opinion	persuade	prove	theory

A. *Use a word or words from the list above to complete each sentence.*

1. Sherlock Holmes is known for his excellent powers of _____, which lead him to the truth.

2. Any detective who wants to _____ a crime would do well to follow Holmes's methods.

3. To _____ that his _____ about a certain crime is correct, Holmes must often take dangerous chances.

4. Holmes always tries to stay _____, keeping his emotions in check.

B. *Follow the directions in responding to each of the items below. Answer in complete sentences.*

1. List two events that occur in nature and seemed mysterious to ancient peoples.

_____

_____

2. Explain how the truth about one of these mysterious events was finally revealed. Use at least two of the Big Question vocabulary words.

_____

_____

_____

C. *In The* Adventure of the Speckled Band, *a detective determines that the truth about a young woman's mysterious death is not what people had previously believed. Complete the sentence below. Then, write a short paragraph in which you connect this statement to the Big Question.*

The truth can be difficult to see, but it can be revealed by _____

_____

_____

_____

_____

"The Adventure of the Speckled Band" by Sir Arthur Conan Doyle

Reading: Recognize Details That Indicate the Author's Purpose

The **author's purpose** is his or her reason for writing. Learn to **recognize details that indicate the author's purpose.** The author's purpose and the types of details in the work affect the way you read the work. Look for these types of details:

- To *inform*, an author might use facts and technical language. Pause frequently to check your understanding, and take notes from material written to inform you.
- To *persuade*, an author might include reasons that lead readers to agree with an opinion. With this kind of writing, question the author's statements and check facts.
- To *entertain*, an author might provide details that amuse, intrigue, horrify, or fascinate readers. With such material, pay attention to descriptions—especially, to images that appeal to the senses.

Frequently, the author has both a general purpose and a specific purpose in mind. In "The Adventure of the Speckled Band," Doyle's *general* purpose is to entertain you with a mystery. As Doyle tells the story, he provides details that entertain in a *particular* way—for instance, by puzzling you or frightening you, as in the following description of Helen Stoner.

> She raised her veil as she spoke, and we could see that she was indeed in a pitiable state of agitation, her face all drawn and gray, with restless, frightened eyes, like those of some hunted animal.

DIRECTIONS: *Read each passage from "The Adventure of the Speckled Band." From the list, choose the item or items that best identify the author's specific purpose in that passage. Alternatively, you may describe the author's specific purpose in words of your own.*

to frighten readers   to make readers curious   to give readers a sense of relief

1. A series of disgraceful brawls took place, two of which ended in the police court, until at last he became the terror of the village, and the folks would fly at his approach, for he is a man of immense strength, and absolutely uncontrollable in his anger.

   _____

2. The lady could not move her bed. It must always be in the same relative position to the ventilator and to the rope—or so we may call it, since it was clearly never meant for a bell-pull.

   _____

3. He had ceased to strike and was gazing up at the ventilator when suddenly there broke from the silence of the night the most horrible cry to which I have ever listened. It swelled up louder and louder, a hoarse yell of pain and fear and anger all mingled in the one dreadful shriek.

   _____

4. "It means that it is all over," Holmes answered. "And perhaps, after all, it is for the best. Take your pistol, and we will enter Dr. Roylott's room."

   _____

"The Adventure of the Speckled Band" by Sir Arthur Conan Doyle
Literary Analysis: Mood

Mood, or atmosphere, is the overall feeling that a literary work or passage creates for the reader. The mood of a work might be somber, joyful, sentimental, and so on. A variety of elements contributes to the mood of a work.

- Words, such as *gloomy*, and images, such as "the wind was . . . splashing against the windows"
- Setting, such as "the windows were broken and blocked with wooden boards"
- Events, such as "our door had been suddenly dashed open"

A writer chooses words carefully in order to create a particular mood. As you read the following passage from "The Adventure of the Speckled Band," notice how the underlined words help create a mood of terror.

> There was something else which she would fain have said, and she <u>stabbed</u> with her finger into the air in the direction of the doctor's room, but a fresh <u>convulsion</u> <u>seized</u> her and <u>choked</u> her words.

DIRECTIONS: *Write the words in each story passage that contribute to the mood of terror.*

1. Imagine, then, my thrill of terror when last night, as I lay awake, thinking over her terrible fate, I suddenly heard in the silence of the night the low whistle which had been the herald of her own death. I sprang up and lit the lamp, but nothing was to be seen in the room. I was too shaken to go to bed again. . . .

   _____

   _____

2. A large face, seared with a thousand wrinkles, burned yellow with the sun, and marked with every evil passion, was turned from one to the other of us, while his deep-set, bile-shot eyes, and his high, thin, fleshless nose, gave him somewhat the resemblance to a fierce old bird of prey.

   _____

   _____

3. How shall I ever forget that dreadful vigil? I could not hear a sound, not even the drawing of a breath, and yet I knew that my companion sat open-eyed, within a few feet of me, in the same state of nervous tension in which I was myself. The shutters cut off the least ray of light, and we waited in absolute darkness.

   _____

   _____

"The Adventure of the Speckled Band" by Sir Arthur Conan Doyle
Vocabulary Builder

Word List

averted   deductions   indiscreetly   invaluable   sinister   tangible

A. DIRECTIONS: *Respond to each numbered item by writing a sentence that uses one word from the Word List. Underline that word.*

1. Describe a reason someone catches the flu.

   _____

2. Describe the costume that one student considered wearing to a masquerade party.

   _____

3. Explain how a detective solved a crime by analyzing clues at a crime scene.

   _____

4. Describe how one person's behavior or words embarrassed another person.

   _____

5. Explain how one city managed to protect itself from a natural disaster.

   _____

6. Tell about some memorable words of advice you once received.

   _____

B. WORD STUDY: The Latin root *-duc-* means "to lead" or "to bring." Explain your answers to the following questions using one of these words containing *-duc-*: *aqueduct, induction, ductile.*

1. Does an *aqueduct* stop water from flowing?

   _____

   _____

2. Why is it useful to us that metals are *ductile*?

   _____

   _____

3. At an *induction* ceremony for a club, what happens?

   _____

   _____

"The Adventure of the Speckled Band" by Sir Arthur Conan Doyle
from **An American Childhood** by Annie Dillard
Integrated Language Skills: Grammar

Personal Pronouns

When you speak and write, you automatically use personal pronouns instead of repeating nouns. Here are the personal pronouns grouped according to their three cases:

Nominative Case: I, we, you, he, she, it, they

Objective Case: me, us, you, him, her, it, them

Possessive Case: my, mine, our, ours, your, yours, his, her, hers, its, their, theirs

The personal pronouns are underlined in the following example.

After Carla and I finished lunch, we rode our bikes to the volleyball game. She rode faster and beat me.

In the example,

- *I*, *we*, and *she* are in the nominative case
- *me* is in the objective case
- *our* is in the possessive case

A. PRACTICE: *First, underline the personal pronouns in each sentence. Next, circle each personal pronoun that shows possession.*

1. One day I want to race my sailboat across the lake.
2. Jim and Carol ordered a pizza while they studied for their math test.
3. When the storm hit, it shook the windows in our house.
4. He watched the rain pound on his garage roof.
5. Have you ever lost your way in the fog?

B. Writing Application: *Revise the following sentences by replacing each italicized word or phrase with the appropriate pronoun.*

1. When Paula was younger, *Paula* was afraid of dogs.

   _____

2. Even though dogs usually liked Paula, *Paula* found *dogs* frightening.

   _____

3. Paula's brother Ray had always wanted a dog of *Ray's* own.

   _____

4. Paula and Ray visited a pet store where *Paula and Ray* watched a puppy playing.

   _____

5. After Paula held a puppy on *Paula's* lap, *Paula* began to lose *Paula's* fear of dogs.

   _____

"The Adventure of the Speckled Band" by Sir Arthur Conan Doyle
from **An American Childhood** by Annie Dillard

Integrated Language Skills: Support for Writing a Personal Narrative

In a **personal narrative,** a writer tells about an event or experience that has happened in his or her life. The writer usually narrates the event in the order in which it occurred, from first incident to last.

Before you begin writing your own personal narrative, think of an event in your life in which you solved a problem using your reasoning skill. Or, think about an event that has led you to an important childhood insight. Maybe you have already told others about this event. The event may be funny, scary, sad, or memorable for some other reason.

When you begin to prepare notes for your personal narrative, list what happened first (the first incident) and continue to the end of the event or experience (the last incident). Reexamine the list, and if necessary, move incidents into the proper order, or add incidents you may have left out. Then, jot down thoughts you had along the way for each incident in the overall event. Use the chart to list each incident and the thoughts you had. Add rows if the event involved more than three incidents.

Incidents (First to Last)	What I Was Thinking at This Point
1.	
2.	
3.	

Now, based on your notes, write a personal narrative about a time you used logic, or reasoning, to solve a problem.

Name _____ Date _____

from **Steinbeck: A Life in Letters**
from **Travels With Charley** by John Steinbeck
Writing About the Big Question

 Is truth the same for everyone?

Big Question Vocabulary

bias	confirm	contradict	doubtful	evidence
factual	fantasy	illogical	investigate	objective
observation	opinion	persuade	prove	theory

A. *Use a word from the list above to complete each sentence.*

1. To have a(n) _____ view of our country, it helps to travel around and see it for yourself.

2. It is _____ that you can learn much about the American people by just reading books and newspapers.

3. John enjoys traveling, so it takes little effort to _____ him to take a long drive.

4. As John travels, he makes one interesting _____ after another.

B. *Follow the directions in responding to each of the items below. Answer in complete sentences.*

1. List two observations that a visitor might make about the area where you live. Use at least two of the Big Question vocabulary words.

   _____

   _____

2. For one of those observations, name two details that would confirm it.

   _____

   _____

C. *In* Travels with Charley, *Steinbeck tours the country to refresh his memory about what Americans are really like. Complete the sentence below. Then, write a short paragraph in which you connect your idea to the Big Question.*

   The objective truth about Americans is _____.

   _____

   _____

   _____

   _____

from **Steinbeck: A Life in Letters**
from **Travels With Charley** by John Steinbeck

Reading: Evaluate Whether the Author Achieves His or Her Purpose

The **author's purpose** is the reason he or she has for writing. A purpose might be to persuade readers, to entertain readers, or to provide information to readers. Keep in mind that sometimes an author may try to achieve more than one purpose. One of your jobs as a reader is to **evaluate whether an author achieves his or her purpose(s).** You must ask yourself if the author has included sufficient support to persuade you of an idea or a position, to entertain you, or to teach you about something. With that question in mind, read these sentences from the first paragraph of the Steinbeck excerpt, which conveys Steinbeck's purpose: to inform himself and his reader about the landscape and people of America.

> I had not heard the speech of America, smelled the grass and trees and sewage, seen its hills and water, its color and quality of light. I knew the changes only from books and newspapers. But more than this, I had not felt the country for twenty-five years. In short, I was writing of something I did not know about, and it seems to me that in a so-called writer this is criminal.

Think about what Steinbeck has to do in the rest of the piece for you to conclude that, becoming informed about his country, he has in turn informed his readers and, therefore, achieved his general purpose.

A. DIRECTIONS: *Read each of the following passages, and tell in what way it helps Steinbeck support the thoughts quoted above and accomplish his general purpose—informing himself and you about the America through which he travels.*

1. "It is some years since I have been alone, nameless, friendless, without any of the safety one gets from family, friends, and accomplices. There is no reality in the danger. It's just a very lonely, helpless feeling at first—a kind of desolate feeling. For this reason I took one companion on my journey—an old French gentleman poodle known as Charley."

   _____

   _____

2. "She was hungry to talk, frantic to talk, about her relatives, her friends, and how she wasn't used to this. For she was not a native and she didn't rightly belong here. Her native clime was a land of milk and honey and had its share of apes and ivory and peacocks. Her voice rattled on as though she was terrified of the silence that would settle when I was gone. As she talked it came to me that she was afraid of this place and, further, that so was I."

   _____

   _____

from **Steinbeck: A Life in Letters**
from **Travels With Charley** by John Steinbeck
Literary Analysis: Author's Style

You express yourself through the clothes you wear, the hairstyle you prefer, and the activities in which you participate. All of these things reflect your individual style. **Style** also refers to the way authors express themselves in their writing. It is the stamp that gives their writing its unique character. Among other things, an author's style is characterized by his or her tone, the way in which the writer views a particular subject. Writers also produce their style by their choice of words and sentence structure.

A. DIRECTIONS: *Complete the chart by providing for each numbered item at least three examples from* Travels With Charley *that reflect Steinbeck's style.*

Author's Style	
1. Word Choice: Mostly, the vocabulary of an educated person, but lots of informal, conversational words and phrases, including unusual, homey modifiers	**Examples:**
2. Sentence Length and Rhythm: A lot of mature sentences, but once in a while short, conversational -sounding sentences pop up to give the piece an informal feel	**Examples:**
3. Tone: Personal, modest, open	**Examples:**

B. DIRECTIONS: *In no more than three sentences, state what you think Steinbeck's style is in this excerpt from* Travels With Charley.

_____

_____

Name _____   Date _____

from **Steinbeck: A Life in Letters**
from **Travels With Charley** by John Steinbeck
Vocabulary Builder

Word List

celestial   concise   desolate   foreboding

impaired   inexplicable   omens   rigorous

A. DIRECTIONS: *From the following alphabetized lists, select one synonym and one antonym for each of the numbered words in the table below. Write your choices in the appropriate boxes.*

Synonyms

deserted

difficult

dread

foreshadowings

heavenly

pithy

unexplainable

weakened

Antonyms

comprehensible

confidence

crowded

earthbound

easy

flashbacks

redundant

strengthened

Vocabulary Word	Synonym	Antonym
1. impaired		
2. rigorous		
3. inexplicable		
4. celestial		
5. concise		
6. desolate		
7. foreboding		
8. omens		

B. WORD STUDY: The Latin root *-sol-* means "alone." Explain your answers to the following questions using one of these words containing *-sol-*: *soloist, solitary, sole.*

1. What do the other orchestra members do when a *soloist* performs?

_____

2. If a person takes *sole* responsibility for painting a room, how many helpers does he or she have?

_____

3. If a prisoner is put into *solitary* confinement, how many others are in the cell?

_____

"The American Dream" by Martin Luther King, Jr.
Writing About the Big Question

 Is truth the same for everyone?

Big Question Vocabulary

bias	confirm	contradict	doubtful	evidence
factual	fantasy	illogical	investigate	objective
observation	opinion	persuade	prove	theory

A. *Use a word or words from the list above to complete each sentence.*

1. The American dream does not allow for _____ against any one group.

2. Slavery and segregation _____ the principles on which this country was founded.

3. You could use an _____ about jet travel to _____ that the world has become a single neighborhood.

4. We should not have to _____ people to care about one another— they should just do it naturally.

B. *Follow the directions in responding to each of the items below. Answer in complete sentences.*

1. List two facts that prove the point that the world is one big neighborhood now.

_____

_____

2. Name one positive result of our being one big neighborhood, and name one negative result.

_____

_____

C. *In "The American Dream," Martin Luther King, Jr., quotes from the Declaration of Independence that "all men are created equal." Write a short paragraph in which you answer the question below.*

How true is "all men are created equal" in America today?

_____

_____

_____

Name _____ Date _____

"The American Dream" by Martin Luther King, Jr.
Reading: Evaluate Whether the Author Achieves His or Her Purpose

The **author's purpose** is the reason he or she has for writing. A purpose might be to persuade readers, to entertain readers, or to provide information to readers. Keep in mind that sometimes an author may try to achieve more than one purpose. One of your jobs as a reader is to **evaluate whether an author achieves his or her purpose(s).** You must ask yourself if the author has included sufficient support to persuade you of an idea or a position, to entertain you, or to teach you about something. With that question in mind, read the opening of "The American Dream," which conveys King's purpose: to persuade you to accept his argument.

> America is essentially a dream, a dream as yet unfulfilled. It is a dream of a land where men of all races, of all nationalities and of all creeds can live together as brothers.

Think about what King has to do in the rest of the piece for you to conclude that he has persuaded you of his opening remark and, therefore, has achieved his general purpose.

A. DIRECTIONS: *Read each passage, and tell in what way it helps support King's opening statement and accomplish his purpose—persuading you to agree with him.*

1. On the one hand, we have proudly professed the principles of democracy, and on the other hand, we have sadly practiced the very antithesis of those principles. Indeed, slavery and segregation have been strange paradoxes in a nation founded on the principle that all men are created equal.

   _____

   _____

2. The hour is late; the clock of destiny is ticking out. It is trite, but urgently true, that if America is to remain a first-class nation she can no longer have second-class citizens. Now, more than ever before, America is challenged to bring her noble dream into reality, and those who are working to implement the American dream are the true saviors of democracy.

   _____

   _____

3. Through our scientific genius, we have made of this world a neighborhood; now, through our moral and spiritual development, we must make of it a brotherhood. In a real sense, we must all learn to live together as brothers, or we will all perish as fools.

   _____

   _____

Name _____ Date _____

"**The American Dream**" by Martin Luther King, Jr.
Literary Analysis: Author's Style

You express yourself through the clothes you wear, the hairstyle you prefer, and the activities in which you participate. All of these things reflect your individual style. **Style** also refers to the way authors express themselves in their writing. It is the stamp that gives their writing its unique character. Among other things, an author's style is characterized by his or her tone, the way in which the writer views a particular subject. Writers also produce their style by their choice of words and sentence structure.

A. DIRECTIONS: *Complete the chart by providing for each numbered item at least three examples from "The American Dream" that reflect King's style.*

King's Style	
1. Word Choice: Many formal, sophisticated words and phrases	Examples:
2. Sentence Length and Rhythm: Repetition in short sentences; some long, complicated but smooth, even sentences	Examples:
3. Tone: Mostly serious, urgent, authoritative, preaching	Examples:

B. DIRECTIONS: *In no more than three sentences, state what you think King's style is in "The American Dream."*

_____

_____

_____

_____

"The American Dream" by Martin Luther King, Jr.
Vocabulary Builder

Word List

antithesis   devoid   exploitation   paradoxes   perish   unequivocal

A. DIRECTIONS: *From the following alphabetized lists, select one synonym and one antonym for each of the numbered words in the table below. Write your choices in the appropriate boxes.*

Synonyms	Antonyms
abuse	agreements
contradictions	doubtful
die	filled
lacking	flourish
opposite	respect
sure	same

Vocabulary Word	Synonym	Antonym
1. antithesis		
2. paradoxes		
3. unequivocal		
4. exploitation		
5. devoid		
6. perish		

B. WORD STUDY: The Latin root *-equi-* means "equal." Revise each sentence so that the underlined word containing the root *-equi-* is used logically. Be sure not to change the underlined word.

1. Because our homes are <u>equidistant</u> from the park, it will take you longer to get there.

_____

2. The <u>equilateral</u> triangle has two six-inch sides and one four-inch side.

_____

3. After dividing the money <u>equitably</u>, Dave had twice as much as Susan.

_____

from **Steinbeck: A Life in Letters**
from **Travels with Charley** by John Steinbeck
"The American Dream" by Martin Luther King, Jr.
Integrated Language Skills: Grammar

Reflexive Pronouns

A reflexive pronoun ends in *-self* or *-selves* and indicates that someone or something performs an action to, for, or upon itself. A reflexive pronoun points back to a noun or pronoun stated or implied earlier in the sentence.

He told *himself* to remember his algebra book. [points back to *He*]

Jacob wrote a poem about *himself.* [points back to *Jacob*]

My father said, "You should be generous to *yourself.*" [points back to *You*]

My father said, "Be generous to *yourself.*" [points back to an unstated *you*]

A reflexive pronoun is formed by adding the suffix *-self* or *-selves* to a personal pronoun.

my + self = myself	her + self = herself
our + selves = ourselves	him + self = himself
your + self = yourself	it + self = itself
your + selves = yourselves	them + selves = themselves

A. PRACTICE: *Write a reflexive pronoun on the line in each sentence below. Be sure that the pronoun is appropriate for the noun or pronoun to which it refers.*

1. Joanna forced _____ to eat the dried beets.

2. Jack and his friends wrote a play about _____.

3. My uncle put a note to _____ next to the phone to remember to call the doctor.

4. The dog barked _____ hoarse.

5. My teacher said, "Have confidence in _____."

6. Herbert hurt _____ climbing the barbed wire fence.

7. We wanted to try solving the problem by _____.

8. Janet repeated the lines to _____.

B. Writing Application: *Use each of the following reflexive pronouns in a complete sentence.*

1. myself _____

2. herself _____

3. ourselves _____

4. itself _____

5. yourself _____

from **Steinbeck: A Life in Letters**
from **Travels With Charley** by John Steinbeck
"The American Dream" by Martin Luther King, Jr.

Integrated Language Skills: Support for Writing an Observation Journal Entry

Notes for an observation journal entry about a favorite place that you have visited and remember well

What I remember: _____	
Details about it	
Anecdotes involving it	
First impressions	
How you feel about it now	

Notes for an observation journal entry about an aspect of today's society that needs improvement

Problem: _____	
Details about it	
Anecdotes involving it	
Examples of it	
Solution: _____	
Actions spurred by it	
Changes in attitude toward it over time	

"The Finish of Patsy Barnes" by Paul Laurence Dunbar
"The Drummer Boy of Shiloh" by Ray Bradbury

Writing About the Big Question
Is truth the same for everyone?

Big Question Vocabulary

bias	confirm	contradict	doubtful	evidence
factual	fantasy	illogical	investigate	objective
observation	opinion	persuade	prove	theory

A. *Use a word or words from the list above to complete each sentence.*

1. What is your _____ about whether a fourteen-year-old should be allowed to ride a race horse?

2. I think it is _____ that a young rider would have the necessary strength and skill to win.

3. _____ reports about the Civil War indicate that some drummer boys were only ten years old.

4. Historical records can _____ that many young drummer boys were killed on the battlefield.

B. *Follow the directions in responding to each of the items below. Answer in complete sentences.*

1. List two truths about growing up that you can confirm by your own experience.

_____

_____

2. Write two sentences in which you give advice to a younger person about growing up. Use at least two of the Big Question vocabulary words.

_____

_____

_____

C. *These stories involve two boys who have to assume serious adult responsibilities. Complete the sentence below. Then, write a paragraph in which you elaborate on your answer.*

When a child is forced to grow up too soon, he or she may later regret it because

_____

_____

_____

_____

"The Finish of Patsy Barnes" by Paul Laurence Dunbar
"The Drummer Boy of Shiloh" by Ray Bradbury
Literary Analysis: Comparing Characters of Different Eras

A **character** is a person who takes part in the action of a literary work.

- A *dynamic character* develops and learns because of events in the story.
- A *static character* does not change. Static characters are often used by writers to develop conflict. These characters are not usually the central characters in a story.

Just as in real life, characters in fiction are affected by the **settings** in which they live. The forces that shape characters can include their jobs, living conditions, and major historical events. When a major historical event—such as a war or an economic downturn—occurs in a story, it can force characters to make difficult decisions for their own survival. Both "The Finish of Patsy Barnes" and "The Drummer Boy of Shiloh" present boys who live through challenging times. In one story, a recent move and a sudden illness have a devastating impact on a poor family. In the other, a war threatens to change the life of a soldier forever.

DIRECTIONS: *Answer the questions about the characters in these stories.*

1. Describe Patsy at the beginning of "The Finish of Patsy Barnes."

   _____

   _____

2. What is life like for Eliza and Patsy Barnes in Dalesford?

   _____

   _____

3. What does Patsy accomplish by the end of the story?

   _____

4. How does Patsy develop and change through events in the story?

   _____

   _____

5. Describe Joby, the drummer boy, at the beginning of "The Drummer Boy of Shiloh."

   _____

   _____

6. What does Joby think of his drum at the beginning of the story?

   _____

7. What causes the general to notice Joby as he walks by?

   _____

8. How has Joby—and his feelings about the drum—changed by the end of the story?

   _____

Name _____ Date _____

"The Finish of Patsy Barnes" by Paul Laurence Dunbar
"The Drummer Boy of Shiloh" by Ray Bradbury
Vocabulary Builder

Word List

> compulsory   diplomatic   immortality   legitimately   meager   resolute

A. DIRECTIONS: *Answer each question, and then explain your answer.*

1. Would a person be able to live extravagantly on a *meager* income?

   _____

2. If Sarah is *resolute* in her decision, is it likely that she will change her mind?

   _____

3. If chorus practice is *compulsory*, would the music teacher let students not attend?

   _____

4. Would a business that is run *legitimately* be likely to break the law?

   _____

5. If Tim is *diplomatic* with classmates, would other students ask him to help settle arguments?

   _____

6. Would someone who believes in *immortality* be afraid of death?

   _____

B. DIRECTIONS: *Fill in the blanks using each Word List word only once.*

1. Shianne was _____ about going to law school; no one could talk her out of it.

2. Before the class trip, students must attend a _____ meeting.

3. The poor boy tried to earn money _____ rather than steal from others.

4. The college student barely survives on his _____ salary at the bookstore.

5. Julio can be very _____ when helping his coworkers resolve a problem.

6. Dan's belief in _____ makes him unafraid of death.

"The Finish of Patsy Barnes" by Paul Laurence Dunbar
"The Drummer Boy of Shiloh" by Ray Bradbury
Integrated Language Skills: Support for Writing to Compare Characters

Before you write an essay that compares and contrasts the characters of Patsy Barnes and Joby, use the graphic organizer below to list ideas about each character.

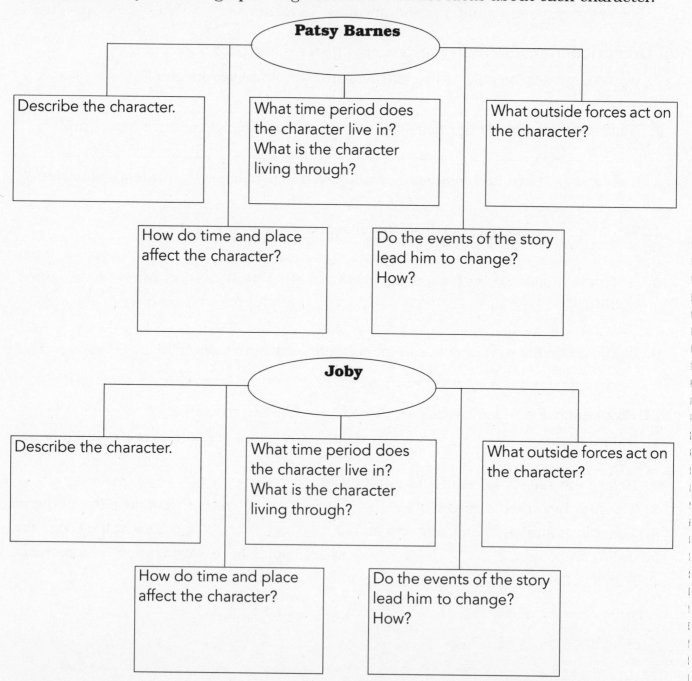

Now, use your notes to write an essay that compares and contrasts Patsy Barnes and Joby.

BQ Tunes

But Can We? performed by Fake Gimms

We find ourselves locked in a **stalemate**

You won't budge - can't work out a **compromise**

An **argument**, can't see eye to eye

A **viewpoint** I can't see

Let's work out a **solution**

But can we?

There's no need, no need for **violence**

Avoiding harm and **injury**

No need to bug and **irritate**

An **argument**, can't see eye to eye

A **viewpoint** I can't see

Let's work out a **solution**

But can we?

Interact, let's work it out face to face

React, speak out,

Lies only **mislead**

An **argument**, can't see eye to eye

But don't **Oppose** me

Let's **negotiate** a **solution**

But can we?

We will be **victorous** when we both win

insecurity plays on our fears

Negotiate a solution

But can we?

Song Title: **But Can We?**

Artist / Performed by Fake Gimms

Vocals & Guitar: Joe Pfeiffer

Bass Guitar: Jared Duncan

Drums: Tom Morra

Lyrics by Joe Pfeiffer

Music composed by the Fake Gimms

Produced by Mike Pandolfo, Wonderful

Unit 2: Short Stories
Big Question Vocabulary—1
The Big Question: Can all conflicts be resolved?

Thematic Vocabulary

argument: *n.* a disagreement, often involving anger; other forms: *argue, arguing, argumentative*

compromise: *n.* a solution in which people agree to accept less than what they originally wanted; other forms: *compromised, compromising*

irritate: *v.* to make someone feel annoyed or impatient; other forms: *irritation, irritated, irritating*

oppose: *v.* to be against or to disagree; other forms: *opposition, opposing, opponent*

viewpoint: *n.* a person's way of thinking about a subject or issue

DIRECTIONS: *Answer the questions using the number of vocabulary words specified. You can use words more than once, but you must use all five Thematic Vocabulary words. You might use the "other forms" of the words, as shown above.*

Rosa and Ellen shared a bedroom at home. Their mother suggested that they repaint the walls, make new curtains, and rearrange the furniture. At first, the sisters were excited about the project. However, their differences of opinion soon brought a conflict.

"I hate the color pink!" Rosa stormed. "Why do we *always* have to do what *you* want?"

1. How might Ellen have responded? Use at least 2 vocabulary words in your answer.

_____

_____

Their older sister Paula heard them speaking angrily to each other. She tried to help.

2. What might Paula have said? Use at least 1 vocabulary word in your answer.

_____

_____

Paula got out a pencil and paper. She took notes as Rosa and Ellen each spoke about how she would like their room to look. Then, she made a suggestion.

3. What did she suggest? Use at least 2 vocabulary words in your answer.

_____

_____

Rosa wasn't totally satisfied, but at least Ellen had listened to some of her ideas.

4. How did the girls resolve their conflict? Use at least 1 vocabulary word in your answer.

_____

_____

Unit 2: Short Stories
Big Question Vocabulary—2

The Big Question: Can all conflicts be resolved?

Thematic Vocabulary

injury: *n.* damage caused by an accident or attack; other forms: *injured, injuring, injuries*

insecurity: *n.* the feeling of being unconfident or unsafe; other forms: *insecure, insecurities*

interact: *v.* to talk or work together; other forms: *interaction, interacting, interacted*

mislead: *v.* to lead in the wrong direction or give false information; other forms: *misled, misleading*

solution: *n.* a way of solving a problem or dealing with a difficult situation; other form: *solve*

A. DIRECTIONS: *On each line, write the Thematic Vocabulary word that best completes the sentence.*

1. Jane's _____ and nervousness before the play caused her to forget her lines.

2. Will the suspect tell the truth, or will he attempt to _____ the detective?

3. The football player had to leave the game due to an unfortunate _____.

4. At the press conference, the president will _____ with members of the news media.

5. A fair compromise is often the best _____ to a conflict.

B. DIRECTIONS: *Write the Thematic Vocabulary word that best completes each group of related words.*

1. communicate, cooperate, _____

2. pain, wound, _____

3. anxiousness, uncertainty, _____

4. answer, resolution, _____

5. deceive, trick, _____

Unit 2: Short Stories
Big Question Vocabulary—3

 The Big Question: Can all conflicts be resolved?

Thematic Vocabulary

negotiate: *v.* to discuss, with the goal of settling a conflict; other form: *negotiation*

reaction: *n.* a response to a statement, event, or situation; other forms: *react, reacting*

stalemate: *n.* a standstill in a conflict, in which neither side can get an advantage

victorious: *adj.* triumphant; on the winning side; other forms: *victor, victory*

violence: *n.* behavior that is intended to cause someone physical harm; other form: *violent*

A. DIRECTIONS: *Respond to each item.*

1. Why is *violence* a poor way to try to solve a conflict? _____
_____

2. What would you do if you reached a *stalemate* while trying to solve a disagreement?
_____

3. Give an example of a situation in which someone might feel *victorious*. _____
_____

4. What skills are important for someone to have in order to *negotiate* successfully?
_____

5. Someone disagrees with you. Give an example of a constructive *reaction* you might express.
_____

B. DIRECTIONS: *Imagine that you are a police officer. On your way home, you see two young boys having a fistfight. You try to help them solve their conflict peacefully. Write a dialogue that takes place between you and the two boys. Use all five Thematic Vocabulary words.*

_____

_____

_____

_____

Name _____ Date _____

Unit 2: Short Stories
Applying the Big Question

 Can all conflicts be resolved?

DIRECTIONS: *Complete the chart below to apply what you have learned about how and if conflicts are resolved. One row has been completed for you.*

Example	Type of Conflict	Opposing forces	Aids/ obstacles to resolution	Outcome	What I learned
From Literature	Charlie's struggle to be normal in "Flowers for Algernon"	Mental disability vs. science	Aid: surgery increases intelligence Obstacle: limits of science and technology	Charlie is still mentally disabled.	Some con-flicts cannot be resolved.
From Literature					
From Science					
From Social Studies					
From Real Life					

Judith Ortiz Cofer
Listening and Viewing

Segment 1: Meet Judith Ortiz Cofer
- As a young child, what did Judith Ortiz Cofer learn about the power of storytelling? In what ways do you see stories as being powerful?

_____

_____

_____

_____

Segment 2: The Short Story
- What truth is revealed in a humorous manner in Judith Ortiz Cofer's short story? What do the themes she discusses in the story reveal about the importance of our elders?

_____

_____

_____

_____

Segment 3: The Writing Process
- What is Judith Ortiz Cofer's writing routine? Why do you think it is important for a writer to establish a routine?

_____

_____

_____

_____

Segment 4: The Rewards of Writing
- What is the goal of Judith Ortiz Cofer's writing? What have you learned about yourself from reading literature?

_____

_____

_____

_____

Learning About Short Stories

A **short story** is a brief work of fiction that contains many of these elements:

Conflict: a struggle between opposing forces In an **external conflict,** a character struggles against an outside force. An **internal conflict** takes place in the mind of a character.
Plot: the sequence of events in the story **Exposition** introduces the characters and setting. The **rising action** introduces the conflict and increases its intensity. The **climax** is the turning point of a story. The **falling action** is the part of the story when the conflict lessens in intensity. The **resolution** is the story's conclusion.
Setting: the time and place of the action in a story **Mood** is the emotional atmosphere that the setting sometimes conveys.
Characters: the people or other beings in a story **Character traits** are a character's qualities and attitudes. **Characterization** is the way the author reveals a character's traits. The author may state traits **directly** ("Ross is strong") or reveal traits **indirectly** by showing what the character says, thinks, and does.
Theme: the central message expressed in a story A theme may be **directly stated** by the author or **implied,** suggested indirectly through what happens to the characters.
Point of View: the perspective from which a story told **First-person point of view** a character in the story tells the story. **Third-person point of view** a narrator outside the story tells the story.
Literary Devices: tools that writers use to enhance their writing **Foreshadowing** uses clues early in the story to hint at future events. A **flashback** interrupts the story to reveal past events. **Irony** is a contradiction between appearance and reality, between expectation and outcome, or between meaning and intention.

A. DIRECTIONS: *For each story detail, circle the letter of the term that best identifies it.*

1. Tom struggles to reach a decision.
   A. external conflict   B. internal conflict   C. mood

2. "Jo is a greedy girl."
   A. direct characterization   B. indirect characterization   C. plot

3. A storm gets worse and worse.
   A. rising action   B. falling action   C. foreshadowing

4. "Kindness is often rewarded."
   A. irony   B. point of view   C. theme

5. "And they all lived happily after."
   A. exposition   B. climax   C. resolution

B. DIRECTIONS: *On a separate sheet of paper, briefly describe the setting, characters, conflict, and theme of a story or fairy tale that you know well.*

"An Hour with Abuelo" by Judith Ortiz Cofer
Model Selection: Short Story

Plot is the sequence of events in a story. The sequence usually unfolds in **chronological order,** the order of time. However, sometimes there is a **flashback** to an earlier time. Flashbacks can provide insight into a character's personality **traits,** or qualities, and **motivation,** the reasons behind the character's behavior.

The events of the plot usually center around one or more **conflicts,** or struggles, that the main character faces. Sometimes the conflict is **external,** pitting the character against an outside force. Sometimes the conflict is **internal,** taking place in the character's mind.

The story's conclusion is the **resolution,** in which the conflict is settled and the outcome is revealed. Sometimes the resolution is a **surprise ending** that the characters or readers do not expect. Surprise endings and other unexpected twists in the plot create **irony,** a contrast between what seems true and what turns out to be the real truth.

The perspective from which a story is told is called the **point of view**. In the **first-person point of view,** the story is told by a character in the story. In the **third-person point of view,** the story is told by a narrator outside the story. An **omniscient** narrator knows everything that each character thinks and feels. A third-person narrator also might be **limited** and only reveal the thoughts and feelings of a single character.

DIRECTIONS: *Answer these questions about "An Hour with Abuelo."*

1. What **internal conflict** does young Arturo have about visiting his grandfather?

   _____

   _____

2. Describe young Arturo's **traits** and **motivation** in life. What does he dislike about the attitude expressed in the Spanish saying *"Así es la vida,"* or "That's the way life is"?

   _____

   _____

   _____

3. In what way does Abuelo's autobiography *Así Es la Vida* serve as a **flashback**? From whose **point of view** is it told, and what does it help you understand about this character?

   _____

   _____

   _____

4. Explain the **irony** in Abuelo's behavior at the story's end. What did Arturo expect about his grandfather, and how did what he expected turn out not to be true?

   _____

   _____

   _____

"Who Can Replace a Man?" by Brian Aldiss
Writing About the Big Question

 Can all conflicts be resolved?

Big Question Vocabulary

argument	compromise	injury	insecurity	interact
irritate	mislead	negotiate	oppose	reaction
solution	stalemate	victorious	viewpoint	violence

A. *Use a word from the list above to complete each sentence.*

1. Humans can avoid personal _____ in certain types of conflicts by using robots.

2. Robots can be programmed to _____ with one another to get jobs done.

3. To solve disagreements, people can _____, with each side giving a little to the other.

4. One _____ to the problem of boring jobs is to have robots do them.

B. *Follow the directions in responding to each of the items below. Answer in complete sentences.*

1. Describe two times when you had a conflict involving a machine. The conflict could be with another person or inside yourself.

   _____

   _____

2. Explain how you found a solution to one of those conflicts. Use at least two Big Question vocabulary words.

   _____

   _____

C. *In "Who Can Replace a Man?" machines in a futuristic world start to fight because they don't know what to do when their human masters disappear. Complete the sentence below. Then, explain how your answer connects to the Big Question.*

When people are not sure what to do, they often _____

_____

_____

_____

"Who Can Replace a Man?" by Brian Aldiss
Reading: Ask Questions to Compare and Contrast

A **comparison** tells how two or more things are alike. A **contrast** tells how two or more things are different. **Asking questions to compare and contrast** helps you notice any similarities and differences in characters, settings, moods, and ideas. When you consider the similarities and differences in a work, you enrich your understanding of it.

Readers of "Who Can Replace a Man?" can tell right away that the character working in the field is not human. When the author refers to the character as "it," readers begin to look for clues as to what this character is, asking questions such as these:

- What does it look like?
- How does it move?
- How does it think?
- Are there any others like it?

As you read and discover more about the machines in the story, you can compare and contrast them with humans.

DIRECTIONS: *Answer the questions by using details given about the machines in the story and facts you know about humans.*

1. What do the machines look like? _____

   _____

   A. How are they similar to humans in appearance? _____

   _____

   B. How are they different? _____

   _____

2. How do the machines communicate with one another? _____

   _____

   A. How is their communication similar to that of humans? _____

   _____

   B. How is it different? _____

   _____

3. What kind of work do the machines do? _____

   _____

   A. How is their work similar to the work of humans? _____

   _____

   B. How is it different? _____

   _____

"Who Can Replace a Man?" by Brian Aldiss
Literary Analysis: Setting

The **setting** is the time and place of a story's action. A setting can create an emotional atmosphere, or *mood.* It also can give readers the sensation of living in a different time and place. As you read, notice details that make up the setting, including

- the customs and beliefs of the characters,
- the physical features of the land,
- the weather or season of the year, and
- the historical era in which the action takes place.

These details help readers not only picture the setting but also understand it better. For example, "Who Can Replace a Man?" takes place in a future time when machines operate at varying levels of independence. The setting changes as the machines act on information that man is extinct. In addition, readers learn about other places that exist in this Earth of the future.

A. DIRECTIONS: *Use the chart to list details you learn about the story's settings.*

Farm in the Country	City	Badlands

B. DIRECTIONS: *Write two or three sentences in which you compare and contrast the farm, where the story begins, and the Badlands, where it ends.*

_____

_____

_____

_____

_____

"Who Can Replace a Man?" by Brian Aldiss
Vocabulary Builder

Word List

debris   deficiency   distinction   erosion   ravaged   respectively

A. DIRECTIONS: *On the line, write the letter of the word whose meaning is closest to that of the word from the Word List.*

____ 1. respectively
   A. orderly   C. gratefully
   B. randomly   D. urgently

____ 2. debris
   A. neatness   C. wreckage
   B. dirt   D. building

____ 3. ravaged
   A. ruined   C. hungry
   B. repaired   D. tired

____ 4. deficiency
   A. abundance   C. defiance
   B. lack   D. satisfaction

____ 5. distinction
   A. similarity   C. closeness
   B. distance   D. difference

____ 6. erosion
   A. devastation   C. formation
   B. production   D. usefulness

B. WORD STUDY   The Latin prefix *de-* means "away" or "from." Answer each of the following questions using one of these words containing *de-*: *debate, decrease, decode.*

1. How can having a *debate* help people avoid having a physical battle?

_____

2. How would a *decrease* in strength affect your ability to run fast?

_____

3. How does the ability to *decode* unfamiliar words help you understand what you read?

_____

Name _____ Date _____

"Tears of Autumn" by Yoshiko Uchida
Writing About the Big Question

 Can all conflicts be resolved?

Big Question Vocabulary

argument	compromise	injury	insecurity	interact
irritate	mislead	negotiate	oppose	reaction
solution	stalemate	victorious	viewpoint	violence

A. *Use a word from the list above to complete each sentence.*

1. In some cultures, families _____ terms for arranged marriages.

2. A matchmaker should not _____ a family about a young man's qualities.

3. If any family members _____ the arranged marriage, it might not take place.

4. A good _____ against an arranged marriage is that love might be lacking.

B. *Follow the directions in responding to each of the items below. Answer in complete sentences.*

1. Write two sentences about a time when you had an inner conflict concerning a big change in your life.

_____

_____

2. In one or two sentences, explain how you resolved this inner conflict. Use at least two of the Big Question vocabulary words.

_____

_____

C. *Complete the sentence below. Then, write a short paragraph in which you discuss the pros and cons of making big changes.*

Making a big change in one's life can cause conflicts because _____

_____

_____

_____

_____

Name _____ Date _____

"Tears of Autumn" by Yoshiko Uchida

Reading: Ask Questions to Compare and Contrast

A **comparison** tells how two or more things are alike. A **contrast** tells how two or more things are different. **Asking questions to compare and contrast** helps you notice similarities and differences in characters, settings, moods, and ideas. When you consider similarities and differences in a work, you enrich your understanding of it.

To compare and contrast characters in "Tears of Autumn," ask these questions:

• What do readers know about Hana's three older sisters?
• How does Hana feel about following the paths of her sisters?
• What do readers know about Taro's life in America? About Taro as a person?

A. DIRECTIONS: *As you read the story, record details you learn about Hana, Hana's sisters, and Taro.*

Hana	Hana's Sisters	Taro

B. DIRECTIONS: *Write two or three sentences in which you compare and contrast Hana, Hana's sisters, and Taro. Use details from the chart.*

_____

_____

_____

"Tears of Autumn" by Yoshiko Uchida
Literary Analysis: Setting

The **setting** is the time and place of a story's action. A setting can create an emotional atmosphere, or *mood*. It also can give readers the sensation of living in a different time and place. As you read, notice details that make up the setting, such as

- the customs and beliefs of the characters,
- the physical features of the land,
- the weather or season of the year, and
- the historical era in which the action takes place.

These details help readers not only picture the setting but also understand it better. For example, "Tears of Autumn" takes place in the past, probably in the early twentieth century. There are three settings: Japan; the Japanese American community of San Francisco, California; and aboard a ship traveling between the two places.

A. DIRECTIONS: *Use the chart to list details you learn about the story's settings.*

Japan	Ship	Japanese American Community

B. DIRECTIONS: *Write two or three sentences in which you compare and contrast the three settings.*

_____

_____

_____

_____

_____

"Tears of Autumn" by Yoshiko Uchida
Vocabulary Builder

Word List

affluence   degrading   radical   recoiled   relentless   turbulent

A. DIRECTIONS: *For each sentence, think about the meaning of the underlined word. Then, answer the question.*

1. Why might someone want more <u>affluence</u> rather than less?

   _____

   _____

2. Why might some people find washing dishes in a restaurant <u>degrading</u>?

   _____

   _____

3. How might a change in the presidency from one political party to another be considered <u>radical</u>?

   _____

   _____

4. Why might a pilot be reluctant to fly in <u>turbulent</u> weather?

   _____

   _____

5. What would explain why a man <u>recoiled</u> at the sight of a rattlesnake?

   _____

   _____

6. Why might a child be <u>relentless</u> in his requests for a new toy?

   _____

   _____

B. WORD STUDY The Latin prefix *de-* means "down." Explain your answers to the following questions using one of these words containing *de-*: *despise, destruction, devalued.*

1. If you *despise* the actions of another person, how do you feel about them?

   _____

2. If you agree to the *destruction* of an old building, do you want it to stay as it is?

   _____

3. If the money of a country is suddenly *devalued*, can you buy more with it?

   _____

Name _____ Date _____

"Who Can Replace a Man?" by Brian Aldiss
"Tears of Autumn" by Yoshiko Uchida

Integrated Language Skills: Grammar

Action and Linking Verbs

An **action verb** expresses physical or mental action.

Action: The man <u>shook</u> his head. The man <u>will say</u> "no."

A **linking verb** expresses a state of being. It links the subject of a sentence with a word or words that rename or describe the subject. Common linking verbs are forms of *be: be, am, is, are, was, were, has been, have been, is being, was being,* and so on.

Linking: His voice <u>was</u> loud and grating. He <u>is being</u> silly.

Other linking verbs are *seem, stay, become, turn, feel, taste, appear, remain, grow, look, sound, smell.* Some of these words also can function as action verbs. To determine whether a verb is an action verb or a linking verb, try replacing it with a form of *to be.* If the sentence still makes sense, the verb is a linking verb.

The car <u>turned</u> the corner. [*The car was the corner* makes no sense: Action Verb.]

The sky <u>turned</u> dark before the storm. [*The sky was dark* makes sense: Linking Verb.]

A. PRACTICE: *Read each sentence, and circle the verb or verb phrase. Then, on the line before the sentence, write* AV *if the verb or verb phrase is an action verb or* LV *if it is a linking verb.*

____ 1. The moon has been full for the past three nights.

____ 2. Our team played in the finals of the city softball tournament.

____ 3. Louisa is the captain of our softball team.

____ 4. The crowd's cheers sounded like a freight train approaching.

____ 5. Alan sounded the bell.

____ 6. Randy stared in wonder at the butterfly and the cocoon.

____ 7. Caterpillars are often beautiful themselves.

____ 8. Dana will become a famous ballerina.

____ 9. Lisle walked quickly home from school.

____10. We will eat lunch at twelve o'clock sharp.

B. Writing Application: *On the lines provided, write sentences in which you use and underline verbs as directed.*

1. a form of *look* as an action verb: _____

_____

2. a form of *look* as a linking verb: _____

_____

3. an action verb of your choice: _____

_____

All-in-One Workbook
© Pearson Education, Inc. All rights reserved.
75

"**Who Can Replace a Man?**" by Brian Aldiss
"**Tears of Autumn**" by Yoshiko Uchida

Integrated Language Skills: Support for Writing a Description

When you **write a description,** it is important to include specific details that help the reader imagine what you are describing. If you are describing a place, details should tell what the place looks like, who lives there, and what the inhabitants do there. If you are describing a person, details should tell about his or her personality, interests, appearance, and reactions.

To prepare for writing a description of your city or town as it might appear at the end of the twenty-first century, consider details about the town as it exists today. Then, imagine ways in which these details might change over the next hundred years. Use the chart to record your ideas.

Category	Detail Today	Detail in 100 Years
Land		
Buildings		
People		
Occupations		
Setting		
Technology		

Now, draft a description of the city or town 100 years in the future.

"Hamadi" by Naomi Shihab Nye

Writing About the Big Question

Can all conflicts be resolved?

Big Question Vocabulary

argument	compromise	injury	insecurity	interact
irritate	mislead	negotiate	oppose	reaction
solution	stalemate	victorious	viewpoint	violence

A. *Use one or more words from the list above to complete each sentence.*

1. Unable to come to a verdict, the jurors told the judge they were at a

   _____.

2. The trial involved a man who had caused a serious _____ to another man.

3. It was unclear which man had let the verbal _____ turn into physical _____.

4. The judge's _____ to the jury's statement was to declare a mistrial.

B. *Follow the directions in responding to each of the items below. Answer in complete sentences.*

1. Write two sentences about a conflict you had concerning a holiday celebration. Use at least two of the Big Question vocabulary words.

   _____

   _____

2. How did you solve the conflict? Explain your solution in two sentences.

   _____

   _____

C. *Complete the sentence below. Then, write a short paragraph in which you state and explain some wise advice to apply to emotional conflict.*

Resolving emotional conflicts can be difficult because _____

_____

_____

_____

_____

"Hamadi" by Naomi Shihab Nye
Reading: Compare and Contrast

When you **compare and contrast characters,** you look for similarities and differences among the people in a story. One strategy for comparing is to **identify each character's perspective**—that is, to consider the way each person understands the world.

- As you read, note details about the main character.
- To compare, consider whether the main character's actions, emotions, and ideas are similar to or different from those of other characters.
- Finally, decide whether you can trust what the character says and does.

One of the main ways readers understand the characters' perspectives in "Hamadi" is by looking closely at the characters' reactions to the same person, topic, or event. Notice the very different reactions to Hamadi in these passages:

Susan's father: "Riddles. He talks in riddles. I don't know why I have patience with him."

Susan: "He says interesting things. He makes me think."

DIRECTIONS: *Answer the following questions. Think about each character's perspective on the topic.*

Topic: staying in touch with friends and relatives

1. How does Susan's father stay in touch with his relatives in the Middle East?

_____

2. How does Hamadi keep in touch with his relatives in the Middle East?

_____

3. How does Susan keep in touch with her friend Hamadi?

_____

Topic: the caroling outing

4. How does Susan's father react when she invites Hamadi to go caroling?

_____

_____

5. How does Hamadi react to the invitation?

_____

_____

6. Why does Susan want to invite Hamadi to carol?

_____

_____

"**Hamadi**" by Naomi Shihab Nye
Literary Analysis: Character Traits

Character traits are the personal qualities, attitudes, and values that make a character unique. For example, one character may be joyless, while another finds pleasure in everything.

- *Round characters* are complex, showing many different character traits.
- In contrast, *flat characters* are one-dimensional, showing just a single trait.

Writers sometimes state character traits directly, but more often they reveal them through details such as a character's actions, appearance, speech, and the reactions of others to the character. In "Hamadi," readers learn about Saleh Hamadi in all these ways. For example, this passage from the story reveals that Hamadi observes closely and enjoys language.

Hamadi liked to use Spanish words. They made him feel expansive, worldly. He'd learned them when he worked at the fruits and vegetables warehouse on Zarzamora Street, marking off crates of apples and avocados on a long white pad.

A. DIRECTIONS: *On the chart below, list at least three details the author gives about Saleh Hamadi and what trait each detail reveals.*

Detail	Trait Revealed

B. DIRECTIONS: *Choose two of the details you recorded about Hamadi. Write a few sentences describing him.*

_____

_____

_____

_____

"**Hamadi**" by Naomi Shihab Nye
Vocabulary Builder

Word List

expansive   melancholy   obscure   refugee   surrogate   tedious

A. DIRECTIONS: *Mark each statement below with T for true or F for false. Then, explain your answers.*

_____ 1. One would expect a *refugee* to have made a personal choice to live away from his or her homeland.

_____

_____

_____ 2. If a good friend moved to another state, you would probably be *melancholy*.

_____

_____ 3. Most people look forward to *tedious* tasks.

_____

_____

_____ 4. A person who is feeling *expansive* would probably donate generously to charity.

_____

_____ 5. Zoos sometimes provide *surrogate* mothers to orphaned baby animals.

_____

_____

_____ 6. An *obscure* fact is one that most people know.

_____

B. WORD STUDY: The suffix *-ee* refers to someone who receives an action or has been put in a certain position. Revise each sentence so that the underlined word containing the prefix *-ee* is used logically. Be sure not to change the underlined word.

1. The *absentee* list included the names of all those who were present at the meeting.

_____

_____

2. The *payee* wrote a check to pay the bill.

_____

_____

3. The *employee* benefits apply only to those who do not work here.

_____

_____

"The Tell-Tale Heart" by Edgar Allan Poe
Writing About the Big Question

Can all conflicts be resolved?

Big Question Vocabulary

argument	compromise	injury	insecurity	interact
irritate	mislead	negotiate	oppose	reaction
solution	stalemate	victorious	viewpoint	violence

A. *Use a word from the list above to complete each sentence.*

1. Sometimes, another person's bad habits can really _____ someone else.

2. Someone's bad habit might cause a serious _____ with a roommate.

3. From my _____, you should try to control bad habits that annoy others.

4. Some bad habits, like nail-biting, suggest that a person suffers from _____.

B. *Follow the directions in responding to each of the items below. Answer in complete sentences.*

1. Describe two things other people do that you find really irritating.

_____

_____

2. In two sentences, explain how you handle one of those situations when it occurs. Use at least two of the Big Question vocabulary words.

_____

_____

C. *Complete the sentence below. Then, write a short paragraph in which you give advice to a person torn between doing right and wrong.*

When torn between doing right and wrong, a person may _____

_____

_____

_____

Name _____ Date _____

"**The Tell-Tale Heart**" by Edgar Allan Poe
Reading: Compare and Contrast

When you **compare and contrast characters,** you look for similarities and differences among the people in a story. One strategy for comparing is to **identify each character's perspective**—that is, to consider the way a person understands the world.

- As you read, note details about the main character.
- To compare, consider whether the main character's actions, emotions, and ideas are similar to or different from those of other characters.
- Finally, decide whether you can trust what the character says and does.

One of the main ways readers understand the characters' perspectives in "The Tell-Tale Heart" is by looking closely at the characters' reactions to the same person, topic, or event. In this story, readers get most of their information about the old man's reactions from the narrator's point of view. Notice the different reactions to the story's events in the following passages.

> The old man (from the narrator's point of view): "Presently I heard a slight groan, and I knew it was the groan of mortal terror. It was not a groan of pain or of grief—oh, no!—it was the low stifled sound that arises from the bottom of the soul when overcharged with awe."

> The narrator: "I knew what the old man felt, and pitied him, although I chuckled at heart."

DIRECTIONS: *Answer the following questions. Think about each character's perspective on the events of the night.*

1. How does the narrator describe his feelings and actions as he looks in on the old man sleeping each night?

   _____

2. How does the old man react on the eighth night when he hears a noise at the door?

   _____

3. How does the narrator feel when he sees the old man's eye in the ray of light? What does the narrator hear?

   _____

   _____

4. What has the old man been doing and feeling during the hour after hearing the noise?

   _____

   _____

5. How does the old man react when the narrator leaps into his room?

   _____

6. How does the narrator describe his feelings after killing the old man?

   _____

"The Tell-Tale Heart" by Edgar Allan Poe
Literary Analysis: Character Traits

Character traits are the personal qualities, attitudes, and values that make a character unique. For example, one character may be joyless, while another finds pleasure in everything.

- *Round characters* are complex, showing many different character traits.
- In contrast, *flat characters* are one-dimensional, showing just a single trait.

Writers sometimes state character traits directly, but more often they reveal them through details such as a character's actions, thoughts, appearance, speech, and the reactions of others to the character. In "The Tell-Tale Heart," readers learn about the narrator through his own description of his thoughts and feelings. For example, this passage from the story reveals that the narrator sees himself as both nervous and calm. He defends his health and sanity, yet refers to things that suggest insanity.

> True!—nervous—very, very dreadfully nervous I had been and am; but why *will* you say that I am mad? The disease had sharpened my senses—not destroyed—not dulled them. Above all was the sense of hearing acute. I heard all things in the heaven and in the earth. I heard many things in hell. How, then, am I mad? Hearken! and observe how healthily—how calmly I can tell you the whole story.

A. DIRECTIONS: *On the chart below, list at least three details the author gives about the narrator and what trait each detail reveals.*

Detail	Trait Revealed

B. DIRECTIONS: *Choose two of the details you recorded about the narrator. Write a few sentences describing him.*

_____

_____

_____

_____

"The Tell-Tale Heart" by Edgar Allan Poe
Vocabulary Builder

Word List

audacity   cunningly   derision   resolved   stealthily   vex

A. DIRECTIONS: *Revise each sentence so that the underlined vocabulary word is used logically. Be sure to keep the vocabulary word in your revision.*

1. When the basketball player made the difficult shot look easy, the crowd shouted with <u>derision</u>.

   _____

   _____

2. Sheila's <u>audacity</u> showed in the way she shyly held back.

   _____

   _____

3. Simon's good behavior continued to <u>vex</u> his mother.

   _____

4. Becca never tried to complete anything she had <u>resolved</u> to do.

   _____

   _____

5. Because Armando had acted so <u>cunningly</u>, everyone knew what he was up to.

   _____

   _____

6. Cindy moved very <u>stealthily</u>, banging on a drum as she went along.

   _____

   _____

B. WORD STUDY: The suffix *-ity* indicates a noun meaning "a quality or state of being." Explain your answers to the following questions using one of these words containing the suffix *-ity*: *possibility, necessity, tranquillity.*

1. Is there a *possibility* that you could travel back in time to before you were born?

   _____

2. What kind of experience would give you a feeling of *tranquillity*?

   _____

3. Why is drinking water a *necessity* when you are taking a long hike?

   _____

   _____

Name _____ Date _____

"**Hamadi**" by Naomi Shihab Nye
"**The Tell-Tale Heart**" by Edgar Allan Poe

Integrated Language Skills: Grammar

Principal Parts of Regular Verbs

Each verb has four **principal parts,** or main forms.

Present (Base Form)	Past	Present Participle	Past Participle
gather(s)	gathered	gathering	gathered
move(s)	moved	moving	moved

- The present participle usually appears after forms of the helping verb *be.* To form the present participle, add *-ing* to the base form. If the verb ends in a consonant plus *e*, drop the *e* before adding *-ing.*

  Ruby is <u>fastening</u> the straps of her backpack.

  Jack is <u>exercising</u> great care with the delicate ship model.

- The past participle is used most often after forms of the helping verb *have.* To form the past participle of regular verbs, add *-ed* to the base form. If the verb ends in a consonant plus *e*, drop the *e* before adding *-ed.*

  No one has <u>warned</u> Eric of the approaching hurricane.

  By Saturday, she had <u>moved</u> into her new apartment.

A. PRACTICE: *Complete each sentence by providing the form of the verb indicated in parentheses.*

1. (present participle of *sell*) Firewood was _____ at forty dollars a cord.

2. (past participle of *notice*) Bart had _____ a used computer at the yard sale.

3. (present participle of *figure*) Cass was _____ out the sum without a calculator.

4. (present form of *tower*) The basketball player _____ over me.

5. (past tense of *halt*) Stanley _____ his dog team before it reached the river.

6. (present form of *search*) Fran always _____ for lost earrings.

B. Writing Application: *Write four sentences to illustrate the principal parts of* shiver. *Your sentences should be about a person who is highly sensitive to cold.*

1. _____

2. _____

3. _____

4. _____

Name _____ Date _____

"**Hamadi**" by Naomi Shihab Nye
"**The Tell-Tale Heart**" by Edgar Allan Poe

Integrated Language Skills: Support for Writing a Character Profile

To prepare for **writing a character profile** of either Saleh Hamadi or the narrator in "The Tell-Tale Heart," use the chart and gather specific details about his personality. Think about Hamadi's choice of lifestyle, the things he says to Susan, and his reaction to Tracy's unhappiness while they are caroling. Alternatively, recall how the narrator describes his relationship with the old man and his reasons for deciding to kill him. Then, think about the various emotions the narrator experiences and describes— nervousness, anxiety, happiness, anger—as he carries out his plan and, finally, confronts the police officers.

Character Trait	How the Trait Affects Plot and Resolution

"**Up the Slide**" by Jack London
"**A Glow in the Dark**" *from* **Woodsong** by Gary Paulsen

Writing About the Big Question

Can all conflicts be resolved?

Big Question Vocabulary

argument	compromise	injury	insecurity	interact
irritate	mislead	negotiate	oppose	reaction
solution	stalemate	victorious	viewpoint	violence

A. *Use a word from the list above to complete each sentence.*

1. For a _____ end to a dangerous situation, you need to be very careful.

2. If a man wants $40 for something and you offer $20, he might _____ at $30.

3. Sled dogs must _____ well as they follow their lead dog.

4. A sudden _____ by a group of sled dogs might indicate danger.

B. *Follow the directions in responding to each of the items below. Answer in complete sentences.*

1. In two sentences, describe your reaction if you realized you were lost in an unfamiliar and icy environment.

   _____

   _____

2. Write two sentences explaining why you would or would not like to work with a sled-dog team in a race. Use at least two of the Big Question vocabulary words.

   _____

   _____

C. *In both of these narrations, an individual struggles against his four of natural dangers. Complete the sentence below. Then, write a short paragraph in which you connect this sentence to the Big Question.*

Nature's beauty can mislead. It often hides dangers for those who _____

_____

_____

_____

_____

"Up the Slide" by Jack London
"A Glow in the Dark" *from* Woodsong by Gary Paulsen
Literary Analysis: Fictional and Nonfictional Narratives

A **narrative** is any type of writing that tells a story. In a **fictional narrative,** the author tells a story about imaginary characters and events. "Up the Slide" is a fictional narrative. Because it does not describe real events, the author had complete control over the basic story elements of *character, setting,* and *plot.*

In a **nonfictional narrative,** such as "A Glow in the Dark," the author tells a story about real characters and events. The author of this work describes an event that actually happened to him. Although he cannot alter any of the details, he does emphasize some of them to give the story a kind of excitement.

DIRECTIONS: *Read each passage, and answer the questions that follow.*

from "Up the Slide" by Jack London

For, coming up from the Siwash village the previous day, he [Clay] had noticed a small dead pine in an out-of-the-way place, which had defied discovery by eyes less sharp than his. And his eyes were both young and sharp, for his seventeenth birthday was just cleared.

A swift ten minutes over the ice brought him to the place, and figuring ten minutes to get the tree and ten minutes to return made him certain that Swanson's dinner would not wait.

Just below Dawson, and rising out of the Yukon itself, towered the great Moosehide Mountain, so named by Lieutenant Schwatka long ere the Yukon became famous.

1. Which elements of this fictional narrative did the author make up? Identify two.

   _____

2. Which details did the author borrow from real life? Identify two. _____

   _____

from "A Glow in the Dark" by Gary Paulsen

They were caught in the green light, curved around my legs staring at the standing form, ears cocked and heads turned sideways while they studied it. I took another short step forward and they all followed me, then another, and they stayed with me until we were right next to the form.

It was a stump.

A six-foot-tall, old rotten stump with the bark knocked off, glowing in the dark with a bright green glow. Impossible. . . . I found out later that it glowed because it had sucked phosphorus from the ground up into the wood and held the light from day all night.

3. What detail provides a clue that this is a nonfictional narrative? _____

   _____

   What kind of detail is this? _____

4. What details give the narrative a fictional feel? Why? _____

   _____

"Up the Slide" by Jack London
"A Glow in the Dark" *from* **Woodsong** by Gary Paulsen
Vocabulary Builder

Word List

ascent   descent   diffused   exertion   maneuver   sustain

A. DIRECTIONS: *Complete each sentence in a way that proves you know the meaning of the italicized word.*

1. When we completed our *ascent,* _____
   _____

2. _____ requires great *exertion.*

3. It is difficult to *sustain* _____
   _____

4. The upward-facing lampshade *diffused* _____
   _____

5. Before our *descent,* _____
   _____

6. Using a careful *maneuver,* _____
   _____

B. DIRECTIONS: *Circle the letter of the word or phrase that is most nearly* opposite *in meaning to the word in CAPITAL LETTERS.*

1. ASCENT
   A. flight
   B. leap
   C. descent
   D. tumble

2. SUSTAIN
   A. let go
   B. strengthen
   C. reject
   D. maintain

3. DIFFUSED
   A. confused
   B. weakened
   C. diluted
   D. condensed

4. MANEUVER
   A. manipulate
   B. bumble
   C. trick
   D. stunt

"**Up the Slide**" by Jack London
"*A Glow in the Dark*" *from* **Woodsong** by Gary Paulsen
Integrated Language Skills: Support for Writing to Compare Use of Details in Narratives

Before you draft your essay comparing and contrasting the use of details in these narratives, complete the graphic organizers below. First, list details that reveal aspects of each character. Then, tell specifically what each detail reveals about the character. Finally, discuss how the details affect your view of the character and his challenges.

Clay Dilham in "Up the Slide"	
Invented Details	**What They Reveal About the Character**
How do these details affect your view of the character's challenge?	

Gary Paulsen in "A Glow in the Dark"	
True Details	**What They Reveal About the Character**
How do these details affect your view of the character's challenges?	

Now, use your notes to write an essay comparing and contrasting the use of details in the two narratives.

"Flowers for Algernon" by Daniel Keyes
Writing About the Big Question

Can all conflicts be resolved?

Big Question Vocabulary

argument	compromise	injury	insecurity	interact
irritate	mislead	negotiate	oppose	reaction
solution	stalemate	victorious	viewpoint	violence

A. *Use a word from the list above to complete each sentence.*

1. Some people interested in animal rights _____ experiments that harm animals.

2. Results of animal experiments can _____ us into thinking the same results would occur in humans.

3. Some experiments can cause a serious _____ to an animal.

4. The conflict between animal-rights activists and some scientists seems to have no good _____.

B. *Follow the directions in responding to each of the items below. Answer in complete sentences.*

1. What are two uses of animals that cause conflict in our society?

   _____

   _____

2. What is your reaction to one of these conflicts? Use at least two of the Big Question vocabulary words.

   _____

   _____

C. *Complete the sentence below. Then, write a short paragraph in which you comment on the conflicts you might feel about a friend who changes.*

When someone I know changes, it is _____

_____

_____

_____

_____

"Flowers for Algernon" by Daniel Keyes
Reading: Notice Details to Make Inferences

Making inferences means **noticing details** that an author provides and using them to make logical assumptions about the events, settings, themes, and other story elements that the author leaves unstated. Consider these details that author Daniel Keyes has Charlie tell us:

> I had a test today. I think I faled it. and I think that maybe now they wont use me. What happind is a nice young man was in the room and he had some white cards with ink spilled all over them. He sed Charlie what do you see on this card. I was very skared even tho I had my rabits foot in my pockit because when I was a kid I always faled tests in school and I spilled ink to.

From these details, you might make the following inferences:

- Charlie is no longer of school age.
- Charlie has a learning disability, so he had a hard time when he was in school.
- Charlie is superstitious.
- Charlie very much wants to pass a test and be used in an experiment.

DIRECTIONS: *In the chart below, the left column gives quotations from the story. Each quotation provides several details. From each group of details, make at least one inference, and list it on the right.*

Details	Inferences
1. They said how come you went to the adult nite scool all by yourself Charlie. How did you find it. I said I askd pepul and sumbody told me where I shud go to lern to read and spell good.	
2. Their really my friends and they like me. Sometimes somebody will say hey look at Joe or Frank or George he really pulled a Charlie Gordon. I dont know why they say that but they always laff.	
3. Dr. Nemur wanted to publish the results of the experiment at the end of this month. Dr. Strauss wanted to wait a while longer to be sure. Dr. Strauss said that Dr. Nemur was more interested in the Chair of Psychology at Princeton than he was in the experiment.	

"Flowers for Algernon" by Daniel Keyes
Literary Analysis: Point of View

Point of view is the perspective from which a story is told. In a story told from the **first-person point of view,** the narrator is a character in the story and refers to himself or herself with first-person pronouns like *I* and *me.* In a story told from the **third-person point of view,** the narrator stands outside the story and refers to all the characters with third-person pronouns like *he, she,* and *they.* A first-person narrator can tell only what he or she sees, hears, knows, thinks, or feels. "Flowers for Algernon" is told from the first-person point of view of its main character, Charlie Gordon, who gives his account in a series of progress reports.

A. DIRECTIONS: *On the lines provided, answer these questions about the story.*

1. Briefly explain the narrator's situation at the start of "Flowers for Algernon" by telling how old he is and how he is different from other people his age.

   _____

   _____

   _____

2. What role do vocabulary and spelling have in showing the changes that take place in the narrator as the story unfolds?

   _____

   _____

   _____

3. Why do you think the author, Keyes, has the narrator, Charlie, tell his story in spaced-out progress reports instead of telling the whole story on a single day in May or in July?

   _____

   _____

   _____

B. DIRECTIONS: *Choose a short progress report or a dated section of a longer report, and then rewrite it from the first-person point of view of Dr. Strauss, Miss Kinnian, or another character. Use a separate sheet of paper, if necessary.*

   _____

   _____

   _____

   _____

   _____

"Flowers for Algernon" by Daniel Keyes
Vocabulary Builder

Word List

deceive   deterioration   intellectual   introspective   naiveté   refute

A. DIRECTIONS: *Answer each question with a sentence that uses one of the Word List words. Each answer must correctly reflect the details in "Flowers for Algernon."*

1. Do Dr. Strauss's experiments prove that an operation can permanently improve intelligence?

_____

_____

2. As the experiment progresses from March through April, does Charlie think less?

_____

_____

3. Are Dr. Nemur and Dr. Strauss trying to fool Charlie by misrepresenting their own intelligence levels?

_____

_____

4. In what way do Charlie's co-workers at the factory take advantage of his simplicity and innocence?

_____

_____

5. What is one example proving that Charlie's level of mental awareness has exceeded those of his doctors?

_____

_____

6. What is the first sign that Algernon's condition is becoming worse?

_____

_____

B. WORD STUDY The Latin root -*spec*- means "to look." Answer the following questions using one of these words containing -*spec*-: *spectator, inspect, respect.*

1. What might you see in a person that would make you *respect* him or her?

_____

2. Why might a detective use a magnifying glass to *inspect* a crime scene?

_____

3. When might a *spectator* use binoculars at a sporting event?

_____

"Charles" by Shirley Jackson
Writing About the Big Question

Can all conflicts be resolved?

Big Question Vocabulary

argument	compromise	injury	insecurity	interact
irritate	mislead	negotiate	oppose	reaction
solution	stalemate	victorious	viewpoint	violence

A. *Use a word from the list above to complete each sentence.*

1. Children often experience a sense of _____ about starting kindergarten.

2. They may find it frightening to _____ with so many new people at once.

3. A normal _____ to this stress is to put on a show of bravado.

4. If this show of bravado becomes too extreme, it can _____ other people.

B. *Follow the directions in responding to each of the items below. Answer in complete sentences.*

1. Describe a conflict you once felt that was related to school. Use at least two of the Big Question vocabulary words.

_____

_____

2. Write two sentences explaining how you dealt with the conflict.

_____

_____

C. *Complete the sentence below. Then, write a short paragraph in which you suggest how a person can handle the inner conflicts that new situations sometimes create.*

Adjusting to new situations is _____

_____

_____

_____

_____

"Charles" by Shirley Jackson
Reading: Notice Details to Make Inferences

Making inferences means **noticing details** that an author provides and using them to make logical assumptions about the events, settings, themes, and other story elements that the author leaves unstated. Consider these details that Shirley Jackson provides about Laurie:

> The day my son Laurie started kindergarten he renounced corduroy overalls with bibs and began wearing blue jeans with a belt; I watched him go off the first morning with the older girl next door, seeing clearly that an era of my life was ended, my sweet-voiced nursery-school tot replaced by a long-trousered, swaggering character who forgot to stop at the corner and wave good-bye to me.

From these details, you might make the following inferences:

- Before starting kindergarten, Laurie was a fairly sheltered and well-behaved child.
- Laurie grows less polite and more self-important, perhaps to mask his nervousness about starting kindergarten.
- Laurie is a strong-willed child able to insist on his own way.
- Laurie's mother feels some regret as she recognizes that her son is growing up.

DIRECTIONS: *In the chart below, the left column gives quotations from the story. Each quotation provides several details. From each group of details, make at least one inference, and list it on the right.*

Details	Inferences
1. He came home the same way, the front door slamming open, his cap on the floor, and the voice suddenly become raucous shouting, "Isn't anybody *here*?"	
2. The third day—it was Wednesday of the first week—Charles bounced a see-saw on the head of a little girl and made her bleed, and the teacher made him stay inside during recess. Thursday Charles had to stand in a corner during story-time because he kept pounding his feet on the floor.	
3. "You know what Charles did today?" Laurie demanded at the lunch table, in a voice slightly awed. "He told a little girl to say a word and she said it and the teacher washed her mouth out with soap and Charles laughed."	

"Charles" by Shirley Jackson
Literary Analysis: Point of View

Point of view is the perspective from which a story is told. In a story told from the **first-person point of view,** the narrator is a character in the story who refers to himself or herself with first-person pronouns like *I* and *me*. In a story told from the **third-person point of view,** the narrator stands outside the story and refers to all the characters with third-person pronouns like *he, she,* and *they*. A first-person narrator can tell only what he or she sees, hears, knows, thinks, or feels. "Charles" is told from the first-person point of view of Laurie's mother.

A. DIRECTIONS: *On the lines provided, answer these questions about the story.*

1. Briefly explain the narrator's situation at the start of "Charles" by telling how she feels about Laurie's going off to school.

   _____

   _____

   _____

2. Would you say the narrator has a sense of humor? Support your answer with details.

   _____

   _____

   _____

3. How does using this particular narrator help create a surprise ending?

   _____

   _____

   _____

B. DIRECTIONS: *Choose one incident that the narrator reports, and retell it from the first-person point of view of Laurie or Laurie's teacher. Use a separate sheet of paper, if necessary.*

   _____

   _____

   _____

   _____

   _____

   _____

   _____

Name _____ Date _____

Word List

cynically   deprived   haggard   insolently   renounced   simultaneously

A. DIRECTIONS: *Answer each question with a sentence that uses one of the Word List words. Each answer must correctly reflect the details in "Charles."*

1. At Laurie's school, do parents go one by one at different times to meet with teachers?

   _____

2. At the end of the story, what does Laurie's teacher report about Laurie's behavior in school?

   _____

3. Why are Charles's blackboard privileges taken away, according to Laurie?

   _____

4. Why does Laurie's mother expect Charles's mother to look worn out?

   _____

5. When Laurie's father hears that Charles has been behaving well, why does he respond with disbelief?

   _____

6. What evidence does Laurie offer to show that Charles behaves disrespectfully toward the teacher?

   _____

B. WORD STUDY: The Latin root *-nounc-/-nunc-* means "report." Answer each of the following questions using one of these words containing this root: *pronunciation, announcer, denounce.*

1. What types of messages would a sports *announcer* be delivering during a game?

   _____

2. For what types of activities might the people *denounce* their political leaders?

   _____

3. What message do you convey to speakers of a foreign language when your *pronunciation* of that language is excellent?

   _____

"Flowers for Algernon" by Daniel Keyes
"Charles" by Shirley Jackson

Integrated Language Skills: Grammar

The Present, Past, and Future Tenses

A **verb tense** tells when the action or condition takes place.

- The **present tense** shows an action or a state of being that occurs regularly.
  These inferences **seem** logical.
  Good readers usually **understand** an author's inferences.

- The **past tense** shows actions that have already happened. Regular verbs form the
  past tense by adding *-ed* or *-d.*
  Yesterday, the story **seemed** a lot more difficult to read.

- The **future tense** shows actions that are going to happen. The future tense is usually formed with the helping verb *will.*
  The lesson **will seem** clearer after you practice the skill.

A. PRACTICE: *On the line after each sentence, identify the underlined verb as present, past, or future. Then, rewrite the sentence in the other two tenses.*

1. The scientists <u>use</u> mice in their experiments. _____

   _____

   _____

2. Some children <u>will behave</u> badly on the first day of school. _____

   _____

   _____

3. He <u>visited</u> a psychologist twice a week. _____

   _____

   _____

B. Writing Application: *Write three sentences about a school subject or field of study that interests you. One sentence should use the past tense, one should use the present tense, and one should use the future tense. Underline the verbs, and label the verb tenses.*

_____

_____

_____

_____

_____

_____

"Flowers for Algernon" by Daniel Keyes
"Charles" by Shirley Jackson

Integrated Language Skills: Support for Writing Dialogue

The dialogue for a movie scene adapted from either "Flowers for Algernon" or "Charles" can start with actual dialogue given in the stories. On the blank lines, write notes for expanding the scene with dialogue that you can imagine. Alternatively, on another sheet of paper, prepare notes for expanding a script that starts with a conversation from elsewhere in one of the stories.

[*Scene: after-dinner conversation between Miss Kinnian and Charlie*]

MISS KINNIAN: I won't go much higher than I am now, but you'll keep climbing up and up, and see more and more, and each step will open new worlds that you never even knew existed. I hope . . . I just hope to God—

CHARLIE: What?

MISS KINNIAN: Never mind, Charles. I just hope I wasn't wrong to advise you to go into this in the first place.

CHARLIE: How could that be? It worked, didn't it? Even Algernon is still smart.

_____

_____

_____

[*Scene: lunchtime after Laurie's first day of kindergarten*]

MOTHER: How *was* school today?

LAURIE: All right.

FATHER: Did you learn anything?

LAURIE: I didn't learn nothing.

MOTHER: Anything. Didn't learn anything.

LAURIE: The teacher spanked a boy, though. For being fresh.

MOTHER: What did he do? Who was it?

LAURIE: It was Charles. He was fresh. The teacher spanked him and made him stand in a corner. He was awfully fresh.

MOTHER: What did he do?

_____

_____

_____

_____

_____

Now, convert your notes into actual dialogue.

Name _____ Date _____

Writing About the Big Question

 Can all conflicts be resolved?

Big Question Vocabulary

argument	compromise	injury	insecurity	interact
irritate	mislead	negotiate	oppose	reaction
solution	stalemate	victorious	viewpoint	violence

A. *Use one or more words from the list above to complete each sentence.*

1. Using _____ is usually the worst way to deal with a problem.

2. When two people cannot agree, they might have a loud _____ about the topic.

3. People who know how to _____ can often find a _____ to a problem.

4. You show respect to someone else when you listen to his or her _____ even though you disagree.

B. *Follow the directions in responding to each of the items below. Answer in complete sentences.*

1. Write two sentences about a person you trust completely. Tell why you trust him or her.

   _____

   _____

2. Suppose a conflict between you and another person hurt your relationship. How might you fix it? Use at least two of the Big Question vocabulary words.

   _____

   _____

C. *Complete the sentence below. Then, write a short paragraph describing a time when you were successful in earning someone's trust.*

The best way to earn trust is _____

   _____

   _____

   _____

   _____

"Thank You, M'am" by Langston Hughes

Reading: Identify the Connections to Make Inferences

An **inference** is a logical assumption that you make about something the writer suggests but does not directly state. You often make inferences by **identifying the connections** between story events and outcomes or between characters' behavior and backgrounds, personalities, or other reasons for the behavior. For example, in "Thank You, M'am," if you connect the detail about the boy's background to his snatching the purse, you can infer that the boy may misbehave because of lack of attention at home.

A young boy snatches a purse.	+	He has a dirty face and no one at home to wash it.	=	The boy misbehaves because of lack of attention at home.

DIRECTIONS: *For each numbered item, connect the two details in order to make the requested inference about a character's behavior or about the outcome of events.*

1. Mrs. Jones lifts Roger by the shirtfront and demands the return of her purse.	+	Roger returns the purse.	=	*Make an inference about why Roger returns the purse:* _____ _____
2. Roger says he has no one at home to wash his face.	+	Mrs. Jones says it will get washed this evening.	=	*Make an inference about how Roger's face will get washed:* _____ _____
3. Roger does not appear to be eating well.	+	Roger snatched the purse to buy blue suede shoes.	=	*Make an inference about the kind of person Roger is:* _____ _____
4. Mrs. Jones leaves her purse out in the open when she prepares food for herself and Roger.	+	Roger sits far away from the purse and does not want to be mistrusted.	=	*Make an inference about how Mrs. Jones has changed Roger's behavior:* _____ _____

Name _____ Date _____

"Thank You, M'am" by Langston Hughes
Literary Analysis: Theme

A **theme** is a central idea, insight, or message that a work of literature conveys. It is usually expressed as a generalization about life or people. A theme is sometimes **stated** directly in a work, either by a character or by the narrator. More often, a theme is **unstated.** That is, it is only **implied,** and you must infer the theme from details in the work.

To determine the theme, consider the experiences of the characters and the outcome of events, and think about the general message to which they point. For example, in a story about a young dancer who practices and practices until she finally lands a starring role in a movie musical, the theme might be "Hard work pays off in the end."

DIRECTIONS: *Create word webs listing details about the story's characters, settings, and events. Then, answer the questions below the word webs.*

_____   Roger **Characters** Mrs. Jones   _____
_____   _____
_____   _____

_____   street/ neigh- borhood **Settings** Mrs. Jones's apartment   _____
_____   _____
_____   _____

_____   purse snatching **Events** taking Roger home   _____
_____   _____
_____   _____

1. Based on the details you listed above, what aspect of life do you think the author is asking you to think about when you read this story? _____

_____

_____

2. Based on the details you listed above, what does the story seem to be saying about that aspect of life? _____

_____

_____

"Thank You, M'am" by Langston Hughes
Vocabulary Builder

Word List

barren   contact   frail   mistrusted   presentable   slung

A. DIRECTIONS: *Write a full-sentence answer using each Word List word only once.*

1. Do people comb their hair in order to look neat enough to be seen?

   _____

   _____

2. Is the frozen sheet of ice near the South Pole an empty part of the world?

   _____

   _____

3. Can you use e-mail to stay in communication with friends who move away?

   _____

   _____

4. What kind of weather would prompt you to take off your jacket and wear it just thrown over your shoulder?

   _____

   _____

5. If you doubted whether it was safe to be friendly to a strange dog, what would you do?

   _____

   _____

6. What is one way a person with weak muscles could improve his or her strength?

   _____

   _____

B. WORD STUDY: The prefix *mis-* means "opposite" or "badly, wrongly." Answer the following questions using one of these words containing the prefix *mis-*: *misrepresent, mislead, misuse.*

1. What is one example of how an ad might *mislead* a potential customer?

   _____

2. What is one way a politician might *misrepresent* himself or herself to the voters?

   _____

3. How might a beginner *misuse* headphones?

   _____

"The Storyteller" by Saki (H. H. Munro)
Writing About the Big Question

 Can all conflicts be resolved?

Big Question Vocabulary

argument	compromise	injury	insecurity	interact
irritate	mislead	negotiate	oppose	reaction
solution	stalemate	victorious	viewpoint	violence

A. *Use one or more words from the list above to complete each sentence.*

1. In most children's stories, good is _____ over evil.

2. The audience's _____ to the shocking story was a loud gasp.

3. There is little _____ over the idea that _____ in children's stories is best avoided.

4. In some children's stories, human characters _____ with talking animals.

B. *Follow the directions in responding to each of the items below. Answer in complete sentences.*

1. Describe a conflict in one of your favorite children's stories.

   _____

   _____

2. Why might a parent have inner conflict about allowing a child to view violence on TV? Use at least two of the Big Question vocabulary words.

   _____

   _____

C. *Complete the sentence below. Then, write a short paragraph in which you comment on the types of conflict commonly found in fairy tales.*

The endings of fairy tales are _____

_____

_____

_____

Name _____   Date _____

"The Story-Teller" by Saki (H. H. Munro)

Reading: Identify Connections to Make Inferences

An **inference** is a logical assumption that you make about something the writer suggests but does not directly state. You often make inferences by **identifying the connections** between story events and outcomes or between characters' behavior and backgrounds, personalities, or other reasons for the behavior. For example, "The Story-Teller" opens with three children cooped up in a hot railway carriage along with their aunt and a bachelor who is a stranger to them. A few sentences later, you read that most of the aunt's remarks seem to begin with "Don't." By connecting these details, you can infer that the children are restless and that the aunt is having trouble controlling them.

| Three children are cooped up in a hot railway carriage. | + | Most of the aunt's remarks begin with "Don't." | = | The children are restless and the aunt is having trouble controlling them. |

DIRECTIONS: *For each numbered item, connect the two details in order to make the requested inference about a character's behavior or the outcome of events.*

| 1. Cyril is smacking the seat cushions of the railway carriage. | + | The aunt invites Cyril to look out the window. | = | *Make an inference about why the aunt tells Cyril to look out the window:* _____ _____ |

| 2. Cyril asks questions about what he sees. | + | Cyril is not satisfied with the aunt's answers and asks more questions. | = | *Make an inference about the kind of boy Cyril is:* _____ _____ |

| 3. The smaller sister recites one line of a poem over and over. | + | The bachelor looks twice at the aunt and once at the train's communication cord. | = | *Make an inference about why the bachelor looks at the aunt and the cord:* _____ _____ |

| 4. The bachelor tells a story about a good little girl who is eaten by a wolf because of her goodness. | + | The children enjoy the story. | = | *Make an inference about why the children enjoy the story:* _____ _____ |

"The Story-Teller" by Saki (H. H. Munro)
Literary Analysis: Theme

A **theme** is a central idea, insight, or message that a work of literature conveys. It is usually expressed as a generalization about life or people. A theme is sometimes **stated** directly in a work, either by a character or by the narrator. More often, a theme is **unstated.** That is, it is only **implied,** and you must infer the theme from details in the work.

To determine the theme, consider the experiences of the characters and the outcome of events, and think about the general message to which they point. For example, in a story about a jewel thief who risks breaking his neck by scaling a building to steal a bracelet that turns out to be fake, the theme might be "Crime does not pay."

DIRECTIONS: *Create word webs about the story that the bachelor tells the children. Then, answer the questions below the word webs.*

1. Based on the details you listed above, what sort of human behavior do you think the bachelor wants listeners to think about when they hear his story? _____

_____

_____

2. Based on the details you listed above, what does the story seem to be saying about the benefits and drawbacks of that kind of behavior?

_____

_____

_____

"**The Story-Teller**" by Saki (H. H. Munro)
Vocabulary Builder

Word List

assail   conviction   immensely   inevitable   persistent   suppressed

A. DIRECTIONS: *Write a full-sentence answer that uses each Word List word only once.*

1. How should you speak about a strong belief that you want others to share?

   _____

   _____

2. If you refuse to give up your habit of saving half your allowance for a year, what will be the result?

   _____

   _____

3. How would you react if your young cousin were to attack you with demands for interesting stories every time you met?

   _____

   _____

4. Describe a school event that is certain to happen sometime in the next week.

   _____

   _____

5. What is one accomplishment of yours that makes you feel extremely proud?

   _____

   _____

6. Describe one situation in which you thought it best to hold back your laughter.

   _____

   _____

B. WORD STUDY: The prefix *per-* means "thoroughly" or "throughout." Revise each sentence so that the underlined word containing the prefix *per-* is used logically. Be sure not to change the underlined word.

1. These plants are <u>perennials</u>, so they will definitely die after one season.

   _____

2. The color red is barely <u>perceptible</u> against a yellow background.

   _____

3. Charlotte's <u>perfect</u> performance was filled with mistakes.

   _____

"Thank You, M'am" by Langston Hughes
"The Story-Teller" by Saki (H. H. Munro)
Integrated Language Skills: Grammar

The Perfect Tenses and the Subjunctive Mood

A **verb tense** tells when the action or state of being takes place. A **perfect tense** describes an action or a state of being that was or will be completed at a certain time. It uses a form of the helping verb *have* and the past participle of the main verb, which in regular verbs ends in *-ed.*

- The **present perfect tense** shows a past action or condition that continues into the present. Example: The gas gauge **has indicated** an empty tank for some time now.
- The **past perfect tense** shows a past action or condition that was completed before another began. Example: Dad **had filled** the tank before we started our vacation.
- The **future perfect tense** shows a future action or condition that will have ended at a certain time. Example: By this time next week, our trip **will have ended.**

The **subjunctive mood** is used to express a wish or a condition contrary to fact, as in this example: If he *were* a dog-owner, he would understand dogs better.

A. PRACTICE: *Complete each sentence with the verb form requested in parentheses.*

1. The teacher _____ our short-answer test papers, and now we are waiting for the class bell to ring. (*collect* in the present perfect)

2. The teacher _____ an essay for us to write before she scheduled this test. (*assign* in the past perfect)

3. By five o'clock, the teacher _____ all our short-answer tests. (*reviewed* in the future perfect)

4. If our teacher _____ any faster, she would set a record. (*be* in the subjunctive mood)

B. Writing Application: *Write four sentences about your education and future plans. One sentence should use the past perfect tense, one should use the present perfect tense, one should use the future perfect tense, and one should use the subjunctive mood. Underline the verbs, and label the verb tenses.*

_____

_____

_____

_____

"Thank You, M'am" by Langston Hughes
"The Story-Teller" by Saki (H. H. Munro)

Integrated Language Skills: Support for Writing a Personal Essay

Use this sheet to do the suggested prewriting for your personal essay. At the top of the graphic, state in your own words what you believe to be the theme of the story. In the boxes below the statement of theme, note thoughts that occur to you as you brainstorm about your own past experiences that relate to this theme. You do not need to fill in all the boxes, but try to examine at least two different experiences. If you cannot think of experiences in your own past, you might consider events and reactions you have heard about through your family or in the local news.

Theme:	
Notes on Experience 1 Relating to Theme:	Notes on Experience 2 Relating to Theme:
Notes on Experience 3 Relating to Theme:	Notes on Experience 4 Relating to Theme:

Now, use your notes to draft your personal essay.

Name _____ Date _____

"The White Umbrella" by Gish Jen
"The Medicine Bag" by Virginia Driving Hawk Sneve

Writing About the Big Question

Can all conflicts be resolved?

Big Question Vocabulary

argument	compromise	injury	insecurity	interact
irritate	mislead	negotiate	oppose	reaction
solution	stalemate	victorious	viewpoint	violence

A. *Use a word from the list above to complete each sentence.*

1. A show-off can really _____ other people by the way he or she acts.

2. The student's _____ to her teacher's praise was to smile broadly.

3. Do not let another person's shabby appearance _____ you about his or her character.

4. The _____ done to the Native Americans took place in a shameful period of history.

B. *Follow the directions in responding to each of the items below. Answer in complete sentences.*

1. List two times when you had to negotiate for something you wanted.

   _____

   _____

2. For one of those times, what was the conflict between you and the person with whom you negotiated? Use at least two of the Big Question vocabulary words.

   _____

   _____

C. *Both of these stories involve characters who struggle with feelings of embarrassment. Complete the sentence below. Then, write a short paragraph in which you* connect this sentence to the Big Question.

People are most likely to react with embarrassment when they _____

_____

_____

_____

_____

_____

"The White Umbrella" by Gish Jen
"The Medicine Bag" by Virginia Driving Hawk Sneve

Literary Analysis: Comparing Symbols

A **symbol** is a person, place, or thing that represents something beyond its literal meaning. For example, a national flag is more than just a colorful rectangle of fabric—it represents a country. Similarly, doves usually symbolize peace. **Symbolism** can add meaning to a literary work. Authors can use symbols in two ways:

- Using existing cultural symbols—such as a dove or a flag—that have commonly understood meanings
- Creating their own symbols and developing their meaning through the descriptions, actions, and events of a story

Appreciating a story's symbolism helps you grasp its main message, or theme.

DIRECTIONS: *Answer the following questions about symbolism in "The White Umbrella" and "The Medicine Bag."*

1. When does the narrator of "The White Umbrella" first see the umbrella?

   _____

   _____

2. What feelings does the white umbrella provoke in the narrator early in the story?

   _____

   _____

3. What significance does the umbrella have in the development of the story?

   _____

   _____

4. At the outset of "The Medicine Bag," whom does the bag belong to? How does Martin feel about this person when he first comes to Martin's house?

   _____

   _____

5. What feelings does the medicine bag provoke in Martin early in the story?

   _____

   _____

6. What significance does the medicine bag have in the development of the story?

   _____

   _____

"The White Umbrella" by Gish Jen
"The Medicine Bag" by Virginia Driving Hawk Sneve
Vocabulary Builder

Word List

authentic   credibility   discreet   procession   revelation   unseemly

A. DIRECTIONS: *Write a complete sentence to answer each question using a Word List word in place of the underlined word.*

1. What is something you could do that would hurt your <u>believability</u>?

   _____

2. At what kind of event have you seen <u>a group moving forward together</u>?

   _____

3. What could you tell others about yourself that would be <u>something that surprises them</u>?

   _____

4. What do you own that is <u>genuine</u>, or real?

   _____

5. What is something that used to be <u>inappropriate</u> but is now considered normal?

   _____

6. In what situation should you be <u>careful about what you say or do</u>?

   _____

B. DIRECTIONS: *Circle the letter of the word or phrase that is most* opposite *in meaning to the word in CAPITAL LETTERS.*

1. UNSEEMLY
   A. improper
   B. prim
   C. sewn well
   D. secretive

2. DISCREET
   A. careless
   B. safe
   C. plain
   D. conservative

3. CREDIBILITY
   A. possibility
   B. lunacy
   C. trustworthiness
   D. improbability

4. AUTHENTIC
   A. dependable
   B. false
   C. real
   D. unfavorable

Name _____ Date _____

Integrated Language Skills:
Support for Writing to Compare Symbols

Before you write your essay that compares the symbols in "The White Umbrella" and "The Medicine Bag," use the graphic organizer below to write ideas about the symbols in each story.

Questions to Answer	"The White Umbrella"	"The Medicine Bag"
What are the main symbols used in the story?		
Does the author use any existing cultural symbols in the story? Name them.		
Do any of the symbols have cultural meanings outside of the story?		
Does the author create her own symbols?		
How does the author develop the meanings of the symbols?		
What does the change in each narrator's attitude toward the symbol tell you?		
What message do the symbols help the story convey?		
Which symbol is more effective and therefore easier for you to understand?		

Now, use your notes to help you write an essay that compares and contrasts these symbols.

Quality Over Quantity, performed by Nina Zeitlin

How much information do we need
To prevent **discrimination**?
That will lead to **inequality** amongst the people
No more unequal treatment of different people

In the world around you
Global issues, know about them
'Cause knowledge always gives some answers
Yeah knowledge always gives an **explanation**, yeah

What's **valuable** to me
When I think of what's worthy
It's hidden truth **revealed** for all to see
It's not how much you know
It's greatness that shows
That it's **quality** over **quantity**

Development and progress come from
Using the right information
Statistics are limited to
Sample numbers of the population
Sample numbers of the population, yeah

Accumulating over time
Thoughts in your brain
That form your mind
Follow the path of **exploration**
Follow down the path of **exploration**, yeah

What's **valuable** to me
What I deem worthy
Is hidden truth **revealed** for all to see
It's not how much you know
It's greatness that shows

Continued

That it's **quality** over **quantity**

La la la, la la la...

How much information do we need
To prevent **discrimination**?
No more **inequality** amongst the people
No more **inequality** amongst the people

The **decisions** that we make
The **challenges** we face
All depend on the **factors** in place
All depend on the **factors** in place

But what's **valuable** to me
When I think of what's worthy
It's hidden truth **revealed** for all to see
It's not how much you know
It's greatness that shows
That it's **quality** over **quantity**

Song Title: **Quality Over Quantity**
Artist / Performed by Nina Zeitlin
Guitar: Josh Green
Drums/Percussion: Vlad Gutkovich
Lyrics by Nina Zeitlin
Music composed by Nina Zeitlin
Produced by Mike Pandolfo, Wonderful
Executive Producer: Keith London, Defined Mind

Unit 3 Types of Nonfiction
Big Question Vocabulary—1

The Big Question: How much information is enough?

Thematic Vocabulary

accumulate: *v.* to gradually get more and more of something; other form: *accumulation*

development: *n.* the process by which someone or something grows or is built up; other forms: *develop, developing*

discrimination: *n.* the act of treating a person or group differently, in an unfair way; other forms: *discriminate, discriminating*

reveal: *v.* to uncover a secret or make something known; other forms: *revealing, revealed*

valuable: *adj.* useful, helpful, or important; other forms: *value, valued*

A. DIRECTIONS: *From the words in the box, choose the correct synonym and antonym for each Thematic Vocabulary word. You will not use every word in the box.*

hide	gather	growth	treasured	fairness	pride
prejudice	expose	deterioration	worthless	scatter	

1. accumulate   **Synonym:** _____ **Antonym:** _____

2. development   **Synonym:** _____ **Antonym:** _____

3. discrimination   **Synonym:** _____ **Antonym:** _____

4. reveal   **Synonym:** _____ **Antonym:** _____

5. valuable   **Synonym:** _____ **Antonym:** _____

B. DIRECTIONS: *Complete each sentence by writing the correct Thematic Vocabulary word on the line.*

1. The _____ of a plant begins with the sprouting of a tiny seed.

2. As a stamp collector, my goal is to _____ a large quantity of valuable stamps.

3. This beautiful portrait is _____ because it was painted by a famous artist.

4. The candidate vowed that she would rule fairly and avoid all forms of _____.

5. When will the judges _____ the identity of the new champion?

All-in-One Workbook

Unit 3 Types of Nonfiction
Big Question Vocabulary—2

The Big Question: How much information is enough?

Thematic Vocabulary

challenge: *n.* a task requiring great strength or effort; other forms: *challenged, challenging*

decision: *n.* a choice that is made after considering the options; other forms: *decide, deciding*

explanation: *n.* the act of making something clear and understandable; other forms: *explain, explaining, explained*

exploration: *n.* the study and observation of a location in order to find facts or make a discovery; other forms: *explore, exploring, explored*

inequality: *n.* an unfair situation in which some people have more money, opportunities, or power than others; other forms: *equal, equality*

A. DIRECTIONS: *Complete the passage by inserting the correct Thematic Vocabulary word on each line.*

In 1620, the Pilgrims faced the mighty (1) _____ of crossing the Atlantic Ocean in the *Mayflower,* a small wooden ship. They suffered greatly along the way, and many died. However, they had great determination. They had left home due to the (2) _____ they faced due to the unfair laws of the British king. He had thrown many Pilgrims into jail because they held religious beliefs that were different from his. Therefore, the Pilgrims' (3) _____ was firm; they would not turn back, despite the suffering. Finally, their battered ship reached the calm waters of Massachusetts Bay, and they dropped anchor. After a small group went ashore for a thorough (4) _____ of the thickly wooded land, they returned and gave the others the following (5) _____ of their settlement plans: They would build a small village, and they would name it Plymouth, after the British port city from which they had sailed.

B. DIRECTIONS: *Answer this question:* If you were President of the United States, what would you do to solve the problem of inequality? *Use as many vocabulary words as you can.*

_____

_____

_____

_____

_____

Name _____ Date _____

Unit 3 Types of Nonfiction
Big Question Vocabulary—3

The Big Question: How much information is enough?

Thematic Vocabulary

challenge: *v.* to question, oppose, or confront in order to dispute a viewpoint; other forms: *challenged, challenging*

global: *adj.* affecting or including the entire world; other forms: *globe, globally*

quality: *n.* the degree to which something is good or bad
　　　　adj. having good qualities

quantity: *n.* an amount of something that can be counted or measured; other form: *quantities*

statistics: *n.* a set of numbers that represent facts or measurements; other forms: *statistical, statistically*

Before the voyage of Christopher Columbus, many people believed that the Earth was flat. Columbus set out to prove them wrong.

A. DIRECTIONS: *Write a proposal that he might have made, trying to persuade King Ferdinand and Queen Isabella to fund his voyage. Use facts about the good qualities of your crew and stress that you will keep a log of facts and measurements throughout the voyage. Use all five Thematic Vocabulary words.*

_____

_____

_____

_____

_____

B. DIRECTIONS: *Okay, Columbus. Now answer these questions. Use the words in parentheses.*

1. Queen Isabella: Tell me, Mr. Columbus, how many ships do you need?

   Answer: (**quantity**): _____

2. King Ferdinand: People say that you'll fall off the edge of the world. What about that?

   Answer: (**challenge**): _____

3. Queen Isabella: Well, why will history ever think this voyage is important?

   Answer: (**global**): _____

Name _____ Date _____

Unit 3 Types of Nonfiction
Applying the Big Question

How much information is enough?

DIRECTIONS: *Complete the chart below to apply what you have learned about quality and quantity of information. One row has been completed for you.*

Example	Type of Information	Useful	Not Useful	What I Learned
From Literature	What Harriet Tubman told the fugitive slaves	Information about success stories	Information that she had never been to Canada	Some information is best left unsaid.
From Literature				
From Science				
From Social Studies				
From Real Life				

Andrew Mishkin
Listening and Viewing

Segment 1: Meet Andrew Mishkin
- Andrew Mishkin uses his experiences as an engineer as the basis for his writing. How does he accomplish this? In your opinion, what aspect of writing might Mishkin find most challenging?

_____

_____

_____

_____

Segment 2: Nonfiction
- Why did Mishkin decide to write a book about the project he worked on? Why was his daily essay writing important to the development of his book?

_____

_____

_____

_____

Segment 3: The Writing Process
- How does Mishkin revise his writing? Is revision important to the process of writing essays and articles? Why or why not?

_____

_____

_____

_____

Segment 4: The Rewards of Writing
- What does Mishkin hope his book conveys to readers? Do you think it is important to tell the stories behind "things of value," as Mishkin does? Why or why not?

_____

_____

_____

_____

Learning About Nonfiction

Nonfiction deals with real people, real events, real places, and ideas. A nonfiction author chooses a method of **organization**. He or she also uses a particular **tone** (his or her attitude toward the audience and the subject) and **voice** (his or her distinctive way of speaking, based on word choice, tone, sound devices, pace, and grammatical structure). This chart names and describes some common types of nonfiction writing:

Type of Nonfiction	Description and Characteristics
Letter	writing addressed to a person or organization
Memoir or journal	writing about one's life that contains thoughts and reflections
Web log (blog)	a journal posted and frequently updated online
Biography	someone's life story written by another person
Autobiography	one's own life story
Media account	writing for newspapers, magazines, television, or radio
Essay or article	a short work on a topic

A. DIRECTIONS: *Write the type of nonfiction that would be most appropriate for the item.*

_____ 1. the story of the writer's life, from childhood to the present

_____ 2. a daily online account of a writer's experiences as a restaurant chef

_____ 3. a short work meant to persuade readers to visit Australia

_____ 4. a request for information about a museum exhibit

_____ 5. a description of the causes and effects of a local fire

_____ 6. reflections on the experience of growing up on a farm

_____ 7. the story of the life of a noted jazz musician

_____ 8. a daily account of a surgeon's thoughts about his or her experiences

B. DIRECTIONS: *Read each sample of nonfiction writing. Indicate whether the author's tone is* formal *or* informal, *and give reasons for your answer.*

Over five weeks, the research team observed a variety of fossils and recorded their findings in a daily journal. The scientists used this journal as the basis for a detailed report on the area's prehistoric animal and plant life.

Tone:_____ **Explanation:** _____

"Making Tracks on Mars" by Andrew Mishkin
Model Selection: Nonfiction

Nonfiction writing is about real people, real events, real places, and ideas. Examples of nonfiction writing include letters, memoirs, journals, Web logs (or blogs), biographies, autobiographies, media accounts, essays, and articles.

Nonfiction writers choose the method of **organization** that best fits their purpose. Methods of organization include **chronological** (presenting details in time order), **comparison and contrast** (showing how subjects are similar and different), **cause and effect** (showing relationships between events), and **problem and solution** (identifying a problem, presenting a solution). The writer of a biography, for example, would most likely present his or her subject's life chronologically, ordering events from earliest to most recent. The writer of a book about a war might use cause-and-effect organization, showing how events led to one another and affected one another.

Nonfiction writers reveal their attitude toward their audience and their subject by using a particular **tone.** Their tone might be formal, informal, playful, or serious.

A. DIRECTIONS: *Answer the following questions about "Making Tracks on Mars."*

1. How do you know that the journal is organized chronologically?

   _____

2. What is the purpose of the journal's subheads?

   _____

3. Would you describe the author's tone as formal or informal? Why?

   _____

4. What major historical event does Mishkin's journal track?

   _____

5. What was Mishkin's job at the time of the events he writes about?

   _____

B. DIRECTIONS: *Andrew Mishkin posted a blog, in which he recorded the progress of the rovers* Spirit *and* Opportunity. *His online audience was able to keep track of the ups and downs of the crafts' experiences on Mars. Was the mission that Mishkin describes in "Making Tracks on Mars" successful? Cite two examples from the selection to support your opinion.*

_____

_____

_____

_____

_____

"Baseball" by Lionel G. García

Writing About the Big Question

 How much information is enough?

Big Question Vocabulary

accumulate	challenge	decision	development	discrimination
explanation	exploration	factor	global	inequality
quality	quantity	reveal	statistics	valuable

A. *Use a word from list above to complete each sentence.*

1. A(n) _____ is one kind of information.

2. Computers have made information instantly _____.

3. Information can _____ more quickly than ever.

4. Computers can lessen _____.

B. *Follow the directions in responding to each of the items below.*

1. In two sentences, describe an important decision you made and explain what made that decision so important to you.

   _____

   _____

2. What was a factor that entered into your decision? Use at least two words from the list in your answer.

   _____

   _____

   _____

C. *Complete the sentence below. Then, write a short paragraph in which you connect this answer to the Big Question. In your answer, consider the kinds of information children might need to play a game.*

Children's games should be _____

_____

_____

_____

_____

_____

_____

"Baseball" by Lionel G. García
Reading: Use Details to Identify the Main Idea

The **main idea** of a work of nonfiction is the central point that the author conveys. Sometimes the author states the main idea directly. More often, the author implies, or suggests, the main idea by giving you details to consider. To **identify the implied main idea,** connect the details that the author provides. The main idea you decide on should cover all the important details in the paragraph, section, or essay.

In "Baseball," the author describes how, as children, he and his friends made up their own rules for playing baseball. He includes details about specific rules, neighborhood observers, and particularly memorable incidents.

Ask: What does the author want me to think or discover as I read these details?

DIRECTIONS: *Read each excerpt from the selection, and summarize its details. The first one is done as an example. Then, add up all the details to identify the main idea of the selection.*

1. The way we played baseball was to rotate positions after every out. First base, the only base we used, was located where one would normally find second base. . . . Aside from the pitcher, the batter and the first baseman, we had a catcher. All the rest of us would stand in the outfield. After an out, the catcher would come up to bat. The pitcher took the position of catcher, and the first baseman moved up to be the pitcher. Those in the outfield were left to their own devices. I don't remember ever getting to bat.

   Summary of details: The players used only one base. Most played in the outfield and never got to bat.

2. First base was wherever Matías or Juan or Cota tossed a stone. They were the law. The distance could be long or short depending on how soon we thought we were going to be called in to eat.

   Summary of details: _____

3. To complicate matters, on the way to home plate the batter had the choice of running anywhere possible to avoid getting hit. . . . Many a time we would wind up . . . in front of the rectory half a block away.

   Summary of details: _____

4. One time we wound up all the way across town before we cornered Juan against a fence, held him down, and hit him with the ball. Afterwards, we all fell laughing in a pile on top of each other, exhausted from the run through town.

   Summary of details: _____

5. What a game! In what enormous stadium would it be played to allow such freedom over such an expanse of ground?

   Summary of details: _____

   Main idea of the selection: _____

"Baseball" by Lionel G. García
Literary Analysis: Narrative Essay

A **narrative essay** tells the story of real events experienced by real people in real places. Narrative essays share these features with fictional stories:

- People's traits and personalities are developed through their words, actions, and thoughts.
- The setting of the action may be an important element.

In "Baseball," Lionel G. García tells a true story about the kind of baseball he and his friends played in their neighborhood while growing up. He includes certain details about people and events during these games. The details help the reader understand the author's personality and the feelings he had about these childhood experiences.

In the essay, the author describes a particular incident in which the players chase Juan across town until they all fall into a laughing heap. These details make it clear that even though the youngsters did not belong to a formal baseball team or follow the traditional rules, they enjoyed the company of friends and playing a fast, unique version of baseball.

DIRECTIONS: *Answer the following questions. Your answers will help you identify the details that the author provides to develop his personality.*

1. Where do the baseball games take place?

   _____

   _____

2. What does the author say to describe Father Zavala's reactions to watching the games?

   _____

   _____

3. Why do you think the author played when he rarely, if ever, got to bat?

   _____

   _____

4. Why was it more interesting and fun if the fielder missed hitting the batter?

   _____

   _____

5. Based on the details the author tells about their game, how do you think the author reacted to Uncle Adolfo's negative comment?

   _____

   _____

Name _____ Date _____

"Baseball" by Lionel G. García
Vocabulary Builder

Word List

devices   evaded   ignorance   option   rotate   scheme   shiftless

A. DIRECTIONS: *Write the letter of the word or phrase that best defines each numbered word.*

____ 1. devices
    A. judgments
    B. duplicates
    C. schemes
    D. licenses

____ 2. evaded
    A. avoided
    B. controlled
    C. lacked
    D. envisioned

____ 3. ignorance
    A. more than enough
    B. knowledge
    C. avoidance
    D. lack of knowledge

____ 4. scheme
    A. plan
    B. problem
    C. mistake
    D. position

____ 5. option
    A. idea
    B. choice
    C. nickname
    D. transaction

____ 6. rotate
    A. turn
    B. rumble
    C. overcome
    D. break down

____ 7. shiftless
    A. tired
    B. foreign
    C. lazy
    D. strange

B. WORD STUDY The suffix *-ance* changes a verb or adjective into a noun that names a condition or state of being. For each sentence, write a synonym of the underlined word with the suffix *-ance*.

1. An excited puppy can cause quite a <u>disturbance</u>.

_____

2. He seems sincere, but do you think his <u>repentance</u> is genuine?

_____

3. <u>Resistance</u> is futile, so don't even dream of trying to escape.

_____

from "Harriet Tubman: Conductor on the Underground Railroad" by Ann Petry

Writing About the Big Question

How much information is enough?

Big Question Vocabulary

accumulate	challenge	decision	development	discrimination
explanation	exploration	factor	global	inequality
quality	quantity	reveal	statistics	valuable

A. *Use a word from the list above to complete each sentence.*

1. Research tells us that slaves enjoyed a lesser _____ of life than white servants did.

2. The _____ to try to escape was difficult for a slave to make.

3. There was _____ disapproval of slavery.

4. Documents show that many spoke out against _____ based on race.

B. *Follow the directions in responding to each of the items below.*

1. Explain why slavery was more common in the South than in the North. Use at least two words from the list in your explanation.

   _____

   _____

2. Do you think slavery will ever disappear completely? Use at least two words from the list in your answer.

   _____

   _____

C. *Complete the sentence below. Then, write a short paragraph in which you connect this answer to the Big Question.*

   The situation of slaves in the United States was _____

   _____

   _____

   _____

Name _____ Date _____

from **"Harriet Tubman: Conductor on the Underground Railroad"** by Ann Petry
Reading: Use Details to Identify the Main Idea

The **main idea** of a work of nonfiction is the central point that the author conveys. Sometimes the author states the main idea directly. More often, the author implies, or suggests, the main idea by giving you details to consider. To **identify the implied main idea,** connect details that the author provides. The main idea you decide upon should cover all the important details in the paragraph, section, or essay.

In "Harriet Tubman: Conductor on the Underground Railroad," the author tells how Tubman led fugitive slaves to freedom in Canada. Harriet Tubman believed strongly in the right of freedom for all. Therefore, she repeatedly risked her own freedom to gain it for others.

Ask: What does the author want me to discover about Harriet Tubman as I read the details of her efforts?

DIRECTIONS: *Read each excerpt from the selection, and summarize its details. The first one is done as an example. Then, add up all the details to identify the main idea of the selection.*

1. In December 1851, when she started out with the band of fugitives that she planned to take to Canada, she had been in the vicinity of the plantation for days, planning the trip, carefully selecting the slaves that she would take with her.

   Summary of details: Tubman planned carefully for each trip.

2. There were eleven in this party. . . . It was the largest group that she had ever conducted, but she was determined that more and more slaves should know what freedom was like.

   Summary of details: _____

3. She had never been in Canada. The route beyond Philadelphia was strange to her. But she could not let the runaways who accompanied her know this. As they walked along she told them stories of her own first flight, she kept painting vivid word pictures of what it would be like to be free.

   Summary of details: _____

4. She lifted the gun, aimed it at the despairing slave. She said, "Go on with us or die." The husky low-pitched voice was grim.

   Summary of details: _____

5. They had come to trust her implicitly, totally. They, too, had come to believe her repeated statement, "We got to go free or die." She was leading them into freedom, and so they waited until she was ready to go on.

   Summary of details: _____

   Main idea of the selection: _____

   _____

from "Harriet Tubman: Conductor on the Underground Railroad" by Ann Petry
Literary Analysis: Narrative Essay

A **narrative essay** tells the story of real events experienced by real people in real places. Narrative essays share these features with fictional stories:

- People's traits and personalities are developed through their words, actions, and thoughts.
- The setting of the action may be an important element.

In "Harriet Tubman: Conductor on the Underground Railroad," the author tells a true story about how a former slave led other slaves to freedom in the mid-1800s. The author provides details about the setting, particular events, and interactions with others. The details help the reader understand Harriet Tubman's personality, her personal strength, and her success as a leader.

DIRECTIONS: *Answer the following questions. Your answers will help you identify the details that the author provides to develop Harriet Tubman's personality.*

1. What kinds of stories does Harriet Tubman tell to the fugitives in order to build their courage?

   _____

   _____

2. What would probably happen to Tubman if she were caught?

   _____

   _____

3. What time of day does the group travel, and what is the weather like?

   _____

   _____

4. After being refused shelter, how does Tubman react?

   _____

   _____

5. Why does Tubman admire the Quaker, Thomas Garrett?

   _____

   _____

6. What does Tubman do when she and her group make it to Canada?

   _____

   _____

from **"Harriet Tubman: Conductor on the Underground Railroad"** by Ann Petry
Vocabulary Builder

Word List

bleak	disheveled	dispel	fastidious
fugitives	incentive	invariably	mutinous

A. DIRECTIONS: *Look at the underlined vocabulary word in each question. Then, answer the question.*

1. Why would <u>fugitives</u> sleep during the day and travel at night?

_____

2. What might be an <u>incentive</u> to apply for a job at a health club?

_____

3. If someone is <u>disheveled</u>, what might he or she look like?

_____

4. If a student is <u>mutinous</u>, what might he or she do?

_____

5. How would you expect a <u>fastidious</u> person's house to look?

_____

6. How might someone <u>dispel</u> a rumor?

_____

7. Why does every class <u>invariably</u> include someone who answers every question?

_____

8. Do you find a desert landscape <u>bleak</u>?

_____

B. WORD STUDY The suffix *-ly* is usually used to create adverbs that describe how, when, or how often something is done. Use what you know about the suffix *-ly* and the meaning of the base word to write whether each adverb describes how, when, or how often.

1. Why doesn't anyone take teenagers <u>seriously</u>?
2. Exercising <u>daily</u> for hours on end is not a wise idea.
3. Answering questions <u>sarcastically</u> is sure to annoy Mr. Kohn.

from "Harriet Tubman: Conductor on the Underground Railroad" by Ann Petry

"Baseball" by Lionel G. García

Integrated Language Skills: Grammar

Adjectives and Articles

An **adjective** is a word that modifies, or describes, a noun or a pronoun. Adjectives make the nouns and pronouns they modify more vivid and precise. They answer questions such as *what kind? which one? how many?* and *how much?* about those nouns and pronouns. The words *a, an,* and *the* are special adjectives, called **articles.** The underlined words below are adjectives. The arrows point to the word each adjective modifies.

what kind? lovely sunset   **which one?** this dog

how many? two pages   **how much?** enough food

An adjective usually comes before the noun it modifies, as in the examples above. Sometimes adjectives come after the nouns or pronouns they modify.

Gold is precious.

A. PRACTICE: *Underline the adjective or adjectives in each sentence. Draw an arrow from every adjective to the noun or pronoun it modifies.*

1. We always played many games after school.
2. Sometimes we made up our own rules for the games.
3. These rules often were complex.
4. One game was a unique version of Hide and Seek.
5. In this game, we all hid in places within fifty feet of the seeker.
6. Seekers wore a big scarf over their eyes.
7. All players made soft sounds to lead the seekers toward them.
8. Games we played were long and fun.

B. Writing Application: *Make the nouns and pronouns in these sentences more vivid and precise by adding adjectives that answer the questions in parentheses. Write each adjective on the line after the question.*

1. The *(what kind?)* _____ cat jumped from the floor to the table.
2. We kicked our feet through the *(what kind?)* _____ leaves that had fallen from the trees.
3. My father brought *(how many?)* _____ CDs to listen to in the car.
4. My little cousin decided she wanted *(which one?)* _____ toy for her birthday.

Name _____ Date _____

Integrated Language Skills: Support for Writing a Biographical Sketch

A **biography** is a written account of a person's life. A **biographical "sketch"** is a much shorter piece of writing in which the author tells something important about a real person.

DIRECTIONS: *Use the graphic organizer below to help plan your biographical sketch about someone who took risks in order to achieve a worthy goal or someone who did something in a new way. Based on the details you generate about the person, come up with a main idea for your sketch.*

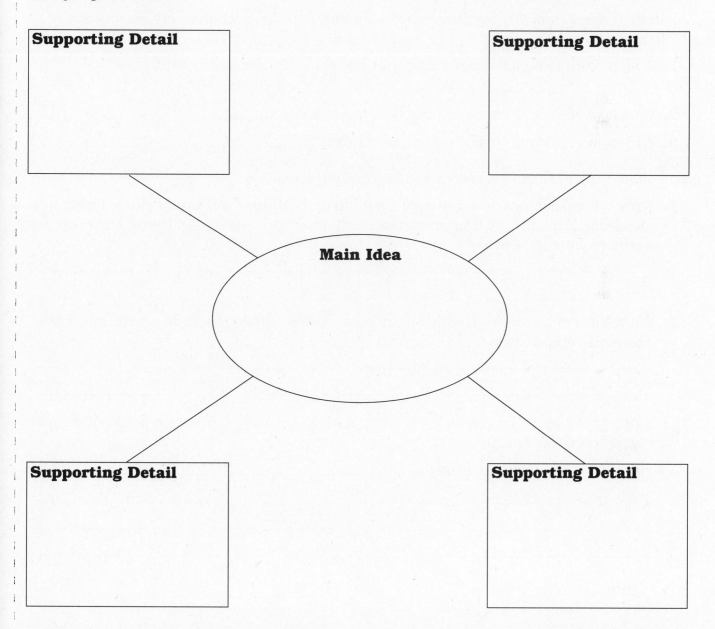

Now, revise your main idea as appropriate, write the body of the biographical sketch, and end with a strong concluding sentence that restates your main idea in different words.

Always to Remember by Brent Ashabranner
Writing About the Big Question

How much information is enough?

Big Question Vocabulary

accumulate	challenge	decision	development	discrimination
explanation	exploration	factor	global	inequality
quality	quantity	reveal	statistics	

A. *Write a word from the Big Question vocabulary list that best answers each question below.*

1. Which word describes something that happens all over the world?

   _____

2. Which word describes something that is hard to do? _____

3. Which word means "make something known"? _____

B. *Follow the directions in responding to each of the items below.*

1. Write a two-sentence description of a person or event that you would like to honor in a memorial. Explain why that person or event deserves a memorial. Use at least two list words in your sentences.

   _____

   _____

2. What kind of memorial should the person or event have? Include one or more list words in your answer.

   _____

   _____

C. *Complete the sentence below. Then, write a short paragraph in which you connect this answer to the Big Question.*

   Exploration of history requires _____

   _____

   _____

   _____

"Always to Remember: The Vision of Maya Ying Lin" by Brent Ashabranner
Reading: Make Connections Between Supporting Paragraphs and the Main Idea

Main ideas are the most important points in a literary work. Writers often organize essays so that main ideas are part of a clear structure. An introduction states the main idea, and then each paragraph supports or develops it. **Make connections between supporting paragraphs and the main idea.**

- Pause to note the main idea of paragraphs or sections.
- Write notes, or complete an organizer to track main ideas and key details.
- Review the main ideas and details in each section to see how they support the essay's main idea.

Read this passage from the selection about Maya Ying Lin.

Announcement of the competition in October, 1980, brought an astonishing response. The Vietnam Veterans Memorial Fund received over five thousand inquiries. They came from every state in the nation and from every field of design.

The details support the main idea: the astonishing support for the competition.

DIRECTIONS: *For each passage, list details that support the stated main idea.*

1. Maya Lin grew up in an environment of art and literature. She was interested in sculpture and made both small and large sculptural figures, one cast in bronze. She learned silversmithing and made jewelry. She was surrounded by books and read a great deal. . . .

   Main idea of whole section: Maya Lin's home was full of art and literature.

   Supporting details: _____

   _____

2. On the day of their visit, Maya Lin remembers, Constitution Gardens was awash with a late November sun; the park was full of light, alive with joggers and people walking beside the lake.

   Main idea of whole section: Maya's visit to the building site was memorable.

   Supporting details: _____

   _____

3. The designs were displayed without any indication of the designer's name so that they could be judged anonymously, on their design merits alone. The jury spent one week reviewing all the designs. . . . On May 1 it made its report to the Vietnam Veterans Memorial Fund; the experts declared Entry Number 1,026 the winner.

   Main idea of whole section: Designs were judged impartially.

   Supporting details: _____

   _____

"Always to Remember: The Vision of Maya Ying Lin" by Brent Ashabranner
Literary Analysis: Biography and Autobiography

- A **biographical essay** is a short work in which a writer tells about an important event in the life of another person.
- An **autobiographical essay** is also a true account, but it is written by the person who experienced the event himself or herself. It includes the writer's thoughts and feelings about an event.

Both types of writing look at the influence of personal experiences, such as schooling, on the later personalities and accomplishments of a person.

DIRECTIONS: *Complete the following outline by providing the details given in the biographical essay about Maya Ying Lin.*

Maya Ying Lin

I. Background and education

   A. Background

      1. _____

      2. _____

      3. _____

   B. Education

      _____

II. The Vietnam Veterans Memorial contest

   A. Steps to winning

      1. _____

      2. _____

   B. Rewards

      1. _____

      2. _____

III. The Vietnam Veterans Memorial

   A. Specifications

      1. _____

      2. _____

      3. _____

   B. Judges' reactions to winning entry

      1. _____

      2. _____

"Always to Remember: The Vision of Maya Ying Lin" by Brent Ashabranner
Vocabulary Builder

Word List

anonymously   authorized   criteria   eloquent   harmonious   unanimous

A. DIRECTIONS: *Complete each of the following sentences with a vocabulary word.*

1. What _____ did the teacher use in grading the research papers?

2. The senator's speech before Congress was _____.

3. The spices created a(n) _____ blend of flavors in the stew.

4. Opinion was _____; everyone agreed to the suggestion.

5. An _____ biography is one that the subject approves.

6. Our newspaper does not print letters people send _____.

B. WORD STUDY The Greek root -*nym*- means "name." Answer each question that follows with one of these words containing the root -*nym*-: *synonym, anonymous, acronym, homonyms.*

1. What is a word formed from the first letters of a phrase?

   _____

2. What is a word that has the same or nearly the same meaning as another word?

   _____

3. What are two words that sound the same but are spelled differently?

   _____

4. What is a word that describes a work whose author is unknown?

   _____

C. DIRECTIONS: *Identify each item as synonyms, homonyms, or an acronym.*

1. their/there _____

2. NATO _____

3. buy/purchase _____

4. do/due _____

5. LOL _____

from **I Know Why the Caged Bird Sings** by Maya Angelou
Writing About the Big Question

How much information is enough?

Big Question Vocabulary

accumulate	challenge	decision	development	discrimination
explanation	exploration	factor	global	inequality
quality	quantity	reveal	statistics	valuable

A. *Use a word from the list above to complete each sentence.*

1. What were the _____ for our team last year?

2. Let's _____ information on stocks for our investment club.

3. Is our information of high _____?

4. Lewis and Clark made a famous journey of _____.

B. *Follow the directions in responding to each of the items below.*

1. Write a two-sentence description of a relative whom you admire. Explain why you hold that person in high esteem. Use at least two list words in your description.

   _____

   _____

   _____

   _____

2. Rate the **quality** and **quantity** of the information about your relative.

   _____

   _____

C. *Complete the sentence below. Then, write a short paragraph in which you connect this answer to the Big Question.*

   The accumulation of knowledge is _____

   _____

   _____

   _____

   _____

from **I Know Why the Caged Bird Sings** by Maya Angelou

Reading: Make Connections Between Supporting Paragraphs and the Main Idea

Main ideas are the most important points in a literary work. Writers often organize essays so that main ideas are part of a clear structure. An introduction states the main idea, and then each paragraph supports or develops it. **Make connections between supporting paragraphs and the main idea.**

- Pause to note the main idea of paragraphs or sections.
- Write notes, or complete an organizer to track main ideas and key details.
- Review the main ideas and details in each section to see how they support the essay's main idea.

Read this passage from the selection by Maya Angelou.

Customers could find food staples, a good variety of colored thread, mash for hogs, corn for chickens, coal oil for lamps, light bulbs for the wealthy, shoestrings, hair dressing, balloons, and flower seeds. Anything not visible had only to be ordered.

The details about the items support the section's main idea: the store fills needs.

DIRECTIONS: *For each passage, list details that support the stated main idea.*

1. Over the years it became the lay center of activities in town. On Saturdays, barbers sat their customers in the shade on the porch of the Store, and troubadours on their ceaseless crawlings through the South leaned across its benches and sang their sad songs. . . .

   Main idea of whole section: The Store is at the center of a thriving community.

   Supporting details: _____

   _____

2. I don't think I ever saw Mrs. Flowers laugh, but she smiled often. A slow widening of her thin black lips to show even, small white teeth, then the slow effortless closing. When she chose to smile on me, I always wanted to thank her. The action was so graceful and inclusively benign.

   Main idea of whole section: The author enjoys Mrs. Flowers's kindness and attention.

   Supporting details: _____

   _____

3. Her voice slid in and curved down through and over the words. She was nearly singing. I wanted to look at the pages. Were they the same that I had read? Or were these notes, music, lined on the pages, as in a hymn book? Her sounds began cascading gently.

   Main idea of whole section: Mrs. Flowers had a beautiful reading voice.

   Supporting details: _____

   _____

from I Know Why the Caged Bird Sings by Maya Angelou
Literary Analysis: Autobiographical Essay

- A **biographical essay** is a short work in which a writer tells about an important event in the life of another person.
- An **autobiographical essay** is also a true account, but it is written by the person who experienced the event himself or herself. It includes the writer's thoughts and feelings about an event.

Both types of writing look at the influence of personal experiences, such as schooling, on the later personalities and accomplishments of a person.

In her autobiographical essay, Maya Angelou describes many of her thoughts and feelings. What does the following passage reveal about the author's feeling toward her grandmother?

> Her crisp meat pies and cool lemonade, when joined to her miraculous ability to be in two places at the same time, assured her business success.

Angelou admires her grandmother's cooking, energy, and talent as a businesswoman.

DIRECTIONS: *Write two thoughts or feelings expressed by the author in each of the following passages from* I Know Why the Caged Bird Sings.

1. Alone and empty in the mornings, it looked like an unopened present from a stranger. Opening the front doors was pulling the ribbon off the unexpected gift. . . . Whenever I walked into the Store in the afternoon, I sensed that it was tired. I alone could hear the slow pulse of its job half done.

   Thoughts or feelings:

   _____

   _____

   _____

2. She pronounced my name so nicely. Or more correctly, she spoke each word with such clarity that I was certain a foreigner who didn't understand English could have understood her.

   Thoughts or feelings:

   _____

   _____

   _____

3. I was liked, and what a difference it made. I was respected not as Mrs. Henderson's grandchild or Bailey's sister but for just being Marguerite Johnson.

   Thoughts or feelings:

   _____

   _____

from **I Know Why the Caged Bird Sings** by Maya Angelou
Vocabulary Builder

Word List

benign   ceaseless   enchantment   fiscal   infuse   intolerant   valid

A. DIRECTIONS: *Revise each sentence so that the underlined vocabulary word is used logically. Be sure to keep the vocabulary word in your version.*

1. Our teacher asked us to write a <u>fiscal</u> report describing the poet's use of rhyme.

   _____

   _____

2. When the children roller-bladed over her garden, Jean responded with a <u>benign</u> look.

   _____

   _____

3. The plot was serious, so the director asked the actors to <u>infuse</u> their lines with humor.

   _____

   _____

4. The easygoing babysitter was <u>intolerant</u> of the children's loud games.

   _____

   _____

5. People used earplugs to block the <u>ceaseless</u> peace and quiet.

   _____

6. His driver's license was <u>valid</u>, so the man got a ticket.

   _____

7. The best way to get good grades is through <u>enchantment</u>.

   _____

B. WORD STUDY The Latin root *-val-* means "strong." Complete the following sentences using one of these words containing the root *-val-*: *value, valor, valedictorian.*

1. Sometimes the cheapest item is not the best _____.

2. The _____ gave a short but powerful speech at graduation.

3. Knights of old demonstrated their _____ in jousting matches.

from **I Know Why the Caged Bird Sings** by Maya Angelou
"Always to Remember: The Vision of Maya Ying Lin" by Brent Ashabranner
Integrated Language Skills: Grammar

Adverbs

An **adverb** modifies, or describes, a verb, an adjective, or another adverb.

Adverbs modifying verbs:

He carefully studied the map.   She walked quietly to her seat.

Adverbs modifying adjectives:

My dog has a very loud bark.   Her hair is extremely long.

Adverbs modifying other adverbs:

She won the race so easily.   Her car accelerates more quickly than mine.

Adverbs, which make the information in a sentence more vivid, usually answer questions such as *when? where? in what way?* and *to what extent?* Note that most words ending in *-ly* are usually adverbs: for example, *carefully* and *finally,* but not *friendly.* Note also that common words *not* ending in *-ly* are adverbs: *rather, always, here, then, only, once.*

A. PRACTICE: *Underline the adverb or adverbs in each sentence, and draw an arrow from every adverb to the word it modifies.*

1. During the Civil War, Lincoln considered his political options very cautiously.

2. He viewed restoration of the Union as an exceedingly important issue.

3. That goal clearly required a victory in the war itself.

4. To that end, he worked quite tirelessly on both the political and military fronts.

5. Border states generally had remained loyal to the Union.

6. Lincoln eventually made his decision about slavery.

B. Writing Application: *Make each sentence more vivid by adding an adverb that answers the question at the end of the sentence. Write each adverb on the blank line.*

1. Rhea is having a party _____. (*when?*)

2. Many people are _____ anxious about getting an invitation. (*to what extent?*)

3. Rhea _____ plans on inviting everyone. (*in what manner?*)

from **I Know Why the Caged Bird Sings** by Maya Angelou

"Always to Remember: The Vision of Maya Ying Lin" by Brent Ashabranner

Integrated Language Skills: Support for Writing a Reflective Essay

Think about a piece of artwork or music that you particularly admire. What makes it linger in your mind? What new ideas does it inspire? Use the chart to organize your thoughts for your composition. First, list some memorable details about the piece of music or the artwork. For each detail, describe briefly why it made an impression on you or what you learned from it.

Memorable Detail From Artwork or Music	What I Learned/Why It Impressed Me

Now, use your notes to generate main ideas, which you will support with details for your draft.

"**Forest Fire**" by Anaïs Nin
"**Why Leaves Turn Color in the Fall**" by Diane Ackerman
"**The Season's Curmudgeon Sees the Light**" by Mary C. Curtis

Writing About the Big Question

How much information is enough?

Big Question Vocabulary

accumulate	challenge	decision	development	discrimination
explanation	exploration	factor	global	inequality
quality	quantity	reveal	statistics	valuable

A. *Use a word from the list above to complete each sentence.*

1. During the fall, leaves _____ their underlying colors.

2. One _____ in the forest fire was dry conditions.

3. What is your _____ for preferring summer to spring?

4. Through _____ you can discover a lot about nature.

B. *Follow the directions in responding to each of the items below.*

1. Write a two-sentence description of your favorite season. Use at least two list words in your sentences.

   _____

   _____

2. Which season do you like least? Use at least two list words in your explanation.

   _____

   _____

C. *These essays highlight different ways of appreciating nature. Complete the sentence below. Then, write a short paragraph in which you connect this sentence to the Big Question.*

   The part of nature that I value the most is _____ because _____

   _____

   _____

   _____

"**Forest Fire**" by Anaïs Nin
"**Why Leaves Turn Color in the Fall**" by Diane Ackerman
"**The Season's Curmudgeon Sees the Light**" by Mary C. Curtis
Literary Analysis: Comparing Types of Organization

Types of Organization

To present information in the most useful way possible, writers can choose among several **types of organization.** Here are three of the most common organizational plans.

- **Chronological order** relates events in the order in which they occurred.
- **Cause-and-effect order** examines the relationship between an event and its result, or results.
- **Comparison and contrast** examines similarities and differences.

DIRECTIONS: *Answer the following questions about the organization of the essays.*

1. List six of the main events in "Forest Fire" in the order that they occur.

   Event 1 _____   Event 4 _____

   Event 2 _____   Event 5 _____

   Event 3 _____   Event 6 _____

2. Why is chronological order the best type of organization for "Forest Fire"?

   _____

   _____

3. Based on "Why Leaves Turn Color in the Fall," explain the causes and effects that make leaves colorful in the fall.

   _____

   _____

   _____

   _____

4. Why is cause-and-effect order the best type of organization for "Why Leaves Turn Color in the Fall"?

   _____

   _____

5. How do the author's feelings change in "The Season's Curmudgeon Sees the Light"?

   _____

   _____

6. Why is comparison and contrast the best type of organization for "The Season's Curmudgeon Sees the Light"?

   _____

   _____

"Forest Fire" by Anaïs Nin
"Why Leaves Turn Color in the Fall" by Diane Ackerman
"The Season's Curmudgeon Sees the Light" by Mary C. Curtis
Vocabulary Builder

A. DIRECTIONS: *Revise each sentence so that it uses the underlined vocabulary word logically. Be sure to keep the vocabulary word in your revision.*

1. The principal is <u>consoling</u> the student by disciplining him.

_____

_____

2. The children are <u>predisposed</u> to illness; they never get sick.

_____

_____

3. I call Lillian <u>capricious</u> because she does not like changing anything.

_____

_____

4. The <u>evacuees</u> left the movie theater laughing and discussing the funny movie.

_____

_____

5. The stage set was <u>macabre</u> and cheerful.

_____

_____

6. Scott has a <u>tenacious</u> personality, so he readily compromises.

_____

_____

B. DIRECTIONS: *Circle the letter of the word that is most nearly* opposite *in meaning to the word in CAPITAL LETTERS.*

1. CONSOLING
   A. scheming
   B. cheering
   C. blending
   D. agitating

2. PREDISPOSED
   A. able
   B. unwilling
   C. ready
   D. upgraded

3. TENACIOUS
   A. relaxed
   B. sturdy
   C. pressure
   D. stretched

4. CAPRICIOUS
   A. inconstant
   B. lighthearted
   C. steadfast
   D. unrealistic

"Forest Fire" by Anaïs Nin
"Why Leaves Turn Color in the Fall" by Diane Ackerman
"The Season's Curmudgeon Sees the Light" by Mary C. Curtis

Support for Writing to Compare Essay Organization

Before you write your essay about the organization of two of the essays, use the graphic organizer below to list ideas about all three essays.

"Forest Fire"	"Why Leaves Turn Color in the Fall"	"The Season's Curmudgeon Sees the Light"
What is the purpose of the essay?	What is the purpose of the essay?	What is the purpose of the essay?
What are key events that occur in the essay?	What are key cause-and-effect relationships in the essay?	What are key negative feelings about spring in the essay?
What is the organization of the essay? How does this organization help the author to achieve her purpose?	What is the organization of the essay? How does this organization help the author to achieve her purpose?	What is the organization of the essay? How does this organization help the author to achieve her purpose?

Now, choose two of the three essays, and explain how the organization of each matches or supports the writer's topic and purpose.

Name _____ Date _____

"The Trouble With Television" by Robert MacNeil
Writing About the Big Question

How much information is enough?

Big Question Vocabulary

accumulate	challenge	decision	development	discrimination
explanation	exploration	factor	global	inequality
quality	quantity	reveal	statistics	valuable

A. *Use a word from the list above to complete each sentence.*

1. Let me _____ some information about television.

2. The _____ of television changed people's lives forever.

3. What is the _____ for why some people watch hours of television a day?

B. *Follow the directions in responding to each of the items below.*

1. How would you rate the quality of television programming? What factors entered into your decision?

   _____

   _____

2. Write two sentences speculating about how your life would change if you stopped watching television. Use at least two Big Question words in your sentences.

   _____

   _____

   _____

C. *Complete the sentence below. Then, write a short paragraph in which you connect this answer to the Big Question.*

The exploration of ideas on TV news shows is usually _____ and

_____

_____

_____

_____

"The Trouble With Television" by Robert MacNeil

Reading: Use Clue Words to Distinguish Fact From Opinion

A **fact** is information that can be proved based on evidence. An **opinion** may be supported by factual evidence, but it cannot be proved. A **generalization** is a conclusion based on facts. Like an opinion, a generalization can be supported by facts. However, an author may sometimes use an **overgeneralization,** a conclusion stated in a more extreme way than can be supported by facts.

Statements may be a combination of opinions and generalizations, or they may be opinions written to sound like facts. As you read, **use clue words** to determine when a statement should be read carefully and evaluated to determine whether it is an opinion, a fact, a generalization, or an overgeneralization.

- Words that communicate judgment, such as *best* and *worst,* or specific words that suggest the writer's good or bad feelings about the topic usually indicate an opinion. Sometimes, opinions are signaled directly with words such as *I believe* or *I think.*
- Words that indicate connections, such as *therefore, so,* and *because,* may signal generalizations or opinions that should be supported by facts. Extreme statements that include words such as *always, everything, anything, nothing, never,* and *only* may be overgeneralizations.

As you read nonfiction, distinguish facts and supported generalizations from opinions and overgeneralizations to evaluate the strengths and weaknesses of a writer's argument.

In "The Trouble With Television," Robert MacNeil makes a strong argument for limiting the time many people spend watching television. He uses a combination of all of these devices to convince his readers. His essay leads to a logical conclusion based on long observation and careful thought.

DIRECTIONS: *Read the passages from the selection, and then answer the questions.*

1. "Yet its dominating communications instrument, its principal form of national linkage, is one that sells neat resolutions to human problems that usually have no neat resolutions."
   On what fact is this generalization based?

   _____

2. "One study estimates that some 30 million adult Americans are 'functionally illiterate' and cannot read or write well enough to answer a want ad or understand the instructions on a medicine bottle."
   How could you prove that this statement is a fact?

   _____

3. "But it has come to be regarded as a given, . . . as though General Sarnoff, or one of the other august pioneers of video, had bequeathed to us tablets of stone commanding that nothing in television shall ever require more than a few moments' concentration."
   Why might this statement be considered an overgeneralization?

   _____

"The Trouble With Television" by Robert MacNeil
Literary Analysis: Persuasive Techniques

Persuasive techniques are the methods that a writer uses to convince an audience to think or act a certain way.

- **Repetition** is an effective way to drive home a point.
- **Rhetorical questions** (questions with obvious answers) make readers more likely to agree with later, more controversial points.

In "The Trouble With Television," Robert MacNeil uses both repetition and rhetorical questioning to drive home a point to his audience. Here is an example of the latter.

> Who can quarrel with a medium that so brilliantly packages escapist entertainment as a mass-marketing tool?

This rhetorical question forces readers to acknowledge the obvious answer: It is hard to argue against such a successful combination of entertainment and marketing.

DIRECTIONS: *Decide whether you find each of the following passages from the selection convincing, and then answer the questions.*

1. "It has become fashionable to think that, like fast food, fast ideas are the way to get to a fast-moving, impatient public."

   A. MacNeil use the word *fast* three times. What three things is he describing?

   _____

   B. How does the repetition in the preceding sentence convey the author's negative attitude toward television?

   _____

2. "When before in human history has so much humanity collectively surrendered so much of its leisure to one toy, one mass diversion?"

   A. How would you answer the rhetorical question?

   _____

   B. Does answering the question help persuade you to support the author's argument? Explain.

   _____

3. "When before in human history has so much humanity collectively surrendered so much of its leisure to one toy, one mass diversion? When before has virtually an entire nation surrendered itself wholesale to a medium for selling?"

   A. Why might MacNeil have repeated the word *surrendered*?

   _____

   B. Do you find the repetition effective? Explain.

   _____

"The Trouble With Television" by Robert MacNeil
Vocabulary Builder

Word List

constructive   diverts   passively   pervading   skeptically   trivial

A. DIRECTIONS: *Circle* T *if the statement is true or* F *if the statement is false. Then, explain your answer.*

1. When you need to concentrate on finishing a complicated project, you should find something that *diverts* your attention.

   T / F _____

2. If a problem with a car is *trivial*, you don't need to repair it immediately.

   T / F _____

3. If a burning smell were *pervading* the room, you would expect it to disappear immediately.

   T / F _____

4. If you respond to a speech *skeptically*, you are likely to trust the speaker.

   T / F _____

5. *Constructive* criticism can help actors improve their performances.

   T / F _____

6. The crowd protested *passively* by lying down in the street.

   T / F _____

B. WORD STUDY The Latin root *-vad-* means "to go." Words with *-vad-* include *pervade,* "go into every part of"; *invade,* "enter for conquest"; and *evade,* "slip away." Use the meaning of the root to help you answer the following questions.

1. What might a home *invader* be doing?

   _____

2. Why might someone *evade* responsibility for a mistake?

   _____

3. What kind of smell might *pervade* an enormous auditorium?

   _____

Name _____ Date _____

"On Woman's Right to Suffrage" by Susan B. Anthony
Writing About the Big Question

How much information is enough?

Big Question Vocabulary

accumulate	challenge	decision	development	discrimination
explanation	exploration	factor	global	inequality
quality	quantity	reveal	statistics	

A. *Use a word from the list above to answer each question.*

1. Which word is an antonym of local? _____

2. When information piles up, what does it do? _____

3. Many people use this word to describe dealing with lots of information.

   _____

B. *Follow the directions in responding to each of the items below.*

1. In two complete sentences, describe Susan B. Anthony's lifelong goal. Use at least two list words in your sentences.

   _____

   _____

   _____

2. How successful was Anthony? Why? Write a two-sentence answer that includes at least one list word.

   _____

   _____

   _____

C. *Complete the sentence below. Consider the source from which Susan B. Anthony drew her ideas about gender discrimination. Then, write a short paragraph in which you connect your answer to the Big Question.*

Discrimination based on gender is _____

_____

_____

_____

_____

"On Woman's Right to Suffrage" by Susan B. Anthony
Reading: Use Clue Words to Distinguish Fact From Opinion

A **fact** is information that can be proved based on evidence. An **opinion** may be supported by factual evidence, but it cannot be proved. A **generalization** is a conclusion based on facts. Like an opinion, a generalization can be supported by facts. However, an author may sometimes use an **overgeneralization,** a conclusion stated in a more extreme way than can be supported by facts.

Statements may be a combination of opinions and generalizations, or they may be opinions written to sound like facts. As you read, **use clue words** to determine when a statement should be read carefully and evaluated to determine whether it is an opinion, a fact, a generalization, or an overgeneralization.

- Words that communicate judgment, such as *best* and *worst*, or specific words that suggest the writer's good or bad feelings about the topic usually indicate an opinion. Sometimes, opinions are signaled directly with words such as *I believe* or *I think*.
- Words that indicate connections, such as *therefore, so,* and *because,* may signal generalizations or opinions that should be supported by facts. Extreme statements that include words such as *always, everything, anything, nothing, never,* and *only* may be overgeneralizations.

As you read nonfiction, distinguish facts and supported generalizations from opinions and overgeneralizations to evaluate the strengths and weaknesses of a writer's argument.

In "On Woman's Right to Suffrage," Susan B. Anthony makes a strong argument for women's constitutional right to vote. Her speech leads to a logical conclusion based on the language of America's Constitution.

DIRECTIONS: *Read the passages from the selection, and then answer the questions.*

1. "Hence, every discrimination against women in the constitutions and laws of the several States is to-day null and void, precisely as in every one against negroes."
   On what fact is this generalization based?

   _____

2. "Webster, Worcester and Bouvier all define a citizen to be a person in the United States, entitled to vote and hold office."
   How could you prove this fact?

   _____

3. "And it is a downright mockery to talk to women of their enjoyment of the blessings of liberty while they are denied the use of the only means of securing them. . . ."
   What makes this statement an opinion?

   _____

4. ". . . this oligarchy of sex . . . carries dissension, discord and rebellion into every home in the nation."
   Why might this statement be considered an overgeneralization?

   _____

"On Woman's Right to Suffrage" by Susan B. Anthony
Literary Analysis: Persuasive Techniques

Persuasive techniques are the methods that a writer uses to convince an audience to think or act a certain way.

- **Repetition** is an effective way to drive home a point.
- **Rhetorical questions** (questions with obvious answers) make readers more likely to agree with later, more controversial points.

In "On Woman's Right to Suffrage," Susan B. Anthony uses both repetition and rhetorical questioning to emphasize her arguments and drive home a point to her audience. These persuasive techniques are especially effective when spoken aloud.

In this passage from the selection, note the repetition of the word *we*.

> It was we, the people; not we, the white male citizens; nor yet we, the male citizens; but we, the whole people, who formed the Union.

By repeating the word *we*, the author emphasizes her point that it was everyone, both males and females, who helped develop our country.

DIRECTIONS: *In each of these passages, Susan B. Anthony uses repetition or a rhetorical question as a persuasive technique. Decide whether you find each passage convincing, and then answer the questions.*

1. "And we formed it, not to give the blessings of liberty, but to secure them; not to the half of ourselves and the half of our posterity, but to the whole people—women as well as men."

   A. Why might the author have repeated the word *half*, followed by the word *whole*?

   _____

   B. Do you find the repetition effective? Why?

   _____

2. "The only question left to be settled now is: Are women persons?"

   A. How would you answer the rhetorical question?

   _____

   B. Does answering the question help persuade you to support the author's argument? Why?

   _____

3. "It is an odious aristocracy; a hateful oligarchy of sex; the most hateful aristocracy ever established on the face of the globe; an oligarchy of wealth, where the rich govern the poor."

   A. What three words are repeated in this sentence?

   _____

   B. What impression of America's leadership do you have, based on this repetition?

   _____

Name _____ Date _____

"On Woman's Right to Suffrage" by Susan B. Anthony
Vocabulary Builder

Word List

derived   dissension   immunities   posterity   rebellion   violation

A. DIRECTIONS: *Write the letter of the word or phrase that best defines each word in CAPITAL LETTERS.*

____ 1. DISSENSION
    A. agreement   C. argument
    B. negotiation   D. imperfect

____ 2. IMMUNITIES
    A. protections   C. contagions
    B. insurances   D. silences

____ 3. POSTERITY
    A. stinginess   C. future generations
    B. forgotten memories   D. peacefulness

____ 4. DERIVED
    A. overturned   C. motored
    B. received   D. framed

____ 5. VIOLATION
    A. rule breaking   C. physical force
    B. misunderstanding   D. nightmare

____ 6. REBELLION
    A. retraining   C. remarking
    B. revision   D. resistance

B. WORD STUDY: The Latin root *-bellum-* means "war." Use the meaning of *-bellum-* to help you answer the questions that follow.

1. Would a *belligerent* person be more likely to fight or cooperate?

_____

2. Would contented people or unhappy people be more likely to favor *rebellion*?

_____

"On Woman's Right to Suffrage" by Susan B. Anthony
"The Trouble With Television" by Robert MacNeil

Integrated Language Skills: Grammar

Conjunctions

Conjunctions are words that connect sentence parts. A **coordinating conjunction** connects words or groups of words of the same kind.

The boy <u>and</u> his dog went everywhere together.

Coordinating Conjunctions:

and	but	or	nor	for	yet	so

Correlative conjunctions connect pairs of equal importance.
Correlative conjunctions come in pairs.

In order to be healthy, you must <u>both</u> eat right <u>and</u> exercise regularly.

Correlative Conjunctions

both/and   either/or   neither/nor

A **subordinating conjunction** connects two ideas by making one dependent on the other.

I bought a stereo system <u>after</u> I had earned enough money.

Common Subordinating Conjunctions:

after	as though	since	until
although	because	so that	when
as	before	than	whenever
as if	even though	though	where
as long as	if	till	wherever
as soon as	in order that	unless	while

A. PRACTICE: *Underline the conjunctions in the following sentences.*

1. My twin brothers and my sister are in elementary school.
2. The twins were cute babies, but they cried a lot.
3. I ran outside whenever they began crying.
4. Neither Kyle nor Kevin slept much at first.
5. As they got older, we started playing together.

B. Writing Application: *Write a short paragraph in which you use at least five conjunctions. Underline the conjunctions.*

_____

_____

_____

_____

"On Woman's Right to Suffrage" by Susan B. Anthony
"The Trouble With Television" by Robert MacNeil

Integrated Language Skills: Support for Writing an Evaluation

An **evaluation** of a writer's arguments should identify specific supporting points that the author uses to defend his or her position. An evaluation should also determine whether each supporting point is effective.

DIRECTIONS: *Fill in the chart with Robert MacNeil's points supporting his negative view of watching television or Susan B. Anthony's points supporting women's right to vote, the persuasive techniques the person uses, and an assessment of whether the overall argument is effective and sound.*

Supporting Points	
Persuasive Techniques	
Assessment	

Now, use your notes in the chart to write your evaluation.

from **"Sharing in the American Dream"** by Colin Powell
Writing About the Big Question

How much information is enough?

Big Question Vocabulary

accumulate	challenge	decision	development	discrimination
explanation	exploration	factor	global	inequality
quality	quantity	reveal	statistics	valuable

A. *Use a word from list above to complete each sentence.*

1. What might help you figure out whether racial discrimination still exists?

   _____

2. Which word might you use to describe tutoring a fidgety kindergarten student?

   _____

3. Which word describes something that is more important than the amount of time a person volunteers? _____

B. *Follow the directions in responding to each of the items below.*

1. Write a two-sentence explanation of how volunteerism can help overcome racial discrimination. Use at least two list words in your explanation.

   _____

   _____

   _____

2. How can volunteering benefit the volunteer? Use at least two list words in your answer.

   _____

   _____

   _____

C. *Complete the sentence below. Then, write a short paragraph in which you connect this answer to the Big Question.*

When there is inequity in society, we should _____

and _____

_____

_____

_____

_____

from **"Sharing in the American Dream"** by Colin Powell
Reading: Use Support for Fact and Opinion

A **fact** is information that can be proved. An **opinion** is a person's judgment or belief. As you read nonfiction, ask questions to evaluate an author's support for his or her opinions.

- A *valid opinion* can be supported by facts or by expert authority.
- A *faulty opinion* cannot be supported by facts. Instead, it is supported by other opinions and often ignores major facts that contradict it. Faulty opinions often show *bias*, an unfair preference or dislike for something.

In this selection from "Sharing in the American Dream," Colin Powell draws on facts and opinions to inspire his audience to step up and volunteer in their communities. His feelings about past and present Americans reflect both pride and hope.

The following statement from Powell's speech about America's founders is a fact because it can be proved.

They pledged their lives, their fortune and their sacred honor to secure inalienable rights. . . .

The following statement is an opinion because it is a judgment or belief.

Yet, despite all we have done, this is still an imperfect world.

Powell supports his opinion with the fact that some Americans, many of whom are children, are in need and at risk.

DIRECTIONS: *Read the following statements of opinion from the selection. Complete the chart with Powell's statements of support for each opinion. Then, decide whether you think the opinion is adequately supported, or valid.*

Opinion	Support	Adequately Supported?
1. "In terms of numbers, the task [of helping children] may seem staggering."		
2. "But if we look at the simple needs that these children have, then the truth is manageable, the goal is achievable."		
3. "There is a spirit of Philadelphia that will leave Philadelphia tomorrow afternoon and spread across this whole nation. . . ."		

from **"Sharing in the American Dream"** by Colin Powell

Literary Analysis: Use Word Choice to Convey Ideas

An author's **word choice** can help him or her convey a certain idea or feeling. An author might choose words that are formal or informal, simple or complex. Factors that influence an author's word choice include the following:

- the author's intended audience and purpose
- the **denotations** of words—their literal or specific meanings
- the **connotations** of words—the negative or positive ideas associated with them

In this passage from his speech to encourage volunteerism, Colin Powell chooses words that he hopes will appeal to his listeners and inspire them to act.

> That is why we are here, my friends. We gather here to pledge that those of us who are more fortunate will not forsake those who are less fortunate.

By calling his listeners *my friends* and using the phrase *those of us*, the speaker creates a feeling of closeness. By using the word *pledge*, he identifies a common goal.

DIRECTIONS: *Read the following passages from the selection. Decide whether the underlined words create a formal feeling or an informal feeling. Then, explain the effect of each passage on listeners and readers.*

1. "We will reach down, we will reach back, we will reach across to help <u>our brothers and sisters</u> who are in need."

   _____

   _____

   _____

2. "These are basic needs that we <u>commit</u> ourselves to today, we <u>promise</u> today."

   _____

   _____

   _____

3. "You heard the governors and the mayors, and you'll hear more in a little minute that says the real answer is . . . <u>for each and every one of us to reach out and touch someone in need</u>."

   _____

   _____

   _____

from **"Sharing in the American Dream"** by Colin Powell
Vocabulary Builder

Word List

  alliance   aspirations   compassionate   deferred   virtue   vulnerable

A. DIRECTIONS: *Use a thesaurus to find a synonym for each Word List word. Then, use each synonym in a sentence that makes the meaning of the synonym clear.*

1. *aspirations*; synonym: _____

   _____

2. *deferred*; synonym: _____

   _____

3. *compassionate*; synonym: _____

   _____

4. *alliance*; synonym: _____

   _____

5. *vulnerable*; synonym: _____

   _____

6. *virtue*; synonym: _____

   _____

B. WORD STUDY The Latin root -*pass*- means "to suffer" or "to endure." Words with -*pass*- include *compassion*, "sympathy for another's hardship"; *impassioned*, "showing intense feeling"; and *dispassionate*, "not influenced by strong feeling." Use the meaning of the root to revise the following sentences so that they make sense.

1. One child had so much *compassion* that she refused to donate a single present.

   _____

2. After she saw the movie, she became so *impassioned* that she fell asleep immediately.

   _____

3. A *dispassionate* teacher can never grade opinion essays fairly.

   _____

Name _____ Date _____

Writing About the Big Question

How much information is enough?

Big Question Vocabulary

accumulate	challenge	decision	development	discrimination
explanation	exploration	factor	global	inequality
quality	quantity	reveal	statistics	valuable

A. *Use a word from the list above to complete each sentence.*

1. Science is more than facts and _____.

2. Scientists' _____ of knowledge about the world continues to grow.

3. Do you think there will come a time when there is a(n) _____ for everything?

B. *Follow the directions in responding to each of the items below.*

1. What two scientific developments would you like to learn more about?

   _____

   _____

2. How might you learn more about these scientific developments? Use at least two list words in your answer.

   _____

   _____

   _____

   _____

C. *Complete the sentence below. Then, write a short paragraph in which you connect this answer to the Big Question.*

The knowledge we gain from space exploration shows us _____

_____

_____

_____

_____

_____

"Science and the Sense of Wonder" by Isaac Asimov
Reading: Use Support for Fact and Opinion

A **fact** is information that can be proved. An **opinion** is a person's judgment or belief. As you read nonfiction, ask questions to evaluate an author's support for his or her opinions.

- A *valid opinion* can be supported by facts or by expert authority.
- A *faulty opinion* cannot be supported by facts. Instead, it is supported by other opinions and may contradict the facts. Faulty opinions often show *bias*.

In "Science and the Sense of Wonder," Isaac Asimov draws on facts and opinions to support his ideas about the limitations of Walt Whitman's poetic view of the stars. He claims that scientific knowledge is necessary to fully appreciate nature's beauty.

The following statement from the essay tells a fact. It can be proved by scientists.

Those other bright spots, which are stars rather than planets, are actually suns.

The following statement is an opinion because it is a judgment or belief.

The trouble is that Walt Whitman is talking through his hat, but the poor soul didn't know any better.

Asimov supports his opinion with scientific descriptions and explanations about our universe.

DIRECTIONS: *Read the following statements of opinion from the selection. Complete the chart with Asimov's statements of support for each opinion. Then, decide whether you think the opinion is adequately supported, or valid.*

Opinion	Support	Adequately Supported?
1. "That is a very convenient point of view since it makes it not only unnecessary, but downright aesthetically wrong, to try to follow all that hard stuff in science."		
2. "There are worlds with thick atmospheres of carbon dioxide and sulfuric acid; . . . each with a weird and unearthly beauty that boils down to a mere speck of light if we just gaze at the night sky."		
3. "Some of them are of incomparable grandeur, each glowing with the light of a thousand suns like ours; some of them are merely red-hot coals doling out their energy stingily."		

"Science and the Sense of Wonder" by Isaac Asimov
Literary Analysis: Use Word Choice to Convey Ideas

An author's **word choice** can help him or her convey a certain idea or feeling. An author might choose words that are formal or informal, simple or complex. Factors that influence an author's word choice include the following:

- the author's intended audience and purpose
- the **connotations** of words—the negative or positive ideas associated with them

In this passage from his essay about the wonders of science, Isaac Asimov chooses words that he hopes will appeal to his listeners and spark their interest in learning about the science behind our universe.

> That is a very convenient point of view since it makes it not only unnecessary, but downright aesthetically wrong, to try to follow all that hard stuff in science. Instead, you can just take a look at the night sky, get a quick beauty fix, and go off to a nightclub.

By using language such as *all that hard stuff* and *get a quick beauty fix*, Asimov creates an informal feeling in his essay. He gets the attention of his audience—as a result, his readers are more likely to continue reading.

DIRECTIONS: *Read the following passages from the selection. Decide whether the underlined words create a formal feeling or an informal feeling. Then, explain the effect of each passage on readers.*

1. "I . . . have in my time <u>spread out</u> on a hillside for hours looking at the stars and being awed by their beauty (and <u>receiving bug-bites</u> whose marks took weeks to go away)."

   _____

   _____

2. "There are stars that <u>pulsate endlessly</u> in a great <u>cosmic breathing</u>; and others that, having <u>consumed</u> their fuel, expand and redden until they <u>swallow up</u> their planets. . . ."

   _____

   _____

3. "And some stars explode in a <u>vast cataclysm</u> whose <u>ferocious blast</u> of cosmic rays . . . reaches across thousands of light years."

   _____

   _____

"Science and the Sense of Wonder" by Isaac Asimov
Vocabulary Builder

Word List

awed   cataclysm   conceivable   contraction   exultantly   radiation

A. DIRECTIONS: *Write the letter of the word that means the* opposite *of the word in* CAPITAL LETTERS.

___ 1. EXULTANTLY
    A. miserably   C. happily
    B. thankfully   D. hopefully

___ 2. CONTRACTION
    A. disappearing   C. shrinking
    B. expansion   D. brightening

___ 3. AWED
    A. scared   C. amused
    B. nervous   D. unimpressed

___ 4. RADIATION
    A. revolving   C. absorption
    B. brightness   D. growth

___ 5. CATACLYSM
    A. success   C. party
    B. challenge   D. event

___ 6. CONCEIVABLE
    A. unimaginable   C. fertile
    B. forgotten   D. initial

B. WORD STUDY The Latin root *-tract-* means "pull or drag." The following questions have words containing the root *-tract-*. Use the meaning of *-tract-* to help you answer the questions.

1. If something *contracts*, is it still or does it move?

  _____

2. Can a *distraction* lure people away from their work?

  _____

Name _____ Date _____

from **"Sharing in the American Dream"** by Colin Powell
"Science and the Sense of Wonder" by Isaac Asimov
Integrated Language Skills: Grammar

Prepositions

A **preposition** relates the noun or pronoun following it to another word in the sentence. Commonly used prepositions are listed in the box below.

about	behind	during	off	to
above	below	except	on	toward
across	beneath	for	onto	under
after	beside	from	opposite	underneath
against	besides	in	out	until
along	between	inside	outside	up
among	beyond	into	over	upon
around	but	like	past	with
at	by	near	since	within
before	down	of	through	without

The group of words beginning with the preposition and ending with the noun or pronoun is called a **prepositional phrase.** The noun or pronoun that follows the preposition is called the **object of the preposition.** Read the following example, and then notice that when identifying the object of a preposition, you do not include any modifiers of the noun or pronoun.

I chased my cat around the house.

Around is the preposition, and *house* is the object of the preposition.

A. PRACTICE: *Underline each preposition, and circle its object.*

1. The teacher enjoyed reading aloud to the class.
2. I watched my dog jump over the fence.
3. If you look through the window, you will see a cardinal sitting on a branch.
4. Of all my friends, Jenny is the funniest.
5. Tom placed his backpack behind the tree.

B. Writing Application: *Choose at least three of the prepositional phrases in the preceding exercise, along with any others you want to include, and write a paragraph using them. Underline the prepositional phrases.*

_____

_____

_____

from **"Sharing in the American Dream"** by Colin Powell
"Science and the Sense of Wonder" by Isaac Asimov

Integrated Language Skills: Support for Writing a Response to Literature

from **"Sharing in the American Dream"**

To prepare for writing a **response** to Colin Powell's statement about volunteering, answer the following questions.

1. What is Colin Powell asking the people in his audience to do for thirty minutes or an hour, once a week?

   _____

2. Could you spare thirty minutes or an hour a week to help another person in some way? If you could spare the time, what are some things you might volunteer to do?

   _____

   _____

3. Do you, or does someone you know, volunteer weekly? If so, doing what?

   _____

4. Does your school have a student organization for community service? If not, how might you start one?

   _____

Now, use your answers to write your response.

"Science and the Sense of Wonder"

To prepare for writing a **response** to Isaac Asimov's idea that a scientist's way of appreciating nature is just as valid as a poet's, answer the following questions.

1. Isaac Asimov's main objection to Walt Whitman's reaction to stars is that it limits one's appreciation of the night sky. Do you agree or disagree with Asimov?

   _____

2. Why do you agree or disagree? _____

   _____

3. Describe any experiences you have had looking at stars.

   _____

   _____

4. Would you describe your response to nature's beauty as more similar to Asimov's or to Whitman's? Explain.

   _____

   _____

Now, use your answers to write your response.

"Emancipation" *from* **Lincoln: A Photobiography** by Russell Freedman
"Brown vs. Board of Education" by Walter Dean Myers

Writing About the Big Question

How much information is enough?

Big Question Vocabulary

accumulate	challenge	decision	development	discrimination
explanation	exploration	factor	global	inequality
quality	quantity	reveal	statistics	valuable

A. *Use a word from list above to complete each sentence.*

1. Did emancipation mean the end of _____?

2. What is the _____ for Lincoln's emancipation of the slaves?

3. Not many children could face the _____ of being the first to integrate a school.

4. It took a long time for the Supreme Court to come to a _____ in *Brown vs. Board of Education.*

B. *Follow the directions in responding to each of the items below.*

1. Give two reasons that Lincoln's decision to emancipate the slaves was difficult for him.

   _____

   _____

2. In two or three sentences, explain what *Brown vs. Board of Education* meant for students. Use at least two list words in your explanation.

   _____

   _____

C. *These works each involve important historical events in the struggle for racial equality. Complete the sentence below. Then, write a short paragraph in which you connect this sentence to the Big Question.*

To learn about inequality in history, I would want to read about _____

because _____

_____

_____

"Emancipation" *from* **Lincoln: A Photobiography** by Russell Freedman
"Brown vs. Board of Education" by Walter Dean Myers
Literary Analysis: Comparing Tone

The **tone** of a literary work is the author's attitude toward his or her audience and subject.

- Tone can often be described by a single adjective, such as *formal, informal, serious, playful, impersonal,* or *personal.*
- Tone is conveyed through an author's choice of words, sentence structure, and details. Tone may vary within a piece of writing.

Both "Emancipation" and "Brown vs. Board of Education" are nonfiction works that describe and explain key figures and events in American history. Both works are serious and aim to make a piece of history interesting. However, these two pieces do have subtle differences in tone, partly because the authors' purposes, or reasons for writing, are different.

DIRECTIONS: *Answer the following questions to discover more about the tone and purpose of the two essays.*

1. What words or details in "Emancipation" suggest the author's tone, or attitude toward his audience and subject?

   _____

   _____

2. What adjectives describe the author's tone, or attitude toward his audience and subject, in "Emancipation"?

   _____

   _____

3. What is the author's purpose, or reason, for writing "Emancipation"?

   _____

   _____

4. What words or details in "Brown vs. Board of Education" suggest the author's tone, or attitude toward his subject and audience?

   _____

   _____

5. What adjectives describe the author's tone, or attitude toward his subject and audience, in "Brown vs. Board of Education"?

   _____

   _____

"Emancipation" *from* Lincoln: A Photobiography by Russell Freedman
"Brown vs. Board of Education" by Walter Dean Myers
Vocabulary Builder

Word List

alienate	compensate	deliberating	humiliating
oppressed	predominantly	unconstitutional	

A. DIRECTIONS: *Write a complete sentence to answer each question. In each sentence, use a vocabulary word from the above Word List in place of the underlined word(s) with similar meanings.*

1. What could you do that would <u>make</u> someone <u>unfriendly</u> to you?

   _____

   _____

2. Based on what you have learned in history class, what action would be <u>not in accordance with or permitted by the U.S. Constitution</u>?

   _____

   _____

3. What group of people could be found <u>thinking and considering</u> something <u>carefully and fully</u>?

   _____

   _____

4. Have you ever done something that was <u>embarrassing</u> or <u>undignified</u>?

   _____

   _____

5. What group of people did slave owners <u>keep down by cruel and unjust power</u>?

   _____

   _____

6. Whom should you <u>repay</u>?

   _____

   _____

7. Are there <u>mainly</u> people under the age of twenty-one living in your neighborhood?

   _____

   _____

Name _____ Date _____

"Emancipation" *from* **Lincoln: A Photobiography** by Russell Freedman
"Brown vs. Board of Education" by Walter Dean Myers

Integrated Language Skills: Support for Writing to Compare Tone

Before you write your essay that compares the tone of "Emancipation" and the tone of "Brown vs. Board of Education," use the graphic organizer below to list details and to make notes about each essay.

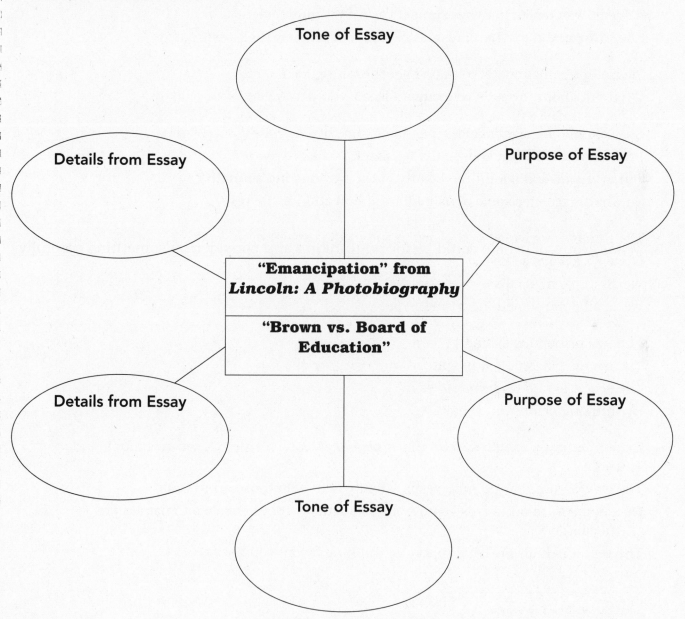

Now, use your notes to write your essay comparing the tone of these two works.

Before You Speak, performed by The Dave Pittenger Band

Something said that's **meaningful** always has importance for those who hear
Express ideas to make them clear maybe they'll **benefit** and help
A friend was down, her **experience** was a frightful incident
She **informed** me of her latest scare and told me how it all went down

Please don't misunderstand don't get the wrong idea
What I'm about to say is **relevant**—I know you can relate

She told me the significance, the importance of what she'd done wrong
I thought about my response the feedback I'd like to share
But everyone is different the beauty of the world is **individuality**
So what is true for some of us might not be **valid** for the rest

The things you've read and heard in the media are wrong
Life isn't always so bad
We all make mistakes
We've all done something wrong

I know our bond is strong
The connection will last in spite of what you've done
The secret is knowing what to say
By thinking before you speak

Explain it in a way that's clear, that's **sensory**—you can almost see and touch and
feel it
The way we live, our cultural responsibility is to help those around us
Ooo, sometimes our words reprove and sometimes they console and sometimes
they forgive
The secret is knowing what to say by thinking before you speak

---

Song Title: **Before You Speak**
Artist / Performed by The Dave Pittenger Band
Vocals & Guitar: Dave Pittenger
Bass Guitar: Jon Price
Drums: Josh Dion
Lyrics by Dave Pittenger
Music composed by Dave Pittenger
Produced by Mike Pandolfo, Wonderful
Executive Producer: Keith London, Defined Mind

Unit 4: Poetry
Big Question Vocabulary—1

The Big Question: What is the secret to reaching someone with words?

Thematic Vocabulary

benefit: *n.* an advantage, an improvement, or a type of help that something offers
     v. to offer an advantage, an improvement, or a type of help; other forms: *beneficial, beneficiary*

cultural: *adj.* belonging or relating to a particular society and its way of life; other form: *culture*

feedback: *n.* advice, praise, or criticism about how successful or useful something is

meaningful: *adj.* serious, important, useful, and valuable; other forms: *mean, meaning*

misunderstand: *v.* to understand someone or something incorrectly; other forms: *understand, misunderstanding*

A. DIRECTIONS: *Write the Thematic Vocabulary word that best completes each group of related words.*

1. comment, observation, _____

2. ethnic, traditional, _____

3. worthwhile, significant, _____

4. confuse, mistake, _____

5. aid, asset, _____

B. DIRECTIONS: *Complete each sentence by writing the correct Thematic Vocabulary word on the line.*

1. It is a _____ tradition to celebrate the Fourth of July in the United States.

2. Was the television program _____, or was it silly?

3. The teacher was careful to give each student helpful _____ regarding their reports.

4. Daily exercise will definitely _____ your health.

5. Listen carefully so that you don't _____ the directions.

Unit 4 Poetry
Big Question Vocabulary—2

The Big Question: What is the secret to reaching someone with words?

Thematic Vocabulary

connection: *n.* a joining together based on common thoughts or interests; other forms: *connect, connecting, connected*

experience: *n.* the act of living through an event

     v. to be involved in an event; other forms: *experiencing, experienced*

express: *v.* to use actions or words to share thoughts and feelings; other forms: *expression, expressing, expressed*

relevant: *adj.* related directly to the subject being discussed; other form: *relevance*

sensory: *adj.* related to or affecting any of the five senses; other forms: *sense, sensing*

Gail's grandmother's birthday was coming up, and Gail wanted to write a poem for her. She asked some friends for advice.

DIRECTIONS: *Use the words and phrases in parentheses to write the dialogue she had with her friends. Use what you have learned about poetry and sensory details.*

Please help me. **(express, connection)**

Gail

(relevant, experience)

Hannah

(sensory details**)**

Maria

All-in-One Workbook
174

Name _____ Date _____

Unit 4 Poetry
Big Question Vocabulary—3

The Big Question: What is the secret to reaching someone with words?

Thematic Vocabulary

individuality: *n.* the sum of personal traits that makes a person unique; other form: *individual*

inform: *v.* to tell, share, or teach facts related to a subject; other forms: *information, informed*

media: *n.* institutions or items that present news and other information, such as newspapers, magazines, television programs, and Internet sources; other form: *medium*

significance: *n.* the meaning or importance of something; other forms: *significant, significantly*

valid: *adj.* believable and reasonable; other forms: *validity, validation*

DIRECTIONS: *For each Thematic Vocabulary word, list three items as instructed. Then, use the vocabulary word in a sentence about one of the things or reasons.*

> **Example:** List three *sensory* details about pizza.
>
> <u>spicy smell</u>   <u>red and yellow color</u>   <u>hot from the oven</u>
>
> **Sentence:** <u>*I love the spicy smell of a pizza cooking in the oven.*</u>

1. List three specific forms of the *media*.

   _____   _____   _____

   Sentence: _____

2. List three things about you that show your *individuality*.

   _____   _____   _____

   Sentence: _____

3. List three *valid* facts about the state in which you live.

   _____   _____   _____

   Sentence: _____

4. List three facts that illustrate the *significance* of good nutrition.

   _____   _____   _____

   Sentence: _____

5. List three facts that you would use to *inform* someone about one of your hobbies or interests.

   _____   _____   _____

   Sentence: _____

Name _____ Date _____

Unit 4: Poetry
Applying the Big Question

What is the secret to reaching someone with words?

DIRECTIONS: *Complete the chart below to apply what you have learned about the secret to reaching others with words. One row has been completed for you.*

Example	Type of communication	Goal of writer or speaker	Effect on reader or listener	How the goal was achieved
From Literature	Poem "Cat!" by Eleanor Farjeon	Share experience of her stubborn cat in an entertaining way	I could see and hear the cat and its owner throughout the action	Alliteration, onomatopoeia, rhyme, choppy rhythm
From Literature				
From Science				
From Social Studies				
From Real Life				

Jacqueline Woodson
Listening and Viewing

Segment 1: Meet Jacqueline Woodson
- How did Jacqueline Woodson's fascination with the "power of words" spark her interest in writing? Jacqueline Woodson tries to keep her writing "real and honest." What do you think that phrase means, and why is "real and honest" important?

_____

_____

_____

_____

Segment 2: Poetry
- Why does Jacqueline Woodson believe that the white space surrounding a poem on its page is important? How do you think poetry can give readers "room for free space" in their lives?

_____

_____

_____

_____

Segment 3: The Writing Process
- Why does Jacqueline Woodson call her writing "character driven"? Which one of Jacqueline Woodson's writing strategies would you use and why?

_____

_____

_____

_____

Segment 4: The Rewards of Writing
- In what way is writing rewarding to Jacqueline Woodson? Jacqueline Woodson thinks a writer must be brave and should welcome any reaction to his or her work. Do you agree or disagree with her? Why?

_____

_____

_____

_____

Learning About Poetry

Poets put words together to create a musical quality and highly charged meaning. A poem combines verbal music and meaning to create a fresh outlook on a subject.

Figurative language is imaginative writing or speech that is not meant to be taken literally. Here are some common figures of speech:

- A **simile** uses a word such as *like* or *as* to compare two apparently unlike things: *Her eyes were like beacons of light.*
- A **metaphor** compares two apparently unlike things but does not use *like* or *as*: *The grass was a carpet of green.*
- **Personification** gives human qualities to nonhuman or inanimate things: *The waves danced in glee.*

Poets use **images**—descriptive, sensory language appealing to the senses: sight, sound, touch, taste, and smell. Poets also use various sound devices:

- **Rhyme** is the repetition of sounds at the ends of words.
- **Meter** is the rhythmical pattern—or the arrangement and number of stressed and unstressed syllables—in a poem.
- **Alliteration** is the repetition of consonant sounds in the beginning of words, as in *fearsome foe.*
- **Assonance** is the repetition of similar vowel sounds in stressed syllables that end in different consonant sounds, as in *made* and *rail.*
- **Consonance** is the repetition of final consonant sounds after different vowel sounds in stressed syllables, as in *lend* and *hand.*
- **Onomatopoeia** is the use of words that imitate sounds, as in *rap, swish,* and *flutter.*
- **Repetition** is the use of any element of language—a sound, word, phrase, clause, or sentence—more than once.

DIRECTIONS: *Circle the letter of the answer that best matches each numbered item.*

1. comparison using *like* or *as*
   A. metaphor   B. personification   C. simile
2. *The snow kissed her nose.*
   A. assonance   B. personification   C. limerick
3. sensory language
   A. consonance   B. imagery   C. alliteration
4. pattern of stressed and unstressed syllables
   A. free verse   B. meter   C. consonance
5. a line of poetry that says, "Their words are trumpet blasts."
   A. simile   B. metaphor   C. personification
6. *buzz, clink, toll, hiss*
   A. personification   B. assonance   C. onomatopoeia

All-in-One Workbook
178

The Poetry of Jacqueline Woodson
Model Selection: Poetry

Two basic elements of poetry are sound and meaning. Poets use **sound devices**—such as rhyme, meter, alliteration, assonance, and onomatopoeia—to create musical effects with words. Poets use **figurative language**—such as simile, metaphor, and personification—to go beyond the ordinary meanings of words to express ideas or feelings in a striking way. Meaning also becomes vivid and memorable when it is conveyed through **imagery,** or words appealing to the senses: sight, sound, smell, taste, and touch.

DIRECTIONS: *Read the following passages from "Describe Somebody" and "Almost a Summer Sky." Then, use the space below each passage to answer the questions.*

I wrote, Ms. Marcus is tall and a little bit skinny. (from "Describe Somebody")

1. Name two sound effects in the preceding line. Which words are involved in each sound effect?

_____

Eric's voice was like something

that didn't seem like it should belong

to Eric.

Seemed like it should be coming out of an angel. (from "Describe Somebody")

2. What figure of speech do the preceding lines contain? What is being compared with what?

_____

_____

You know what I love about trees, Rodney says.

It's like . . . It's like their leaves are hands reaching

out to you. Saying Come on over here, Brother.

Let me just . . . Let me just . . .

Rodney looks down at me and grins.

Let me just give you some shade for a while. (from "Almost a Summer Sky")

3. What figure of speech is most prominent in the preceding passage?

_____

4. In the second line of the preceding passage from "Almost a Summer Sky," which two words create the sound effect called assonance? Which words create alliteration?

_____

Poetry Collection: Eleanor Farjeon, Walter de la Mare, Georgia Douglas Johnson

Writing About the Big Question

What is the secret to reaching someone with words?

Big Question Vocabulary

benefit	connection	cultural	experience	express
feedback	individuality	inform	meaningful	media
misunderstand	relevant	sensory	significance	valid

A. *Use one or more words from the list above to complete each sentence.*

1. When Kirsten wrote her summary, she included only _____ information.

2. Justin hoped that Sarah didn't _____ his question.

3. To paint a picture with words, poetry uses _____ details.

4. Jasmine chose to express her _____ through her writing.

5. Zoe appreciated the _____ she received from her teacher.

B. *Follow the directions in responding to each of the items below.*

1. Write two sentences describing a personal connection you have formed in the last year.

   _____.

   _____.

2. Write two sentences explaining how to resolve conflicts over cultural differences. Use at least two of the Big Question vocabulary words.

   _____

   _____

C. *Complete the sentence below. Then, write a short paragraph in which you connect this idea to the Big Question.*

Poets use sounds and rhythms to _____

_____

_____

_____

Poetry Collection: Eleanor Farjeon, Walter de la Mare, Georgia Douglas Johnson
Reading: Preview to Determine Meanings From Context

Poetry often contains unusual words with which you may not be familiar. When you read a poem, it is a good idea to **preview** it, or examine it in advance, to identify any unfamiliar words. Then, as you read the poem more closely, look for clues in the **context** that can help you determine the meanings of these words. The **context** consists of the other words and phrases that surround a particular word. The following chart shows common types of context clues and an example of each. In the examples, the possibly unfamiliar words are underlined, and the context clues are in italics.

Clue	**Synonym/Definition:** words that mean the same as the unfamiliar word
Example	Knowing the importance of *exercise*, she does calisthenics every day.
Clue	**Antonym/Contrast:** words that mean the opposite of the unfamiliar word
Example	She does calisthenics every day, *but her brother is a couch potato.*
Clue	**Explanation:** words that give more information about the unfamiliar word
Example	Calisthenics *can improve your muscle tone and breathing.*
Clue	**Example:** a word or words that illustrate the unfamiliar word
Example	Calisthenics include *pushups and situps.*
Clue	**Sentence Role:** structural clue that indicates the unfamiliar word's part of speech
Example	Joanna *does* calisthenics every morning. [clearly a noun; seems to be an activity]

DIRECTIONS: *Answer these questions about words in the three poems in this collection.*

1. What synonym later in the poem shows the meaning of *git* in line 11 of "Cat!"? ___

   _____

2. A. In lines 26–27 of "Cat!" what does the context suggest that a *sycamore* is?

   _____

   B. What other word is a clue to the meaning of *sycamore*? _____

3. In line 3 of "Silver," what synonym shows the meaning of *peers*? _____

4. In lines 5–6 of "Your World," what words give an explanation of *horizon*? _____

5. A. Looking at the role of *reaches* in line 11, what part of speech is it? _____

   B. From the context, what do you think *reaches* means here? _____

   _____

Poetry Collection: Eleanor Farjeon, Walter de la Mare, Georgia Douglas Johnson
Literary Analysis: Sound Devices

Poets often use **sound devices** to make their poems more musical and memorable. Four of the most popular sound devices are rhythm, rhyme, alliteration, and onomatopoeia.

- **Rhythm** is the pattern of strong and weak beats, as in TWINkle TWINkle LITtle STAR.
- **Rhyme** is the repetition of sounds at the ends of words, as in *star* and *far*.
- **Alliteration** is the repetition of consonant sounds at the beginnings of nearby words, as in *twinkle* and *twist*.
- **Onomatopoeia** is the use of words that imitate sounds, such as *bang* and *sizzle*.

DIRECTIONS: *As you read the three poems in this collection, record on this chart examples of rhythm, rhyme, alliteration, and onomatopoeia.*

Poem	Rhythm	Rhyme	Alliteration	Onomatopoeia
"Cat!"				
"Silver"				
"Your World"				

Poetry Collection: Eleanor Farjeon, Walter de la Mare, Georgia Douglas Johnson
Vocabulary Builder

Word List

flatterer   horizon   immensity   kennel   rapture   reeds   scampering

A. DIRECTIONS: *Using your knowledge of the underlined Word List words, circle* T *if the statement is true or* F *if the statement is false.*

T / F   1. Someone experiencing <u>rapture</u> is probably frowning.

T / F   2. A <u>flatterer</u> always tells the truth.

T / F   3. Dogs may be housed in a <u>kennel</u>.

T / F   4. You might find <u>reeds</u> along the banks of a pond.

T / F   5. An elephant is likely to be seen <u>scampering</u> through the savannah.

T / F   6. The <u>immensity</u> of a task can be overwhelming.

T / F   7. The sun appears to set on the <u>horizon</u>.

B. DIRECTIONS: *Answer each question with a sentence that uses one of the Word List words. Use each Word List word only once.*

1. What sort of person lavishly praises someone else?

_____

_____

2. Where might you keep your pet?

_____

_____

3. How might a person who is feeling absolutely wonderful describe his or her state?

_____

_____

C. WORD STUDY: *The prefix* im- *means "not." Use the context of the sentences and what you know about the Latin prefix* im- *to explain your answer to each question.*

1. Would talking with your mouth full be consider *improper*? Explain.

_____

_____

2. How would an *impatient* person likely act?

_____

_____

Poetry Collection: Eve Merriam; Nikki Giovanni; Alfred, Lord Tennyson

Writing About the Big Question

What is the secret to reaching someone with words?

Big Question Vocabulary

benefit	connection	cultural	experience	express
feedback	individuality	inform	meaningful	media
misunderstand	relevant	sensory	significance	valid

A. Use one or more words from the list above to complete each sentence.

1. The politician wrote a speech to _____ his audience about his positions.

2. Amanda wanted a career in print _____,—at a newspaper, for example.

3. One _____ of written works is that they can be reviewed.

4. Barb had a hard time expressing the personal _____ she found in the poem.

5. To form a _____ argument, one must base it on facts.

B. Follow the directions in responding to each of the items below.

1. Write two sentences using sensory details to describe an object.

   _____.

   _____.

2. Describe the possible results of a misunderstanding. Use at least two of the Big Question vocabulary words.

   _____

   _____

C. Complete the sentence below. Then, write a short paragraph in which you connect this experience to the big question.

Poetry and songs touch people in ways that are _____

_____

_____

_____

Poetry Collection: Eve Merriam; Nikki Giovanni; Alfred, Lord Tennyson
Reading: Preview to Determine Meanings From Context

Context consists of the words and phrases that surround a particular word. When you read a poem, first **preview** it, or examine it in advance, to identify any unfamiliar words. Then, as you read the poem more closely, look for clues in the **context** that can help you determine the meanings of those words. The following list shows common types of context clues and an example of each. In the examples, the possibly unfamiliar words are underlined, and the context clues are in italics.

- **Synonym or Definition:** words that mean the same as the unfamiliar word
  It will soon be time to <u>commence</u> the race, so please get ready to *start*.
  She shopped in a <u>boutique</u>, *a small specialty store*.

- **Antonym or Contrast:** words that mean the opposite of the unfamiliar word or tell what the unfamiliar word is *not*
  The race will <u>commence</u> at 6 o'clock and *end* three hours later.
  Did you buy that in a <u>boutique</u> or in *a large chain store?*

- **Explanation:** words that give more information about an unfamiliar word
  A <u>feline</u> is *any animal of the cat family*.

- **Example:** words that illustrate the unfamiliar word
  <u>Felines</u> include *lions, tigers, and leopards*.

- **Sentence Role:** structural clue that indicates the unfamiliar word's part of speech. For example, in the following sentence, a reader can figure out that a *boutique* is a noun and that it is not abstract, since it can be entered.
  The two friends *entered* the <u>boutique</u>.

DIRECTIONS: *The chart below lists three words from this collection's poems. You may not be certain of their meanings. Use context clues to help you understand the words, and on the chart, write the clues you use and your best guess about each word's meaning. Then, check a dictionary to see if you were right about the meaning.*

Word	*unique*	*kettles*	*slander*
Location	"Thumbprint," line 3	"The Drum," line 4	"Ring Out, Wild Bells," line 22
Context Clues			
Likely Meaning			
Dictionary Meaning			

Name _____ Date _____

Poetry Collection: Eve Merriam; Nikki Giovanni; Alfred, Lord Tennyson
Literary Analysis: Sound Devices

Poets often use **sound devices** to make their poems more musical and memorable. The chart below shows four of the most popular sound devices.

Sound Device	Definition	Example
rhythm	the pattern of strong and weak beats	HICKory DICKory DOCK
rhyme	the repetition of sounds at the ends of words	dock and clock
alliteration	the repetition of consonant sounds at the start of nearby words	clock and close
onomatopoeia	the use of words that imitate sounds	fizz, bubble

DIRECTIONS: *Answer these questions about the sound devices used in the poems in this collection. Include the line numbers of any examples you list.*

1. What are two examples of alliteration in "Thumbprint"? _____

    _____

2. List two examples of onomatopoeia in "The Drum." Also, explain what sound each example imitates. _____

    _____

3. List one example of alliteration and one example of onomatopoeia in "Ring Out, Wild Bells." Also, explain what the onomatopoeia imitates. _____

4. Of the three poems in this collection, which one follows a pattern of rhymes at the ends of lines? Describe that pattern. _____

    _____

5. Focus on the rhythm of "The Drum" as you say the lines to yourself. What rhythm is the poet trying to imitate? _____

    _____

6. Given the subject, why is it appropriate that "Ring Out, Wild Bells" is such a musical poem? _____

    _____

Poetry Collection: Eve Merriam; Nikki Giovanni; Alfred, Lord Tennyson
Vocabulary Builder

Word List

 imprint   modes   resounding   singularity   spite   strife

A. DIRECTIONS: *Answer each question with a sentence that uses one of the Word List words. Use each Word List word only once.*

1. Was there a lot of misery in the world during the twentieth century?

   _____

   _____

2. What quality might an independent person display?

   _____

   _____

3. What sort of music might you hear at a loud concert?

   _____

   _____

4. How might a person feel toward his enemy?

   _____

   _____

5. What do publishers use to identify themselves in books?

   _____

   _____

6. What can you call different ways of doing something, such as learning?

   _____

   _____

B. WORD STUDY: *The Latin prefix* im- *means "in" or "into." Use the context of the sentences and what you know about the Latin prefix* im- *to explain your answer to each question.*

1. What is something that can be *implanted*?

   _____

   _____

2. Is someone who is *imperiled* safe? Explain.

   _____

   _____

Poetry Collections: Eleanor Farjeon, Walter de la Mare, Georgia Douglas Johnson; Eve Merriam; Nikki Giovanni; Alfred, Lord Tennyson

Integrated Language Skills: Grammar

Subject Complements

A **subject complement** is a word that follows a linking verb and tells something about the subject. One kind of subject complement is called a *predicate adjective*. It describes the subject. Other kinds of subject complements are called a *predicate noun* and a *predicate pronoun*. They further identify the subject. A predicate pronoun uses the subject, not object, form.

Predicate Adjective:	The visitor seems lost. [*Lost* describes the subject, *visitor.*]
Predicate Noun:	He was the best *player* on the team. [*Player* further identifies the subject, *He.*]
Predicate Pronoun:	The winner is *she.* [*She* further identifies the subject, *winner.*]

A. PRACTICE: *Circle the subject complement in each sentence that contains a subject complement. On the line before the sentence, write* PN *if the subject complement is a predicate noun,* PP *if it is a predicate pronoun, and* PA *if it is a predicate adjective. If the sentence does not contain a subject complement, write* none *on the line.*

____ 1. Poems are often very musical.

____ 2. That word is an example of onomatopoeia.

____ 3. The last speaker in the choral reading was I.

____ 4. The rhythm of the poem sounded familiar to me.

____ 5. The bell sounded at the end of English class.

B. Writing Application: *Add to each subject in the items below to build a sentence that includes a linking verb and a subject complement. Include at least one predicate noun, one predicate pronoun, and one predicate adjective in your sentences.*

1. The cat _____

_____

2. Martin Luther King, Jr., _____

_____

3. The fingerprint _____

_____

4. The bravest person _____

_____

5. The bells _____

_____

Poetry Collection: Eleanor Farjeon, Walter de la Mare, Georgia Douglas Johnson;
Eve Merriam; Nikki Giovanni; Alfred, Lord Tennyson

Integrated Language Skills: Support for Writing a Poem That Uses Rhythm and Sound Devices

Use this chart to jot down your ideas about what to include in your poem.

Title	
Author	
Subject	
Main Idea	
Sound Devices	Rhyme:
	Meter:
	Alliteration:
	Other:

Poetry Collection: Patricia Hubbell, Richard García, Langston Hughes

Writing About the Big Question

What is the secret to reaching someone with words?

Big Question Vocabulary

benefit	connection	cultural	experience	express
feedback	individuality	inform	meaningful	media
misunderstand	relevant	sensory	significance	valid

A. *Use one or more words from the list above to complete each sentence.*

1. Jamie recorded her camping _____ for her friends to enjoy.

2. Alex wanted to _____ his gratitude for his parents' help.

3. Meg and her grandson had a _____ conversation about her history.

4. After their conversation, Lynn and Ronnie felt the _____ of true friendship.

5. The poet reading his work aloud provided a true _____ experience: we felt as though we were there.

B. *Follow the directions in responding to each of the items below.*

1. Write two sentences about the media. Consider media's role in society.

   _____.

   _____.

2. Write about a way you express your individuality. Use at least two of the Big Question vocabulary words.

   _____

   _____

C. *Complete the sentence below. Then, write a short paragraph in which you connect this idea to the Big Question.*

The sounds of language influence meaning in literature by _____

_____

_____

_____

Poetry Collection: Patricia Hubbell, Richard García, Langston Hughes

Reading: Reread and Read Ahead to Determine Meanings From Context

Poetry often contains unusual words with which you may not be familiar. Nevertheless, you can often understand these words if you examine the **context**—the words and phrases surrounding an unfamiliar word. When you find an unfamiliar word, **reread and read ahead** for context clues that will help you figure out the meaning. When you think you have come up with a possible meaning, insert the meaning in place of the unfamiliar word, and reread the sentence. If it does not make sense, look for more context clues, or consult a dictionary.

In "Concrete Mixers" by Patricia Hubbell, for example, the word *ponderous* may be unfamiliar, but the context provides clues to its meaning.

> Tough gray-skinned monsters standing *ponderous,*
>
> Elephant-bellied. . . .

If you reread the line with *ponderous* and focus on "monsters standing" and then read ahead to "elephant-bellied," you can figure out from these clues that *ponderous* probably means "big and heavy."

DIRECTIONS: *Reread the poem "Concrete Mixers," looking for clues to the meaning of the underlined word in each item below. On the lines provided, write your best guess about the meaning of the word, and write the clue, if any, that pointed you to that meaning. When you have finished, you can check the meanings in a dictionary.*

1. Likely meaning of <u>hose</u> in line 2: _____

   Clue(s): _____

2. Likely meaning of <u>muck</u> in line 5: _____

   Clue(s): _____

3. Likely meaning of <u>perch</u> in line 7: _____

   Clue(s): _____

4. Likely meaning of <u>bellow</u> in line 14: _____

   Clue(s): _____

5. Likely meaning of <u>urban</u> in line 16: _____

   Clue(s): _____

Poetry Collection: Patricia Hubbell, Richard García, Langston Hughes
Literary Analysis: Figurative Language

Poets often use imaginative **figures of speech,** or **figurative language,** to make their poems more musical and memorable. Figures of speech often compare unlike things. A **simile** directly states the comparison of two unlike things by using a word such as *like* or *as.* A **metaphor** suggests a comparison between two unlike things by saying that one *is* the other. **Personification** compares something nonhuman to a human being by giving it human characteristics.

Similes:　　　　　Life is like a dance. The ocean is as moody as a child.

Metaphor:　　　　Life is a dance.

Personification:　　The ocean laughs and cries.

DIRECTIONS: *On the chart below, record the desired examples.*

	Line Number(s)	**What Two Things Are Compared**
1. Simile in "Concrete Mixers"		
2. Metaphor in "Concrete Mixers"		
3. Personification in "Concrete Mixers"		
4. Personification in "The City Is So Big"		

Poetry Collection: Patricia Hubbell, Richard García, Langston Hughes
Vocabulary Builder

Word List

    bellow   dew   ponderous   roam   urban

A. DIRECTIONS: *Answer each question with a sentence that uses one of the Word List words. Use each Word List word only once.*

1. What might a suitcase with lots of travel labels show about its owner?

   _____

   _____

2. What kind of suitcase would be hard to carry?

   _____

   _____

3. How might you describe a roar of a lion?

   _____

   _____

4. What might cover flowers' petals on a spring morning?

   _____

   _____

5. How might you describe a photograph of a city?

   _____

   _____

B. WORD STUDY: *The suffix -ous means "characterized by" or "full of." Use the context of the sentences and what you know about the suffix -ous to explain your answer to each question.*

1. Does something *instantaneous* take a long time? Explain.

   _____

   _____

2. Is something *frivolous* necessary? Explain.

   _____

   _____

Poetry Collection: Pablo Neruda, Elizabeth Bishop, Emily Dickinson

Writing About the Big Question

What is the secret to reaching someone with words?

Big Question Vocabulary

benefit	connection	cultural	experience	express
feedback	individuality	inform	meaningful	media
misunderstand	relevant	sensory	significance	valid

A. *Use one or more words from the list above to complete each sentence.*

1. The _____ of his message was expressed through his heartfelt emotion.

2. Everyone can _____ from communication.

3. Shawna made a _____ point when she said I didn't listen to her.

4. My _____ with communication suggests that my words must reflect my true feelings.

5. The _____ the poet received from the critics was positive.

B. *Follow the directions in responding to each of the items below.*

1. Write two sentences about a topic relevant to your communication with others.

   _____.

   _____.

2. Write two sentences that use sensory details to describe a conversation. Use at least two of the Big Question vocabulary words.

   _____

   _____

C. *Complete the sentence below. Then, write a short paragraph in which you connect this idea to the Big Question.*

   Writers often respond to nature in poetry because _____

   _____

   _____

   _____

Poetry Collection: Pablo Neruda, Elizabeth Bishop, Emily Dickinson

Reading: Reread and Read Ahead to Determine Meanings From Context

Poetry often contains unusual words with which you may not be familiar. Nevertheless, you can often understand these words if you examine the **context**—the words and phrases surrounding an unfamiliar word. When you find an unfamiliar word, **reread and read ahead** for context clues that will help you figure out the meaning. When you think you have come up with a possible meaning, insert the meaning in place of the unfamiliar word, and reread the sentence. If it does not make sense, look for more context clues, or consult a dictionary.

DIRECTIONS: *The chart below lists three words from this collection's poems that you may not immediately be able to define. Use context clues to help you understand the words, and on the chart, write the clues you find and your best guess about each word's meaning. Then, check a dictionary to see if you were right about the meaning.*

Word	*latticework*	*heron*	*uninjured*
Location	"Ode to Enchanted Light," line 5	"Little Exercise," line 7	"Little Exercise," line 21
Context Clues			
Likely Meaning			
Dictionary Meaning			

Poetry Collection: Pablo Neruda, Elizabeth Bishop, Emily Dickinson
Literary Analysis: Figurative Language

Poets often use **figures of speech,** or **figurative language,** to make their poems more musical and memorable. The chart below lists and explains three common figures of speech.

Figure of Speech	Definition	Example
simile	a comparison of two unlike things as if they were alike, using a comparing word such as *like* or *as* to state the comparison	The wind is like a cheerleader.
metaphor	a comparison of two unlike things as if they were alike, suggested by stating one thing *is* another	The wind is a cheerleader.
personification	a comparison of something nonhuman with something human, suggested by giving the nonhuman thing human characteristics	The wind sang in a loud, cheerful voice.

DIRECTIONS: *Answer these questions about the figurative language in "Ode to Enchanted Light." Include the line numbers of any examples you list.*

1. List two similes that help the reader picture the light in "Ode to Enchanted Light."

   _____

2. Which simile in the first nine lines do you think best captures the enchanted mood the poet wants to convey? Why? _____

   _____

3. Explain how the details about the cicada involve personification. _____

   _____

4. With what metaphor does "Ode to Enchanted Light" conclude? _____

   _____

5. What feelings, or mood, does the final metaphor help convey? _____

   _____

Poetry Collection: Pablo Neruda, Elizabeth Bishop, Emily Dickinson
Vocabulary Builder

Word List

boulevard   cicada   debates   rut   uneasily   unresponsive

A. DIRECTIONS: *Circle* T *if the statement is true or* F *if the statement is false.* Then, explain your answer.

T / F   1. A nightmare can make someone sleep <u>uneasily</u>.

_____

_____

T / F   2. Daydreamers are sometimes <u>unresponsive</u> when you ask them a question.

_____

_____

T / F   3. Every homeowner likes a big <u>rut</u> in the driveway.

_____

_____

T / F   4. Someone who <u>debates</u> all her decisions probably acts much too quickly.

_____

_____

T / F   5. It is hard to locate a <u>cicada</u> because it is so quiet.

_____

_____

T / F   6. Most <u>boulevards</u> are lined with trees.

_____

_____

B. WORD STUDY: *The suffix* -ive *indicates a tendency toward a certain kind of action. Use the context of the sentences and what you know about the suffix* -ive *to explain your answer to each question.*

1. What is another way to describe a person who is *indecisive*?

_____

_____

2. How might an *impulsive* person act?

_____

_____

All-in-One Workbook
197

Poetry Collections: Patricia Hubbell, Richard García, Langston Hughes;
Pablo Neruda, Elizabeth Bishop, Emily Dickinson

Integrated Language Skills: Grammar

Direct and Indirect Objects

A **direct object** is a noun or pronoun that follows an action verb and receives the action of the verb. It answers the question *What?* or *Whom?* after the action verb. (A direct object does not appear after a linking verb.)

Sonya brewed some *tea*. [*What* did Sonya brew?]

The aroma tempted *them*. [*Whom* did the aroma tempt?]

An **indirect object** is a noun or pronoun that comes between an action verb and a direct object. It answers the question *To or for whom?* or *To or for what?* after an action verb. You cannot have an indirect object without a direct object.

Sonya brewed her *guests* some tea. [*For whom* did Sonya brew some tea?]

Sonya gave each *cup* a different flavor. [*To what* did Sonya give a different flavor?]

Pronouns used as direct or indirect objects require the object form of the pronoun.

Incorrect: We visited *Sue and he*. **Correct:** We visited *Sue and him*.

Incorrect: Sal gave *Dave and I* help. **Correct:** Sal gave *Dave and me* help.

A. PRACTICE: *Underline the direct object and circle the indirect object in each sentence that contains one or both. If the pronoun form is incorrect, cross it out and write the correct form on the line after the sentence. If there is no direct or indirect object in the sentence, write* none *on the line.*

1. Nature plays a strong role in her poetry. _____

2. The poem's speaker gives us advice about human relationships.

   _____

3. The last poem really impressed Nancy and I. _____

4. The images show readers the speaker's feelings. _____

5. The biggest fans of her poetry are Celia and Mary. _____

B. Writing Application: *Add to each subject below to create a sentence that includes an action verb and a direct object. Also, include an indirect object in two of your sentences.*

1. The heavy machinery _____

2. Great poets _____

3. My thoughts _____

4. The glowing light _____

5. The islanders _____

Poetry Collections: Patricia Hubbell, Richard García, Langston Hughes;
Pablo Neruda, Elizabeth Bishop, Emily Dickinson

Integrated Language Skills: Support for Writing a Study for a Poem

Use this chart to jot down ideas about the figurative language that you hope to include in your poem about a natural or city setting.

Comparison to Make	Wording to Use	Type of Figurative Language

"Snake on the Etowah" by David Bottoms
"Vanishing Species" by Bailey White
Writing About the Big Question

What is the secret to reaching someone with words?

Big Question Vocabulary

benefit	connection	cultural	experience	express
feedback	individuality	inform	meaningful	media
misunderstand	relevant	sensory	significance	valid

A. *Use one or more words from the list above to complete each sentence.*

1. Animals are often able to _____ emotions without words.

2. Their gestures and movements form _____ messages.

3. Both Bottoms and White write about an _____ with animal communication.

B. *Follow the directions in responding to each of the items below.*

1. Write two sentences about ways to express yourself through different media.

   _____.

   _____.

2. Write about a meaningful experience you have had communicating with another person or animal. Use at least two of the Big Question vocabulary words.

   _____

   _____

C. *Complete the sentence below. Then, write a short paragraph in which you connect this idea to the Big Question.*

Sensory details can help make an experience real by _____

_____

_____

_____

Name _____   Date _____

"Snake on the Etowah" by David Bottoms
"Vanishing Species" by Bailey White

Literary Analysis: Comparing Poetry and Prose

Literature comes in two major forms—prose and poetry.

- **Prose** is the ordinary form of written language. Prose is usually presented in paragraphs and runs continuously. It includes both fiction and nonfiction. Essays, stories, and novels are all forms of prose.

- **Poetry** is distinguished from prose by its use of precise words, deliberate line lengths, and sound devices such as rhyme and alliteration. Poetry is organized in stanzas and often uses line breaks to emphasize meaning. Poetry is abbreviated, so poets must choose precise words to express their ideas. Poems can rhyme, can be written in free verse, can be lyric, or can tell a story.

Though the two kinds of literature take different form, the writers of both often have the same task—to choose words and images that appeal to the reader and express precise meaning or emotion.

DIRECTIONS: *Use the following chart to identify the similarities and differences between the presentation of the poem "Snake on the Etowah" and that of "Vanishing Species."*

	Form	Literary Techniques/ Language	Setting/Mood	Events
"Snake on the Etowah"				
"Vanishing Species"				

DIRECTIONS: *Use the information from the chart to write a compare-and-contrast paragraph about the differences in the presentation of ideas in the poem and in the prose selection.*

"Snake on the Etowah" by David Bottoms
"Vanishing Species" by Bailey White
Vocabulary Builder

Word List

acquire   extinction   resurgence   rituals   sidling   undulation

A. DIRECTIONS: *Write a complete sentence to answer each question.*

1. If a plant or animal is facing *extinction*, what is likely to happen to it?

_____

_____

2. What happens if there is a *resurgence* of a fashion from a previous decade?

_____

_____

3. When you *acquire* something, what happens?

_____

_____

4. Where or when are you likely to participate in *rituals?*

_____

_____

5. What is a dog doing if it is *sidling* up to you?

_____

_____

6. Where might you witness an *undulation?*

_____

_____

B. DIRECTIONS: *Circle* T *if the statement is true or* F *if the statement is false.*

T / F   1. If I want to *acquire* something, I will try to avoid it.

T / F   2. The child is *sidling* because he has just learned to walk.

T / F   3. *Rituals* are formed over many years.

T / F   4. *Resurgence* is the same as *extinction*.

T / F   5. *Undulations* are often violent.

"**Snake on the Etowah**" by David Bottoms
"**Vanishing Species**" by Bailey White

Integrated Language Skills: Support for Writing to Compare Poetry and Prose

Before you write your essay comparing poetry and prose, use the graphic organizer below to jot down your ideas and answers to questions.

How do narrative and poetry differ?	
Narrative	Poetry

How are the two selections similar? List their common characteristics.	
"Snake on the Etowah"	"Vanishing Species"

How do the two selections differ? List their individual characteristics.	
"Snake on the Etowah"	"Vanishing Species"

What possibilities do the genres allow in expressing nature themes?	
Narrative	Poetry

Poetry Collection: Robert Hayden, William Shakespeare, Ricardo Sánchez

Writing About the Big Question

What is the secret to reaching someone with words?

Big Question Vocabulary

benefit	connection	cultural	experience	express
feedback	individuality	inform	meaningful	media
misunderstand	relevant	sensory	significance	valid

A. *Use one or more words from the list above to complete each sentence.*

1. "I have called this meeting to _____ you of our new dress code," said Principal McNut.

2. The community was a spectrum of different _____ influences reflected in the people and food from around the world.

3. One way Clarissa expressed her _____ was through her art and writing.

B. *Follow the directions in responding to each of the items below.*

1. What is the benefit of talking about meaningful experiences? Use at least two Big Question Vocabulary words in your answer.

_____

_____

2. Write about a time when you received feedback that made you uncomfortable.

_____

_____

C. *Complete the sentence below. Then, write a short paragraph in which you connect this idea to the Big Question.*

Reading about other people's feelings and experiences may benefit people and help them _____

_____

_____

_____

Poetry Collection: Robert Hayden, William Shakespeare, Ricardo Sánchez
Reading: Reread to Paraphrase

To make their poems more powerful and memorable, poets often use language that is rarely used in everyday speech. To understand a poem, it may therefore be helpful to paraphrase it in simple, everyday language. When you **paraphrase,** you restate text in your own words. First, **reread the poem to clarify** the writer's meaning. Identify the most basic information in each sentence or phrase—what is being done and who or what is doing it. Use a dictionary or text aids like footnotes, if provided, to help you with unfamiliar terms. Once you understand the poet's meaning, restate the sentences in everyday English. Eliminate repetition, use simpler synonyms, and put unusual sentence structures into a word order that is easier to understand.

DIRECTIONS: *Use this chart to paraphrase the poems by Shakespeare and Sánchez in this collection. One example has been provided for you.*

Poem	Original Lines	Paraphrased Lines
"Blow, Blow, Thou Winter Wind"	Line 1: "Blow . . . wind."	Winter wind, go ahead and blow.
	Lines 2–3: "Thou . . . ingratitude."	
	Lines 4–6: "Thy . . . rude."	
	Line 7: "Heigh-ho! . . . holly."	
	Line 8: "Most . . . folly."	
	Lines 9–10: "Then . . . jolly."	
	Lines 11–13: "Freeze . . . forgot."	
	Lines 14–16: "Though . . . not."	
	Lines 17–20: "Heigh-ho . . . jolly."	
"Old Man"	Lines 1–6: "old . . . freely;"	
	Lines 7–14: "old . . . life . . ."	
	Lines 15–21: "you . . . albuquerque . . ."	
	Lines 22–28: "old . . . there:"	
	Lines 29–36: "some . . . painful . . ."	
	Lines 37–47: "old . . . you . . ."	

Poetry Collection: Robert Hayden, William Shakespeare, Ricardo Sánchez
Literary Analysis: Lyric and Narrative Poetry

A **lyric poem** expresses the thoughts and feelings of a single speaker and uses images and other details to create a single, unified impression. A **narrative poem** tells a story in verse and has all the elements of a short story, including plot, conflict, setting, characters, and theme.

DIRECTIONS: *Choose one lyric poem and one narrative poem in this collection. Write the title of each poem on the line provided, and then answer the questions about it.*

A. Lyric Poem Title: _____

1. Why is this poem a lyric poem? _____

   _____

2. What are two feelings or emotions that the speaker expresses? _____

   _____

3. List two images that the speaker uses and the ideas they convey. _____

   _____

   _____

4. What main impression would you say the poem conveys? _____

   _____

B. Narrative Poem Title: _____

1. Why is this poem a narrative poem? _____

   _____

2. Summarize the plot in one or two sentences. _____

   _____

   _____

3. What is the main conflict or struggle, and how is it resolved in the end?

   _____

   _____

4. As specifically as possible, identify the poem's main setting.

   _____

   _____

5. Who is the main character? What minor characters does the poem feature?

   _____

   _____

Poetry Collection: Robert Hayden, William Shakespeare, Ricardo Sánchez
Vocabulary Builder

Word List

    aromas   beckoning   ingratitude   legacy   shackles   supple

A. DIRECTIONS: *Answer each question with a sentence that uses one of the Word List words. Use each Word List word only once.*

1. What might someone get from a rich relative when that relative dies?

_____

_____

2. How would you describe a person who fails to give thanks to those who help him or her?

_____

_____

3. How would you describe a light in the darkness?

_____

_____

4. What might you call the smells of different coffees?

_____

_____

5. How could you restrain a criminal?

_____

_____

6. How could you describe a person's muscular body?

_____

_____

B. WORD STUDY: *The prefix* in- *means "not" or "lacking." Use the context of the sentences and what you know about the prefix* in- *to explain your answer to each question.*

1. What might a student do if he were *incapable* of solving a problem?

_____

_____

2. Are *indefinite* plans fixed? Explain.

_____

_____

Poetry Collection: Emma Lazarus, Henry Wadsworth Longfellow, Paul Laurence Dunbar

Writing About the Big Question

What is the secret to reaching someone with words?

Big Question Vocabulary

benefit	connection	cultural	experience	express
feedback	individuality	inform	meaningful	media
misunderstand	relevant	sensory	significance	valid

A. *Use one or more words from the list above to complete each sentence.*

1. Dunbar communicates the African American _____ experience through his poetry.

2. Lazarus understands that all people _____ a need for home.

3. Longfellow commemorates the _____ of a historical icon's brave deeds.

4. The _____ that Americans feel surpasses cultural differences.

B. *Follow the directions in responding to each of the items below.*

1. What do you include if you want to inform someone about a significant event?

   _____.

   _____.

2. What kind of feedback would you give one of the poets you have read? Use at least two of the Big Question vocabulary words.

   _____

   _____

C. *Complete the sentence below. Then, write a short paragraph in which you connect this idea to the Big Question.*

Someone who has contributed greatly to the history of our country is _____

_____

_____

_____

Name _____ Date _____

Reading: Reread to Paraphrase

To understand a poem, it often helps to paraphrase it in simple, everyday language. When you **paraphrase,** you restate text in your own words. First, **reread the poem to clarify** the writer's meaning. Identify the most basic information in each sentence or phrase—what is being done and who or what is doing it. Use a dictionary or text aids like footnotes, if provided, to help you with unfamiliar terms. Once you understand the poet's meaning, restate the sentences in everyday English. Eliminate repetition, use simpler synonyms, and put unusual sentence structures into a word order that is easier to understand.

DIRECTIONS: *Use this chart to paraphrase the two shorter poems in this collection. An example has been provided for you.*

Poem	Original Lines	Paraphrased Lines
"The New Colossus"	Lines 1–2: "Not . . . land;"	Unlike the giant bronze statue on the Greek island of Rhodes, with its image of conquest,
	Lines 3–6: "Here . . . Exiles."	
	Lines 6–8: "From . . . frame."	
	Lines 9–10: "Keep . . . lips."	
	Lines 10–12: "Give . . . shore."	
	Lines 13–14: "Send . . . door!"	
"Harriet Beecher Stowe"	Lines 1–3: "She . . . alone."	
	Line 4: "She . . . slept:"	
	Lines 5–6: "Her message . . . throne."	
	Lines 7–8: "Command . . . leapt."	
	Lines 9–10: "Around . . . flame"	
	Lines 11–13: "Blest . . . priestess!"	
	Lines 13–14: "At . . . fame."	

Poetry Collection: Emma Lazarus, Henry Wadsworth Longfellow, Paul Laurence Dunbar

Literary Analysis: Lyric and Narrative Poetry

A **lyric poem** expresses the thoughts and feelings of a single speaker and uses images and other details to create a single, unified impression. A **narrative poem** tells a story in verse and has all the elements of a short story, including plot, conflict, setting, characters, and theme.

DIRECTIONS: *Choose one lyric poem and one narrative poem in this collection. Write the title of each poem on the line provided, and then answer the questions about it.*

A. Lyric Poem Title: _____

1. Why is this poem a lyric poem? _____

_____

2. What are two feelings or emotions that the speaker expresses? _____

_____

3. List two images that the speaker uses and the ideas they convey. _____

_____

_____

4. What main impression would you say the poem conveys? _____

_____

B. Narrative Poem Title: _____

1. Why is this poem a narrative poem? _____

_____

2. Summarize the plot in one or two sentences. _____

_____

_____

3. What is the main conflict or struggle, and how is it resolved in the end?

_____

_____

4. As specifically as possible, identify the poem's main setting.

_____

_____

5. Who is the main character? What minor characters does the poem feature?

_____

_____

Poetry Collection: Emma Lazarus, Henry Wadsworth Longfellow, Paul Laurence Dunbar

Vocabulary Builder

Word List

defiance   exiles   peril   somber   transfigured   yearning

A. DIRECTIONS: *Answer each question with a sentence that uses one of the Word List words. Use each Word List word only once.*

1. What is the mood at a funeral usually like?

   _____

   _____

2. What adjective describes a person who craves a piece of candy?

   _____

   _____

3. How can you describe danger?

   _____

   _____

4. What do you call people who are forced to leave their homelands?

   _____

   _____

5. How could you describe a child's refusing to listen to his or her parent?

   _____

   _____

6. If something is changed, what can it be said to be?

   _____

   _____

B. WORD STUDY: *The prefix* trans- *means "change." Use the context of the sentences and what you know about the prefix* trans- *to explain your answer to each question.*

1. What is a *translator's* job?

   _____

   _____

2. What might happen to someone who experiences *translocation*?

   _____

   _____

Poetry Collections: Robert Hayden, William Shakespeare, Ricardo Sánchez;
Emma Lazarus, Henry Wadsworth Longfellow, Paul Laurence Dunbar

Integrated Language Skills: Grammar

Prepositions and Prepositional Phrases

A **preposition** is a word that relates a noun or pronoun to another word in the
sentence. The noun or pronoun is called the **object of the preposition**. A
prepositional phrase consists of a preposition, its object, and any words that modify
the object. The entire phrase serves as an adjective or an adverb. Study this example:

> The boy *with Mary* danced *around the empty room.*

The first preposition, *with,* relates its object, the noun *Mary,* to another word in the
sentence, *boy.* The preposition and its object form the prepositional phrase *with Mary.*
The phrase serves as an adjective, describing the noun *boy*—it tells you *which* boy. The
second preposition, *around,* relates its object, the noun *room,* to another word in the
sentence, *danced.* The preposition, its object, and the words *the* and *empty,* which modify
the object, form the prepositional phrase *around the empty room.* The phrase serves as an
adverb, describing the verb *danced*—it tells you *where* the boy danced.

The chart shows some words that are often used as prepositions.

Sequence	Location	Direction	Other Relationships
after	above	around	about
before	in	down	at
during	near	from	for
until	under	up	of

A. PRACTICE: *Circle the prepositional phrase in each sentence, labeling the preposition* P
and its object OP. *Draw an arrow to the word that the phrase modifies. On the line
before the sentence, indicate whether the phrase serves as an* adjective *or an* adverb.

_____ 1. The study of poetry is not always easy.

_____ 2. To understand a poem, you often read between the lines.

_____ 3. I enjoyed that poem by an African American poet.

_____ 4. He wrote poetry after the Civil War.

_____ 5. Read it with me as I recite it aloud.

B. Writing Application: *Expand each sentence by adding a prepositional phrase to
describe the underlined word. Write the new sentence on the line.*

1. The <u>dog</u> barked all night. _____

2. The moonlight <u>streamed</u>. _____

3. We <u>sat</u> together. _____

Name _____ Date _____

Integrated Language Skills: Support for Writing
a Lyric or Narrative Poem

Use this sheet to jot down your notes for your lyric or narrative poem. If you plan to write a lyric poem, fill in the information called for on the first chart. If you plan to write a narrative poem, fill in the information called for on the second chart.

Lyric Poem
Person:
Qualities:
Achievements:

Narrative Poem
Events:
Characters:
Details of Setting:

Name _____ Date _____

Writing About the Big Question

What is the secret to reaching someone with words?

Big Question Vocabulary

benefit	connection	cultural	experience	express
feedback	individuality	inform	meaningful	media
misunderstand	relevant	sensory	significance	valid

A. *Use one or more words from the list above to complete each sentence.*

1. In his poem "January," Updike uses _____ details to appeal to sight and feeling.

2. In Alice Walker's poem, she expresses the _____ experiences she had with her sister.

3. N. Scott Momaday examines the _____ between man and nature in "New World."

B. *Follow the directions in responding to each of the items below.*

1. Write two sentences about the benefit of observing nature. Consider how observation affects your life.

   _____.

   _____.

2. Write about a significant experience you had at a particular time of the year. Use at least two of the Big Question vocabulary words.

   _____

   _____

C. *Complete the sentence below. Then, write a short paragraph in which you connect this idea to the Big Question.*

   Poetry written about nature helps us discover _____

   _____

   _____

   _____

Name _____ Date _____

Reading: Read According to Punctuation to Paraphrase

When you **paraphrase** a poem, you restate it in your own words. First, read the poem through carefully and try to determine the complete thoughts it contains. **Use the punctuation** on the page—as well as the words themselves—to help you identify complete thoughts. Next, restate the meaning of each complete thought in your own words. Eliminate unneeded repetition. Mentally fill in any missing words to complete thoughts that are not fully stated. If the vocabulary is difficult, use simpler synonyms. Put unusual sentence structures into a word order that is easier to understand.

DIRECTIONS: *Use this chart to paraphrase the first two parts of "New World" by N. Scott Momaday. An example has been provided for you.*

Complete Thoughts	Paraphrased Lines
Lines 1–2: "First Man, behold:"	Look, First Man
Lines 3–5: "the earth . . . leaves;"	
Lines 6–8: "the sky . . . rain."	
Lines 9–15: "Pollen . . . mountains."	
Lines 16–19: "Cedars . . . pines."	
Lines 20–28: "At . . . pools."	
Lines 29–31: "Grasses . . . shine."	
Lines 32–36: "Shadows . . . smoke."	

Name _____ Date _____

Literary Analysis: Imagery

Poetry often makes use of **imagery,** language that appeals to one or more of the five senses. Each instance of imagery is called an **image**. If you take note of the images as you read a poem, you will often understand it better. As you read, imagine that you are actually seeing, smelling, hearing, tasting, or touching the things described by the poet. Put yourself at the scene mentally, and experience the images.

DIRECTIONS: *Use this chart to help you focus on the imagery in the three poems in this collection. From each poem, list words or phrases that appeal to the senses in the corresponding boxes. Remember that many images appeal to more than one sense.*

	Sight	**Sound**	**Touch**	**Smell**	**Taste**
"January"					
"New World"					
"For My Sister Molly . . ."					

Poetry Collection: John Updike, N. Scott Momaday, Alice Walker
Vocabulary Builder

Word List

extinguished   inexpressible   pollen   recede   remote   wearisome

A. DIRECTIONS: *Circle* T *if the statement is true or* F *if the statement is false.* Then, explain your answer.

T / F **1.** After a wave comes up on the shore, it begins to <u>recede</u>.

    _____

T / F **2.** A <u>remote</u> land is close by.

    _____

T / F **3.** A <u>wearisome</u> task is easily completed.

    _____

T / F **4.** Flowers produce <u>pollen</u>.

    _____

T / F **5.** An <u>extinguished</u> fire is no longer a danger.

    _____

T / F **6.** An <u>inexpressible</u> emotion cannot be described.

    _____

B. WORD STUDY: *The roots -cede- and -ceed- mean "go" or "yield." Use the context of the sentences and what you know about the roots -cede- and -ceed- to explain your answer to each question.*

1. If a line *proceeds* quickly, what happens?

    _____

    _____

2. If someone *exceeds* expectations at work, what will likely happen?

    _____

    _____

C. DIRECTIONS: *Circle the letter of the word that is closest in meaning to the Word List word in CAPITAL LETTERS.*

1. RECEDE
  A. triumph   B. grow   C. retreat   D. increase

2. REMOTE
  A. distant   B. near   C. connected   D. clear

3. EXTINGUISHED
  A. forgotten   B. empty   C. extinct   D. alive

4. WEARISOME
  A. old   B. tiring   C. soothing   D. fashionable

Poetry Collection: Amy Ling, Wendy Rose, E. E. Cummings
Writing About the Big Question

What is the secret to reaching someone with words?

Big Question Vocabulary

benefit	connection	cultural	experience	express
feedback	individuality	inform	meaningful	media
misunderstand	relevant	sensory	significance	valid

A. *Use one or more words from the list above to complete each sentence.*

1. Karl hoped to _____ from his practice in speech class.

2. Jasmine realized too late the _____ of the harsh words she spoke.

3. "Make sure you include only _____ details in your essay," Ms. Brennan said.

B. *Follow the directions in responding to each of the items below.*

1. Express your ideas about a relevant issue in your school or community. Use at least two Big Question vocabulary words.

   _____.

   _____.

2. Make a connection between literature and life, referring to a poem, story, or novel you have read recently.

   _____

   _____

C. *Complete the sentence below. Then, write a short paragraph in which you connect this idea to the Big Question.*

   Stimulating the senses with familiar smells can stir up memories of _____

   _____

   _____

   _____

Poetry Collection: Amy Ling, Wendy Rose, E. E. Cummings
Reading: Read According to Punctuation to Paraphrase

When you **paraphrase** a poem, you restate it in your own words. First, read the poem through carefully and try to determine the complete thoughts it contains. **Use the punctuation** on the page—as well as the words themselves—to help you identify complete thoughts. Next, restate the meaning of each complete thought in your own words. Eliminate unneeded repetition. Mentally fill in any missing words to complete thoughts that are not fully stated. If the vocabulary is difficult, use simpler synonyms. Put unusual sentence structures into a word order that is easier to understand.

DIRECTIONS: *Because the poem "your little voice" does not use standard punctuation or capitalization to make complete thoughts clear, try to figure them out from the poem's words and the spacing of the words on the page. On the chart below, list your paraphrase on the right. An example has been provided for you.*

Complete Thoughts	Paraphrased Lines
Lines 1–2: "your . . . leaping"	I heard your little voice over the telephone.
Lines 3–4: "and . . . dizzy"	
Lines 5–10: "With . . . faces"	
Line 11: "floating . . . me"	
Lines 12–17: "I . . . moon"	
Lines 18–19: "dear . . . crazy"	
Lines 19–24: "how . . . voice"	

All-in-One Workbook
219

Poetry Collection: Amy Ling, Wendy Rose, E. E. Cummings
Literary Analysis: Imagery

Poetry often makes use of **imagery,** language that appeals to one or more of the five senses. Each instance of imagery is called an **image.** If you take note of the images as you read a poem, you will often understand it better. As you read, imagine that you are actually seeing, smelling, hearing, tasting, or touching the things described by the poet. Put yourself at the scene mentally, and experience the images.

DIRECTIONS: *Use this chart to help you focus on the imagery in the three poems in this collection. From each poem, list words or phrases that appeal to the senses in the corresponding boxes. Remember that many images appeal to more than one sense.*

	Sight	**Sound**	**Touch**	**Smell**	**Taste**
"Grandma Ling"					
"Drum Song"					
"your little voice"					

Poetry Collection: Amy Ling, Wendy Rose, E. E. Cummings
Vocabulary Builder

Word List

burrow   exquisite   impertinently   jostling   tongue   vertical

A. DIRECTIONS: *Circle* T *if the statement is true or* F *if the statement is false. Then, explain your answer.*

T / F 1. An animal that makes its home in a passage underground lives in a <u>burrow</u>.
_____

T / F 2. Most teachers like students who speak <u>impertinently</u>.
_____

T / F 3. A <u>jostling</u> ride is comfortable.
_____

T / F 4. If you hold your <u>tongue</u>, you don't speak.
_____

T / F 5. An <u>exquisite</u> diamond will be really expensive.
_____

B. WORD STUDY: *The root* -vert- *means "turn." Use the context of the sentences and what you know about the root* -vert- *to explain your answer to each question.*

1. What happens to a person who suffers *vertigo*?
_____
_____

2. What function do *vertebrae* play in your spinal column?
_____
_____

C. DIRECTIONS: *Circle the letter of the word that is closest in meaning to the Word List word in capital letters.*

1. VERTICAL
   A. normal   **B.** upright   **C.** green   **D.** horizontal
2. BURROW
   A. hole   **B.** whole   **C.** lend   **D.** donkey
3. IMPERTINENTLY
   A. relevantly   **B.** intelligently **C.** rudely   **D.** eagerly

Poetry Collections: John Updike, N. Scott Momaday, Alice Walker;
Amy Ling, Wendy Rose, E. E. Cummings
Integrated Language Skills: Grammar

Infinitives and Infinitive Phrases

An **infinitive** is the form of a verb that includes the word *to* and acts as a noun, an adjective, or an adverb. Each of these sentences contains the infinitive *to dance.*

Noun:	*To dance* is difficult for some people. [serves as the subject of the sentence]
Noun:	Many people love *to dance.* [serves as the direct object of the verb *love*]
Adjective:	That catchy music is an invitation *to dance.* [modifies the noun *invitation*]
Adverb:	It is easy *to dance* to that music. [modifies the adjective *easy*]

An **infinitive phrase** is an infinitive with modifiers or a complement. The entire phrase acts as a single part of speech. The following sentences show some ways in which infinitives are expanded into infinitive phrases. In each sentence, the infinitive phrase is in italics.

With Adverb:	I would love *to dance well.* [phrase serves as noun (direct object)]
With Direct Object:	He gave me an invitation *to dance a mambo.* [phrase serves as adjective (modifies *invitation*)]
With Prepositional Phrase:	I find it easy *to dance to that music.* [phrase serves as adverb (modifies *easy*)]

A. PRACTICE: *Circle the infinitive phrase in each sentence. On the line after the sentence, indicate whether the phrase serves as a* noun, *an* adjective, *or an* adverb. *If it serves as a noun, tell whether it is a subject, a direct object, or another part of the sentence. If it serves as an adjective or an adverb, tell what it modifies.*

1. I like to read poetry aloud._____

2. It is easiest to recite poetry with a strong rhythm._____

3. We had an assignment to do a poetry reading._____

4. To set the poem to music was difficult._____

5. We were able to rehearse twice._____

B. Writing Application: *Complete each sentence by adding an infinitive phrase on the line.*

1. I really want _____

2. It is fun _____

3. My cousin gave me tips _____

Poetry Collections: John Updike, N. Scott Momaday, Alice Walker;
Amy Ling, Wendy Rose, E. E. Cummings

Integrated Language Skills: Support for Writing a Review of Poetry

Use this chart to help you evaluate the poems in Collection 7 or 8. To rate each element, use *A+, A, A-, B+, B,* and so on. Consider *C* a passing grade and *F* failure. In the third column, include examples as well as your general comments. Then, use the information on the chart to help you write your review.

Poem Title:

Element	Rating	Details
sound		
word choice		
imagery		

Poem Title:

Element	Rating	Details
sound		
word choice		
imagery		

Poem Title:

Element	Rating	Details
sound		
word choice		
imagery		

Name _____ Date _____

Writing About the Big Question

What is the secret to reaching someone with words?

Big Question Vocabulary

benefit	connection	cultural	experience	express
feedback	individuality	inform	meaningful	media
misunderstand	relevant	sensory	significance	valid

A. *Use one or more words from the list above to complete each sentence.*

1. Whitman makes a _____ between a ship and the government of the country.

2. Whitman expresses the _____ of the history of our country in his poem.

3. Frost examines a _____ experience that reflects the choices we make in life.

B. *Follow the directions in responding to each of the items below.*

1. How would you best express your opinion of the choices you have made thus far in life?

   _____.

   _____.

2. Who has reached you with his or her words? Write two sentences explaining the experience. Use at least two of the Big Question vocabulary words.

   _____

   _____

C. *Complete the sentence below. Then, write a short paragraph in which you connect this idea to the Big Question.*

   Choosing words carefully when we write helps us to _____

   _____

   _____

   _____

Name _____   Date _____

"The Road Not Taken" by Robert Frost
"O Captain! My Captain!" by Walt Whitman
Literary Analysis: Comparing Types of Description

Descriptive writing paints word pictures for readers. A variety of descriptions can be used in poetry to present **levels of meaning.**

- **Literal meaning** is the actual, everyday meaning of words.
- **Figurative meaning** relies on figures of speech and the symbolic nature of language.

An **analogy** is a figurative description that compares two or more things that are similar in some ways, but otherwise unalike. For example, a poem that literally describes the ocean also can be read as an analogy: It may compare the ocean to life because both are vast, deep, and ever-changing. The poem, therefore, has two levels of meaning—one literal and one figurative.

DIRECTIONS: *On the following chart, for each quotation from a poem, note words and images that give you clues about its figurative meaning. The first one is done for you.*

Passages from "The Road Not Taken"	Which words and images give you clues about the figurative meaning of the passage?
1. "Two roads diverged in a yellow wood,"	Two roads = choices; yellow wood = life
2. "Then took the other, as just as fair, / And having perhaps the better claim, / Because it was grassy and wanted wear;"	

Passages from "O Captain! My Captain!"	Which words and images give you clues about the figurative meaning of the passage?
3. "O Captain! my Captain! our fearful trip is done, / The ship has weather'd every rack, the prize we sought is won,"	
4. "My Captain does not answer, his lips are pale and still, / My father does not feel my arm, he has no pulse nor will."	

"The Road Not Taken" by Robert Frost
"O Captain! My Captain!" by Walt Whitman
Vocabulary Builder

Word List

  diverged   exulting

A. DIRECTIONS: *Complete the following word map by filling in the appropriate information.*

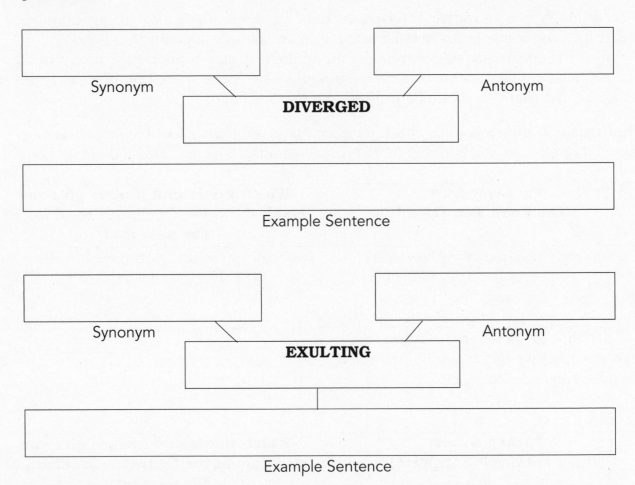

Synonym   Antonym

DIVERGED

Example Sentence

Synonym   Antonym

EXULTING

Example Sentence

B. DIRECTIONS: *Circle the letter of the pair that best expresses a relationship similar to that expressed in the pair in CAPITAL LETTERS.*

1. DIVERGED : SEPARATED ::
   A. converged : split
   B. removed : extracted
   C. weighed : calculated
   D. dressed : appeared

2. EXULTING : LAMENTING ::
   A. talk : converse
   B. barrel : basket
   C. seldom : often
   D. dwindle : decrease

"**The Road Not Taken**" by Robert Frost
"**O Captain! My Captain!**" by Walt Whitman

Integrated Language Skills: Support for Writing to Compare Description in Literary Works

Before you write your essay, use the graphic organizer below to list ideas about each poem.

"The Road Not Taken"

How common are the experiences the poets describe?	How universal are the emotions that prompt the descriptions?	Which poet better expresses his emotions through the descriptions? Why?	Which message is easier for you to interpret? Why?

"O Captain! My Captain!"

Now, use your notes to write your essay comparing the descriptions in "The Road Not Taken" and "O Captain! My Captain!"

BQ Tunes

Joe's Flo / Similar Souls, performed by Queen Godls

I.

This is a story about a girl named Flo

Had school everyday

Everyday she wouldn't go

She was so shy

Found it hard to **unify**

With her other classmates

She felt **separate**

Like two different worlds

From the other boys and girls

and she couldn't hide

She felt a **divide**

She was from another part of town

far away from school

She didn't own a car

So she thought she wasn't cool

Inside she was afraid other kids would to

They had

fancy clothes

fancy cars

fancy things

Flo couldn't afford fancy

to be her middle name

So, to play it safe

She stayed far away

Couldn't bare the thought that they might **discriminate**

Rash decisions out of hate -

based upon their fake

artificial

superficial

unofficial take

Continued

of who she was -

simply just because

of what she didn't have

Flo was from a small family

they all worked hard

Her parents were ill

her sister couldn't get a job

She was injured overseas

So Flo was in charge

Of the bills and the chores

And everything seemed hard

Flo loved her family

felt alone and ashamed

The rich kids at school

Wouldn't understand her pain

Was this the truth

or a hasty presumption ?

caused Flo to make a very very bad **assumption**?

II.

Now this is a story about a boy named Joe

Had school everyday

Everyday he wouldn't go

he was so shy

Found it hard to **unify**

With his other classmates

He felt **separate**

Like two different worlds

From the other boys and girls

and he couldn't hide

He felt a **divide**

He was from another part of town

very close to class

But he owned a car

His parents bought it for him last

day of the month

Continued

They always bought him what he wanted

fancy trips

fancy clothes

and other fancy things to flaunt

Joe had an older brother who died overseas

His parents bought him things out of (pity) pain and **sympathy**

Joe always took-

everything they'd buy

He couldn't bear the thought of having to see his parents cry

He knew what they meant

What all the gifts **represent**

Symbols of their fear, of their loss and their love

But he was afraid the other kids at school might **judge** . . .

Him for what he had

and not because of who he was

He thought these opinions

just might

one day

complicate his friendships

so he stayed far away

couldn't bare to **tolerate**

deal with or embrace

artificial

superficial

people who were fake

Was this the truth, or a hasty presumption

that caused Joe to make a very very bad **assumption**?

III.

One day Flo

She bumped into Joe

thought they recognized each other

Continued

but at first they weren't sure

Could not **identify**

where they met before

They were from a different **class**

socially and cultural

Economically too

If you judged by what they wore

He **assumed** that she was rich

and she **assumed** that he was poor -

He was dressed down because he had to fix his ride

She <u>was</u> dressed up because she had church that night

They started talking even though they both were shy

They shared a **common** bond when she looked into his eyes

Something familiar, in tune and similar

Joe could not hide that he was really into her

So they sat down, started talking over soda

She was really moved by all the things that he told her

They could not **distinguish** (identify)

or make sense..of the feelings manifested-

everything was intense

But He was not afraid

and She no longer felt alone

Although two strangers from two different homes

Every **assumption** and **generalization**

every thought, feeling and action made from pure speculation

started to fade away with the connection they were making

Something amazing suddenly happened inside

Flo was so moved, tears welled up in her eyes

Joe told Flo about his brother who had died

His brother was the soldier who had saved her sister's life.

IV.

This is a story about Flo and Joe

very different but similar also

Continued

They got to know each other

Found one another cool

Became best friends when they both went back to school . . .

Song Title: **Joe's Flo / Similar Souls**

Artist / Performed by Queen GodIs

Lyrics by Queen GodIs

Music composed by Mike Pandolfo, Wonderful

Produced by Mike Pandolfo, Wonderful

Executive Producer: Keith London, Defined Mind

Unit 5: Drama
Big Question Vocabulary—1

The Big Question: Is it our differences or our similarities that matter most?

Thematic Vocabulary

assumption: *n.* the act of supposing that something is true, without seeking proof; other form: *assume*

class: *n.* a group in society, separate from others, often based on jobs, income, or level of education; other forms: *classify, classification*

distinguish: *v.* to separate or classify according to special features or differences

represent: *v.* to personify a special quality or value; other forms: *representative, representation*

sympathy: *n.* a feeling of sorrow for someone who is in a bad situation; other forms: *sympathize, sympathetic*

A. DIRECTIONS: *Write the Thematic Vocabulary word that best completes each sentence.*

1. Because Carlos is very tall, I made the _____ that he was a basketball player.

2. How will the judges _____ between the very talented and the less talented singers?

3. John and Ramon _____ the highest level of academic achievement.

4. I felt a great deal of _____ for the player who was hurt during the game.

5. Members of each social _____ should have equal opportunities for quality education.

B. DIRECTIONS: *Write the Thematic Vocabulary word that best completes each group of related words.*

1. compassion, support, _____

2. group, division, _____

3. exemplify, embody, _____

4. divide, judge, _____

5. guess, idea, _____

Unit 5: Drama
Big Question Vocabulary—2

The Big Question: Is it our differences or our similarities that matter most?

Thematic Vocabulary

common: *adj.* shared with others, such as mutual ideas or interests; other form: *commonly*

discriminate: *v.* to treat someone differently and unfairly; other forms: *discrimination, discriminated*

divide: *v.* to separate objects or people into groups; other forms: *division, divided, divisive*

generalization: *n.* a statement that may be true sometimes but not always; other form: *generalize*

superficial: *adj.* uninterested in important matters; shallow; other form: *superficially*

DIRECTIONS: *Read the passage, and then answer the question below. Use the vocabulary words in parentheses for your responses.*

"I don't want to be on a study committee with Grace," Peg said to her friend Ilene. "She's too quiet, and you know that people who are quiet tend to be sneaky and mean. If you're my friend, Ilene, you'll refuse to work with her, too." Ilene wasn't sure what to say. Should she go along with her friend or stand up for Grace, whom she hardly knew? What was Ilene thinking?

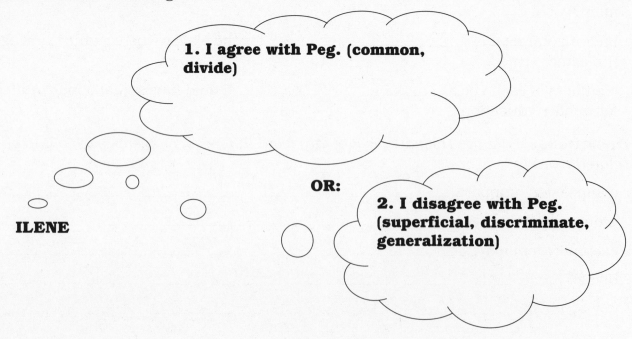

1. I agree with Peg. (common, divide)

OR:

2. I disagree with Peg. (superficial, discriminate, generalization)

ILENE

Unit 5: Drama
Big Question Vocabulary—3

The Big Question: Is it our differences or our similarities that matter most?

Thematic Vocabulary

identify: *v.* to connect with another person, based on shared qualities or thoughts; other forms: *identity, identification*

judge: *v.* to have or express a strong opinion as to the value of something; other forms: *judgment, judging*

separate: *v.* to move apart or divide two or more things into different groups
 adj. different or apart from something else; other form: *separation*

tolerance: *n.* a willingness to accept and respect others, despite differences; other forms: *tolerate, tolerant*

unify: *v.* to bring things or people together into a workable group; other forms: *unity, union*

DIRECTIONS: *Answer each question. Use the word or words in parentheses.*

1. What are the most important aspects of friendship? **(judge, identify)**

 _____

 _____

 _____

 _____

2. If you were the President of the United States, what would you do to encourage different groups of people to work together? **(unify, separate)**

 _____

 _____

 _____

 _____

3. Why is it important to teach children the importance of respecting and accepting others, regardless of differences? **(tolerance)**

 _____

 _____

 _____

 _____

Name _____ Date _____

Unit 5: Drama
Applying the Big Question

Is it our differences or our similarities that matter most?

DIRECTIONS: *Complete the chart below to apply what you have learned about differences and similarities, and which matter most. One row has been completed for you.*

Example	Type of difference or similarity	How did it matter?	Effect on the people involved	What I learned
From Literature	Working-class governess feels inferior to upper-class employer in "The Governess"	Governess would not stand up for herself and allowed employer to walk all over her	Employer was using the situation to instruct the governess about asserting herself, and so treated her fairly	It is possible to recognize and overcome class differences.
From Literature				
From Science				
From Social Studies				
From Real Life				

Cherie Bennett
Listening and Viewing

Segment 1: Meet Cherie Bennett
• How did Cherie Bennett become a writer of young adult novels? What young adult books have you read that had an impact on you?

_____

_____

_____

_____

Segment 2: Drama
• Why do you think Cherie Bennett first chose to write *Anne Frank & Me* as a play? How did the reaction of a young New York audience show that this play successfully affected its audience? Explain.

_____

_____

_____

_____

Segment 3: The Writing Process
• When Cherie Bennett writes collaboratively with her husband, Jeff Gottesfeld, what is the most important step of their writing process? Why do you think that it is important to outline a story?

_____

_____

_____

_____

Segment 4: The Rewards of Writing
• According to Cherie Bennett, how are reading and writing empowering to young people? Why do you think it is important to begin writing while still in school?

_____

_____

_____

_____

Learning About Drama

The following chart lists and defines some common elements of drama.

Elements	Definition
Playwright	the author of a drama
Acts	units of the action in a drama
Characterization	the technique of creating believable characters
Dialogue	a character's words set after the character's name
Stage directions	bracketed information about sound effects, sets, and actions (including gestures and emotions)
Props	small, portable items that actors use to make their actions look realistic

DIRECTIONS: *Read the following dialogue, and answer the questions that follow.*

How He Got a Life by Morgan O'Neil

Act 1, Scene 1

[Charlie and Monica are walking into a living room, talking animatedly. It is an exceptionally neat room with landscapes on the wall and vases of flowers on tables.]

Monica [laughing while tossing her book bag onto the couch]. So what magic tricks do *you* know how to do?

Charlie. A few, OK? [He drops his stuffed backpack on the floor and flops into a chair.]

Monica [with skepticism]. And how did you learn them?

Charlie [a bit defensively]. My uncle taught me. He was a professional magician once.

Monica. Well, this I'll have to see. When is the birthday party?

Charlie [excited now]. Saturday morning. Twelve 7-year-olds. Look at all this stuff. . . . (CHARLIE begins to pull out several items from his backpack, including an old and crumpled top hat, a stuffed rabbit, and a faded deck of cards.)

Monica. Hey, I think you need an assistant!

1. Who is the playwright?

   _____

2. What does the set look like in this act?

   _____

3. Based on the dialogue, what is Charlie's plan for Saturday?

   _____

4. Judging from the stage directions, what is Monica's first reaction to Charlie's plan?

   _____

5. What props are necessary in this scene?

from **Anne Frank & Me** by Cherie Bennett
Model Selection: Drama

Drama is written to be performed. Like other types of fiction such as short stories and novels, dramas have a **setting, plot,** and **conflict. Playwrights**—writers of dramas—use **characterization** to create believable characters.

You learn much about the characters, plot, and events through the **dialogue,** or conversation among characters. Bracketed **stage directions** may describe the setting, sound effects, or a character's emotions while speaking.

The **set** of a drama is the stage construction that represents the time and place of the action. **Props** are small, portable items that actors use to make their actions look realistic.

A. DIRECTIONS: *Answer the following questions about* Anne Frank & Me.

1. What is the setting of this excerpt from the play?

_____

2. In what language are Anne and Nicole having a dialogue?

_____

3. How does Anne react when Nicole knows her name and the name *Van Daan*?

_____

4. What explanations does Anne offer for Nicole's knowledge of her diary?

_____

5. What props would be necessary in this scene?

_____

B. DIRECTIONS: *Describe how you imagine the inside of the cattle car to look, sound, and smell. Use information from the stage directions and the characters' dialogue to help form your answer. Then, compare your description with a partner's.*

_____

_____

_____

_____

_____

All-in-One Workbook

"The Governess" by Neil Simon
Writing About the Big Question

Is it our differences or our similarities that matter most?

Big Question Vocabulary

assumption	class	common	discriminate	distinguish
divide	generalization	identify	judge	represent
separate	superficial	sympathy	tolerance	unify

A. *Use one or more words from the list above to complete each sentence.*

1. It can be hard to communicate with someone from a different

   _____.

2. People show _____ when they accept that other
   people may not always share their views.

3. It is not fair to _____ against people just
   because they are different from you.

B. *Respond to the following item, using full sentences.*

   Describe a time when someone showed **sympathy** to you.

   _____

   _____

   _____

   _____

C. *Complete the sentence below. Then, write a short paragraph in which you connect the
completed sentence to the Big Question.*

   People sometimes **identify** themselves as part of a group on the basis of _____

   _____

   _____

   _____

   _____

   _____

   _____

The Governess by Neil Simon
Reading: Draw Conclusions

When you **draw conclusions** about something, you reach decisions or opinions after considering facts and details. To draw conclusions from a play, observe what characters say and do.

- Look for statements that reveal underlying ideas and attitudes.
- Analyze interactions that show how characters treat one another.
- Notice actions that create a clear pattern of behavior.

Make connections among these items to learn about the character.
In this excerpt from the play, Julia's actions and words tell you about her.

JULIA. [Lifts her head up] Yes, madame. [But her head has a habit of slowly drifting down again]

Julia's words tell you that Julia is Mistress's inferior; her actions tell you that Julia is either shy or afraid.

DIRECTIONS: *Fill in the graphic below with examples of Mistress's statements, actions, and treatment of Julia. In the center, write conclusions you can draw about Mistress.*

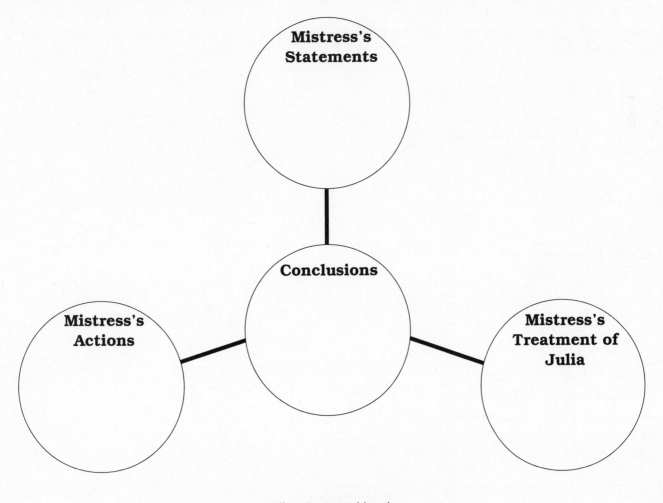

The Governess by Neil Simon
Literary Analysis: Setting and Character

Playwrights have few tools with which to develop **characters** and establish **setting**. **Stage directions** describe the scenery, costumes, lighting, and sound, and tell how the characters feel, move, and speak. Stage directions are usually printed in italics and set in brackets. The following stage directions describe the setting of a play.

[*It is late evening. The stage is dark, except for the glow of a small lamp beside the bed.*]

When you read a play, use the stage directions to create a mental image of how a stage production would look and sound.

DIRECTIONS: *Fill in this chart with the information the stage directions give you.*

Stage Direction	What It Describes (scenery, costumes, lighting, sound; characters' feelings, movements, tone of voice)	What It Tells You
1. [*A young governess, Julia, comes rushing in. She stops before the desk and curtsies*]	Scenery Character's movements	The room probably belongs to someone important. Julia is young, a governess; she is energetic and humble.
2. [*But her head has a habit of slowly drifting down again*]		
3. [*She turns away, softly crying*]		
4. [*She curtsies again and runs off. The mistress looks after her a moment, a look of complete bafflement on her face. The lights fade.*]		

Name _____ Date _____

The Governess by Neil Simon
Vocabulary Builder

Word List

bafflement   discharged   discrepancies   guileless
inferior   satisfactory   supervisor

A. DIRECTIONS: *Use the underlined word in your answer to each question. Your answer should show you know the meaning of the word.*

1. If the stories told by two witnesses to a crime have serious <u>discrepancies</u>, what should the investigating officer do?

   _____

2. If you got to work late each day, would it be surprising if your boss <u>discharged</u> you?

   _____

3. Who is more likely to believe a lie, someone who is <u>guileless</u> or someone who is not?

   _____

4. If a supervisor finds a worker's performance <u>satisfactory</u>, is she likely to fire the worker?

   _____

5. Who was considered <u>inferior</u> in a medieval kingdom, the king or his subjects?

   _____

6. If someone expresses <u>bafflement</u> about instructions for a task, will the person be able to do the task well?

   _____

7. Which is a more likely measure of how likely you are to get a raise at work—the opinion of your coworkers or the opinion of your <u>supervisor</u>?

   _____

B. WORD STUDY: The **suffix -ory** means "of," "relating to," or "characterized by." Think about the meaning of *-ory* in each italicized word. On the line before each sentence, write T if the statement is true and F if the statement is false. Then explain your answer.

1. _____ A *mandatory* payment is one that you can make or not make according to your preference.

   _____

2. _____ A *hortatory* statement is one that urges you to do something.

   _____

3. _____ Hearing a sound is a form of *sensory* perception.

   _____

The Governess by Neil Simon
Integrated Language Skills: Grammar

Participial Phrases

A **participle** is a verb form that is used as an adjective. Participles commonly end in *-ing* (present participle) or *-ed* (past participle). A **participial phrase** is made up of a participle with its modifiers and complements, such as adverbs or objects. The entire participial phrase is used as an adjective.

> **Example:** The tourist, *confused by the signs*, got lost.
>
> *Traveling quickly*, we got to the game on time.
>
> Lila, *loving hot weather*, visits Santa Fe each August.

A. PRACTICE: *In each sentence, underline the participial phrase.*

1. Sitting behind her desk, Mistress questions Julia.
2. Julia, worried about her job, answered hesitantly.
3. Mistress, asking questions repeatedly, made Julia more nervous.
4. Julia, weeping quietly, stared at the ground.
5. Lifting Julia's head, Mistress made her look up.
6. Mistress gave Julia the rest of her money, insisting that she take it.
7. Baffled by the encounter, Mistress sat alone onstage.

B. Writing Application: *Write sentences about the characters in* The Governess *using each participial phrase shown.*

1. curtsying to Mistress

   _____

   _____

2. writing in her book

   _____

   _____

3. confused by the questions

   _____

   _____

4. handing Julia the envelope

   _____

   _____

5. angered by Julia's humility

   _____

   _____

Name _____ Date _____

The Governess by Neil Simon
Support for Writing a Public-Service Announcement

To prepare for writing a public-service announcement (PSA) on workers' rights, fair payment for workers, or worker safety, use the graphic organizer below:

Choose a public figure who will be your spokesperson:	Summarize, in one or two sentences, the points you will use to persuade your audience:	Make a list of words, phrases, images, or symbols you might use in your message:
_____ _____	_____ _____ _____	_____ _____ _____

Write a rough draft or sketch out the main ideas for a radio or television message to be delivered by your spokesperson, using elements from your notes and lists. Use sound effects and images as part of your message. Write or continue your draft on a separate sheet of paper if you wish.

_____

_____

_____

_____

_____

_____

_____

_____

The Governess by Neil Simon
"The Ninny" by Anton Chekhov
Writing About the Big Question

THE BIG
?

Is it our differences or our similarities that matter most?

Big Question Vocabulary

assumption	class	common	discriminate	distinguish
divide	generalization	identify	judge	represent
separate	superficial	sympathy	tolerance	unify

A. *Circle the more appropriate word from each pair listed to complete each sentence.*

1. You might make a mistaken assumption/class if you do not know all the facts.

2. Miguel felt sympathy/tolerance for his friend when her dog died.

3. It is not always easy to distinguish/represent between facts and opinions.

B. *Use complete sentences to respond to each item.*

1. How would you **identify** yourself when meeting a new neighbor for the first time?

   _____

   _____

2. Does this introduction focus more on what you and your neighbor have in **common** or on your differences?

   _____

   _____

C. *Complete the sentence below. Then, write a short paragraph in which you connect the completed sentence to the Big Question.*

When people focus only on their differences, _____

_____

_____

_____

_____

_____

_____

The Governess by Neil Simon
"The Ninny" by Anton Chekhov

Literary Analysis: Comparing an Adaptation With an Original

A literary **adaptation** is a work that has been changed or adjusted to fit a different form or genre. For example, a novel may be adapted into a play or a movie. Adapting a literary work usually means changing or leaving out some parts of the original to suit the new form. For instance, a play depends almost entirely on dialogue, without the narration or description that is often included in a story. Neil Simon's play *The Governess* is an adaptation of "The Ninny," a short story by the Russian writer Anton Chekhov.

To compare an adaptation with the original work, keep in mind the differences in the two literary forms.

DIRECTIONS: *Answer the following questions to compare an adaptation with an original.*

1. What form is "The Ninny" written in? What form is *The Governess* written in?

   _____

   _____

2. What important information do we learn from both the original and the adaptation?

   _____

   _____

3. Which details in the original are left out of the adaptation or are changed?

   _____

   _____

   _____

4. What elements has the writer of the adaptation introduced?

   _____

   _____

   _____

5. Are the styles of the two authors similar, or is one style lighter or funnier?

   _____

   _____

6. Which form do you find more engaging? Why do you like one better than the other?

   _____

   _____

The Governess by Neil Simon
"The Ninny" by Anton Chekhov
Vocabulary Builder

Word List

account   carelessness   dock   ninny   spineless   timidly

A. DIRECTIONS: *Revise each sentence so that the underlined vocabulary word is used logically. Be sure not to change the vocabulary word.*

1. At the end of each month, companies <u>dock</u> employees' paychecks to show appreciation for the employees' hard work.

   _____

   _____

2. The student is a <u>ninny</u> who works very hard and does well in all of her classes.

   _____

   _____

3. The building contractor settled his <u>account</u> with the carpenter but forgot to pay him.

   _____

   _____

4. Yulya <u>timidly</u> approached the assembled student body and gave her speech with confidence and ease.

   _____

   _____

5. The <u>spineless</u> crowd of people helped to free a man trapped in his car.

   _____

   _____

6. The chemist's <u>carelessness</u> about small details is what enabled him to succeed with the complicated experiment.

B. DIRECTIONS: *Circle the letter of the word or phrase most opposite the word in CAPITAL LETTERS.*

1. SPINELESS
   A. weak   B. ineffectual   C. strong-willed   D. furious
2. NINNY
   A. fool   B. clot   C. caretaker   D. serious person
3. TIMIDLY
   A. boldly   B. fearfully   C. wisely   D. firmly
4. DOCK
   A. help   B. reward   C. boat ramp   D. rank

Name _____ Date _____

The Governess by Neil Simon
"The Ninny" by Anton Chekhov
Support for Writing to Compare Literary Works

In addition to a comparison chart, you may find the graphic organizer presented here helpful for answering the final question of the writing assignment:

Do you think that one version—the story or the play—is more effective than the other? Why?

For each question on the graphic, place a check in either the column for Chekhov's story "The Ninny" or the column for Simon's play *The Governess*.

Criteria	The Chekhov Story	The Simon Play
1. Which work tells you more about the setting?		
2. Which work gives you a fuller portrait of the employer?		
3. In which work do you feel more empathy for the governess?		
4. Which work makes you think more as you read and/or as you reflect on the work?		

Now, combining your notes from this sheet and from your comparison chart, write an essay in which you compare and contrast the adaptation, *The Governess*, with the original, "The Ninny."

The Diary of Anne Frank, *Act I,* by Frances Goodrich and Albert Hackett
Writing About the Big Question

 Is it our differences or our similarities that matter most?

Big Question Vocabulary

assumption	class	common	discriminate	distinguish
divide	generalization	identify	judge	represent
separate	superficial	sympathy	tolerance	unify

A. *Use one or more words from the list above to complete each sentence.*

1. Their shared feelings of support for a local sports team helped
_____ the people of the town.

2. The color of a person's hair is an example of a _____
characteristic.

3. Someone who claims that all kids hate vegetables is making a
_____ .

B. *Use complete sentences to respond to each of the items below.*

1. Describe a time when you witnessed or experienced an act of **discrimination.**

_____

_____

_____

2. How did this experience make you feel?

_____

_____

_____

C. *Use the sentence starter below as the lead-in to a paragraph that deals with the Big Question.*

When people must face danger together, it tends to make them focus on _____

_____

_____

_____

_____

_____

The Diary of Anne Frank, *Act I,* by Frances Goodrich and Albert Hackett

Reading: Use Background Information to Link Historical Causes With Effects

A **cause** is an event, action, or feeling that produces a result, or an **effect.** When you read a work that is set in a particular time and place, you can **use background information to link historical causes with effects.** This background information includes the following:

- the introduction to a literary work
- information provided in footnotes
- facts you learned in other classes
- information you already know about the topic

In *The Diary of Anne Frank*, Act I, Anne states the following in her diary:

As my family is Jewish, we emigrated to Holland when Hitler came to power.

You already know that Adolph Hitler was a German dictator who persecuted the Jews of Europe. The effect of his persecution on Anne and her family was their forced immigration to Holland and then more than two years in a hideout—the attic rooms where the play is set.

DIRECTIONS: *In the right column of the chart, write the effects on Anne Frank and the others of each historical cause noted in the play.*

Historical Cause	Effect on Anne and Others
1. Jews were treated badly in Holland when the Germans took over.	
2. Jews had to hide if they were to survive.	
3. Goods were rationed in wartime.	
4. Some people escaped to Switzerland.	

All-in-One Workbook
251

The Diary of Anne Frank, *Act I,* by Frances Goodrich and Albert Hackett
Literary Analysis: Dialogue

Dialogue is a conversation between or among characters. In the *script*, or text, of a play, lines of dialogue follow the name of the speaker who delivers them. Dialogue can reveal character traits. It also advances the plot, and it shows conflict between characters or against outside forces.

DIRECTIONS: *Explain what each example of dialogue from the play reveals about the characters and events.*

1. **MR. KRALER.** I never thought I'd live to see the day when a man like Mr. Frank would have to go into hiding. When you think—

_____

_____

_____

2. **MR. FRANK.** It'll be hard, I know. But always remember this, Anneke. There are no walls, there are no bolts, no locks that anyone can put on your mind. Miep will bring us books. We will read history, poetry, mythology.

_____

_____

_____

3. **MR. VAN DAAN.** [*restraining himself with difficulty*] Why aren't you nice and quiet like your sister Margot? Why do you have to show off all the time? Let me give you a little advice, young lady. Men don't like that kind of thing in a girl. You know that? A man likes a girl who'll listen to him once in a while . . . a domestic girl, who'll keep her house shining for her husband . . . who loves to cook and sew and . . .
ANNE. I'd cut my throat first! I'd open my veins! I'm going to be remarkable! I'm going to Paris . . .

_____

_____

_____

4. **ANNE.** Things have changed. People aren't like that any more. "Yes, Mother." "No, Mother." "Anything you say, Mother." I've got to fight things out for myself! Make something of myself!

_____

_____

_____

The Diary of Anne Frank, *Act I,* by Frances Goodrich and Albert Hackett
Vocabulary Builder

Word List

bewildered   conspicuous   fatalist   insufferable   resent   tension

A. DIRECTIONS: *Use the underlined word in your answer to each question. Your answer should show you know the meaning of the word.*

1. Would a <u>fatalist</u> believe that good acts can change a person's fate?

   _____

2. How would you react if a friend's behavior was <u>insufferable</u>?

   _____

3. If you have a <u>conspicuous</u> rip in your jacket, can others see it?

   _____

4. Would you be likely to <u>resent</u> someone who was constantly bragging about how much bigger his house is than yours?

   _____

5. If the owner's manual of your new DVD player left you <u>bewildered</u>, would you be likely to have an easy time setting up the machine?

   _____

6. If there were a lot of <u>tension</u> at a business meeting, would the participants probably be agreeing or disagreeing on most points?

   _____

B. WORD STUDY: The **suffix -*ist*** means "one who performs, makes, practices, is skilled in, or believes in." Think about the meaning of -*ist*- in each italicized word. On the line before each sentence, write T if the statement is true and F if the statement is false. Then, explain your answer.

1. _____ A *soloist* is someone who plays an equal role with other musicians in a band.

   _____

2. _____ A *pharmacist* can help you fill a prescription for medicine from your doctor.

   _____

3. _____ A *finalist* is someone who is eliminated in the first round of a competition.

   _____

The Diary of Anne Frank, *Act I,* by Frances Goodrich and Albert Hackett

Integrated Language Skills: Grammar—
Dangling and Misplaced Modifiers

A **modifier** is a word, phrase, or clause that clarifies the meaning of a word or group of words in a sentence. A phrase or clause that acts as a modifier should be placed as close as possible to the word it modifies. If it is placed far away, it might seem to modify the wrong word or no word at all.

A dangling **modifier** is one that cannot sensibly modify any word in the sentence.

Dangling: Obtaining fake ration books, there was enough food for all. (Who obtained the ration books?)

Correct: Obtaining fake ration books, **the family** had enough food.

A **misplaced modifier** seems to modify the wrong word.

Misplaced: Starting a spice business, success soon followed for Mr. Frank. (*Success* did not start the business; Mr. Frank did.)

Correct: Starting a spice business, **Mr. Frank** soon found success.

A. PRACTICE: *In each sentence, circle the misplaced modifier. Draw an arrow pointing to the word it should be placed close to.*

1. A beautiful girl of eighteen, Mrs. Frank was proud of her daughter Margaret.

2. A neat and fussy man, the Franks and the Van Daans made room for Mr. Dussel.

3. Anne hurt Mrs. Frank preferring her father to her mother.

B. PRACTICE: *Using the names in parentheses, rewrite each sentence to correct the dangling modifier.*

1. Opening the door a crack, nothing could be seen. (Mr. Frank)

   _____

2. Putting her ear to the floor, the sound of the bombers faded away. (Anne)

   _____

3. Making room for Mr. Dussel, the annex became even more crowded. (the Franks)

   _____

Writing Application

Write a sentence in which you use each of the following phrases or clauses as a modifier. Keep the modifier in the right place.

1. as they were looking at the moon _____

   _____

2. when writing in the diary _____

   _____

The Diary of Anne Frank, Act I, by Frances Goodrich and Albert Hackett
Support for Writing Diary Entries

To prepare for writing diary entries from the points of view of two other characters, choose the event you will write about and the two characters besides Anne. Enter this information on the lines below. Then, write details about the scene as each character you have chosen might experience or see them.

Event: _____

Details as Experienced or Seen by Characters Besides Anne	
Character 1: _____	Character 2: _____

Now, use the details you have gathered to write your diary entries.

The Diary of Anne Frank, **Act II,** by Frances Goodrich and Albert Hackett

Writing About the Big Question

Is it our differences or our similarities that matter most?

Big Question Vocabulary

assumption	class	common	discriminate	distinguish
divide	generalization	identify	judge	represent
separate	superficial	sympathy	tolerance	unify

A. *Circle the more appropriate word from each pair listed to complete each sentence.*

1. My friend Etta and I get along well because we have many <u>common/separate</u> interests.

2. Having different political views is an example of something that might <u>divide/unify</u> people.

3. The people of our town elected a new official to <u>represent/judge</u> us in Congress.

B. *Respond to the following item, using full sentences.*

Describe a situation in which you might have to show **tolerance.**

_____

_____

_____

_____

C. *Use the sentence starter below as the lead-in to a paragraph that deals with the Big Question.*

People who face persecution can maintain their humanity and dignity by _____

_____

_____

_____

_____

_____

_____

_____

_____

Name _____ Date _____

The Diary of Anne Frank, *Act II,* by Frances Goodrich and Albert Hackett

Reading: Ask Questions to Analyze Cause-and-Effect Relationships

Cause-and-effect relationships explain the connection between events, but they do not always follow the simple pattern of a single cause producing a single effect. Sometimes, a single cause produces multiple effects. Alternatively, multiple causes can produce a single effect. A chain of causes and effects, in which one cause triggers an effect that becomes the cause of another effect, also is common. **Ask questions to analyze cause-and-effect relationships** in a literary work. Here are examples:

- What are all the possible causes that might have triggered this event?
- What are the various effects that might result from this cause?
- Are these events really related in a cause-and-effect way? Just because two events occur in chronological, or time, order does not mean they are a cause and an effect. They may be coincidental or random occurrences.

DIRECTIONS: *Fill in the diagrams with the answers to these questions.*

1. What are all the possible causes that might have triggered the effect shown?

Cause 1: _____

Cause 2: _____

Cause 3: _____

Effect: The tension in the attic grows in Act II, Scene 4.

2. What are the various effects that result from the cause shown?

Cause: News comes of the invasion of Normandy

Effect 1: _____

Effect 2: _____

Effect 3: _____

The Diary of Anne Frank, *Act II,* by Frances Goodrich and Albert Hackett
Literary Analysis: Character Motivation

A **character's motivation** is the reason he or she takes a particular action. Motivation may be internal, external, or a combination of both.

- **Internal** motivations are based on emotions, such as loneliness or jealousy.
- **External** motivations are sparked by events or situations, such as a fire or poverty.

In *The Diary of Anne Frank*, Act II, Peter Van Daan kisses Anne on the cheek. His internal motivation is a strong feeling of affection for her. His external motivation is his mother's disapproval of his feelings and of Anne.

DIRECTIONS: *Fill in the chart with examples of internal and external motivations for each character's actions.*

Character's Action	Internal Motivation	External Motivation
1. Miep helps the families in the attic.		
2. Margot wishes for the end to come (Act II, Scene 1).		
3. Mr. Van Daan steals food (Act II, Scene 3).		
4. Anne confides in Peter (Act II, Scenes 1 and 2).		

Name _____ Date _____

The Diary of Anne Frank, *Act II,* by Frances Goodrich and Albert Hackett
Vocabulary Builder

Word List

apprehension   blackmail   forlorn   inarticulate   ineffectually   intuition

A. DIRECTIONS: *Circle* T *if the statement is true or* F *if the statement is false. Then, explain your answer.*

1. If you *blackmail* another person, you are showing kindness and generosity.

   T / F _____

2. A violinist who practices *ineffectually* will become a much better player.

   T / F _____

3. If you have a strong *intuition*, you can sense something that has happened or will happen.

   T / F _____

4. If your friend looks *forlorn*, she has probably just done unexpectedly well on an exam.

   T / F _____

5. When you feel *apprehension* about a test, you are fearful about it.

   T / F _____

6. An *inarticulate* speaker can easily move or persuade an audience.

   T / F _____

B. WORD STUDY: The prefix *in-* can mean "into" or "within." Think about the meaning of *in-* in each italicized word. On the line before each sentence, write T if the statement is true and F if the statement is false. Then explain your answer.

1. _____ An *injection* involves taking blood from the body. _____

   _____

2. _____ The *infield* is the part of the baseball field that is closest to the batter.

   _____

3. _____ If you were *inflating* a tire, you would be taking air out of it. _____

   _____

The Diary of Anne Frank, *Act II,* **by Frances Goodrich and Albert Hackett**
Integrated Language Skills: Grammar

Clauses: Independent and Subordinate

A **clause** is a group of words with its own subject and verb. There are two basic types of clauses, which are easy to distinguish. An *independent clause* has a subject and a verb and can stand by itself as a complete sentence. A *subordinate clause* has a subject and a verb, but it cannot stand by itself because it does not express a complete thought.

A. PRACTICE: *Underline the independent clauses once and the subordinate clauses twice.*

1. After they spent two years in the attic, all the adults and teenagers had frayed nerves.
2. Anne and Peter spent a lot of time together, and they grew close.
3. Everyone got nervous when the telephone rang.
4. The person supplying food for the attic was arrested, and the food stopped coming.
5. Hunger made them irritable, and they became more likely to argue.
6. Although Anne had seen horrifying behavior, she still believed in people's goodness.

B. Writing Application: *Answer the following questions using independent and subordinate clauses as indicated in parentheses.*

1. What did Miep do for the people in the attic? (two independent clauses)

   _____

   _____

2. What happened when Mrs. Frank caught Mr. Van Daan stealing food? (subordinate clause followed by independent clause)

   _____

   _____

3. What did Mr. Frank do when he returned from the war? (independent clause followed by subordinate clause)

   _____

   _____

The Diary of Anne Frank, *Act II*, by Frances Goodrich and Albert Hackett
Integrated Language Skills:
Support for Writing an Advertisement

Use the chart below to help you to write a script for an advertisement to air on the Internet, television, or radio for a film adaptation of *The Diary of Anne Frank*. Incorporate the elements featured in the chart:

Emotional Appeal: Select scenes for the trailer that will appeal to viewers' emotions.	
Appeal to Authority: In the script, include quotes from people who have seen the movie or from experts testifying to its authenticity.	
Movie Rating (G, PG, PG-13, etc.): Explain the reason for the rating.	
Tagline for the Movie: The tagline should be a catchy slogan that explains why people should go see the movie.	

Now, use the details you have collected to write your advertisement.

from **Anne Frank: "The Diary of a Young Girl"** by Anne Frank
and *from* **Anne Frank Remembered** by Miep Gies
Writing About the Big Question

Is it our differences or our similarities that matter most?

Big Question Vocabulary

assumption	class	common	discriminate	distinguish
divide	generalization	identify	judge	represent
separate	superficial	sympathy	tolerance	unify

A. *Circle the more appropriate word from each pair listed to complete each sentence.*

1. The team members are easy to <u>divide/identify</u> by the uniforms they wear.

2. I tend to <u>discriminate/judge</u> a restaurant based on the quality of its food.

3. I use a multisection ring binder to <u>separate/unify</u> my school notes and papers for different classes.

B. *Respond to the following items, using full sentences.*

1. Describe one thing you have in **common** with other people you know.

   _____

   _____

2. Describe one thing that **distinguishes** you from other people you know.

   _____

   _____

C. *Complete the sentence below. Then, write a short paragraph in which you connect this idea to the Big Question.*

Different people may tell the same story in different ways because _____

_____

_____

_____

_____

The Diary of Anne Frank by Frances Goodrich and Albert Hackett
from **Anne Frank: The Diary of a Young Girl** by Anne Frank
from **Anne Frank Remembered** by Miep Gies

Literary Analysis: Comparing Sources With a Dramatization

When Anne Frank's diary was published, it became a bestseller, inspiring Albert Hackett and Frances Goodrich to develop the diary into a play that could reach an even wider audience. Later, Miep Gies, the woman who helped to hide the Franks, told her version of the story in a memoir.

A **primary source** document is a firsthand account in which the writer reports or describes real events that took place at the time he or she was writing. Primary sources include memoirs, letters, diaries, and legal documents.

A **secondary source** interprets information gathered from primary sources. Secondary sources include biographies and textbooks.

A **dramatization** is a play that has been adapted from another work. When a playwright dramatizes a primary source, such as a diary, he or she may also draw on other sources to add information not known by the original author. In addition, the playwright might choose to fictionalize aspects of certain events for dramatic effect.

All primary sources tell something about their author and their time. Readers can learn about Anne Frank's personality, her circumstances, and the time in which she lived from her diary. Compare the information that the excerpts from Anne's diary and the memoir contain with the type of information presented in the dramatization.

DIRECTIONS: *Answer the following questions to help you compare Anne Frank's diary with the dramatization.*

1. In general, what is reported in the excerpts written by Anne Frank herself on June 20, 1942, and on November 19, 1942?

   _____

   _____

2. What is revealed about Anne's personality in the two excerpts from her diary? What is revealed about others' personalities in Anne's diary?

   _____

   _____

   _____

3. How is information revealed differently in the dramatization than in the memoir and in the diary excerpts?

   _____

   _____

4. Is Anne's personality portrayed similarly or differently in the dramatization than in her diary excerpts? Give examples.

   _____

   _____

from **Anne Frank: The Diary of a Young Girl** by Anne Frank
from **Anne Frank Remembered** by Miep Gies
Vocabulary Builder

Word List

decrees   emigrated   enhance   liberated   succumbed

A. DIRECTIONS: *Answer each of the following questions. Then, provide an explanation for your answer to each question.*

1. Will wearing platform shoes *enhance* a person's height?

   Answer: _____

   Explanation: _____

2. Would a servant issue *decrees* to the king of a country?

   Answer: _____

   Explanation: _____

3. If you have *emigrated* somewhere, does that mean you have lived in one place your whole life?

   Answer: _____

   Explanation: _____

4. If a mother makes sacrifices for her children, would she be acting in a selfish way?

   Answer: _____

   Explanation: _____

5. If armed forces liberated a country, does that mean that they conquered it?

   Answer: _____

   Explanation: _____

6. If a person succumbed to a disease, does that mean he was cured?

   Answer: _____

   Explanation: _____

B. DIRECTIONS: *Complete the following sentences with the appropriate vocabulary word.*

1. My grandparents, who were born in Scotland, _____ to America in 1913.

   A. sacrifices   B. succumbed   C. emigrated   D. enhance

2. Some women use false eyelashes or mascara to _____ their eyes.

   A. sacrifices   B. succumbed   C. emigrated   D. enhance

3. On Memorial Day, the United States honors the _____ made by members of its armed forces.

   A. sacrifices   B. succumbed   C. emigrated   D. enhance

4. Even though she was on a strict diet, she _____ to temptation and ordered a large ice cream sundae.

   A. sacrifices   B. succumbed   C. emigrated   D. enhance

Name _____ Date _____

The Diary of Anne Frank by Frances Goodrich and Albert Hackett
from **Anne Frank: The Diary of a Young Girl** by Anne Frank
from **Anne Frank Remembered** by Miep Gies

Integrated Language Skills: Support for Writing to Compare Literary Works

In addition to a comparison chart, as suggested in the anthology, you may find the graphic organizer presented here helpful for answering the final question of the writing assignment:

> Which form—the dramatization, the diary, or the memoir—do you think is the most powerful? Why?

For each question on the graphic, place a check in the column for the original work: *Anne Frank: The Diary of a Young Girl*; the column for Goodrich and Hackett's play *The Diary of Anne Frank*; or the column for Miep Gies's memoir, *Anne Frank Remembered*.

Criteria	The Original Diary	The Play	The Memoir
1. Which work tells you the most about the setting?			
2. Which work is most capable of giving you a portrait of Anne?			
3. In which work do you feel more empathy for Anne? For Dussel? For the other Franks and the Van Daans?			
4. Which work makes you think the most as you reflect on the work?			
5. Which version would you recommend to other readers?			

Now, combining your notes from this sheet and from your comparison chart, write an essay in which you compare and contrast the dramatic adaptation of Anne Frank's story with the diary and the memoir.

BQ Tunes

Heroes Yesterday, performed by DogDay

She said "Judge a man by his **accomplishments**"

What he's done show more than his eyes reveal

Do his works **endure** the test of time?

What do they represent and **symbolize?**

In with the new, sterile and cold

Outdated courtesies, are the tell you're old

Deeds of **bravery**, loyal and true

Saving the day, that was the rule

Now I'm looking for

Some inspiration

Heroes yesterday

Defined their

Generations

I followed her where she led

She had to **emphasize** what she said

She said it twice to get it through my head

"**Influence**, change the world, lead, don't be led"

Create something new, don't **imitate**

Don't repeat the mistakes they make

The **effect** is easy to see

There's no heroism in celebrity

I'm searching for

Some inspiration

Heroes yesterday

Defined their

Generations

Courageously face **suffering** and sacrifice

They endured the pain, it's a part of life

Continued

The challenges of their time conquered, **overcome**

Admirably rising above

My time with her drew to a close

Each **aspect** reviewed, each angle exposed

She wished me well and said, "I won't **exaggerate**"

"Each new day, the choice is ours to make"

I'm looking back

To find

Some inspiration

Yesterday's Heroes

Blazed the path for

Generations

Song Title: **Heroes Yesterday**
Artist / Performed by DogDay
Vocals & Guitar: Joe Pascarell
Lyrics by Keith London
Music composed by Keith London, Joe Pascarell & Mike Pandolfo
Produced by Mike Pandolfo, Wonderful
Executive Producer: Keith London, Defined Mind

All-in-One Workbook
267

Unit 6: Themes in American Stories
Big Question Vocabulary—1

The Big Question: Are yesterday's heroes important today?

Thematic Vocabulary

admirably: *adv.* in a way that earns respect and high praise; other forms: *admire, admiration*

bravery: *n.* courage and confidence in the face of danger; other form: *brave*

emphasize: *v.* to stress or show that something is very important; other forms: *emphasis, emphasizing*

endure: *v.* to continue to exist for a long time; other forms: *endurance, endurable, enduring*

outdated: *adj.* not useful or valuable anymore

A. DIRECTIONS: *From the words in the box, choose the correct synonym and antonym for each Thematic Vocabulary word. You will not use every word in the box.*

| old-fashioned | strong | survive | heavily | excellently | fearlessness | downplay |
| poorly | die | modern | cowardice | pride | pretend | highlight |

1. admirably   **Synonym:** _____   **Antonym:** _____

2. bravery   **Synonym:** _____   **Antonym:** _____

3. emphasize   **Synonym:** _____   **Antonym:** _____

4. endure   **Synonym:** _____   **Antonym:** _____

5. outdated   **Synonym:** _____   **Antonym:** _____

B. DIRECTIONS: *Complete each sentence by writing the correct Thematic Vocabulary word on the line.*

1. The soldier received a medal for his outstanding _____.

2. Use an exclamation point to _____ your character's strong feelings.

3. My love for the beauty of this island will _____ for the rest of my life.

4. Even though he lost the contest, he performed _____.

5. Grandma writes letters on a computer, but Grandpa still uses his _____ typewriter.

Unit 6: Themes in American Stories
Big Question Vocabulary—2

 The Big Question: Are yesterday's heroes important today?

Thematic Vocabulary

accomplishments: *n.* successful or impressive achievements; other form: *accomplish*

aspects: *n.* parts of a situation, idea, or plan; other form: *aspect*

courage: *n.* bravery; other form: *courageous*

exaggerate: *v.* to make something seem better, larger, or worse than it actually is; other forms: *exaggeration, exaggerating*

imitate: *v.* to copy or duplicate another's actions; other forms: *imitation, imitating, imitated*

DIRECTIONS: *Respond to each of the items below.*

1. Rewrite this sentence so that it exaggerates the situation described: *He has a huge dog.*

   _____

2. Name a historical figure who you feel exhibited great *courage*. Explain your choice.

   _____

   _____

3. List the *aspects* of the task of making a sandwich.

   _____

   _____

4. What steps would you follow to *imitate* a robot?

   _____

   _____

5. What do you consider to be one of your greatest *accomplishments*? Explain your choice.

   _____

   _____

Unit 6: Themes in American Stories
Big Question Vocabulary—3

The Big Question: Are yesterday's heroes important today?

Thematic Vocabulary

cultural: *adj.* belonging or relating to a particular society and its way of life; other form: *culture*

influence: *v.* to have an effect on the thinking or behavior of another person; other forms: *influential, influencing*

overcome: *v.* to successfully control or do away with a harmful feeling or problem; other form: *overcame*

suffering: *v.* having serious mental or physical pain; other forms: *suffer, suffered*

symbolize: *v.* to represent something large or intangible; other forms: *symbol, symbolized*

A. DIRECTIONS: *Write the Thematic Vocabulary word that best completes each sentence.*

1. The people of many different societies use a dove to _____ peace.

2. If you want to be a successful actor, you will have to _____ your stage fright.

3. My kindergarten teacher worked hard to _____ us to have a lifelong love of reading.

4. In Great Britain, the queen's birthday is a widely celebrated _____ holiday.

5. Many students in our school are _____ from colds this winter.

B. DIRECTIONS: *Answer each question.*

1. Which animal would you choose to *symbolize* strength and courage? Explain.

_____

2. If a friend were *suffering* from a lack of confidence, what would you do to help him or her *overcome* this problem? _____

_____

3. What is your favorite holiday, and what *cultural* tradition makes it so special?

_____

4. What family member, famous person, or historical figure has *influenced* your thinking or values? Explain. _____

_____

Name _____ Date _____

Unit 6: Themes in American Stories
Applying the Big Question

 Are yesterday's heroes important today?

DIRECTIONS: *Complete the chart below to apply what you have learned about yesterday's heroes and their importance today. One row has been completed for you.*

Example	Hero's action	Cause of hero's action	Effect of hero's action	What I Learned
From Literature	Daddy in "Out of the Dust" continues to work and hope while other families leave.	Dust storms ravage the land, but he is a farmer and chooses to be true to his work.	Narrator's family stays behind while others flee to faraway places.	The odds against success may be high, but perseverance may lead to triumph.
From Literature				
From Science				
From Social Studies				
From Real Life				

Lan Samantha Chang
Listening and Viewing

Segment 1: Meet Lan Samantha Chang
- How has Lan Samantha Chang's experiences with music affected her writing? Why do you think it is important to practice writing every day?

_____

_____

_____

Segment 2: Themes in Literature
- According to Lan Samantha Chang, why was storytelling important to the Chinese culture? Why do you think folk tales and fairy tales are important to society?

_____

_____

_____

Segment 3: The Writing Process
- Through writing, how does Lan Samantha Chang "make a riddle out of an answer"? How do you think writing can help you learn more about something that you do not understand?

_____

_____

_____

Segment 4: The Rewards of Writing
- How has writing stories based on her own family experiences been rewarding to Lan Samantha Chang? How do you think writing stories could be rewarding for you?

_____

_____

_____

Learning About Themes in American Stories

Folk tradition includes the manners, customs, sayings, and stories of a culture. The American folk tradition grew out of **oral tradition**—stories and histories that were originally shared by word of mouth rather than in print. Here are some characteristics of oral tradition:

- A **theme** is an idea revealed in a tale. A **universal theme**—for example, the power of love—shows up in stories of different cultures and periods.
- **Heroes** and **heroines** are larger-than-life figures whose virtues and achievements are celebrated in the oral tradition.
- **Storytelling techniques** maintain the interest of live audiences. Techniques include

  - **Hyperbole:** exaggeration or overstatement, either to create humor or to express heightened emotion
  - **Personification:** figurative language that gives a personality and human characteristics to nonhuman subjects, such as animals or natural elements
  - **Idioms:** in a language, region, community, or class, the expressions that cannot be understood literally—for example, "cut the mustard"

Here are types of literature that began in the oral tradition:

- **Myths:** tales that use gods, goddesses, and heroes to explain the causes of natural phenomena. Every culture has its own collection of myths, or **mythology.**
- **Epics:** long narrative poems about larger-than-life heroes who engage in dangerous journeys, or **quests,** that are important to the history of a nation or culture
- **Fables:** brief stories with animals that speak and act like humans. Fables often end with a directly stated **moral,** or message.
- **Tall tales:** folk tales that use **hyperbole.** Featuring a hero who performs impossible feats, tall tales are forms of **legends,** which are based on facts but that become more fictionalized with each telling.

DIRECTIONS: *Circle the letter of the answer choice that best matches each numbered item.*

1. a story about the Greek goddess Athena
   A. myth   B. tall tale   C. fable
2. a long narrative poem about a hero's journey home from a war
   A. fable   B. epic   C. idiom
3. the description of nonhuman subjects as if they were human
   A. personification   B. hyperbole   C. symbolism
4. story about a sly fox who outwits a crow
   A. epic   B. tall tale   C. fable
5. fictionalized, exaggerated story with a factual or historical basis
   A. legend   B. fable   C. epic
6. collection of myths
   A. folk tradition   B. mythology   C. oral tradition

Name _____ Date _____

"**Water Names**" by Lan Samantha Chang
Model Selection: American Stories

By its very nature, **folk tradition** is a living body of customs, manners, stories, and sayings that constantly changes. For example, as a story is retold over generations—either orally or in writing—new characters may appear. In the United States, nineteenth-century folk heroes included patriots, soldiers, farmers, and cowboys. A century later, American heroes came to include sports figures, politicians, businesspeople, and astronauts.

A. DIRECTIONS: *Use the space below each question about "Water Names" to write your answer.*

1. As noted above, a folk tale was often passed along orally before it was written down. When and where did Waipuo herself first hear the tale she tells her granddaughters?

   _____

   _____

2. Waipuo and her granddaughters live on the American prairie, far from a river such as the one in the story. So of what use is the story about the river to the girls?

   _____

   _____

3. Which details in "Water Names" show Waipuo's pride in the family heritage? Which details show that the family has a special relationship with the Yangtze River?

   _____

   _____

   _____

   _____

4. Identify at least two specific times when Lily reacts to or asks a question about Waipuo's story. What do these interruptions of Lily's remind us about the folk tradition?

   _____

   _____

5. What elements of Waipuo's story might explain why it has been told and retold as part of the family's folk tradition?

   _____

   _____

   _____

   _____

"Coyote Steals the Sun and Moon" retold by Richard Erdoes and Alfonso Ortiz
Writing About the Big Question
Are Yesterday's Heroes Important Today?

Big Question Vocabulary

accomplishments	admirably	aspects	bravery	courage
cultural	emphasize	endure	exaggerate	imitate
influence	outdated	overcome	suffering	symbolize

A. *Use a word or words from the list above to answer each question.*

1. Myths from different countries differ because they emphasize what kinds of values?
   _____

2. If a mythical hero faces a challenge, what does the hero always do?
   _____

3. To create a hero of myth, what would a storyteller do to the hero's personality traits? _____

B. *Write two or three sentences in response to each item below.*

1. List your ideas about why myths explain **aspects** of nature and **emphasize courage.**
   _____
   _____
   _____

2. Explain why you believe myths are **outdated** or whether mythical heroes can still **influence** people.
   _____
   _____
   _____

C. *Complete the sentence below. Then, write a short paragraph in which you connect this answer to the Big Question.*

Myths have endured throughout the ages because they _____
   _____
   _____

"Coyote Steals the Sun and Moon" retold by Richard Erdoes and Alfonso Ortiz
Reading: Create a Summary

A **summary** is a short statement that presents the main points in a piece of writing. Summarizing helps you focus on the most important information and remember it better. You also may need to summarize a work as part of your discussion of it.

Follow this strategy when you summarize a work that tells a story:

- Reread the work to identify the main events.
- Restate these events in complete sentences.
- Put the sentences in chronological order.
- Cross out any minor details that do not seem important enough to include.
- Be sure that your sentences mention all the major points, including the main characters and settings.
- Revise your sentences so that they use as few words as possible.

A. DIRECTIONS: *Answer the questions about a summary of "Coyote Steals the Sun and Moon."*

1. Which two characters would be most important to mention in your summary?

   _____   _____

2. What are three settings that should be mentioned in your summary?

   _____   _____   _____

3. Restate two things a character says that should be included in your summary.

   _____

   _____

4. List two things the characters do that should be included in your summary.

   _____

   _____

B. DIRECTIONS: *Based on the guidelines and your answers to items 1–4 above, write a summary of "Coyote Steals the Sun and Moon." Use the space below or a separate sheet of paper.*

_____

_____

_____

_____

_____

_____

"Coyote Steals the Sun and Moon" retold by Richard Erdoes and Alfonso Ortiz

Literary Analysis: Myth

In ancient times, people wondered about the world, just as people do today. Sometimes they told stories to try to explain it. These stories are called myths. A **myth** is an ancient tale that presents the beliefs or customs of a culture. Most myths try to explain an aspect of nature, history, or human behavior. They usually feature supernatural creatures and often contain animals or forces of nature that display human qualities.

You can usually understand a myth better if you know something about the culture that produced it. For example, when you read the Zuñi myth "Coyote Steals the Sun and Moon," it helps to know that the Zuñi are a Native American people from the American Southwest. The myth itself also reveals information about the culture or landscape in which it is set.

DIRECTIONS: *Use this chart to show what "Coyote Steals the Sun and Moon" tells you about Native American people like the Zuñi and their life in the Southwest. For each detail in the left column, list at least one insight it gives you into the culture or setting. The insight from the first detail has been given as an example.*

Detail	Insight
1. Coyote and Eagle hunt rabbits.	• Coyotes and eagles are found in the Southwest. • Southwestern tribes sometimes hunted.
2. Coyote and Eagle come to a village called a pueblo.	
3. The people in the pueblo watch Kachinas do a sacred dance.	
4. Coyote says to Eagle, "You're my chief."	
5. Eagle gives Coyote the box because "if someone asks four times, you'd better give him what he wants."	
6. Peaches, squashes, and melons shrivel up with the cold.	

"Coyote Steals the Sun and Moon" retold by Richard Erdoes and Alfonso Ortiz
Vocabulary Builder

Word List

curiosity   lagged   pestering   pursuit   sacred   shriveled

A. DIRECTIONS: *Answer the questions with complete sentences, using each World List word only once and underlining it.*

1. What is one book that many people consider holy?

   _____

2. What small, wrinkled fruit is made by drying grapes in the sun?

   _____

3. What does a police car do when chasing a criminal?

   _____

4. How do most people react to being annoyed constantly?

   _____

5. What is something about which people have lots of questions?

   _____

6. How might someone react after trailing behind everyone else in a race?

   _____

B. WORD STUDY: *The word root -sacre- means "sacred" or "holy." Use what you know about -sacre- to answer the questions.*

1. Do all religions have the same *sacred* book?

   _____

2. In what kind of building will you find a room called a *sacristy*, which holds sacred items?

   _____

3. What do *sacraments* such as baptism and communion have in common?

   _____

"Why the Waves Have Whitecaps" by Zora Neale Hurston
Writing About the Big Question

Are Yesterday's Heroes Important Today?

Big Question Vocabulary

accomplishments	admirably	aspects	bravery	courage
cultural	emphasize	endure	exaggerate	imitate
influence	outdated	overcome	suffering	symbolize

A. *Use a word or words from the list above to complete each sentence.*

1. Two traits that nearly all heroes display are _____ and _____.

2. Someone might _____ a beloved hero.

3. A person today might think a hero from ages past is _____.

4. People still enjoy reading ancient myths about heroes' _____.

B. *Follow the directions in responding to each of the items below. Use at least one Big Question vocabulary word in each answer.*

1. In one Greek myth, Orpheus loved Eurydice so much that after she died he figured out a way to enter the underworld to try to rescue her. In two sentences, describe the heroic traits Orpheus displayed.

   _____

   _____

2. In two sentences, describe a hero from American history whose life story has become like a myth.

   _____

   _____

C. *Complete the sentence below. Then, write a short paragraph in which you connect this answer to the Big Question.*

Things that we might use today to symbolize disturbances in the natural world include _____.

   _____

   _____

"Why the Waves Have Whitecaps" by Zora Neale Hurston
Reading: Create a Summary

A **summary** is a short statement that presents the main points in a piece of writing. Summarizing helps you focus on the most important information and remember it better. You also may need to summarize a work as part of your discussion of it.

Follow this strategy when you summarize a work that tells a story:

- Reread the work to identify the main events.
- Restate these events in complete sentences.
- Put the sentences in chronological order.
- Cross out any minor details that do not seem important enough to include.
- Be sure that your sentences mention all the major points, including the main characters and settings.
- Revise your sentences so that they use as few words as possible.

DIRECTIONS: *Follow the numbered instructions to revise this paragraph into a good summary of "Why the Waves Have Whitecaps."*

The wind and the water are both characters. They used to speak proudly and boastfully about their children. Mrs. Wind said one thing and Mrs. Water said another.

Mrs. Water got so sick and tired of hearing about Mrs. Wind's children that one day, when the children came to drink her water, she drowned them. When Mrs. Wind went to look for her children, Mrs. Water said she had not seen them. Mrs. Wind searched high and low. Mrs. Wind passed over the water calling for her children. Whitecaps came to the top. _____

_____

1. Add a key detail to the first sentence.
2. Replace the phrase "speak proudly and boastfully" with a single word.
3. Remove two unnecessary words from the fourth sentence.
4. Cross out the two sentences that most clearly do not belong in the summary.
5. Reword the last two sentences to make the relationship between them clear.
6. On the lines at the end, add a sentence that makes clear what the myth explains.

"Why the Waves Have Whitecaps" by Zora Neale Hurston
Literary Analysis: Myth

A **myth** is an ancient tale that presents the beliefs or customs of a culture or people. Most myths try to explain an aspect of nature, history, or human behavior. They often feature supernatural creatures like gods and goddesses or contain animals or forces of nature that display human qualities. "Why the Waves Have Whitecaps" is Zora Neale Hurston's retelling of an African American myth.

DIRECTIONS: *Answer these questions about the retold myth "Why the Waves Have Whitecaps."*

1. What does the myth try to explain?

   _____

2. Sum up the explanation in three or four sentences.

   _____

   _____

   _____

   _____

3. What supernatural creatures, humanlike animals, or forces of nature does the myth feature as characters?

   _____

4. What human qualities do these characters display?

   _____

   _____

   _____

5. What does the myth suggest about the role of nature in African American life in times past? Explain.

   _____

   _____

   _____

6. What else does the myth suggest about African American life?

   _____

   _____

   _____

"Why the Waves Have Whitecaps" by Zora Neale Hurston
Vocabulary Builder

To make "Why the Waves Have Whitecaps" seem like authentic oral storytelling, Hurston tells it in African American dialect. **Dialect** is the vocabulary and grammar used in a particular region or by a particular group. Because it differs from **standard English,** the most widely known and accepted form of the language, it may contain terms that are puzzling at first. To understand a puzzling dialect term, follow these steps:

- Consider whether it might mean the same as a more familiar word or phrase that it sounds like.
- Use its position in a sentence to help you determine what part of speech it might be.
- Look for other clues about the term in its **context,** or surrounding words.
- Once you guess the meaning, replace the term with your guess to see if it makes sense.

For example, in the sentence "They useter talk together a whole heap," you can figure out that *useter* probably means "used to" because it sounds like those words, its position in the sentence suggests that it functions as a verb, and "used to" makes sense in the context.

A. DIRECTIONS: *Use the sound, position, and other context clues to figure out the meaning of each underlined dialect term. Then, circle the letter of the correct meaning.*

1. De wind is a woman, and de water is a woman too.
   A. day   B. did   C. the   D. deed

2. They was jus' like all lady people. They loved to talk about their chillun, and brag on 'em.
   A. chill out   B. child   C. children   D. killing

3. One day a whole passle of her chillun come to Mrs. Wind. . . .
   A. large group B. small coin C. pass out   D. people

4. "Mama, wese thirsty. Kin we go git us a cool drink of water?"
   A. I am   B. we are   C. wheeze   D. become

5. When them chillun went to squinch they thirst Mrs. Water grabbed 'em all. . . .
   A. squint   B. spinach   C. crunch   D. quench

B. DIRECTIONS: *Rewrite this dialect passage in standard English.*

"Oh, but Ah got mo' different chilluns than anybody in de world. They flies, they walks, they swims, they sings, they talks, they cries. They got all de colors from de sun. Lawd, my chillun sho is a pleasure. 'Tain't nobody got no babies like mine."

_____

_____

_____

_____

"Coyote Steals the Sun and Moon" retold by Richard Erdoes and Alfonso Ortiz
"Why the Waves Have Whitecaps" by Zora Neale Hurston
Integrated Language Skills: Grammar

Independent Clauses	Subordinate Clauses
S V	S V
The school bell rang.	When the school bell rang
S S V V	S S V V
The boys and girls shouted and cheered.	As the boys and girls shouted and cheered

Sentence Structures

A **clause** is a group of words with at least one subject (*S*) and one verb (*V*). An **independent clause** can stand on its own as a sentence; a **subordinate clause** cannot.

Sentences are classified by their clauses. A **simple sentence** includes one independent clause:

The school bell rang.   The boys and girls shouted and cheered.

A **compound sentence** has two or more independent clauses joined by a comma (or commas) and a coordinating conjunction (*and, or, but, so, nor, for,* or *yet*) or by a semicolon. In these examples, each independent clause is underlined.

The school bell rang, *but* class continued. The school bell rang; class continued.

A **complex sentence** has one independent clause (indicated by one underline) and one or more subordinate clauses (indicated by a double underline).

When the school bell rang, the children raced to the bus that stood by the curb.

A **compound-complex** sentence has at least two independent clauses and at least one subordinate clause.

When the clock chimed three, the school bell rang, and the children raced to the bus.

A. PRACTICE: *Underline each independent clause once and each subordinate clause twice. Label the sentence* simple, compound, complex, *or* compound-complex.

_____ 1. The Northwest is damp and rainy, but the Southwest is dry.

_____ 2. When it rains, many desert flowers bloom.

B. Writing Application: *Rewrite the sentences as instructed.*

1. The beach traffic is usually heavy in summer. This weekend was an exception. (Combine into a compound sentence.) _____

_____

2. I stood on the beach. The waves rushed to shore. The seagulls flew overhead. (Combine into a compound-complex sentence.) _____

_____

"Coyote Steals the Sun and Moon" retold by Richard Erdoes and Alfonso Ortiz
"Why the Waves Have Whitecaps" by Zora Neale Hurston
Integrated Language Skills: Support for Writing

Use the chart below to help you gather details for the myth you will create. For statements by the characters, use dialect, idioms, and humor. They will make the myth seem authentic.

Subject (Natural Feature or Event to Be Explained)	
Main Characters	
Setting (Time and Place)	
Main Events of the Myth	
Statements by Characters (include Dialect, Idioms, and Humor)	

Name _____ Date _____

"Brer Possum's Dilemma" by Jackie Torrence
"John Henry" Traditional
Writing About the Big Question

Are Yesterday's Heroes Important Today?

Big Question Vocabulary

accomplishments	admirably	aspects	bravery	courage
cultural	emphasize	endure	exaggerate	imitate
influence	outdated	overcome	suffering	symbolize

A. *Use a word or words from the list above to complete each sentence.*

1. Cartoons based on tall tales help regional folk heroes _____ a whole country.

2. Tellers of tall tales often _____ the dialect of the region a tale comes from.

3. Beloved folk heroes _____ difficulties in ways that are clever and humorous.

4. The dialect of some folk tales has disappeared, so the tales can sound _____.

B. *Write two sentences to respond to each of the items below.*

1. What do folk heroes stand for, or **symbolize**, to you?

   _____

   _____

   _____

2. Have all the folk heroes you have read about behaved **admirably**? Would they be more interesting if they did or didn't?

   _____

   _____

   _____

C. *Complete the sentence below. Then, write a short paragraph in which you connect this answer to the Big Question.*

Although the accomplishments of folk heroes are exaggerated, folk heroes have value because _____.

_____

_____

"Brer Possum's Dilemma" by Jackie Torrence
"John Henry" Traditional

Reading: Use a Graphic to Summarize Literature

A **summary** is a short statement that presents the main points of a piece of writing. Since a summary leaves out the less important details, it provides a quick way to preview or review a much longer work and focus on what is most important in it. You will also use a summary of a work as part of your discussion of the work.

Before you write a summary of a work of literature, determine whether an event or idea is important enough to include in your summary. Then, use a graphic aid such as a cluster diagram or a timeline to organize the important events or ideas. For example, for a summary of the selection from "John Henry," you might use a timeline like this one:

JH as baby ● predicts death at Big Bend Tunnel
JH as worker ● steam drill brought in
● JH claims he'll beat steam drill or die.
● JH points out captain's drill broke.
● JH hurts himself.
● JH dies from injuries.

DIRECTIONS: *Write a summary of "Brer Possum's Dilemma." Before you write, determine which events or ideas are important enough to include in the summary. Use a graphic aid such as a cluster diagram or a timeline to organize the important events or ideas.*

Graphic Aid

Summary

_____

_____

_____

_____

_____

_____

"Brer Possum's Dilemma" by Jackie Torrence
"John Henry" Traditional
Literary Analysis: Oral Tradition

Both "Brer Possum's Dilemma" and "John Henry" come from the American **oral tradition,** which is the body of stories, poems, and songs passed down by word of mouth from one generation to the next. Even when they are written down, the tales, poems, and songs from the oral tradition often use dialect to make them seem like spoken English. **Dialect** is the vocabulary and grammar spoken in a particular region or by a particular group. Because it differs from **standard English,** the most widely known and accepted form of the language, it may contain terms that puzzle you at first. To understand a puzzling dialect term, follow these steps:

- Consider whether it might mean the same as a more familiar word or phrase that it sounds like.
- Use its position in the sentence to help you determine its likely part of speech.
- Look for other clues about the term in its **context,** or surrounding words.
- Once you guess the meaning, replace the term with your guess to see if it makes sense.

A. DIRECTIONS: *Use the sound, position, and other context clues to figure out the meaning of each underlined dialect term. Then, circle the letter of the correct meaning.*

1. Back in the days when the animals could talk, there lived ol' Brer Possum. He was a fine <u>feller</u>.
   A. filler   B. fellow   C. dropper   D. cutter

2. Why, he never liked to see no <u>critters</u> in trouble. He was always helpin' out, a-doin' somethin' for others.
   A. quitters   B. critics   C. creatures   D. makers

3. <u>Cap'n</u> says to John Henry, "Gonna bring me a steam drill 'round."
   A. Captain   B. cap in   C. cape   D. Corporal

4. The rock so tall an' John Henry so small, / That he <u>lied</u> down his hammer an' he cried.
   A. told a falsehood   C. went to sleep
   B. sang   D. laid

B. DIRECTIONS: *Write your reaction to the use of dialect in the two selections. Do you find that dialect makes each selection more or less effective? Why?*

_____

_____

_____

_____

_____

Name _____ Date _____

"Brer Possum's Dilemma" by Jackie Torrence
"John Henry" Traditional
Vocabulary Builder

Word List

coiled   commenced   flagged   pitiful

A. DIRECTIONS: *Answer the questions with complete sentences, using each Word List word only once.*

1. Is a motherless kitten a sight that arouses sympathy?

   _____

2. Has the twenty-first century started yet?

   _____

3. Would you wave down a man who has just dropped his wallet?

   _____

4. How would you react if you saw a snake curled up in a corner?

   _____

B. WORD STUDY: *The suffix -ful means "full of." Complete the following sentences using one of these words with the suffix -ful: beautiful, careful, deceitful, successful, thankful.*

1. If someone makes a lot of money, does that make the person _____ ?
2. What a _____ oil painting!
3. Be _____ when you hike in the desert after dark.
4. Do you try to be _____ for something every day?
5. Is it _____ to tell your friend that you like her new haircut if you really don't?

"Chicoria" by José Griego y Maestra and Rudolfo A. Anaya
from **The People, Yes** by Carl Sandburg
Writing About the Big Question
Are Yesterday's Heroes Important Today?

Big Question Vocabulary

accomplishments	admirably	aspects	bravery	courage
cultural	emphasize	endure	exaggerate	imitate
influence	outdated	overcome	suffering	symbolize

A. *Write the word from the list above that best completes each sentence.*

1. Tall tales always _____ the hero's actions.

2. In tall tales, the heroes _____ are generally outrageous.

3. Tall tales reveal the _____ background of the people they come from.

4. Tall tale heroes _____ unbelievable difficulties.

B. *Write two- or three-sentence answers to each of the following questions.*

1. What aspects of a hero's character might the teller of a tall tale exaggerate? Why?

_____

_____

_____

2. What would a writer have to do to **imitate** the style of a tall tale?

_____

_____

_____

C. *Complete the sentence below. Then, write a short paragraph in which you connect this answer to the Big Question.*

In today's stories, qualities such as _____ are still admired in a heroic character. _____

_____

_____

"Chicoria" adapted by José Griego y Maestas, retold by Rudolfo A. Anaya
from **"The People, Yes"** by Carl Sandburg
Reading: Use a Graphic to Summarize Literature

A **summary** is a short statement that presents the main points of a piece of writing. Since a summary leaves out the less important details, it provides a quick way to preview or review a much longer work and focus on what is most important in it. You also will use a summary of a work as part of your discussion of the work.

In the passage from "The People, Yes," Carl Sandburg presents summaries of more than twenty American folk tales, which he calls "yarns." Each summary can complete his opening statement, "They have yarns. . . ." For example, lines 1–7 can read as "They have yarns of a skyscraper. . . . They have yarns of one corn crop. . . . They have yarns of pancakes so thin. . . ."

DIRECTIONS: *Write a summary of "Chicoria" that could have appeared as an item in "The People, Yes." Before you write the summary, determine which events or ideas from "Chicoria" are important enough to include. Use a graphic aid such as a cluster diagram or a timeline to organize the important events or ideas.*

Graphic Aid

Summary

They have yarns _____

_____

_____

_____

_____

_____

Name _____ Date _____

"Chicoria" adapted by José Griego y Maestas, retold by Rudolfo A. Anaya
from **"The People, Yes"** by Carl Sandburg
Literary Analysis: Oral Tradition

Although "The People, Yes" is a piece of written literature, it pulls together many stories from the American **oral tradition,** which is the body of stories, poems, and songs passed down by word of mouth from one generation to the next. The yarns and legends of oral tradition often contain exaggeration, references to magic, and other invented details that do not reflect reality. At the same time, they often have some basis in actual fact. Consider, for example, Sandburg's summary of a yarn about a corn crop:

> They have yarns . . .
>
> Of one corn crop in Missouri when the roots
>
> Went so deep and drew off so much water
>
> The Mississippi riverbed that year was dry. . . .

Although no corn crop could cause the Mississippi riverbed to go dry, it is a fact that corn was grown in Missouri along the Mississippi River, and the yarn probably had its origins in a time when a Mississippi drought followed a good corn crop.

DIRECTIONS: *Identify another yarn that Sandburg summarizes in "The People, Yes." Then, from the summary, list one exaggerated detail and one factual detail.*

"Chicoria" adapted by José Griego y Maestas, retold by Rudolfo A. Anaya
from **"The People, Yes"** by Carl Sandburg
Vocabulary Builder

Word List

cordially   cyclone   haughty   mutineers   self-confident   straddling

A. DIRECTIONS: *Answer the questions with complete sentences, using each Word List word only once.*

1. In some fairy tales, is the queen proud and superior?

   _____

2. Could a rotating windstorm destroy a farmer's crops?

   _____

3. Does a good receptionist usually greet visitors in a friendly way?

   _____

4. What might increase the chances of success for sailors who plan to overthrow their ship's commander?

   _____

5. When might you be standing over your bicycle with your legs wide apart?

   _____

6. Can people who have too strong a belief in their own abilities and judgment ever have problems as a result?

   _____

B. WORD STUDY: *The suffix -eer means "one who does something." Explain what the person referred to in each sentence does.*

1. I think working as a *puppeteer* would be an enjoyable job.

   _____

2. The best *charioteer* in a film is sure to be the hero.

   _____

3. The *mountaineer* tried to reach the highest peak without needing extra oxygen.

   _____

"**Brer Possum's Dilemma**" by Jackie Torrence
"**John Henry**" Traditional
"**Chicoria**" adapted by José Griego y Maestas, retold by Rudolfo A. Anaya
from "**The People, Yes**" by Carl Sandburg

Integrated Language Skills: Grammar

Commas

Use a **comma** in the following situations:

- before a conjunction that separates two independent clauses:
    Cats are my favorite pet, but my sister prefers dogs.
- between items in a series:
    We own a cat, a dog, and a hamster.
- after introductory words, phrases, or clauses:
    Yes, our cat is very shy and quiet.
    Walking on her soft paws, she rarely makes a sound.
- to set off appositives, participial phrases, or adjective clauses that interrupt a sentence:
    Bobo, our dog, is friendly.
    Bobo, welcoming us home, always expects a pat.
- to set off other parenthetical words and expressions that interrupt a sentence:
    Did you know, John, that our house caught fire?
    It was our cat, not our dog, that woke us up.

A. PRACTICE: *Insert one or more commas in each sentence, as needed.*

1. When I read I prefer humorous yarns.

2. Annie Oakley a famous sharpshooter appeared in one tale that I read.

3. I also read folk tales about Brer Possum Paul Bunyan and Pecos Bill.

B. Writing Application: *Expand each sentence according to the instructions in parentheses. Use commas where necessary.*

1. People enjoy all kinds of music. (Add an independent clause.) _____

_____

2. I like the singers Nanci Griffith and Natalie Merchant. (Add another singer.) _____

_____

3. I thought that song was beautiful. (Add an introductory clause that begins with *When*.)

_____

4. Those lyrics are in dialect. (Add an appositive to explain what *dialect* is.) _____

_____

Name _____ Date _____

"Brer Possum's Dilemma" by Jackie Torrence
"John Henry" Traditional
"Chicoria" adapted by José Griego y Maestas, retold by Rudolfo A. Anaya
from **The People, Yes** by Carl Sandburg

Integrated Language Skills: Support for Writing

Use this chart to gather examples of dialect, folk idioms, hyperbole, and other elements of the oral tradition that you plan to discuss in your **critical analysis**. For the location of an example from "Brer Possum's Dilemma," use *BPD* and a line number; for an example from "John Henry," use *JH* and a line number; for an example from "Chicoria," use *Chic* and a paragraph number; for an example from "The People, Yes," use *TPY* and a line number. An example has been done for you.

Type	Example	Location	Effect on Tone or Mood
Dialect	ol' Brer Possum	BPD 4	creates a folksy, familiar quality that makes the character more appealing
Idiom (expression that has a meaning particular to a language or region)			
Hyperbole (exaggeration)			
Other element of oral tradition			

Now, explain how the examples you collected affect the tone, meaning, and mood of folk literature.

"Davy Crockett's Dream" by Davy Crockett
"Paul Bunyan of the North Woods" by Carl Sandburg
"Invocation" *from* **John Brown's Body** by Stephen Vincent Benét

Writing About the Big Question

Are Yesterday's Heroes Important Today?

Big Question Vocabulary

accomplishments	admirably	aspects	bravery	courage
cultural	emphasize	endure	exaggerate	imitate
influence	outdated	overcome	suffering	symbolize

A. *Use a word or words from the list above to complete each sentence.*

1. The pioneers behaved _____ as they traveled West.

2. But no pioneer could match the _____ of folk tale heroes.

3. However a pioneer could _____ _____ of the traits of those heroes, such as courage and grit.

B. *Follow the directions in responding to the items below.*

1. Write a two-sentence comparison of the tales about Davy Crockett and Paul Bunyan. Use at least two Big Question vocabulary words in your comparison.

   _____

   _____

   _____

2. In two sentences, explain why you think Davy Crockett and Paul Bunyan were such appealing folk heroes to the pioneers. Use at least two Big Question vocabulary words.

   _____

   _____

   _____

C. *In different ways, these selections look back to the heroes of an earlier America. Complete the sentence below. Then, write a short paragraph in which you connect this sentence to the Big Question.*

To be a hero today, a person can win admiration through such actions as
_____ and _____.

_____

_____

_____

"Davy Crockett's Dream" by Davy Crockett
"Paul Bunyan of the North Woods" by Carl Sandburg
"Invocation" *from* **John Brown's Body** by Stephen Vincent Benét
Literary Analysis: Comparing Heroic Characters

Heroic characters are men and women who show great courage and overcome difficult challenges. A heroic character can be fictional or real. Often, the hero in a tall tale or legend is a combination of both—a real historical figure whose actions have become so exaggerated over time that he or she becomes a legend.

Many American legends and stories focus on the pioneers of the western frontier. Because survival in such a harsh setting depended on skill and strength, many tall tales and legends exaggerate these admirable qualities.

DIRECTIONS: *Answer the questions about each heroic character in the following chart.*

Questions	Davy Crockett	Paul Bunyan
1. In what ways did the hero(es) show great courage?		
2. Did these characters overcome difficult challenges? How?		
3. What actions, if any, by the character(s) are exaggerated?		
4. Label the characters with one of these three phrases: real historical figure, fictional legend, or combination of both.		

"**Davy Crockett's Dream**" by Davy Crockett
"**Paul Bunyan of the North Woods**" by Carl Sandburg
"**Invocation**" *from* **John Brown's Body** by Stephen Vincent Benét
Vocabulary Builder

Word List

arrogant   commotion   kindled   shanties   squatter   subdued

A. DIRECTIONS: *Write a sentence to answer each question. Your answer must show that you know the meaning of the italicized word.*

1. Would a camper want to have a fire *kindled* just before he or she packs up and leaves a campsite?

   _____

2. Would young business executives like to live in *shanties*?

   _____

3. Would *squatters* want to be discovered living where they are by the police or the government?

   _____

4. During a movie, would you prefer for the people sitting in front of you to create a *commotion* or sit still?

   _____

5. Would someone feel *subdued* after winning a contest?

   _____

6. Why might an *arrogant* person be difficult to live with?

   _____

B. DIRECTIONS: *For each related pair of words in CAPITAL LETTERS, circle the lettered pair that best expresses a similar relationship.*

1. SHANTIES : MANSIONS ::
   A. fire : cook
   B. glass : diamonds
   C. flower : spring
   D. construction : building

2. ARROGANT : PROUD ::
   A. child : adult
   B. pleasant : nasty
   C. voter : election
   D. ecstatic : happy

"Davy Crockett's Dream" by Davy Crockett
"Paul Bunyan of the North Woods" by Carl Sandburg
"Invocation" *from* **John Brown's Body** by Stephen Vincent Benét

Integrated Language Skills: Support for Writing

Before you write your essay that compares and contrasts the way in which these three selections present heroic characters, use the graphic organizer below to list ideas about each character.

How does each writer use exaggeration? What is the effect?	David Crockett	Paul Bunyan	The American Muse

How important is humor in each selection?	David Crockett	Paul Bunyan	The American Muse

What do these selections show about the American character and what we admire in our heroes?	David Crockett	Paul Bunyan	The American Muse

Now, use your notes to write an essay comparing the presentations of the different heroic characters.

Name _____ Date _____

from **Out of the Dust** by Karen Hesse
Writing About the Big Question

Are Yesterday's Heroes Important Today?

Big Question Vocabulary

accomplishments	admirably	aspects	bravery	courage
cultural	emphasize	endure	exaggerate	imitate
influence	outdated	overcome	suffering	symbolize

A. *Use a word or words from the list above to answer each question.*

1. What qualities did Dust Bowl farmers of the 1930s often display?

   _____

2. What did some farm families do when a dust storm hit? _____

3. What caused some Dust Bowl farm families to move West? _____

B. *Write two sentences in response to each item below. Use at least two Big Question vocabulary words in your sentences.*

1. Which reacted more heroically, Dust Bowl farm families of the 1930s that stayed on their farms or the ones that left? Explain.

   _____

   _____

   _____

2. What importance do stories of heroic farm families of the Dust Bowl era hold for us today?

   _____

   _____

   _____

C. *Complete the sentence below. Then, write a short paragraph in which you connect this answer to the Big Question.*

   The ability to endure tough challenges shows that _____.

   _____

   _____

from **Out of the Dust** by Karen Hesse
Reading: Ask Questions to Set a Purpose for Reading

Setting a purpose for reading helps you focus your attention as you read a literary work. One way to set a purpose is to **ask questions** about the topic of the work, questions that you can answer as you read. Use a K-W-L chart to ask questions, and then answer them. See the example below, using material from *Out of the Dust*.

"K" (What I already know about the topic): I know that the Dust Bowl during the Great Depression made farming life on the Great Plains almost impossible.	"W" (What I want to know): How did people keep going when their crops were so often destroyed in the Dust Bowl?	"L" (What I learned): I will answer this question after I have read the selection.

DIRECTIONS: *Read each passage from* Out of the Dust, *and then answer each question.*

Debts
Daddy is thinking
of taking a loan from Mr. Roosevelt and his men,
to get some new wheat planted
where the winter crop has spindled out and died.
Mr. Roosevelt promises
Daddy won't have to pay a dime
till the crop comes in.

1. What is one solution the Roosevelt administration set up to help farmers?

_____

Migrants
We'll be back when the rain comes,
they say,
pulling away with all they own,
straining the springs of their motor cars.
Don't forget us.

And so they go,
fleeing the blowing dust . . .

2. What did some Dust Bowl farmers do instead of trying to grow another wheat crop?

_____

Name _____ Date _____

from **Out of the Dust** by Karen Hesse
Literary Analysis: Cultural Context

The **cultural context** of a literary work is the social and historical environment in which the characters live. Major historical events can shape people's lives in important ways. Consider this passage from *Out of the Dust:* "While Ma and Daddy slept, / the dust came, / tearing up fields where the winter wheat, / set for harvest in June, / stood helpless. / I watched the plants, / surviving after so much drought and so much wind, / I watched them fry . . ."

This passage describes the onset of a dust storm, narrated by a character who lived in the Dust Bowl in the 1930s. The Dust Bowl era, in which failed crops led to poverty and hunger, is the historical context of the passage.

DIRECTIONS: *Read this example from* Out of the Dust, *and answer the questions.*

Daddy says, / "I can turn the fields over, / start again. / It's sure to rain soon. / Wheat's sure to grow."

Ma says, "Bay, / it hasn't rained enough to grow wheat in / three years."

I ask Ma / How, / After all this time, / Daddy still believes in rain.

"Well, it rains enough," Ma says, / "now and again, / to keep a person hoping. / But even if it didn't / your daddy would have to believe. / It's coming on spring, / And he's a farmer."

1. How do the father and mother respond to the event that rules their lives?

_____

_____

_____

_____

2. According to the mother, why does the father continue to hope for rain?

_____

_____

_____

_____

from **Out of the Dust** by Karen Hesse
Vocabulary Builder

Word List

drought   feuding   grateful   rickety   sparse   spindly

A. DIRECTIONS: *For each item below, think about the meaning of the italicized Word List word, and then answer the question.*

1. Would you expect a pair of *feuding* brothers to live together? Why or why not?

   _____

   _____

2. Does a hippopotamus or a rhinoceros have *spindly* legs? Explain.

   _____

   _____

3. Is a *drought* a good period in which to plant vegetables and flowers? Why or why not?

   _____

   _____

4. Would you expect the hair on a newborn baby to be *sparse*? Explain.

   _____

   _____

5. Is a *rickety* stepladder one that needs repair before you use it? Explain.

   _____

   _____

6. Is a *grateful* person more likely to be happy or unhappy? Explain.

   _____

   _____

B. WORD STUDY: *The Latin root -grat- means "thankful" or "pleased." Use the meaning of -grat- to help you answer the following questions.*

1. Would you express *gratitude* by thanking someone or by complaining?

   _____

2. What are some occasions for which *congratulations* are expected?

   _____

3. Who might accept a *gratuity*, and why?

   _____

Name _____ Date _____

Writing About the Big Question

Are Yesterday's Heroes Important Today?

Big Question Vocabulary

accomplishments	admirably	aspects	bravery	courage
cultural	emphasize	endure	exaggerate	imitate
influence	outdated	overcome	suffering	symbolize

A. *Use a word or words from the list above to complete each sentence.*

1. The speaker's ancestors had a great _____ on him.

2. The ancestors on both sides of the speaker's family had to _____ _____ .

3. The speaker did not think a visit to Ellis Island was _____ .

B. *Answer the questions. Use at least two Big Question vocabulary words in each answer.*

1. How would you compare the speaker's feelings about his Slovak ancestors to his feelings about his Native American ancestors?

_____

_____

2. Why do you think the speaker visited Ellis Island?

_____

_____

C. *Complete the sentence below. Then, write a short paragraph in which you connect this answer to the Big Question.*

A person's cultural background can be important because _____ .

_____

_____

"**Ellis Island**" by Joseph Bruchac
Reading: Ask Questions to Set a Purpose for Reading

Setting a purpose for reading helps you focus your attention as you read a literary work. One way to set a purpose is to **ask questions** about the topic of the work, questions that you can answer as you read. Using the K-W-L chart can help you to ask questions that can be answered by reading the work. Consider this example using "Ellis Island":

"K" (What I already know about the topic): I know that Ellis Island was the site at which hundreds of thousands of European immigrants entered the United States in the late 1800s and early 1900s.	"W" (What I want to know): I want to know what kinds of experiences people had while they were at Ellis Island.	"L" (What I learned): I will answer this question after I have read the poem.

DIRECTIONS: *Read each passage from "Ellis Island" below. As you read, think about what you knew before you read the poem and what you learn from reading the poem. Then, write an answer to each question.*

> Beyond the red brick of Ellis Island
> where the two Slovak children
> who became my grandparents
> waited the long days of quarantine,

1. What kinds of experiences did people have at Ellis Island?

   _____

   _____

> Yet only one part of my blood
>   loves that memory.
> Another voice speaks
> of native lands
> within this nation.

2. What other historical context plays a role in the writer's personal background?

   _____

   _____

   _____

"Ellis Island" by Joseph Bruchac
Literary Analysis: Cultural Context

The **cultural context** of a literary work is the social and historical environment in which the characters live. Major historical events such as a war or bad economic times can shape people's lives in important ways. As you read, look for details that show how characters respond to cultural and historical events. Consider the following passage from "Ellis Island":

> Beyond the red brick of Ellis Island
>
> where the two Slovak children
>
> who became my grandparents
>
> waited the long days of quarantine,

The poet describes the entrance of two of his grandparents into the United States. They entered Ellis Island from the part of Europe that is now called Slovakia. At Ellis Island, they had to wait in quarantine to be checked for illnesses that could infect the people already living in America. The cultural context here is an important historical event—the massive immigration of people into the United States.

DIRECTIONS: *Read the passage from "Ellis Island," and then answer the questions.*

> Yet only one part of my blood
>
>   loves that memory.
>
> Another voice speaks
>
> of native lands
>
> within this nation.
>
> Lands invaded
>
> when the earth became owned.
>
> Lands of those who followed
>
> the changing Moon,
>
> knowledge of the seasons
>
> in their veins.

1. To whom does the author refer as his other ancestors, besides those who came from Slovakia?

   _____

2. What does the poet tell readers about Native American people?

   _____

   _____

3. What is the major cultural context of this poem? Explain your answer.

   _____

   _____

"Ellis Island" by Joseph Bruchac
Vocabulary Builder

Word List

empires   invaded   meadows   native   quarantine

A. DIRECTIONS: *For each item below, think about the meaning of the italicized Word List word, and then answer the question.*

1. If a person were *native* to Sweden, would he or she be called a German? Explain.

   _____

2. If you were in *quarantine* with the measles, could you visit your friends? Why or why not?

   _____

3. If you prefer the seashore to anyplace else, why might *meadows* not be your favorite spots?

   _____

4. Why do *empires* often have strong leaders?

   _____

5. If your town were about to be *invaded*, what might the citizens do?

   _____

B. WORD STUDY: *The Latin root -nat- means "to be born." Fill in the blank in each sentence below with one of the following words with the root -nat-: innate, natal, nation, native.*

1. Do you think a person's musical ability is _____, or is it learned?

2. Another word for *native* is _____.

3. A _____ is made up of its citizens.

4. Students in our classroom are _____ of several different states.

from **Out of the Dust** by Karen Hesse
"**Ellis Island**" by Joseph Bruchac
Integrated Language Skills: Grammar

Semicolons and Colons

Use a **semicolon (;)** to join independent clauses that are not already joined by the conjunctions *and, but, or, nor, for, so,* or *yet.*

> The ship passed the Statue of Liberty and sailed to the pier at Ellis Island.

> The ship passed the Statue of Liberty; it docked at the pier on Ellis Island.

Use a **colon (:)** to set off a list of items that follow an independent clause.

> The immigrants came from a variety of European countries: Ireland, Germany, England, France, and Russia.

A. DIRECTIONS: *Decide whether each of the following sentences needs a semicolon or a colon. Insert each punctuation mark where it belongs. You will not need to change the punctuation of every sentence.*

1. Immigrants come to American for several reasons many are looking for economic opportunity.
2. The young boy took his favorite items out of his trunk photographs of his family, a cap knitted by his grandmother, and a small telescope.
3. The immigrants spoke many languages, so they could not communicate with one another.
4. Each immigrant was examined by a doctor those who were healthy were cleared to go.
5. The immigrant family unwrapped their lunch potato pie, cheese, and apples.

B. DIRECTIONS: *Write a short paragraph about one of your grandparents or an older person in your family. Use at least one sentence with a semicolon and one sentence with a colon in your paragraph.*

_____

_____

_____

_____

_____

_____

_____

_____

from **Out of the Dust** by Karen Hesse
"Ellis Island" by Joseph Bruchac
Integrated Language Skills: Support for Writing

To prepare a **research proposal** for a report on immigrant experiences passing through Ellis Island or how farmers in the 1930s were affected by the Dust Bowl, use the Internet and library resources, and enter data into the chart below.

Research Proposal	
Three questions about the topic	_____ _____ _____ _____ _____ _____ _____
Three sources that contain information to answer questions	_____ _____ _____ _____ _____ _____ _____
Points to make in proposal	_____ _____ _____ _____ _____ _____

On a separate page, write a draft of your research proposal. Include a description of the sources you found, and explain why they will be useful.

"Choice: A Tribute to Martin Luther King, Jr." by Alice Walker

Writing About the Big Question

Are Yesterday's Heroes Important Today?

Big Question Vocabulary

accomplishments	admirably	aspects	bravery	courage
cultural	emphasize	endure	exaggerate	imitate
influence	outdated	overcome	suffering	symbolize

A. *Use a word from the list above to complete each sentence.*

1. In honor of his _____ in fighting for equal rights for African Americans, Martin Luther King, Jr., won the Nobel Peace Prize.

2. In his speeches and writings, Dr. King would always _____ nonviolence.

3. It is hard to overstate the _____ Dr. King had on young civil rights leaders.

4. Today King is a _____ hero not only of African Americans but also of all Americans.

B. *Answer the questions below. Use at least two Big Question vocabulary words in your answers.*

1. Why do you think Martin Luther King, Jr., continues to inspire people today?

   _____

   _____.

2. Who is one of your heroes? Why do you regard that person as a hero?

   _____

   _____.

C. *Complete the sentence below. Then, write a short paragraph in which you connect this answer to the Big Question.*

Those who have overcome difficult challenges can show us _____.

_____

_____

All-in-One Workbook
309

"Choice: A Tribute to Dr. Martin Luther King, Jr." by Alice Walker

Reading: Set a Purpose for Reading and Adjust Your Reading Rate

When you **set a purpose for reading,** you determine your focus before reading a written work. Once you have set a purpose, **adjust your reading rate** according to that goal. When you read to learn new information, read slowly and carefully. Take time to think about what you have read. Reread, if necessary, to clarify your understanding. When you read for entertainment, you may read more quickly.

DIRECTIONS: *Answer the questions below about setting a purpose and adjusting your reading rate.*

1. What purpose might you set for reading a speech by Dr. Martin Luther King, Jr.?
   _____

2. What reading rate might you set for reading this speech? _____
   _____

3. What purpose might you set for reading a collection of short stories by Alice Walker? _____
   _____

4. What reading rate might you set for reading the stories? _____
   _____

5. What purpose might you set for reading a magazine article about Dr. King in a popular magazine? _____

6. What reading rate might you set for reading the article? _____
   _____

7. What purpose might you set for reading a detailed review of Alice Walker's novels?
   _____

8. What reading rate might you set for reading the detailed review? _____
   _____

"Choice: A Tribute to Dr. Martin Luther King, Jr." by Alice Walker

Literary Analysis: Author's Influences

An **author's influences** are the cultural and historical factors that affect his or her writing. These factors include the time and place of an author's birth and life, the author's cultural background, or world events that happened during the author's lifetime. Read biographical information to learn about an author's influences. When reading an author's work, look for references to details that show cultural or historical attitudes. Consider these passages from "Choice: A Tribute to Dr. Martin Luther King, Jr."

> My great-great-great-grandmother walked as a slave from Virginia to Eatonton, Georgia—which passes for the Walker ancestral home—with two babies on her hips.

> In 1960, my mother bought a television set, and each day after school I watched Hamilton Holmes and Charlayne Hunter as they struggled to integrate—fair-skinned as they were—the University of Georgia.

The first passage tells you that the writer, Alice Walker, is an African American woman descended from slaves. The second passage tells you that during her school years, she watched other African American students struggle for the right to enter college. These passages locate Alice Walker in time (during the 1960s) and place (the South) and suggest that the selection reflects on the civil rights movement.

DIRECTIONS: *Read the passage below from "Choice: A Tribute to Martin Luther King, Jr.," and then answer the questions.*

> At the moment I first saw [Dr. Martin Luther King, Jr.] he was being handcuffed and shoved into a police truck. He had dared to claim his rights as a native son, and had been arrested. He displayed no fear, but seemed calm and serene, unaware of his own extraordinary courage. . . . At the moment I saw his resistance I knew I would never be able to live in this country without resisting everything that sought to disinherit me . . .

1. Who inspired Alice Walker to resist the racism against African American people in America? _____

2. What impressed Walker about Dr. King?

   _____

3. How did America see Alice Walker and other African Americans in this historical period, according to the author's words in the passage?

   _____

   _____

   _____

"Choice: A Tribute to Dr. Martin Luther King, Jr." by Alice Walker
Vocabulary Builder

Word List

ancestral   brutal   disinherit   integrate   revolutionary   sensibility

A. DIRECTIONS: *For each item below, think about the meaning of the italicized Word List word, and then answer the question.*

1. If your aunt has an artistic *sensibility*, how would she feel about going to plays?

   _____

2. Did Dr. King make *revolutionary* changes in America's social structure? Explain.

   _____

   _____

3. To *disinherit* a group, how would you change its rights?

   _____

   _____

4. How might discovering one's *ancestral* lands affect a person?

   _____

   _____

5. What qualities would someone need to successfully *integrate* into a group of another race?

   _____

   _____

6. Is *brutal* treatment of prisoners ever appropriate?

   _____

   _____

B. WORD STUDY: *The Latin root -her- means "heir" or "inheritor." Use the meaning of the root to help you answer the following questions.*

1. Which aspects of your personality have you *inherited* from a parent?

   _____

   _____

2. Do you think someone will ever prove whether *heredity* or environment is more important? Explain.

   _____

   _____

3. How might someone benefit from knowing his or her *heritage*?

   _____

   _____

Name _____ Date _____

"An Episode of War" by Stephen Crane
Writing About the Big Question

 Are Yesterday's Heroes Important Today?

Big Question Vocabulary

accomplishments	admirably	aspects	bravery	courage
cultural	emphasize	endure	exaggerate	imitate
influence	outdated	overcome	suffering	symbolize

A. *Use a word or words from the list above to complete each sentence.*

1. Many people believe that soldiers' _____ will never be
   _____ .

2. Their commanders _____ the way soldiers
   respond to war.

3. Soldiers hope to _____ the enemy.

4. There are many _____ of war that soldiers do not like to
   discuss.

B. *Follow the directions in responding to each item.*

1. Do you think a heroic Civil War soldier would make a good soldier today? In two or
   three sentences, explain why or why not. Use at least one Big Question vocabulary
   word in your sentences.

   _____

   _____ .

2. Write two or three sentences in which you describe an important way that warfare
   is different today from long ago. Use at least one Big Question vocabulary word in
   your sentences.

   _____

   _____ .

C. *Complete the sentence below. Then, write a short paragraph in which you connect this
answer to the Big Question.*

The experience of suffering is _____ .

_____

_____

"An Episode of War" by Stephen Crane

Reading: Set a Purpose for Reading and Adjust Your Reading Rate

When you **set a purpose for reading,** you determine your focus before reading a written work. Once you have set a purpose, **adjust your reading rate** according to that goal. You might read fiction for both entertainment and information. Entertainment does not always mean amusement or enjoyment. It can also mean that you learn about characters and why they act as they do. When you read fiction that is written more formally than today's writing, read slowly and carefully. Reread long sentences, or material with unfamiliar facts and content. When you read modern fiction, you can usually read faster. Nonfiction, both older and modern, needs careful reading and rereading so that you can understand important information.

DIRECTIONS: *Answer the questions about setting purpose and adjusting reading rate.*

1. What purpose might you set for reading Stephen Crane's famous novel of the Civil War, *The Red Badge of Courage,* published in 1895?

   _____

   _____

2. What reading rate might you set for reading this novel?

   _____

3. What purpose might you set for reading nonfiction accounts of Civil War battles?

   _____

4. What reading rate might you set for reading about Civil War battles?

   _____

5. What purpose might you set for reading a short story about the Vietnam War?

   _____

6. What reading rate might you use for reading this story?

   _____

7. What purpose might you set for reading a modern novel about war?

   _____

8. What reading rate might you use for reading a modern novel about war?

   _____

"An Episode of War" by Stephen Crane
Literary Analysis: Author's Influences

An **author's influences** are the cultural and historical factors that affect his or her writing. These factors may include the time and place of an author's birth and life, the author's cultural background, or world events that happened during the author's lifetime. Read the following facts about the Civil War and Stephen Crane.

A. Civil War field hospitals were unclean and crowded with wounded soldiers.

B. Medical practices included cutting off injured limbs to keep soldiers from dying from infection.

C. Crane was fascinated by war. He interviewed Civil War veterans, and studied battlefield maps and accounts of the fighting.

DIRECTIONS: *Read each passage from "An Episode of War." Decide which of the historical and cultural factors above is reflected in the passage. Write the correct letter or letters in the blank.*

1. _____ As the wounded officer passed from the line of battle, he was enabled to see many things which as a participant in the fight were unknown to him.

2. _____ An interminable [unending] crowd of bandaged men were coming and going. Great numbers sat under the trees nursing heads or arms or legs.

3. _____ "Nonsense, man! Nonsense! Nonsense!" cried the doctor. "Come along, now. I won't amputate it. Come along. Don't be a baby."

    "Let go of me," said the lieutenant, holding back wrathfully, his glance fixed upon the door of the old schoolhouse, as sinister to him as the portals of death.

4. _____ A battery, a tumultuous and shining mass, was swirling toward the right. The wild thud of hoofs, the cries of the riders shouting blame and praise, menace and encouragement, and last, the roar of the wheels, the slant of the glistening guns, brought the lieutenant to an intent pause.

"An Episode of War" by Stephen Crane
Vocabulary Builder

Word List

audible   compelled   contempt   disdainfully   hostile   tumultuous   winced

A. DIRECTIONS: *For each item below, think about the meaning of the italicized Word List word, and then answer the question.*

1. How would you feel if a friend *compelled* you to go to a party you didn't want to go to?

   _____

2. How would someone in the grip of *tumultuous* emotions handle a surprise event? Explain.

   _____

3. What kind of behavior would cause you to have *contempt* for a person?

   _____

4. If someone *winced*, what sort of thing happened to him or her?

   _____

5. What might you do if the music on the radio was barely *audible*?

   _____

6. What might make a dog *hostile* toward its owner?

   _____

7. How would you feel if you were treated *disdainfully*?

   _____

B. WORD STUDY: *The Latin root -aud- means "to hear." Use the meaning of the root -aud- to help you complete the following sentences.*

1. Use the *audio* control to _____

   _____

2. We should hold the concert in an *auditorium* because _____

   _____

3. I want to *audition* for _____

"Choice: A Tribute to Dr. Martin Luther King, Jr." by Alice Walker
"An Episode of War" by Stephen Crane
Integrated Language Skills: Grammar

Capitalization

Use a capital letter at the beginning of a sentence. Also, use a capital for the first letter of a proper noun or proper adjective.

Stephen **C**rane is a well-known **A**merican short-story writer.

A. DIRECTIONS: *Rewrite each sentence below. Substitute capital letters or lowercase letters where they belong.*

1. Alice walker's life was deeply affected by dr. martin luther king, jr., the civil rights Leader.

   _____

2. she loved to hear him preach at ebenezer baptist church.

   _____

3. alice was changed when she watched two African American Students try to Enroll at the university of georgia.

   _____

4. she says that many black Americans feel more comfortable in the south because of Dr. king's Life.

   _____

B. DIRECTIONS: *Write a short paragraph about a person, a place, or an event that has affected you. Be sure to capitalize the first word of each sentence as well as proper nouns and proper adjectives.*

   _____

   _____

   _____

   _____

   _____

   _____

   _____

   _____

   _____

All-in-One Workbook
317

"Choice: A Tribute to Dr. Martin Luther King, Jr." by Alice Walker
"An Episode of War" by Stephen Crane
Integrated Language Skills: Support for Writing

"Choice: A Tribute to Dr. Martin Luther King, Jr."
To prepare to write a persuasive **speech** in favor of building a memorial in honor of
Dr. Martin Luther King, Jr., enter important information into the chart below.

Dr. King and His Legacy	
Why Dr. King's ideas are important in today's world	_____ _____
Why Dr. King should be remembered	_____ _____
Vivid words and phrases	_____ _____
Vivid words and phrases to be repeated	_____ _____

On a separate page, write a draft of your speech.

"An Episode of War"
To prepare to write a persuasive **speech** in favor of building a memorial in honor of
soldiers of the Civil War, enter important information into the chart below.

The Common Soldier: Courage and Determination	
Details from "An Episode of War" about hardships of war on soldiers	_____ _____
Why Civil War soldiers deserve to be remembered and honored	_____ _____
Vivid words and phrases	_____ _____

On a separate page, write a draft of your speech.

Name _____ Date _____

"**Poetry**" by Pablo Neruda
from "**My Own True Name**" by Pat Mora
"**Words to Sit On, Like Chairs**" by Naomi Shihab Nye
Writing About the Big Question

Are Yesterday's Heroes Important Today?

Big Question Vocabulary

accomplishments	admirably	aspects	bravery	courage
cultural	emphasize	endure	exaggerate	imitate
influence	outdated	overcome	suffering	symbolize

A. *Use a word or words from the list above to complete each sentence.*

1. In a story with a sad beginning, the hero might _____
   _____.

2. If the hero behaves _____, the hero will likely
   _____ his or her difficulties.

3. A story might _____ certain heroic qualities
   and not others.

B. *Follow the directions in responding to each item.*

1. In two sentences, explain which hero from history you would like to meet most and
   why. Use at least two Big Question vocabulary words in your sentences.

   _____

   _____

2. What questions would you like to ask the hero? Use at least one Big Question
   vocabulary word in each question.

   _____

   _____

C. *Complete the sentence below. Then, write a short paragraph in which you connect this
answer to the Big Question.*

   Writing about one's feelings takes **courage** because _____.

   _____

   _____

Name _____ Date _____

"**Poetry**" by Pablo Neruda

from "**My Own True Name**" by Pat Mora

"**Words to Sit In, Like Chairs**" by Naomi Shihab Nye

Literary Analysis: Comparing Works on a Similar Theme

The **theme** of a literary work is the insight, major idea, or underlying message that it communicates. Certain themes are common across cultures and historical eras. These recurring ideas are known as **universal themes** because they appear in many cultures. Examples of universal themes include the power of love and the importance of freedom.

"Poetry," the excerpt from "My Own True Name," and "Words to Sit In, Like Chairs" all take as their theme the importance of self-expression. Even when authors choose to write on a similar theme, they frequently produce different results. The reason is that writers draw on different life experiences, use different structures, have different opinions, and explore different aspects of the same theme.

DIRECTIONS: *For each work, answer the following questions about the presentation of theme:*

1. What literary form did each writer choose?
2. What main points does each writer make about the theme?
3. What are the similarities in the three writers' approaches to the theme?
4. What are the differences in the three writers' approaches to the theme?

"Poetry"	*from* "My Own True Name"	"Words to Sit In, Like Chairs"

All-in-One Workbook

Name _____ Date _____

"Poetry" by Pablo Neruda
from **"My Own True Name"** by Pat Mora
"Words to Sit In, Like Chairs" by Naomi Shihab Nye
Vocabulary Builder

A. DIRECTIONS: *Find a synonym or definition as directed for each vocabulary word below. Then, use the vocabulary word in a sentence that makes the meaning of the word clear.*

1. **Vocabulary Word:** intimidating   **Synonym:** _____

   Sample Sentence: _____

   _____

2. **Vocabulary Word:** deciphering   **Definition:** _____

   Sample Sentence: _____

   _____

3. **Vocabulary Word:** eavesdropping   **Definition:** _____

   Sample Sentence: _____

   _____

4. **Vocabulary Word:** abyss   **Synonym:** _____

   Sample Sentence: _____

   _____

5. **Vocabulary Word:** turmoil   **Synonym:** _____

   Sample Sentence: _____

   _____

6. **Vocabulary Word:** beacons   **Synonym:** _____

   Sample Sentence: _____

B. DIRECTIONS: *Circle the letter of the word that is most* opposite *in meaning to the word in CAPITAL LETTERS.*

1. SOBERLY
   A. loudly
   B. seriously
   C. flippantly
   D. conscientiously

2. TURMOIL
   A. heartache
   B. confusion
   C. trouble
   D. calm

3. INTIMIDATING
   A. bulldozing
   B. welcoming
   C. smiling
   D. counting

4. BEACONS
   A. darkness
   B. light
   C. runway
   D. warning

"Poetry" by Pablo Neruda
from **"My Own True Name"** by Pat Mora
"Words to Sit In, Like Chairs" by Naomi Shihab Nye

Integrated Language Skills: Support for Writing

Before you write your **essay** comparing "Poetry," the excerpt from "My Own True Nature," and "Words to Sit In, Like Chairs," use the graphic organizer below to list ideas about how each author develops the theme of self-expression and its importance.

1. How much does the author reveal about himself or herself?

NERUDA	MORA	SHIHAB NYE

2. Based on what the writer says, how does writing help him or her?

NERUDA	MORA	SHIHAB NYE

3. Which writer is most compelling to you?

NERUDA	MORA	SHIHAB NYE

Now, use your notes to write your essay comparing the development of theme in these works.

Tips for Improving Your Reading Fluency

You've probably heard the expression "Practice makes perfect." Through your own experiences, you know that practice improves all types of skills. If you play a guitar, you know that practicing has made you a better player. The same is true for sports, for crafts, and for reading. The following tips will help you to practice skills that will lead to reading **fluency**—the ability to read easily, smoothly, and expressively.

Choose your practice materials carefully.

Make reading fun! Make a list of subjects that interest you. Then, search for reading materials—books, magazines, newspapers, reliable Web sites. As you learn more about your interests, you will also be practicing your reading skills.

Choose your practice space and time carefully.

Help your concentration skills. Find a quiet, comfortable place to read—away from the television and other distractions. Get in the habit of treating yourself to an hour of pleasure reading every day—apart from homework and other tasks. Reading about interesting topics in a quiet, comfortable place will provide both pleasure and relaxation.

Practice prereading strategies.

A movie preview gives viewers a good idea about what the movie will be about. Before you read, create your own preview of what you plan to read. Look at pictures and captions, subheads, and diagrams. As you scan, look for unfamiliar words. Find out what those words mean before you start reading.

Use punctuation marks.

Think of punctuation marks as stop signs. For example, the period at the end of a sentence signals the end of a complete thought. From time to time in your reading, stop at that stop sign. Reread the sentence. Summarize the complete thought in your own words.

Read aloud.

Use your voice and your ears as well as your eyes. Read phrases and sentences expressively. Pause at commas and periods. Show emphasis in your voice when you come to an exclamation point. Let your voice naturally rise at the end of a question. If possible, record your reading. Then listen to the recording, noting your pacing and expression.

All-in-One Workbook
323

Pause to ask questions.

Stop reading after a short amount of time (for example, five minutes) or at the end of a meaty paragraph. Look away from the text. Ask yourself questions—What are the main ideas? What message does the author want me to get? What might happen next? If the answers seem unclear, reread—either silently or aloud. Find the answers!

Use what you know.

As you read an informational article, think about what you already know about the topic. Use your knowledge and ideas as background information. Doing so will help you to understand new ideas. As you read fiction or a personal narrative, think about your own experiences. If you have been in a situation that is similar to that of a fictional character, you will be better able to understand his or her feelings, actions, and goals.

Talk about it.

Ask a friend or family member to read what you have read. Take turns reading aloud together, listening to both content and expression. Then discuss what you read. Share, compare, and contrast your ideas. Doing so will reinforce your knowledge of the content of what you read, and may provide new and interesting perspectives about the topic.

Reading Fluency Assessment Passage 1

So you want to be a detective?

Many things about being a detective have changed since the fictional Sherlock Holmes prowled the streets of London. The basic principles of detection, however, remain the same.

Perhaps the most important quality that any detective must possess is intuition about human nature. Detectives[50] rely on their natural instincts to know when people are lying and when they are telling the truth. They observe a suspect closely and listen carefully to his or her narrative. In this way, they pick up important clues that an untrained observer would be unlikely to recognize.

Detectives must[100] conceal any uncertainty they may have. They must behave as if they have no doubts at all about the truthfulness of a suspect's story. By showing belief in the suspect, a detective might get him or her to reveal secrets never meant to be spoken aloud!

Each case is unique[150] and distinctive. Detectives investigate everything from murders to missing persons. Detectives may be hired to locate witnesses or track down old friends. Business owners may seek help with thefts and other crimes related to commerce.

Unlike Holmes, modern detectives utilize computer skills to be fully effective in their work. Databases[200] allow them to quickly gather information that was beyond the reach of detectives just a few decades ago.

Detectives must also be skilled in the art of surveillance. Whether in a car or on foot, a detective must watch someone without that person knowing he or she is being watched.[250] Detectives now have access to electronic spying devices that Holmes and real-life detectives in the past could never have imagined.

Above all, detectives must be relentless in their search for the truth. Like Holmes, a good detective is driven by natural curiosity to pursue each case to its conclusion.[299]

1000L

Check Your Understanding

1. Write *T* for "true" or *F* for "false" next to each statement.

_____ Detectives should always rely on clues rather than instinct.

_____ Pretending to trust a suspect might make the suspect reveal secrets.

_____ Shelock Holmes predicted electronic surveillance.

2. Name two things detectives investigate.

_____

_____

Reading Fluency Assessment Passage 2

During the 1500s, the practice of medicine was quite different from that of modern medicine. Most doctors had no formal education, having taught themselves through trial and error. Because of the lamentable lack of knowledge in this time, most doctors actually harmed more patients than they helped. When people became[50] ill or suffered an injury, they had few choices for treatment. Unfortunately, making the wrong choice usually meant a patient would get worse rather than better.

The best choice was to see a physician. Physicians were well-educated men with up-to-date methods of treatment, however pitiful these treatments may seem compared[100] to those used today. Physicians had been to university and studied both medicine and philosophy. Diagnoses were made only after examining the patient.

This examination, however, was not nearly as thorough and advanced as those done by doctors today. Physicians had no X-ray machines, for example. Still, there is no[150] doubt that going to a physician was the best option for a sick person. Physicians were few in number, and consequently charged a lot of money.

For the desperate patient unable to afford a physician, the alternative was to find a surgeon, who doubled often as dentist and barber. Most[200] of these "surgeons" were self-taught. They worked without painkillers and used equipment that was not sterilized, which, detrimental to the patient's health, left the patient prone to infection. He or she usually ended up in a miserable condition, with an untreatable infection and no cure in sight.

A patient could[250] also see an herbalist who used various homemade concoctions to relieve pain or disease. It was not uncommon for the herbalist to concoct a remedy out of newts' tongues or worms' livers. Most of the ingredients used by herbalists were ineffective, but some were beneficial.[295]

1010L

Check Your Understanding

1. Physicians in the 1500s had numerous ways of treating illnesses and injuries.

   True / False? Explain:

   _____

   _____

2. Briefly explain the education of physicians and surgeons.

   _____

   _____

Reading Fluency Assessment Passage 3

Many people believe that Abraham Lincoln freed the slaves during the Civil War, but that is only partly true. On January 1, 1863, he boldly declared that the slaves in the southern states were free. However, Lincoln had no authority over the eleven southern states that had pulled out of,[50] or seceded from, the Union. They had their own laws, their own government, and their own president so, as a result, Lincoln's action had no immediate impact in their jurisdiction.

Did Lincoln's action immediately outlaw slavery in the North? No, it didn't. Slaves in the so-called Border States—Delaware, Maryland[100], Kentucky, and Missouri— were still bound to their masters. Lincoln was afraid that setting slaves free in the Border States would turn their slave owners against the Union.

In view of all this, does Lincoln's declaration seem absurd? In fact, Lincoln's action was quite sensible. It encouraged free blacks and escaped[150] slaves to join the northern army. With heavy losses, the Union army needed more and more soldiers, and only with the help of blacks was the North was able to win the war.

As Lincoln had hoped the Border States remained loyal to the Union. England and France, which depended[200] on southern cotton, refused to help the South when the Civil War became a war against slavery.

Perhaps the most important and honorable event that Lincoln's action prompted was the Thirteenth Amendment to the Constitution, which passed on December 18, 1865. From that time forward, slavery was not legal anywhere[250] in the Union. Former slaves now could begin walking down that long road toward equality. They could hope that someday, their children's children would enjoy the same rights that others took for granted.[283]

1020L

Check Your Understanding

1. On January 1, 1863, Lincoln declared that all slaves were free.

   True / False? Explain:

   _____

2. Why did the Union army need free blacks and escaped slaves to join the northern army?

   _____

   _____

Reading Fluency Assessment Passage 4

San Francisco's Chinatown is the second largest Chinese community in the United States. Rebuilt after the 1906 earthquake, it became a major tourist attraction in the 1920s. Today, tourists from all over flock to Chinatown to visit the many fascinating shops and superb restaurants that line the crowded streets.

Begin[50] your tour at the Chinatown Gate. Stroll along Grant Avenue and peek into some of the crowded shops you pass along the way. You'll find that the shop windows display unusual objects of every description. Some shops sell everything from valuable antiques to inexpensive trinkets. Others concentrate on one specific[100] kind of item. The Clarion Music Center, for example, has long specialized in selling traditional musical instruments from China and Tibet. Other shops specialize in everything from kites and art supplies to fine linens and cookware. The Ten Ren Tea Shop offers more than fifty kinds of regional teas imported from[150] different areas of China.

With so many tempting restaurants to choose from, deciding where to have[200] lunch can be a problem. Be sure to look at the menu displayed outside the restaurant before making your choice. After lunch, stroll past the Buddhist temples on Waverly Place. Breathe deep and enjoy[200] the pungent smell of incense that wafts out onto the street. Look toward the bay and you might even see the Golden Gate Bridge if the city's famous thick fog hasn't completely obscured it.

The most interesting part of a visit to Chinatown, of course, is seeing the people who[250] live there. Portsmouth Square is a good place for people watching. There you'll see elderly grandparents keeping a close watch over the children who run around on the busy playground. Like mothers and fathers everywhere, the parents and grandparents of Chinatown are fiercely protective of their children![297]

1030L

Check Your Understanding

1. San Francisco's Chinatown was rebuilt after the 1906 earthquake.

   a. True

   b. False

2. Name three things you can find in the shops in San Francisco's Chinatown.

   _____

   _____

   _____

Reading Fluency Assessment Passage 5

The life of an actor is not all glamour, as popular magazines would have you believe. On the contrary, those actors who achieve success in their chosen profession must put in long hours and go through numerous hardships. For many, the training begins in drama classes in high school, though[50] this no guarantee of future success on a professional level.

Successful actors must be able to imagine themselves living other lives. They must be able to assume the personalities of characters that are completely different from themselves. Actors use body language and voice to express their interpretation of a role.[100]

Acting classes are usually recommended for aspiring actors. These sessions can be time consuming, and often the young actor will also have to work at a regular job while attending classes part-time.

Finding roles is not easy. When directors issue "casting calls," mobs of actors line up to try out[150] for only a few roles. Many will not be considered as eligible candidates for a particular role because of appearance. For example, the director might be looking for someone of a certain height and weight. Consequently, to save time and avoid disappointment, most actors generally try to make inquiries[200] about the director's requirements beforehand.

Once an actor lands a role, he or she must be available at odd times for filming. Suppose a scene needs to be shot outdoors at night, and the actor has a night job as a waiter. A determined actor will not let minor hardships[250] get in the way.

An acting career brings with it fulfilling rewards. One of the greatest is working with interesting colleagues—directors, producers, and fellow actors. Determination, mixed with luck, can pay off. One "right" role might turn an unknown actor into a Hollywood star.[295]

Check Your Understanding

1. Name two things that successful actors must do.

   _____

   _____

2. Name two things that make an aspiring actor's life hard.

   _____

   _____

1030L

Reading Fluency Assessment Passage 6

No one knows for sure when chess was invented. An early version of the game was popularized by the end of the tenth century, then further developed in southern Europe a few centuries later.

Players in the sixteenth century wanted others to study their games and become better players. The[50] best players were proclaimed "masters" and were highly honored. Chess masters who were at first reluctant to divulge their secrets soon relented. At last, they allowed their games to be recorded. Instruction books were essential to the growing popularity of the game. Books on chess were soon being read internationally.[100]

Paul Morphy was the first acclaimed American chess player. He defeated all his American rivals at an early age before traveling to Europe in 1858. There, he was triumphant over the greatest players of his time. The onset of mental illness brought an abrupt end to Morphy's brilliant career.

After[150] the Russian Revolution, the Russian government deliberately set out to dominate world chess. It set up a program of chess education for children. It offered financial support to the country's best players. Russian players dominated the game throughout the twentieth century. Russian dominance was briefly interrupted when the American chess[200] master Bobby Fischer took home the world championship trophy in 1972.

Computer programs that play chess first appeared in the 1960s, but these programs were no match for the top human players. It was not until 1997 that a chess computer called Deep Blue was able to narrowly defeat the world[250] chess champion in a series of games.

The champion concealed his disappointment as best he could, but he could not hide the embarrassment he felt over losing to a machine.

Today, computers have revolutionized the game of chess, allowing players at all skill levels to practice and improve.[298]

Check Your Understanding

1. The best chess players are called _____.

2. Who briefly ended Russia's dominance in the game of chess?

   _____

   _____

   _____

1040L

Reading Fluency Assessment Passage 7

Eleanor Roosevelt, first lady and human rights champion, left a record of inspiring quotes that reveal her character.

"No one can make you feel inferior without your consent," she said.

Eleanor was the plain child of a beautiful mother, her youth marked by the sensation that she did not measure[50] up. Then she lost both of her parents prematurely, before the age of ten. Their early and unexpected deaths increased her insecurity, and subsequently, she kept to herself as a child.

However, as she grew up, encouraged by a teacher, she recognized her own strengths and her demeanor changed dramatically.[100] Her willingness to rally in the support of others was a testament to her generosity and newfound belief in herself.

Eleanor Roosevelt said, "People grow through experience if they meet life honestly and courageously. This is how character is built."

Despite the tragic death of parents, and the paralysis of[150] her husband, Franklin, by a disease called polio, Eleanor demonstrated courage in the face of tragedy. She helped her husband to keep going by becoming "his legs": With her support, Franklin never wavered in his determination to overcome his disability.

While he was president, from 1933 to 1945, Eleanor traveled[200] widely to investigate the country's needs. She constantly pushed the president to develop programs that would benefit the disadvantaged. She is viewed as an exemplary first lady, due to the respect she earned from her contemporaries.

She said, "You must do the thing you think you cannot do."

Eleanor Roosevelt's[250] life was a series of contrasts, of opportunity and difficulty: She was deeply shy as a girl, yet grew up to be one of the most outspoken women of her time. She fought for civil and human rights everywhere, never giving up the fight. By that measure, she was victorious.[300]

Check Your Understanding

1. Eleanor Roosevelt was always secure and outspoken.

   True / False? Explain:

   _____

   _____

2. How did Eleanor Roosevelt help her husband while he was president?

   _____

   _____

Reading Fluency Assessment Passage 8

Warren Faidley has an unusual job as a professional storm chaser. As other people scurry away from extreme weather conditions, he gets up close, capturing the excitement on film and video. The pictures he takes have made him famous. You have probably seen some of his photographs of tornadoes, hurricanes[50], and jagged bolts of lightning. They have appeared in newspapers, magazines, books, films, and advertisements in almost every country of the world.

Faidley's interest in tornadoes began at a young age when he would notice gusts of wind forming into whirlwinds in the dusty vacant lots of his neighborhood.[100] These spinning columns of dust resembled small tornadoes. He had recently seen the movie *The Wizard of Oz*, which gave him the idea of riding his bike into the middle of one of these so-called "dust devils." He says that he was able to get into the middle of a[150] dust devil where the air was still and almost dust free. A wall of dirt full of newspaper and tumbleweed debris spun around him. As he looked up, he could see the blue sky.

In 1991, Faidley pursued his first real tornado. It was rated an F5, the most violent[200] of all tornadoes. The F5 rating means that the winds are between 261 and 318 miles per hour. Such a storm picks up boulders as if they were pebbles and tosses them with ease through the air. As Faidley shot the video of this violent storm, his emotions ran from[250] excitement to terror. Since then, he has had many terrifying moments, but these haven't stopped him from chasing tornadoes. Sometimes he has even had to outrun tornadoes that started to chase him, but the thrill of the adventure is what keeps him going.[293]

1050L

Check Your Understanding

1. Faidley first became interested in tornadoes through _____

   a. magazines, newpapers, and advertisements.

   b. the movie *The Wizard of Oz*.

   c. a video of a violent storm.

2. Briefly describe Faidley's first real tornado.

   _____

   _____

Reading Fluency Assessment Passage 9

Almost every country in the world tells stories about dragons. Dragon myths have circulated for thousands of years in various cultures throughout the world.

Most of us are familiar with the fire-breathing dragon of European folklore. This gigantic, snakelike monster is almost always portrayed as a menace to society. Eventually,[50] the outraged citizens raise a clamor, and some valiant individual must step forward and battle the dreadful beast.

In medieval tales, it is usually a courageous knight who volunteers to slay the dragon and free the maiden it holds captive. The dragon has no intention of relinquishing without a fight.[100] In the end, however, the knight's attempt to vanquish his opponent is invariably successful. Despite its cunning and great physical strength, the wicked dragon is eventually outmaneuvered by the clever and fearless knight. The dragon is vanquished, and his assassin returns with the treasure and the heart of the rescued maiden.[150]

The dragons of Asia are usually portrayed as wise and likable creatures—this gentler dragon seldom has wings and rarely exhales flames. Asian dragons can be distinguished by their number of toes: A three-toed dragon is Japanese; a four-toed dragon is Indonesian or Korean; and a five-toed dragon, or[200] Lung, is Chinese.

The Chinese dragon is a mosaic of different animals: the body of a snake, the head of a camel, the scales of a fish, the horns of a stag, the eyes of a hare, the paws of a tiger, and the claws of an eagle. As a[250] rule, Chinese dragons generally bring good fortune but can be dangerous if not treated with the proper respect. Chinese dragons that feel unrespected may express displeasure by causing storms or floods. Fortunately, they are less likely than European dragons to start fires as the result of an imprudent sneeze.[299]

Check Your Understanding

1. In medieval stories, who usually kills the dragon, and what does he win?

   _____

   _____

2. What is the main difference between European dragons and Asian dragons.

   a. Asian dragons are friendly, but European dragons are menacing.

   b. European dragons have five toes, but Asian dragons have four toes.

   c. Asian dragons are menacing, but European dragons are wise and friendly.

1070L

Reading Fluency Assessment Passage 10

In 1782, the Second Continental Congress selected the bald eagle, found only in North America, as the symbol of the newly formed United States. It was agreed upon by most members. One famous dissenter, Benjamin Franklin, preferred the wild turkey, calling the bald eagle "too lazy to fish for himself."[50]

Franklin, a usually discerning thinker, was incorrect in his judgment of the bald eagle. Contrary to his belief, it feeds on fish, water birds, and small mammals. Interestingly, what and how it eats has had a negative impact on its survival.

When a bald eagle feeds, it descends at up[100] to 100 miles per hour, but it can lift only about five pounds with its sharp talon claws. A determined bald eagle will swim to shore dragging its prey.

The bald eagle's feeding habits gave it a bad reputation. Early settlers believed it attacked their livestock and were afraid their[150] animals would be killed or injured. They began to hunt the bird, hoping to be rid of the eagle forever.

In the mid-1900s, pesticides got into the food chain and hurt bald eagles. By the 1960s, fewer than a thousand eagles lived in the continental United States.

The eagle is[200] the outside of the food chain. The loss of the eagle hurt plants and animals in the chain. It was not only important as a national symbol. Scientists saw that something had to be done.

In 1973, President Richard Nixon signed the Endangered Species Act. It led to reforms of[250] the use of some pesticides and helped the bald eagle survive.

Today the bald eagle population has soared to more than 12,000 in the 48 states, with some 50,000 birds flourishing in Alaska. If those numbers continue to rise, the bald eagle will prevail.[294]

1080L

Check Your Understanding

1. What did Benjamin Franklin have against the bald eagle as a symbol of the United States?

   a. It killed livestock.

   b. It was weak and could lift only about five pounds.

   c. It was too lazy to fish for itself.

2. What caused most eagles in the United States to disappear?

   _____

   _____

Reading Fluency Assessment Passage 11

When Chief Dan George appeared in the movie *Little Big Man* in 1970, he portrayed a Native American, seemingly a right choice. Traditionally, however, most Native American film roles were taken by white actors and actresses. Films presented Native Americans in a narrow way. Placed in their natural surroundings on[50] the Great Plains or in the Southwest, viewers saw only where the tribal people lived. Filmmakers omitted realistic detail about how they lived. Each group of Native American peoples, such as the Sioux and the Navajo, had a rich and complex society. Yet in the movies, family life and[100] cultural traditions and beliefs were seldom shown.

In the moviemakers' defense, the common view of Native Americans was filled with stereotypes. In the 1800s, inexpensive "dime novels" were filled with exaggerated tales of life in the West. Even some Native Americans contributed to a violent depiction of their people. The[150] frontiersman Buffalo Bill Cody and his Wild West Show toured America and Europe with Native American performers. To secure large audiences, Cody's extravaganza included a crowd-pleasing highlight: there was always a staged Indian "attack."

Over time, different images began to emerge. Indian performers were determined to improve the portrayal of[200] Native Americans. One example is Jay Silverheels, who played the native character Tonto in the popular 1950s series *The Lone Ranger*. Silverheels, who was a Mohawk from Canada, formed the Indian Actors Workshop. Strong training in acting created moving performances and increased the popularity of Native American screen actors.

Today[250] the endurance of actors like Silverheels and George has paid off. Their fight for change led to breakthroughs in film. Movies that show deeper view of Native American life and history have been widely successful, much to the contentment of those depicted in the films.[295]

1090L

Check Your Understanding

1. In the early days of film, films portrayed realistic Native Americans play by Native American actors.

   True / False? Explain:

   _____

   _____

2. Which person helped change the image of Native Americans in movies?
   a. Wild Bill Cody
   b. The Lone Ranger
   c. Jay Silverheels

Reading Fluency Assessment Passage 12

More than fifteen million people in the United State today identify themselves as Mexican Americans. Although this is the fastest-growing ethnic group, the history and culture of Mexican Americans may be unfamiliar to many.

From the time it was first settled, much of what is now the American Southwest[50] was claimed by Spain. After Mexico won its independence from Spain, these lands belonged to Mexico. The people who lived there were Mexicans until Mexico signed a treaty giving up the territory to the United States. Those who chose to stay suddenly had a new national identity—Mexican American.[100]

After 1848, Americans of European descent grew to become a majority in the lands that had once belonged to Mexico. The nation began to react with concern over the large number of foreign immigrants entering the United States. Mexican Americans came to be held in the same low esteem as[150] foreign-born immigrants. This view was especially illogical as many Mexican Americans had lived in this country longer than the people who regarded them as outsiders.

Despite the discrimination they faced, many Mexican Americans have overcome these challenges. They have made an outstanding contribution to many areas of society, including[200] art, music, literature, film, politics, and the sciences.

Recently, Mexican American communities have shown a revival of interest in the Mexican holiday known as Day of the Dead. Actually, many non-Mexican Americans have also come to appreciate this celebration as an alternative to Halloween. The holiday honors the humanity of[250] all departed loved ones. It helps people stay connected to their ancestors. It is also much healthier to eat tamales and hot chocolate than pounds of Halloween candy![278]

1120L

Check Your Understanding

1. Mexican Americans are the fastest-growing ethnic group in the United States.

   a. True
   b. False

2. Name at least three Mexican Americans who have contributed to the arts and sciences

   _____

   _____

   _____

Screening Test

Directions: Read the following passages. Then answer the questions. On the answer sheet, fill in the bubble for the answer that you think is correct.

> Telephones, faxes, and computers are company property and should be used for company business only. This includes voice mail, electronic mail, and computer files. Employees may need to use these communication tools for personal reasons from time to time. If and when that time comes, employees should keep their personal use to a minimum and should do so only during non-work hours such as lunchtime.

1 **According to the passage, which of the following is *true*?**
A Employees can use computers for personal use only.
B Employees are never allowed to use computers for personal reasons.
C Employees should keep their personal use of computers to a minimum.
D Employees cannot use computers during their non-work hours.

2 **When are employees at this company allowed to use the telephone for personal reasons?**
F when work is slow
G when taking an official break
H whenever they need to
J whenever their boss approves

3 **This paragraph describes —**
A how to use computers for personal reasons
B how to fix a fax machine
C the rules for taking a lunchtime break
D the rules for using office communication tools

> **To Start Your Washer:**
> 1. Measure detergent and add to basin.
> 2. Set water temperature control and number of rinses.
> 3. Close lid and pull wash cycle knob out to begin washing.

4 **What information do you find in this passage?**
F descriptions of temperature settings for a washer
G speeds and controls for a washer
H directions for starting a washer
J instructions for care and service of a washer

5 **What is the first step in using the washer?**
A setting the water temperature
B setting the number of rinses
C pulling the wash cycle knob
D measuring detergent and adding it to the basin

6 **What should you do immediately before pulling the wash cycle knob?**
F measure the detergent
G set the number of rinses
H close the washer lid
J add the detergent to the basin

What could chocolate and Coca-Cola possibly have in common? Both contain caffeine and are popular around the world. The main ingredient in chocolate comes from the beans of the cacao tree, and the flavoring for Coca-Cola originally came from the nuts of the kola tree. Although they grow in different parts of the world, the cacao tree and the kola tree are part of the same plant family.

7 One ingredient chocolate and Coca-Cola have in common is —

A kola nuts
B caffeine
C cacao beans
D cocoa

8 Chocolate's main ingredient —

F grows in a different part of the world than Coca-Cola's flavoring
G is more popular around the world than Coca-Cola's flavoring
H is derived from a different plant family than Coca-Cola's flavoring
J is less popular around the world than Coca-Cola's flavoring

1 "Who's that?" asked Jamey.

2 Karyn looked at the tall, athletic woman with gray hair tied back in a short ponytail. "Oh, that's my grandmother. She's training for the City Run next week."

3 The two girls finished their run and sat on the sidelines. The older woman joined them shortly.

4 "How's it going, Nanna?" Karyn asked.

5 "Pretty good," her grandmother replied. "I cut three seconds off my best time."

6 Jamey looked at the older woman. "How long have you been running?" she asked.

7 "Most of my life," Nanna replied. "But not on a team. You girls are lucky."

8 "What do you mean?" Jamey asked, confused.

9 Nanna told the girls about the old days when women had few opportunities to race. She explained how things changed when Kathryn Switzer entered the Boston Marathon in 1967. "She registered as K. Switzer so no one would know she was a woman," Nanna said. "She finished in four hours and 20 minutes, better than some men."

10 Nanna rose to her feet and said good-bye to the girls. The girls watched Nanna as she jogged to the parking lot. "Your grandma is pretty cool," Jamey said.

9 What causes Karyn to look over at the woman who was running?

A The woman is running fast.
B Jamey asks who the woman is.
C Karyn is looking for another friend.
D The woman is talking about Kathryn Switzer.

10 What effect do you think meeting Nanna will have on Jamey?

F She will like Karyn more as a friend.
G She will want to enter the Boston Marathon.
H She will appreciate being able to participate in sports.
J She will come back to the track more often.

1   Rebecca moved around in her seat nervously. Her teacher had asked the students to give oral reports on family history. All the students had wonderful stories. Robbie said his great-grandfather had been a cowboy. Angelica's ancestors had come from Ireland on a ship.

2   When her turn came, Rebecca rose slowly and walked to the front of the class. She took a deep breath and began. "My family is from Germany," she started. "They were Jewish, and in the 1930s, Adolf Hitler and the Nazis were rounding up Jews and putting them in work camps."

3   She told of how her great-grandparents decided to flee to America. "They had to walk to Germany's border," Rebecca said. "It was more than a hundred miles. They traveled at night and slept during the day. It was very hard."

4   Rebecca held up a tiny doll. "My grandmother carried this in her pocket for weeks. It's still dirty from the trip because my grandmother never washed it. She said that it reminded her of what she and her family endured for freedom."

5   The class was silent for a moment, then the students asked many questions about Rebecca's story and her family. At that moment, the butterflies in Rebecca's stomach were replaced with a glow of pride. The teacher's encouraging smile told her that she had helped her classmates learn about courage.

11 What is this story *mostly* about?
   A a teacher who asks her students to give reports
   B a girl who tells how her family came to America
   C a class of students who have nice stories
   D why some people tried to escape from the Nazis

12 What is the main idea of the last paragraph?
   F The teacher decides that Rebecca needs help.
   G The class doesn't understand Rebecca's story.
   H Students often ask too many questions about families.
   J Rebecca changes from being afraid to feeling proud.

13 Which of these is a *fact* from the story?
   A The teacher had asked the students to give oral reports.
   B Adolf Hitler and the Nazis were rounding up Jews and putting them in work camps.
   C Rebecca rose slowly and walked to the front of the class.
   D all of the above

14 Which of these is an *opinion* in the story?
   F Rebecca moved around in her seat nervously.
   G All the students had wonderful stories.
   H Rebecca's great-grandparents decided to flee to America.
   J Rebecca held up a tiny doll.

One of the most breathtaking places in the world, the Grand Canyon, lies in northwestern Arizona. It is about 277 miles long, 1 mile deep, and anywhere from 1 to 18 miles wide. In 1869, an American geologist named John Wesley Powell led a river expedition through the canyons of the Green and Colorado Rivers. Powell named the area the Grand Canyon, and his exploration of the area was one of the greatest adventures in American history. Few people remember Powell today, but he and his fellow explorers accomplished an extraordinary feat that would be difficult even with today's technology.

15 Which of the following statements is *not* supported by the paragraph?

A John Wesley Powell was lazy.

B John Wesley Powell was curious.

C John Wesley Powell was brave.

D John Wesley Powell was determined.

16 After reading this paragraph, Connie thinks that a trip through the Grand Canyon would be harder than she first thought. Which words from the story cause her to think this?

F ". . . feat that would be difficult even with today's technology."

G "One of the most breathtaking places in the world . . ."

H "Powell named the area the Grand Canyon . . ."

J ". . . Powell led a river expedition through the canyons . . ."

Directions: Read the following questions. On the answer sheet, fill in the bubble for the answer that you think is correct.

17 Which of these describes poetry?

A Facts are presented so that you can understand them easily.

B The setting is described in great detail.

C Stage directions show the placement of characters.

D Rhyme and rhythm help you understand the meaning.

18 What is a great advantage of writing fiction?

F You can write about things that haven't happened.

G You always write about history or real people.

H You just tell facts and don't have to worry about a story.

J You can use rhyme to make things sound more important.

Name _____ Date _____

Directions: Read the following passages. Then answer the questions. On the answer sheet, fill in the bubble for the answer that you think is correct.

> Daniel Parsons lives just four blocks from the hospital. Neighbors call him "Doc" and often stop to visit the retired doctor. Doc was a great doctor because he truly cared about people. When he first retired, he missed his patients. So he moved a big comfortable chair to his front porch, and he sits there when the weather permits. Doc visits with the people who pass by. Many of them are his former patients.

19 According to the story, being a good doctor means —
A living near the hospital
B having a caring personality
C getting plenty of fresh air
D enjoying many houseguests

20 Why does Daniel Parsons visit with former patients?
F He feels obligated.
G He misses them.
H He has nothing better to do.
J none of the above

Directions: Read each sentence. Choose the correct meaning of the underlined word. On the answer sheet, fill in the bubble for the answer that you think is correct.

21 Most people described Paul's personality as being <u>rough</u>.
A uneven
B approximate
C stormy
D harsh

22 Many of us had learned to be cautious in dealing with representatives of the <u>press</u>.
F push against
G news media
H a large machine
J move forward

Directions: Find the meaning of each sentence. On the answer sheet, fill in the bubble for the answer that you think is correct.

23 All hands on deck!
A a card player's demand
B a request for help
C an order to hold onto safety railing
D a command to people to show their palms

24 All the world's a stage, / And all the men and women merely players.
F Live your life while you have the chance.
G In real life, everybody has a part to play.
H Drama gives us insight into the purpose of life.
J Do not be too serious about life's meaning.

Directions: Read the following phrases. Then decide which of the four answers has most nearly the same meaning as the underlined word. Then fill in the bubble for the answer that you think is correct.

25 A **jaunt** in the park
  A game
  B parade
  C pony ride
  D short trip

26 A **massive** building
  F large
  G brick
  H empty
  J important

Directions: Read the following words. Look for mistakes in spelling. For each item on the answer sheet, fill in the bubble for the answer that has the mistake. If there is no mistake, fill in the last answer choice.

27 **A** argue
  B vauge
  C bounty
  D *(No mistakes)*

28 **F** drums
  G music
  H radeo
  J *(No mistakes)*

Directions: Read the following sentences. Look for mistakes in punctuation. For each item on the answer sheet, fill in the bubble for the answer that has the mistake. If there is no mistake, fill in the last answer choice.

29 **A** Following the Civil War, Congress passed
  B many laws protecting the rights of African
  C Americans. Most of them werent followed.
  D *(No mistakes)*

30 **F** Born in San Francisco California
  G Russell Freedman published his
  H first book in 1961.
  J *(No mistakes)*

Practice Test 1

Suppose that you are going to interview your town's mayor about her experiences as a junior high school student years ago. You will use the interview to help you write an article for the school newspaper.

Answer the questions that follow.

1. What should you do before arriving at the mayor's office?
   A. Wonder what the mayor is like.
   B. Write a list of questions to ask.
   C. Remember to bring your eighth grade class picture with you.
   D. Interview another person.

2. During the interview, how should you use a notebook?
   A. Write the questions you want to ask in it.
   B. Have the mayor autograph it for you.
   C. Take notes in it as the mayor talks.
   D. Begin writing your article for the newspaper in it.

3. What should you do when you quote the mayor in your article?
   A. Try to write exactly what she says.
   B. Use quotation marks.
   C. Add to what she says to make it more interesting.
   D. both A and B

4. Which of the following shows that you have asked good interview questions?
   A. The mayor compliments you on them.
   B. They help you answer the questions *who, what, where, when, why,* and *how.*
   C. You can use them to make up interesting stories about the mayor.
   D. They are questions that many people have asked the mayor before.

Suppose that you and your classmates will work in small groups to write speeches about the importance of wearing seat belts while riding in an automobile. You will travel to elementary schools to deliver your speeches to fourth-grade students. Answer the questions that follow.

5. What should be the specific purpose of this speech?
   A. to persuade listeners to wear their seat belts whenever they drive
   B. to explain to listeners why seat belts should be optional
   C. to persuade listeners to wear seat belts whenever they ride in an automobile
   D. to inform listeners of what to do in case they are in a car accident

6. What should be the tone of your speech?
   A. serious and professional
   B. serious and frightening
   C. humorous and light-hearted
   D. mysterious and vague

7. Which of the following should you do during your speech?
   A. Use slang and a quick pace.   C. Mumble and say "um" a lot.
   B. Make eye contact with the audience. D. Slouch and keep your head down.

8. What is the point of letting the audience ask questions or make comments after you have finished your speech?
   A. to provide more information and clarify your points
   B. to fill time if your speech runs too short
   C. to make the audience feel important
   D. to demonstrate your listening skills

9. When you write your speech, which of the following should you avoid doing?
   A. Observe the rules of grammar.
   B. Use vocabulary and sentence structure that your audience will understand.
   C. Stay focused on your main idea.
   D. Include statistics and other facts that you aren't sure are accurate.

10. What is the **best** way to help other groups improve on their presentation skills?
   A. Read their speeches before they present them to the audience.
   B. Observe their performances, taking notes on strengths and weaknesses.
   C. Compare their speeches to your own group's speech.
   D. Listen to the kinds of questions and comments the audience makes.

Read the following passage. Then answer the questions that follow.

SNEAKER SALE!

On sale this week only!

•The best sneakers money can buy—each pair is made especially to fit YOUR feet.

•Improve your performance in all sports: jump higher, run faster, kick harder. You'll feel as though you are flying!

•Sneakers come in 10 cool colors, for boys and girls.

Don't be the only kid in your school who wears old-fashioned sneakers.

Buy a new pair TODAY.

11. Which statement from the sneaker ad tries to appeal to your emotions?
   A. Each pair is made especially to fit YOUR feet.
   B. Improve your performance in all sports.
   C. Don't be the only kid in your school who wears old-fashioned sneakers.
   D. all of the above

12. What is the **primary** purpose of the sneaker ad?
   A. to persuade   C. to describe
   B. to entertain   D. to inform

Answer the questions that follow.

13. Which of the following sentences contains a metaphor?
    A. The long hall was dark, dreary, and frightening.
    B. Sun shone through the south window of the little house.
    C. The spotlight was a great eye looking down upon us.
    D. Marlene flung her clothes carelessly over the furniture.

14. Which of the following sentences contains a simile?
    A. The ball connected crisply with Lili's bat and shot into center field like a jet.
    B. Red and yellow apples were piled in brown bushel baskets.
    C. Across the gym, the "away" team's fans filled the bleachers, an array of colors, lacking features.
    D. Savory meat, flavorful beans, crisp lettuce, even a crispy taco shell—they're nothing without salsa.

15. Which of the following sentences contains a hyperbole?
    A. Juanita was so surprised to see Dan that you could have knocked her over with a feather.
    B. Charles said that he lost his appetite when he saw the dirty floor of the restaurant.
    C. "Do your best work of the year on this test," Mr. Harper warned.
    D. Rita loved to dance and sing songs from her native Scotland.

16. What is the correct meaning of the underlined word in the sentence below?

    The outcome of the game was <u>even</u> worse than any of us had feared.

    A. divisible by two   C. flat or smooth
    B. equal in number   D. none of the above

17. What is the correct meaning of the underlined phrase in the sentence below?

    Mom and I feel it is unfair to simply <u>string him along</u>.

    A. give him a job   C. make fun of him
    B. ask him to volunteer   D. fool or deceive him

Read the following passages. Then answer the questions that follow.

The Price of Beauty

According to legend, the peacock did not always have such beautiful feathers. He was just an average bird who wanted to stand out. When the peacock's wish was granted, and he got his new feathers, he visited his old friends. The pheasant, the swan, and the heron all admitted that the peacock was by far the most beautiful. On his way home, the peacock saw an eagle soaring overhead, as he used to do. Lifting his wings, the peacock tried to rise, but the weight of his new feathers held him down. He knew then that he would no longer fly up to greet the morning but instead walk the ground like a common beast.

18. What lesson can be learned from this story?
    A. There is always someone less fortunate than you.
    B. Do not give up freedom for something less important.
    C. The most precious things in life cannot be bought.
    D. Do not take credit for something you did not do.

First Steps Concert

Jason watched with wide eyes as the four singers approached the stage. He had been looking forward to this moment for six weeks. When his choir director, Mr. Nelson, announced that the group First Steps would be performing for the school, Jason almost jumped out of his seat. He had all their CDs and dreamed of singing with the group someday. Mr. Nelson told the class that they could watch the group warm up before the performance, and Jason was the first one in the auditorium. He leaned forward, mesmerized, as they tuned to each other's voices. Suddenly they burst into an old spiritual. Jason had never heard anything so beautiful.

Lesson Plan

It was my favorite class of the day. Not only that, Ms. Peeler had asked *me* to come up with a lesson plan to teach the class! Today was the day I was supposed to present it. I could hardly wait to stand in front of the class and tell them what I had learned. I stayed up until 12 o'clock the night before preparing. When I walked into class, Ms. Peeler pulled me aside. She told me that the school was having a special assembly and that I would have to wait until next class time to present my lesson. I tried not to act disappointed, but I wanted to cry. As the class filed into the hall, I was the last to leave. I walked slowly to the auditorium and sat in the back row. Some group I'd never heard of called First Steps was going to sing. All I could think about was my lesson.

The Return

Chris, Randy, Mark, and Abel had never performed at a high school before. Abel's high school choir director called him after their last tour. Mr. Nelson suggested that they do a concert for Abel's school. Abel hadn't been back to his old school for ten years. When they arrived, Abel gave the guys a tour of the place. Memories from his past flooded back

"This was my old locker. My friends and I would meet here after school every Wednesday to have jam sessions. Students would crowd around while we started to sing all kinds of fun stuff."

In the choir room, Abel hugged Mr. Nelson and said, "This is the man who made me fall in love with music." Abel and the guys followed Mr. Nelson into the auditorium where students were waiting to listen to the group warm up.

19. In *First Steps Concert*, why is Jason excited about the concert?
    A. He gets to go into the auditorium first.
    B. He enjoys music and likes the group's work.
    C. The group sings Jason's favorite spiritual.
    D. The group wants to hear Jason sing.

20. Which of the following *best* describes the points of view in *Lesson Plan* and *The Return*?

    A. *Lesson Plan* is in first person; *The Return* is in third person.

    B. *Lesson Plan* is in third person; *The Return* is in first person.

    C. *Lesson Plan* is in second person; *The Return* is in third person.

    D. *Lesson Plan* is in first person; *The Return* is in second person.

21. Why does the poet repeat the word *knock* so often in these lines of poetry?

What was the constant knock,

knock, knocking

Waking me before dawn?

    A. to show that the speaker is expecting a visitor

    B. to show that the speaker has been asleep

    C. to show that there is no doorbell

    D. to show that the knocking is continuous

First Trip

I was happy to be taking my first cross-country trip with my cousin, Beth. As the hours passed, we covered hundreds of miles. The states passed by one after the other, and at the end of the week, we stood on the shore of an ocean that neither of us had ever seen before.

Freedom

Freedom rode in the car with my cousin Beth and me as we painted a bright red line across the map of our country. After many moons, we stood at a new coast.

22. How are the two passages above *similar*?

    A. Both describe road maps.

    B. Both describe an airplane flight taken by the narrator and Beth.

    C. Both describe a long trip by car.

    D. Both describe the items packed by the narrator and Beth.

23. How are the two passages above *different*?

    A. They tell two different stories.

    B. *First Trip* has two characters, and *Freedom* has three.

    C. *Freedom* has more metaphors.

    D. *First Trip* is told in first person, and *Freedom* is not.

*Read each of the sentences that follow. Then choose the word that **best** expresses the meaning of the underlined word.*

24. The forks and spoons <u>cascaded</u> to the floor.

    A. broke into pieces   **C.** rushed

    B. slid across   **D.** fell like water

25. The <u>nimble</u> mouse evaded the cat's claws.

    A. hungry   **C.** tame

    B. quick   **D.** naughty

Practice Test 2

Read the following passages. Then answer the questions that follow.

Better Morning

Waking up to a fresh cup of coffee has never been so easy. Percolite Plus offers an auto timer feature that allows you to prepare your coffee the night before. Just pour in the water, fill the filter with coffee, and set the timer. The next morning, the aroma of fresh coffee will awaken you. Percolite Plus is your answer to waking up happy.

Instructions for Percolite Plus Coffeemaker

1. Fill the coffee pot with the desired amount of water (using the numbers on the pot as a guide) by pouring the water into the chamber at the top of the coffeemaker.

2. Place a small filter in the basket at the top of the coffeemaker.

3. Measure the desired amount of ground coffee and place in the filter.

4. Set the timer, if using the auto timer feature.

5. Move switch to ON or AUTO.

1. What is the purpose of the passage *Better Morning*?
   - A. to sell a product
   - B. to explain a process
   - C. to state a fact
   - D. to make an agreement

2. What does *Instructions for Percolite Plus Coffeemaker* explain?
   - A. what to do if the coffeemaker breaks
   - B. why the coffeemaker is a good product
   - C. when the coffeemaker can be fixed
   - D. how to operate the coffeemaker

3. From the information in *Better Morning*, what you can conclude about its author?
   - A. The author wants the details to persuade you to use the coffeemaker.
   - B. The author is someone who knows a lot about coffee.
   - C. The author knows how you can have a happier morning.
   - D. The author drinks coffee every morning.

The Truth About *The Wizard Walks*

Recently, some parents tried to remove *The Wizard Walks* from the shelves of the local public library. These foolish people are entitled to decide for themselves what they will read, but *The Wizard Walks* should not be banned.

The people who object to *The Wizard Walks* believe that it is unsuitable for children. However, a poll showed that most people who want to ban *The Wizard Walks* haven't even read the book. They are mindlessly repeating what they have heard from others without taking the trouble to research the subject themselves.

Name _____ Date _____

The main argument for banning *The Wizard Walks* is that it is almost a textbook on magic. But anyone who has actually read the book knows that it does not teach witchcraft. Although the main character of *The Wizard Walks* has magical powers, the story is obviously fictional. Most children have no trouble figuring out that this book describes an imaginary world.

Perhaps *The Wizard Walks* is not good for every child, but banning it from the public library goes too far. If ignorant people start banning books, soon our libraries will be empty. Every book is offensive to someone for some reason.

Parents who do not want children to read *The Wizard Walks* can ban it from their homes. To ban it from the public library would take away the right of other parents to make that decision for their own children.

4. Why is the author offended by the attempt to ban *The Wizard Walks*?
   A. Many supporters of the ban have not read the book.
   B. The author used *The Wizard Walks* to learn witchcraft.
   C. The author enjoyed reading *The Wizard Walks* very much.
   D. Supporters of the ban are prejudiced against witchcraft.

5. Which of these is the *first* clue that the author does not respect the supporters of the ban?
   A. The author calls the supporters "foolish people."
   B. The author says the supporters are acting "mindlessly."
   C. The author says the book is "not good" for all children.
   D. The author suggests that parents "ban [the book] from their homes."

6. Based on the evidence in this essay, what can you infer that the author believes?
   A. Only a few books should ever be banned from the library.
   B. All children should be required to read *The Wizard Walks*.
   C. *The Wizard Walks* is the best children's book of our time.
   D. Public libraries should have a wide variety of books.

7. How does the author of the passage make the argument effective?
   A. The author says negative things about the people who ban books.
   B. The author states the issues, gives examples, and presents a solution.
   C. The author agrees that the book may not be good for every child.
   D. The author says that those who ban books are wrong.

Using Your Chef's Gourmet Hand Mixer

Before using your mixer for the first time, wash and dry the beaters and the mixing bowl. Make sure that the speed control is in the OFF position and the mixer is not plugged in. Insert the beaters into the openings on the bottom of the mixer. Push until each beater clicks into position. Then plug the cord into a standard household electrical outlet (120 volt, 60 Hz A.C.).

8. What should you do just before inserting the beaters?
   A. Plug the mixer into an outlet.
   B. Check that the mixer is turned off and unplugged.
   C. Set the speed control to "1."
   D. Rock the mixer back onto its base.

9. What should you do before using the mixer for the first time?
   A. Wash and dry the beaters and mixing bowl.
   B. Wash and dry the electrical outlet.
   C. Wash and dry the cord.
   D. Wash and dry the speed control.

10. Which of the following is the **best** explanation of the purpose of this passage?
    A. The passage describes how to buy The Chef's Gourmet Hand Mixer.
    B. The passage informs how to use The Chef's Gourmet Hand Mixer.
    C. The passage informs how to plug in The Chef's Gourmet Hand Mixer.
    D. The passage describes how to wash The Chef's Gourmet Hand Mixer.

11. Based on the information in this passage, what you can conclude?
    A. The mixer should be operated without the beaters.
    B. The mixer should be operated by professional chefs.
    C. The mixer should be operated near an electrical outlet.
    D. The mixer should be operated outdoors.

Lake Louise

Lake Louise is part of Banff National Park in southern Alberta, Canada. The lake is about a mile and a half long and a third of a mile wide. Visitors find it quiet and peaceful at Lake Louise. The smooth waters mirror the surrounding mountains, creating breathtaking views. More people visit Lake Louise than anywhere else in the Canadian Rockies.

12. Suppose you are writing an essay persuading people to visit Lake Louise. Which of the following statements would be **most** effective?
    A. Lake Louise is part of Banff National Park in southern Alberta, Canada.
    B. The lake is about a mile and a half long and a third of a mile wide.
    C. The smooth waters mirror the surrounding mountains, creating breathtaking views.
    D. More people visit Lake Louise than anywhere else in the Canadian Rockies.

13. Which of these statements can be inferred from the paragraph?
    A. Lake Louise is close to the United States.
    B. People enjoy the spectacular scenery at Lake Louise.
    C. Lake Louise is the largest lake in Canada.
    D. The Canadian Rockies have many beautiful lakes.

Modern Bandage

Although many people don't even know his name, Earle Dickson was responsible for creating one of today's most common household items. Dickson was the genius behind Band-Aids®.

In 1917, Dickson was a newly married man and a cotton buyer for a successful bandage company in New Jersey called Johnson & Johnson.

As the story goes, Dickson's wife, Frances, was accident-prone. She often cut herself or nicked her fingers doing various household tasks. The regular bandages were too big and clumsy for Frances, so Dickson devised something better.

He folded pads of cotton gauze and placed them on long strips of surgical tape. He covered this with a material called crinoline. This prevented the tape from sticking to itself when it was rolled back together. Frances could unroll the bandage and cut off as much as she needed.

One day, Dickson mentioned his creation to a friend at work. Soon, Dickson was before the Johnsons, showing them what he had come up with. The Johnsons were especially impressed with the fact that you could put the new bandage on yourself. Up until that point, bandages had been difficult to apply without help.

Johnson & Johnson began producing Band-Aids®, but the bandages didn't take off until the mid-1920s when the company gave thousands of samples to the Boy Scouts. After that, Band-Aids® were a hit. Dickson was made vice president of Johnson & Johnson, and when he died in 1961, the company was selling $30,000,000 dollars' worth of Band-Aids® a year.

Here is a partial outline of the passage.

The Invention of Band-Aids®

    I.   Who Earle Dickson was

    II.   _____

    III. How Dickson made his own bandage

    IV. What happened at Johnson & Johnson

    V.   The success of Band-Aids®

14. Which answer would fit **best** in the blank in the outline?
   A. Where Johnson & Johnson was
   B. What Dickson's wife's name was
   C. Why Dickson made his own bandage
   D. How Dickson met with Johnson & Johnson

15. If you were taking notes about this passage, which of these ideas should you **omit**?
   A. Dickson became vice president.
   B. Band-Aids® were popular right away.
   C. Early bandages were difficult to put on.
   D. Dickson worked for Johnson & Johnson.

16. Which of these statements gives the **best** summary of the passage?
   A. The Boy Scouts make Band-Aids® more popular.
   B. A housewife is finally able to bandage herself.
   C. A cotton inventor becomes head of a company.
   D. One man's homemade bandages become Band-Aids®.

The Growing Popularity of Tennis

The sport of tennis is becoming more popular with children and teenagers.

Part 1

Young stars such as Andy Roddick and Serena Williams to look up to. Many schools are adding tennis.

Part 2

To their physical education programs. Community centers have recognized the growing popularity of tennis.

Part 3

Added tennis courts to their existing facilities.

17. If you were assigned to write a research report based on information from the passage, what would be the ***best*** information or vocabulary to include?
   A. community centers
   B. growing popularity of tennis
   C. physical education programs
   D. existing facilities

18. Which is the ***best*** way to revise Part 1?
   A. The sport of tennis is becoming more popular with children and teenagers; young stars such as Andy Roddick and Serena Williams to look up to.
   B. With young stars such as Andy Roddick and Serena Williams to look up to, the sport of tennis is becoming more popular with children and teenagers.
   C. Young stars such as Andy Roddick and Serena Williams have made the sport of tennis more popular with children and teenagers.
   D. Young stars such as Andy Roddick and Serena Williams. Have made the sport of tennis more popular with children and teenagers.

19. Suppose that the writer wanted to use the material in this passage to write two paragraphs, with Part 2 appearing at the beginning of the second paragraph. Which of the following would be the *best* transition to the second paragraph?
   A. For instance,   C. As a result,
   B. After all,   D. On the contrary,

20. If you were typing this paragraph into a computer's word-processing program, which of the following would be helpful?
   A. The computer can automatically add additional research for you.
   B. You can make corrections easily.
   C. You can move text around easily.
   D. both B and C

Answer the following question.

21. In the sentence, "Maria read many books," which of the following words is the direct object?
   A. Maria   C. many
   B. read   D. books

Read the following passages. Then answer the questions that follow.

Techniques of Fiction Writers

Fiction writers use a variety of techniques to _____1_____ their characters seem like real people. One such technique is to have characters use dialects when they speak. Some writers use first-person narration so that the reader knows how one of the characters feels, as well as what _____2_____ says.

22. Suppose you were to make a web showing the sentence that contains the main idea in the center and the sentences that contain details in circles that connect to the center. Which sentence would you place in the center?
    A. Fiction writers use a variety of techniques to _____1_____ their characters seem like real people.
    B. One such technique is to have characters use dialects when they speak.
    C. Some writers use first-person narration so that the reader knows how one of the characters feels, as well as what _____2_____ says.
    D. This paragraph does not contain a main idea.

23. Which of the following words belongs in space 1 as shown in question 22 above?
    A. makes   C. make
    B. made   D. making

24. Which word or group of words belongs in space 2 as shown in question 22 above?
    A. he or she   C. the narrator
    B. they   D. the author

The newspapers in my town and your city _____ the championship games.

25. Which word or group of words belongs in the space shown in the sentence above?
    A. covers
    B. covering
    C. cover
    D. has covered

Museum Visit

When we went to the museum, we didn't expect to have a very good time. It was crowded, and my brother said to me, "Do you want me to tell Dad that I'm sick?" I'm glad that I said "no," because within five minutes, we *are* interested in what we saw.

26. Which of the following verbs correctly replaces the italicized, boldfaced verb in the passage above?
    A. was   C. had been
    B. were   D. was being

Of the two O'Connor brothers, Chris is the _____.

27. Which word or group of words belongs in the space shown in the sentence above?
    A. most athletic   C. athleticest
    B. athletic   D. more athletic

Carolyn is the sophomore who has the _____ grade point average.

28. Which word or group of words belongs in the space shown in the sentence above?
- **A.** higher
- **B.** highest
- **C.** high
- **D.** more high

Devon failed to pass the lifeguard test the first time _____ therefore, he studied harder before his second attempt.

29. Which mark of punctuation belongs in the space shown in the sentence above?
- **A.** semi-colon
- **B.** exclamation mark
- **C.** period
- **D.** colon

Writing Prompt #1

Imagine that the community center in your town will soon be adding something new. What do you think should be added? It may be a new piece of equipment, a new club, or a new class that you would like to take. It might be something you can use or take part in after school, on weekends, or during summer vacation. Write to convince the director of the community center that your idea is the one that should be added. Be sure to be specific and explain your reasons.

Writing Prompt #2

If you had three wishes, what you wish for and why? Think about your three wishes and why you chose them. Perhaps your wishes have to do with a place or an event that you remember from your past. Maybe your wishes would make you and/or other people happy. You might think also about how the wishes could help change the world for the better. Write an essay in which you explain what you wish for and why. Support your ideas with examples and details.

Practice Test 3

Part 1: Textual Analysis

Read the following narrative and then answer the questions that follow.

from *The Pioneers* by James Fenimore Cooper

James Fenimore Cooper wrote action-filled adventure stories that were very popular. The central character in five of his novels is a wilderness hunter named Natty Bumppo, or Leather-stocking, who lives between the Indian and white worlds. Bumppo has learned the forest skills of the Indians. This selection is from The Pioneers. In this scene, Leather-stocking realizes that the wilderness is fast falling to settlers.

1)   The heavens were alive with pigeons; the whole village seemed equally in motion, with men, women, and children. Every species of fire-arms, from the French ducking-gun, with a barrel near six feet in length, to the common horseman's pistol, was to be seen in the hands of the men and boys; while bows and arrows, some made of the simple stick of a walnut sapling, and others in a rude [simple] imitation of the ancient cross-bows, were carried by many of the latter. . . .

2)   Amongst the sportsmen was the tall, gaunt form of Leather-stocking, walking over the field, with his rifle hanging on his arm, his dogs at his heels; the latter now scenting the dead or wounded birds, that were beginning to tumble from the flocks, and then crouching under the legs of their master, as if they participated in his feelings, at this wasteful and unsportsmanlike execution.

3)   The reports of the fire-arms became rapid, whole volleys rising from the plain, as flocks of more than ordinary numbers darted over the opening, shadowing the field, like a cloud; and then the light smoke of a single piece would issue from among the leafless bushes on the mountain, as death was hurled on the retreat of the affrighted birds, who were rising from a volley, in a vain effort to escape.

4)   Arrows, and missiles of every kind, were in the midst of the flocks; and so numerous were the birds, and so low did they take their flight, that even long poles, in the hands of those on the sides of the mountain, were used to strike them to the earth. . . .So prodigious was the number of birds, that the scattering fire of the guns, with the hurling of missiles, and the cries of the boys, had no other effect than to break off small flocks from the immense masses that continued to dart along the valley, as if the whole of the feathered tribe were pouring through one pass.

5)   None pretended to collect the game, which lay scattered over the fields in such profusion, as to cover the very ground with the fluttering victims. Leather-stocking was a silent, but uneasy spectator of all these proceedings, but was able to keep his sentiments to himself until he saw the introduction of the swivel [cannon] into the sports.

6)   "This comes of settling a country!" he said — "here have I known the pigeons to fly for forty long years, and, till you made your clearings, there was nobody to skear [scare]or to hurt them. I loved to see them come into the woods, for they were company to a body; hurting nothing; being, as it was, as harmless as a garter-snake. But now it gives me sore thoughts when I hear the frighty things whizzing through the air, for I know it's only a motion to bring out all the brats in the village. Well! the Lord won't see the waste of his creators for nothing, and right will be done to the pigeons, as well as others, by-and-by. . . .

7) "Among the sportsmen was Billy Kirby, who, armed with an old musket, was loading, and, without even looking into the air, was firing, and shouting as his victims fell even on his own person. He heard the speech of Natty, and took upon himself to reply, "What! old Leather-stocking," he cried, "grumbling at the loss of a few pigeons! If you had to sow your wheat twice, and three times, as I have done, you wouldn't be so massy-fully [mercifully] feeling'd towards the divils.—Hurrah, boys! scatter the feathers. This is better than shooting at a turkey's head and neck, old fellow.""

8) "It's better for you, maybe, Billy Kirby," replied the indignant old hunter, "and all them that don't know how to put a ball down a rifle-barrel, or how to bring it up ag'in with a true aim; but it's wicked to be shooting into flocks in this wastey manner; and none do it, who know how to knock over a single bird. If a body has a craving for pigeon's flesh, why! it's made the same as all other creator's, for man's eating, but not to kill twenty and eat one."

1 **Which of the following best describes Leather Stocking?**

A pioneer clothing

B an old Indian

C a wilderness hunter

D a young farmer

2 **What is the main idea of the selection?**

A Leather Stocking does not like the pioneers.

B Leather Stocking thinks you should never kill pigeons.

C Leather Stocking does not believe wildlife should be killed for sport.

D Leather Stocking does not like guns.

3 **Which of the following best describes Billy Kirby?**

A A pioneer that does not like Leather Stocking.

B A farmer who thinks he is protecting his crops.

C A pioneer who thinks it is fun to kill the pigeons.

D A farmer who wants to show off for his friends.

4 **Why most likely did the author use the word "skear" instead of scare?**

A He did not know the correct spelling.

B He likes to write dialogue.

C He is showing Leather Stocking's dialect.

D He is showing how the word was written in pioneer days.

5 **How *most likely* did Natty Bumppo get the name Leather Stocking?**

A because of his clothing

B because he lived with the Indians

C because he wanted to change his name

D because the pioneers did not like him

6 **Which of the following relationships is most similar to the relationship below?**

Leather Stocking : pigeons

A Indians :pioneers

B Pioneers : Indians

C Billy Kirby :crops

D Crops : Billy Kirby

7 **Which of the following best describes the conflict in the selection?**

A man versus man

B wildlife versus wilderness

C nature versus wilderness

D man versus environment

8 **Based on paragraph 4, what is the meaning of the word *prodigious*?**

A birds

B angry

C enormous

D weak

9 **Based on paragraph 8, what is the meaning of *indignant*?**

A uneasy

B unfair

C anxious

D angry

10 **Which of the following best fits the Venn diagram?**

Leather Stocking	**Bill Kirby**
Hunter	farmer
Old	young
Lives in the woods	lives in a community

A gaunt

B sportsman

C pioneer

D lonely

Jabberwocky by Lewis Carroll

"Jabberwocky" is generally considered the greatest of all nonsense poems. It can be found in the first chapter of <u>Through the looking Glass and What Alice Found There</u>. You may know this novel better as <u>Alice in Wonderland</u>. The following quote follows the poem in the novel:

"It sees very pretty," she said when she had finished it, "but it's rather hard to understand!" (You see she didn't like to confess even to herself, that she couldn't make it out at all.)

Humpty Dumpty explained some of the words. Read the following definitions and answer the questions after the poem.

Brillig : 4:00pm, the time to cook dinner

Slithy: Smooth and active

Tove: something like a bagger; something like a lizard

Gyre: to go round and around

Gimble: to make holes

Wabe : a grass plot beside a sundial

Mimsy : flimsy and miserable

Borogove: a shabby looking bird

Mome raths : lost green pigs

Outgrabe : something between bellowing and whistling with a sneeze in the middle.

1)   'Twas brillig, and the slithy toves
        Did gyre and gimble in the wabe;
        All mimsy were the borogoves,
        And the mome raths outgrabe.

2)   "Beware the Jabberwock, my son!
        The jaws that bite, the claws that catch!
        Beware the Jubjub bird, and shun
        The frumious Bandersnatch!"

3)   He took his vorpal sword in hand:
        Long time the manxome foe he sought—
        So rested he by the Tumtum tree,
        And stood awhile in thought.

4)   And, as in uffish thought he stood,
        The Jabberwock, with eyes of flame,
        Came whiffling through the tulgey wood,
        And burbled as it came!

5)   One two! One two! And through and through
        The vorpal blade went snicker-snack!
        He left it dead, and with its head
        He went galumphing back.

6) "And hast thou slain the Jabberwock?
Come to my arms, my beamish boy!
O frabjous day! Callooh! Callay!"
He chortled in his joy.

7) 'Twas brillig, and the slithy toves
Did gyre and gimble in the wabe;
All mimsy were the borogoves,
And the mome raths outgrabe.

11 What *most likely* is the Jabberwock?

A a person

B a creature

C a type of food

D a kind of bird

12 Which of the following would be *most* like Alice's experience in the selection?

A being given asked to read a very difficult book.

B being asked to read a book in a foreign language

C talking to an imaginary character

D reading a fantasy novel

13 Which of the following is *most likely* the meaning of frabjous in stanza 6?

A fabulous

B wonderful and beautiful

C fabulous and joyous

D joyous

14 Which is the *best* restatement of stanzas 1 and 7?

A I was cooking troves for dinner and listening to the green pigs as they cried for help.

B I was cooking dinner, the troves were making holes in the grass and the green pigs were making noises.

C I was looking for something to cook for dinner when I saw the monster.

D I was cooking dinner when I heard strange noises coming from the woods.

15 What most likely is the meaning of *manx-ome* in stanza 3?

A large and fierce

B small and strong

C mythical and loud

D unusual and silent

16 What is the author's tone?

A serious

B ironic

C sarcastic

D humorous

17 Which of the following is *most similar* to the selection?

A a science fiction poem

B a poem about slaying a dragon

C a poem about the Renaissance

D a realistic poem

Fine Art: Remembering the work of Maya Ying Lin

1) Maya Lin competed with over 1,400 other entrants to design the Vietnam Veterans Memorial. When the board of directors of the Southern Poverty Law Center (SPLC) in Montgomery, Alabama decided they wanted a Civil Rights memorial, they called every Lin in the New York City phone book looking for Maya. They knew exactly who they wanted to design their memorial.

2) The SPLC was founded in 1971 to protect and advance the legal rights of minorities and poor people, and it remains one of the nation's leading Civil Rights organizations.

3) Maya, inspired by the historical significance of the civil rights movement, agreed to design the monument. In researching the background of the Civil Rights movement, she came across these words by Martin Luther King, Jr.:

"We will not be satisfied until justice rolls down like waters, and righteousness like a mighty stream."

4) King used these words from the Bible in several of his speeches. The words inspired Maya to use water as a main design element of the monument. The plan was to memorialize those individuals who had been killed in the cause of marching for civil rights.

5) The SPLC came up with 53 entries they wanted etched in stone. Maya decided to create a huge, twelve-foot disk, or table of granite, and to inscribe the names around the perimeter. The entries would be listed in chronological order from 17 May 1954, the date of the Supreme Court ruling outlawing school segregation, to 4 April 1968, the assassination of Martin Luther King, Jr.

6) A black granite wall behind the disk rising nine feet would be inscribed with the words that inspired Maya, *"until justice rolls down like waters, and righteousness like a mighty stream."* Water would flow down the wall and across the disk, touching each name in the timeline. The disk would be close to the ground so people could walk around it and touch the inscriptions.

18 **Why *most likely* did the SPLC know they wanted Maya Lin to create their memorial?**

 A They like Asian art.

 B They liked her other work.

 C They knew where she lived.

 D They wanted someone famous.

19 **Why was the SPLC founded?**

 A to become civil rights organization.

 B to honor Martin Luther King, Jr.

 C to protect the legal rights of the poor and minorities

 D to research and protect civil rights

20 **What is the meaning of the figurative language in paragraph 3?**

 A We will not stop until there is justice for everyone.

 B We will roll down the river until it stops.

 C We will not let the water stop us.

 D We will not be satisfied with current civil rights.

21 **Why most likely did Lin use water in her monument?**

 A It symbolized Civil Rights.

 B It was restful to watch

 C It symbolized King, Jr.'s, determination.

 D It was what the SPLC asked her to do.

How I Became a Printer By Benjamin Franklin

This excerpt from Benjamin Franklin's autobiography describes his early education and his apprentice-ship to his brother James, a Boston printer. Franklin also writes about the role printers played in bringing attention to colonial opposition to British rule.

From Social Studies © Prentice-Hall, Inc.

1)   I was put to the grammar-school at eight years of age, my father intending to devote me, as the tithe of his sons, to the service of the Church. My early readiness in learning to read (which must have been very early, as I do not remember when I could not read), and the opinion of all his friends, that I should certainly make a good scholar, encouraged him in this purpose of his.

2)   But my father, in the mean time, from the view of the expense of a college education, which having so large a family he could not well afford . . . took me from the grammar-school, and sent me to a school for writing and arithmetic. . . . At ten years old, I was taken home to assist my father in his business, which was that of a tallow-chandler and soap boiler. . . .

3)   Accordingly, I was employed in cutting wick for the candles, filling the dipping mold and the molds for cast candles, attending the shop, going of errands etc.

4)   I disliked the trade, and had a strong inclina-tion for the sea, but my father declared against it. However, living near the water, I was much in and about it, learned early to swim well, and to manage boats; and when in a boat or canoe with other boys, I was commonly allowed to govern, especially in any case of difficulty; and upon other occasions I was generally a leader among the boys. . . .

5)   From a child I was fond of reading, and all the little money that came into my hands was ever laid out in books. . . . This bookish inclination at length determined my father to make me a printer, though he had already one son (James) of that profession.

6)   In 1717 my brother James returned from England with a press and letters to set up his business in Boston. I liked it much better than that of my father, but still had a hankering for the sea. To prevent the apprehended effect of such an inclination, my father was impatient to have me bound to my brother. I stood out some time, but at last was persuaded, and signed the indenture when I was yet but twelve years old. I was to serve as an apprentice till I was twenty-one years of age, only I was to be allowed journeyman's wages dur-ing the last year.

7)   In a little time I made great proficiency in the business, and became a useful hand to my brother. Though as brother, he considered himself as my master, and me as his apprentice, and accordingly, expected the same services from me as he would from another, while I thought he demeaned me too much in some he required of me, who from a brother expected more indulgence.

8)   Our disputes were often brought before our father, and I fancy I was either generally in the right, or else a better pleader, because the judg-ment was generally in my favor. But my brother was passionate, and had often beaten me, which I took extremely amiss; and, thinking my appren-ticeship very tedious, I was continually wishing for some opportunity of shortening it, which at length offered in a manner unexpected.

9)   One of the pieces in our newspaper on some political point, which I have now forgotten, gave offense to the Assembly. He [James] was taken up, censured, and imprisoned for a month, by the speaker's warrant, I suppose, because he would not discover [reveal] his author. I too was taken up and examined before the council; but, though I did not give them any satisfaction, they contented themselves with admonishing me, and dismissed me, considering me, perhaps, as an apprentice, who was bound to keep his master's secrets.

10)   During my brother's confinement, which I resented a good deal, not withstanding our private differences, I had the management of the paper; and I made bold to give our rulers some rubs in it, which my brother took very kindly, while others began to consider me in an unfavorable light, as a young genius that had a turn for libeling and satire. My brother's discharge was accompanied with an order of the House (a very odd one), that "James Franklin should no longer print the paper called the New England Courant."

11)   There was a consultation held in our printing-house among his friends, what he should do in this case. Some proposed to evade the order by changing the name of the paper; but my brother, seeing inconveniences in that, it was finally concluded on as a better way, to let it be printed for the future under the name of BENJAMIN FRANKLIN; and to avoid the censure of the Assembly, that might fall on him as still printing it by his apprentice, the contrivance was that my old indenture should be returned to me, with full discharge on the back of it, to be shown on occasion, but to secure to him the benefit of my service, I was to sign new indentures for the remainder of the term, which were to be kept private. A very flimsy scheme it was; however, it was immediately executed, and the paper went on accordingly, under my name for several months.

22 Why *most likely* did Benjamin's father send him to school?

A He wanted one of his children to be educated.

B He wanted his son to help him in his business.

C He wanted Benjamin to become famous.

D He believed that Benjamin was smart.

23 What is the meaning of *govern* in paragraph 4?

A swim

B row

C control

D trade

24 Why did Benjamin's father want him to go to work with his brother?

A to keep him from becoming a sailor.

B to keep him working for the family.

C because his brother needed help.

D because his brother wanted an indentured servant.

25 Why *most likely* did Benjamin resent his brother's imprisonment?

A It made his work harder.

B He believed in free speech.

C He wanted to run the paper

D It made their father mad.

26 Why was the name of the paper changed to BENJAMIN FRANKLIN?

A Benjamin named the new paper after himself.

B Benjamin bought the paper from his brother.

C The government would not let James continue to print his paper.

D The government made James change the name of his paper.

27 Why did James release Benjamin from his indenture?

A because he had helped him

B because he wanted to trick the government.

C because his father asked for Franklin's freedom.

D because his time was up

28 What is the meaning of *admonishing* in paragraph 9?

A imprisoning

B dismissing

C managing

D warning

29 How were Benjamin and James similar?

A They both owned newspapers.

B They were both put in jail.

C They both wanted to be sailors.

D They both liked to write.

30 Why *most likely* did Benjamin think he was right when he and his brother had a dispute?

A His brother always gave in.

B His father liked him best.

C His brother had gone to jail.

D His father usually agreed with him.

Drama Critical Reading

Read the selection and answer the following questions based on the reading.

After the death of her parents, Mary has recently moved into the home of her uncle. She is awoken by the sounds of someone crying.

from The Girl Whose Fortune Sought Her by Patricia Clapp

from The Secret Garden by Frances Hodgson Burnett

"Who are you?" he said at last in a half-frightened whisper. "Are you a ghost?"

"No, I am not," Mary answered, her own whisper sounding half frightened. "Are you one?"

He stared and stared and stared. Mary could not help noticing what strange eyes he had. They were agate gray and they looked too big for his face because they had black lashes all round them.

"No," he replied after waiting a moment or so. "I am Colin."

"Who is Colin?" she faltered.

"I am Colin Craven. Who are you?"

"I am Mary Lennox. Mr. Craven is my uncle."

"He is my father," said the boy.

"Your father!" gasped Mary. "No one ever told me he had a boy! Why didn't they?"

"Come here," he said, still keeping his strange eyes fixed on her with an anxious expression.

She came close to the bed and he put out his hand and touched her.

"You are real, aren't you?" he said. "I have such real dreams very often. You might be one of them."

Mary had slipped on a woolen wrapper before she left her room and she put a piece of it between his fingers.

"Rub that and see how thick and warm it is," she said. "I will pinch you a little if you like, to show you how real I am. For a minute I thought you might be a dream too."

"Where did you come from?" he asked.

"From my own room. The wind wuthered so I couldn't go to sleep and I heard some one crying and wanted to find out who it was. What were you crying for?"

"Because I couldn't go to sleep either and my head ached. Tell me your name again."

"Mary Lennox. Did no one ever tell you I had come to live here?"

He was still fingering the fold of her wrapper, but he began to look a little more as if he believed in her reality.

"No," he answered. "They daren't."

"Why?" asked Mary.

"Because I should have been afraid you would see me. I won't let people see me and talk me over."

"Why?" Mary asked again, feeling more mystified every moment.

"Because I am like this always, ill and having to lie down. My father won't let people talk me over either. The servants are not allowed to speak about me. If I live I may be a hunchback, but I shan't live. My father hates to think I may be like him."

"Oh, what a queer house this is!" Mary said. "What a queer house! Everything is a kind of secret. Rooms are locked up and gardens are locked up—and you! Have you been locked up?"

"No. I stay in this room because I don't want to be moved out of it. It tires me too much."

"Does your father come and see you?" Mary ventured.

"Sometimes. Generally when I am asleep. He doesn't want to see me."

"Why?" Mary could not help asking again.

A sort of angry shadow passed over the boy's face.

"My mother died when I was born and it makes him wretched to look at me. He thinks I don't know, but I've heard people talking. He almost hates me."

"He hates the garden, because she died," said Mary half speaking to herself.

"What garden?" the boy asked.

"Oh! just—just a garden she used to like," Mary stammered. "Have you been here always?"

"How old are you?" he asked.

"I am ten," answered Mary, forgetting herself for the moment, "and so are you."

"How do you know that?" he demanded in a surprised voice.

"Because when you were born the garden door was locked and the key was buried. And it has been locked for ten years."

Colin half sat up, turning toward her, leaning on his elbows.

"What garden door was locked? Who did it? Where was the key buried?" he exclaimed as if he were suddenly very much interested.

"It—it was the garden Mr. Craven hates," said Mary nervously. "He locked the door. No one—no one knew where he buried the key."

"What sort of a garden is it?" Colin persisted eagerly.

"No one has been allowed to go into it for ten years," was Mary's careful answer.

But it was too late to be careful. He was too much like herself. He too had had nothing to think about and the idea of a hidden garden attracted him as it had attracted her. He asked question after question. Where was it? Had she never looked for the door? Had she never asked the gardeners?

"They won't talk about it," said Mary. "I think they have been told not to answer questions."

"I would make them," said Colin.

"Could you?" Mary faltered, beginning to feel frightened. If he could make people answer questions, who knew what might happen!

"Every one is obliged to please me. I told you that," he said. "If I were to live, this place would sometime belong to me. They all know that. I would make them tell me."

Mary had not known that she herself had been spoiled, but she could see quite plainly that this mysterious boy had been. He thought that the whole world belonged to him. How peculiar he was and how coolly he spoke of not living.

Name _____ Date _____

31 **Which of the following statements best describes Colin?**

A He is always excited to see his father.

B He is happy and likes to have visitors.

C He is a sad boy and angry with his father.

D He is timid and afraid of the servants in the house.

32 **Which of the following statements *best* describes how Colin feels?**

A At first he is happy to meet Mary, but later he is afraid of Mary's plans.

B At first he is happy, but later he is worried the servants will discover his meeting with Mary.

C At first he is unsure of Mary, and later he is very excited about the garden.

D At first he is unsure of Mary, and later he is unsure of the garden.

33 **Based on the title of this passage, what do you predict will happen in the story?**

A Soon Mary and Colin will forget about the garden.

B Colin's father will surprise them with a trip to the garden.

C Mary and Colin will try to find the garden.

D The servants will offer to tell Mary and Colin about the garden.

34 **What is the setting of this scene?**

A Mary's room

B the hallway of the great house

C Colin's bedroom

D outside the garden

35 **Based on the context of this selection, why *most likely* do you think the garden was locked?**

A Colin's mother died in the garden.

B Since Colin's mother died, there was no one to care for the garden.

C For Colin's father, having the garden open was a sad reminder of his wife's death.

D Because Colin was young and ill, the garden was too dangerous for him.

36 **Which of the following phrases best describes Colin's father?**

A a man who does not enjoy nature

B a kind man who shows great care for his son

C a man who spends a lot of time with his son

D a man who is still suffering after his wife's death

37 **How are Colin and Mary similar?**

A They are both ten years old and dealing with a serious illness.

B They are attracted to the garden.

C They both have fathers who love them.

D They are both very spoiled.

Casey at the Bat by Ernest Lawrence Thayer

(1)   The outlook wasn't brilliant for the Mudville nine that day:
The score stood four to two, with but one inning more to play,
And then when Cooney died at first, and Barrows did the same,
A pall-like silence fell upon the patrons of the game.

(2)   A straggling few got up to go in deep despair. The rest
Clung to that hope which springs eternal in the human breast;
They thought, "If only Casey could but get a whack at that—
We'd put up even money now, with Casey at the bat.

(3)   But Flynn preceded Casey, as did also Jimmy Blake,
And the former was a hoodoo, while the latter was a cake;
So upon that stricken multitude grim melancholy sat,
For there seemed but little chance of Casey getting to the bat.

(4)   But Flynn let drive a single, to the wonderment of all,
And Blake, the much despised, tore the cover off the ball;
And when the dust had lifted, and men saw what had occurred,
There was Jimmy safe at second and Flynn a-hugging third.

(5)   Then from five thousand throats and more there rose a lusty yell;
It rumbled through the valley, it rattled in the dell;
It pounded on the mountain and recoiled upon the flat,
For Casey, mighty Casey, was advancing to the bat.

(6)   There was ease in Casey's manner as he stepped into his place;
There was pride in Casey's bearing and a smile lit Casey's face.
And when, responding to the cheers, he lightly doffed his hat,
No stranger in the crowd could doubt 'twas Casey at the bat.

(7)   Ten thousand eyes were on him as he rubbed his hands with dirt;
Five thousand tongues applauded when he wiped them on his shirt;
Then while the writhing pitcher ground the ball into his hip,
Defiance flashed in Casey's eye, a sneer curled Case's lip.

(8)   And now the leather-covered sphere came hurtling through the air,
And Casey stood a-watching it in haughty grandeur there.
Close by the sturdy batsman the ball unheeded sped—
"That ain't my style," said Casey. "Strike one!" the umpire said.

(9)   From the benches, black with people, there went up a muffled roar, Like the beating of the storm-
waves on a stern and distant shore;
"Kill him! Kill the umpire!" shouted someone on the stand;
And it's likely they'd have killed him had not Casey raised his hand.

(10) With a smile of Christian charity great Casey's visage shone;
He stilled the rising tumult; he bade the game go on;
He signaled to the pitcher, and once more the dun sphere flew;
But Casey still ignored it and the umpire said, "Strike two!"

(11) "Fraud!" cried the maddened thousands, and echo answered "Fraud!"
But one scornful look from Casey and the audience was awed.
They saw his face grow stern and cold, they saw his muscles strain,
And they knew that Casey wouldn't let that ball go by again.

(12) The sneer is gone from Casey's lip, his teeth are clenched in hate,
He pounds with cruel violence his bat upon the plate;
And now the pitcher holds the ball, and now he lets it go,
And now the air is shattered by the force of Casey's blow.

(13) Oh, somewhere in this favored land the sun is shining bright,
The band is playing somewhere, and somewhere hearts are light;
And somewhere men are laughing, and somewhere children shout,
But there is no joy in Mudville—mighty Casey has struck out.

All-in-One Workbook: Standardized Test Practice
368

38 **Why is the selection a narrative poem?**

   A It has a rhyming beat.

   B It is about a person.

   C It only has one speaker.

   D It tells a story.

39 **What is the speaker's opinion of Flynn and Blake in stanza 3?**

   A He does not want them on the team.

   B He thinks they are good players.

   C He thinks they are weak players.

   D He wants them thrown out of the game.

40 **Based on stanza 5, what happened when Casey walked to home plate to bat?**

   A The crowd became very quiet.

   B The crowd yelled wildly.

   C People all around the country side started yelling.

   D People became very concerned.

41 **Which of the following *best* describes Casey**

   A A good player who never misses the ball.

   B The best player on the team.

   C A good player who is overly confident.

   D The only player who smiles at the crowd.

42 **What is ironic about the poem?**

   A The players that the speaker thought were weak hit the ball and Casey did not.

   B The crowd was yelling at the umpire not at the players.

   C The very loud crowd became very quiet at the end of the poem.

   D The crowd changed from very happy with Casey to very angry with him.

43 **Based on the context of stanza 10, what is the meaning of visage?**

   A baseball term

   B umpire's term

   C facial expression

   D happy expression

44 **Why *most likely* did Casey not try to hit the first two balls?**

   A The balls were no good.

   B He was showing off.

   C He wanted to frighten the crowd.

   D The balls were hard to hit.

45 **Why was it important for Casey to hit the ball at the time described in the selection?**

   A The team was losing badly.

   B The team had a chance to make one or possibly two runs.

   C It was the last chance for Casey to play with the team.

   D It was the last game of the season.

Dracula by Bram Stoker 1897 Edition

1)   *Fictional stories about vampires have always fascinated readers. You may have read a vampire story or possibly you have seen the movie Buffy the Vampire Slayer or an episode of the television series of the same name. Almost everyone enjoys a good scary story. Read the following excerpt from chapter two of Bram Stoker's Dracula the 1897 edition. Most readers would agree that Dracula is the "Grand-daddy" of the vampire stories.*

CHAPTER 2

Jonathan Harker's Journal Continued

2)   5 May.—I must have been asleep, for certainly if I had been fully awake I must have noticed the approach of such a remarkable place. In the gloom the courtyard looked of considerable size, and as several dark ways led from it under great round arches, it perhaps seemed bigger than it really is. I have not yet been able to see it by daylight.

3)   When the caleche stopped, the driver jumped down and held out his hand to assist me to alight. Again I could not but notice his prodigious strength. His hand actually seemed like a steel vice that could have crushed mine if he had chosen. Then he took my traps, and placed them on the ground beside me as I stood close to a great door, old and studded with large iron nails, and set in a projecting doorway of massive stone. I could see even in the dim light that the stone was massively carved, but that the carving had been much worn by time and weather. As I stood, the driver jumped again into his seat and shook the reins. The horses started forward, and trap and all disappeared down one of the dark openings.

4)   I stood in silence where I was, for I did not know what to do. Of bell or knocker there was no sign. Through these frowning walls and dark window openings it was not likely that my voice could penetrate. The time I waited seemed endless, and I felt doubts and fears crowding upon me. What sort of place had I come to, and among what kind of people? What sort of grim adventure was it on which I had embarked?....

5)   ... I heard a heavy step approaching behind the great door, and saw through the chinks the gleam of a coming light. Then there was the sound of rattling chains and the clanking of massive bolts drawn back. A key was turned with the loud grating noise of long disuse, and the great door swung back.

6)   Within, stood a tall old man, clean-shaven save for a long white moustache, and clad in black from head to foot, without a single speck of colour about him anywhere. He held in his hand an antique silver lamp, in which the flame burned without a chimney or globe of any kind, throwing long quivering shadows as it flickered in the draught of the open door. The old man motioned me in with his right hand with a courtly gesture, saying in excellent English, but with a strange intonation.

7)   "Welcome to my house! Enter freely and of your own free will!" He made no motion of stepping to meet me, but stood like a statue, as though his gesture of welcome had fixed him into stone. The instant, however, that I had stepped over the threshold, he moved impulsively forward, and holding out his hand grasped mine with a strength which made me wince, an effect which was not lessened by the fact that it seemed cold as ice, more like the hand of a dead than a living man. Again he said,

8)   "Welcome to my house! Enter freely. Go safely, and leave something of the happiness you

bring!" The strength of the handshake was so much akin to that which I had noticed in the driver, whose face I had not seen, that for a moment I doubted if it were not the same person to whom I was speaking. So to make sure, I said interrogatively, "Count Dracula?"

9) He bowed in a courtly way as he replied, "I am Dracula, and I bid you welcome, Mr. Harker, to my house. Come in, the night air is chill, and you must need to eat and rest." As he was speaking, he put the lamp on a bracket on the wall, and stepping out, took my luggage. He had carried it in before I could forestall him. I protested, but he insisted.

10) "Nay, sir, you are my guest. It is late, and my people are not available. Let me see to your comfort myself." He insisted on carrying my traps along the passage, and then up a great winding stair, and along another great passage, on whose stone floor our steps rang heavily. At the end of this he threw open a heavy door, and I rejoiced to see within a well-lit room in which a table was spread for supper, and on whose mighty hearth a great fire of logs, freshly replenished, flamed and flared.

11) The Count halted, putting down my bags, closed the door, and crossing the room, opened another door, which led into a small octagonal room lit by a single lamp, and seemingly without a window of any sort. Passing through this, he opened another door, and motioned me to enter. It was a welcome sight. For here was a great bedroom well lighted and warmed with another log fire, also added to but lately, for the top logs were fresh, which sent a hollow roar up the wide chimney. The Count himself left my luggage inside and withdrew, saying, before he closed the door.

12) "You will need, after your journey, to refresh yourself by making your toilet. I trust you will find all you wish. When you are ready, come into the other room, where you will find your supper prepared."

13) The light and warmth and the Count's courteous welcome seemed to have dissipated all my doubts and fears. Having then reached my normal state, I discovered that I was half famished with hunger. So making a hasty toilet, I went into the other room.

14) I found supper already laid out. My host, who stood on one side of the great fireplace, leaning against the stonework, made a graceful wave of his hand to the table, and said, "I pray you, be seated and sup how you please. You will I trust, excuse me that I do not join you, but I have dined already, and I do not sup."

15) The count himself came forward and took off the cover of a dish, and I fell to at once on an excellent roast chicken. This, with some cheese and a salad and a bottle of old tokay, of which I had two glasses, was my supper. During the time I was eating it the Count asked me many questions as to my journey, and I told him by degrees all I had experienced.

16) By this time, I had finished my supper, and by my host's desire had drawn up a chair by the fire and begun to smoke a cigar, which he offered me, at the same time excusing himself that he did not smoke. I had now an opportunity of observing him, and found him of a very marked physiognomy.

17) His face was a strong, a very strong, aquiline, with high bridge of the thin nose and peculiarly arched nostrils, with lofty domed forehead, and hair growing scantily round the temples but profusely elsewhere. His eyebrows were very massive, almost meeting over the nose, and with bushy hair that seemed to curl in its own profusion. The mouth, so far as I could see it under the heavy moustache, was fixed and rather cruel-looking, with peculiarly sharp white teeth. These protruded over the lips, whose remarkable ruddiness showed astonishing vitality in a man of his years. For the rest, his ears were pale, and at the tops extremely pointed. The chin was broad and strong, and the cheeks firm though thin. The general effect was one of extraordinary pallor.

18) Hitherto, I had noticed the backs of his hands as they lay on his knees in the firelight, and they

had seemed rather white and fine. But seeing them now close to me, I could not but notice that they were rather coarse, broad, with squat fingers. Strange to say, there were hairs in the centre of the palm. The nails were long and fine, and cut to a sharp point. As the Count leaned over me and his hands touched me, I could not repress a shudder. It may have been that his breath was rank, but a horrible feeling of nausea came over me, which, do what I would, I could not conceal.

19) The Count, evidently noticing it, drew back. And with a grim sort of smile, which showed more than he had yet done his protuberant teeth, sat himself down again on his own side of the fireplace. We were both silent for a while, and as I looked towards the window I saw the first dim streak of the coming dawn. There seemed a strange stillness over everything. But as I listened, I heard as if from down below in the valley the howling of many wolves. The Count's eyes gleamed, and he said,

20) "Listen to them, the children of the night. What music they make!" Seeing, I suppose, some expression in my face strange to him, he added, "Ah, sir, you dwellers in the city cannot enter into the feelings of the hunter." Then he rose and said.

21) "But you must be tired. Your bedroom is all ready, and tomorrow you shall sleep as late as you will. I have to be away till the afternoon, so sleep well and dream well!" With a courteous bow, he opened for me himself the door to the octagonal room, and I entered my bedroom.

22) I am all in a sea of wonders. I doubt. I fear. I think strange things, which I dare not confess to my own soul. God keep me, if only for the sake of those dear to me!

46 Based on the context of paragraph 3, what is the meaning of caleche?

   A a coachman

   B a castle

   C a carriage

   D a door

47 What did Jonathan find unusual about the Count's behavior in paragraph 7?

   A He had very cold hands.

   B He moved quickly for an old man.

   C He had great strength.

   D He did not step to meet his visitor.

48 Which of the following best describes the author's purpose for paragraph 17?

   A It lets the reader know how the Count looked.

   B It lets the reader know that the Count had bad breath.

   C It lets the reader know that the Count seemed friendly.

   D It lets the reader know that the Count was very strong.

49 Which best describes the Count's feelings towards the wolves in paragraph 20?

   A He appreciates the wolves.

   B He fears the wolves.

   C He feels the wolves are his children.

   D He considers himself a hunter.

50 Which of the following best describe the Count in the selection?

   A evil and frightening

   B strong and very pale

   C cold and talkative

   D mysterious and courteous

51 Which of the following best describes how Jonathan reacts to this meeting?

   A He is cold and frightened.

   B He likes his food and his nice sleeping quarters.

   C He is confused and fearful of his own thoughts.

   D He doesn't understand what is happening.

52 Which of the following does the author use most often in the selection to create reader interest?

   A vivid descriptions

   B suspense

   C figurative language

   D sounds

Thank You Letters *are always appreciated*

Has someone done something nice for you recently? Are you planning to look for a summer job? Well, if you answered yes to either of these questions this news is for you.

Many people forget or overlook writing a thank you note. However, they are appropriate, show good manners and are a sincere way to show your interest.

Personal thank you notes should be sent when someone has done something special for you. It could be that they went out of their way to help you with a project or maybe they took time from their busy schedule to take you somewhere. Thank you notes aren't just for presents, but of course, you would want to send a note if you did receive a gift.

Before you begin to write think about the person you are planning to thank. It is always nice to mention something in the note that you have in common. Thank you notes don't have to be long. A short, to the point note that is sincere will have meaning for the person that receives your letter. In this very busy world, a hand written thank you note is a pleasant surprise to find in the mailbox.

A thank you note after a job interview can reap great rewards. Often, this step is overlooked. The note will make your name stand out in the interviewers mind and might help you land a great summer job. The note should be written the day after your interview. Unlike the personal thank you note, the business thank you should be written on your typewriter or computer. The paper should be nice but not fancy. Address the recipient with a formal Mr. or Ms. Thank the interviewer for a great interview, and then describe what made it great. For example, you might mention the good exchange of ideas or that you see the job as a wonderful opportunity. Add in a few of your ideas or mention something that you said in the interview that the interviewer liked. Complete your letter with the appropriate type of closing. "Sincerely", "Yours truly", or "Gratefully" are acceptable for business letters.

In many ways, thank you letters may seem old-fashioned to you. You may be thinking a short email or a phone call will work just as well as a letter. This can be true when you need to correspond to someone that you know very well, but don't underestimate the power of a well written thank you note. Letters go a long way to show your manners, sincerity, and attitude. They are easy to write and a great way to make a good impression.

53 **What is the main idea of the selection?**

A Handwritten notes are better than emails.

B Always write a thank you note after a job interview.

C Thank you notes are a good way to show sincere appreciation.

D Thank you notes are hard to write but they show good manners.

54 **How is a business note different from a personal note?**

A A business note is more formal.

B A personal note is shorter.

C A business note should be handwritten.

D A personal note should always be an email.

55 **Why is it to your advantage for the interviewer to remember your name?**

A They only hire people they know.

B They don't keep records of interviews.

C It will ensure that you get the job.

D It may increase your chances for getting the job.

ITBS PRACTICE TEST

Vocabulary

DIRECTIONS

This is a test about words and their meanings.

■ For each question, you are to decide which one of the four answers has most nearly the same meaning as the underlined word above it.

■ Then, on your answer folder, find the row of answer spaces numbered the same as the question. Fill in the answer space that has the same letter as the answer you picked.

The sample on this page shows you what the questions are like and how to mark your answers.

SAMPLE

S1 Getting enough <u>exercise</u>
   A excitement
   B work finished
   C enjoyment of life
   D movement of the body

ANSWER
S1 A B C **D**

Vocabulary

1 To <u>cease</u> fighting

A enjoy
B avoid
C receive
D halt

2 To tell an <u>anecdote</u>

J funny story
K strong argument
L riddle
M untruth

3 Discovered a <u>rarity</u>

A something underground
B anything difficult
C something uncommon
D anything remembered

4 A <u>genteel</u> officer

J polite
K well-trained
L well-armed
M gruff

5 The <u>nimble</u> mouse

A hungry
B quick
C tame
D naughty

6 He showed great <u>valor</u>.

J dancing skill
K courage
L sense of adventure
M understanding

7 A <u>petite</u> girl

A having good manners
B dressing with style
C short and thin
D long and lean

8 An <u>oath</u> given

J promise
K gift
L support
M alarm

9 <u>Genuine</u> leather

A tough
B real
C new
D sold

10 The police <u>relented</u>.

J patrolled
K softened
L continued
M chased

11 To <u>wreak</u> destruction

A break
B escape
C add to
D carry out

12 The glasses <u>cascaded</u>.

J broke into pieces
K slid across
L were cleaned
M fell like water

13 Full of <u>mirth</u>

A mixture
B danger
C happiness
D togetherness

14 An <u>outstanding</u> job

J difficult
K long waited for
L high quality
M serious

Reading Comprehension

DIRECTIONS

This is a test of how well you understand what you read.

■ This test consists of reading passages followed by questions.

■ Read each passage and then answer the questions.

■ Four answers are given for each question. You are to choose the answer that you think is better than the others.

■ Then, on your answer folder, find the row of answer spaces numbered the same as the question. Fill in the answer space for the best answer.

The sample on this page shows you what the questions are like and how to mark your answers.

SAMPLE

> Demi watched her new treasure sink beneath the surface of the lake. She was not in a hurry to get home because she knew she would have to tell her father what happened. He had spent quite a bit of money on that doll.

S1 **Why is Demi not in a hurry to get home?**

   A She wants to go and buy another doll.
   B She is afraid her father will be angry.
   C She is having a lot of fun at the lake.
   D She wants to look for her doll in the lake.

ANSWER
S1 A B C D

This is an excerpt from an adaptation of a speech by American Indian speaker and diplomat, Chief Seattle. Originally delivered in the 1850s, Chief Seattle's message was modified by screenwriter Ted Perry for use in a 1972 film about ecology.

¶1   The President in Washington sends word that he wishes to buy our land. But how can you buy or sell the sky? The land? The idea is strange to us. If we do not own the freshness of the air and the sparkle of the water, how can you buy them?

¶2   Every part of the earth is sacred to my people. Every shining pine needle, every sandy shore, every mist in the dark woods, every meadow, every humming insect. All are holy in the memory and experience of my people. . . .

¶3   The shining water that moves in the streams and rivers is not just water, but the blood of our ancestors. If we sell you our land, you must remember that it is sacred. Each ghostly reflection in the clear water of the lake tells of events and memories in the life of my people. The water's murmur is the voice of my father's father.

¶4   The rivers are our brothers. They quench our thirst. They carry our canoes and feed our children. So you must give the rivers the kindness you would give any brother.

¶5   If we sell you our land, remember that the air is precious to us, that the air shares its spirit with all the life it supports. The wind that gave our grandfather his first breath also receives his last sigh. The wind also gives our children the spirit of life. So if we sell you our land, you must keep it apart and sacred, as a place where man can go to taste the wind that is sweetened by the meadow flowers. . . .

¶6   This we know: The earth does not belong to man, man belongs to the earth. All things are connected like the blood which unites us all. Man did not weave the web of life, he is merely a strand in it. Whatever he does to the web, he does to himself. . . .

¶7   Your destiny is a mystery to us. What will happen when the buffalo are all slaughtered? The wild horses tamed? What will happen when the secret corners of the forest are heavy with the scent of many men and the view of the ripe hills is blotted by talking wires? Where will the thicket be? Gone! Where will the eagle be? Gone! And what is it to say goodbye to the swift pony and the hunt? The end of living and the beginning of survival.

¶8   When the last Red Man has vanished with his wilderness and his memory is only the shadow of a cloud moving across the prairie, will these shores and forests still be here? Will there be any of the spirit of my people left?

1 **What is the main idea of this essay?**

A The memories of people are connected to their homeland.

B People should never try to sell land that belongs to their family.

C The spirits of Native Americans live on in the water and air.

D People should respect the land because it gives them life.

2 **What is the effect of the writer asking questions in paragraphs 1, 7, and 8?**

J It forces the reader to think more carefully about the ideas in the passage.

K It makes the reader wonder how much the writer knows about his subject.

L It challenges the reader to look for the answers somewhere in the paragraph.

M It persuades the reader to agree with the ideas in the passage.

3 **What prompts the narrator to discuss how important the earth is to his people?**

A Determination not to sell his land

B Appreciation for the beauty of the dark woods

C Concern for what whites will do to it

D Hope that his father's spirit will remain

4 **Why does the narrator think the idea of buying land is so strange?**

J The narrator has inherited land, not bought it.

K It is too hard to set a price on water and air.

L The narrator does not understand money.

M You cannot buy what is not owned.

5 **How does the author of this essay feel about the earth?**

A He is puzzled by its mysteries.

B He believes that it is sacred.

C He is worried that it will vanish.

D He wishes that he owned it.

6 **What does the narrator think the white people will do after they have bought the land?**

J Sell it

K Ruin it

L Work it

M Worship it

7 **How does the author feel about white people?**

A He does not know any of them.

B He does not believe them.

C He does not understand them.

D He does not like them.

8 **In paragraph 7, what does "talking wires" mean?**

J Television cables

K Clothes lines

L Telephone wires

M Radio wires

9 **The tone of this essay is one of**

A anger.

B melancholy.

C humor.

D mystery.

Little Boy Blue by Eugene Field

The little toy dog is covered with dust,
  But sturdy and stanch he stands;
And the little toy soldier is red with rust,
  And his musket molds in his hands.
Time was when the little toy dog was new
  And the soldier was passing fair,
And that was the time when our Little Boy Blue
  Kissed them and put them there.

"Now, don't you go till I come," he said,
  "And don't you make any noise!"
So toddling off to his trundle-bed
  He dreamed of the pretty toys.
And as he was dreaming, an angel song
  Awakened our Little Boy Blue,—
Oh, the years are many, the years are long,
  But the little toy friends are true.

Ay, faithful to Little Boy Blue they stand,
  Each in the same old place,
Awaiting the touch of a little hand,
  The smile of a little face.
And they wonder, as waiting these long years through,
  In the dust of that little chair,
What has become of our Little Boy Blue
  Since he kissed them and put them there.

10 What *most likely* is the setting of the poem?

J a shop with old toys

K a bedroom which was used by a little boy many years ago

L an old playground

M a bedroom of a little boy who just went to sleep

11 In line 3, why is the little toy soldier red with rust?

A No one has played with the toy soldier for a long time.

B The toy soldier was left out in the rain.

C Little Boy Blue painted his toys red.

D The toy soldier was thrown away with the trash.

12 How does the little boy feel about the toys?

J He loves them and treats them like they are his friends.

K He thinks they are too noisy.

L He has out-grown them.

M He doesn't like them because they are old.

13 Based on the context of this poem, who is Little Boy Blue?

A the little boy who just went to bed

B the boy in the nursery rhyme

C a sad little boy

D the boy who owns the toys

14 Based on the context of the poem, which of the following statements *could be true*?

J The toys are waiting for someone to play with them.

K The little boy has grown up, and this is his old room.

L The little boy dreamed of his toys and angels.

M all of the above

Statement of Senator Obama on the Death of Rosa Parks

On Tuesday, October 25, 2005, Senator Obama spoke from the Senate Floor. He spoke about Rosa Parks, a black woman whose actions helped bring about freedom for all people in America.

1)   Mr. President, today the nation mourns a genuine American hero. Rosa Parks died yesterday in her home in Detroit. Through her courage and by her example, Rosa Parks helped lay the foundation for a country that could begin to live up to its creed.

2)   Her life, and her brave actions, reminded each and every one of us of our personal responsibilities to stand up for what is right and the central truth of the American experience that our greatness as a nation derives from seemingly ordinary people doing extraordinary things.

3)   Rosa Parks' life was a lesson in perseverance. As a child, she grew up listening to the Ku Klux Klan ride by her house and lying in bed at night fearing that her house would be burnt down. In her small hometown in Alabama, she attended a one-room school for African-American children that only went through the sixth grade. When she moved to Montgomery, Alabama, to continue her schooling, she was forced to clean classrooms after school to pay her tuition. Although she attended Alabama State Teachers College, Rosa Parks would later make her living as a seamstress and housekeeper.

4)   But she didn't accept that her opportunities were limited to sewing clothes or cleaning houses. In her forties, Rosa Parks was appointed secretary of the Montgomery branch of the NAACP and was active in voter registration drives with the Montgomery Voters League. In the summer of 1955, she attended the Highlander Folk School, where she took classes in workers' rights and racial equality. Well before she made headlines across the country, she was a highly respected member of the Montgomery community and a committed member of the civil rights effort.

5)   Of course, her name became permanently etched in American history on December 1, 1955, when she was arrested for refusing to give up her seat to a white passenger on a Montgomery bus. It wasn't the first time Rosa Parks refused to acquiesce to the Jim Crow system. The same bus driver who had her arrested had thrown her off a bus the year before for refusing to give up her seat.

6)   Some schoolchildren are taught that Rosa Parks refused to give up her seat because her feet were tired. Our nation's schoolbooks are only getting it half right. She once said: "The only tired I was, was tired of giving in."

7)   This solitary act of civil disobedience became a call to action. Her arrest led a then relatively unknown pastor, Martin Luther King, Jr., to organize a boycott of the Montgomery bus system. That boycott lasted 381 days and culminated in a landmark Supreme Court decision finding that the city's segregation policy was unconstitutional.

8)   This solitary act of civil disobedience was also the spark that ignited the beginning of the end for segregation and inspired millions around the country and ultimately around the world to get involved in the fight for racial equality.

9)   Rosa Parks' persistence and determination did not end that day in Montgomery, nor did it end with the passage of the Civil Rights Act and Voting Rights Act years later. She stayed active in the NAACP and other civil rights groups for years. From 1965 to 1988, Ms. Parks continued her public service by working for my good friend Congressman John Conyers. And in an example of her low-key demeanor, her job in Congressman Conyers' office did not involve appearances as a figurehead or celebrity; she helped homeless folks find housing.

10)   At the age of 74, she opened the Rosa and Raymond Parks Institute for Self-Development, which offers education and job training programs for disadvantaged youth. And even into her 80s, Rosa Parks gave lectures and attended meetings with civil rights groups.

11)   At the age of 86, Rosa Parks' courage and fortitude was recognized by President Bill Clinton, who awarded her the nation's highest honor for a civilian—the Congressional Gold Medal.

12)   As we honor the life of Rosa Parks, we should not limit our commemorations to lofty eulogies. Instead, let us commit ourselves to carrying on her fight, one solitary act at a time, and ensure that her passion continues to inspire as it did a half-century ago. That, in my view, is how we can best thank her for her immense contributions to our country.

15 **Where did Senator Obama make his statement about Rosa Parks?**

A at the White House

B at Rosa Parks's house

C on the Senate Floor

D on the Freedom Trail

16 **What is one reason Rosa Parks's childhood was difficult?**

J She didn't know how to read.

K Her parents were killed by the Ku Klux Klan.

L She feared that her house would be burned down by the Ku Klux Klan.

M She was forced to work in a factory after school.

17 **Which of the following statements best describes Rosa Parks?**

A a brave woman who was determined to make a difference in the lives of others

B an uneducated woman who unknowingly started a change

C a good friend of Dr. Martin Luther King, Jr., even before she refused to give up her bus seat

D a brave woman who was qualified only to be a seamstress or housekeeper

18 **According to the passage, why did Rosa Parks refuse to give up her bus seat?**

J She was tired after a long day at work.

K She was tired of unfair treatment.

L Martin Luther King, Jr., had encouraged her to act.

M She was following the lead of others on the bus who did not give up their seats

19 **How did Rosa Parks stay active in civil rights causes?**

A She gave lectures.

B She helped homeless people find housing.

C She was active with the NAACP.

D all of the above

20 **Based on the context of paragraph 5, what does the word *acquiesce* mean?**

J give in to

K protest

L stand up to

M notice

21 **Why did President Clinton award Rosa Parks with the Congressional Medal of Honor?**

A to recognize her courage and fortitude

B to recognize her solitary act that made a difference

C to recognize her as a leader in the fight for people's rights

D all of the above

22 **Which of the following would Rosa Parks *most likely* recommend?**

J Work with community-based organizations to help others.

K Forcefully demand service if it has been denied.

L Enjoy the rights that you have been given and do not expect more.

M Work together to make changes; individuals cannot make a difference.

from Famous Female Mathematicians

Florence Nightingale

1)   Florence Nightingale is usually remembered for her groundbreaking work as a nurse. It is less well known that she was also a highly respected mathematician. In her life, she successfully combined these two interests. As a consequence, she was able to accomplish some extremely important goals.

2)   **Early Years** Nightingale was born on May 12, 1820, in Florence, Italy. Her English parents were touring Europe at the time, and they decided to name their baby after the city where she was born. As a young girl, Nightingale was fascinated by math, according to her sister. Her father served as the children's tutor for much of their childhood, teaching the children history, the classics, and math. Nightingale's mother felt that as a young woman of a certain position Florence should learn the subjects that would make her a good wife and household manager. By the time Nightingale was 20, she pleaded with her parents to free her from studying needlework and dancing so she could focus on what really interested her. She finally convinced her parents. They agreed to hire tutors for Florence's studies in arithmetic, geometry, and algebra.

3)   As a young woman, Nightingale tutored children in math. She felt that the standard education for young girls at that time was too confining, with its focus on domestic skills. She was concerned that most girls did not receive a satisfactory education in mathematics. Nightingale wanted very much to improve the way math was taught. She used a strategy of posing questions to her students, called the Socratic method. Socrates, for whom this teaching technique is named, was a famous Greek philosopher and teacher. Nightingale hoped that by constantly questioning assumptions, her students would not only solve math problems, but they would also learn how to think for themselves.

4)   **Years As a Nurse** In addition to her interest in mathematics, Nightingale had also developed an interest in many social issues of the time. She decided to study nursing to help other people. At the time, nursing was not considered a respectable career, and her parents tried to dissuade her from it. Nightingale was determined, though, and took on the challenge of pursuing a nursing career.

5)   After completing her nursing studies, Nightingale was asked by the British Secretary for War to become a nursing administrator. It was 1854, and the Crimean War had begun when France, Turkey, and Britain declared war on Russia. Nightingale's assignment was to train nurses in the military hospitals that tended to wounded soldiers. She traveled to Istanbul, Turkey, to oversee the hospital there. What she found once she got there was shocking! Wounded soldiers were kept in very unsanitary conditions. Sheets and bandages were seldom washed. Wounded soldiers were sleeping on the floor. Rats ran freely throughout the hospital. Nightingale tried to convince the British military to do something about these terrible conditions, but she was not able to sway them at first.

6)   Finally, she used her mathematical ability to collect data and organize records. She believed unclean conditions were a factor in the high number of deaths of the wounded. She then set out to use mathematics, specifically statistics, to convince others of her point of view. She developed a visual, called a *polar-area chart*. The chart showed the statistical relationship between the hospital deaths and the conditions. In this sort of chart, a statistic is represented by a proportional wedge-shaped area in a circular diagram. Through the use of these charts, Nightingale was able to prove her point. The death rate of the wounded would decrease as the result of more sanitary conditions.

7)   Statistics shown in charts were a dramatic way to emphasize the unnecessary deaths that were taking place. Nightingale's approach was able to convince the military to change their methods in caring for the wounded. Her predictions for survival rates proved accurate after the reforms took place.

23 Based on the context of paragraph 4, what is the meaning of the word *dissuade*?

  A to persuade someone not to do something

  B to convince someone to do something

  C to encourage

  D to challenge

24 Which of the following best describes Florence Nightingale's view of education?

  J Students needed to learn to think for themselves.

  K Math education for girls needed to be strengthened.

  L Girls were spending too much time learning needlework.

  M all of the above

25 Why did Nightingale use the Socratic method of teaching?

  A She felt that the constant questioning would teach students to think for themselves.

  B This was the method her father used as a tutor, and he found it very successful.

  C She felt that asking questions was easier than answering the questions.

  D She was both a philosopher and a nurse.

26 What is the purpose of this selection?

  J to entertain the reader

  K to persuade any reader who is considering nursing to study math as well

  L to inform the reader of Nightingale's successful combination of math and nursing skills

  M to question the sanitary conditions in hospitals

27 Which of the following best describes Nightingale's parents?

  A They wanted their daughter to marry at a young age.

  B They agreed to let their daughter study mathematics.

  C They encouraged Florence to choose a career like nursing so she could help others.

  D Her father provided her a math tutor because he was not as skilled in math himself.

28 What is the main idea of the "Year As a Nurse" section?

  J Using math, Nightingale proved that soldiers were dying because of unsanitary hospital conditions.

  K To be successful in nursing, it is important to make charts and diagrams.

  L Nightingale led a protest against a hospital in Istanbul, Turkey that had unsanitary conditions.

  M Nightingale was not able to convince the British military of the problem of unsanitary hospital conditions.

29 Based on the context of paragraph 5, what does the word *unsanitary* mean?

  A uncomfortable

  B painful

  C unclean

  D poor

30 What *most likely* happened after reforms took place?

  J Fewer soldiers died unnecessarily.

  K More hospitals were built in Europe.

  L The military gave Nightingale a medal of honor.

  M The death rate of wounded soldiers continued to increase.

Spelling

DIRECTIONS

This test will show how well you can spell.

- Many of the questions in this test contain mistakes in spelling. Some do not have any mistakes at all.

- You should look for mistakes in spelling.

- When you find a mistake, fill in the answer space on your answer folder that has the same letter as the **line** containing the mistake.

- If there is no mistake, fill in the last answer space.

The samples on this page show you what the questions are like and how to mark your answers.

SAMPLES

S1 A   crisp
       B   bright
       C   washed
       D   appel
       E   (No mistakes)

S2 J   silver
       K   copper
       L   bronze
       M   nickel
       N   *(No mistakes)*

ANSWERS

S1 A B C **D** E

S2 J K L M **N**

Spelling

1
A ligten
B glitch
C thorough
D borrow
E *(No mistakes)*

2
J stallion
K oriental
L accidentel
M tournament
N *(No mistakes)*

3
A trophy
B ability
C catastrophe
D commitee
E *(No mistakes)*

4
J reproduce
K proportion
L installation
M lettuce
N *(No mistakes)*

5
A indignant
B severance
C preparation
D allowense
E *(No mistakes)*

6
J tremendous
K torrential
L pourous
M emperor
N *(No mistakes)*

7
A tremble
B tenous
C extend
D delirious
E *(No mistakes)*

8
J incidental
K practicing
L galactic
M significant
N *(No mistakes)*

9
A gaget
B rocket
C hatchet
D college
E *(No mistakes)*

10
J invisible
K fairy
L totalety
M entirety
N *(No mistakes)*

11
A nibbled
B antelope
C cantalope
D builder
E *(No mistakes)*

12
J energize
K anesthesia
L gypsy
M incapible
N *(No mistakes)*

13
A dabbling
B gossiped
C irresistible
D graple
E *(No mistakes)*

14
J hereditary
K ordinery
L intrigue
M boredom
N *(No mistakes)*

Capitalization

DIRECTIONS

This is a test on capitalization. It will show how well you can use capital letters in sentences.

■ You should look for mistakes in capitalization in the sentences on this test.

■ When you find a mistake, fill in the answer space on your answer folder that has the same letter as the **line** containing the mistake.

■ Some sentences do not have any mistakes at all. If there is no mistake, fill in the last answer space.

The samples on this page show you what the questions are like and how to mark your answers.

SAMPLES

S1 A My birthday is on
     B june 25, and I am
     C having a party.
     D *(No mistakes)*

S2 J My Aunt asked
     K my cousin to bring
     L his pet horse.
     M *(No mistakes)*

S3 A The horse's name
     B is Lightfoot, and he
     C is an Arabian.
     D *(No mistakes)*

ANSWERS

S1 A **B** C D
S2 **J** K L M
S3 A B C **D**

Capitalization

1
A Although Mark Twain traveled
B widely, his boyhood experiences
C on the Mississippi river affected
   him most.
D *(No mistakes)*

2
J The Congress avenue bridge
K is home to the largest urban colony
   of bats.
L I have tried but never suceeded in
   seeing them.
M *(No mistakes)*

3
A Every Saturday night, more than
   two million
B listeners tune in to Garrison
   Keillor's
C radio show, "A Prairie Home
   Companion."
D *(No mistakes)*

4
J For years, astronauts have
   conducted
K experiments to learn about
   living in
L space, maybe even on the Moon.
M *(No mistakes)*

5
A The underground Railroad was a
   network
B of people who helped slaves escape
   from
C the South in the mid-1800s.
D *(No mistakes)*

6
J Many of the Pilgrims who first
   came to
K America were members of the
   puritan
L sect, who were unpopular in
   England.
M *(No mistakes)*

7
A I find some of the strangest people
B enjoy listening to AM radio.
   stranger
C ones still listen to the FM stuff.
D *(No mistakes)*

8
J The Yukon Territory is in the
K northwestern corner of Canada,
L just beside alaska.
M *(No mistakes)*

9
A History's largest gold rush took
   place
B in august of 1896 near a river
C called Dawson's Creek.
D *(No mistakes)*

10
J Taiwan has been occupied by
   Portugal,
K China, Holland, and Japan. Today,
   it is
L home to many who fled Mainland
   China.
M *(No mistakes)*

11
A Langston Hughes published his
   first
B collection of poetry, *The Weary
   blues,*
C in 1926. By 1930, he was famous.
D *(No mistakes)*

12
J One of Russia's, and perhaps the
   world's,
K greatest writers, Leo Tolstoy, died
L seven years before the Russian
   revolution.
M *(No mistakes)*

Punctuation

DIRECTIONS

This is a test on punctuation. It will show how well you can use periods, question marks, commas, and other kinds of punctuation marks.

■ You should look for mistakes in punctuation in the sentences on this test.

■ When you find a mistake, fill in the answer space on your answer folder that has the same letter as the **line** containing the mistake.

■ Some sentences do not have any mistakes at all. If there is no mistake, fill in the last answer space.

The samples on this page show you what the questions are like and how to mark your answers.

SAMPLES

S1 A When he spotted the
B water fountain, Bill
C said, "Finally!"
D *(No mistakes)*

S2 J How long had he been
K running? He was too
L tired to remember?
M *(No mistakes)*

S3 A He knew he had started
B at 8:00 A.M, but what
C time was it now?
D *(No mistakes)*

ANSWERS

S1 A B C **D**

S2 J K **L** M

S3 A **B** C D

Punctuation

1   **A**   Carved into a peak, Mount Rushmore has the
    B   heads of four U.S. presidents Washington,
    C   Jefferson, Lincoln, and Teddy Roosevelt.
    D   *(No mistakes)*

2   **J**   In 1936, the United States was in
    K   the middle of the Great Depression a time
    L   of economic struggle.
    M   *(No mistakes)*

3   **A**   Between 1892 and 1924 more than
    B   12,000,000 immigrants entered the
    C   United States through Ellis Island.
    D   *(No mistakes)*

4   **J**   Carl Sandburg said of Americans
    K   during the Great Depression "The people
    L   will live on . . . and come back."
    M   *(No mistakes)*

5   **A**   On a trip from California to New York,
    B   John Steinbeck passed through the Mojave
    C   Desert; Texas; and the Deep South.
    D   *(No mistakes)*

6   **J**   Carhenge is a replica of Stonehenge.
    K   It is built entirely out of American
    L   cars stacked on top of each other
    M   *(No mistakes)*

7   **A**   Dear Allan and Julia Stiles.
    B   I am very sorry for your loss,
    C   and I know things will be better soon.
    D   *(No mistakes)*

8   **J**   "Tell them I hope the funeral is just
    K   beautiful, was what Mom said, and
    L   then she just started crying again.
    M   *(No mistakes)*

9   **A**   Skippy was a good friend and a loyal
    B   companion. so full of life and love that
    C   it seemed he would live forever.
    D   *(No mistakes)*

10   **J**   Can you ever love another dog
    K   I certainly hope so because
    L   I'm sending along a new friend for you.
    M   *(No mistakes)*

11   **A**   The puppy's name is Winston, and he
    B   licks your face just the way Skippy did.
    C   He eats puppy food now, but he's growing.
    D   *(No mistakes)*

12   **J**   Try to write back and tell me what you think.
    K   With much love
    L   Wendy Jackson
    M   *(No mistakes)*

Usage and Expression

PART 1 DIRECTIONS

This is a test on the use of words. It will show how well you can use words according to the standards of correctly written English.

■ You should look for mistakes in the sentences on this test.

■ When you find a mistake, fill in the answer space on your answer folder that has the same letter as the **line** containing the mistake.

■ Some sentences do not have any mistakes at all. If there is no mistake, fill in the last answer space.

The samples on this page show you what the questions are like and how to mark your answers.

SAMPLES

S1 **A** If dogs are called man's
B best friend, shouldn't
C it be nice to men?
D *(No mistakes)*

S2 **J** I have had three dogs
K in my life, and not one
L of them has liked me.
M *(No mistakes)*

ANSWERS

S1 A B C D
S2 J K L M

Usage

1
A A symbolic shadow fell across the country
B when war breaks out between the northern
C and southern states in 1861.
D *(No mistakes)*

2
J The couple stopped to look at
K the flock of gooses rising from the pond
L in one tremendous swoop.
M *(No mistakes)*

3
A Eated for hours made Edward so
B thirsty that he drank four sodas,
C three milkshakes, and a gallon of milk.
D *(No mistakes)*

4
J Mushrooms are a type of fungus. As long as
K much needed minerals, climate, and moisture
L are provided, mushrooms can live for years.
M *(No mistakes)*

5
A Whenever I make a mistake, I try to get
B the grip on where was it I went wrong.
C This helps me figure out how to fix it.
D *(No mistakes)*

6
J Alice was very tired after she bringed
K fifteen bags of groceries back from the
L store and put them all away.
M *(No mistakes)*

7
A The recipe called for two cups of Swiss
B cheese, so Maria searched in the top
C cupboard for her cheese grater.
D *(No mistakes)*

8
J "Try not to eat them tomatoes," Gary's
K father warned him. "They've been sitting
L in the chicken coop for hours."
M *(No mistakes)*

9
A A bat is a mammal, meaning that its
B young are born live, not hatched, and get
C its milk from its mothers.
D *(No mistakes)*

10
J Evan was being made tired and cranky
K by the constant spinning and whirling
L of the empty clothes dryer.
M *(No mistakes)*

11
A Creative more than a hundred years ago,
B Sherlock Holmes is as popular as ever,
C appearing in countless films and plays.
D *(No mistakes)*

12
J One of those brand new gelatin machines
K are being delivered to my parents' house,
L and they said I get to try it first.
M *(No mistakes)*

Expression

PART 2 DIRECTIONS

This is Part 2 of the test about the use of words. It will show how well you can express ideas correctly and effectively. There are several sections to this part of the test. Read the directions to each section carefully. Then mark your answers on your answer folder.

Directions: In questions 13–19, choose the best way to express the idea.

13 **A** The two boys hunted through the entire toy store without finding the dolls.
B The two boys through the entire toy store hunted without finding the dolls.
C The two boys hunted, without finding, through the entire toy store the dolls.
D The two boys, without finding the dolls, hunted through the entire toy store.

14 **J** Before going to bed, he finished his sandwich.
K He finished his sandwich, and then he decided to go to bed.
L Even though he was going to bed, he felt like he needed to finish his sandwich.
M Before going to bed, his sandwich was finished.

15 **A** Beth saw a woman looking at her mother, who was too good for this world.
B Beth saw a woman looking at her mother who was too good for this world.
C Looking at her mother, Beth saw a woman too good for this world.
D Too good for this world, Beth's mother saw a woman looking.

16 **J** Going on a hike and bike riding are Joan's favorite outdoor activities.
K Hiking and bike riding are Joan's favorite outdoor activities.
L Joan's favorite outdoor activities are hiking and a ride on her bike.
M Joan's favorite outdoor activities are a hike and a bike.

17
A. The door shut with a crash. The door squeaked loudly.
B. The door shut with a crash, loudly squeaking.
C. Crashing loudly, the door squeaked shut.
D. The door squeaked loudly and then shut with a crash.

18
J. Running in the park, Dave's son saw a squirrel, and he chased him.
K. Dave's son saw a squirrel, and Dave chased him in the park.
L. Running in the park, Dave's son chased him and a squirrel.
M. Dave chased his son running after a squirrel in the park.

19
A. Clowns that don't have big noses, usually has huge feet.
B. Clowns without big noses usually have huge feet.
C. Clowns that had huge feet usually end up not having big noses.
D. Clowns without big noses were clowns without having huge feet.

20 **Which of these is the best advertisement for a big shoe sale?**

J. All sneakers, pumps, and boots in the store are up to 75% off.

K. Up to 75 shoes are on sale, from sneakers to boots to pumps.

L. If you go one place to buy shoes, come to the place where they are cheap.

M. A 75% off sale is going on this weekend only; everything must go.

TERRANOVA PRACTICE TEST

Reading and Language Arts

Sample Passage

Volunteers

In communities across the nation, people volunteer and improve the lives of others. Some volunteering opportunities can be found through organizations—serving food in a soup kitchen, working with a group to teach adults to read, or joining others to build houses for those who might not otherwise be able to afford them. In contrast, some volunteering opportunities are not organized. People may take groceries to their elderly neighbors, or a few adults might get together to help a mother of triplets manage her newborns.

Sample A

This passage is mostly about

Ⓐ why people volunteer

Ⓑ how people can volunteer

Ⓒ how people benefit from volunteering

Ⓓ why volunteer programs save money

Directions

A student wrote a paragraph about volunteering at a local nursing home. There are some mistakes that need correcting.

> ¹Last summer I volunteered one day a week at the Sunshine Retirement Center. ²Some days I helped change sheets and deliver meals, and other days I just spending time talking to the residents. ³Even though the summer volunteer program is over and I'm back in school, I still stop by to spend time with the people there.

Sample B

Choose the best way to write Sentence 2.

Ⓕ Some days I helped change sheets and deliver meals, and other days I just spent time talking to the residents.

Ⓖ Some days I helped change sheets and delivered meals, and other days I just spending time talking to the residents.

Ⓗ Some days I helping change sheets and delivering meals, and other days I just spending time talking to the residents.

Ⓙ Best as it is

Sample C

Which sentence would best follow Sentence 2?

Ⓐ It took a lot of my time.

Ⓑ It was more rewarding than I could have ever imagined.

Ⓒ I don't like doing that much work if I'm not being graded.

Ⓓ I think that next year I'll do some other kind of volunteering.

from The Growth of the Internet

Directions

In this excerpt, the history of the Internet is discussed. Read the excerpt. Then do numbers 1 through 6.

Global Warming

The debate is over. In June of 2006, the National Academy of Sciences confirmed the findings of many earlier studies. The conclusion? Our planet definitely has a fever. In February of 2007, delegates from 113 countries came together to identify the causes of current climate changes. After sharing their research and observations, they all agreed. Global warming is a fact.

In the past 100 years, average global temperatures have risen by 1° F (Fahrenheit). That may not sound like much. But it's enough to cause global climate change. Already parts of the world have experienced hotter summers, colder winters, increased flooding and other weather related disasters. Climatologists say that by 2099, temperatures will rise by *at least* 3°. They emphasize that it could get worse. Temperatures *may* rise by 9° or 10°! When that happens, Earth will be an unpleasant place live.

Greenhouse Gases

Carbon dioxide (CO_2) and other so-called "greenhouse gases" occur naturally in Earth's atmosphere. Greenhouse gases trap the sun's warmth and make life on Earth possible. Without them, Earth would be covered in ice. Until recently, our planet's natural recycling processes have kept the amount of greenhouse gases in balance. Because of this, most of our global climate stays temperate.

CO_2 gets into the air because of the "carbon cycle." Plants and animals absorb a chemical element called carbon from the environment. Plants take in carbon from the air, soil, and water. Animals, including humans, take in carbon from food. When plants and animals die, they return carbon to the soil and water. The carbon is stored there the way water is stored in a reservoir. Eventually, some of it is released as carbon dioxide. Trees store a lot of carbon, too. So, during a forest fire, lots of carbon is released into the atmosphere. Logging also releases carbon. Fossils and fossil fuels like coal and oil store carbon inside them. When we burn them, they release carbon. All this carbon rises into the atmosphere as CO_2.

Too Much of a Good Thing

In natural amounts, greenhouse gases are essential to life. The problem today is we have too much of a good thing. In the past 100 years, we've been releasing too much CO_2 and other gases. Our planet's natural systems can only get rid of about one-third of the amount of CO_2 we emit daily. In other words, greenhouse gases are trapping too much heat. This promotes climate changes around the globe.

Human activity is also releasing too much of other greenhouse gases into the atmosphere. These gases include water vapor, methane (CH_4), and nitrous oxide (N_2O). Industries, such as coal mining, release methane. The nitrogen fertilizers farmers spread on their crops release nitrous oxide.

Effects Will Vary

Global warming is creating climate change. Still, not every place will experience warmer temperatures. The impact of global warming will vary across the globe. Many areas, such as Sub-Saharan Africa will experience higher temperatures and less rain, causing extended drought. Southeast Asia, on the other hand, will experience more storms and flooding. Hurricanes and tropical storms in other parts of the globe are likely to become stronger.

The Arctic

The effect of global warming in the Arctic regions is breathtaking. Arctic sea ice is forming later and melting earlier. Scientists predict that if nothing changes, by 2050, there will be no sea ice at all during the summer months. Glaciers all over the world are retreating. It's happening in the Alps, the Himalayas, and here in the United States. If, in 2030, you take your children to Glacier National Park you may not see any glaciers. Some scientists predict that by that time those glaciers will be gone.

Lately, scientists have been compelled to adjust their predictions. They see that we are losing polar ice at a much faster rate. Why? As ice melts, water runs into cracks in the glaciers. Water in the cracks warms the ice deeper down, causing it to melt faster.

Here's another reason. Broad sheets of ice reflect heat back out of Earth's atmosphere. Exposed land and water don't. They hold the heat in. Where there is less ice, less heat is reflected away from land. The land gets warmer, thus, more ice melts.

To illustrate global warming effects let's focus on two examples.

Focus on Greenland

What would happen if the world's largest island melted away? That's what appears to be happening in Greenland. Greenland's ice mass extends 600,000 cubic miles. In 2006, Greenland lost 52 cubic miles of ice. That may seem like a small amount compared to the total mass, but the speed of loss is increasing. If –or when– Greenland's entire ice sheet melts, sea levels across the world would rise by 20 feet, flooding all coastal areas. That will put a lot of real estate underwater.

In addition, the increase in fresh water will make the ocean less salty. Scientists believe that a change in saltiness, along with rising seawater temperatures could change the Gulf Stream, causing it to shift. The Gulf Steam is largely responsible for the mild temperatures in northwestern Europe. A shift in the Gulf Stream could bring about revolutionary climate changes to England and several other countries. Animal and human life would be deeply affected.

Focus on Polar Bears

Polar bears are already affected by changes in the Arctic. In 2004, researchers found four drowned polar bears in the Beaufort Sea. They were shocked. Polar bears are strong swimmers! What happened? Well, polar bears cross sheets of floating ice to hunt for seals. It appears these four bears drowned trying to swim the great distances between the melting ice sheets.

Other threats to polar bears include chemical toxins in their food and potential oil spills caused by deep sea drilling. These threats affect all the wildlife in the Arctic.

Here is a time line of what happen in the passage.

Global warming is creating climate changes	Artice sea ice is forming later and melting earlier	?	Seerval polar been have drowned

1. **Which of these should go into the empty box in the timeline?**
   - Ⓐ There are fewer sheets of floating ice upon where polar bears can hunt.
   - Ⓑ Ocean is becoming less salty.
   - Ⓒ Seawater temperatures rise.
   - Ⓓ Toxins are in the polar bear's diet.

2. **Choose the sentence that best describes what the passage is mainly about.**
   - Ⓕ Polar bears need to develop better swimming skills to survive.
   - Ⓖ Greenland is losing ice at a dangerous rate.
   - Ⓗ Global warming is causing a climate change that is negatively affecting our world.
   - Ⓙ Our use of fossil fuels should be decreased.

3. **What are the effects of "greenhouse gases"?**
   - Ⓐ They trap the sun's warmth
   - Ⓑ They prevent Earth from being covered with ice.
   - Ⓒ They make life on Earth possible.
   - Ⓓ All of the above.

4. **In the "Too Much of a Good Thing" section, the author says that greenhouse gases trap too much heat, and this effect "promotes climate changes around the globe." The word *promotes* means**
   - Ⓕ eliminates
   - Ⓖ develops
   - Ⓗ encourages
   - Ⓙ sells

5. **According to the passage, the effects of global warming will**
   - Ⓐ create climate changes worldwide.
   - Ⓑ raise temperatures in all areas of the world.
   - Ⓒ lessen the strength of most hurricanes and tropical storms.
   - Ⓓ all of the above.

6. **According to the passage, carbon dioxide**
   - Ⓕ is released into the atmosphere as soon as a plant or animal dies.
   - Ⓖ is released into the atmosphere during a forest fire.
   - Ⓗ is not found in fossil fuels.
   - Ⓙ is increasing, and will cause a build up of ice.

The Internet

Directions

Mrs. Anderson's class is writing about different kinds of technology. Josh wrote about the Internet, a worldwide computer network. There are several mistakes that need correcting. Here is the first part of his report.

---

¹What is the Internet? ²I have to admit that before I started writing this report. ³I really wasn't sure. ⁴The Internet is the largest computer network on the planet. ⁵A network is a group of computers linked together to share information. ⁶The network of computers grouped together to make up the Internet connects over 20 million computers!

---

7 **Sentence 2 is not a complete sentence. Which of these best combines it with Sentence 3?**

 Ⓐ Before I started writing this report, I really wasn't sure I have to admit.

 Ⓑ Before I started writing this report, I have to admit that I really wasn't sure of that.

 Ⓒ I have to admit that before I started writing this report, I really wasn't sure.

 Ⓓ I have to admit that I really wasn't sure and that's why I started writing this report.

8 **Which is the best way to write Sentence 6?**

 Ⓕ The computer network that makes up the Internet connects over 20 million computers!

 Ⓖ The Internet connects over 20 million computers with the computers that make up its network.

 Ⓗ The network of computers that are grouped together to form the Internet connects over 20 million computers!

 Ⓙ Best as it is

Now read the second part of the report.

---

¹The United States Department of Defense started the Internet in the 1960s so that researchers in different parts of the country could communicate and exchange information. ²In addition to work, these researchers discussed all kinds of things on the Internet. ³It wasn't long before their friends started using the Internet. ⁴Some of their families used it too. ⁵By the 1990s, the Internet was huge and real popular. ⁶Today, anyone with a computer and a modem can access the Internet.

---

9 Where would this sentence best fit in the paragraph?

They talked about the Rolling Stones, flying kites, friends, and other things that interested them.

- Ⓐ after Sentence 1
- Ⓑ after Sentence 2
- Ⓒ after Sentence 3
- Ⓓ after Sentence 5

10 Which is the best way to write Sentence 5?

- Ⓕ Huge and popular the Internet was by the 1990s.
- Ⓖ By the 1990s, the huge Internet was real popular.
- Ⓗ By the 1990s, the Internet was huge and really popular.
- Ⓙ Best as it is

Here is the last part of the report.

---

¹Today, you can use the Internet for all kinds of things. ²I used it to research this report. ³I also used it to help me with a science project. ⁴The Internet is like having a gigantic library at your fingertips—all you have to do to enter it is click your mouse! ⁵Researchers believe that in the future every single house on the planet has a computer and will have access to the Internet.

---

11 **Which is the best way to combine Sentences 2 and 3 into one?**

Ⓐ I used the Internet to research this report and help me with a science project.

Ⓑ I used the Internet to research this report, I also used it to help me with a science project.

Ⓒ I used the Internet to research this report, but I also used it to help me with a science project.

Ⓓ While I used the Internet to research this report, I also used it to help me with a science project.

12 **The best way to write Sentence 5 is**

Ⓕ Researchers believe that in the future every house on the planet will have a computer and access to the Internet.

Ⓖ Researchers believe that in the future every house on the planet, having a computer and access to the Internet.

Ⓗ Researchers believe that, on the planet, most houses in the future will have a computer and will have access to the Internet.

Ⓙ Best as it is

from **Welcome to the Blogosphere by David Heath**

Directions

Here is an excerpt from an essay by David Heath. In the essay, Heath discusses the development of blogs and how they are used to communicate.

What Is a Blog?

The word *blog* is a blending of two words—*Web* and *log*. *Web* is short for the World Wide Web, and a log is a type of journal or diary where information is recorded. A blog is an on-line journal or diary, published on the World Wide Web. Keeping a log, journal, or diary is nothing new, however.

People have kept journals and diaries for hundreds of years. Some of the earliest journals were kept for business and travel. Merchants generated a daily record of their inventories, sales, and purchases. Sea captains kept daily logs of their ships' movements, the weather, and other important information. Travelers also kept journals detailing the places they went, the routes they took, and the people they encountered.

Along with business logs and journals, individuals started recording their personal thoughts and experiences in diaries and journals. It was a form of self-expression. One of the most famous journalists was Samuel Pepys (PEEPS) of England, who became head of the Royal Navy. From 1660 to 1669, Pepys kept a personal diary that described his daily life in great detail. In his diary, he told about his interests, his career, the restoration of the English king, the Great Plague, and the Great Fire of London in 1666. Through Pepys's words, we can see history in an entirely different context from what you get in history books. Pepys words reflect his point of view and the emotions that he experienced.

Almost 300 years later, the diary kept by Anne Frank tells how she and her family reacted to the horrors of Nazi occupation during World War II. Anne's diary shows how a teenage girl perceived the world of fear caused by the Nazi invasion of the Netherlands.

Blog Characteristics

So what are some of the common characteristics of blogs, and what sets them apart from traditional journals, email, chat rooms, or even personal Web pages?

Blogs Are Public Most people who write in diaries appreciate privacy. They don't want anyone else to read what they write. Blogs, on the other hand, are published on the Internet and are meant to be read (potentially, by millions of people). Publishing their writing online appeals to bloggers. Bloggers can, however, limit who can read their blogs with passwords or by having people subscribe to their blog.

Blogs Aren't Just Words Blogs may have a lot of text or verbal content, but there are visual elements to them as well. This can include simple things, such as the background pattern or frame, the choice of fonts, and the template provided by the blog host. Like personal Web pages, blogs can include photos, slide shows, audio clips, and videos.

Blogs Are Interactive Readers can comment on the things that they read, and bloggers can send comments back. This back and forth communication becomes an online dialog between bloggers and their readers.

Blogs Are Dynamic Blogs are constantly changing. Some bloggers update their blogs daily or even more often than that. Comments are also posted that add to the blog.

As you've read, blogging can be rewarding for both the blogger and the reader. Blogs have created a brand new way of communicating and conveying information that allows anyone connected to the Internet to share his or her thoughts and ideas with thousands of people.

As the blogosphere has grown, there have been opportunities as well as problems. The Wild-West, no-holds-barred attitude of many bloggers has led to as much misinformation as it has valuable information. In fact, Internet guru Tim O'Reilly has suggested that bloggers follow a code of conduct that respects the rights of others and avoids spreading false or harmful information.

No one has a crystal ball to look into the future, but blogs are here to stay. They are yet another tool to help people communicate. And they are a lot faster than painting a picture on the wall of a cave.

13. What is the major purpose of this essay?
- Ⓐ to inform the readers about blogs
- Ⓑ to convince readers to start a blog
- Ⓒ to entertain readers with stories from diaries and blogs
- Ⓓ to persuade readers that blogs contain a lot of misinformation and should be avoided

14. In this passage, the author says that Anne Frank's diary shows how she "*perceived* the world..." What does the word *perceived* mean?
- Ⓕ recreated
- Ⓖ observed
- Ⓗ hated
- Ⓙ ignored

15. According to the passage, diaries and blogs
- Ⓐ are the same except that a blog is online.
- Ⓑ are both expression of one's ideas.
- Ⓒ are both read and enjoyed by others.
- Ⓓ all of the above

16. In the passage, the author says that online writing "appeals to bloggers." What does the word *appeal* mean?
- Ⓕ to increase awareness
- Ⓖ to be attractive
- Ⓗ to bother
- Ⓙ to boost readership

17. The author of this passage would agree that
- Ⓐ Blogs help people communicate and share information.
- Ⓑ Because of misleading information found on blogs, usage of blogs will decrease.
- Ⓒ Blogs should be private rather than public.
- Ⓓ Blogs and diaries are virtually the same.

from The Growth of the Internet

Directions

In this excerpt, the history of the Internet is discussed.

A "Net" is Born

The Internet was born in the 1960s, and like most newborns, it started off really small. There was no such thing as global emailing or a gazillion websites hanging out in cyberspace. All of that fun stuff was yet to come. The Internet originated as a modest research project carried out by the Department of Defense.

Bringing Up the Net

During the 1970s and 1980s, other networks were created, but they involved only a few computers each. Just a handful of people used them, mainly computer scientists working for governments or for universities.

The 70s and 80s was a time of great innovation. In the 1970s, scientists developed the first electronic mail, or what we now call email. (On March 26, 1976, Queen Elizabeth II of England visited the Royal Signals and Radar Establishment, and sent her first email.)

Researchers also developed computer protocols, a fancy word for *ways to do something*. These protocols established standardized ways for computers to send information to other computers. Once the protocols were wired into the system, they enabled small networks to link up to each other, creating larger harmonious networks.

Linking up networks is known as "inter-networking." That's where the term "Internet" comes from. The Internet is a network of networks. Just as networks consist of computers joined up to share information, the Internet consists of many smaller networks joined together.

The Net Neighborhood

It was also during these early days of the Internet that computer scientists developed the system of domain names. (Domain means *a particular area of influence*) Domains are the areas in which the hosts exist, i.e., government, commercial, education, and so on.

Hosts are the computers that actually contain the information you find on the Internet. Hosts send email between computers. Hosts also maintain websites. So when you access a website online, you are connecting to a distant host computer which sends the information on its website back to your computer.

The Internet Grows Up

In the late 1980s, the government, who up to then had restricted use of the Internet to the military and scientists, opened the Internet to the public. Internet service providers, which serve as relay stations between hosts, sold their services to private computer owners. Here's the cool part. The service providers allowed any computer network to connect: the very large, the very small, the very fast, and the very slow. Now people within any network could obtain information on computers in other networks. It was an "open" system, meaning every computer user was allowed to benefit from the new technology.

Suddenly everyone who signed on with a service provider could connect or *get online*. Almost as suddenly, millions of people began participating in online activities. The number of website hosts within different domains increased. Commercial enterprises, news affiliations, educational institutions, and special interest groups for every known topic established websites that informed, entertained, and sold products.

People responded enthusiastically. They used the Internet increasingly to find books, articles, entertainment, news, maps and directions, and even deals on products and services. And of course, the Internet allowed a quick, easy way to communicate with friends and family through email. The world was literally at our fingertips!

The World Wide Web

The rapid growth of the Internet in the 1990s was the result of another technological breakthrough: the browser (as in *browse*, which means to look around for something in a leisurely manner). It's an apt name, because an online browser is a program that assists users in their search for websites over the Internet. The first online browser, created in 1990, was the only way to visit the web. It was called World-WideWeb. Later the program name was changed to Nexus. The abstract space where websites reside, was renamed World Wide Web with spaces between the words.

Websites quickly became interactive, offering many online options. Today, users can go to a website and find a menu of links (connections). With a "point and click" of a mouse, a user can access additional images, music, services, and other related sites. This is a giant leap from simply transferring data between computers. So the World Wide Web (often referred to as "The Web") grew rapidly. At the beginning of 1993 there were just 130 websites online. Three years later there were 230,000, and the number continued to grow.

Sometimes people use the terms "Web" and "Internet" as if they were the same. It's important to emphasize the difference between them. The Internet is the global network of computers connected by Internet service providers. It is used to send email or transfer files. The Internet is made from real stuff: computers and cables. The Web is an intangible space. It refers to all the websites that pervade the Internet, but it has no material qualities. It exists within the programs that communicate between computers on the Net.

Growing Beyond Tomorrow

More people are becoming Internet users and creating new websites every day. That means more people are sharing more information with a wider audience. As a result, traffic on the information highway is becoming crowded. If the Internet is to continue to grow, Internet capacity must increase to accommodate the increased traffic. Luckily, researchers are constantly developing new technologies that increase the speed, capacity and utility of the Net.

So how will this bigger, faster, more efficient Internet affect your world? Think about it: an ever-expanding universe of knowledge, ideas, and services, right at your fingertips—anytime, anywhere.

Table 1 captures the yearly number of host computers online plus the ratio to the previous year. These statistics show that at the beginning of 1993 there were a little over a million Internet hosts. By the beginning of 1996, there were nearly 10 million hosts.

Table 1

Month/Year	# of Websites	Ratio to previous year
January 1993	1,300,000	------
January 1994	2,200,000	1.69
January 1995	4,900,000	2.23
January 1996	9,500,000	1.94

It's not just the number of hosts online that's growing. The number of *new* hosts added every year is growing, too. The right-hand column in **Table 2** shows the number of new hosts added each year between 1993 and 1996.

Table 2

Year	Hosts	New hosts
1993	1,300,000	------
1994	2,200,000	900,000
1995	4,900,000	2,700,000
1996	9,500,000	46,00,000

18. **Look over the passage again. Choose a sentence that gives a clue about the continued growth of the Internet. Write the sentence on the lines below.**

_____

_____

Now write the sentence in your own words.

_____

_____

Write whether or not you think the number of websites and new hosts increased in 1997. Use at least one piece of data from each of the tables to support your answer.

_____

_____

_____

_____

19. **A student used the Internet to research and write this paragraph about volcanoes. She made five mistakes in grammar, capitalization, and punctuation. Draw a line through each part that has mistake, and write the correction above it.**

A volcano is a vent in the surface of the earth through which hot gases and ashes sometimes flows. When the gases and ashes flow out of the top of a volcano. It's said to be active. When this activity stops, the volcano is considered dormant. One of the most famousest volcanoes is Mt. St. Helen's in Washington. After being dormant for over 120 years, the volcano erupted on May 18, 1980. While the major activity has stop, Mt. St. Helen's is still considered active.

20. Look back at the essay "Welcome to the Blogosphere" and think about the problems that arise due to blogging. Now think about "The Growth of the Internet." When can it be dangerous or harmful to share information on the Internet? Write a paragraph explaining your answer. Be sure to support your opinion with examples from either "Welcome to the Blogosphere" or "The Growth of the Internet."

For this answer, make sure you use complete sentences and check your work for correct spelling, Capitalization, and punctuation.

_____

_____

_____

_____

_____

_____

_____

_____

_____

_____

SAT 10 PRACTICE TEST

Vocabulary

Directions:

Look at each underlined word. Choose the word or group of words that means about the same thing.

1 A <u>volume</u> is a—

A bottle

B book

C storm

D map

2 To <u>remain</u> is to—

F stay

G keep

H travel

J buy

3 <u>Circumference</u> refers to—

A how tall

B how long

C how far around

D how heavy

4 <u>Speedily</u> means—

F quickly

G recently

H accurately

J carefully

Directions:

Read each boxed sentence. Then read the sentences that follow. Choose the sentence that uses the underlined word in the same way as in the box.

5

> Steel contains <u>iron</u> and carbon.

In which sentence does the word <u>iron</u> mean the same thing as in the sentence above?

A Use an <u>iron</u> to press your skirt.

B <u>Iron</u> is a metallic element.

C Greg was stubborn and had an <u>iron</u> will.

D The ranchers marked the cattle with a branding <u>iron</u>.

6

> The playground is in a bad <u>state</u> of repair.

In which sentence does the word <u>state</u> mean the same thing as in the sentence above?

F Alabama was the 22nd <u>state</u> to join the union.

G Please <u>state</u> your name and age.

H Keiko was in a <u>state</u> of excitement on her birthday.

J You should <u>state</u> your intentions.

Directions

Here is an excerpt from "Vanishing Forests." The essay discusses some of the reasons that our forestlands are disappearing. Read the excerpt. Then complete numbers 1 through 3 by choosing the best answer.

Here's another disturbing statistic. Nearly half of the earth's forestlands are gone, wiped out, vanished. Grasslands, wetlands, riverside habitats, and coastal scrublands are disappearing, too. As a result, many habitats for Earth's species are disappearing, too. And, yes, it is mostly our fault.

It isn't that humans have contempt for the natural world. Actually, most of us love it, but the natural world is consistently being challenged by the necessities of our modern lifestyles. Housing, commercial development, industry, off-road vehicles, expansion of large-scale agriculture, road construction, and grazing all contribute to the loss of natural habitats.

For animals and plants that are endemic to one part of the world, things are especially hard. *Endemic* means the animals are restricted to a certain area and can survive nowhere else. If their habitat disappears, they have no place else to go. If unfavorable conditions transform their home, they may not be able to adapt.

It now appears that the endemic wildlife in the Atlantic Forest is in critical danger. The Atlantic Forest, which runs along the coast of Brazil, is a "biodiversity hotspot." Biodiversity hotspots are considered essential to the survival of thousands of plant and animal species.

Deforestation of the Atlantic Forest has been going on since Europeans arrived in the 1500s. It sped up in the 1800s when forests were cleared for timber, cattle ranches, and coffee plantations. Between 1960 and 1984, heavy industry arrived. Forests were subjected to air and water pollution as well as tree cutting.

Today, only about 3% of the original coastal forest remains in northeastern Brazil. The hotspot includes 55 threatened birds, 21 threatened mammals, and 14 threatened amphibians. All of these species are endemic to the area. Once their habitation is gone, they will become extinct. Other species are barely hanging on.

1 **Which of the following is the best definition of endemic wildlife?**

A animals that can only live and survive in certain areas of our world

B animals that are on the endangered species list

C animals found in remote tropical regions

D wildlife found in the Atlantic Forest

2 **Based on the context of the passage, what is the meaning of the word *contempt*?**

F approval

G lack of awareness

H comfort

J disrespect

3 **Why did the author write this passage?**

A to make readers aware of the danger our forests face

B to entertain readers with a story about the forests

C to persuade readers to take a particular action to help our forests

D to inform readers about the problems in northeastern Brazil's forest

Reading Comprehension

from "Up the Slide" by Jack London

Directions:

Read this excerpt from "Up the Slide" by Jack London. Then complete numbers 4 through 7 by choosing the best answer.

When Clay Dilham left the tent to get a sled-load of firewood, he expected to be back in half an hour. So he told Swanson, who was cooking the dinner. Swanson and he belonged to different outfits, located about twenty miles apart on the Stewart River, but they had become traveling partners on a trip down the Yukon to Dawson to get the mail.

Swanson had laughed when Clay said he would be back in half an hour. It stood to reason, Swanson said, that good, dry firewood could not be found so close to Dawson; that whatever firewood there was originally had long since been gathered in; that firewood would not be selling at forty dollars a cord if any man could go out and get a sled-load and be back in the time Clay expected to make it.

Then it was Clay's turn to laugh, as he sprang on the sled and *mushed* the dogs on the river-trail. For, coming up from the Siwash village the previous day, he had noticed a small dead pine in an out-of-the-way place, which had defied discovery by eyes less sharp than his. And his eyes were both young and sharp, for his seventeenth birthday was just cleared.

4 Why does Swanson laugh at Clay?

   F Swanson thinks that Clay is trying to trick him.

   G Swanson believes that firewood should be cheaper.

   H Swanson thinks Clay's trip will be much longer.

   J Swanson thinks that Clay is being lazy.

5 Why does Clay laugh at Swanson?

   A Clay is nervous about traveling on the ice alone.

   B Clay knows where to find a dead tree for firewood.

   C Clay thinks Swanson is too old to be camping.

   D Clay thinks Swanson is too easily worried.

6 From what literary point of view is this passage told?

   F first-person limited

   G first-person omniscient

   H third-person limited

   J third-person omniscient

7 Which of the following is the best evidence that this passage is a work of fiction?

   A The places described exist in the real world.

   B It describes events that took place in the past.

   C It does not contain extensive dialogue.

   D The thoughts of a main character are revealed.

Reading Comprehension

from *Travels with Charley* by John Steinbeck

Directions:

In this excerpt from *Travels with Charley*, John Steinbeck discusses his need to get back in touch with something that means a great deal to him. Read the excerpt. Then complete numbers 8 and 9 by choosing the best answer.

My plan was clear, concise, and reasonable, I think. For many years I have traveled in many parts of the world. In America I live in New York, or dip into Chicago or San Francisco. But New York is no more America than Paris is France or London is England. Thus I discovered that I did not know my own country. I, an American writer, writing about America, was working from memory, and the memory is at best a faulty, warpy reservoir. I had not heard the speech of America, smelled the grass and trees and sewage, seen its hills and water, its color and quality of light. I knew the changes only from books and newspapers. But more than this, I had not felt the country for twenty-five years. In short, I was writing of something I did not know about, and it seems to me that in a so-called writer this is criminal. My memories were distorted by twenty-five intervening years.

8 **Which of the following statements best summarizes the passage?**

F The author does not believe that his memories are accurate.

G The author feels he has been writing about America without knowing it.

H The author wants to be concise in what he writes about America.

J The author feels that New York is to America as Paris is to France.

9 **What does the author mean when he says, "New York is no more America than Paris is France"?**

A New York does not represent the truth about America.

B New York and Paris are approximately the same size.

C New York is more like France than Paris is like America.

D New York is more French than American.

Reading Comprehension

from *The Story-Teller* by Saki

Directions:

Read this excerpt from "The Story-Teller" by Saki. Then complete numbers 10 and 11 by choosing the best answer.

It was a hot afternoon, and the railway carriage was correspondingly sultry, and the next stop was at Templecombe, nearly an hour ahead. The occupants of the carriage were a small girl, and a smaller girl, and a small boy. An aunt belonging to the children occupied one corner seat, and the further corner seat on the opposite side was occupied by a bachelor who was a stranger to their party, but the small girls and the small boy emphatically occupied the compartment. Both the aunt and the children were conversational in a limited, persistent way, reminding one of the attentions of a housefly that refused to be discouraged. Most of the aunt's remarks seemed to begin with "Don't," and nearly all of the children's remarks began with "Why?" The bachelor said nothing out loud.

10 **What in this excerpt indicates that the remainder of the story is most likely to be about the bachelor?**

F The story is told from his point of view.

G The aunt and the children are soon leaving the carriage.

H He gets the other characters to react to him.

J He is the most mysterious character.

11 **Which characteristic is the narrator referring to when he compares the conversation of the aunt and children to a housefly?**

A the housefly's buzzing sound

B the housefly's circular flight

C the housefly's persistent nature

D the housefly's small size

Reading Comprehension

Directions:

Read this excerpt from a brochure. Then, complete number 12 by choosing the best answer.

> In communities across the nation, people volunteer and improve the lives of others. Some volunteering opportunities can be found through organizations—serving food in a soup kitchen, working with a group to teach adults to read, or joining others to build houses for those who might not otherwise be able to afford them. In contrast, some volunteering opportunities are not organized. People may take groceries to their elderly neighbors, or a few might get together to help a mother of triplets manage her newborns.

12 What is this passage mostly about?

　F why people volunteer

　G how people can volunteer

　H how people benefit from volunteering

　J why volunteer programs save money

Directions:

Read the following announcement. Then, complete number 13 by choosing the best answer.

JOIN THE EIGHTH GRADE DRAMA CLUB!

Whatever talent you have, the Drama Club has a part for you in its upcoming production of Mark Twain's *Tom Sawyer and Huckleberry Finn*.

The Drama Club is searching for the following members:

Actors
Cast members must memorize script and attend all rehearsals and performances.

Set Designers, Artists, and Assistants
Design scenery and props. Attend mandatory meetings. Design and produce stage props and scrim layouts. Drawing and painting skills are required.

Backstage Crew
Members set up and change scenes; construct props; and manage the voice system, curtains, and lighting.

Writers, Editors, and Clerical Staff
Members produce the playbill, posters, newspaper stories, and advertising brochures. Research in encyclopedias and other sources is a required activity.

Please attend our meeting in the auditorium on Friday, March 19, at 3:00 P.M.

Reading Comprehension

13 Why are writers and editors required to research information in encyclopedias and other sources?

    A These members help the people who sell advertisements.

    B These members have to persuade the audience to see the play.

    C These members must report on how the audience liked the play.

    D These members need to create factual materials.

Directions:

Read the following passage. Then, complete number 14 by choosing the best answer.

> The recently proposed plan to create a curbside recycling program for the community of Summerstown is a bad idea. It will be very expensive to hire a recycling company to pick up and sort the recyclable materials. As a result, citizens of Summerstown will be required to pay more taxes. In addition, the program may be unnecessary. People who want to recycle may already do so by taking recyclable materials to a local recycling center.

14 The main argument of this passage is that—

    F the curbside recycling program is too expensive

    G the curbside recycling program is necessary

    H the curbside recycling program needs to be stopped

    J the curbside recycling program is a good idea

Spelling

Directions:

Read each group of sentences. For each item on the answer sheet, fill in the bubble for the answer that has a mistake in spelling. If there is no mistake, fill in the last answer choice.

1 A The magazine had an <u>advertisement</u> for skates.

    B Two <u>buses</u> go to the stadium.

    C Cut the paper with <u>scissors</u>.

    D No mistake

2 F Add that <u>colum</u> of numbers.

    G Ling tripped over the door's <u>threshold</u>.

    H The traffic noise is a <u>nuisance</u>.

    J No mistake

3 A <u>Nickel</u> is a metallic element.

    B I like watermelon for <u>desert</u>.

    C You can use the computers in the <u>library</u>.

    D No mistake

4 F <u>Rehersals</u> for the play start today.

    G A holiday is a happy <u>occasion</u>.

    H Liars try to <u>deceive</u> people.

    J No mistake

5 A Things you own are your <u>possessions</u>.

    B Murray <u>usualy</u> eats peanut butter and jelly for lunch.

    C The race was <u>canceled</u> because of rain.

    D No mistake

6 F Jack and Jill had a wedding <u>banquet</u>.

    G Please <u>answer</u> the phone.

    H The month on the <u>calander</u> is June.

    J No mistake

7 A It is said that "<u>beggars</u> can't be choosers."

    B The baby sleeps in her <u>carriage</u>.

    C What is the <u>explanation</u> for an eclipse?

    D No mistake

8 F There are <u>various</u> toppings on the pizza.

    G Carla's <u>bycicle</u> has ten speeds.

    H That kite is <u>guaranteed</u> to fly.

    J No mistake

9 A Choose a <u>catagory</u>: fiction or nonfiction.

    B Be sure your answer is <u>accurate</u>.

    C Tony got a <u>bruise</u> when he fell.

    D No mistake

10 F The new student is <u>likeable</u>.

    G Sunset will <u>occur</u> at 7:30.

    H Jerry plays the <u>bass</u>.

    J No mistake

11 A Acid rain has a bad <u>effect</u> on the environment.

    B Mr. Kelly is <u>chief</u> of police.

    C I do not <u>beleive</u> in UFOs.

    D No mistake

Spelling

12 F Dental <u>hygiene</u> keeps teeth healthy.

   G It is <u>necessary</u> to brush and floss every day.

   H A dentist is a <u>physician</u> who fixes teeth.

   J No mistake

13 A The fallen tree was an <u>obstacle</u> to drivers.

   B <u>Nucular</u> accidents are very rare.

   C She did not <u>recognize</u> the stranger.

   D No mistake

14 F A <u>cilinder</u> is a solid figure.

   G The flood was <u>disastrous</u>.

   H Display your graph on the <u>bulletin</u> board.

   J No mistake

15 A The quarterback has <u>athletic</u> ability.

   B The <u>comittee</u> chose the music for the dance.

   C A <u>census</u> takes place every ten years.

   D No mistake

16 F *Pride and <u>Prejudis</u>* is a book by Jane Austen.

   G 100¢ is <u>equivalent</u> to $1.00.

   H It takes <u>patience</u> to learn to play piano.

   J No mistake

17 A The project is easier if you <u>cooperate</u>.

   B Are the lines <u>parallel</u> or perpendicular?

   C Oak <u>Bulevard</u> is two blocks north.

   D No mistake

18 F Diamonds are <u>valuable</u> stones.

   G Betsy moved to a new <u>nieghborhood</u>.

   H The <u>previous</u> month was April.

   J No mistake

19 A Thomas Jefferson wrote the Declaration of <u>Independance</u>.

   B You can return the CD if you have the <u>receipt</u>.

   C Heat and humidity make me <u>irritable</u>.

   D No mistake

20 F The muffins have a <u>pleasant</u> aroma.

   G The meeting is <u>scheduled</u> for Friday.

   H The movie <u>theatre</u> sells popcorn.

   J No mistake

21 A Bryce's cold turned into <u>pneumonia</u>.

   B Practice will improve your <u>pronounciation</u>.

   C Is that a <u>genuine</u> moon rock?

   D No mistake

22 F Carmen was a <u>defendant</u> in court.

   G The flashlight needs a new <u>battery</u>.

   H I <u>apologize</u> for interrupting you.

   J No mistake

Language

Directions:

Read the passage. Then, choose the word or group of words that belongs in each space. For each item on the answer sheet, fill in the bubble for the answer that you think is correct.

One of the greatest American artists was Charles M. Russell, ____(1)____ was born in St. Louis in 1866. Russell ____(2)____ to Montana at the age of 15 to become a cowboy, and he never left. By the age of 29, Russell ____(3)____ his living as an artist. During the course of ____(4)____ career, Russell created more than 3,000 paintings, drawings, and sculptures that captured the splendor of the American West. Art critics ____(5)____ Frederic Remington and him to be the most authentic of the western painters. Today, his works ____(6)____ in galleries throughout the world, displayed in the same galleries as works by the world's greatest painters. This is quite an achievement for a Montana cowboy!

---

1 A which

   B that

   C he

   D who

2 F moved

   G will move

   H had been moving

   J is moving

3 A was making

   B will make

   C makes

   D can make

4 F its

   G their

   H his

   J your

5 A considering

   B considers

   C consider

   D will be considering

6 F hangs

   G hang

   H were hanging

   J will hang

Language

Directions:

Read the passage. Then, decide which type of error, if any, appears in each underlined section. For each item on the answer sheet, fill in the bubble for the answer that you think is correct. If there is no error, fill in the last answer choice.

<u>Dear Aunt Jen</u>
7

   I am really looking forward to your visit this summer. We always have so much fun when

you are here. Are you ready to go on another <u>picnic down by the creek. I found</u> a great spot!
                                              8

   I have a question to ask you. When I was looking at a box of <u>your childhood toys in</u>
                                                                  9

<u>the attic,</u> I found an antique skeleton key. It looks so mysterious; I'm dying to know what

<u>it's for. My Mother said she</u> had never seen it before. When you visit, will you <u>tell me the</u>
10   11

<u>storey of the key?</u>

   I guess I had better go now, since I have so much homework to do. I just wanted to

let you know that <u>I'm looking foreword to your visit.</u>
                    12

                                                              Love,

                                                              Patricia

---

7 A Spelling error

   B Capitalization error

   C Punctuation error

   D No error

8 F Spelling error

   G Capitalization error

   H Punctuation error

   J No error

9 A Spelling error

   B Capitalization error

   C Punctuation error

   D No error

10 F Spelling error

    G Capitalization error

    H Punctuation error

    J No error

11 A Spelling error

    B Capitalization error

    C Punctuation error

    D No error

12 F Spelling error

    G Capitalization error

    H Punctuation error

    J No error

Name _____ Date _____

Language

Many people have fond memories of <u>childhood games. What some people may not</u>
<u>13</u>

<u>realize, however, is</u> how old these games actually are. Follow-the-leader dates back to the

twelfth century. Others, <u>especially those involveing rhyme,</u> have long histories as well.
14

The rhyme chanted for ring-around-the-rosey, for example, dates back to at least the

sixteenth century. Not only do games remain popular over the centuries, passed down

from generation to <u>generation, but they also cross National and cultural</u> boundaries.
15

Marbles, hide-and-seek, and spinning tops are <u>only a few of the games, that are played</u>
16

<u>around the world.</u>

Although some games go out of fashion and new ones are constantly <u>emerging, there</u>
17

<u>appeal is timeless.</u> It seems likely that the games that will still be played four <u>centuries</u>
18

<u>from now are the ones that have entertained kids'</u> for the past four centuries.

---

13 A Spelling error
   B Capitalization error
   C Punctuation error
   D No error

14 F Spelling error
   G Capitalization error
   H Punctuation error
   J No error

15 A Spelling error
   B Capitalization error
   C Punctuation error
   D No error

16 F Spelling error
   G Capitalization error
   H Punctuation error
   J No error

17 A Spelling error
   B Capitalization error
   C Punctuation error
   D No error

18 F Spelling error
   G Capitalization error
   H Punctuation error
   J No error

Language

Directions:

Read each passage. Some sections are underlined. The underlined sections may be one of the following:

- **Incomplete sentences**
- **Run-on sentences**
- **Correctly written sentences that should be combined**
- **Correctly written sentences that do not need to be rewritten**

Choose the best way to write each underlined section and mark the letter for your answer. If the underlined section needs no change, mark the choice "Correct as is."

If you are afraid of spiders, it may comfort you to learn that only two spiders in the

United States can be truly dangerous to humans. <u>One is the brown recluse spider. Also</u>
                                                  19

<u>called the violin spider.</u> <u>It is a shy creature. Often found among rocks or in unused</u>
                                  20

<u>corners of houses.</u> <u>If you want to avoid this unfriendly little creature, you should know</u>
                        21

<u>that it is easily identified by a distinct violin-shaped patch on its head and body.</u>

---

19 A One is the brown recluse spider, also called the violin spider.

   B One is the brown recluse spider: also called the violin spider.

   C One is the brown recluse spider; also called the violin spider.

   D Correct as is

20 F It is a shy creature, often found among rocks or in unused corners of houses.

   G It is a shy creature, often found. Among rocks or in unused corners of houses.

   H It is a shy creature. This creature is often found among rocks or in unused corners of houses.

   J Correct as is

21 A If you want to avoid this unfriendly little creature. You should know that it is easily identified by a distinct violin-shaped patch on its head and body.

   B If you want to avoid this unfriendly little creature you should know that it is easily identified. By a distinct violin-shaped patch on its head and body.

   C You should know, if you want to avoid this unfriendly little creature. That it is easily identified by a distinct violin-shaped patch on its head and body.

   D Correct as is

Language

> Almost everyone has heard of the unlucky dodo bird. Which has been extinct for a
> 22
>
> long time. It was first reported in 1598 by Dutch colonizers on the island of Mauritius.
>
> The dodo received its name from the Portuguese word *duodo*, meaning "silly" or "stupid."
> 23
>
> There are drawings and even engravings of the dodo, so we have a pretty good idea of
>
> what it looked like. It was quite large. It had short legs. It also had a large, curved beak.
>   24
>
> However, not much is known of its habits, except that it was flightless. Apparently a
>
> dodo would make a nest on the ground, out in the open. In the nest, it laid a single large
>   25
>
> egg, the egg was at the mercy of whatever might walk by. The last dodo was observed in
>
> 1681. They were the victims of careless hunters. They were also the victims of imported
>   26
>
> domestic animals that destroyed their unprotected eggs.

22 F Almost everyone has heard of the unlucky dodo bird. The dodo bird has been extinct for a long time.

    G Almost everyone has heard of the unlucky dodo bird, of which it has been extinct for a long time.

    H Almost everyone has heard of the unlucky dodo bird, which has been extinct for a long time.

    J Correct as is

23 A The dodo received its name. From the Portuguese word *duodo*, meaning "silly" or "stupid."

    B Meaning "silly or stupid." The dodo received its name from the Portuguese word *duodo*.

    C The dodo received its name from the Portuguese word. *Duodo* means "silly" or "stupid."

    D Correct as is

Language

24 F It was quite large, it had short legs, it also had a large, curved beak.

  G It was quite large, with short legs and a large, curved beak.

  H It was quite large and it had short legs and had a large, curved beak.

  J Correct as is

25 A In the nest, it laid a single large egg and it was at the mercy of whatever might walk by.

  B In the nest, it laid a single large egg that was at the mercy of whatever might walk by.

  C At the mercy of whatever might walk by, the dodo laid a single large egg. The egg was in the nest.

  D Correct as is

26 F They were the victims of careless hunters and imported domestic animals that destroyed their unprotected eggs.

  G They were the victims of careless hunters and they were also the victims of imported domestic animals that destroyed their unprotected eggs.

  H They were the victims of careless hunters, and victims of imported domestic animals that destroyed their unprotected eggs.

  J Correct as is

Language

Directions:

Complete number 27 by choosing the best answer.

27 Which of the following would be the most appropriate tool to help you plan an essay?

   A a graphic organizer

   B a sentence diagram

   C a scoring rubric

   D a bibliography

Directions:

The following report contains several mistakes. Read the following passage. Then, complete numbers 28 through 30 by choosing the best answer.

¹Poets use language imaginatively to create images, tell stories, explore feelings, and suggest meanings. ²The greatest poets have never made much money from their work. ³They choose and combine words carefully to enable you to see your world in a fresh, new way. ⁴To appreciate and enjoy poetry fully, use the following reading strategies.

⁵Read the lines according to punctuation. ⁶Punctuation marks are like traffic signals to a reader of poetry. ⁷Then, identify the speaker in the poem. ⁸The speaker was the voice that the poet creates to communicate his or her message. ⁹Finally, you should try to use your senses as fully as possible when you read a poem. ¹⁰Identify the images that appeal to your senses; and pause to experience and appreciate them.

28 Which sentence does not support the main idea of the passage?

   F Sentence 2

   G Sentence 3

   H Sentence 4

   J Sentence 6

29 What is the best way to write Sentence 8?

   A The speaker had been the voice that the poet creates to communicate his or her message.

   B The speaker had the voice that the poet creates to communicate his or her message.

   C The speaker is the voice that the poet creates to communicate his or her message.

   D best as it is

30 Which transition best fits at the beginning of Sentence 5?

   F However,

   G Next,

   H Then,

   J First,

Listening

Directions:

Suppose that the following poem is being read aloud. Read the poem. Then, complete numbers 1 through 3 by choosing the best answer.

> Dark hills at evening in the west,
> Where sunset <u>hovers</u> like a sound
> Of golden horns that sang to rest
> Old bones of warriors under ground,
> Far now from all the bannered ways
> Where flash the legions of the sun,
> You fade—as if the last of days
> Were fading, and all wars were done.
> —"The Dark Hills" by Edwin Arlington Robinson

1 **You can tell from the poem that the word <u>hovers</u> means—**

A glows

B sinks

C hangs

D flashes

2 **What do the "golden horns" sing "to rest"?**

F the bannered ways

G the old bones of warriors

H the dark hills

J the legions of the sun

3 **What is the mood of this poem?**

A joyful

B humorous

C anxious

D serious

Listening

Directions:

Read the following passage from an oral report. Then, complete number 4 by choosing the best answer.

Wetlands are areas of land on which the water level remains near or above the surface of the ground for most of the year. Types of wetlands include bogs, fens, marshes, and swamps. Wetlands are home to many types of plants and animals, including several endangered species. They also help control flooding by retaining large amounts of water. Although wetlands in the United States are protected by the Federal Clean Water Act and by various state and local laws, many environmentalists are asking for stronger laws to preserve these important water features.

4 This passage is mostly about—

   F the Federal Clean Water Act

   G the importance of wetlands

   H endangered plants and animals

   J the importance of controlling flooding

Directions:

Read the following message left on Mr. Jackson's answering machine. Then, complete number 5 by choosing the best answer.

Hello, Mr. Jackson, this is Carla calling from Dr. Avery's office. I just wanted to confirm your appointment with Dr. Avery on September 9 at 8:00 A.M. You should not eat or drink anything for eight hours before your exam. When you arrive at the office, you'll need to give your insurance card to the receptionist. Please call me at 555-1926 if you have any questions. Thank you.

5 In order to dictate this message for Mr. Jackson, you would—

   A wait for Carla to call back

   B listen only for names you know

   C ignore the information that you think is unimportant

   D listen carefully to the entire message

Answer Sheet: Screening Test

1. Ⓐ Ⓑ Ⓒ Ⓓ	16. Ⓕ Ⓖ Ⓗ Ⓙ
2. Ⓕ Ⓖ Ⓗ Ⓙ	17. Ⓐ Ⓑ Ⓒ Ⓓ
3. Ⓐ Ⓑ Ⓒ Ⓓ	18. Ⓕ Ⓖ Ⓗ Ⓙ
4. Ⓕ Ⓖ Ⓗ Ⓙ	19. Ⓐ Ⓑ Ⓒ Ⓓ
5. Ⓐ Ⓑ Ⓒ Ⓓ	20. Ⓕ Ⓖ Ⓗ Ⓙ
6. Ⓕ Ⓖ Ⓗ Ⓙ	21. Ⓐ Ⓑ Ⓒ Ⓓ
7. Ⓐ Ⓑ Ⓒ Ⓓ	22. Ⓕ Ⓖ Ⓗ Ⓙ
8. Ⓕ Ⓖ Ⓗ Ⓙ	23. Ⓐ Ⓑ Ⓒ Ⓓ
9. Ⓐ Ⓑ Ⓒ Ⓓ	24. Ⓕ Ⓖ Ⓗ Ⓙ
10. Ⓕ Ⓖ Ⓗ Ⓙ	25. Ⓐ Ⓑ Ⓒ Ⓓ
11. Ⓐ Ⓑ Ⓒ Ⓓ	24. Ⓕ Ⓖ Ⓗ Ⓙ
12. Ⓕ Ⓖ Ⓗ Ⓙ	27. Ⓐ Ⓑ Ⓒ Ⓓ
13. Ⓐ Ⓑ Ⓒ Ⓓ	28. Ⓕ Ⓖ Ⓗ Ⓙ
14. Ⓕ Ⓖ Ⓗ Ⓙ	29. Ⓐ Ⓑ Ⓒ Ⓓ
15. Ⓐ Ⓑ Ⓒ Ⓓ	30. Ⓕ Ⓖ Ⓗ Ⓙ

Answer Sheet: Practice Test 1

1. Ⓐ Ⓑ Ⓒ Ⓓ	14. Ⓐ Ⓑ Ⓒ Ⓓ
2. Ⓐ Ⓑ Ⓒ Ⓓ	15. Ⓐ Ⓑ Ⓒ Ⓓ
3. Ⓐ Ⓑ Ⓒ Ⓓ	16. Ⓐ Ⓑ Ⓒ Ⓓ
4. Ⓐ Ⓑ Ⓒ Ⓓ	17. Ⓐ Ⓑ Ⓒ Ⓓ
5. Ⓐ Ⓑ Ⓒ Ⓓ	18. Ⓐ Ⓑ Ⓒ Ⓓ
6. Ⓐ Ⓑ Ⓒ Ⓓ	19. Ⓐ Ⓑ Ⓒ Ⓓ
7. Ⓐ Ⓑ Ⓒ Ⓓ	20. Ⓐ Ⓑ Ⓒ Ⓓ
8. Ⓐ Ⓑ Ⓒ Ⓓ	21. Ⓐ Ⓑ Ⓒ Ⓓ
9. Ⓐ Ⓑ Ⓒ Ⓓ	22. Ⓐ Ⓑ Ⓒ Ⓓ
10. Ⓐ Ⓑ Ⓒ Ⓓ	23. Ⓐ Ⓑ Ⓒ Ⓓ
11. Ⓐ Ⓑ Ⓒ Ⓓ	24. Ⓐ Ⓑ Ⓒ Ⓓ
12. Ⓐ Ⓑ Ⓒ Ⓓ	25. Ⓐ Ⓑ Ⓒ Ⓓ
13. Ⓐ Ⓑ Ⓒ Ⓓ	

Name _____ Date _____

Answer Sheet: Practice Test 2

1. (A)(B)(C)(D)	16. (A)(B)(C)(D)
2. (A)(B)(C)(D)	17. (A)(B)(C)(D)
3. (A)(B)(C)(D)	18. (A)(B)(C)(D)
4. (A)(B)(C)(D)	19. (A)(B)(C)(D)
5. (A)(B)(C)(D)	20. (A)(B)(C)(D)
6. (A)(B)(C)(D)	21. (A)(B)(C)(D)
7. (A)(B)(C)(D)	22. (A)(B)(C)(D)
8. (A)(B)(C)(D)	23. (A)(B)(C)(D)
9. (A)(B)(C)(D)	24. (A)(B)(C)(D)
10. (A)(B)(C)(D)	25. (A)(B)(C)(D)
11. (A)(B)(C)(D)	26. (A)(B)(C)(D)
12. (A)(B)(C)(D)	27. (A)(B)(C)(D)
13. (A)(B)(C)(D)	28. (A)(B)(C)(D)
14. (A)(B)(C)(D)	29. (A)(B)(C)(D)
15. (A)(B)(C)(D)	

Name _____ Date _____

Writing Prompt 1:

_____

_____

_____

_____

_____

_____

_____

_____

_____

_____

_____

_____

_____

_____

_____

_____

_____

_____

_____

_____

_____

_____

_____

_____

_____

Practice Test 2, *Continued*

Name _____ Date _____

Writing Prompt 2:

_____

_____

_____

_____

_____

_____

_____

_____

_____

_____

_____

_____

_____

_____

_____

_____

_____

_____

_____

_____

_____

_____

_____

_____

_____

_____

_____

_____

_____

_____

_____

Name _____ Date _____

Answer Sheet: Practice Test 3

1. Ⓐ Ⓑ Ⓒ Ⓓ	20. Ⓐ Ⓑ Ⓒ Ⓓ	39. Ⓐ Ⓑ Ⓒ Ⓓ
2. Ⓐ Ⓑ Ⓒ Ⓓ	21. Ⓐ Ⓑ Ⓒ Ⓓ	40. Ⓐ Ⓑ Ⓒ Ⓓ
3. Ⓐ Ⓑ Ⓒ Ⓓ	22. Ⓐ Ⓑ Ⓒ Ⓓ	41. Ⓐ Ⓑ Ⓒ Ⓓ
4. Ⓐ Ⓑ Ⓒ Ⓓ	23. Ⓐ Ⓑ Ⓒ Ⓓ	42. Ⓐ Ⓑ Ⓒ Ⓓ
5. Ⓐ Ⓑ Ⓒ Ⓓ	24. Ⓐ Ⓑ Ⓒ Ⓓ	43. Ⓐ Ⓑ Ⓒ Ⓓ
6. Ⓐ Ⓑ Ⓒ Ⓓ	25. Ⓐ Ⓑ Ⓒ Ⓓ	44. Ⓐ Ⓑ Ⓒ Ⓓ
7. Ⓐ Ⓑ Ⓒ Ⓓ	26. Ⓐ Ⓑ Ⓒ Ⓓ	45. Ⓐ Ⓑ Ⓒ Ⓓ
8. Ⓐ Ⓑ Ⓒ Ⓓ	27. Ⓐ Ⓑ Ⓒ Ⓓ	46. Ⓐ Ⓑ Ⓒ Ⓓ
9. Ⓐ Ⓑ Ⓒ Ⓓ	28. Ⓐ Ⓑ Ⓒ Ⓓ	47. Ⓐ Ⓑ Ⓒ Ⓓ
10. Ⓐ Ⓑ Ⓒ Ⓓ	29. Ⓐ Ⓑ Ⓒ Ⓓ	48. Ⓐ Ⓑ Ⓒ Ⓓ
11. Ⓐ Ⓑ Ⓒ Ⓓ	30. Ⓐ Ⓑ Ⓒ Ⓓ	49. Ⓐ Ⓑ Ⓒ Ⓓ
12. Ⓐ Ⓑ Ⓒ Ⓓ	31. Ⓐ Ⓑ Ⓒ Ⓓ	50. Ⓐ Ⓑ Ⓒ Ⓓ
13. Ⓐ Ⓑ Ⓒ Ⓓ	32. Ⓐ Ⓑ Ⓒ Ⓓ	51. Ⓐ Ⓑ Ⓒ Ⓓ
14. Ⓐ Ⓑ Ⓒ Ⓓ	33. Ⓐ Ⓑ Ⓒ Ⓓ	52. Ⓐ Ⓑ Ⓒ Ⓓ
15. Ⓐ Ⓑ Ⓒ Ⓓ	34. Ⓐ Ⓑ Ⓒ Ⓓ	53. Ⓐ Ⓑ Ⓒ Ⓓ
16. Ⓐ Ⓑ Ⓒ Ⓓ	35. Ⓐ Ⓑ Ⓒ Ⓓ	54. Ⓐ Ⓑ Ⓒ Ⓓ
17. Ⓐ Ⓑ Ⓒ Ⓓ	36. Ⓐ Ⓑ Ⓒ Ⓓ	55. Ⓐ Ⓑ Ⓒ Ⓓ
18. Ⓐ Ⓑ Ⓒ Ⓓ	37. Ⓐ Ⓑ Ⓒ Ⓓ	
19. Ⓐ Ⓑ Ⓒ Ⓓ	38. Ⓐ Ⓑ Ⓒ Ⓓ	

Name _____ Date _____

Answer Sheet for ITBS

Vocabulary

1. Ⓐ Ⓑ Ⓒ Ⓓ	5. Ⓐ Ⓑ Ⓒ Ⓓ	9. Ⓐ Ⓑ Ⓒ Ⓓ	13. Ⓐ Ⓑ Ⓒ Ⓓ
2. Ⓙ Ⓚ Ⓛ Ⓜ	6. Ⓙ Ⓚ Ⓛ Ⓜ	10. Ⓙ Ⓚ Ⓛ Ⓜ	14. Ⓙ Ⓚ Ⓛ Ⓜ
3. Ⓐ Ⓑ Ⓒ Ⓓ	7. Ⓐ Ⓑ Ⓒ Ⓓ	11. Ⓐ Ⓑ Ⓒ Ⓓ	
4. Ⓙ Ⓚ Ⓛ Ⓜ	8. Ⓙ Ⓚ Ⓛ Ⓜ	12. Ⓙ Ⓚ Ⓛ Ⓜ	

Reading Comprehension

1. Ⓐ Ⓑ Ⓒ Ⓓ	7. Ⓐ Ⓑ Ⓒ Ⓓ	13. Ⓐ Ⓑ Ⓒ Ⓓ	19. Ⓐ Ⓑ Ⓒ Ⓓ	25. Ⓐ Ⓑ Ⓒ Ⓓ
2. Ⓕ Ⓖ Ⓗ Ⓙ	8. Ⓕ Ⓖ Ⓗ Ⓙ	14. Ⓕ Ⓖ Ⓗ Ⓙ	20. Ⓕ Ⓖ Ⓗ Ⓙ	26. Ⓕ Ⓖ Ⓗ Ⓙ
3. Ⓐ Ⓑ Ⓒ Ⓓ	9. Ⓐ Ⓑ Ⓒ Ⓓ	15. Ⓐ Ⓑ Ⓒ Ⓓ	21. Ⓐ Ⓑ Ⓒ Ⓓ	27. Ⓐ Ⓑ Ⓒ Ⓓ
4. Ⓕ Ⓖ Ⓗ Ⓙ	10. Ⓕ Ⓖ Ⓗ Ⓙ	16. Ⓕ Ⓖ Ⓗ Ⓙ	22. Ⓕ Ⓖ Ⓗ Ⓙ	28. Ⓕ Ⓖ Ⓗ Ⓙ
5. Ⓐ Ⓑ Ⓒ Ⓓ	11. Ⓐ Ⓑ Ⓒ Ⓓ	17. Ⓐ Ⓑ Ⓒ Ⓓ	23. Ⓐ Ⓑ Ⓒ Ⓓ	29. Ⓐ Ⓑ Ⓒ Ⓓ
6. Ⓕ Ⓖ Ⓗ Ⓙ	12. Ⓕ Ⓖ Ⓗ Ⓙ	18. Ⓕ Ⓖ Ⓗ Ⓙ	24. Ⓕ Ⓖ Ⓗ Ⓙ	30. Ⓕ Ⓖ Ⓗ Ⓙ

Spelling

1. Ⓐ Ⓑ Ⓒ Ⓓ Ⓔ	4. Ⓙ Ⓚ Ⓛ Ⓜ Ⓝ	7. Ⓐ Ⓑ Ⓒ Ⓓ Ⓔ	10. Ⓙ Ⓚ Ⓛ Ⓜ Ⓝ	13. Ⓐ Ⓑ Ⓒ Ⓓ Ⓔ
2. Ⓙ Ⓚ Ⓛ Ⓜ Ⓝ	5. Ⓐ Ⓑ Ⓒ Ⓓ Ⓔ	8. Ⓙ Ⓚ Ⓛ Ⓜ Ⓝ	11. Ⓐ Ⓑ Ⓒ Ⓓ Ⓔ	14. Ⓙ Ⓚ Ⓛ Ⓜ Ⓝ
3. Ⓐ Ⓑ Ⓒ Ⓓ Ⓔ	6. Ⓙ Ⓚ Ⓛ Ⓜ Ⓝ	9. Ⓐ Ⓑ Ⓒ Ⓓ Ⓔ	12. Ⓙ Ⓚ Ⓛ Ⓜ Ⓝ	

Capitalization

1. Ⓐ Ⓑ Ⓒ Ⓓ	4. Ⓙ Ⓚ Ⓛ Ⓜ	7. Ⓐ Ⓑ Ⓒ Ⓓ	10. Ⓙ Ⓚ Ⓛ Ⓜ
2. Ⓙ Ⓚ Ⓛ Ⓜ	5. Ⓐ Ⓑ Ⓒ Ⓓ	8. Ⓙ Ⓚ Ⓛ Ⓜ	11. Ⓐ Ⓑ Ⓒ Ⓓ
3. Ⓐ Ⓑ Ⓒ Ⓓ	6. Ⓙ Ⓚ Ⓛ Ⓜ	9. Ⓐ Ⓑ Ⓒ Ⓓ	12. Ⓙ Ⓚ Ⓛ Ⓜ

Punctuation

1. Ⓐ Ⓑ Ⓒ Ⓓ	4. Ⓙ Ⓚ Ⓛ Ⓜ	7. Ⓐ Ⓑ Ⓒ Ⓓ	10. Ⓙ Ⓚ Ⓛ Ⓜ
2. Ⓙ Ⓚ Ⓛ Ⓜ	5. Ⓐ Ⓑ Ⓒ Ⓓ	8. Ⓙ Ⓚ Ⓛ Ⓜ	11. Ⓐ Ⓑ Ⓒ Ⓓ
3. Ⓐ Ⓑ Ⓒ Ⓓ	6. Ⓙ Ⓚ Ⓛ Ⓜ	9. Ⓐ Ⓑ Ⓒ Ⓓ	12. Ⓙ Ⓚ Ⓛ Ⓜ

Usage and Expression

1. Ⓐ Ⓑ Ⓒ Ⓓ	5. Ⓐ Ⓑ Ⓒ Ⓓ	9. Ⓐ Ⓑ Ⓒ Ⓓ	13. Ⓐ Ⓑ Ⓒ Ⓓ	17. Ⓐ Ⓑ Ⓒ Ⓓ
2. Ⓙ Ⓚ Ⓛ Ⓜ	6. Ⓙ Ⓚ Ⓛ Ⓜ	10. Ⓙ Ⓚ Ⓛ Ⓜ	14. Ⓙ Ⓚ Ⓛ Ⓜ	18. Ⓙ Ⓚ Ⓛ Ⓜ
3. Ⓐ Ⓑ Ⓒ Ⓓ	7. Ⓐ Ⓑ Ⓒ Ⓓ	11. Ⓐ Ⓑ Ⓒ Ⓓ	15. Ⓐ Ⓑ Ⓒ Ⓓ	19. Ⓐ Ⓑ Ⓒ Ⓓ
4. Ⓙ Ⓚ Ⓛ Ⓜ	8. Ⓙ Ⓚ Ⓛ Ⓜ	12. Ⓙ Ⓚ Ⓛ Ⓜ	16. Ⓙ Ⓚ Ⓛ Ⓜ	20. Ⓙ Ⓚ Ⓛ Ⓜ

Name _____ Date _____

Answer Sheet for SAT 10

Vocabulary

1. Ⓐ Ⓑ Ⓒ Ⓓ	4. Ⓕ Ⓖ Ⓗ Ⓙ
2. Ⓕ Ⓖ Ⓗ Ⓙ	5. Ⓐ Ⓑ Ⓒ Ⓓ
3. Ⓐ Ⓑ Ⓒ Ⓓ	6. Ⓕ Ⓖ Ⓗ Ⓙ

Reading Comprehension

1. Ⓐ Ⓑ Ⓒ Ⓓ	6. Ⓕ Ⓖ Ⓗ Ⓙ	11. Ⓐ Ⓑ Ⓒ Ⓓ
2. Ⓕ Ⓖ Ⓗ Ⓙ	7. Ⓐ Ⓑ Ⓒ Ⓓ	12. Ⓕ Ⓖ Ⓗ Ⓙ
3. Ⓐ Ⓑ Ⓒ Ⓓ	8. Ⓕ Ⓖ Ⓗ Ⓙ	13. Ⓐ Ⓑ Ⓒ Ⓓ
4. Ⓕ Ⓖ Ⓗ Ⓙ	9. Ⓐ Ⓑ Ⓒ Ⓓ	14. Ⓕ Ⓖ Ⓗ Ⓙ
5. Ⓐ Ⓑ Ⓒ Ⓓ	10. Ⓕ Ⓖ Ⓗ Ⓙ	

Spelling

1. Ⓐ Ⓑ Ⓒ Ⓓ	6. Ⓕ Ⓖ Ⓗ Ⓙ	11. Ⓐ Ⓑ Ⓒ Ⓓ	16. Ⓕ Ⓖ Ⓗ Ⓙ	21. Ⓐ Ⓑ Ⓒ Ⓓ
2. Ⓕ Ⓖ Ⓗ Ⓙ	7. Ⓐ Ⓑ Ⓒ Ⓓ	12. Ⓕ Ⓖ Ⓗ Ⓙ	17. Ⓐ Ⓑ Ⓒ Ⓓ	22. Ⓕ Ⓖ Ⓗ Ⓙ
3. Ⓐ Ⓑ Ⓒ Ⓓ	8. Ⓕ Ⓖ Ⓗ Ⓙ	13. Ⓐ Ⓑ Ⓒ Ⓓ	18. Ⓕ Ⓖ Ⓗ Ⓙ	
4. Ⓕ Ⓖ Ⓗ Ⓙ	9. Ⓐ Ⓑ Ⓒ Ⓓ	14. Ⓕ Ⓖ Ⓗ Ⓙ	19. Ⓐ Ⓑ Ⓒ Ⓓ	
5. Ⓐ Ⓑ Ⓒ Ⓓ	10. Ⓕ Ⓖ Ⓗ Ⓙ	15. Ⓐ Ⓑ Ⓒ Ⓓ	20. Ⓕ Ⓖ Ⓗ Ⓙ	

Language

1. Ⓐ Ⓑ Ⓒ Ⓓ	7. Ⓐ Ⓑ Ⓒ Ⓓ	13. Ⓐ Ⓑ Ⓒ Ⓓ	19. Ⓐ Ⓑ Ⓒ Ⓓ	25. Ⓐ Ⓑ Ⓒ Ⓓ
2. Ⓕ Ⓖ Ⓗ Ⓙ	8. Ⓕ Ⓖ Ⓗ Ⓙ	14. Ⓕ Ⓖ Ⓗ Ⓙ	20. Ⓕ Ⓖ Ⓗ Ⓙ	26. Ⓕ Ⓖ Ⓗ Ⓙ
3. Ⓐ Ⓑ Ⓒ Ⓓ	9. Ⓐ Ⓑ Ⓒ Ⓓ	15. Ⓐ Ⓑ Ⓒ Ⓓ	21. Ⓐ Ⓑ Ⓒ Ⓓ	27. Ⓐ Ⓑ Ⓒ Ⓓ
4. Ⓕ Ⓖ Ⓗ Ⓙ	10. Ⓕ Ⓖ Ⓗ Ⓙ	16. Ⓕ Ⓖ Ⓗ Ⓙ	22. Ⓕ Ⓖ Ⓗ Ⓙ	28. Ⓕ Ⓖ Ⓗ Ⓙ
5. Ⓐ Ⓑ Ⓒ Ⓓ	11. Ⓐ Ⓑ Ⓒ Ⓓ	17. Ⓐ Ⓑ Ⓒ Ⓓ	23. Ⓐ Ⓑ Ⓒ Ⓓ	29. Ⓐ Ⓑ Ⓒ Ⓓ
6. Ⓕ Ⓖ Ⓗ Ⓙ	12. Ⓕ Ⓖ Ⓗ Ⓙ	18. Ⓕ Ⓖ Ⓗ Ⓙ	24. Ⓕ Ⓖ Ⓗ Ⓙ	30. Ⓕ Ⓖ Ⓗ Ⓙ

Listening

1. Ⓐ Ⓑ Ⓒ Ⓓ	4. Ⓕ Ⓖ Ⓗ Ⓙ
2. Ⓕ Ⓖ Ⓗ Ⓙ	5. Ⓐ Ⓑ Ⓒ Ⓓ
3. Ⓐ Ⓑ Ⓒ Ⓓ	

Answer Sheet

Short Answer/Essay

_____

_____

_____

_____

_____

_____

_____

_____

_____

_____

_____

_____

_____

_____

_____

_____

_____

_____

_____

_____

_____

_____

_____

_____

_____

_____

_____

_____

_____

Cracking the

AP®

U.S. HISTORY EXAM
PREMIUM

2020 Edition

By the Staff of The Princeton Review

PrincetonReview.com

Penguin
Random
House

The Princeton Review
110 East 42nd St, 7th Floor
New York, NY 10017
Email: editorialsupport@review.com

Published in the United States by Penguin Random House LLC,
New York, and in Canada by Random House of Canada,
a division of Penguin Random House Ltd., Toronto.

ISBN: 978-0-525-56838-4
eBook ISBN: 978-0-525-56874-2
ISSN: 2572-827X

AP is a trademark registered and owned by the College Board, which is not affiliated with, and does not endorse, this product.

The Princeton Review is not affiliated with Princeton University.

The material in this book is up-to-date at the time of publication. However, changes may have been instituted by the testing body in the test after this book was published.

If there are any important late-breaking developments, changes, or corrections to the materials in this book, we will post that information online in the Student Tools. Register your book and check your Student Tools to see if there are any updates posted there.

Editor: Meave Shelton
Production Editors: Wendy Rosen and Emma Parker
Production Artist: Gabriel Berlin
Content Contributor: Gina Donegan

Printed in the United States of America.

10 9 8 7 6 5 4 3 2 1

2020 Edition

Acknowledgments

The Princeton Review would like to thank Gina Donegan for her valuable contributions to the 2020 edition of this book.

As always, we are also very grateful to Gabriel Berlin, Wendy Rosen, and Emma Parker for their time and attention to each page.

Contents

(Free) Content
at **PrincetonReview.com/cracking**

As easy as **1·2·3**

1 Go to PrincetonReview.com/cracking and enter the following ISBN for your book:
9780525568384

2 Answer a few simple questions to set up an exclusive Princeton Review account. *(If you already have one, you can just log in.)*

3 Enjoy access to your **FREE** content!

Once you've registered, you can...

- Get our take on any recent or pending updates to the AP U.S. History Exam

- Access and print out Practice Test 5 as well as the corresponding Answers and Explanations

- Get valuable advice about the college application process, including tips for writing a great essay and where to apply for financial aid

- If you're still choosing between colleges, use our searchable rankings of *The Best 385 Colleges* to find out more information about your dream school.

- Access comprehensive study guides and a variety of printable resources, including bubble sheets for the practice tests in this book, and a handy list of key concepts, people, policies, and events

- Check to see if there have been any corrections or updates to this edition

Need to report a potential **content** issue?

Contact **EditorialSupport@review.com** and include:

- full title of the book
- ISBN
- page number

Need to report a **technical** issue?

Contact **TPRStudentTech@review.com** and provide:

- your full name
- email address used to register the book
- full book title and ISBN
- Operating system (Mac/PC) and browser (Firefox, Safari, etc.)

Look For These Icons Throughout The Book

 ONLINE ARTICLES

 ONLINE PRACTICE TESTS

 PROVEN TECHNIQUES

 APPLIED STRATEGIES

 TIME-SAVING TIP

 ASK YOURSELF

 OTHER REFERENCES

Part I
Using This
Book to Improve
Your AP Score

- Preview: Your Knowledge, Your Expectations
- Your Guide to Using This Book
- How to Begin

PREVIEW: YOUR KNOWLEDGE, YOUR EXPECTATIONS

Your route to a high score on the AP U.S. History Exam depends a lot on how you plan to use this book. To help you determine your approach, respond to the following questions.

1. Rate your level of confidence about your knowledge of the content tested by the AP U.S. History Exam:

    A. Very confident—I know it all
    B. I'm pretty confident, but there are topics for which I could use help
    C. Not confident—I need quite a bit of support
    D. I'm not sure

2. Circle your goal score for the AP U.S. History Exam:

    5   4   3   2   1   I'm not sure yet

3. What do you expect to learn from this book? Circle all that apply to you.

    A. A general overview of the test and what to expect
    B. Strategies for how to approach the test
    C. The content tested by this exam
    D. I'm not sure yet

YOUR GUIDE TO USING THIS BOOK

This book is organized to provide as much—or as little—support as you need, so you can use this book in whatever way will be most helpful to improving your score on the AP U.S. History Exam.

- The remainder of **Part I** will provide guidance on how to use this book and help you determine your strengths and weaknesses.

- **Part II** of this book contains Practice Test 1, and its answers and explanations. (Bubble sheets can be found in the very back of the book for easy tear-out.) We strongly recommend that you take this test before going any further, in order to realistically determine:
  o your starting point right now
  o which question types you're ready for and which you might need to practice
  o which content topics you are familiar with and which you should carefully review

Once you have nailed down your strengths and weaknesses with regard to this exam, you can focus your test preparation, build a study plan, and be efficient with your time.

Access your Student Tools for a free diagnostic answer key for Practice Test 1, which includes targeted study recommendations. See pages viii–ix for more information.

- **Part III** of this book will:
  - o provide information about the structure, scoring, and content of the AP U.S. History Exam
  - o help you to make a study plan
  - o point you toward additional resources

- **Part IV** of this book will explore the following strategies:
  - o attacking multiple-choice and short-answer questions
  - o writing effective essays
  - o managing your time to maximize the number of points available to you

- **Part V** of this book covers the content you need for the AP U.S. History Exam.

- **Part VI** of this book contains Practice Tests 2, 3, and 4, and their answers and explanations. (Bubble sheets can be found in the very back of the book for easy tear-out.) If you skipped Practice Test 1, we recommend that you take both Practice Tests 1 and 2 (with at least a day or two between them) so that you can compare your progress between the two. Additionally, this will help to identify any external issues. If you answered a certain type of question wrong both times, you probably need to review it. If you answered it wrong only once, you may have run out of time or been distracted by something. In either case, comparing the two exams will allow you to focus on the factors that caused the discrepancy in scores and to be as prepared as possible on the day of the test.

You may choose to use some parts of this book over others, or you may work through the entire book. Your approach will depend on your needs and how much time you have. Let's now look at how to make this determination.

Don't Forget!
To take Practice Test 5, be sure to register your book online following the instructions on pages viii–ix. You'll also gain access to a wealth of other helpful Student Tools, including study guides, printable bubble sheets, and the Chapter 15 Key Terms list.

HOW TO BEGIN

1. **Take a Test**

    Before you can decide how to use this book, you need to take a practice test. Doing so will give you insight into your strengths and weaknesses, and the test will also help you make an effective study plan. If you're feeling test-phobic, remind yourself that a practice test is a tool for diagnosing yourself—it's not how well you do that matters but how you use information gleaned from your performance to guide your preparation.

    So, before you read further, take Practice Test 1 starting at page 9 of this book. Be sure to do so in one sitting, following the instructions that appear before the test.

2. **Check Your Answers**

Using the answer key on page 36, count the number of multiple-choice questions you answered correctly and the number you missed. Don't worry about the explanations for now, and don't worry about why you missed questions. We'll get to that soon.

3. **Reflect on the Test**

After you take your first test, respond to the following questions:

- How much time did you spend on the multiple-choice questions?
- How much time did you spend on the short-answer questions?
- How much time did you spend on each essay?
- How many multiple-choice questions did you miss?
- Do you feel you had the knowledge to address the subject matter of the short-answer questions and essays?
- Do you feel you wrote well-organized, thoughtful essays?
- Circle the content areas that were most challenging for you, and draw a line through the ones in which you felt confident/did well.

Puritanism/Early Colonization
Colonial Era
English Oppression and the Revolutionary War
The U.S. Constitution and Early American Politics
The Louisiana Purchase and Westward Expansion
The War of 1812
Woman's Rights and Suffrage Movement
Slavery and the Abolitionist Movement
Manifest Destiny
Civil War
Reconstruction
The Gilded Age (Reconstruction–1900)
The Industrial Revolution
World War I
Prohibition
The Great Depression and New Deal
World War II
The Cold War
McCarthyism
The Civil Rights Movement
Great Society
Vietnam War
The 1970s—Clash of Cultures and Political Scandals
The Reagan Revolution and the New Right
End of the Cold War
America's Rise as a Global Power and 21st Century Challenges

4. Read Part III of this Book, and Complete the Self-Evaluation

As discussed in "Your Guide to Using this Book," Part III will provide information on how the test is structured and scored. It will also set out areas of content that are tested.

As you read Part III, reevaluate your answers to the questions above. At the end of Part III, you will revisit and refine the questions you answered on page 4. You will then be able to make a study plan based on your needs and time available that will allow you to use this book most effectively.

5. Engage with Parts IV and V as Needed

Notice the word *engage*. You'll get more out of this book if you use it intentionally than if you read it passively, hoping for an improved score through osmosis.

Strategy chapters in Part IV will help you think about your approach to the question types on this exam. This part opens with a reminder to think about how you approach questions now and then closes with a reflection section asking you to think about how/whether you will change your approach in the future.

Content chapters in Part V are designed to provide a review of the content tested on the AP U.S. History Exam, including the level of detail you need to know and how the content is tested. You will have the opportunity to assess your mastery of the content of each chapter through test-appropriate questions and a reflection section.

6. Take Practice Tests 2 Through 5, and Assess Your Performance

Once you feel you have developed the strategies you need and gained the knowledge you lacked, you should take Practice Test 2, which starts at page 385 of this book. You should do so in one sitting, following the instructions at the beginning of the test.

When you finish, check your answers to the multiple-choice sections. See if a teacher will read your essays and provide feedback.

Once you have taken the test, reflect on what areas you still need to work on, and revisit the chapters in this book that address those deficiencies. Repeat this process with Practice Tests 3, 4, and 5. Through this type of reflection and engagement, you will continue to improve.

7. Keep Working

As we'll discuss in Part III, there are other resources available to you, including a wealth of information on AP Students (apstudent. collegeboard.org/home). You can continue to explore areas that can stand improvement and engage in those areas right up to the day of the test.

Part II
Practice Test 1

Practice Test 1

AP® United States History Exam

SECTION I, PART A: Multiple Choice

DO NOT OPEN THIS BOOKLET UNTIL YOU ARE TOLD TO DO SO.

At a Glance
Time
55 minutes
Number of Questions
55
Percent of Total Score
40%
Writing Instrument
Pencil required

Instructions

Section I, Part A, of this exam contains 55 multiple-choice questions. Fill in only the ovals for numbers 1 through 55 on your answer sheet. Because this section offers only four answer options for each question, do not mark the (E) answer circle for any question.

Indicate all of your answers to the multiple-choice questions on the answer sheet. No credit will be given for anything written in this exam booklet, but you may use the booklet for notes or scratch work. After you have decided which of the suggested answers is best, completely fill in the corresponding oval on the answer sheet. Give only one answer to each question. If you change an answer, be sure that the previous mark is erased completely. Here is a sample question and answer.

Sample Question

The first president of the United States was
(A) Millard Fillmore
(B) George Washington
(C) Benjamin Franklin
(D) Andrew Jackson

Sample Answer

Ⓐ ● Ⓒ Ⓓ

Use your time effectively, working as rapidly as you can without losing accuracy. Do not spend too much time on any one question. Go on to other questions and come back to the ones you have not answered if you have time. It is not expected that everyone will know the answers to all of the multiple-choice questions.

Your total score on the multiple-choice section is based only on the number of questions answered correctly. Points are not deducted for incorrect answers or unanswered questions.

SECTION I, PART B: Short Answer

At a Glance
Time
40 minutes
Number of Questions
3
Percent of Total Score
20%
Writing Instrument
Pen with black or dark blue ink
Questions 1 and 2
Mandatory
Question 3 or 4
Choose One Question

Instructions

For Section I, Part B of this exam, answer Question 1 and Question 2 and **either** Question 3 **or** Question 4. Write your responses in the Section I, Part B: Short-Answer Response booklet. You must write your response to each question on the lined page designated for that response. Each response is expected to fit within its designated page. Fill in the circle on the Section I, Part B: Short-Answer Response booklet indicating whether you answered Question 3 or Question 4. Failure to do so may delay your score.

GO ON TO THE NEXT PAGE.

UNITED STATES HISTORY
SECTION I, Part A
Time—55 minutes
55 Questions

Directions: Each of the questions or incomplete statements below is followed by four suggested answers or completions. Select the one that is best in each case and then blacken the corresponding space on the answer sheet.

Questions 1 - 4 refer to the excerpts below.

"Those whose condition is such that their function is the use of their bodies and nothing better can be expected of them, those, I say, are slaves of nature. It is better for them to be ruled thus."

Juan de Sepulveda, *Politics*, 1522

"When Latin American nations gained independence in the 19th century, those two strains converged, and merged with an older, more universalist, natural law tradition. The result was a distinctively Latin American form of rights discourse. Paolo Carozza traces the roots of that discourse to a distinctive application, and extension, of Thomistic moral philosophy to the injustices of Spanish conquests in the New World. The key figure in that development seems to have been Bartolomé de Las Casas, a 16th-century Spanish bishop who condemned slavery and championed the cause of Indians on the basis of a natural right to liberty grounded in their membership in a single common humanity. 'All the peoples of the world are humans,' Las Casas wrote, and 'all the races of humankind are one.' According to Brian Tierney, Las Casas and other Spanish Dominican philosophers laid the groundwork for a doctrine of natural rights that was independent of religious revelation 'by drawing on a juridical tradition that derived natural rights and natural law from human rationality and free will, and by appealing to Aristotelian philosophy.'"

Mary Ann Glendon, "The Forgotten Crucible: The Latin American Influence on the Universal Human Rights Idea," 2003

1. The above excerpts support which one of the following generalizations?

   (A) After European and Latin American populations interacted economically, most Europeans were more compassionate toward the interests of non-whites.
   (B) There was some degree of debate by Spanish explorers over how to treat natives in the New World.
   (C) The appeal to natural rights and natural law succeeded in abolishing slavery in the New World.
   (D) The European belief in white superiority was used to justify the doctrine of natural rights.

2. Which one of the following statements about the Spanish conquest of the Americas is most accurate?

   (A) African slavery was a direct result of Spanish settlements in Florida.
   (B) Early native civilizations in Mexico introduced Spanish explorers to cattle ranching and wheat cultivation.
   (C) Christopher Columbus was not the first European to have explored North America.
   (D) Because of racial prejudice, Spanish explorers shunned intermarriage with native people.

3. Which of the following presidents was most involved in Latin American politics in the twentieth century?

   (A) James K. Polk
   (B) James Monroe
   (C) Theodore Roosevelt
   (D) Chester Arthur

4. Maize cultivation among the native peoples of Mexico is most analogous to which of the following?

   (A) Buffalo hunting among the Lakota Sioux
   (B) Wolf domestication by the Algonquians
   (C) Mixed agriculture among the Iroquois
   (D) Seal hunting among the Inuit

GO ON TO THE NEXT PAGE.

Questions 5 - 9 refer to the excerpt below.

"I observe the great and wonderful mistake, both our own and our fathers, as to the civil powers of this world, acting in spiritual matters. I have read…the last will and testament of the Lord Jesus over many times, and yet I cannot find by one tittle of that testament that if He had been pleased to have accepted of a temporal crown and government that ever He would have put forth the least finger of temporal or civil power in the matters of His spiritual affairs and Kingdom. Hence must it lamentably be against the testimony of Christ Jesus for the civil state to impose upon the souls of the people a religion, a worship, a ministry, oaths (in religious and civil affairs), tithes, times, days, marryings, and buryings in holy ground…"

Roger Williams, *The Hireling Ministry None of Christ's,* 1652

5. The Puritans believed that the freedom to practice religion should be extended to

(A) Puritans only
(B) all Protestants only
(C) all Christians only
(D) all Jews and Christians only

6. Consistent with the excerpt above, Roger Williams was banished from Massachusetts Bay in 1636 for advocating

(A) the separation of church and state
(B) women's suffrage
(C) bigamy
(D) the export of tobacco

7. The "First Great Awakening" can be seen as a direct response to which of the following?

(A) Puritanism
(B) The Enlightenment
(C) Transcendentalism
(D) Existentialism

8. Puritan emigration from England came to a near halt between the years 1649 and 1660 because, during that period,

(A) most English Puritans were imprisoned for heresy
(B) most Puritans converted to Catholicism
(C) the New England settlement had become too overcrowded, and colonial legislatures strongly discouraged immigration
(D) the Puritans controlled the English government

9. Which of the following documents encouraged church membership in the Massachusetts Bay Colony?

(A) The Mayflower Compact
(B) The Fundamental Orders
(C) The Halfway Covenant
(D) The Cambridge Agreement

GO ON TO THE NEXT PAGE.

Questions 10 and 11 refer to the excerpt below.

"Permit us, then, earnestly to recommend these articles to the immediate and dispassionate attention of the legislatures of the respective states. Let them be candidly reviewed under a sense of the difficulty of combining in one system the various sentiments and interests of a continent divided into so many sovereign and independent communities, under a conviction of the absolute necessity of uniting all our councils and all our strength, to maintain and defend our common liberties...."

Journals of the Continental Congress, 1777

10. A major weakness of the Articles of Confederation was that they

   (A) created a too-powerful chief executive
   (B) did not include a mechanism for their own amendment
   (C) made it too difficult for the government to raise money through taxes and duties
   (D) denied the federal government the power to mediate disputes between states

11. The most notable achievement of the United States under the Articles of Confederation was

   (A) the creation of a strong executive office to lead the national government
   (B) the empowerment of Congress to regulate commerce
   (C) the empowerment of Congress to collect taxes
   (D) the provision for land sales in the Northwest that would benefit the entire nation

Questions 12 - 14 refer to the excerpt below.

"Whereas it is expedient that new provisions and regulations should be established for improving the revenue of this kingdom, and for extending and securing the navigation and commerce between Great Britain and your Majesty's dominions in America, which, by the peace, have been so happily enlarged: and whereas it is just and necessary, that a revenue be raised, in your Majesty's said dominions in America, for defraying the expenses of defending, protecting, and securing the same; we, your Majesty's most dutiful and loyal subjects, the commons of Great Britain, in parliament assembled, being desirous to make some provision, in this present session of parliament, towards raising the said revenue in America, have resolved to give and grant unto your Majesty the several rates and duties herein after-mentioned...."

The Sugar Act of 1764

12. The Sugar Act of 1764 represented a major shift in British policy toward the colonies in that, for the first time, the British

   (A) attempted to control colonial exports
   (B) offered the colonists the opportunity to address Parliament with grievances
   (C) required the colonies to import English goods exclusively
   (D) levied taxes aimed at raising revenue rather than regulating trade

13. In harmony with the sentiments expressed in the excerpt, which of the following does NOT represent the views of Prime Minister Grenville after the French and Indian War?

   (A) He felt that the Crown needed to control trade and raise revenue.
   (B) He felt that the colonists should help pay the debt incurred by the war.
   (C) He felt that Parliament had the right to increase taxes on the colonies.
   (D) He wanted to reward the colonies through his extension of "salutary neglect."

14. The goals presented in the excerpt have the most in common with which of the following?

   (A) Antitrust reforms of the Progressive Era
   (B) Free trade policies of the 1970s
   (C) Increasing federal income tax rates after World War I
   (D) Decreasing federal income tax rates in the 1980s

GO ON TO THE NEXT PAGE.

Questions 15 and 16 refer to the excerpt below.

"Society in every state is a blessing, but government even in its best state is but a necessary evil; in its worst state an intolerable one; for when we suffer, or are exposed to the same miseries *by a government,* which we might expect in a country *without government,* our calamity is heightened by reflecting that we furnish the means by which we suffer. Government, like dress, is the badge of lost innocence; the palaces of kings are built on the ruins of the bowers of paradise. For were the impulses of conscience clear, uniform, and irresistibly obeyed, man would need no other lawgiver; but that not being the case, he finds it necessary to surrender up a part of his property to furnish means for the protection of the rest; and this he is induced to do by the same prudence which in every other case advises him out of two evils to choose the least. *Wherefore,* security being the true design and end of government, it unanswerably follows that whatever *form* thereof appears most likely to ensure it to us, with the least expense and greatest benefit, is preferable to all others."

Thomas Paine, *Common Sense,* 1776

15. Which of the following is most harmonious with the sentiment expressed in the excerpt?

(A) Government is unnecessary, since humanity is capable of guiding itself by personal conscience.

(B) A limited republican government is preferable to a monarchy.

(C) Government is a necessary check against the corrupting influence of society.

(D) Security is the only justification for government.

16. Which of the following "miseries" alluded to above were most condemned by Anti-Federalists of the post-Revolutionary era?

(A) Organized response to Bacon's Rebellion

(B) Federal response to Shays's Rebellion

(C) Federal response to the Whiskey Rebellion

(D) Federal response to Pontiac's Rebellion

GO ON TO THE NEXT PAGE.

Questions 17 - 22 refer to the excerpt below.

"The far-reaching, the boundless future will be the era of American greatness. In its magnificent domain of space and time, the nation of many nations is destined to manifest to mankind the excellence of divine principles; to establish on earth the noblest temple ever dedicated to the worship of the Most High—the Sacred and the True. Its floor shall be a hemisphere— its roof the firmament of the star-studded heavens, and its congregation a Union of many Republics, comprising hundreds of happy millions, calling, owning no man master, but governed by God's natural and moral law of equality, the law of brotherhood—of 'peace and good will amongst men.'"

John L. O'Sullivan, "The Great Nation of Futurity," 1839

17. Which of the following best states the principle described above?

   (A) Colonists were destined to leave the British Empire because of the distance between the New World and England.
   (B) Women are biologically predestined to lives of child rearing and domestic labor.
   (C) America's expansion to the West Coast was inevitable and divinely sanctioned.
   (D) The abolition of slavery in the United States was certain to come about because slavery was immoral.

18. Between 1820 and 1854, the greatest number of immigrants to the United States came from

   (A) France
   (B) Russia
   (C) England
   (D) Ireland

19. Which of the following best describes the effect of the American rail system in the nineteenth century?

   (A) Government subsidy of the railroads enabled markets to expand and production to become more efficient.
   (B) The entire national system was planned before the first railway was constructed.
   (C) The development of the rails had little effect on the development of American industry.
   (D) A more highly developed rail system gave the Confederacy a decided advantage in the Civil War.

20. Which of the following changes in westward migration is most likely to have occurred in the 1840s?

   (A) The number of pioneers headed for the Oregon territory decreased while the number headed for California greatly increased.
   (B) The first great wave of migration ended, and the number of migrants remained extremely low until after the Civil War.
   (C) For the first time, pioneers began to settle areas west of the Mississippi River.
   (D) Large numbers of free blacks, unwelcome in the East, began to resettle in the West.

21. By what means did the United States take possession of the Oregon Territory?

   (A) The United States was granted the territory in a postwar treaty with France.
   (B) The United States bought it from the Native Americans who lived there.
   (C) U.S. settlers were the first to arrive in the region; they claimed it for their country.
   (D) Great Britain ceded it to the United States as part of a negotiated treaty.

22. Which of the following presidents is most closely associated with the concept of Manifest Destiny?

   (A) James K. Polk
   (B) Andrew Johnson
   (C) Woodrow Wilson
   (D) Ronald Reagan

GO ON TO THE NEXT PAGE.

Questions 23 - 27 refer to the excerpt below.

"In one view the slaveholders have a decided advantage over all opposition. It is well to notice this advantage—the advantage of complete organization. They are organized; and yet were not at the pains of creating their organizations. The State governments, where the system of slavery exists, are complete slavery organizations. The church organizations in those States are equally at the service of slavery; while the Federal Government, with its army and navy, from the chief magistracy in Washington, to the Supreme Court, and thence to the chief marshalship at New York, is pledged to support, defend, and propagate the crying curse of human bondage. The pen, the purse, and the sword, are united against the simple truth, preached by humble men in obscure places."

Frederick Douglass, "The Dred Scott Decision," 1857

23. In his opinion on the case *Dred Scott v. Sandford,* Chief Justice Roger Taney upheld the sentiment above by stating that

   (A) "separate but equal" facilities for people of different races was constitutional
   (B) corporations were entitled to the same protections guaranteed to individuals under the Fourteenth Amendment
   (C) school prayer violated the principle of "separation of church and state"
   (D) Congress had no right to regulate slavery in United States territories

24. In what way did the actions of Abraham Lincoln in 1860 contradict Douglass's sentiments in the excerpt above?

   (A) Lincoln promoted the freedom of settlers within territories to determine the slave status of their new state.
   (B) Lincoln passed the Homestead Act to give free land to all western settlers.
   (C) Lincoln favored the exclusion of slavery from any of the new territories.
   (D) Lincoln enacted the policy of giving newly freed slaves "forty acres and a mule."

25. The excerpt from Frederick Douglass is most clearly an example of which of the following developments in the mid-nineteenth century?

   (A) The gradual replacement of indentured servants with African slaves
   (B) The preservation of African culture through cultural adaptation
   (C) Southern influence upon the federal government to defend the institution of slavery
   (D) The success of abolitionists to sway majority public opinion

26. Which of the following groups would be most likely to support the perspective of Frederick Douglass?

   (A) Southern Democrats in the 1880s
   (B) Western ranchers in the 1850s
   (C) Southern farmers in the 1830s
   (D) Northern Republicans in the 1860s

27. Frederick Douglass was most influenced by which of the following social movements?

   (A) First Great Awakening
   (B) Second Great Awakening
   (C) Manifest Destiny
   (D) Popular Sovereignty

GO ON TO THE NEXT PAGE.

Questions 28 - 32 refer to the excerpt below.

"We have witnessed for more than a quarter of a century the struggles of the two great political parties for power and plunder, while grievous wrongs have been inflicted upon the suffering people. We charge that the controlling influences dominating both these parties have permitted the existing dreadful conditions to develop without serious effort to prevent or restrain them. Neither do they now promise us any substantial reform. They have agreed together to ignore, in the coming campaign, every issue but one. They propose to drown the outcries of a plundered people with the uproar of a sham battle over the tariff, so that capitalists, corporations, national banks, rings, trusts, watered stock, the demonetization of silver and the oppressions of the usurers may all be lost sight of. They propose to sacrifice our homes, lives, and children on the altar of mammon; to destroy the multitude in order to secure corruption funds from the millionaires.

"Assembled on the anniversary of the birthday of the nation, and filled with the spirit of the grand general and chief who established our independence, we seek to restore the government of the Republic to the hands of 'the plain people,' with which class it originated. We assert our purposes to be identical with the purposes of the National Constitution; to form a more perfect union and establish justice, insure domestic tranquillity, provide for the common defence, promote the general welfare, and secure the blessings of liberty for ourselves and our posterity."

Populist Party Platform, 1892

28. The sentiments expressed in the excerpt above about political parties are most similar to those expressed by

   (A) George McGovern, Democratic Party, 1972
   (B) Theodore Roosevelt, Progressive Party, 1912
   (C) Andrew Jackson, Democratic Party, 1829
   (D) H. Ross Perot, Reform Party, 1996

29. The "free silver" campaign of 1896 received its greatest popular support from

   (A) New England businessmen, who were discriminated against under the existing banking system
   (B) Southern women, who incorporated it into a larger campaign for economic equality
   (C) bankers, who had run out of paper currency to invest
   (D) farmers, who hoped that a more generous money supply would ease their debt burdens

30. Which one of the following political movements most closely shared many of the goals outlined by the Populist Party?

   (A) Progressivism of the early 1900s
   (B) Neoconservatism of the 1980s
   (C) Federalism of the late 1700s
   (D) Jacksonian Democracy of the early 1800s

31. Which of the following is LEAST associated with the Populist movement?

   (A) Support of labor unions
   (B) Secret ballot elections
   (C) Free coinage of silver
   (D) Deregulation of railroads and utilities

32. Which of the following was most directly a cause of the success of the Populist party?

   (A) Western farmers and ranchers favored conservation and organized to promote the National Parks system.
   (B) The growth of corporate power and banking interests inspired rural activists to lobby for political reform.
   (C) Western farmers resisted the mechanization of agriculture and resented government interference in rural affairs.
   (D) After the Civil War, westward migration slowed, causing a long-term recession in many Western territories.

GO ON TO THE NEXT PAGE.

Questions 33 and 34 refer to the excerpt below.

"With 78 percent of the Union electorate casting ballots, Lincoln was reelected in an Electoral College landslide, 212 to McClellan's 21. The 55% popular vote for the president was the third largest in the nineteenth century, surpassed only by Jackson's first victory in 1828 and Grant's reelection in 1872. McClellan won only New Jersey, Delaware, and Kentucky. Republicans drew support from native-born farmers, skilled and professional workers, those of New England descent, younger voters, and military personnel. Democrats were strongest in the cities and among Irish- and German-Americans (the most populous immigrant groups). It has been estimated that Lincoln received 78% of the vote of Union soldiers and sailors. The figure was not necessary for his reelection, but was perhaps the margin of victory in a few close states and, more importantly, of great symbolic value. Republicans also gained seats in Congress to retain unassailable control, 149 to 42 in the House and 42 to 10 in the Senate; took back several state legislatures; and lost only the governorship of New Jersey (McClellan's home state)."

"1864: Lincoln v. McClellan," Harpweek.com

33. Which of the following conclusions is best supported by the excerpt above?

(A) Lincoln received more votes in the heavily populated states of the North, while McClellan won more sparsely populated states.

(B) Lincoln won the Election of 1864 because of Union successes during the Civil War.

(C) The Emancipation Proclamation mobilized black voters in the South to vote for Lincoln in the Election of 1864.

(D) Republicans managed to gain control of Congress through the efforts of Lincoln to campaign on their behalf.

34. Which of the following provides the best explanation for why Radical Republicans opposed Lincoln in 1861?

(A) Lincoln's decision to issue the Emancipation Proclamation was done without congressional oversight.

(B) The Radical Republicans wanted immediate emancipation of slaves, but Lincoln refused to cooperate.

(C) Lincoln's Ten Percent Plan provided no assurance of black suffrage.

(D) Lincoln's appointment of Andrew Johnson as vice president clashed with the Reconstruction goals of the Senate.

GO ON TO THE NEXT PAGE.

Questions 35 - 39 refer to the excerpt below.

"The conscience of the people, in a time of grave national problems, has called into being a new party, born of the nation's sense of justice. We of the Progressive party here dedicate ourselves to the fulfillment of the duty laid upon us by our fathers to maintain the government of the people, by the people and for the people whose foundations they laid. We hold with Thomas Jefferson and Abraham Lincoln that the people are the masters of their Constitution, to fulfill its purposes and to safeguard it from those who, by perversion of its intent, would convert it into an instrument of injustice. In accordance with the needs of each generation the people must use their sovereign powers to establish and maintain equal opportunity and industrial justice, to secure which this Government was founded and without which no republic can endure.

"This country belongs to the people who inhabit it. Its resources, its business, its institutions and its laws should be utilized, maintained or altered in whatever manner will best promote the general interest. It is time to set the public welfare in the first place."

Progressive Party Platform, 1912

35. Of the following policies, which was NOT a main objective of American Progressives?

(A) Passage of the Pure Food and Water Act
(B) Creation of national forests and protected wildlife reserves
(C) Initiation of antitrust lawsuits against various corporate monopolies
(D) Intervention in the affairs of Central American governments

36. "Muckraking" author Jacob A. Riis's *How the Other Half Lives* best exemplifies which of the following quotes from the excerpt above?

(A) "the duty laid upon us by our fathers"
(B) "masters of their Constitution"
(C) "an instrument of injustice"
(D) "without which no republic can endure"

37. Which of the following regulatory laws was passed as a result of Upton Sinclair's *The Jungle*?

(A) The Clayton Antitrust act
(B) The Hepburn Act
(C) The Sherman Antitrust Act
(D) The Pure Food and Drug Act

38. In harmony with the sentiments of the excerpt above, which of the following best characterizes the "Square Deal" of Theodore Roosevelt?

(A) Conservation, trust-busting, consumer protection
(B) Protective tariffs, centralized banking, conservation
(C) Equal opportunity, women's suffrage, laissez-faire economics
(D) Laissez-faire economics, support of labor unions, conservation

39. Would the Underwood-Simmons Tariff of 1913 be generally endorsed by Progressives of that era?

(A) Yes, because they were largely supporters of Teddy Roosevelt's "Square Deal"
(B) Yes, because most Democrats advocated lower duties
(C) No, because they were largely supporters of Teddy Roosevelt's "New Nationalism"
(D) No, because they were largely opponents of Woodrow Wilson

GO ON TO THE NEXT PAGE.

Questions 40 - 44 refer to the cartoon below.

Strike-Breaking

40. The 1933 political cartoon shown above makes the point that

   (A) infighting within and among unions prevented their rise to economic power
   (B) government inspectors turned their backs to illegal repression of labor unions
   (C) attacks on unions were so well concealed that the government did not know where to begin its investigations
   (D) from their beginnings, labor unions were controlled by organized crime

41. Which of the following acts was the most beneficial to the labor movement?

   (A) The Clayton Antitrust Act, which legalized strikes and picketing
   (B) The Sherman Antitrust Act, which prevented corporations from monopolizing markets
   (C) The Elkins Act, which provided greater regulation of railroads
   (D) The Hepburn Act, which regulated public modes of transportation

42. Which of the following best accounts for the successes of labor unions?

   (A) Throughout the early 1900s, Congress promoted the interests of labor unions over captains of industry.
   (B) Immigrants helped to promote a more diverse workforce less reliant on child labor.
   (C) Sharecroppers in the South largely voted for Democrats who championed labor causes.
   (D) Locally and nationally, organizations such as the American Federation of Labor negotiated directly with corporations to effect change in the workplace.

GO ON TO THE NEXT PAGE.

43. Which of the following best describes the conflict between management and labor illustrated in the cartoon?

    (A) Tradition vs. innovation

    (B) Native-born vs. immigrant

    (C) Christian vs. atheist

    (D) Urban vs. rural

44. How was the Red Scare in post–World War I America connected to organized labor movements?

    (A) Unrestricted immigration after World War I flooded the job markets with low-wage workers, leading to resentment by union members and accusations of communist sympathies.

    (B) California migrant workers were largely Italian immigrants, many of whom had anarchist leanings.

    (C) Labor unions were largely thought to be controlled by liberals with Marxist sympathies.

    (D) Senator Joseph McCarthy, a Wisconsin Republican, was hostile to both Communism and labor unions, fueling suspicion among American Conservatives.

GO ON TO THE NEXT PAGE.

Questions 45 - 48 refer to the excerpt below.

"We conclude that, in the field of public education, the doctrine of "separate but equal" has no place. Separate educational facilities are inherently unequal. Therefore, we hold that the plaintiffs and others similarly situated for whom the actions have been brought are, by reason of the segregation complained of, deprived of the equal protection of the laws guaranteed by the Fourteenth Amendment."

Brown v. Board of Education, 1954

45. In which decision did the Supreme Court validate the practice of "separate but equal" facilities for blacks and whites?

   (A) *Marbury v. Madison*
   (B) *Bradwell v. Illinois*
   (C) *Plessy v. Ferguson*
   (D) *Holden v. Hardy*

46. Which of the following best represents an effect of the legal decision described above?

   (A) Continuing white resistance slowed efforts at desegregation, sparking a series of social conflicts throughout the South.
   (B) The Supreme Court decision *Brown v. Board of Education* led to increased enrollment in colleges and universities.
   (C) During the 1960s, increasing numbers of high school graduates rejected the notion that a college education was desirable.
   (D) In the twentieth century, jobs in advanced technical and medical industries generally require postgraduate degrees.

47. All of the following are social movements inspired by the Civil Rights movement EXCEPT

   (A) women's rights
   (B) gay and lesbian rights
   (C) states' rights
   (D) Native American rights

48. Desegregation of schools was, in part, a response to unfulfilled promises from which of the following initiatives?

   (A) The Great Society
   (B) The Square Deal
   (C) The New Deal
   (D) Reconstruction

GO ON TO THE NEXT PAGE.

Questions 49 and 50 refer to the excerpt below.

"If you analyze it I believe the very heart and soul of conservatism is libertarianism. I think conservatism is really a misnomer just as liberalism is a misnomer for the liberals—if we were back in the days of the Revolution, so-called conservatives today would be the Liberals and the liberals would be the Tories. The basis of conservatism is a desire for less government interference or less centralized authority or more individual freedom and this is a pretty general description also of what libertarianism is. Now, I can't say that I will agree with all the things that the present group who call themselves Libertarians in the sense of a party say, because I think that like in any political movement there are shades, and there are libertarians who are almost over at the point of wanting no government at all or anarchy. I believe there are legitimate government functions. There is a legitimate need in an orderly society for some government to maintain freedom or we will have tyranny by individuals. The strongest man on the block will run the neighborhood. We have government to ensure that we don't each one of us have to carry a club to defend ourselves. But again, I stand on my statement that I think that libertarianism and conservatism are traveling the same path."

Ronald Reagan, Interview published in *Reason* magazine, 1975

49. All of the following are factors that contributed to the prominence of conservatism in the late 1970s and 1980s EXCEPT

   (A) the success of the Libertarian party in national elections
   (B) the growth of religious fundamentalism
   (C) perceived economic and foreign policy failures under President Carter
   (D) social changes following the Civil Rights movement and Vietnam War

50. Which of the following groups would be most opposed to the sentiments expressed in the excerpt above?

   (A) Neoconservatives
   (B) Reagan Democrats
   (C) Progressive Liberals
   (D) Populists

GO ON TO THE NEXT PAGE.

Questions 51 - 55 refer to the excerpt below.

"The challenge of the next half century is whether we have the wisdom to use wealth to enrich and elevate our national life, and to advance the quality of our American civilization…. The Great Society rests on abundance and liberty for all. It demands an end to poverty and racial injustice, to which we are totally committed in our time. But that is just the beginning. The Great Society is a place where every child can find knowledge to enrich his mind and to enlarge his talents. It is a place where leisure is a welcome chance to build and reflect, not a feared cause of boredom and restlessness. It is a place where the city of man serves not only the needs of the body and the demands of commerce but the desire for beauty and the hunger for community. It is a place where man can renew contact with nature. It is a place which honors creation for its own sake and for what it adds to the understanding of the race. It is a place where men are more concerned with the quality of their goals than the quantity of their goods. But most of all, the Great Society is not a safe harbor, a resting place, a final objective, a finished work. It is a challenge constantly renewed, beckoning us toward a destiny where the meaning of our lives matches the marvelous products of our labor."

Lyndon Johnson, Remarks at the University of Michigan, Ann Arbor, 1964

51. Which of the following programs is most related to Johnson's claim that the Great Society is "a place where man can renew contact with nature"?

(A) Urban Mass Transportation Act
(B) Endangered Species Preservation Act
(C) Public Broadcasting Act
(D) Higher Education Act

52. All of the following were part of Johnson's Great Society program EXCEPT

(A) the Civil Rights Act of 1964
(B) Medicare and Medicaid
(C) the establishment of the Department of Housing and Urban Development
(D) the balanced budget mandate

53. Along with his goals of establishing a Great Society, Johnson was also engaged in which of the following initiatives?

(A) Undermining Communism in Cuba with the Bay of Pigs Invasion
(B) Undermining Communism in Vietnam after the Tet Offensive
(C) Undermining Communism in Turkey and Greece using economic aid
(D) Undermining Communism in the Eastern Block by demanding a removal of the Berlin Wall

54. Johnson's Great Society most represented an extension of which of the following initiatives?

(A) The New Deal
(B) The Square Deal
(C) The Truman Doctrine
(D) The Monroe Doctrine

55. Which one of the following was an unintended consequence of the liberal successes of the 1960s?

(A) Liberal Democrats abandoned antiwar protests in a show of support for President Johnson.
(B) Conservative Republicans mobilized to defend traditional mores and curb government authority.
(C) Economic recession catalyzed by increased government spending causing "stagflation."
(D) A majority of Northern black voters abandoned the Democrat party, siding with Republicans.

GO ON TO THE NEXT PAGE.

**UNITED STATES HISTORY
SECTION I, Part B
Time—40 minutes**

Directions: Answer Question 1 **and** Question 2. Answer **either** Question 3 **or** Question 4.

Write your responses in the Section I, Part B: Short-Answer Response booklet. You must write your response to each question on the lined page designated for that response. Each response is expected to fit within the space provided.

In your responses, be sure to address all parts of the questions you answer. Use complete sentences; an outline or bulleted list alone is not acceptable. You may plan your answers in this exam booklet, but no credit will be given for notes written in this booklet.

Question 1 is based on the excerpts below.

"Constitutionalism is descriptive of a complicated concept, deeply imbedded in historical experience, which subjects the officials who exercise governmental powers to the limitations of a higher law. Constitutionalism proclaims the desirability of the rule of law as opposed to rule by the arbitrary judgment or mere fiat of public officials.… Throughout the literature dealing with modern public law and the foundations of statecraft the central element of the concept of constitutionalism is that in political society government officials are not free to do anything they please in any manner they choose; they are bound to observe both the limitations on power and the procedures which are set out in the supreme, constitutional law of the community. It may therefore be said that the touchstone of constitutionalism is the concept of limited government under a higher law."

> Philip P. Wiener, Ed., *Dictionary of the History of Ideas: Studies of Selected Pivotal Ideas*, 1973

"I do not say that democracy has been more pernicious on the whole, and in the long run, than monarchy or aristocracy. Democracy has never been and never can be so durable as aristocracy or monarchy; but while it lasts, it is more bloody than either.… Remember, democracy never lasts long. It soon wastes, exhausts, and murders itself. There never was a democracy yet that did not commit suicide. It is in vain to say that democracy is less vain, less proud, less selfish, less ambitious, or less avaricious than aristocracy or monarchy. It is not true, in fact, and nowhere appears in history. Those passions are the same in all men, under all forms of simple government, and when unchecked, produce the same effects of fraud, violence, and cruelty. When clear prospects are opened before vanity, pride, avarice, or ambition, for their easy gratification, it is hard for the most considerate philosophers and the most conscientious moralists to resist the temptation. Individuals have conquered themselves. Nations and large bodies of men, never."

> John Adams, letter to John Taylor, 1814

1.   Using the excerpts above, answer parts (a), (b), and (c).

  a)   Briefly explain the point of view made by Passage 1.

  b)   Briefly explain the point of view made by Passage 2.

  c)   Provide ONE piece of evidence about New England government before 1800, and explain how it either supports the interpretation in the first passage OR refutes the interpretation in the second passage.

GO ON TO THE NEXT PAGE.

Question 2 is based on the following image.

2. Use the image above and your knowledge of history to answer parts (a), (b), and (c).

a) Explain the point of view in the image regarding ONE of the following:
    * Commerce
    * American Indians
    * European exploration

b) Explain how ONE element of the image expresses the point of view you identified in part a.

c) Explain how a SECOND element of the image expresses the point of view you identified in part a.

Question 3 or 4

Directions: Answer **either** Question 3 **or** Question 4.

3.   Answer parts (a), (b), and (c).

    a)   Briefly explain ONE example of how freedom of religion brought about new ideas in politics and society at any time prior to 1800.

    b)   Briefly explain a SECOND example of how freedom of religion brought about new ideas in politics and society in the same period.

    c)   Briefly explain ONE example of how religious people or groups resisted new ideas in politics and society in the same period.

4.   United States historians have debated the role of collective security in determining U.S. foreign policy in the late twentieth century. Using your knowledge of United States history, answer parts (a), (b), and (c).

    a)   Briefly explain the basic principles of collective security.

    b)   Choose ONE of the organizations listed below and explain to what extent membership in this organization was a continuation or departure from U.S. foreign policy earlier in the century. Provide at least ONE piece of evidence to support your explanation.

       • The UN

       • NATO

       • SEATO

    c)   Briefly explain why ONE of the other options is not as persuasive as the one you chose.

END OF SECTION I

AP® United States History Exam

SECTION II: Free Response

DO NOT OPEN THIS BOOKLET UNTIL YOU ARE TOLD TO DO SO.

At a Glance

Total Time
1 hour, 40 minutes
Number of Questions
2
Percent of Total Score
40%
Writing Instrument
Pen with black or dark blue ink

Question 1 (DBQ): Mandatory

Suggested Reading and Writing Time
60 minutes

Reading Period
15 minutes. Use this time to read Question 1 and plan your answer. You may begin writing your response before the reading period is over.
Suggested Writing Time
45 minutes
Percent of Total Score
25%

Question 2, 3, or 4: Choose One Question

Answer Question 2, Question 3, or Question 4
Suggested Writing Time
40 minutes
Percent of Total Score
15%

Instructions

The questions for Section II are printed in the orange Questions and Documents booklet. You may use that booklet to organize your answers and for scratch work, but you must write your answers in this Section II: Free Response booklet. No credit will be given for any work written in the Questions and Documents booklet.

The proctor will announce the beginning and end of the reading period. You are advised to spend the 15-minute period reading the question and planning your answer to Question 1, the document-based question. If you have time, you may also read Questions 2, 3, and 4. Do not begin writing in this booklet until the proctor tells you to do so.

Section II of this exam requires answers in essay form. Write clearly and legibly. Circle the number of the question you are answering at the top of each page in this booklet. Begin each answer on a new page. Do not skip lines. Cross out any errors you make; crossed-out work will not be scored.

Manage your time carefully. The proctor will announce the suggested time for each part, but you may proceed freely from one part to the next. Go on to Question 2, 3, or 4 if you finish Question 1 early. You may review your responses if you finish before the end of the exam is announced.

After the exam, you must apply the label that corresponds to the long-essay question you answered—Question 2, 3, or 4. For example, if you answered Question 2, apply the label ②. Failure to do so may delay your score.

GO ON TO THE NEXT PAGE.

UNITED STATES HISTORY
SECTION II
Total Time—1 hour, 40 minutes

Question 1 (Document-Based Question)
Suggested reading and writing time: 1 hour

It is suggested that you spend 15 minutes reading the documents and 45 minutes writing your response.

Note: You may begin writing your response before the reading period is over.

Directions: Question 1 is based on the accompanying documents. The documents have been edited for the purpose of this exercise.

In your response you should do the following.

- Respond to the prompt with a historically defensible thesis or claim that establishes a line of reasoning.
- Describe a broader historical context relevant to the prompt.
- Support an argument in response to the prompt using at least six documents.
- Use at least one additional piece of specific historical evidence (beyond that found in the documents) relevant to an argument about the prompt.
- For at least three documents, explain how or why the document's point of view, purpose, historical situation, and/or audience is relevant to an argument.
- Use evidence to corroborate, qualify, or modify an argument that addresses the prompt.

GO ON TO THE NEXT PAGE.

1. When World War I broke out, the United States declared its policy of neutrality. To what extent did the United States follow a policy of neutrality between 1914 and 1917?

Document 1

Source: President Woodrow Wilson, message to Congress (August 19, 1914)

The effect of the war upon the United States will depend upon what American citizens say and do. Every man who really loves America will act and speak in the true spirit of neutrality, which is the spirit of impartiality and fairness and friendliness to all concerned.

The people of the United States are drawn from many nations, and chiefly from the nations now at war. It is natural and inevitable that there should be the utmost variety of sympathy and desire among them with regard to the issues and circumstances of the conflict.

Such divisions amongst us would be fatal to our peace of mind and might seriously stand in the way of the proper performance of our duty as the one great nation at peace, the one people holding itself ready to play a part of impartial mediation and speak the counsels of peace and accommodation, not as a partisan, but as a friend.

Document 2

Source: Hugo Munsterberg, Harvard University professor, letter to Woodrow Wilson (November 19, 1914)

Dear Mr. President:

[I] ask your permission to enter into some detail with regard to the neutrality question. But let me assure you beforehand that I interpret your inquiry as referring exclusively to the views which are expressed to me by American citizens who sympathize with the German cause or who are disturbed by the vehement hostility to Germany on the part of the American press. My remarks refer in no way to the views of official Germany....

First, all cables sent by and received by wire pass uncensored, while all wireless news is censored. This reacts against Germany, because England sends all her news by cable, whereas Germany alone uses the wireless....

Second, the policy of the administration with regard to the holding up, detaining and searching of Germans and Austrians from neutral and American vessels is a reversal of the American policy established in 1812. It has excited no end of bitterness.

Third, the United States permitted the violation by England of the Hague Convention and international law in connection with conditional and unconditional contraband.... [O]n former occasions the United States has taken a spirited stand against one-sided interpretations of international agreements. The United States, moreover, [previously] insisted that conditional contraband can be sent in neutral or in American [ships] even to belligerent nations, provided it was not consigned to the government, the military or naval authorities.... By permitting this new interpretation the United States practically supports the starving out policy of the Allies [and seriously handicapping] Germany and Austria in their fight for existence....

Many of the complaints refer more to the unfriendly spirit than to the actual violation of the law. Here above all belongs the unlimited sale of ammunition to the belligerents....

GO ON TO THE NEXT PAGE.

Document 3

Source: Robert Lansing, *War Memoirs* (1935)

The author was acting secretary of state during the period described below.

The British authorities…proceeded with their policy [of blockading American ships headed for mainland Europe] regardless of protests and complaints. Neutral ships were intercepted and, without being boarded or examined at sea, sent to a British port, where their cargoes were examined after delays, which not infrequently lasted for weeks. Even a vessel which was finally permitted to proceed on her voyage was often detained so long a time that the profits to the owners or charterers were eaten up by the additional expenses of lying in port and by the loss of the use of the vessels during the period of detention.

Document 4

Source: Secretary of State William Jennings Bryan, letter to the Chairman of the Senate Committee on Foreign Relations (January 20, 1915)

Dear Mr. Stone:

I have received your letter…referring to frequent complaints or charges made…that this Government has shown partiality to Great Britain, France, and Russia against Germany and Austria during the present war…. I will take them up…

(1)   Freedom of communication by submarine cables versus censored communication by wireless.

The reason that wireless messages and cable messages require different treatment by a neutral government is as follows: Communications by wireless can not be interrupted by a belligerent. With a submarine cable it is otherwise. The possibility of cutting the cable exists…. Since a cable is subject to hostile attack, the responsibility falls upon the belligerent and not upon the neutral to prevent cable communication.

A more important reason, however, at least from the point of view of a neutral government is that messages sent out from a wireless station in neutral territory may be received by belligerent warships on the high seas. If these messages…direct the movements of warships…the neutral territory becomes a base of naval operations, to permit which would be essentially unneutral.

(4)   Submission without protest to British violations of the rules regarding absolute and conditional contraband as laid down in the Hague conventions, the Declaration of London, and international law.

There is no Hague convention which deals with absolute or conditional contraband, and, as the Declaration of London is not in force, the rules of international law only apply. As to the articles to be regarded as contraband, there is no general agreement between nations….

The United States has made earnest representations to Great Britain in regard to the seizure and detention by the British authorities of all American ships…. It will be recalled, however, that American courts have established various rules bearing on these matters.

(9)   The United States has not interfered with the sale to Great Britain and her allies of arms, ammunition, horses, uniforms, and other munitions of war, although such sales prolong the conflict.

There is no power in the Executive to prevent the sale of ammunition to the belligerents.

The duty of a neutral to restrict trade in munitions of war has never been imposed by international law….

(20)   General unfriendly attitude of Government toward Germany and Austria. If any American citizens, partisans of Germany and Austria-Hungary, feel that this administration is acting in a way injurious to the cause of those countries, this feeling results from the fact that on the high seas the German and Austro-Hungarian naval power is thus far inferior to the British. It is the business of a belligerent operating on the high seas, not the duty of a neutral, to prevent contraband from reaching an enemy….

I am [etc.]

W.J. Bryan

GO ON TO THE NEXT PAGE.

Document 5

Source: *New York Times*, notice (May 1, 1915)

NOTICE!

TRAVELLERS intending to embark on the Atlantic voyage are reminded that a state of war exists between Germany and her allies; that the zone of her waters includes the waters adjacent to the British Isles; that, in accordance with formal notice given by the Imperial German Government, vessels flying the flag of Great Britain, or of any of her allies, are liable to destruction in those waters and that travellers sailing in the war zone on ships of Great Britain or her allies do so at their own risk.

IMPERIAL GERMAN EMBASSY

Document 6

Source: Report from the American Customs Inspector in New York (1915)

Q: Did the *Lusitania* have on board on said trip 5400 cases of ammunition? If so, to whom were they consigned?

A: The *Lusitania* had on board, on said trip, 5468 cases of ammunition. The Remington Arms-Union Metallic Cartridge Co. shipped 4200 cases of metallic cartridges, consigned to the Remington Arms Co., London, of which the ultimate consignee was the British Government. G. W. Sheldon & Co. shipped three lots of fuses of 6 cases each, and 1250 cases of shrapnel, consigned to the Deputy Director of Ammunition Stores, Woolwich, England.

GO ON TO THE NEXT PAGE.

Document 7

Source: Woodrow Wilson, speech to Congress (March 24, 1916)

…I have deemed it my duty, therefore, to say to the Imperial German Government, that if it is still its purpose to prosecute relentless and indiscriminate warfare against vessels of commerce by the use of submarines, notwithstanding the now demonstrated impossibility of conducting that warfare in accordance with what the Government of the United States must consider the sacred and indisputable rules of international law and the universally recognized dictates of humanity, the Government of the United States is at last forced to the conclusion that there is but one course it can pursue; and that unless the Imperial German Government should now immediately declare and effect an abandonment of its present methods of warfare against passenger and freight carrying vessels, this Government can have no choice but to sever diplomatic relations with the Government of the German Empire altogether.

This decision I have arrived at with the keenest regret; the possibility of the action contemplated I am sure all thoughtful Americans will look forward to with unaffected reluctance. But we cannot forget that we are in some sort and by the force of circumstances the responsible spokesmen of the rights of humanity, and that we cannot remain silent while those rights seem in process of being swept utterly away in the maelstrom of this terrible war. We owe it to a due regard to our own rights as a nation, to our sense of duty as a representative of the rights of neutrals the world over, and to a just conception of the rights of mankind to take this stand now with the utmost solemnity and firmness….

END OF DOCUMENTS FOR QUESTION 1

GO ON TO THE NEXT PAGE.

Question 2, 3, or 4 (Long Essay)

Suggested writing time: 40 minutes

Directions: Answer Question 2 **or** Question 3 **or** Question 4.

In your response you should do the following.

- Respond to the prompt with a historically defensible thesis or claim that establishes a line of reasoning.
- Describe a broader historical context relevant to the prompt.
- Support an argument in response to the prompt using specific and relevant examples of evidence.
- Use historical reasoning (e.g., comparison, causation, continuity or change over time) to frame or structure an argument that addresses the prompt.
- Use evidence to corroborate, qualify, or modify an argument that addresses the prompt.

2. To what extent did the American Revolution represent change and/or continuity over time in relation to how colonists reacted to the British imperial authority?

3. Evaluate the extent to which the assassination of James Garfield marked a turning point in the Gilded Age.

   In the development of your argument, explain what changed and what stayed the same from the period immediately before James Garfield's assassination (1870s) to the period immediately after his assassination (1880s).

4. To what extent did the social and political actions of Americans during the 1960s represent change and/or continuity over time?

WHEN YOU FINISH WRITING, CHECK YOUR WORK ON SECTION II IF TIME PERMITS

STOP

END OF EXAM

Practice Test 1: Answers and Explanations

ANSWER KEY

Section I, Part A: Multiple-Choice Questions

1. B	20. A	39. B
2. C	21. D	40. B
3. C	22. A	41. A
4. C	23. D	42. D
5. A	24. C	43. A
6. A	25. C	44. C
7. B	26. D	45. C
8. D	27. B	46. A
9. C	28. D	47. C
10. C	29. D	48. D
11. D	30. A	49. A
12. D	31. D	50. C
13. D	32. B	51. B
14. C	33. A	52. D
15. B	34. B	53. B
16. C	35. D	54. A
17. C	36. C	55. B
18. D	37. D	
19. A	38. A	

Once you have checked your answers, remember to return to page 4 and respond to the Reflect questions.

Access your Student Tools for a free diagnostic answer key for Practice Test 1, which includes targeted study recommendations.

SECTION I, PART A: MULTIPLE-CHOICE QUESTIONS

Questions 1–4

Early interactions among native peoples and Europeans challenged the worldviews of each group. European overseas expansion and sustained contacts with native peoples shaped European views of social, political, and economic relationships among and between white and non-white peoples. With little experience dealing with people who were different from themselves, Spanish and Portuguese explorers poorly understood the native peoples they encountered in the Americas, leading to debates over how natives should be treated and how "civilized" these groups were compared to European standards. Many Europeans developed a belief in white superiority to justify their subjugation of Africans and American Indians, while others took a more humanitarian approach.

1. **B** The two quotations represent two vastly different views of non-white natives. The quote by Juan de Sepulveda rules out (A). Neither quote mentions the abolition of slavery, so rule out (C), and the concept of natural rights would tend to discourage white supremacy, so rule out (D).

2. **C** Although many people assume Columbus to be the first European to explore North America, Scandinavians had previously explored areas in the northern part of this continent. The Spanish were not directly responsible for slavery, so rule out (A). Early Mexicans did not raise cattle or wheat, so rule out (B). And the Spanish did, in fact, intermarry extensively with native peoples throughout Mexico and South America, so rule out (D).

3. **C** Theodore Roosevelt was most known for key foreign policy strategies in Latin America, particularly the Spanish-American War. Choice (A), Polk, was more concerned with domestic expansion. Choice (B), James Monroe, originator of the Monroe Doctrine, may have inspired Roosevelt, but Monroe was not involved in Latin American affairs during his presidency from 1817 to 1825. Chester Arthur is irrelevant to this question, so rule out (D). (Additionally, if you know that all choices but (C) are 19th-century presidents, "twentieth century" is a giveaway.)

4. **C** The spread of maize cultivation from present-day Mexico northward into the American Southwest and beyond supported economic development in these areas and allowed tribes to remain in fixed communities. This is most similar to the fixed agricultural and fishing communities of the Iroquois. Buffalo and seal hunting would require some degree of migration, so rule out (A) and (D), while (B), wolf domestication, would not provide a steady supply of food.

Questions 5–9

The Puritans came to the New World to escape religious and political persecution in England. In their communities, freedom of worship was solely a Puritan right. Non-Puritans were limited politically as well: only property-owning male Puritans were allowed to vote in the colonial assemblies (which, oddly, were quite democratic, within the extremely limited parameters of their membership). Those who questioned the church too aggressively—as did Roger Williams and Anne Hutchinson—were banished from the community. Williams went on to found the colony of Rhode Island, which for decades was the only place in New England where religious liberty was granted.

5. **A** Believing that theirs was the one true church, the Puritans saw no contradiction in denying others the same rights they had sought in England.

6. **A** Williams was quite a radical thinker for his time and place. After accepting a position as teacher in the Salem Bay settlement, Williams both taught and published a number of controversial principles. He believed, for example, that the king of England had no power to give away land that clearly belonged to the Native Americans. He also felt that the state was an imperfect vehicle for the imposition of God's will on Earth, so he advocated religious tolerance and the separation of church and state. Such ideas were pure anathema to the Puritans, who had settled Massachusetts Bay to establish precisely the type of state that Williams preached against. Neither easygoing nor good sports, the Puritans eventually banished Williams. Williams moved to what is now Rhode Island, received a charter, and founded a new colony. Rhode Island's charter allowed for the free exercise of religion; it did not require voters in its legislature to be church members.

7. **B** The term "First Great Awakening" refers to a period of resurgence of religious fundamentalism that took place between the 1730s and the 1760s. Its most prominent spokesmen were Congregationalist preacher Jonathan Edwards and Methodist preacher George Whitefield. From 1739 until his death in 1770, Whitefield toured the colonies preaching what has since come to be known as "revivalism." The period was marked by the creation of a number of evangelical churches, emphasis on the emotional power of religion, and briefly, a return of the persecution of witches. Whitefield was a native of England, where the Enlightenment was in full swing; its effects were also beginning to be felt in the colonies. The Enlightenment was a natural outgrowth of the Renaissance, during which Europe rediscovered the great works of the ancient world and began to assimilate some of its ideals. While European thinkers of the time did not turn their backs on religion, they also entertained ideas about the value of empirical thought and scientific inquiry that were not entirely consonant with contemporary religious beliefs. Further, they began to view humanity as a more important—and God as a less important—force in shaping human history. The First Great Awakening is usually characterized as a response to the threats posed by the intellectual trends of the Enlightenment.

8. **D** The period between 1649 and 1660 is often referred to as the "Interregnum," Latin for "between kings," because during that brief period England had no king. Rather, it was governed as a republican Commonwealth, with its leader, Oliver Cromwell, named "lord protector." The English Civil Wars, between 1642 and 1648, are often called the Puritan Revolution because they pitted the Puritans against the Crown. Royalists fought for the divine right of the king to rule and the maintenance of the Church of England (which later became known as the Episcopal Church in the United States) as the official church of state. The Puritans fought for a republican Commonwealth and a greater level of state tolerance for freedom of religion. The Puritans won and, for a little over a decade, ruled England. The death of Cromwell (1658) robbed the Puritans of their best-known and most respected leader, and by 1660 the Stuarts were restored to the throne. During the Interregnum, Puritans had little motive to move to the New World. Everything they wanted—freedom to practice their religion, representation in the government—was available to them in England. With the restoration of the Stuarts, many Puritans sought the opportunities and freedoms of the New World, bringing with them the republican ideals of the revolution.

9.　**C**　The Halfway Covenant extended the privilege of baptism to all children of baptized people, not just those who had the personal experience of conversion. The Covenant was an attempt to bring more people into the church and do away with some of the distinctions between the "elect" and all others.

Questions 10–11

During the fight for liberation against the English monarchy, the colonists were leery of establishing a too-powerful national government. They erred too much on the side of caution, however; by severely limiting the government's ability to levy taxes and duties, the framers of the Articles essentially hobbled the fledgling government. The Articles also curtailed the government's ability to regulate international trade, enforce treaties, and perform other tasks necessary to international relations. Havoc ensued. The British refused to abandon military posts in the states, and the government was powerless to expel them. Furthermore, the British, French, and Spanish began to restrict U.S. trade with their colonies. That, coupled with the government's reluctance and inability to tax its citizens, nearly destroyed the country's economy.

10.　**C**　Choice (A) is incorrect because the Articles did not create an executive, just a unicameral legislature. Choice (B) is incorrect because the Articles could be amended, but only by unanimous approval of the states. Choice (D) is incorrect; the Articles gave the government the power to mediate such disputes, on appeal raised by the states.

11.　**D**　The land sales in the Northwest were structured so that they would benefit the entire nation and gave newly created states equal status with the older states. None of the other choices were actually accomplished under the Articles of Confederation, which did not provide for a strong central government.

Questions 12–14

Throughout the colonial period, the English subscribed to the economic theory of mercantilism, which held, among other things, that a nation's wealth rested on colonial holdings, a favorable balance of trade, and a large store of precious metals. Mercantilists held that governments must regulate trade through taxes so as to preserve their self-interest. Accordingly, English taxes and levies on the colonists (prior to the Sugar Act) were proposed and accepted as acts of mercantilist protectionism. The Sugar Act was something different.

12.　**D**　England accrued a large war debt during the French and Indian War. Since, it was argued, the war was fought to protect the colonists, the colonists should share in its expense. Revenues from the Sugar Act were earmarked toward repaying that debt. The colonists saw things differently, however. Many argued that Englishmen could not be taxed without their consent, and since the colonists had no representatives in Parliament, they simply could not be taxed. The Sugar Act is often regarded as a major catalyst in the chain of events that led to the Revolutionary War.

13.　**D**　British treatment of the colonies during the period preceding the French and Indian War (also called the Seven Years' War) is often described as "salutary neglect" (or "benign neglect"). Although England regulated trade and government in its colonies, it interfered in colonial affairs as little as possible. Grenville's policies put an end to salutary neglect, rather than extending it.

14.　**C**　Since the Sugar Act was designed to raise funds necessary to pay off war debts, increased taxes following World War I would be most similar to this.

Questions 15–16

Before the Revolution, the rebels needed a masterpiece of propaganda that would rally colonists to their cause. They got it in *Common Sense*, a pamphlet published in January of 1776 by an English printer named Thomas Paine. Paine not only advocated colonial independence but also argued for the merits of republicanism over monarchy.

15. **B**   Since Paine describes government as a "*necessary* evil," (A) is too extreme. Choice (C) is wrong because Paine states that society is a "blessing." The word "only" makes (D) too extreme.

16. **C**   The key to this question is its reference to the Anti-Federalists. The Anti-Federalists were suspicious of centralized government power and were leery of Washington's military response to the Whiskey Rebellion in 1794. The response to Shays's Rebellion was weak; it would not have posed a perceived threat, so eliminate (B). Choice (A), Bacon's Rebellion, and (D), Pontiac's Rebellion, occurred prior to the Revolution, so these answers can be ruled out immediately.

Questions 17–22

The idea of Manifest Destiny was originally advanced by a newspaper editor in the 1840s, and it quickly became a part of the public's—and government's—vocabulary. Part and parcel with the doctrine of Manifest Destiny was the notion that Europeans, especially English-speaking Europeans, were culturally and morally superior to those whom they supplanted, and so they were entitled to the land even if others were already living on it. Manifest Destiny was later invoked as a justification for the Spanish-American War.

17. **C**   O'Sullivan makes reference to God and the tone of the passage is clear and confident, so (C) is the best choice. No mention is made of distances, so rule out (A). Neither women nor slaves are mentioned, so rule out (B) and (D), respectively.

18. **D**   Overpopulation and poor harvests in Ireland fueled a steady stream of immigration to the United States. Between the years 1820 and 1854, the Irish made up the single largest immigrant group for all but two of the years. The peak immigration period was between 1847 and 1854, when the potato famine struck Ireland; during those years, well over one million Irish left for America. In 1854, German immigrants began to outnumber the Irish, although Irish immigration remained at such a level that, by 1900, there were more Irish in the United States than in Ireland.

19. **A**   During the century, the federal government gave over 180 million acres to railroad companies; state and local governments gave away another 50 million. For the federal government, the goal was the completion of a national rail system in order to promote trade. Local governments often wanted the railroad to come to a specific town because a rail station was a great boon to growth.

The incorrect answers are all entirely false. The nation's railroads grew haphazardly, and frequently different lines could not be joined because the tracks were of different gauges, so rule out (B). The transcontinental railroad was the single greatest factor in the growth of the American steel industry, so rule out (C). The North had a much more sophisticated rail system than the South, which gave the Union a great advantage in the Civil War, so rule out (D).

20. **A**   In January 1848, a carpenter discovered gold at Sutter's Mill, California. Word spread quickly, and soon the Gold Rush was on. Western migrants continued to travel west on the Oregon Trail until they reached Fort Hall (in modern Idaho), but then they turned south on the California Trail and headed for where the gold was supposed to be. Most wound up disappointed, as only a very few found much gold. In seven years, California's population grew from 15,000 to 300,000. One observer noted that, by 1849, the western section of the Oregon Trail (which led into the Oregon Territory) "bore no evidence of having been much traveled."

21. **D**   The United States almost fought a war over the Oregon Territory, which consisted of present-day Oregon, Washington, and parts of Montana and Idaho. Originally, American expansionists and settlers demanded all the territory up to the 54°40′ boundary, and they were willing to fight the British (who held it as part of their Canadian territories) to get it. Contemporaneous conflicts near Mexico caused President Polk to reconsider war with Great Britain; he feared that two wars would spread forces dangerously thin, as well as damage his popularity with voters. Therefore, Polk decided to negotiate a settlement with the British—the United States accepted a boundary at the 49th parallel—and directed his military activities southward. The United States subsequently entered a war with Mexico, which netted them much of the territory that makes up the Southwestern states.

22. **A**   James K. Polk is known as the "Manifest Destiny" president; it was during his term that the country extended so many of its borders.

Questions 23–27

In the 1840s, Frederick Douglass began publishing his influential newspaper *The North Star*. Douglass, an escaped slave, gained fame as a gifted writer and eloquent advocate of freedom and equality.

23. **D**   Dred Scott was a slave whose owner had traveled with him into the free state of Illinois and also into the Wisconsin Territory, where slavery was prohibited. Scott declared himself a free man, and a series of court cases ruled variously for and against his claim. The case finally reached the Supreme Court in 1857. Taney's ruling was remarkable in that it far exceeded the scope of the case. Taney could simply have ruled on the merits of the case; instead, he decided to establish a wide-ranging precedent. Slaves, he said, were property, and as such could be transported anywhere. Because slaves were not citizens, Taney further reasoned, they could not sue in federal court (thereby eliminating the possibility of the court reviewing any such cases in the future). Taney topped off his decision by stating that Congress could neither prevent settlers from transporting their slaves to western territories nor could it legislate slavery in those areas, thus nullifying the Missouri Compromise and rendering the concept of popular sovereignty unconstitutional. Taney's decision is infamous for its lack of compassion for Scott and slaves, and it is significant in that it hastened the inevitable Civil War. Choice (A) describes *Plessy v. Ferguson,* (B) describes many Supreme Court cases of the 1890s, and (C) describes *Engle v. Vitale.* You should know the *Plessy* and Dred Scott decisions, but not *Engle,* by name.

24. **C** In the excerpt, Douglass asserts that slaveholders have an advantage because they control all aspects of government. He states that "the Federal Government…is pledged to support, defend, and propagate the crying curse of human bondage." This may have been true in 1857, but Lincoln turned the tables in 1860 by running on a Free-Soil platform, thus opposing the institution of slavery. He did not promote popular sovereignty, so rule out (A). The Homestead Act is irrelevant to this question, so rule out (B). The slaves were not freed in 1860, so rule out (D).

25. **C** Many white Americans in the South asserted their regional identity through pride in the institution of slavery, insisting that the federal government should defend that institution. Indentured servants had long been replaced by slaves before 1857, so rule out (A). Douglass does not appear to be "adapting," so rule out (B). And, although Douglass was an abolitionist, he has not apparently swayed the opinion of Southerners, according to his own words, so rule out (D).

26. **D** Northern Republicans were most prone to abolitionist sentiments in 1857. Southerners in general were more likely to defend or tolerate slavery, so rule out (A) and (C). Western ranchers, (B), were not known for having strong abolitionist views, although many were no doubt sympathetic to Douglass. Choice (D) is a better answer.

27. **B** In the Northeast, the Second Great Awakening gave birth to numerous societies dedicated to the task of saving humanity from its own worst impulses. Much of the language of reform had a religious tone. For example, drinking and poverty were considered social evils. The religious and moral fervor that accompanied the Second Great Awakening also persuaded more and more Northerners that slavery was a great evil.

Questions 28–32

The Populists fought for the rights of the farmers and supported the free coinage of silver instead of the traditional reliance on the gold standard (which was seen as favoring bankers and lenders). Their leader, William Jennings Bryan, gave his most memorable speech in which he stated that the poor were being "crucified on a Cross of Gold." The Populists also believed in government ownership of railroads and utilities and opposed the tariff policies of William McKinley.

28. **D** The excerpt specifically decries the "two great political parties" and asserts that "grievous wrongs have been inflicted upon the suffering people." This is most similar to the third-party presidential candidate H. Ross Perot, who ran for office twice in the 1990s, lambasting both Democrats and Republicans in his bid for independent-minded voters. Choices (A), George McGovern, and (C), Andrew Jackson, were not critics of political parties per se. Theodore Roosevelt is a close choice, since Progressives did adopt some Populist ideals, but he was not as much of an outlier as Perot. Choice (D) is the best choice.

29. **D** The "free silver" campaign aimed to increase the money supply through the free coinage of silver. It was the great cause of the Populist party, which argued that the existing monetary practices favored the wealthy and elite, particularly in the Northeast. Free coinage of silver, the party argued,

would cause inflation but would also put more money in circulation, making it easier for farmers to pay off their debts. Furthermore, Populists felt that a larger money supply was appropriate to the United States' tremendous growth rate at that time. The policy was naturally quite popular with farmers, but not with bankers, who would have had their loans repaid with devalued currency. Free silver was a central issue in the 1896 election, during which the Populists and the Democratic party joined forces.

30.   **A**   Progressives adopted some Populist causes, such as better conditions for working people and government regulation of certain industries, so (A) is the best choice. Although some Populists had conservative leanings, neoconservatism is a very different ideology, so rule out (B). Jackson was not reform-minded in the same way Populists were, so rule out (D).

31.   **D**   Western Populists resented the control that the railroads exerted over transportation of goods across the country and wished to see railroads more tightly controlled by the federal government. All other answers represent Populist causes.

32.   **B**   The Populists generally resented big business and banking interests and saw their power as working contrary to the interests of farmers, ranchers, and working people in general. Most Populists lived in rural areas, although later Populists championed the causes of urban factory workers. Conservation was not a prominent concern for Populists, so rule out (A). Western farmers did not resent government interference; in fact, they often welcomed it, so rule out (C). Westward migration did not slow after the Civil War; it increased, so rule out (D).

Questions 33–34

Abraham Lincoln ran as the Republican nominee against Democratic candidate George B. McClellan, who ran as the "peace candidate" without personally believing in his party's platform. Lincoln was re-elected president. Electoral College votes were counted from 25 states. Since the election of 1860, the Electoral College had expanded with the admission of Kansas, West Virginia, and Nevada as free-soil states. As the American Civil War was still raging, no electoral votes were counted from any of the eleven Southern states. Lincoln won by more than 400,000 popular votes on the strength of the soldier vote and military successes such as the Battle of Atlanta.

33.   **A**   This question is all about Process of Elimination (POE). There is no mention of black voters, so rule out (C). Choice (D) is tempting, but we don't know for sure if Lincoln was campaigning for any other Republicans. Choice (B) is likewise unsupported. Choice (A) must be true because Lincoln won so many Electoral College votes. New Jersey and Delaware are relatively small states, while Kentucky was rural in 1864.

34.   **B**   When the Union dissolved and the South left Congress, Lincoln was faced with a legislature much more progressive in its thoughts on slavery than he was. The Radical Republican wing of Congress wanted immediate emancipation. Choices (A), (C), and (D) are all post-1861.

Questions 35–39

Progressives were primarily concerned with domestic reform; their agenda was the greater empowerment of labor, women, and the poor. The successes of the Progressive Era include those mentioned in the answer choices, the beginning of direct elections for the U.S. Senate, and the establishment of three popular political tools: the ballot initiative, the referendum, and the recall.

35. **D** The Progressives pursued no coherent foreign policy per se. Although Theodore Roosevelt was interested in Central American affairs, he was not representing primarily Progressive ideals with this initiative.

36. **C** Photojournalist Jacob Riis exposed the misery of tenement life in his book *How the Other Half Lives*, published in 1890. Muckrakers in general were concerned with "injustice," so the answer is (C).

37. **D** The Pure Food and Drug Act was passed after Sinclair wrote *The Jungle*, which exposed the filth and disease that was rampant throughout the slaughterhouses of Chicago.

38. **A** Theodore Roosevelt's "Square Deal" program was designed to conserve the earth's resources, control corporations through government regulation, and protect the consumer.

39. **B** The Underwood-Simmons Tariff was passed under Woodrow Wilson. (Hint: "Under," then "w" for Wilson.) Although Wilson was one of the three Progressive presidents (Roosevelt and Taft being the other two), he was the only Democrat. The Republican Party has supported big business since the end of the 19th century, and therefore, high protective tariffs are usually enacted when Republicans are in office. The Underwood-Simmons Tariff, however, actually *lowered* duties on imported goods; thus the answer is (B).

Questions 40–44

Labor unions have had a very rough go of it for many decades. At first, government policy and law were directed only at the protection of corporations and their property. Eventually, legislature passed bills protecting the rights of workers to organize and to bargain collectively. Enforcement of those protections, however, was lax to nonexistent; as a result, many union workers were subject to all sorts of harassment. The use of scabs and strike-breaking thugs was common; workers who dared to organize could lose their jobs and even their lives.

40. **B** The cartoon depicts the government conducting a misdirected fact-finding mission at a time when abuses against labor unions were obvious. The attack is not "well-concealed," so rule out (C).

41. **A** Samuel Gompers once referred to the Clayton Antitrust Act as "The Magna Carta of Labor," because in addition to strengthening the Sherman Antitrust Act, it also exempted labor unions from antitrust prosecution and legalized strikes and picketing.

42. **D** Congress did not consistently promote the interests of labor unions, so rule out (A); Republicans, in particular, tended to try to curb the power of labor. Immigrants were not a large part of labor union membership, nor did they displace child workers (laws banning child labor accomplished this), so rule out (B). Black sharecroppers may have voted for Democrats, but they did not have a direct influence, so rule out (C). Thus, the success of labor unions was largely due to their own efforts.

43.   **A**   Labor unions met with resistance, in part, because they were new to America, a change from the traditional relationship between employer and employee. Many conservatives did not trust this new attempt to organize the workforce. Both union organizers and employers tended to be largely native-born, so (B) does not represent a contrast. Religion is not a factor here, so rule out (C). And most union AND employers were urban, so (D) does not represent a contrast.

44.   **C**   Although it was by no means universal, many early 20th-century union leaders were, in fact, Communists, or sympathetic to socialist ideologies. (This tendency reversed after World War II.) Choice (A) may have some kernel of truth, but is not the primary cause of the antilabor sentiment. Choice (D) is incorrect because McCarthy was most vocal in the 1950s.

Questions 45–48

In 1954, the Supreme Court ruled invalid the "separate but equal" standard approved by the court in *Plessy v. Ferguson* (1896). In a 9 to 0 decision, the court ruled that "separate educational facilities are inherently unequal." The suit was brought on behalf of Linda Brown, a black school-age child, by the NAACP. Then-future Supreme Court Justice Thurgood Marshall argued the case.

45.   **C**   About the other cases mentioned here: (A), *Marbury v. Madison*, is the case that established the principle of judicial review. Choice (B), *Bradwell v. Illinois*, is an 1873 decision in which the court upheld the right of the state of Illinois to deny a female attorney the right to practice law simply on the basis of gender. That case represented a setback for both women's rights and the Fourteenth Amendment. In (D), *Holden v. Hardy*, the Court ruled that states could pass laws regulating safety conditions in privately owned workplaces.

46.   **A**   Liberalism, based on a firm belief in the efficacy of governmental and especially federal power to achieve social goals at home, reached its apex in the mid-1960s and generated a variety of political and cultural responses. Southern Conservatives did not accept the goals of Civil Rights liberals without a struggle. Riots and protests erupted throughout the South, while Little Rock, Arkansas, refused to integrate its high school for some time. Choices (B) and (C) are unsupportable, while (D) cannot be directly attributed to *Brown*.

47.   **C**   Many formerly oppressed groups were inspired to take action after the successes of the Civil Rights movement. States' rights, however, was never a social movement in the same manner as the others.

48.   **D**   Reconstruction had originally intended to integrate freed slaves into Southern white society, but it largely failed to do so. Civil Rights leaders picked up the banner and sought to get the equal rights they had legally earned after the Civil War.

Questions 49–50

In the 1980s, a new conservatism grew to prominence in U.S. culture and politics, defending traditional social values and rejecting liberal views about the role of government. Reduced public faith in the government's ability to solve social and economic problems, the growth of religious fundamentalism, and the dissemination of neo-conservative thought all combined to invigorate conservatism.

49. **A** Public confidence and trust in government declined in the 1970s in the wake of economic infla-tion, political scandals, and foreign policy crises, such as the Iranian hostage crisis, so rule out (C). The rapid and substantial growth of evangelical and fundamentalist Christian churches and organizations, as well as increased political participation by some of those groups, encouraged sig-nificant opposition to liberal social and political trends—rule out (B) and (D). Libertarians never had much success in national elections, so (A) is the exception.

50. **C** Progressive Liberals would have been most opposed to Reagan's conservative principles. Choice (B), Reagan Democrats, were more moderate in their views, while (D), Populists, were not entirely liberal in their views.

Questions 51–55

The legislation passed during 1965 and 1966 represented the most sweeping change to U.S. government since the New Deal. Johnson's social agenda was termed the "Great Society."

51. **B** The mention of renewing "contact with nature" should call to mind wildlife and the preservation of natural habitats. Choice (B) is the only answer that connects to these ideas. An act related to mass transportation would not likely renew contact with nature. Eliminate (A). The Public Broad-casting Act and Higher Education Acts also have aims that are not directly related to nature, so (C) and (D) are incorrect.

52. **D** All choices, except (D), were indeed part of the Great Society program. Rather than balancing the budget, the Great Society reforms meant a significant increase in federal spending, which grew faster than government revenues through taxes.

53. **B** Under the Lyndon B. Johnson Administration, U.S. involvement in Vietnam accelerated. Choice (A) is associated with Kennedy. Choice (C) is associated with Truman and Eisenhower. Choice (D) occurred in the late 1980s and early 1990s under Reagan and George H.W. Bush.

54. **A** Today's social welfare system stems from the New Deal; those who feel that the current American system has failed can point to Roosevelt as the man who started it all.

55. **B** Liberal ideals were realized in Supreme Court decisions that expanded democracy and individual freedoms, Great Society social programs and policies, and the power of the federal government, yet these unintentionally helped energize a new conservative movement that mobilized to defend traditional visions of morality and the proper role of state authority.

SECTION I, PART B: SHORT-ANSWER QUESTIONS

Question 1

a) American constitutionalism is a group of ideas elaborating upon the principle that the authority of government derives from the people, and it is limited by a body of fundamental law. Constitutionalism is a bulwark against monarchy, totalitarianism, or pure democracy. In the first excerpt, Philip Wiener mentions such key ideas as the "rule of law," "officials are not free to do anything they please," "limitations on power," and "limited government."

b) Democracy is a form of government in which all eligible citizens participate equally—either directly or indirectly through elected representatives—in the proposal, development, and creation of laws. In his letter, John Adams seems to presuppose the drawbacks of pure democracy. He likens it to monarchy, though acknowledging that it is more short-lived. Democracy, "when unchecked, produces the same effects of fraud, violence, and cruelty...it is hard for the most considerate philosophers and the most conscientious moralists to resist the temptation" to descend into tyranny.

c) In your response to this question, you could have mentioned any one of the following:

Constitutionalism

- The Mayflower Compact—This document is not a constitution in the strictest sense because it does not provide for an actual government. Still, it was an important forerunner to constitutional government in the New World. Those who signed it agreed to self-government and to abide by the laws they passed.
- The Fundamental Orders of Connecticut—the formal constitution written by Connecticut settlers and enacted in 1639. (If you knew its name and date, give yourself bonus points.) You do have to know that this document was the first formal constitution in the New World and that it stated that the power of government rests in the consent of those being governed. In this assertion, the Connecticut settlers distinguished themselves from the royalists, who often argued that the king, and therefore the government, ruled by Divine Right (that is, that the king's power came from God, who chose the king).

Give yourself extra credit for mentioning the following:

- The Massachusetts Bay Charter—Acting as a constitution of sorts, it provided the mechanism for self-government. As mentioned above, Massachusetts Bay was technically ruled by the king, but actually, it was governed by the company's general court, established in the company charter. All property holders—thus, nearly all the white males in the settlement—voted for deputies (representatives) to the general court. The charter also required the company's proprietors to seek the advice and consent of all freemen before making laws.
- English traditions—(1) The Magna Carta (1215) established a few fundamental, inalienable rights for property holders. (2) The concept of limited government—the idea that the king ruled by the people's consent, and not by Divine Right—was gaining wider acceptance in England at the time. (3) The existence of a bicameral legislature—the House of Lords and the House of Commons— gave the colonists a tradition in both representative government and constitutional government.
- The English Civil War—In the early 17th century, Parliament, backed by reform forces that included the Puritans, began to demand changes to make government more responsive to and

representative of the people. King Charles responded by dissolving Parliament in 1629. When he finally recalled Parliament in 1640 (because his government was failing), Puritans demanded major constitutional reforms. Charles refused and a long, bloody war followed. When Puritan forces won in 1649, Charles lost his head and England, briefly, had a constitution. The whole episode demonstrates that the Puritans were strongly committed to constitutionalism.

- The New England Confederation—Founded in 1643, the confederation of New England colonies was mostly powerless because it had no executive power. However, it did settle some border disputes, and it represented the people's willingness to create governmental agencies and to (sort of) abide by their decisions.

Democracy

- All the New England colonies had elected legislatures by 1650.
- Most had bicameral legislatures, with a lower house elected by all freemen and an upper house usually made up of appointees. Freemen also usually elected the governor.
- New England had a tradition of town meetings at which many of the decisions concerning local government were made.
- Women, indentured servants, and slaves could not vote.
- Except in Rhode Island, only Puritans had the right to vote.
- Otherwise, voting rights were extended to all property holders. Because most settlers were enticed to the New World by the prospect of owning land and because in the early years land was plentiful, nearly all the white male colonists could vote.

Give yourself extra credit for mentioning the following:

- The Massachusetts Bay Company, while technically controlled by the king, had little contact with England. It was empowered to make almost all important decisions. It set an early precedent for self-government in the New World.
- Although initially governed by the owners of the company, Massachusetts Bay's governors soon extended democratic rights to all Puritan property-owning settlers. The colony was ruled by a general court to which all towns were allowed to elect delegates.
- The Plymouth settlement formed a legislature as soon as the settlement expanded beyond a couple of towns.
- The Puritans valued the ideal of the covenant. They believed they had a covenant with God, and they used the covenant as a model for their secular behavior. Accordingly, the Puritans expected everyone to work for the communal good and that everyone would have a voice in how the community was run.
- When settlers moved into the Connecticut Valley, they had their first run-in with Native Americans. The settlers essentially tried to bully the natives out of their land. In the resulting Pequot War, settlers torched villages and killed women and children. You might mention this as evidence of the settlers' rather limited sense of fair play and justice, which are usually considered democratic ideals.

About the Structure of Your Essay

For part (c), you want a short statement that allows you to discuss both of the basic characteristics of early American democracy. One way to achieve this is to discuss these developments in the context of their contribution to later developments in American self-governance. For example, you might phrase your statement in the following manner: "Because of their distance from England, the English colonists in New England were in a situation that largely allowed them to govern themselves. Other factors—English traditions, Puritan beliefs, the wide availability of land—helped create the communities that in many ways laid the foundation for American government. However, these communities also differed in significant ways from what we usually identify as the "American ideal." Then follow it up with ONE pertinent fact with regard to your chosen themes (supporting the first excerpt or refuting the second excerpt). A one-sentence conclusion, perhaps mentioning the similarities and differences between Puritan society and the more pluralistic democratic societies that followed it, would also be helpful.

Question 2

The name of this work is "English Trade with Indians" by Theodor de Bry, painted in 1634. (Notice that the College Board does not tell you this; they want to see if you can interpret the drawing on your own.)

This picture shows you one interpretation of a trading session between the English and Native Americans. Theodor de Bry was one of the first to create such drawings of the New World. Are there any European biases about Native Americans in this drawing? That might make good fodder for your essay.

a) For this question, you may have mentioned some of the following:

Commerce

- Make a nod to the Columbian Exchange, a series of interactions and adaptations among societies across the Atlantic.
- The Spanish introduced new crops and livestock to natives.

American Indians

- Iroquois and Algonquian Indians were not nomadic. They had permanent villages built around agriculture and fishing. This enabled them to engage in serious commerce with the English.
- Many Europeans had deeply ingrained beliefs about racial superiority.
- The English eventually established American colonies based on agriculture; large numbers of settlers came, often having relatively hostile relationships with American Indians.
- Early conflicts: The Beaver Wars, the Chickasaw Wars, King Philip's War.

European Exploration

- Spanish and Portuguese exploration and conquest of the Americas led to widespread deadly epidemics.
- New sources of mineral wealth facilitated the European shift from feudalism to capitalism.
- New sailing technology: the sextant.

b) and c) For these questions, describe the contrasts in how each group is portrayed, Indian and English traders. Explain the significance of any objects depicted. The traders seem to be interacting in a positive way, but we know that relationships between the English and native peoples were not always easy. What might have happened after the exchange depicted?

Question 3

a) and b) For these questions, you may have discussed some of the following:

- Spain was particularly successful in converting much of Meso-America to Catholicism through the Spanish mission system, thus introducing the idea that Natives could be Europeanized through religion. Christians in the Northeast tried this tactic and largely failed.
- The Puritans sought a new life and religious freedom in Massachusetts, thus setting the stage for the eventual republic.
- The Pilgrims created the Mayflower Compact, which is important not only because it created a legal authority and an assembly, but also because it asserted that the government's power derives from the consent of the governed.
- John Winthrop delivered a now-famous sermon, "A Model of Christian Charity," urging the colonists to be a "city upon a hill"—a model for others to look up to. All Puritans believed they had a covenant with God. Government was to be a covenant among the people.
- The First Great Awakening: Congregationalist minister Jonathan Edwards and Methodist preacher George Whitefield came to exemplify the period. Edwards preached the severe doctrines of Calvinism and became famous for his graphic depictions of Hell; his most famous speech was "Sinners in the Hands of an Angry God." Whitefield preached a Christianity based on emotionalism and spirituality, which today is most clearly manifested in Southern evangelism. The First Great Awakening is often described as the response of devout people to the Enlightenment.

c) For this question, you may have mentioned some of the following:

- Explorers, such as Juan de Oñate, swept through the American Southwest, determined to create Christian converts by any means necessary—including violence. Oñate was resisted by the natives.
- The Salem Witch Trials are often thought to be a product of the Puritan resistance to changes in their power within Massachusetts and declining support for Puritanism within the younger generation.
- Even though the Puritans had fled England because of religious persecution, they did not allow freedom of religion in their colonies.
- Roger Williams—Williams came to the New World to teach in the Salem Bay settlement (part of the Massachusetts Bay colony). His writings and teachings advocated separation of church and state and the free practice of all religions in the New World. He also had some other radical ideas, such as suggesting that the English had no right to take land away from Native American tribes. The Puritans banished Williams from the colony in 1636. He moved to modern-day Providence and received a charter for the colony of Rhode Island in 1642. The charter specified that Rhode Island would protect the freedom of religion. By 1650 Rhode Island was still the only New England colony that allowed individuals to follow their religious faiths in freedom.
- Anne Hutchinson—Hutchinson fell from favor with the Puritans because of her ideas. She believed in the power of grace and also that God spoke directly to certain, chosen people. Those people, she argued, did not need Puritan ministers or the Church because God assured those He spoke to that they would be saved. Her position was known as "antinomianism." Hutchinson's message appealed to many Puritans because of its assurances of salvation. She was considered dangerous, doubly so because she was becoming a powerful woman in a society in which women were definitely second-class citizens. The General Court of Massachusetts brought her up on charges of defaming the ministry, found her guilty, and banished her. She started a settlement in Portsmouth, Rhode Island.
- There was no separation of church and state, as evidenced by the charges against Anne Hutchinson.

Question 4

This essay requires you to demonstrate an understanding of the concept of collective security and then provide historical examples that illustrate the role of collective security in the formation of U.S. foreign policy in the postwar period. That's the easy part, however. Remember that if you're aiming to get a 4 or 5 on this exam, you need to write analytical, not merely descriptive, essays. The College Board often utilizes this continuation/departure format in a social or foreign policy question, asking you to determine if the U.S. government is doing the same thing it always has or if this is a new policy. A really strong essay will not only answer the last part of this question but also discuss why the United States chose to alter its course at this time in history.

a) For this part, you merely have to describe what is meant by *collective security*. In simple terms, it is the cooperation of multiple nation-states for mutually beneficial security. To move your score higher, give an example or two on how this has been used by the United States. You may touch on the alliance systems from the two world wars, for instance.

b) For this question, you may have mentioned some of the following:

- In his Farewell Address, George Washington had urged the new nation to avoid permanent entangling alliances. Subsequent administrations followed Washington's advice throughout the entire 19th and early 20th centuries. We did not enter a major military alliance until World War I, and even then, we attempted to retreat to our traditional policy of isolationism when the war was over.
- How about the Senate's defeat of the Treaty of Versailles and the failure of the United States to join the League of Nations? This will enable you to argue that U.S. foreign policy following World War II was a *departure* from previous policy.
- If you choose the UN as one of the two alliances about which to write in your essay, you should mention the wartime conferences that established the UN at the conclusion of World War II.
- If you plan to write about NATO, then you should mention the uneasy alliance between the Soviet Union and the United States during World War II. You should also discuss the decisions reached at Yalta and the subsequent Soviet takeover of Eastern Europe. Be careful not to go into too much detail here. This is only a short essay! But this information answers the "Why at this time?" question and will strengthen your essay.
- It is not necessary to provide the historical background to SEATO. A brief discussion of NATO, however, might provide the rationale as to why the United States formed SEATO in 1954.
- Be sure to include a definition of collective security somewhere in your essay. It is usually a good idea to define the terms you will use in whatever essay you are writing. For example, it never hurts to define terms such as *democracy, nationalism,* and *imperialism*.
- A strong essay should answer a why question; so in this case, you should not only state that these international alliances were a clear departure from previous U.S. foreign policy, but you might also blame them on Stalin, for example. Don't be afraid to say something slightly unusual, as long as you have historical evidence to support what you are writing. Don't just say "We created the UN because we didn't join the League of Nations after World War I." This is a weak and boring statement.

Here is some in-depth info on each organization:

The UN

Many historians believe that the Treaty of Versailles was one of the major causes of World War II. Others see the failure of collective security to prevent another world war and blame the impotence of the League of Nations for its failure to stop German, Italian, and Japanese aggression throughout the 1930s. Some critics argue the

Cracking the AP U.S. History Exam

League would have been stronger had the United States been a member. You should remember that the League of Nations was proposed by Woodrow Wilson in his Fourteen Points as a means of maintaining world peace. The United Nations was formed after World War II in part to replace the League of Nations and in response to the horrors committed during World War II.

The most obvious choice here is the Korean War. You should begin this paragraph with a brief discussion of the Truman Doctrine and the articulation of the policy of containment by George Kennan. The Korean conflict is often considered the first test case of containment. Mao's forces won a victory in China in 1949, and when Soviet-supported North Korean troops invaded South Korea the following year, the UN Security Council declared North Korea an aggressor and voted to send in troops. Although the United States provided the majority of manpower, we went into Korea in 1950 under the protective umbrella of the United Nations. The Soviets had successfully tested an atomic bomb in 1949. Given the threat of atomic warfare, the United States felt more secure as part of an international peacekeeping organization.

NATO

In 1949, the United States, Canada, Great Britain, France, Italy, Belgium, the Netherlands, Luxembourg, Portugal, Denmark, Norway, and Iceland signed the North Atlantic Treaty. Each nation agreed that it would view an attack on any one nation as an attack on them all. Greece and Turkey were admitted to the Organization three years later. Unlike the UN, which is an international peacekeeping organization, NATO is an international, defensive military alliance. The United States' entrance into NATO was a significant departure from traditional U.S. foreign policy and marked the first peacetime military alliance in U.S. history. If the Truman Doctrine was an ideological response to the establishment of Soviet satellites following World War II, and the Marshall Plan "put our money where our mouth is," then NATO may be seen as the military component of this equation. You might mention either the war in Bosnia or the Persian Gulf War to illustrate NATO in action.

SEATO

In 1954, eight nations—including the United States and its major western allies, Great Britain and France—signed a collective defense treaty with the Philippines, Thailand, and Pakistan to form what became known as the Southeast Asia Treaty Organization. In essence, it was basically a Southeast Asian version of NATO. Each member nation pledged to come to the defense of another member nation in the event it was attacked. However, unlike NATO, an attack on one nation would not necessarily be viewed as an attack on them all. The United States agreed to the provisions of the treaty on the condition that the aggressor be a member of the communist bloc. Although the organization was intended to provide an "anticommunist shield" to the nations of Southeast Asia, SEATO was not invoked to protect Cambodia, Laos, or Vietnam during the Vietnam War, as one would have suspected. In fact, the Geneva Accords specifically precluded South Vietnam, Cambodia, and Laos from joining the organization. France lost interest almost immediately and did not feel bound to the other member nations after Vietnam gained its independence following the French defeat in the battle of Dien Bien Phu. The United States tried to make the situation in Vietnam a collective security issue, as evidenced by the rhetoric of the domino theory, but was unsuccessful. In effect, SEATO never had the teeth or muscle that NATO had, and it was dissolved in 1977.

c) This question can be answered by using any of the facts cited for part (a), while demonstrating that the organization was NOT a strong continuation or departure from prior U.S. foreign policy OR by simply explaining why it is LESS of a continuation or departure from the choice you made in part (a).

SECTION II, QUESTION 1: DOCUMENT-BASED QUESTION

The document-based question begins with a mandatory 15-minute reading period. During these 15 minutes, you should (1) come up with some information not included in the given documents (your outside knowledge) to include in your essay, (2) get an overview of what each document means, (3) decide what opinion you are going to argue, and (4) write an outline of your essay.

This DBQ concerns U.S. neutrality prior to World War I. You will have to explore to what extent the United States followed a policy of neutrality between 1914 and 1917. On the following pages, we will talk about how you might successfully explore this topic.

The first thing you want to do, BEFORE YOU LOOK AT THE DOCUMENTS, is brainstorm for a minute or two. Try to list everything you remember about the period leading up to the United States' entry into World War I. This list will serve as your reference to the outside information you must provide in order to earn a top grade.

Next, read over the documents. As you read them, take notes in the margins and underline those passages that you are certain you are going to use in your essay. If a document helps you remember a piece of outside information, add that information to your brainstorming list. If you cannot make sense of a document or it argues strongly against your position, relax! You may omit mention of <u>one</u> of the documents and still score well on the DBQ.

You need to look for the following in each document to get the most out of it:

- the author
- the date
- the audience (for whom was the document intended?)
- the significance

Remember: while readers are looking for as much in-depth document analysis as possible, it does help to bring in some outside information. They will not be able to give you a high score unless you have both! What readers really don't like is a laundry list of documents: that is, a paper in which the student merely goes through the documents, explaining each one. Those students are often the ones who forget to bring in outside information, because they are so focused on going through the documents.

Here is what you might see in the time you have to look over the documents.

The Documents

Document 1 is an excerpt from Wilson's declaration of neutrality. It makes several important points you can use.

Neutrality is defined as "impartiality and fairness and friendliness to all concerned." This standard will enable you to argue that the United States was, or was not, neutral.

The American people come from the different nations at war. The political implication is that even if the U.S. government wanted to enter World War I, the varied national backgrounds of the electorate would make it difficult to rally the nation to one side or the other. Even before Vietnam, American politicians knew the risks of entering an unpopular war.

Wilson envisions a prominent role for the United States resulting from neutrality. He sees the United States as "the one people holding itself ready to play a part of impartial mediation and speak the counsels of peace and accommodation, not as a partisan, but as a friend." This point argues that the United States entered the war as a neutral force, or, at the very least, intended to.

Document 2 is an excerpt from a letter a respected German-American intellectual wrote to Wilson early in the war. It describes German-American perceptions of U.S. favoritism toward the Allies.

This document persuasively argues that U.S. policies at the time favored the Allies. The details are important, but they are less important than the overall point; the document illustrates that an intelligent critique of U.S. policy, held up to its own definition of neutrality, is possible. In fact, when Wilson received this letter, he sent it to his secretary of state with a note essentially saying, "This letter makes a pretty strong case."

Munsterberg's second point, regarding the detention and searching of Germans and Austrians, is not often mentioned in discussions of the events leading up to World War I, and you are not expected to have heard of this policy. However, it does provide ammunition for those arguing that the United States was never neutral; searching civilians is, at the very least, an act of aggressive mistrust. If Allied travelers were not being treated the same way—and the letter implies they were not—then it indicates favoritism.

The issue of contraband could lead you to discuss the British blockade. (Document 3 provides more evidence of the effect of the British blockade.) Contraband is illegal merchandise. During war, contraband always includes weapons and other supplies necessary to the successful execution of war. The notion that contraband is illegal does not preclude the United States from selling arms to Europe; this same document demonstrates that the United States did just that. It does mean, however, that a country executing a successful blockade has the right to confiscate contraband. Munsterberg is saying that England defined contraband very broadly, including on its list of contraband items supplies that the German civilian population needed to survive. He complains that the United States was not aggressive enough in protesting this practice.

The last paragraph talks about the U.S. sale of arms to belligerents. This information can be interpreted in many ways. You could argue that to sell arms is essentially non-neutral, even if you sell to both sides. To make this argument, you would have to equate neutrality with pacifism (something Wilson does in Document 1) and then assert that arms sales prolong the war, and so they are counterproductive to the goals of neutrality. On the other hand, you could argue that because of the successful British blockade, arms sales were predominantly to the Allies; arms shipments to Germany never made it through the blockade. Again, Document 3 will help bolster this position.

Document 3, an often-quoted passage, comes from the memoirs of Robert Lansing, acting secretary of state and, later, secretary of state under Wilson.

Lansing describes the effects of the British blockade. Note that merchants are losing profits, and Americans are being terribly inconvenienced.

You might use this to argue favoritism toward the British. Since the British were interfering with U.S. trade, why didn't we go to war against them? To the contrary, you could point out that as it became clear that U.S. commercial interests were at stake, U.S. involvement in the war became more likely. In other words, the United States started out neutral, but the British blockade and German submarine warfare slowly forced America into the war. (See Documents 5, 6, 7, and 8.) You can also use this document to further discuss the effects of the British blockade on (1) the Allies and (2) the Central Powers. As you do, ask yourself whether the United States' response to the blockade was consistent with its policy of neutrality.

Document 4, a report from then-Secretary of State William Jennings Bryan (he would soon resign in protest) to the Senate. It is still early in the war.

Do not be intimidated by the length of this passage! The main point is simple. The government felt that its actions were neutral. This letter can be seen as a response to the complaints voiced in Munsterberg's letter.

Bryan discusses communication, the blockade, arms sales, and perceived hostility toward the governments of the Central Powers. In almost every case, he argues that England's advantages in geographic location and naval power are causing America's perceived breaches of neutrality.

If you are arguing that the United States was neutral, you might mention (if you remember) that Bryan, a pacifist, was committed to neutrality. His feeling that U.S. actions were neutral could be presented as strong evidence for your case.

If you are arguing that the United States was not neutral, you might contend that because Bryan is reporting to the Senate, he paints the rosiest picture he can. You might also mention (if you remember) that Bryan resigned not long after because of his disagreements with U.S. policy.

Document 5 is an advertisement that ran in fifty American newspapers just before the *Lusitania* sailed.

This document gives you the opportunity to discuss German submarine warfare. The British blockade was too effective for the Germans to fight it conventionally. The Germans therefore turned to the U-boat, or submarine. Submarines gave the Germans the advantage of surprise, as the British had no means of detecting them. You could argue that because submarine attacks resulted in the deaths of U.S. citizens, the use of submarines constituted a hostile act that ultimately forced the neutral United States into war. You might mention that Wilson regarded submarines as a violation of international law (see Chapter 11) and, as such, repeatedly asked the Germans to curtail their usage.

On the contrary, you might claim that the British blockade forced Germany to use submarines, and that by not opposing the blockade more aggressively, the United States was essentially siding with the Allies.

This document, along with Document 6, also gives you the opportunity to discuss the sinking of the *Lusitania* and its effects, both on U.S. policy and on anti-German sentiments in the general population. The shift in American public opinion away from neutrality is a factor you might mention in your discussion of U.S. entry into the war.

Document 6 is a customs report that provides evidence that the *Lusitania* carried weapons.

This document can be paired with Munsterberg's complaint about arms sales (Document 2) to support the argument that the United States was not neutral. Note that the shipment is headed for England. Your outside knowledge that the sinking of the *Lusitania* led to William Jennings Bryan's resignation as secretary of state would also be helpful here. Remember, the United States protested the sinking vigorously and demanded reparations. Bryan pointed out that the ship carried arms and quietly assured the Germans that the United States understood why the ship was sunk. In short, Bryan was at odds with official government policy, and he resigned when he realized that his advice to the president was going unheeded. His replacement, Robert Lansing, more active in defending American interests than Bryan, was willing to trade a reduction in American commerce for peace.

If you are arguing for neutrality, it is best to mention this document only in passing. Note that in Document 4, Bryan explains how the United States reconciles arms sales and neutrality. His justification, in short, is that international law does not outlaw such sales.

Document 7: Wilson gave this speech after the Germans sank the *Sussex*, an unarmed French channel steamer. The document is from 1916, almost a year after the sinking of the *Lusitania*.

Wilson threatens to break off diplomatic relations with Germany—a first step toward war.

Wilson invokes international law. Because Wilson interpreted international law as severely restricting submarine warfare, submarine attacks by Germany particularly angered him. Wilson considered himself and the United States the defenders of international law.

Wilson continues to declare America's international role as a mediator and peacemaker, as he did in his neutrality speech (Document 1). This insistence indicates that Wilson still considers the United States a neutral force.

You might point out that a year after the sinking of the *Lusitania* and that of several other ships, the United States is still not at war. This fact strongly argues for neutrality through early 1916.

Outside Information

We have already discussed much more than you could possibly include in a 45-minute essay. Do not worry. You will not be expected to mention everything or even most of what we have covered in the section above. You will, however, be expected to include some outside information—that is, information not mentioned directly in the documents.

Here is some outside information you might have used in your essay. The information is divided into two groups: general concepts and specific events.

General Concepts

- Even before the war, the United States relied more on trade with the British than with Germany. After the war began, this dependence became even heavier as the British blockade decreased American trade with Germany. The war effort also resulted in an increase in British orders for American goods. This increase occurred because the war had decreased British productivity. The British had taken men out of factories and put them in the army, and they also had converted some commercial manufacturing to munitions manufacturing.

- When the war started, official U.S. policy stated that American banks should not lend money to any nation at war. However, bankers pressured the administration to change this policy because Europe did not have the money to pay for the American goods it was ordering. Also, the loans were profitable, and American banks feared losing a lucrative opportunity to banks in other neutral nations. The majority of these loans went to the Allies.

- Wilson hoped the war would end in a draw. He thought a victorious Germany "would change the course of our civilization and make the United States a military nation." He also felt that an Allied victory would shift the balance of power too favorably toward England and France. Many of Wilson's advisors, however, were both pro-British and anti-German.

- "Wilsonianism," Wilson's idealized vision of the future, included universal, nonexploitative, free market capitalism; universal political constitutionalism, which would lead to the disappearance of empires; and universal cooperation and peace through the offices of the League of Nations. Wilson was also anxious to create a world leadership role for the United States. Many of his actions can be explained as the pursuit of these goals.

- Wilson held very strong views concerning international law, and those views favored the British. According to international law, an attacker had to warn a passenger or merchant ship before attacking. Submarines did not do this, for the obvious reason that it would cancel the greatest advantage submarines had—the element of surprise. Germany argued that submarines provided their only means of breaking British control of shipping channels, but this assertion did not persuade Wilson.

Specific Events

- The British blockade—From the beginning of the war, the British used their advantage at sea. They blocked shipping channels and confiscated any contraband headed for a Central Power country. Furthermore, England defined contraband very broadly, including some food and commercial products on its contraband list. The United States lodged numerous complaints against the practice, but the British government always paid for what it confiscated. The payment satisfied merchants and took enough pressure off Washington that the U.S. government never forced the issue.

- The sinking of the *Lusitania*, May 7, 1915—You will lose big points if you say that this event caused the United States to enter the war; the United States waited another two years before it started to fight. The *Lusitania* was a luxury liner that sailed from New York to England. When it sank, it took with it 1,198 passengers, among them 128 Americans. As

Document 6 illustrates, the *Lusitania* was carrying a considerable amount of contraband, including over 4 million rounds of rifle ammunition. Still, Wilson and most of his advisors considered Germany's attack on the ship barbaric. As a result of the attack, anti-German sentiments among voters grew stronger and more widespread.

- William Jennings Bryan's resignation—Bryan resigned in the aftermath of the *Lusitania* incident. An ardent pacifist, Bryan wanted the United States to respond to the incident with a strongly worded letter of protest to both the English and the Germans. Bryan also suggested that the United States ban American passengers from any ship flying the flag of a belligerent country. Wilson rejected both recommendations. He sent a letter of protest only to the Germans, and he refused to restrict American travel abroad. Bryan resigned in protest. In response to Wilson's letter, the Germans temporarily halted U-boat attacks on passenger ships.

- The sinking of the *Arabic*—In mid-August 1915, the Germans sank another passenger liner. This time only two Americans died, but the government was furious about the breach of etiquette. The Germans pledged again never to attack a passenger liner without advance warning, a promise they did not keep.

- Gore-McLemore resolution—After the sinking of the *Arabic*, Congress began to seriously consider a resolution prohibiting Americans from traveling on armed merchant ships or on ships carting contraband. Wilson fought this Gore-McLemore resolution. Wilson remained adamant that neutral nations should have free access to international waters. The resolution was defeated.

- The sinking of the *Sussex* and the Sussex Agreement—In February 1917, the Germans sank a French channel steamer called the *Sussex*. No Americans died, although four were injured. However, the incident had a big impact because the *Sussex* was neither armed nor was it carrying contraband. In short, its sinking convinced many people that either (1) German submarines could not tell what they were shooting at, or (2) the Germans did not care that they were killing civilians. Either way, it supported the widespread sentiment that submarine warfare was barbaric. Germany again agreed not to attack passenger ships without warning. Wilson was still resolutely determined to stay out of the war, so he accepted the agreement.

- The presidential election of 1916—Despite the many quarrels with England and Germany, most Americans still wanted no part of the European hostilities. All the major candidates campaigned against entry into the war. The Republican, Hughes, courted German-American votes and depicted Wilson as partial to the Allies. Wilson campaigned on the slogan "He kept us out of war." As the campaign wore on, however, he also began to stress "preparedness" for the possibility of war. Wilson won by a narrow margin.

- Details about the Zimmermann note—By the time this telegram was leaked to the press, Germany had already warned the United States of its plans to resume unrestricted submarine warfare. The reason for the shift in policy is that the Germans realized that without the submarines they would soon lose the war. The resumption of submarine warfare greatly angered Wilson. When the British intercepted the telegram, Wilson had already severed diplomatic ties with Germany and was considering his future options. Wilson received the telegram on February 24, 1917, and the newspapers received it four days later.

The telegram represents a last-ditch effort on Germany's part to keep the United States out of the war. Germany knew that its resumption of submarine warfare would draw the United States into the war. Planning to distract the United States with a border skirmish, Germany hoped to buy enough time to win the war in Europe before U.S. reinforcements could arrive. Because the Mexican Revolution had just replaced a government friendly to the United States with one much more hostile, the U.S. government took the threat of a German-backed Mexican attack in the Southwest very seriously.

It particularly galled the United States that Zimmermann sent the telegram through U.S. State Department channels. The United States had opened those channels to him in hopes of bringing the Germans back to the negotiating table. When he used those same channels to plot war against the United States, it was regarded as an act of extreme hostility and bad manners.

The United States did not immediately declare war. In the weeks that followed, Wilson asked Congress for a policy of "armed neutrality," which would allow American merchant ships to mount offensive weapons. Debate was fierce, showing how strong antiwar sentiment was even at the time. The United States did not officially declare war until the following month, on April 2, 1917.

- The Nye Commission investigations of 1933—The Nye Commission, investigating American business practices in the years leading up to World War I, revealed that American arms merchants had lobbied intensely for entry into the war. The commission also discovered that these merchants had reaped enormous profit from arms sales, first from whomever they could get them to in Europe and then from the U.S. government.

Choosing a Side

We have just covered an intimidating amount of material. Do not worry; your essay has to cover only some of the points mentioned above. This review mentions nearly everything you might include in a successful essay, not everything that must be in a successful essay.

Your next task is to choose a position to argue and then construct a strong justification from your notes on the documents and outside information. Document-based questions are written so that there is no one right answer, and there are many different defensible positions to this question. There are also many different ways to argue the same point; that is, there is no one right way to write an essay for any given argument.

Here are some positions you might argue:

- The United States was neutral at the beginning of the war, but a combination of factors— such as economic interests, German transgressions of international law, and America's predisposition toward England—ultimately drew America into the war.

- The United States was neutral at the beginning of the war but was provoked to fight by German aggression.

- The United States claimed neutrality, and maybe its leaders even convinced themselves that their actions were neutral, but in reality, U.S. actions helped the Allies. Consequently, the United States was never really neutral.

- The United States was correct in claiming neutrality because its policies adhered to its standards of neutrality. However, the Central Powers legitimately accused the United States of acting in a way that assisted the Allies and so were justified in regarding the United States as non-neutral. The question is semantic; whether the United States was neutral depends on how you define neutrality.

The only position you should certainly avoid is the claim that the United States had always sided fully with the Allies and lied about neutrality in order to help them. There is simply too much evidence of Wilson's commitment to neutrality to support that argument.

Planning Your Essay

Unless you read extremely quickly, you probably will not have time to write a detailed outline for your essay during the 15-minute reading period. However, it is worth taking several minutes to jot down a loose structure of your essay; it will actually save you time when you write. First, decide on your thesis and write it down in the test booklet. (There is usually some blank space below the documents.) Then, take a minute or two to brainstorm all the points you might put in your essay. Choose the strongest points and number them in the order you plan to present them. Lastly, note which documents and outside information you plan to use in conjunction with each point. If you organize your essay before you write, the actual writing process will go much more smoothly. More importantly, you will not write yourself into a corner and suddenly find yourself making a point you cannot support or heading toward a weak conclusion (or worse still, no conclusion at all).

For example, if you are going to argue that the United States was neutral at the start of the war, but a combination of factors eventually forced America's entry, you might write down an abbreviated version of that thesis, such as the following:

> *Started neutral, forced into war*

Then you would brainstorm a list of ideas and events you wanted to mention in your essay, such as these.

> *Started neutral*
> *British blockade*
> *Business losing money from blockade*
> *Wilson didn't want Germany to win war*
> *U-boats violate international law*
> *U-boats kill U.S. civilians*
> *Zimmermann telegram*
> Lusitania
> Sussex
> *American people were against war*
> *Americans a little more favorable to war by 1917*

Next, you would want to figure out which of your brainstorm ideas could be the main idea of a paragraph, which could be used as evidence to support a point, and which should be eliminated. You would probably want to begin your first paragraph by stating your thesis and then discussing how the United States was neutral at the start of the war. Your first point, "Started neutral," could be the main idea of that paragraph. That the "American people were against the war" would help explain why the United States was neutral, so you could use that as evidence. At this point, your list might look like this.

Started neutral	1
British blockade	
Business losing money from blockade	
Wilson didn't want Germany to win war	
U-boats violate international law	
U-boats kill U.S. civilians	
Zimmermann telegram	
Lusitania	
Sussex	
American people were against war	evidence for point 1
Americans a little more favorable to war by 1917	

What else would you want to mention in this paragraph? Certainly refer to Document 1, Wilson's statement of American neutrality and his definition of neutrality. Use that definition to explain how each of America's ensuing actions was either neutral or favorable to the Allies. You might also mention Wilson's desire to turn the United States into a world power and how he viewed neutrality as a means toward that end. Mentioning this point helps you fulfill the requirement to include outside information.

Next you might want to discuss the British blockade and America's response to it. That would make "British blockade" the subject of paragraph 2; "business losing money from blockade" is something you might want to mention in this paragraph. Now your list might look like this:

Started neutral	1
British blockade	2
Business losing money from blockade	evidence for point 2
Wilson didn't want Germany to win war	
U-boats violate international law	
U-boats kill U.S. civilians	
Zimmermann telegram	
Lusitania	
Sussex	
American people were against war	evidence for point 1
Americans a little more favorable to war by 1917	

In this paragraph you probably also want to mention Documents 2, 3, and 4. Document 4, Bryan's letter to the Senate, gives the strongest evidence of U.S. neutrality. You might want to use Documents 2 and 3 (Munsterberg's complaint to Wilson and Lansing's description of the effects of the blockade) to explain how the United States found itself more involved in Europe's war than it perhaps had expected to be.

Proceed in this way until you have finished planning your strategy. Try to fit as many of the documents into your argument as you can, but do not stretch too far to fit one in. An obvious, desperate stretch will only hurt your grade.

As you write, remember that you do not have to fall entirely on one side or another of this issue. History is complex, and simple explanations are rarely accurate ones. If your essay argues that the United States intended to remain neutral and then discusses the events referred to by the documents in the context of neutrality, you will get a 9 on your DBQ essay, even if it does not characterize each U.S. action as neutral or non-neutral.

Arguing Against Neutrality

If you choose to argue that the United States was not neutral, you should concentrate on Documents 1, 2, and 3. Use Document 1, Wilson's congressional address, for the definition of neutrality, and then use the other documents and outside knowledge to argue that the United States did not meet its own definition. Document 2, Munsterberg's letter, really helps your position as it points out how U.S. actions appeared non-neutral at the time these events were taking place. Use Document 3, Lansing's criticism of the British blockade, to argue that the United States put up with abuses from the British at the same time they were denouncing Germany for similar abuses. Focus also on Document 6, which describes the substantial arms shipment aboard the *Lusitania*. You might then incorporate the other documents by claiming that Germany responded reasonably to its situation and that the United States, as a neutral nation, should have understood its actions. That position, by the way, is how William Jennings Bryan felt; if you knew that and included it in your essay, you would have gotten major bonus points for outside knowledge.

What You Should Have Discussed

Regardless of what side of the issue you argued, your essay should have discussed all of the following:

- Wilson's declaration of neutrality and his definition of neutrality
- Munsterberg's letter
- Bryan's response to Munsterberg
- the British blockade
- German submarine warfare
- the sinking of the *Lusitania*
- Zimmermann telegram

Give yourself very high marks for outside knowledge if you mentioned any three of the following:

- Wilsonianism
- U.S. balance of trade with the Allies and the Central Powers
- U.S. loans to England and France
- Wilson's cabinet and its predisposition toward England
- Wilson's interpretation of international law regarding submarine warfare
- Bryan's resignation
- the sinking of the *Sussex*
- the Gore-McLemore resolution
- the sinking of the *Arabic*
- "armed neutrality"
- the Nye Commission

SECTION II: THE LONG ESSAY QUESTION

Question 2

If you choose this question, keep in mind the three major theories concerning the issue. One holds that the Revolution was truly radical in its ideological quest for liberty and in the social and economic changes it brought about. A second theory holds that, on the contrary, simple economic and material interests, led by the colonists' desire to control their own economy, propelled the Revolution. A third holds that both ideology and material interests inspired our Revolution and that only by understanding the relationship between the two can we fully comprehend it.

If you decide to write about how the American Revolution was a radical break with the past, your essay pretty much has to mention the following:

- the establishment of representative government in the new United States and the expansion of voting rights
- the political changes that resulted from our new republican form of government, including the concept of Federalism, a written constitution, and the delicate balance between the rights of the state and those of the individual
- the notion that the colonists were spurred to revolution by their study of the ideas of the Enlightenment and their dislike of British rule

Give yourself extra points for mentioning any of the following:

- Thomas Paine's *Common Sense* and how it swayed public opinion in favor of independence by stating that it was against common sense for people to pledge loyalty to a corrupt and distant king whose laws were unreasonable
- the social changes brought about by the Revolution, such as the abolition of aristocratic titles and the separation of church and state

- the economic opportunities that resulted from our no longer being a British colony and the rise our independence gave to free enterprise and capitalism
- any of the relevant Revolutionary theorists or historians, such as Bailyn, Beard, Nash, or Boorstin

If you decide to write about how the American Revolution was a conservative attempt to maintain the status quo, then your essay pretty much has to mention the following:

- that some of the colonists' most important motives for seeking independence were based on economic self-interest, such as their desire to escape British taxes and British control of trade
- that the colonists sought to maintain the same social structure that existed under British rule, which included patronage and a devotion to patriarchal authority
- that the status of women and blacks remained pretty much unchanged after the Revolution

Give yourself bonus points for mentioning any of the following:

- the class aspect of the Revolution, including the idea that the Revolution wasn't only about "home rule" but about "who should rule at home" (in other words, the Revolutionaries thought that American aristocrats should rule instead of British aristocrats)
- the issue of slavery and how this war "for freedom" did nothing to abolish it, and, in fact, gave rise to a nation that enshrined slavery in its Constitution, with the notorious "Three-Fifths Clause" in Article I
- that the Revolution did not make great strides in the status of women. Extra bonus points for including Abigail Adams's letter to her husband, John, in which she writes, "Remember the ladies, and be more generous and favorable to them than your ancestors."
- that American distribution of wealth was not radically changed by the Revolution, which meant that those at the top of the social ladder were able to hold on to what they had

About the Structure of Your Essay

Remember that the best essays make the reader aware that you know both sides of the argument, even though you support one side more than the other. Try to take one side, and support it with as many details as you can (names, dates, documents, publications). Before your conclusion, you should include a paragraph in which you explain why the other side is wrong. For instance, if you were to write a glowing essay about how revolutionary the American Revolution was, one of your paragraphs should include the fact that, yes, certain lives, like those of women and blacks, were not radically altered by the Revolution, but that nonetheless this doesn't undermine the Revolution's many other radical achievements, because…. You are showing here that you understand the question well enough to have taken either side, but have chosen one over the other because you are an AP student who has learned to think for yourself! Don't forget to end with a strong conclusion that reinforces your original thesis.

Question 3

James Garfield's violent death no doubt placed a spotlight on corruption in both federal and local governments. Your job in this essay is to both enumerate the ways and analyze why this event was a catalyst for change. Your essay should describe the corruption caused by the spoils system. While the president's assassination was the act of a lone (perhaps crazed) gunman, it is a symptom of the frustration felt by many toward an unfair system. You will also discuss how reforms were necessary after the event: it was the newly appointed president, Chester A. Arthur, who was tasked with starting to clean up the mess.

Begin the essay with a brief discussion of the Gilded Age—both the wealth and the corruption. Then, lead your introduction to a claim that establishes how much the system changed following the 1881 assassination. Your body paragraphs should elaborate on the American system both before and after James Garfield's presidency.

What you may want to write about the Gilded Age before Garfield's assassination:

Rutherford B. Hayes

- Tammany Hall was the center of New York's Democratic political machine. Tammany Hall provided resources to local residents, particularly immigrants, in exchange for electoral loyalty.
- Graft, or using a political office for personal gain, was rampant in 19th-century politics.
- Boss Tweed was the most notorious of political bosses. As head of Tammany Hall, Tweed engaged in fraud and even received kickbacks from large government projects, such as the Erie Railroad. Tweed was arrested in 1871 for profiting from city contracts.
- In the spoils system, each new president would be tasked with filling hundreds of jobs. These appointments were not required to be based on merit, and were often a result of political loyalty.
- Those with opinions on the spoils system could be categorized into one of two groups: Stalwarts, who supported the system of appointing political supporters to government jobs, and Half-Breeds, who advocated civil service reform toward a merit-based system.

Give yourself bonus points for mentioning any of the following:

- George Washington Plunkitt was another boss of Tammany Hall. He distinguished between dishonest graft (motivated by selfish aims) and honest graft (for the good of the community).
- The New York Custom House, where federal duties on imports were collected, was an important symbol in the spoils system debate. The Custom House was employed entirely by political appointees.
- Roscoe Conkling, a New York senator, resigned from the body after feuding with James Garfield over New York Custom House patronage.

Things to mention about the Gilded Age following the assassination:

- President Garfield, shortly after handing out political appointments to his supporters, was killed by a supporter who was denied a job that he desired. The murder led to widespread calls for civil service reform.

- Chester A. Arthur, a longtime beneficiary of the spoils system was in the awkward position of rising to the presidency when Americans wanted nothing more from the government than to end the spoils system. Arthur ultimately signed the Pendleton Act, which was intended to do just that.
- The weak presidency that continued in the years immediately following the Pendleton Act shows us the little power the office held in the Gilded Age when the spoils system was eliminated.
- The corporate control of Congress throughout the Gilded Age, as evidenced by a toothless Sherman Antitrust Act, shows us that perhaps little had changed following the assassination.

Give yourself extra points for mentioning the following:

- Perhaps you want to make it clear that Muckrakers fixed the corrupt system, not the Pendleton Act. Lincoln Steffens's *Shame of the Cities* makes it clear that local corruption was alive and well into the early 20th century.
- Thomas Nast, the cartoonist, took great pride in exposing corruption. His cartoons of Boss Tweed were heavily influential to later satirists.

About the Structure of Your Essay

This topic can be tricky because, while some things did change following Garfield's assassination, much stayed the same. Don't worry—that can actually be your claim. If you feel that the Pendleton Act is not enough change to argue a clear difference before and after the assassination, then claim that little changed in terms of government corruption. On the other hand, the severity of misdeeds from political bosses such as Plunkett and Tweed were not as blatant following civil service reform. If you choose to say that little changed, be sure to mention what did, in fact, change the deep corruption of the Gilded Age. Perhaps you want to chalk it up to the Progressives and Muckrakers, after all.

Keep your facts plentiful, but relevant. Let your analysis do the hard work, though. Convince your reader of the power (or ineffectiveness) of the events surrounding James Garfield's assassination.

Question 4

This essay asks you to discuss that amazing decade, the 1960s. In it, you should describe the politics and social fabric of the country, giving specific examples, and then choose which two or three issues had the most impact on this decade. The 1960s are often described as a "turbulent" decade, and the reasons for that turbulence are where you want to begin. The social upheaval that was brought about by domestic and international issues, combined with the "generation gap" that defined the era, needs to be discussed. Although both the civil rights movement and the war in Vietnam began in the 1950s, the 1960s were defined by a rising tide of change and resistance to what had been readily accepted during the decades before. In contrast to the 1950s, known for its conformity and cold war jitters, the decade that followed, ushered in by the youngest president, John F. Kennedy, was one of the most mercurial in U.S. history.

You would have to begin with a solid description of the "stormy" sixties, with specific examples of the social changes that came about, and then move on to an in-depth analysis of two or three major issues. You would also be wise to mention the assassinations of John F. Kennedy, Robert F. Kennedy, and Martin Luther King, Jr., and the difficult presidency of Lyndon B. Johnson.

NOTE: It is much easier to build a case that the 1960s *did* represent a time of great change. In order to support the opposite position, you would need to find examples of turbulent events that began before the 1960s, a MUCH more difficult task. Go with the task that you can more easily defend!

The Civil Rights Movement

- Martin Luther King Jr., and his "I Have a Dream" speech
- Malcolm X and the Black Muslims
- the Southern Christian Leadership Conference, CORE, the Student Nonviolent Coordinating Committee, the NAACP, and the Black Panthers
- the voter registration drives, the "sit-ins" in the South, and the Freedom Riders
- Johnson's War on Poverty and Great Society programs
- the desegregation attempts made by Kennedy and Johnson, as compared with those made by Eisenhower and previous leaders
- the segregationist politicians and law "enforcers" in the South
- the Civil Rights Act of 1964
- the Voting Rights Act of 1965
- urban violence, "race riots"
- the shift to a more militant movement after the death of King

Give yourself extra points for mentioning the following:

- King's "Letter from a Birmingham Jail"
- the march from Selma to Montgomery, Alabama
- "Freedom Summer" in Mississippi
- the Greensboro, North Carolina, sit-ins at Woolworths
- the assassinations of Medgar Evers, Emmett Till, the three civil rights workers in Mississippi (Schwerner, Chaney, and Goodman), and the four little girls at the 16th St. Baptist Church in Birmingham
- the integration of "Ole Miss" by James Meredith, and Mississippi Governor Ross Barnett, who tried to stop him
- Governor George Wallace (and his candidacy for president in 1968), police chief Eugene "Bull" Connor, and the use of police dogs and fire hoses in Alabama
- the Mississippi Freedom Democratic Party (MFDP) at the Democratic Convention of 1964
- Stokely Carmichael, H. Rap Brown, Huey Newton, Bobby Seale, Eldridge Cleaver, and the Black Power movement
- Robert Weaver, who became the first black cabinet member (secretary of housing and urban development)
- the 1967 Kerner Commission, which concluded that black riots were a result of poverty and lack of job opportunities

The Vietnam War

- "Hawks" vs. "Doves"
- John F. Kennedy, Lyndon Johnson, Richard Nixon, Eugene McCarthy, Robert Kennedy
- Vietminh, Ho Chi Minh, South Vietnam, and Diem

- the Tet Offensive
- the war being broadcast on television to a national audience
- the Pentagon Papers
- Johnson's decision not to seek reelection
- the moratoriums and other demonstrations against the war
- the student antiwar movement

Give yourself extra points for mentioning the following:

- the Berkeley Student Movement, "hippies"
- the Students for a Democratic Society (SDS)
- "The Weathermen" (and you can add two points if you mentioned the fact that they got their name from a line in a Dylan song: "You don't need a weatherman to know which way the wind blows.")
- Hubert Humphrey
- the Democratic National Convention, Mayor Daley, the Chicago Seven
- Laos, Cambodia
- "Vietnamization"
- the burning of draft cards and the draft resistance movement
- antiwar music and Woodstock

The Women's Movement

- "Feminism" and the "Women's Liberation Movement"
- the Equal Rights Amendment and the Equal Pay Act
- National Organization for Women (NOW)
- abortion rights controversy (though *Roe v. Wade* wasn't until 1973)
- "Sexual Revolution," the birth control pill, "free love"

Give yourself extra points for mentioning the following:

- Betty Friedan's *The Feminine Mystique*
- the "glass ceiling"
- "Sexual Politics" (and the book by Kate Millett that gave it its name)
- the Kinsey Report
- Gloria Steinem, Bella Abzug, Shirley Chisholm (Chisholm could be mentioned under civil rights also)
- Woodstock and the "Counterculture"

About the Structure of Your Essay

You would need to describe the times by delving into the issues that caused the changes. But don't forget: the essays that look "easy" are often the most difficult. Don't forget to include *lots of facts* (don't let them go "blowin' in the wind…") that focus on how society and politics changed so dramatically in the 1960s.

Part III
About the AP U.S. History Exam

THE STRUCTURE OF THE AP U.S. HISTORY EXAM

The AP U.S. History Exam consists of two main sections: a multiple-choice and short-answer section and an essay questions section.

Changes to the AP U.S. History Course and Exam

The College Board recently announced that the course and exam have undergone revision beginning with the 2019–2020 academic year and the 2020 exam administration.

While this book was updated to align with the most recent information from the College Board as of Summer 2019, we recommend that you check your online Student Tools for any late-breaking news. See pages viii–ix for details.

You can also visit the College Board's AP Central page for this course: https://apcentral.collegeboard.org/courses/ap-united-states-history

The multiple-choice and short-answer section comprises 55 multiple-choice questions covering the breadth of U.S. history, and three short-answer questions. Students are provided with a total time of 95 minutes to complete this section. The multiple-choice questions are arranged in sets of two to five questions, which are tied to a primary- or secondary-source material. Students are allowed to spend 55 minutes completing the multiple-choice questions. The short-answer questions will explore one or more of the course thematic learning objectives. Students are expected to write a short response to three of four questions centered on a provided primary source, secondary source, or a prompt with no stimulus provided. Students are allowed to spend 40 minutes completing the short-answer questions.

The essay questions section of the exam consists of two essays to be completed in a total of 100 minutes. After a 15-minute reading period, students may divide up the remaining time as desired, spending more or less time on each essay. AP recommends 45 minutes for the document-based question (DBQ) and 40 minutes for the long essay. The document-based question is an essay for which students will have to answer a question based on seven primary source documents provided. For the long essay, students will be asked to select an essay prompt from three different options. Unlike the DBQ, there will be no outside sources provided. This question requires the development of a thesis and/or historical argument supported by student-provided evidence.

	Structure of the AP United States History Exam			
Section	Description	Number of Questions	Time Allotted	Percentage of Total Exam Score
Section I	Part A: Multiple-choice	55	55 min	40%
	Part B: Short-answer	3	40 min	20%
Reading Period			15 min	
Section II	Part A: DBQ	1	45 min	25%
	Part B: Long essay	1	40 min	15%

HOW THE AP U.S. HISTORY EXAM IS SCORED

AP U.S. History Exam scoring is based on the performance of the student on each of the four exam parts. The raw scores from each section will be weighted and summed to generate an overall AP grade of 1–5. Scoring of the multiple-choice section is based solely on the raw score of the number of correct answers. There is no penalty for guessing. The multiple-choice question section constitutes 40 percent of the total exam score. The short-answer questions will be evaluated for accuracy and useful application of historical thinking skills to address each question. The short-answer questions represent 20 percent of the total exam score.

The essay questions are graded against very clear rubrics outlined by the College Board, which we'll show you in Chapter 3. Both essays will be evaluated for development of a central thesis, contextualization, evidence, and analysis. The document-based question is scored with a maximum score of 7 possible points allocated across the following areas: thesis (1 point), contextualization (1 point), historical evidence (3 points), and analysis (2 points). The DBQ score represents 25 percent of the total exam score. The long essay is scored with a maximum score of 6 points allocated across the following areas: thesis (1 point), use of evidence in support of argument (2 points), contextualization (1 point), and analysis (2 points). The long essay constitutes 15 percent of the total exam score.

Incorporating the depth and content necessary to get high scores on the AP Exam requires practice and good time management. We will discuss approaches to maximize your score in Chapter 4.

For your reference, here is the College Board's score distribution data from the 2019 AP U.S. History Exam administration.

Score	Percentage
5	12.1%
4	18.7%
3	23.5%
2	22.0%
1	23.7%
Total	100%

OVERVIEW OF CONTENT TOPICS

The College Board provides a breakdown of assessment weighting of material for the exam by historical periods. These periods and their relative weights are shown below. It is important to remember that many events in history span multiple periods and are connected by overarching themes. You will notice that in the table below, several of the periods recognized by the College Board overlap. As you begin to evaluate the material, strive to make adequate connections between the periods rather than treating them as separate isolated entities. We will begin to look at how the College Board views connections in the next section about thematic learning objectives.

Historical Periods Covered on the AP U.S. History Exam			
Historical Period	Date Range	Suggested Instructional Time	Approximate Percentage of Questions on the AP Exam
1	1491–1607	6%	4–6%
2	1607–1754	10%	6–8%
3	1754–1800	12%	10–17%
4	1800–1848	12%	10–17%
5	1844–1877	12%	10–17%
6	1865–1898	13%	10–17%
7	1890–1945	15%	10–17%
8	1945–1980	14%	10–17%
9	1980–Present	6%	4–6%

Excelling on the AP U.S. History Exam requires a thorough knowledge of the events of American history and their significance. We have provided a review of this material in Part V of this text. Listed below is an overview of the specific topics that will be covered on the AP U.S. History Exam and should be reviewed in a course.

1. Pre-Columbian Societies
2. Transatlantic Encounters and Colonial Beginnings, 1492–1690
3. Colonial North America, 1690–1754
4. The American Revolutionary Era, 1754–1789
5. The Early Republic, 1789–1815
6. Transformation of the Economy and Society in Antebellum America
7. The Transformation of Politics in Antebellum America
8. Religion, Reform, and Renaissance in Antebellum America
9. Territorial Expansion and Manifest Destiny
10. The Crisis of the Union
11. Civil War
12. Reconstruction

13. The Origins of the New South
14. Development of the West in the Late 19th Century
15. Industrial America in the Late 19th Century
16. Urban Society in the late 19th Century
17. Populism and Progressivism
18. The Emergence of America as a World Power
19. The New Era: 1920s
20. The Great Depression and the New Deal
21. The Second World War
22. The Home Front During the War
23. The United States and the Early Cold War
24. The 1950s
25. The Turbulent Sixties
26. Politics and Economics at the End of the 20th Century
27. Society and Culture at the End of the 20th Century
28. The United States in the Post–Cold War World

UNDERSTANDING CONTENT WITH THEMATIC LEARNING OBJECTIVES

The College Board has focused the breadth of historical developments and events covered in the AP U.S. History course and exam into eight key themes. All questions on the AP U.S. History Exam will evaluate student understanding of one or more of these learning objectives. As you begin to review the content covered in Part V, pay particular attention to these themes. The following are the thematic learning objectives:

1. **American and National Identity.** This theme explores how the American identity has formed and been transformed by the development of group identities throughout U.S. history. Particular emphasis is placed on understanding developments in gender, racial, class, and ethnic identities and how different groups have interacted with each other to form the modern American identity.

2. **Work, Exchange, and Technology.** This theme evaluates the development of American economies based on advances and developments in the fields of agriculture, commerce, and manufacturing. The exam will evaluate your understanding of how different economic and labor platforms and technological developments have revolutionized and shaped American society.

3. **Geography and the Environment: Physical and Human.** This theme explores how the environment, weather, and geography have transformed decisions that have shaped the country.

4. **Migration and Settlement.** This theme targets the movement and transformation of peoples over time. Particular emphasis is placed on understanding the motivating factors for migration and the impact of movement on American society today.

5. **Politics and Power.** This theme explores the relationship between political views and processes and society. You should have a firm understanding of the powers of different levels of government and how those powers are important in providing rights and freedoms to the American public.

6. **America and the World.** This theme investigates the influence of other cultures on American development, society, and culture and, alternatively, the impact of America on the rest of the world.

7. **American Regional Culture.** This theme explores how various regions of the United States have developed their own distinct identities and cultures and how those differences have impacted American history.

8. **Social Structures.** This theme focuses on how and why systems of social organization develop and change as well as the impact that these systems have on the broader society.

HOW AP EXAMS ARE USED

Different colleges use AP exams in different ways, so it is important that you go to a particular college's website to determine how it uses AP exams. The three items below represent the main ways in which AP exam scores can be used:

- **College Credit.** Some colleges will give you college credit if you score well on an AP Exam. These credits count toward your graduation requirements, meaning that you can take fewer courses while in college. Given the cost of college, this could be quite a benefit, indeed.

- **Satisfy Requirements.** Some colleges will allow you to "place out" of certain requirements if you do well on an AP Exam, even if they do not give you actual college credits. For example, you might not need to take an introductory-level course, or perhaps you might not need to take a class in a certain discipline at all.

- **Admissions Plus.** Even if your AP Exam will not result in college credit or even allow you to place out of certain courses, most colleges will respect your decision to push yourself by taking an AP Course or even an AP Exam outside of a course. A high score on an AP Exam shows mastery of content more difficult than that taught in many high school courses, and colleges may take that into account during the admissions process.

OTHER RESOURCES

There are many resources available to help you improve your score on the AP U.S. History Exam, not the least of which are your teachers. If you are taking an AP class, you may be able to get extra attention from your teacher, such as obtaining feedback on your practice essays. If you are not in an AP course, reach out to a teacher who teaches U.S. History (or another AP history teacher) and ask if the teacher will review your essays or otherwise help you with content.

Another wonderful resource is **AP Students**, the official site of the AP Exams. The scope of the information at this site is quite broad and includes the following materials:

Check out The Princeton Review's college guide-books, including *The Best 385 Colleges, The Complete Book of Colleges, Paying for College,* and many more!

- A comprehensive course description, which includes details on what content is covered and sample questions
- Essay prompts, answers, and grading suggestions from previous years
- Several helpful links to websites containing era-specific information
- The official 2017 AP U.S. History Practice Exam
- Past AP U.S. History Exams for purchase through the College Board. Although these will not be aligned with the recent updates to the exam, they are still good practice.
- Updates on future changes to the AP U.S. History Exam

The AP Students home page address is
apstudent.collegeboard.org/home

The AP U.S. History Exam Course home page address is
apstudent.collegeboard.org/apcourse/ap-united-states-history

Finally, **The Princeton Review** offers tutoring and small group instruction for the AP U.S. History Exam. Our expert instructors can help you refine your strategic approach and add to your content knowledge. For more information, call 1-800-2REVIEW.

Break up your review into manageable portions. Download our helpful study guide for this book, once you register online (see pages viii–ix for details).

DESIGNING YOUR STUDY PLAN

In Part I, you identified some areas of potential improvement. Let's now delve further into your performance on Practice Test 1, with the goal of developing a study plan appropriate to your needs and time commitment.

Read the answers and explanations associated with the multiple-choice questions (starting at page 35). After you have done so, respond to the following questions:

- Review the content topics on pages 72–73 and, next to each one, indicate your rank of the topic as follows: "1" means "I need a lot of work on this," "2" means "I need to beef up my knowledge," and "3" means "I know this topic well."

- How many days/weeks/months away is your AP U.S. History Exam?

- What time of day is your best, most focused study time?

- How much time per day/week/month will you devote to preparing for your AP U.S. History Exam?

- When will you do this preparation? (Be as specific as possible: Mondays and Wednesdays from 3:00 to 4:00 p.m., for example.)

- Based on the answers above, will you focus on strategy (Part IV) or content (Part V) or both?

- What are your overall goals in using this book?

Part IV
Test-Taking Strategies for the AP U.S. History Exam

PREVIEW

Understanding your current testing approach is an integral part of finding ways to maximize your efficiency and improve your studying effectiveness. Review your responses to the questions on page 4 of Part I and then respond to the following questions:

- How many multiple-choice questions did you miss even though you knew the answer?

- On how many multiple-choice questions did you guess blindly?

- How many multiple-choice questions did you miss after eliminating some answers and guessing based on the remaining answers?

- For how many of the short-answer questions did you have no clue where to start?

- Did you plan out your essay prompts before writing them? Did you create an outline for either of them?

- How did you approach the long essay question?

- Did you find any of the essay prompts easier or harder than the others—and, if so, why?

HOW TO USE THE CHAPTERS IN THIS PART

Before you read the following Strategy chapters, think about what you are doing now. As you read and engage in the directed practice, be sure to appreciate the ways you can change your approach. At the end of Part IV, you will have the opportunity to reflect on how you will change your approach.

Chapter 1
How to Approach
Multiple-Choice
Questions

THE BASICS

The multiple-choice part of the test will consist of sets of two to five questions, which are tied to primary sources, secondary sources, or historical issues. The directions will be pretty simple. They will read something similar to the following:

> **Directions:** Each of the questions or incomplete statements below is followed by four suggested answers or completions. Select the one that is best in each case and then fill in the corresponding space on the answer sheet.

In short, you are being asked to evaluate a provided document or source and answer a series of questions. Once you select an answer, you will fill in the appropriate bubble on a separate answer sheet. You will *not* be given credit for answers you record in your test booklet (e.g., by circling them) but not on your answer sheet. Part A of Section I consists of 55 questions, which are expected to take you approximately 55 minutes to complete. Time management will be a key part of this section, as you are also expected to complete three of four short-answer questions (in Part B) in the 105 minutes allotted for the entire section.

TYPES OF SOURCES

Unlike several of the other AP Exams, the multiple-choice questions on this test appear in sets associated with a primary source, secondary source, or historical issue. Primary sources are original materials, which provide a firsthand account or perspective. Many of the primary sources that you are likely to see on the exam will include direct excerpts from famous works, legislation, or speeches. Secondary sources are pieces of information, which relate to or are discussed in reference to information presented elsewhere (not firsthand information). Examples of secondary sources include historical perspectives on events, historical criticisms, artworks or cartoons, books or perspectives on historical events, or retrospective analyses. Additional sources used on the exam may include charts or graphs, which depict key historical relationships.

Here is an example of a primary source as it may appear on the AP Exam.

Questions 9 - 11 refer to the excerpt below.

"Can we forge against these enemies a grand and global alliance, North and South, East and West, that can assure a more fruitful life for all mankind? Will you join in that historic effort?

In the long history of the world, only a few generations have been granted the role of defending freedom in its hour of maximum danger. I do not shrink from this responsibility—I welcome it. I do not believe that any of us would exchange places with any other people or any other generation. The energy, the faith, the devotion which we bring to this endeavor will light our country and all who serve it—and the glow from that fire can truly light the world.

And so, my fellow Americans: ask not what your country can do for you—ask what you can do for your country.

John F. Kennedy, Inaugural Address, 1961

The speech by President Kennedy, excerpted above, outlines the American dream and the American vision. On the exam, you will be given primary sources that address key events or issues in U.S. history and be given questions that will evaluate these sources from the perspective of the thematic learning objectives described in Part III of this book. Throughout this section, we have provided additional examples, which represent the diversity of different sources you may see on the exam. We will now discuss how to tackle the questions stemming from these sources.

TYPES OF QUESTIONS

The questions in the multiple-choice section will center on one or more key themes addressed by the source document provided for each set of questions. The majority of the questions will be pretty straightforward once the context of the source is understood. For instance, an example question stemming from the Kennedy excerpt may appear as follows:

10. The excerpt provided discusses global turbulence and the desire for freedom of mankind in reference to which of the following events?

   (A) Civil Rights Movement
   (B) Women's Suffrage Movement
   (C) The Cold War
   (D) The Great Depression

However, the College Board often makes the questions a little trickier. One way it does this is by phrasing a question so that three answers are correct and one is incorrect. We call these questions "NOT/EXCEPT" questions because they usually contain one of those words (in capital letters, so they're harder to miss). A simple way to handle these types of problems is by treating them as "true" or "false." The answer choice that is false is correct. Here is an example of another primary source and an EXCEPT-type question:

Questions 6 - 10 refer to the excerpt below.

"Two months ago we were facing serious problems. The country was dying by inches. It was dying because trade and commerce had declined to dangerously low levels; prices for basic commodities were such as to destroy the value of the assets of national institutions such as banks, savings banks, insurance companies, and others. These institutions, because of their great needs, were foreclosing mortgages, calling loans, refusing credit. Thus there was actually in process of destruction the property of millions of people who had borrowed money on that property in terms of dollars which had had an entirely different value from the level of March, 1933. That situation in that crisis did not call for any complicated consideration of economic panaceas or fancy plans. We were faced by a condition and not a theory...."

Franklin Delano Roosevelt, Fireside Chat, 1933

6. The New Deal included programs for achieving all of the following goals EXCEPT

   (A) developing an interstate highway system
   (B) stabilizing agricultural prices
   (C) insuring bank deposits
   (D) providing employment for the unemployed

A few times during the multiple-choice section, you will be asked to interpret an illustration source, often a map or a political cartoon. These are usually pretty easy. The key is not to try to read too much between the lines. To save time, read the question first, and then go to the illustration, map, or political cartoon. This way you know what you are looking for!

Here is an example of a political cartoon source and associated question.

Questions 29 - 30 refer to the illustration below.

Hanna to McKinley: That Man Clay was an Ass.
It's Better to be President than to be Right!

29. The political cartoon above implies that

   (A) McKinley was the first president to favor big business interests openly
   (B) by the 1890s, Henry Clay's political approach had lost favor with the electorate
   (C) McKinley's presidential campaign was masterminded by Marcus Hanna
   (D) Marcus Hanna single-handedly controlled all three branches of the federal government

Finally, there will be a few questions on your test asking you to interpret a graph or chart source. Again, these are usually very straightforward, unless they are "EXCEPT" or "NOT" questions. Those tend to be time-consuming, and even strong students should probably do those at the end, if time permits. When you answer one of these chart or graph questions, realize that more than one answer might be valid, but only one will be supported by the information in the chart or graph.

An example of a chart source and question is shown below.

Questions 41 - 45 refer to the table below.

Average, Highest, and Lowest Approval Ratings, by Percentage of All Eligible Voters, for American Presidents, 1953 to 1974			
	Average	High	Low
Eisenhower	65	79	48
Kennedy	70	83	56
Johnson	55	79	35
Nixon	49	67	24

Source: Gallup Polls

43. Which of the following conclusions can be drawn from the information presented in the chart above?

(A) Eisenhower was the most consistently popular president in the nation's history.

(B) Kennedy received greater congressional support for his program than did any other president during the period in question.

(C) Nixon's approval rating was the result of the Watergate scandal.

(D) The difference between Johnson's highest and lowest approval ratings was the greatest for any president during the period in question.

Answers to these and other sample questions appear at the end of this chapter.

No Military History and No Trivial Pursuit

Here's some good news: the AP U.S. History Exam doesn't ask about the details of military history, such as the military strategy or exact death toll of a specific battle. You will never see a question on the AP Exam like the one below:

14. Union general Ulysses S. Grant was intent on capturing Vicksburg, Mississippi, because

(A) Vicksburg was the munitions capital of the Confederacy

(B) whoever controlled the city could control transportation along the Mississippi River

(C) Grant hoped to use the city as a supply depot for Union troops stationed throughout the South

(D) the city was poorly defended, and the Union desperately needed a victory for morale purposes

Although Grant's siege of Vicksburg in 1863 marked an important moment in the Civil War, you won't be asked about it on the test. The AP U.S. History Exam does not ask about important battles, military strategy, or advances in weapons technology. When it asks about war, the questions concern the political, diplomatic, or social implications of a war or battle, rather than the details of warfare. For example, you might have a question about the significance of the battle of

Saratoga in the Revolutionary War. (It helped lead to the French providing direct aid to the colonists.) The correct answer, to the question above, by the way, is (B).

Also, AP U.S. History questions never test rote memorization *only*. While you have to know your facts to do well on this test, the questions always ask for information in the context of larger historical trends. Therefore, you will never see a question like this one:

15. The treaty that ended the War of 1812 was called the

(A) Treaty of Versailles
(B) War of 1812 Treaty
(C) Jay Treaty
(D) Treaty of Ghent

The Big Picture

One of the most important characteristics of the AP U.S. History multiple-choice section is that the questions and answers are designed to illustrate **basic principles** of American history. These principles are evaluated through the seven thematic learning objectives described in Part III. Multiple-choice questions will NOT ask about exceptions to historical trends; the test ignores these because the test writers are trying to find out whether you have mastered the important generalizations that can be drawn from history. They do not want to know whether you have memorized your textbook (they already know that you haven't). Talk of historical exceptions is welcome in the essay section, though. Students who discuss exceptions in their essays often impress the readers. More on that later.

Always keep the big picture in mind.

Overall, you should always keep the **big picture** in mind as you take this exam. As you approach questions, use the sources provided to help you focus on the key points or themes that are being questioned. Even if you cannot remember the specific event or concept being tested, you should be able to answer the question by remembering the general social and political trends of the era and using the information that may be ascertained from the source.

Let's look at a couple of illustrative examples.

Questions 52 - 54 refer to the excerpt below.

"Whenever the [Federal Trade] Commission shall have reason to believe that any such person, partnership, or corporation has been or is using any unfair method of competition or unfair or deceptive act or practice in or affecting commerce, and if it shall appear to the Commission that a proceeding by it in respect thereof would be to the interest of the public, it shall issue and serve upon such person, partnership, or corporation a complaint stating its charges in that respect and containing a notice of a hearing upon a day and at a place therein fixed at least thirty days after the service of said complaint."

Excerpted from 15 U.S. Code § 45—*Unfair methods of competition unlawful; prevention by Commission*

53. During the Harding and Coolidge administrations, the Federal Trade Commission

   (A) greatly increased the number of court cases it brought against unethical business

   (B) controlled the rationing of food, rubber, and gasoline

   (C) generally worked to assist businesses, rather than regulate them

   (D) saw its regulatory powers expanded

Here's How to Crack It

At first glance, this question appears to require you to remember the history of the Federal Trade Commission. It's not that tricky, though. To answer this question correctly, you really need only to remember the big picture. What was the attitude of the Harding and Coolidge administrations toward business? Harding and Coolidge were presidents after both the Progressive Era and World War I ended; the country grew more conservative during their administrations, and both pursued policies favorable to business. Because pro-business governments weaken regulations, you should have been able to eliminate (A) and (D). Now let's look at the remaining answer choices. Was there rationing during the 1920s? No, rationing occurred during World War II, in the early 1940s. Eliminate (B). The correct answer is (C), which illustrates a "big picture" principle; the 1920s were a pro-business era.

Apply the Strategy
Use the big picture to help you find the correct answer!

Questions 17 - 18 refer to the excerpt below.

"[This legislative body declares] that it views the power of the Federal Government as resulting from the compact to which states are parties, as limited by plain sense and intention of the instrument constituting the compact…and that, in case of a deliberate, palpable, and dangerous exercise of other powers, not granted by the said compact, the states…have the right, and are duty bound, to interpose, for arresting the progress of the evil, and for maintaining…the authorities, rights, and liberties, pertaining to them."

17. The quotation above appears in which of the following?

    (A) The Wealth of Nations
    (B) *Common Sense*
    (C) Virginia Resolutions of 1798
    (D) *The Liberator*

Here's How to Crack It

The first thing you may notice is that this question is pretty difficult; the quotation is one long sentence filled with archaic language and syntax. However, if you key in on the big picture, this question isn't all that hard, provided you've prepared for the exam. The central concept of the quotation is that the states have the right to try to stop the federal government when it tries to exercise too much power (particularly when it exceeds the constitutional limitations on it). Sound familiar? It's the doctrine of *nullification*. If you remembered that the source of the doctrine of nullification was the Virginia and Kentucky Resolutions, you would already be on your way to the next question. If not, look at the other answer choices. *The Wealth of Nations* is a treatise on capitalism; *Common Sense* was written before there even were states, let alone state assemblies; and *The Liberator* was an abolitionist newspaper. Looking at the big picture, you should realize that only the Virginia Resolutions and *The Liberator* could conceivably be right. If you don't know, guess. A fifty-fifty shot is pretty good on question 17. (Only about 30 percent of students taking the test will get this question right.)

Proven Technique
Use POE to boost your score!

PROCESS OF ELIMINATION (POE)

If it seems that we are focusing more on eliminating incorrect answers than on finding the correct answers, it is because that is the most efficient way to take a multiple-choice exam. Use **Process of Elimination (POE)** to whittle down the answer choices to one on all but the easiest questions (on easy questions, the correct answer will be obvious), because incorrect answers are much easier to identify than correct ones. When you look for the correct answer among the answer choices, you have a tendency to try to justify how each answer *might* be correct. You'll adopt a forgiving attitude in a situation in which tough assertiveness is rewarded. Eliminate incorrect answers. Terminate them with extreme prejudice. Remember that half wrong is all wrong, and mark up the test as you do this. You are probably used to teachers telling you not to write on the test. This test, however, is yours to mark up, and that will make it easier for you to decide what to guess. If you have done your job well, only the correct answer will be left standing at the end.

Common Sense Can Help

Sometimes an answer on the multiple-choice section contradicts common sense. Eliminate those answers. Common sense works on the AP U.S. History Exam. Evaluate the question below, which stems from a source on early farming. Which of the answer choices to the question below don't make common sense?

19. Which of the following best explains the most important effect tobacco cultivation had on the development of the Chesapeake Bay settlements during the seventeenth century?

   (A) Because tobacco cultivation requires large tracts of fertile land, it led to the rapid expansion of settled areas in the region.
   (B) The immediate commercial success of tobacco forced the settlers to defend against attacks by Spanish and French settlers, who wanted to take control of the tobacco trade.
   (C) Tobacco provided the settlers a lucrative crop to trade with nearby Native American tribes.
   (D) British customs houses established in the region to regulate tobacco trade led to widespread resentment of the British by the colonists.

Here's How to Crack It

Common sense should allow you to eliminate (C) immediately. Nearby Native American tribes lived on farmland similar to that held by the Chesapeake Bay settlers; why would they trade for something they could have easily grown themselves? Now let's consider the other answer choices. Did the Spanish or the French attack the Maryland/Virginia region during the 17th century? It would have been a pretty big deal if they had, right? You would remember if there had been a war for the control of Virginia in the 1600s, wouldn't you? You don't remember it because it didn't happen; eliminate (B). Choice (D) is anachronistic. The period of colonial resentment toward England was still 100 years away during the 17th century. The correct answer is (A).

Context Clues

Some questions contain context clues or vocabulary words that will either lead you to the correct answer or at least help you eliminate an incorrect answer. Look at the passage and question below.

Questions 36 - 39 refer to the excerpt below.

"It has been enacted by the Senate and House of Representatives of the United States of America in Congress assembled, That if, during the present or any future insurrection against the Government of the United States, after the President of the United States shall have declared, by proclamation, that the laws of the United States are opposed, and the execution thereof obstructed,...any person or persons, his, her, or their agent, attorney, or employee, shall purchase or acquire, sell or give, any property of whatsoever kind or description, with intent to use or employ the same, or suffer the same to be used or employed, in aiding, abetting, or promoting such insurrection or resistance to the laws, or any person or persons engaged therein;...all such property is hereby declared to be lawful subject of prize and capture wherever found; and it shall be the duty of the President of the United States to cause the same to be seized, confiscated, and condemned."

Section 1, The Confiscation Act of 1861

37. The Confiscation Act of 1861 authorized the Union to

(A) divert commercial production in the North toward the war effort

(B) negotiate a settlement to the Civil War with ambassadors from the Confederacy

(C) liberate those slaves used by the Confederacy "for insurrectionary purposes"

(D) stop merchant ships headed for Europe and seize their cargo

Here's How to Crack It

If you don't remember the exact purpose of the Confiscation Act of 1861, the word *confiscation* might give you enough of a context clue to answer this question correctly anyway. Which answer choices have nothing to do with confiscation? Clearly, (B). The dictionary definition of confiscation is "the seizure of private property." Choice (A) seems pretty unlikely too. It indicates that the government used industry for the war effort, not that it confiscated the factories. Choice (D) looks good, except when you ask "For what purpose would the Union be stopping ships headed away from the Confederacy?" This answer would much more likely be correct if it discussed the confiscation of property headed for the Confederacy. The correct answer, (C), is a little tricky because we don't normally think of human beings as private property. Slaves, however, were exactly that: the private property of slave holders. In order to liberate them, the Union had to "confiscate" them.

———————◯———————

Finally, here are the answers to the questions that appear in this chapter.
10: (C); 6: (A); 29: (C); 43: (D); 53: (C); 17: (C); 19: (A); 37: (C).

Summary

o The multiple-choice section consists of sets of two to five questions, which are tied to primary sources, secondary sources, or historical issues.

o Familiarize yourself with the different types of questions that will appear on the multiple-choice section. Be aware that you will see many questions about political and social history, some questions about international relations, and relatively few about economic and cultural trends. Tailor your studies accordingly.

o Look for "big picture" answers. Correct answers on the multiple-choice section confirm important trends in American history. This section will not ask you about weird exceptions that contradict those trends. It also will not ask you about military history featured on the History Channel. You will not be required to perform miraculous feats of memorization; however, you must be thoroughly familiar with all the basics of American history. (And there are a lot of them! See our content review later in the book.)

o Use Process of Elimination (POE) on all but the easiest questions. Once you have worked on a question, eliminated some answers (by scratching them out in your packet of questions), and convinced yourself that you cannot eliminate any other incorrect answers, you should guess and move on to the next question.

o Use common sense. Look for context clues.

Chapter 2
How to Approach
Short-Answer
Questions

OVERVIEW

The short-answer part of Section I involves answering three of four short-answer questions. Two of the four provided questions will involve an element of choice, which will allow you to pick the topic or theme you feel most confident writing about. All of the questions will be tied to a primary source, historical argument, data or maps, or general propositions of U.S. history. Since these are short-answer prompts, you are not required to develop and support a thesis statement.

TIME CRUNCH

Probably the biggest challenge you have in answering the short-answer essays is the time allotment. You have a total of 40 minutes to answer three short-essay prompts, which means you have about 3 minutes to brainstorm ideas and about 10 minutes in which to write each one. You'll be given up to a page to write on. It is not necessary to fill all the allotted space. Quality matters more than quantity, though a longer essay will look more impressive to the reader. So there is no time to dawdle on the short essays. You must keep brainstorming to a minimum, and keep your pencil moving!

Here are the steps you should follow for each short-answer essay:

Choose, think, write: your short-answer strategy!

1. **Choose.** For one of the four essays you can choose a topic that best fits your knowledge base. Chances are, one of the choices will resonate more with your level of expertise. You can also decide in what *order* you wish to write the essays.

2. **Think**. Write down all the facts and details that you know about the topic. Try to rank them according to their importance in history and their relevance to the prompt question.

3. **Write.** Steps 1 and 2 should not take much more than 2 minutes. Writing is where you will spend the bulk of your time. Each of your essays should be two to three paragraphs, though the paragraphs need not be long. You have about 10 minutes of writing time, so don't feel the need to get too bogged down in minutiae.

STRATEGY FOR THE SHORT-ANSWER QUESTIONS

The short-answer questions will consist of multiple parts, which center on a key learning objective. You are required to answer questions 1 and 2 and are allowed to *choose* between questions 3 and 4. Many of these questions will resemble the example shown below.

> "Convinced that the Revolution was the work of a full few miscreants who had rallied an armed rabble to their cause, they expected that the revolutionaries would be intimidated.... Then the vast majority of Americans, who were loyal but cowed by the terroristic tactics...would rise up, kick out the rebels, and restore loyal government in each colony."
>
> Jeremy Black, *Crisis of Empire: Britain and America in the Eighteenth Century* (2008)

Answer parts a, b, and c.

a) Briefly explain ONE example of rebellion during the time period described in Black's quote.
b) Briefly explain ONE cause of the rebellion you chose.
c) Briefly explain ONE effect of the rebellion you chose.

Here's How to Crack It

1. **Choose.** If you remember all those Revolutionary War notes from the beginning of the year, then this one should be a slam dunk. There were many events during the period of 1754–1775 that prompted anti-British sentiment and ultimately led to the push for independence including the Stamp Act (1765), the Townshend Revenue Act (1767), the Sugar Act (1764), and the Tea Act of 1773. Let's say you don't remember what the Townshend Revenue Act was (two tax laws imposed on imports of common products into the colonies), but you remember the Stamp Act and the Tea Act. Which one provoked a strong response from the colonists and an even stronger counter-response from the British? I'll have my tea with lemon and sugar, please!

Apply the three-step strategy to answer this question

2. **Think.**
    • East India Tea Company
    • Boston Tea Party
    • Sons of Liberty
    • Intolerable Acts
    • Closing of Boston Harbor

3. **Write.** Here is a sample essay using some of the ideas outlined above:

> Under the principle of mercantilism, Britain frequently put the interests of its corporations ahead of the interests of American colonists. The Tea Act of 1773 was an attempt to force colonists to purchase tea from the East India Company rather than from cheaper sources. This hurt many colonial merchants, so the Sons of Liberty, dressed as Indians, initiated the Boston Tea Party; the protesters boarded Company ships and dumped many pounds of tea into Boston Harbor, thus sending a message to the King that his economic tactics were not welcome.
>
> The King did not ignore the Boston Tea Party. Governor George Grenville implemented the Intolerable Acts, which were designed to punish Massachusetts for its willful spirit and included such harsh measures as closing the port of Boston and required the quartering of soldiers in private homes. Little did Grenville realize that the people of Massachusetts would soon become instrumental in the defeat of British rule in North America.

Freedom of Choice

One beneficial aspect of the short-answer section in Part I is that you are allowed to choose between Questions 3 and 4. This allows you to play up your strengths, while avoiding topics that are less familiar. Questions 3 and 4 will always draw from different time periods (Question 3 always from an earlier time period than Question 4) and subjects, so you can choose the time period or subject that you know the most about.

Consider the following two prompts. Which one would be most suitable for you based upon your own knowledge?

—————————○—————————

Directions: Answer **either** Question 3 **or** Question 4

3. Answer (a), (b), and (c). Confine your response to the period from 1600 to 1800.

    a) Briefly describe ONE specific historical difference between the types of people who settled and colonized New England and those who settled the South.

    b) Briefly describe ONE specific historical similarity between the types of people who settled and colonized New England and those who settled the South.

    c) Briefly describe ONE specific historical effect of the differences between the types of people who settled and colonized New England and those who settled the South.

4. Answer (a), (b), and (c).

    a)   Briefly describe ONE specific historical difference between the immigration policies of the United States in the period 1920-1965 and the immigration policies in the period 1965 to the present.

    b)   Briefly describe ONE specific historical similarity between the immigration policies of the United States in the period 1920-1965 and the immigration policies in the period 1965 to the present.

    c)   Briefly explain ONE specific historical impact of the immigration policies in either time period.

Here's How to Crack It

1. **Choose.** Perhaps you're a little foggy about immigration policies throughout the 20th century. Sure, they changed, but how is 1965 significant? If you have no idea, then Question 3 is safer. The differences between the New England colonies and the Southern colonies were fairly well-defined, and the "South" could even include the Chesapeake region, if you so choose. And there had to be similarities, too. The most obvious one might be that most colonists in both the North and South were from the British Isles. One important thing to note is that this prompt limits you to the years 1600 to 1800. So, the "historical effect" you choose for part (c) should be relevant to this time period.

2. **Think.**

Similarity: mostly Protestant, with the exception of Maryland. Difference: Puritans in New England

New England: religious freedom; South: cash crops, leading to widespread use of indentured servants and slaves

Both North and South maintained cultural separation from Indians. New England had more early conflicts with and made more of an attempt to convert Indians to Christianity.

Focus on town-meeting-style democracy in New England

Mercantilism

Joint-stock companies in the South

Similarity: strong British identity

Effects: more New England independence from the crown, fewer economic strings; dependence on slavery in the South; differences in views on French and Indian War and Northwest Ordinance

3. **Write.** Here is a sample essay using some of the ideas outlined above:

The English started to emigrate to the New World in the early 1600s. The first successful colony was Jamestown, Virginia, settled in 1607 by a joint-stock company. Not too long after, the Pilgrims and Puritans settled The Massachusetts Bay area in order to seek religious freedom. From then on, the New England colonies and the colonies from the Chesapeake south were characterized by cultural and economic differences. While New Englanders were largely subsistence farmers and merchants who had left England to seek religious and political freedom, the colonists in southern areas were either wealthy farmers, agricultural investors, or, at the bottom of society, indentured servants and slaves. Though most of the colonists in the North and South were Protestant Christians, the Pilgrims and Puritans were more devout, perhaps even radical, in their vision of a perfect Christian society. John Winthrop's admonition to Puritan society to establish themselves as a "city upon a hill" would not have been delivered by a tobacco farmer whose goals were more mercenary. Despite religious differences, though, almost all colonists in the North and South had a strong sense of themselves as English citizens. Loyalty to the crown persisted in both regions. These loyalties were tested later, though, when the differences between New England and the remaining colonies became more apparent: talk of Revolution began in independent Massachusetts, while many Loyalists in the South were uncomfortable with the notion of risking trading partnerships with England.

Summary

o   Spend a few minutes reading the questions carefully, and choose a historical event, perspective, or view that addresses the questions completely and for which you have a thorough understanding.

o   When you have an option, think carefully about which would be easiest to write about in reference to all parts of the question.

o   Make sure your responses are clear, succinct, and fully address all parts of the questions.

o   Be mindful of your time. The first section of the test is shared with the multiple-choice questions. Consider doing the short-answer questions first before attempting the multiple-choice questions.

Chapter 3
How to Approach the Document-Based and Long Essay Questions

OVERVIEW

There are two types of essay questions on the AP U.S. History Exam. The first is the document-based question (DBQ), which requires you to answer a question based on six or seven primary source documents and your knowledge of the subject and time period. The second is the long essay question, which is more like typical essay questions on any other history exam. The era addressed in the long essay question shifts depending on what era the DBQ covers. Hence, if the DBQ concerns progressivism, then the long essay prompt might concern the road to the Civil War and elections in the mid-20th century. You are provided a total of 100 minutes to read the documents for the DBQ question, choose your long essay prompt from three available options, and write both essays. We will discuss each of these question types in greater detail in this chapter. First, let's talk about the basics of writing a successful AP essay.

What Are the AP Essay Graders Looking For?

Here is what one AP grader said:

> "My most basic advice to students taking the AP U.S. History Exam would be the same advice I give to college students facing an essay exam: ANSWER THE QUESTION, begin with a thesis, and follow a reasonable outline. Questions usually suggest a basic thesis statement and a logical outline, so look for them and follow them. The less a writer confuses his or her reader, the better."
>
> Pamela Riney-Kehrberg, Illinois State University

In other words, be straightforward. Do not try to fudge your way through the essay; the graders are all experts in history, and you will not be able to fool them into thinking you know more than you actually do.

It is also very important to focus on the phrasing of the question. Some students are so anxious to get going that they start writing as soon as they know the general subject of the question, and many of these students lose points because their essays do not answer the question being asked. Take, for example, an essay question that asks you to discuss the effects of the Great Depression on working-class citizens. The overanxious test taker might start rattling off everything he or she knows about the Depression: its causes, its effect on the presidential election of 1932, the New Deal programs that helped alleviate its effects, and so on. No matter how well this essay is written, points are going to be lost for one simple reason—the writer did not answer the question!

Second, a good essay does more than rattle off facts. It reveals an understanding of the general principles or the "big picture" of American history. Professor Keith Edgerton at Montana State University in Billings grades AP essays, and here's what he says:

"The best essays that I encountered were the ones that wove an understanding of content with some critical analysis. I am impressed with some originality of thought too; so few students possess it these days. Students should be willing to take something of a chance with the essays and not simply provide recitation of the few 'facts' that they have memorized. Longer essays, though not necessarily better, are usually more thorough in their coverage rather than the quick, I-need-to-get-this-done-because-I'm-tired-and-sick-of-this-test essays. It is a cliché, to be sure, but there still is no substitute for hard work. It can be painful and awfully grinding sometimes to learn history well, and it seems that there are not many students who want to devote much time to it. It does not provide instant gratification and cannot be mastered quickly, and it certainly does not happen in 23 minutes with appropriate commercial interruption. Students should read everything they can get their hands on and turn off the television. That is the best advice I can give."

If all this sounds intimidating, read on! There are a few simple things you can do to improve your grade on your AP essays.

Reasons to Be Cheerful

AP graders know that you are given only 100 minutes to plan and write two separate essays. They also know that is not enough time to cover the subject matter tested by the question. The fact is, many very long books have been written about any subject that you might be asked about on the DBQ and the long essay questions. That is why the College Board includes this statement:

> "As with the long essay, responses to the document-based question will be judged on students' ability to formulate a thesis and support it with relevant evidence."

In other words, expressing good ideas and presenting valid evidence in support of those ideas are important. Making sure you mention every single relevant piece of historical information is not so important, or even possible.

Remember that the graders are not given a lot of time to read your essays. One of them explains the grading experience this way:

> "There were about 545 graders drawn from colleges, universities, high schools, and prep schools. We had about 70 tables of readers. A table leader presides over each group. A typical schedule looks like this: 8:30 A.M. to 10:00 reading; 10:00 to 10:20 break; 10:20 to 12:00 reading; 12:00 to 1:00 lunch; 1:00 to 3:00 reading; 3:00 to 3:20 break; 3:20 to 5:00 reading. We read for six and a half days. Before grading the essays, we read sample packets selected by the table leaders, who arrive a few days before the rest of us.

With the sample packets we try to establish standards using a 0 to 9 scale. When the table leader believes we all have 'locked into' the standards, we commence reading. The table leader occasionally samples our finished product in order to ensure accuracy. Also, a computer correlates the essay scores with the grade received on the multiple-choice section. The AP authorities emphasize accuracy rather than speed. In the six and a half days, I read 995 essays. I do not know how this rate relates to other readers.... We look for responsiveness to the question. For the DBQ, we seek a clear thesis statement and supporting evidence."

Charles Quirk, University of Northern Iowa

Think about it. Professor Quirk averaged almost 150 essays a day—a little more than two minutes per essay. True, they are not writing comments, but at any rate, readers cannot look for anything profound or subtle. What they can do is look for evidence that you have something reasonably intelligent to say and that you know how to say it. Furthermore, the graders read many awful essays. (Not everyone, remember, is preparing for this test as well as you are.)

It is true that you can get the best possible score only if you have mastered the material. However, regardless of how well-prepared you are, you can improve your score if you follow the guidelines on the following pages. They will tell you how to avoid the mistakes all graders hate and how to use writing and organizational techniques they love.

Before we get to those guidelines, a final word from Darril Wilburn, a high school history teacher in Bardstown, New York. We think it is inspirational:

"On essay questions I stress two things: using detail and staying positive. You must be able to substantiate your ideas and thoughts with detail (factual, of course). This will go very far in impressing the reader that you do indeed know what you are talking about....On staying positive, I ask the students not to think of the essay questions (or any part of the exam for that matter) as something you lose points on. Think of each question and each bit of detail and each morsel of fact as an addition to your score; do not think of everything you leave out as being a subtraction from your score. This helps you stay focused and keeps stress levels lower (unless, of course, you do not know anything; then you deserve to be nervous). You can also play a mind game with yourself: 'How many points can I gather on this question?' This also keeps stress low."

Focus on what you know, rather than on what you do not know. Turn the test into a game.

Things That Make Any Essay Better

There are two essential components to writing a successful timed essay. First, plan what you are going to write before you start writing! Second, use a number of tried-and-true writing techniques that will make your essay appear better organized, better thought-out, and better written. This section is about those techniques. Remember: an essay that is better written and better organized usually earns a higher score than an essay that rambles but is packed with facts.

Choose, think, outline, write: your essay strategy!

1. Choose

Read the question carefully. For the DBQ, read each of the documents. You will be required to write one DBQ and one long essay. While there is no choice regarding the DBQ, you will be asked to select one question from a pair of long essay questions. The DBQ requires you to interpret a variety of documents and integrate your interpretation of these documents with your knowledge of the topic or time period. Being familiar with these instructions is useful in preparing for the exam, but you should reread all of the instructions very carefully on the actual day you take the exam to ensure that you are doing what is required of you.

2. Think

Brainstorm for one or two minutes. In your test booklet, write down everything that comes to mind about the subject. (There is room in the margins and at the top and bottom of the pages.) Look at your notes, and consider the results of your brainstorming session as you decide what point you will argue in your essay; that argument is going to be your thesis. Remember: your thesis must respond to the question. Utilize your notes to prove your thesis, but do not choose an argument that you know is wrong or with which you disagree. Finally, sort the results of your brainstorm. Some of what you wrote down will be "big picture" conclusions, some will be historical facts that can be used as evidence to support your conclusions, and some will be garbage.

3. Outline

Try to have at least three body paragraphs. You should go into special detail in each of the paragraphs on the DBQ. (Remember: you will have the documents and your outside knowledge to discuss on the DBQ.) Your first paragraph should contain your thesis statement as the last sentence. Your second, third, and fourth paragraphs (if there are three topics in the prompt) should contain three arguments that support that statement, along with historical evidence to back those arguments. The fifth paragraph should contain your conclusion, and you must specifically answer the question here if you have not already done so. Before you start to write your outline, you will have to decide what type of argument you are going to make. The following is a list of some classic arguments:

- **Three Good Points**

  This is the simplest strategy. Look at the results of your brainstorming session, and pick the three best points supporting your position. Make each of these points the subject of one paragraph, respectively. Make the weakest of the three points the subject of the second paragraph, and save the strongest point for the fourth paragraph. If your three points are interrelated and there is a natural sequence to arguing them, then by all means use that sequence, but otherwise, try to save your strongest point for last. Begin each paragraph with a topic sentence that tells the reader which topic you are going to address in that paragraph. Then spend the rest of the paragraph supporting it. Use specific historical examples whenever possible. Your first paragraph should state what you intend to argue; your final paragraph should explain why you have proven what you set out to prove. Don't forget to use transitions to make your examples and argument more cohesive and stronger.

- **The Chronological Argument**
  Many questions lend themselves to a chronological treatment. Questions about the development of a political, social, or economic trend can hardly be answered any other way. When you make a chronological argument, look for important transitions and use them to start new paragraphs. A five-paragraph essay about the events leading up to the Civil War, for example, might start with an introductory discussion of slavery and regional differences in the early 19th century. This is also where you should state your thesis. The second paragraph might then discuss the Missouri Compromise and other efforts to avoid the war. The third paragraph might mention the expansionism of the Polk era and how it forced the slavery issue, and the fourth paragraph might cover the collapse of the Missouri Compromise and how the events that followed—the Compromise of 1850, the Kansas-Nebraska Act, and the Dred Scott case—led the country into war. Your conclusion in this type of essay should restate the essay question and answer it. For example, if the question asks whether the war was inevitable, you should answer "yes" or "no" in this paragraph. However, remember that simply writing "The Civil War was inevitable" is not a thesis.

- **Comparison**
  Some questions, particularly on the free-response section, ask you to compare events, issues, and/or policies. Very often, the way the question is phrased will suggest the best organization for your essay. Take, for example, a question asking you to compare the impact of three events and issues on the United States' decision to enter World War II. This question pretty much requires you to start by setting the historical scene prior to the three events/issues you are about to discuss. Continue by devoting one paragraph to each of the three, and conclude by comparing and contrasting the relative importance of each.

Other questions will provide options. If you are asked to compare the political philosophies of two presidents, you might use each paragraph to compare and contrast both presidents' views on a single subject. For example, you might compare the two presidents' philosophies regarding the interpretation of the Constitution (loose or strict) in one paragraph, their differing approaches to foreign policy in one paragraph, and their ideas about the American economy in another paragraph. In the final paragraph, you can draw your conclusion (e.g., "their similarities were more significant than their differences," or vice versa), but be certain you state your argument in your thesis at the beginning of the essay.

- **The "Straw Man" Argument**
  In this essay-writing technique, choose a couple of arguments that someone taking the position opposite yours would take. State their arguments, and then tear them down. Remember that proving that your opposition is wrong does not mean that you have proved you are correct; that is why you should choose only a few opposing arguments to refute. Summarize your opponent's arguments in paragraph two, dismiss them in paragraph three, and use paragraph four to make the argument for your side. Or, use one paragraph to summarize and dismiss each of your opponent's arguments, and then make the case for your side in your concluding paragraph. Acknowledging both sides of an argument, even when you choose one over the other, is a good indicator that you understand that historical issues are complex and can be interpreted in more than one way—which teachers and readers like to see.

No matter which format you choose, remember to organize your essay so that the first paragraph addresses the question and states how you are going to answer it. (That is your thesis.) The second, third, and fourth paragraphs should each be organized around a single argument that supports your thesis, and each of these arguments must be supported by historical evidence. Your final paragraph then ties the essay up into a nice, neat package. Your concluding paragraph should also answer the question.

4. Write

- **Keep sentences as simple as possible.** Long sentences get convoluted very quickly and will give your graders a headache, putting them in a bad mood. Do not antagonize your reader! Remember that good writing does not have to be complicated; some great ideas can be stated simply. NEVER use a word if you are unsure of its definition or proper usage. A malapropism might give your graders a good laugh, but it will not earn you any points, and it will probably cost you.

- **Write clearly and neatly.** As long as we are discussing your graders' moods, here is an easy way to put them in good ones. Graders look at a lot of chicken scratch; it strains their eyes and makes them grumpy. Neatly written essays make them happy. When you cross out, do it neatly. If you are making any major edits—if you want to insert a paragraph in the middle of your essay, for example—make sure you indicate these changes clearly.

- **Define your terms.** Most questions require you to use terms that mean different things to different people. One person's "conservative" is another person's "liberal" and yet another person's "radical." What one person considers "expansionism," another might call "colonialism" or "imperialism." The folks who grade the test want to know what you think these terms mean. When you use them, define them. Take particular care to define any such terms that appear in the question. The introductory paragraph is a good place to include any definitions. Almost all official College Board materials stress this point, so do not forget it. Be sure to define any term that you suspect can be interpreted in more than one way.

- **Use transition words between paragraphs and within paragraphs to show where you are going.** When continuing an idea, use words such as *furthermore, also,* and *in addition*. When changing the flow of thought, use words such as *however* and *yet*. Transition words make your essay easier to understand by clarifying your intentions. Better yet, they indicate to the graders that you know how to make a coherent, persuasive argument.

- **Use structural indicators to organize your paragraphs.** Another way to clarify your intentions is to organize your essay around structural indicators. For example, if you are making a number of related points, number them ("First… Second… And last…"). If you are writing a compare/contrast essay, use the indicators "on the one hand" and "on the other hand."

- **Stick to your outline.** Unless you get an absolutely brilliant idea while you are writing, do not deviate from your outline. If you do, you will risk winding up with an incoherent essay.

- **Try to prove one "big picture" idea per paragraph.** Keep it simple. Each paragraph should make one point and then substantiate that point with historical evidence.

- **Back up your ideas with examples.** Yes, we have said this already, but it bears repeating. Do not just throw ideas out there and hope that you are right (unless you are absolutely desperate). You will score big points if you substantiate your claims with specific, historical examples.

- **Try to fill the essay form.** An overly short essay will hurt you more than one that is overly long. Try to write five solid paragraphs.

- **Make sure your first and last paragraphs directly address the question.** Nothing will cost you points faster than if the graders decide you did not answer the question. It is always a safe move to start your final paragraph by answering the question. If you have written a good essay, that answer will serve as a legitimate conclusion.

CRACKING THE DOCUMENT-BASED QUESTION

The DBQ is an essay question that requires you to interpret a mix of textual and visual *primary source* documents. (There are six or seven documents in a DBQ.) These documents will include many, if not all, of the following: newspaper articles and editorials, letters, diaries, speeches, excerpts from legislation, political cartoons, charts, and graphs. The documents will *not* include excerpts from current textbooks. Occasionally, one or two of the documents will be taken from something "classic" that you may have previously seen, but generally the documents will be new to you. However, they will discuss events and ideas with which you should be familiar. All the documents will pertain to a single subject. The documents are usually between a quarter and a half page long, although occasionally you will see something longer.

The DBQ, which is approximately 60 minutes long, is part of the second section of the test. At the beginning of the DBQ, you will be handed a green booklet, in which the essay question and documents are printed, as well as a separate form on which to write your essay. You are advised to spend the first 15 minutes of the section reading the documents and planning your essay.

To give you an idea of what you can expect on your DBQ, let's look at what appeared on a recent test. The question asked students to decide whether liberal opponents, conservative opponents, or President Woodrow Wilson bore the responsibility for the Senate's defeat of the Treaty of Versailles. The seven documents included excerpts from the following:

- A speech by a conservative senator, denouncing the League of Nations

- A letter from Herbert Hoover to Wilson, urging him to compromise with the Senate

- An editorial cartoon from a newspaper, opposing the League of Nations

- An article by economist John Maynard Keynes, discussing the European victors' opposition to Wilson's Fourteen Points

- A 1920 speech by Wilson, asking voters to support the League of Nations

- A 1921 article by W. E. B. Du Bois, criticizing Wilson for his handling of the treaty negotiations with the Senate

- A 1922 article by Jane Addams, discussing the necessity of the League of Nations

As you can see, a typical DBQ may contain documents you might have seen prior to the exam. However, the DBQ also includes documents you certainly have not seen before. Each of the documents, though, represents a political position you have studied. Many are written by famous people about whom you should know quite a bit (Keynes, Addams, Du Bois, Hoover), even if you do not know precisely how they felt about the Treaty of Versailles before reading the documents. In other words, you will not be starting from square one, even when the documents are new to you. Each document should trigger a memory of some historical figure, event, or trend in U.S. history.

Is There a "Right" Answer to Each DBQ?

No. DBQs are worded in such a way that you can argue any number of positions, and often the question is a historiographical one that historians have been debating for years. In the example on the previous page, the documents provide evidence for those who would blame the failure of the Treaty of Versailles on Wilson, liberals, conservatives, or some combination of the three. So long as you support your argument with evidence, you can argue whatever thesis you want. Often, however, the documents will "drive" a particular thesis, and it becomes more difficult to try to argue the other side.

Similarly, there is no "checklist" of facts and ideas against which DBQs are graded. Here's an excerpt from the College Board's official material:

> "The document-based question will typically require students to relate the documents to a historical period or theme and, thus, to focus on major periods and issues."

Readers are supposed to take into account the strength of your argument and the evidence you offer in support of it. In other words, if you forget to mention a good, illustrative historical event but manage to back up your point in some other way, you will not be penalized.

However, in order to earn the most credit for your essay, you must include *outside information*. You will notice that your DBQ contains the following instruction:

> Use at least one additional piece of specific historical evidence
> (beyond that found in the documents) relevant to an argument about the prompt.

Use the Documents AND Your Knowledge of the Subject

The outside information includes historical facts and ideas that are relevant to the question but not mentioned in the DBQ documents. For example, in the Treaty of Versailles DBQ described on the previous page, any information offered about the writers' backgrounds would count as outside information, as would information about the war itself. Of course, to receive credit, that information would have to help explain who was responsible for the failure of the Treaty of Versailles in the United States. Some students make the mistake of throwing everything they know about a subject into their essays, whether or not it pertains to the question. That type of information receives partial credit, at best.

GETTING STARTED ON THE DBQ: THE QUESTION

Start by reading the question. This direction may seem obvious, but it obviously is not, given the number of students who write essays on subjects that are only marginally related to the question being asked. Students miss the question because they become anxious during the exam. They panic. They think they are going too slowly. In an effort to speed up, they read half the question, say to themselves, "A-ha! I know what they're going to ask!" and stop reading. Do NOT make this mistake! The question is probably the shortest thing you have to read on the DBQ. Take your time; savor it. Explore its nuances. Essays that address the question fully earn huge bonuses; essays that ignore parts of the question are doomed to much lower scores.

Here's a sample question:

1. To what extent did the constituencies and agenda of the Progressive movement of the early 1900s represent continuity and/or change in relation to both the reform movements of the 1830s and 1840s and the Populist movement of the 1890s?

The first question you should ask yourself is this: do I have an opinion about this subject? The second question is this: what must I discuss in order to write a successful essay?

Of the two questions, the second is much more important. You can construct a position later, after you have gathered the information you want to include in your essay. First, you need to figure out what issues you must address and what data you will use in your discussion.

To begin with, you should notice that the question asks you to compare three movements—the Progressives, the Populists, and the reformers of the 1830s and 1840s. Your essay will obviously have to mention all three groups. Equally important, the question asks you to consider the constituencies and the agendas of these three groups in drawing your comparisons. Also, you must decide whether the Progressives were more similar to the Populists or to the reformers. Finally, you must include a discussion of the given documents and your outside knowledge in your essay.

Some people find it helpful to circle and underline key elements of an essay question. If you did that, your question probably looked something like this:

1. To what extent did the (constituencies) and (agenda) of the <u>Progressive</u> movement of the early 1900s represent continuity and/or change in relation to both the <u>reform</u> movements of the 1830s and 1840s and the <u>Populist</u> movement of the 1890s?

However you decide to approach the question, it is essential that you do not rush. Read carefully to make sure that you understand what issues must be addressed in your essay. Then determine how to organize the information you are going to collect from the documents and from memory for inclusion in the essay.

Drawing a grid can help you to quickly organize your ideas.

Organizing Your Essay: Grids and Columns

Many DBQs ask you to draw comparisons. For those questions, you can always organize your thoughts in a grid. Drawing a grid helps in seeing all sides of an argument, which is important because DBQ graders will reward you for acknowledging arguments other than your own. Consider the question from earlier; here is how you could grid this question:

	Constituency	Agenda
Antebellum Reformers		
Populists		
Progressives		

As you remember appropriate outside information and as you read the documents, take notes in the appropriate boxes. When it comes time to write your essay, you will find it easier to compare and contrast the three movements because your information will already be organized in a way that makes similarities and differences more obvious.

If you cannot draw a grid for a question, you can instead set up column headings. Because every DBQ can be argued from at least two different positions, you can always set up two (or more) columns, designating one for each position. Consider the DBQ about the Treaty of Versailles, which we discussed earlier in the chapter. You could create one column entitled "It was Wilson's fault," one entitled "It was liberals' fault," a third entitled "It was conservatives' fault," and even a fourth for information that you know belongs in your essay but that you cannot yet classify (give that the title "To be classified").

Good essays do not just flow out of your pen by accident. They happen when you know what you are going to say *before you start writing*. Although, given the time constraints, it is difficult (if not impossible) to prepare your entire DBQ essay before you begin writing, pre-organization and a good outline will get you much closer to that goal.

A Sample Question

Let's take a look at another question. Circle and/or underline the key elements of the question; then create a grid (or columns) in which to organize your information.

1. From the end of World War II through the Eisenhower administration, many Americans feared that communism threatened the existence of the United States. Using BOTH the documents AND your knowledge of the 1940s and 1950s, assess the reasons for and the validity of those fears.

Your question should look something like this:

1. From the end of World War II through the Eisenhower administration, many Americans feared that communism threatened the existence of the United States. Using BOTH the documents AND your knowledge of the 1940s and 1950s, assess the reasons for and the validity of those fears.

Your thesis must address the reasons for and validity of the Cold War fears, and your essay will have to address the Red Scare, the widespread fear of a communist takeover that Americans experienced during the early Cold War. (Remember that the second Red Scare in the age of McCarthyism during the 1950s followed the first Red Scare in the 1920s.) You will, of course, have to include analysis of both the documents and outside information, and your essay should cover the years between the end of the war and the end of the Eisenhower administration. Last (and what most students miss), you must answer two questions: Why did Americans fear a communist takeover? And, how valid were their fears?

Because the question does not ask you to draw any comparisons, you might want to organize your information in columns titled "Valid reason," "Not a valid reason," and "Maybe valid/maybe not." However, the question naturally lends itself to comparisons among the various perceived and real threats to the United States, which means that you could use a grid instead. Americans feared communist attacks both from communist nations and from subversives in the government. You could, therefore, draw a grid, giving your rows the headings "Threats from other countries" (e.g., the USSR and China), and "Threats from within the United States" (e.g., the Communist Party of the United States of America). This analysis would leave you with a grid that looks like the following:

	Valid	Not valid	Maybe valid/maybe not
Threats from other countries			
Threats from within the United States			

Once you have created your grid, begin collecting information for your essay. At this point, you are probably eager to start reading the documents. Resist the temptation. You have one more important job to do before you start reading.

Gather Outside Information

Most students read the DBQ documents first and then try to think of outside information to supplement their essays. This is a mistake. The reason? *The power of suggestion*. Once you have read the documents—a chore that can take six to eight minutes—those documents will be on your mind. If you wait until after you have read them to think of outside information, you will not be able to get the documents out of your head. Invariably, you will think of things you have already read about, rather than things you *have not* read about, which is precisely what outside information means.

Plus, reading and processing the documents is a big task. Once you have accomplished that, you will want to get started right away on organizing and writing your essay while the documents are fresh in your mind. You *do not* want to stop to think of outside information to include in your essay. And you certainly do not want to be trying to come up with outside information *while* you are writing your essay. So do it *before* you read the documents. The only exception to this strategy is the unlikely event that you are totally unfamiliar with a topic. In that case, the documents might jog your memory.

Look at your grid or columns and brainstorm. In a separate blank space in your green booklet (*not* in your grid/columns), write down everything you can think of that relates to the question. Spend two or three minutes on this task, then look at what you have written, cross out what you know you cannot use, and enter the rest into your grid/columns in the appropriate spaces.

Chances are that some of the outside information you think of will be mentioned in the documents, which means that it will not be outside information anymore.

That is no big deal. In fact, you should think of it as something good. If some of what you remembered shows up in the documents, that means you are on the right track toward answering the question!

This is what a brainstorming grid for the communism question might look like:

	Valid	Not valid	Maybe valid/ maybe not
Threats from other countries	−Soviets develop H-bomb −U.S.-Soviet confrontations: containment, Greece, Marshall Plan, Truman Doctrine −Korean War heightens tensions −fall of Cuba		−Chinese revolution −fall of Hungary: Soviet aggression, or Soviets protecting border? −U.S. involvement in Vietnam −Guatemala's ties to USSR
Threats from within the United States	−there was an American Communist party −though small, party was influential in powerful labor unions −some evidence of espionage: the Rosenbergs	−Rosenbergs' punishment too great for crime, shows U.S. paranoia −Loyalty Review Board; McCarthy's list of State Dept. subversives; blacklisting; bomb shelters −postwar affluence made Americans more conservative	−Alger Hiss case

1. Choose

After you have gathered outside information to include in your essay, you are ready to read the documents. As you read, keep the following things in mind:

- **The order in which documents appear is almost always helpful.**
  Very often, the documents in the DBQ appear in chronological order.
  When they do, it often indicates that the College Board wants you to
  trace the historical development of the DBQ subject. On such questions, you do not have to write an essay that adheres strictly to chronological order, but chronology should play an important part in the development of your thesis. When the documents appear in an order other than chronological, they are usually organized so that you can easily compare and contrast different viewpoints on a particular event or issue. On these questions, one of your main goals should be to draw those comparisons.

- **Watch for inconsistencies within and among the documents.** The documents will not necessarily agree with one another. In fact, they are almost certain to present different viewpoints on issues and almost as certain to present conflicting accounts of a historical event. Some documents might even contradict themselves! This is intentional. The AP is testing your ability to recognize these contradictions. You are expected to resolve these conflicts in your essay. To do so, you will have to identify the sources of the documents. (See below.)

- **Identify the sources of the documents.** Why do two accounts of the same event contradict each other? Why do two economists, looking at the same data, come up with dissimilar interpretations? It is because the people giving these accounts—the sources of the documents—have different perspectives. Identify the sources and explain why their opinions differ. As you explain these differences, look for the following differences between sources:

    o political ideology
    o class
    o race
    o religion
    o gender

    Consider the question of whether communism posed a serious threat to the United States in the 1940s and 1950s. An urban Northeastern intellectual, a wealthy Midwestern industrialist, and a Chinese immigrant on the West Coast would offer very different answers to that question. The graders will be looking specifically to see if you have tried to explain those differences.

- **Look for evidence that could refute your argument.** Once you have decided what your thesis will be, you will be looking through the documents for evidence to support your argument. Not all the documents will necessarily back you up. Some may appear to contradict your argument. Do not simply ignore those documents! As you read them, try to figure out how you might incorporate them into your argument. Again, let's consider the communism DBQ. Suppose you argue that Americans overreacted to the communist threat. Now suppose that one of the documents presents evidence of subversive communist activity in the United States. You might be tempted to pretend that the document does not exist. However, you will be better off if you incorporate the document into your essay. For example, acknowledge that America was not immune to communist subversion but that the threat was nowhere near as great as most anticommunists claimed. By doing this, you will be acknowledging that this historical issue, like all historical issues, is complex and multifaceted. This acknowledgment is good. AP readers are instructed to look for evidence that you understand that history has no simple answers and to reward you for it.

To make sure you're giving an in-depth document analysis (and the best way to get full credit!) use HIPA.

H – historical context
I – intended audience
P – purpose
A – author or artist's point of view

As you read the documents, be aware that each one holds a few morsels of information for your essay. Do not fixate on any one document, as you can't afford to waste the time. Try to use all, or all but one, of the documents. Don't panic if you are initially confused by a document. Remember: the AP puts each document in the DBQ to serve one or two purposes, rather than five. Think about it and try to figure out why they've included this document, and you'll have a pretty good idea of why it's in the DBQ and how to fit it into your essay. Unless you are clueless (which is unlikely), you will be able to find a way to include each document in your essay, which is better than leaving it out entirely. However, it is better to leave a document out than to misinterpret it. And be confident. If you're in an AP History course, you're smart enough to figure out why the document has been included in the DBQ. Often, the documents "speak" to one another. You, the historian, should enter that dialogue.

Also, as you read the documents, take note of any outside information that the document reminds you of, scribble it into the margins around the document, and enter it into your grid/columns. Again, don't panic if, after you read the question, you can't think of any outside information. Stay calm; you will remember more after looking at the documents. Even though brainstorming first is best, if you freeze, you should go to the documents, and let the documents get you going on the outside info.

2. Think

As you finish reading the documents and prepare to formulate your thesis, remember that while you do not have to answer this question by falling squarely on one side or the other of the issue, it's best to lean one way, with a nod to the other side. A safe, effective route to take on your DBQ essay is to indicate that there is evidence to support both sides of the argument. A good lawyer acknowledges there is other evidence, but he or she is confident that there is stronger evidence to support his or her side of the case. Try to develop a case as you write your essay, using the documents and outside knowledge as mounting evidence. "To what extent" questions should prompt you to determine if something is more this way than that way. Most questions can be rephrased as "to what extent" questions and doing so is often a useful strategy in developing a thesis.

Before you decide on your thesis, GO BACK AND READ THE QUESTION ONE MORE TIME! Make sure that your thesis addresses all the pertinent aspects of the question.

3. Outline

Having a distinct outline for your essay will better ensure that all of the material flows properly and that you address all of the parts of the essay questions. Create an outline with one Roman numeral for each paragraph. Decide on the subject of each paragraph and on what information you will include in each paragraph. Do not rely on your grid/columns if you do not have to. The grid/columns are good for organizing your information but are less efficient for structuring an essay.

4. Write

Go back and reread the section in this chapter titled "Things That Make Any Essay Better" to review good essay-writing techniques. Follow this advice: don't write flowery introductions or conclusions—just say what you are going to say. The readers want to get right to the point and see how much you know. Remember to back up your thesis statement with lots of facts, even if you are stretching it, because the graders want to hear solid evidence and not a lot of fluff. Also, make sure to remember what is being asked in the question, and refer to the question several times during the essay writing, as it is easy to wander away from your main point.

Stay confident. Everyone else taking the test, all across the country, is at least as nervous about it as you are.

GRADING OF YOUR DBQ ESSAY

The document-based question (DBQ) is scored with a maximum score of 7 possible points allocated across the following areas: thesis (1 point), contextualization (1 point), evidence (3 points), and analysis (2 points). The DBQ score represents 25 percent of the total exam score. Your essay is being graded with a rubric similar to the one shown below. Remember that the graders are looking quickly for the elements of the essay, which address the core themes in this rubric.

The general grading approach is described in Part III of this book. We have included the rubric here to assist you in optimizing your writing approach.

DBQ Scoring Rubric		
Task	**Points Possible**	**Description**
Thesis	1	Respond to the prompt by creating a logically and historically defensible claim. **(1 point)**
Contextualization	1	Offer a larger historical context that is rooted in the prompt. **(1 point)**
Evidence	3	1. Connecting at least three documents to the **topic** will yield 1 point, whereas… 2. Developing an **argument** with at least six documents will yield 2 points. Incorporating at least one relevant piece of evidence outside those offered in the documents will earn the third point.
Analysis	2	1. Explain the relevance of at least three of the documents in terms of the thesis. (1 point). 2. Show a complex understanding of the issue (comparison, causation, and continuity and change over time) with the use of relevant evidence. (1 point).

CRACKING THE LONG ESSAY QUESTION

The other essay question in Section II of the test is a long essay question. You will be asked to choose one of three different essay prompts. The options for the essay prompts fall under three time periods: option one is 1491–1800, option two is 1800–1898, and option three is 1890–present. These questions will usually take the form of a historical statement or stance. You must support, modify, or refute its interpretation in a written essay. Similar to the DBQ, you are expected to develop and defend a relevant thesis. Many of the design and outlining approaches for the DBQ described earlier in this chapter are applicable for this essay. However, unlike the DBQ, you are provided no documents. In other words, all information you use will be that which you come up with. You are expected to take approximately 40 minutes to write your essay, and the long essay question will constitute 15 percent of your total AP Exam score.

A simple, defendable thesis, accompanied by an organized essay filled with strong analysis of the given subject, should result in a high score. Do not write an essay that is simply descriptive, in which you regurgitate everything you know about the essay prompt. Purely descriptive essays rarely get scored well as they fail to analyze, assess, and evaluate the given subject.

Here is an example of a long essay question:

1. Compare and contrast the impact of religion on the American colonies during the First Great Awakening and in the Second Great Awakening (1800–1860).

   In the development of your argument, explain the reasons for the similarities and differences.

As you can see, long essay questions are designed to prompt analysis and evaluation of subject matter that you have learned in class. The subjects should be familiar; the questions are straightforward. The long essay is scored with a maximum score of 6 points allocated across the following areas: thesis (1 point), use of evidence in support of argument (2 points), contextualization (1 point), and analysis (2 points). Similar to the DBQ, a grading rubric is available and will be similar to the one shown on the following page.

Long Essay Scoring Rubric		
Task	Points Possible	Description
Thesis	1	Respond to the prompt by creating a logically and historically defensible claim. **(1 point)**
Contextualization	1	Offer a larger historical context that is rooted in the prompt. **(1 point)**
Evidence	2	1. Offering evidence related to the **topic** will yield 1 point, whereas… 2. Developing an **argument** with specific, relevant pieces of evidence will yield 2 points.
Analysis	2	1. Structuring the argument around historical reasoning will yield 1 point, whereas… 2. Showing a complex understanding (comparison, causation, and continuity and change over time) of the issue that is backed up with relevant evidence will yield 2 points.

Choose

Choose the question about which you know the most, NOT the one that looks easiest at first glance. The more you know about the subject, the better your final grade will be.

Think, Outline, Write

Because we have already covered this information, here are brief directions to structure your essay. First, read the question and analyze it. Second, create a grid or columns and take notes. Third, assess your information and devise a thesis. Fourth, write a quick outline. Lastly, write your essay. If any of these instructions are unclear, reread the previous parts of this chapter.

A Final Note

This section is short because we have already discussed what you need to know to write successful AP essays, not because the long essay questions are unimportant. The long essay question is worth 15 percent of your total test score and is very important. Many students are tempted to ease up or invest all of their time in the DBQ, because it is so challenging. Do not make this mistake. Reach down for the last bit of energy and finish strong.

Summary

Overview

o Read the questions carefully. You must answer the specific question asked in order to receive full credit.

o Do not start writing until you have brainstormed, developed a thesis, and written an outline.

o Follow your outline. Stick to one important idea per paragraph (say, comparisons only or social issues only). Support your ideas with historical evidence.

o Write clearly and neatly. Do not write in long, overly complex sentences. When in doubt, stick to simple syntax and vocabulary.

o Use transition words to indicate continuity of thought and changes in the direction of your argument.

o Proofread your essay to make sure you have answered the question and to catch any errors or omissions. Watch out for any careless errors in names or years. Did you write Theodore Roosevelt when you meant to write Franklin Roosevelt? Did you say that the Declaration of Independence was written in 1876 when you meant to write 1776?

The Document-Based Question

o The DBQ consists of an essay question and 6 or 7 historical documents. Most likely, you will not have seen most of the documents before, but they will all relate to major historical events and ideas and will remind you of what you have learned about this topic. The DBQ is expected to take you 1 hour (including the time of planning and reading the documents).

o There is no single "correct" answer to the DBQ. DBQs are framed so that they can be successfully argued from many different viewpoints.

- o Read the essay question carefully. Circle and/or underline important words and phrases. Once you understand the question, create a grid or columns in which to organize your notes on the essay.

- o Before you start reading the documents, brainstorm about the question. This way you will gather the all-important outside information before you submerge yourself in the documents.

- o Read the documents. Read them in order, as there is usually a logic to the order in which they are presented. Pay attention to contradictions within and among the documents and to who is speaking and what sociopolitical tradition he or she represents. If you have already decided on a thesis, keep an eye out for information that might refute your thesis, and be prepared to address it in your essay.

- o Decide on a thesis; then write an outline for your essay.

- o Try to summarize key points from as many of the documents as you can in your essay. Weave in as much outside information as you can.

The Long Essay Question

- o The long essay section consists of three questions. You must answer one question from the three. The eras covered in this section will depend upon what eras were covered on your DBQ.

- o Choose the questions about which you know the most, not the ones that look easiest.

- o Analyze each question you choose. Circle and/or underline important words and phrases. Once you understand the question, create a grid or columns in which to organize your notes on the essay.

- o Decide on a thesis; then write an outline for your essay.

- o Follow your outline. Stick to one important idea per paragraph. Support your ideas with historical evidence.

- o Write clearly and neatly. Do not write in overly complex sentences. Toss in a couple of "big" words that you know you will not misuse. When in doubt, stick to simple syntax and vocabulary.

- o Use transition words to indicate continuity of thought and changes in the direction of your argument.

Chapter 4
Using Time
Effectively to
Maximize Points

Very few students stop to think about how to improve their test-taking skills. Most assume that if they study hard, they will test well, and if they do not study, they will do poorly. Most students continue to believe this even after experience teaches them otherwise. Have you ever studied really hard for an exam and then blown it on test day? Have you ever aced an exam for which you thought you weren't well prepared? Most students have had one, if not both, of these experiences. The lesson should be clear. Factors other than your level of preparation influence your final test score. This chapter will provide you with some insights that will help you perform better on the AP U.S. History Exam and on other exams as well.

PACING AND TIMING

A big part of scoring well on an exam is working at a consistent pace. The worst mistake made by inexperienced or unsavvy test takers is that they come to a question that stumps them, and rather than just skip it, they panic and stall. Time stands still when you're working on a question you cannot answer, and it is not unusual for students to waste five minutes on a single question (especially a question involving a graph or the word EXCEPT) because they are too stubborn to cut their losses. It is important to be aware of how much time you have spent on a given question and on the section you are working. There are several ways to improving your pacing and timing for the test:

- **Know your average pace.** While you prepare for your test, try to gauge how long you take on 5, 10, or 20 multiple-choice questions. Knowing how long you spend on average per question will help you identify the number of questions you can answer effectively and how best to pace yourself for the test.

- **Have a watch or clock nearby.** You are permitted to have a watch or clock nearby to help you keep track of time. It is important to remember, however, that constantly checking the clock is in itself a waste of time and can be distracting. Devise a plan. Try checking the clock after every 15 or 30 questions to see if you are keeping the correct pace or whether you need to speed up; this will ensure that you're cognizant of the time but will not permit you to fall into the trap of dwelling on it.

- **Know when to move on.** Since all multiple-choice questions are scored equally, investing appreciable amounts of time on a single question is inefficient and can potentially deprive you of the chance to answer easier questions later on. If you are able to eliminate answer choices, do so, but don't worry about picking a random answer and moving on if you cannot find the correct answer. Tests are like marathons; you do best when you work through them at a steady pace. You can always come back to a question you don't know. When you do, very often you will find that your previous mental block is gone, and you will wonder why the question perplexed you the first time around (as you gleefully move on to the next question). Even if you still don't know the answer, you will not have wasted valuable time you could have spent on easier questions.

- **Be selective.** You don't have to do any of the questions in a given section in order. If you are stumped by an essay or multiple-choice question, skip it or choose a different one. In the section below, you will see that you may not have to answer every question correctly to achieve your desired score. Select the questions or essays that you can answer, and work on them first. This will make you more efficient and give you the greatest chance of getting the most questions correct.

- **Use Process of Elimination on multiple-choice questions.** Many times, one or more answer choices can be eliminated. Every answer choice that can be eliminated increases the odds that you will answer the question correctly. The section on multiple-choice questions (Chapter 1) presented strategies to find these incorrect answer choices and increase your odds of getting the question correct.

Remember: when all the questions on a test are of equal value, no one question is that important; your overall goal for pacing is to get the most questions correct. Finally, you should set a realistic goal for your final score. In the next section, we will break down how to achieve your desired score and ways of pacing yourself to do so.

GETTING THE SCORE YOU WANT

Depending on the score you need, it may be in your best interest *not* to try to work through every question. Check with the schools to which you are applying. Do you need a 3 to earn credit for the test? With the recently updated formatting of the test, it remains unclear how the College Board will calculate score distributions. However, you will likely be able to skip one or two of the sets of questions in the multiple-choice section completely and still be able to attain a 3. The key to scoring what you need is knowing approximately how many questions you, on average, get correct out of the number of questions attempted. For instance, do you normally get 75 percent of the multiple-choice questions correct? If so, then you would need to attempt far fewer questions than someone who averages only 50 percent correct. The only way to know for sure is practice. Remember, however, that you are not penalized for guessing, so you should never leave a question blank. If, for example, you do not attempt 12 questions but rather guess at random, you would expect to get an additional 3 questions correct based on random chance.

Of course, obtaining a 5 is not impossible, but it will require good performance on all sections of the test. As described in Part III, there are a lot of different ways to score points. The test evaluates your understanding of AP U.S. History from multiple perspectives. Scoring a 5 requires a thorough understanding of the material (which we will address in the next part of this text) and the ability to utilize provided sources and historical perspectives to synthesize a thesis around a central question or argument.

You have nothing to lose by guessing.

More Great Books
Check out The Princeton Review's test prep titles for ACT and SAT: *Princeton Review ACT Premium Prep, Cracking the SAT Premium, ACT Elite, SAT Elite,* and many more!

TEST ANXIETY

Everybody experiences anxiety before and during an exam. To a certain extent, test anxiety *can* be helpful. Some people find that they perform more quickly and efficiently under stress. If you have ever pulled an all-nighter to write a paper and ended up doing good work, you know the feeling.

However, *too much* stress is definitely a bad thing. Hyperventilating during the test, for example, almost always leads to a lower score. If you find that you stress out during exams, here are a few preemptive actions you can take.

- **Take a reality check.** Evaluate your situation before the test begins. If you have studied hard, remind yourself that you are well prepared. Remember that many others taking the test are not as well prepared, and (in your classes, at least) you are being graded against them, so you have an advantage. If you didn't study, accept the fact that you will probably not ace the test. Make sure you get to every question you know something about. Don't stress out or fixate on how much you don't know. Your job is to score as high as you can by maximizing the benefits of what you do know. In either scenario, it is best to think of a test as if it were a game. How can you get the most points in the time allotted to you? Always answer questions you can answer easily and quickly before you answer those that will take more time.

- **Try to relax.** Slow, deep breathing works for almost everyone. Close your eyes, take a few, slow, deep breaths, and concentrate on nothing but your inhalation and exhalation for a few seconds. This is a basic form of meditation, and it should help you to clear your mind of stress and, as a result, concentrate better on the test. If you have ever taken yoga classes, you probably know some other good relaxation techniques. Use them when you can (obviously, anything that requires leaving your seat and, say, assuming a handstand position won't be allowed by any but the most free-spirited proctors).

- **Eliminate as many surprises as you can.** Make sure you know where the test will be given, when it starts, what type of questions are going to be asked, and how long the test will take. You don't want to be worrying about any of these things on test day or, even worse, after the test has already begun.

The best way to avoid stress is to study both the test material and the test itself. Congratulations! By buying or reading this book, you are taking a major step toward a stress-free AP U.S. History Exam.

Chapter 5
Pacing Drills

In this chapter, you'll have the opportunity to put to use the strategies you've learned. Let's get cracking!

Multiple-Choice Drill

As you work through the following questions, try to apply everything you learned in Chapter 1. Make sure to keep the big picture in mind as you consider the answer choices. Use POE. If you can get rid of one or more answer choices and can go no further, guess and move on. Use common sense and context clues. Answers and explanations for these questions follow the drills in this chapter.

Questions 1 - 3 refer to the excerpt below.

"As for the lawfulness of keeping slaves, I have no doubt, since I hear of some that were bought with Abraham's money, and some that were born in his house.—And I cannot help thinking, that some of those servants mentioned by the Apostles in their epistles, were or had been slaves. It is plain, that the Gibeonites were doomed to perpetual slavery, and though liberty is a sweet thing to such as are born free, yet to those who never knew the sweets of it, slavery perhaps may not be so irksome."

George Whitefield, 1751

1. Whitefield's statements suggest that many colonists' opinions on slavery in the 1700s were most directly shaped by

   (A) Christian biblical interpretations
   (B) commerce and business interests
   (C) trade with the Gibeonites
   (D) agricultural interests

2. Whitefield's revival meetings contributed most directly to which of the following trends?

   (A) Republican Motherhood
   (B) Political and religious independence
   (C) Back-to-the-land migration
   (D) Progressive social reforms

3. The speaker above would be most associated with which of the following social or political movements?

   (A) Republicanism
   (B) Abolitionism
   (C) The Age of Reason
   (D) The First Great Awakening

Questions 4 - 6 refer to the excerpt below.

"Neither here, nor in any other part of the world, is the right of suffrage allowed to extend beyond one of the sexes. This universal exclusion of woman…argues, conclusively, that, not as yet, is there one nation so far emerged from barbarism, and so far practically Christian, as to permit woman to rise up to the one level of the human family."

U.S. Representative Gerrit Smith, 1848

4. The ideas expressed in the excerpt most directly challenged the prevailing ideal in the nineteenth century that

(A) women should enjoy full and equal rights with men
(B) women's political interests were sufficiently represented by their husbands and fathers
(C) the presence of women in industry and agriculture was a positive step toward independence
(D) women were responsible for the education of their children

5. According to the sentiments expressed, which of the following trends in the late nineteenth century would Gerrit most support?

(A) Women's suffrage
(B) The Gospel of Wealth
(C) Prohibition
(D) The Second Great Awakening

6. Many supporters of the sentiments expressed above would also ally themselves with which of the following ideologies?

(A) Social Darwinism
(B) States' rights
(C) Abolitionism
(D) Isolationism

Questions 7 - 9 refer to the excerpt below.

"The battle, sir, is not to the strong alone; it is to the vigilant, the active, the brave. Besides, sir, we have no election. If we were base enough to desire it, it is now too late to retire from the contest. There is no retreat but in submission and slavery! Our chains are forged! Their clanking may be heard on the plains of Boston! The war is inevitable—and let it come! I repeat it, sir, let it come!

"It is in vain, sir, to extenuate the matter. Gentlemen may cry, 'Peace! Peace!'—but there is no peace. The war is actually begun! The next gale that sweeps from the north will bring to our ears the clash of resounding arms! Our brethren are already in the field! Why stand we here idle? What is it that gentlemen wish? What would they have? Is life so dear, or peace so sweet, as to be purchased at the price of chains and slavery? Forbid it, Almighty God! I know not what course others may take; but as for me, give me liberty, or give me death!"

7. The excerpt above was from a speech by which of the following?

   (A) Dred Scott
   (B) John Brown
   (C) Patrick Henry
   (D) Samuel Adams

8. The excerpt is most clearly an example of advocating for which of the following?

   (A) Abolition of slavery
   (B) Equal civil rights for African Americans
   (C) Freedom from Great Britain
   (D) Joining the war effort during World War II

9. Which of the following groups would be most likely to support the perspective presented in the excerpt?

   (A) Northern abolitionists
   (B) Southern plantation owners
   (C) Loyalists
   (D) Patriots

Short-Answer Drill

Question 1 is based on the following image.

XVth Amendment—"Shoo, fly, don't bother me!"

1. Use the image above to answer parts (a), (b), and (c).

    a) Briefly explain the point of view expressed through the image about ONE of the following:
        • Voting Rights
        • Emancipation
        • The Constitutional Amendment process

    b) Briefly explain ONE outcome of the Civil War that led to the historical change depicted in the image.

    c) Briefly explain ONE way in which the historical change you explained in part b was challenged in the period between 1866 and 1896.

"It is a solemn sight to see so many Christians lying in their blood, some here, and some there, like a company of sheep torn by wolves, all of them stripped naked by a company of hell-hounds, roaring, singing, ranting, and insulting, as if they would have torn our very hearts out; yet the Lord by His almighty power preserved a number of us from death, for there were twenty-four of us taken alive and carried captive."

Mary Rowlandson, taken captive during King Philip's War, 1675

"How different would be the sensation of a philosophic mind to reflect that instead of exterminating a part of the human race by our modes of population that we had persevered through all difficulties and at last had imparted our Knowledge of cultivating and the arts, to the Aboriginals of the Country by which the source of future life and happiness had been preserved and extended."

Henry Knox to George Washington, 1790s

2. Using the excerpts above, answer parts (a), (b), and (c).

a) Briefly explain ONE major difference between Rowlandson's and Knox's interpretations.

b) Briefly explain how someone supporting Rowlandson's interpretation could use ONE piece of evidence from the period between 1600 and 1800 not directly mentioned in the excerpt.

c) Briefly explain how someone supporting Knox's interpretation could use ONE piece of evidence from the period between 1600 and 1800 not directly mentioned in the excerpt.

DBQ Drill

1. From the end of World War II through the Eisenhower administration, many Americans feared that communism threatened the existence of the United States. Using BOTH the documents AND your knowledge of the 1940s and 1950s, assess the reasons for and the validity of those fears.

Document 1

Source: Decoded telegram from a KGB agent, New York to Moscow. Intercepted by U.S. intelligence.

November 14, 1944

To VIKTOR,

LIBERAL has safely carried through the contracting of Kh'YuS. Kh'YuS is a good pal of METR's. We propose to pair them off and get them to photograph their own materials having given them a camera for this purpose… LIBERAL will receive the film from METR for passing on….

OSA has agreed to cooperate with us in drawing in ShMEL'…with a view to ENORMOUS. On summons from KALIER she is leaving on 22 November for the Camp 2 area….

_____

Notes:

VIKTOR = Lt. Gen. P. M. FITIN [KGB Moscow]

LIBERAL = Julius ROSENBERG

Kh'YuS = probably Joel BARR or Alfred SARANT

OSA = Ruth GREENGLASS

ShMEL'/KALIER = David GREENGLASS

ENORMOUS = Atomic Energy Project

Document 2

Source: Representative John F. Kennedy, speech to Congress, January 1949.

Mr. Speaker, over this weekend we have learned the extent of the disaster that has befallen China and the United States. The responsibility for the failure of our foreign policy in the Far East rests squarely with the White House and the State Department.

The continued insistence that aid would not be forthcoming unless a coalition government with the Communists was formed, was a crippling blow to the National Government.

So concerned were our diplomats and their advisers…with the imperfection of the democratic system in China…and the tales of corruption in high places that they lost sight of our tremendous stake in a non-Communist China….

This House must now assume the responsibility of preventing the onrushing tide of communism from engulfing all of Asia.

Document 3

Source: President Harry Truman, speech, July 29, 1951.

This malicious propaganda has gone so far that on the Fourth of July…people were afraid to say they believed in the Declaration of Independence. A hundred and twelve people were asked to sign a petition that contained nothing except quotations from the Declaration of Independence and the Bill of Rights. One hundred and eleven of these people refused to sign that paper—many of them because they were afraid that it was some kind of subversive document and that they would lose their jobs or be called Communists.

Document 4

Source: Advertisement, *Civil Defender* magazine, 1955.

TO: CIVIL DEFENSE AUTHORITIES, EDUCATORS, AND PARENT-TEACHER ASSOCIATIONS

STUDENT IDENTIFICATION DURING AN "ATOMIC" ALERT

NEED: Is Civil Defense needed? If the answer to this question is yes, then we must entertain the thought of evacuation. Since the advent of the Hydrogen Bomb, the only safety lies in not being "there."

EVACUATION: Should it be necessary to evacuate the children during school hours, it is also necessary to identify them. Many educators feel that this identification is more necessary for the grades from sixth down through kindergarten.

IDENTIFICATION: Identification must be positive, practical, and nontransferable. Identification must be kept in the school, to be used only during the time of the actual alert or drill. Identification must be inexpensive, since neither the schools nor the Civil Defense people have a lot of money to spend.

How do we of NATIONAL SCHOOL STUDIOS fit into this picture?

We offer the solution to the Identification problem...

We will furnish the Identification Card, chain, and pin (pictured in this ad) for the small sum of sixty cents per student.... We will furnish the Identification Card...free of charge if we are permitted to submit our envelopes of pictures to the parents for possible purchase of these envelopes by the parents. Incidentally, this entails absolutely NO OBLIGATION on the part of the parent to purchase the envelope of pictures. We submit the envelope of pictures 100% on speculation....

Document 5

"COME UNTO ME, YE OPPREST!"

Document 6

Source: Senator Joseph McCarthy, Lincoln Day speech to the Republican Women's Club of Wheeling, West Virginia, 1950.

The State Department is infested with communists. I have here in my hand a list of 205—a list of names that were made known to the Secretary of State as being members of the Communist Party and who nevertheless are still working and shaping policy in the State Department.

Document 7

Source: Edward R. Murrow, broadcast journalist, 1954.

No one familiar with the history of this country can deny that congressional committees are useful. It is necessary to investigate before legislating, but the line between investigating and persecuting is a very fine one, and the junior Senator from Wisconsin has stepped over it repeatedly. His primary achievement has been in confusing the public mind, as between the internal and the external threats of Communism. We must not confuse dissent with disloyalty. We must remember always that accusation is not proof and that conviction depends upon evidence and due process of law. We will not walk in fear, one of another. We will not be driven by fear into an age of unreason, if we dig deep in our history and our doctrine, and remember that we are not descended from fearful men—not from men who feared to write, to speak, to associate and to defend causes that were, for the moment, unpopular.

Long Essay Drill

Below is a drill based upon a long essay question. During the actual exam, you will have the option to choose between one of three different questions. Since the long essay questions provide no outside information, you will have to provide all of the relevant outside information you can come up with. Develop an outline and an approach to how you would write an essay based on the following prompt:

1.   Assess the causes and consequences of the abolition movement of the 1840s and 50s.

EXPLANATIONS FOR THE MULTIPLE-CHOICE DRILL

1. **A** Along with Jonathan Edwards, George Whitefield was a leading Methodist preacher and star of the First Great Awakening, a religious movement that gained in popularity in the mid-18th century. He was known for leading revival tent meetings. He was known mostly for his evangelism, but as you can see from this quote, he was also tolerant of slavery. Notice that Whitefield makes frequent references to the Bible ("Abraham," "apostles," "Gibeonites") and claims that slavery is not so "irksome" to those who have been born into it.

2. **B** This one is pure Process of Elimination (POE). Choices (A) and (C) are unrelated to both the First Great Awakening and the issue of slavery. Choice (D), progressive social reforms, don't come until many years later. Choice (B) is the best answer because the First Great Awakening did encourage a more personal experience of religious faith. Preachers tended to be charismatic individuals rather than formally educated drones.

3. **D** If you recognized Whitefield's name, then this one is a slam dunk. Otherwise, use POE. Choice (B) is the opposite of what we're looking for. Choices (A) and (C) are unrelated to the topic.

4. **B** Gerrit Smith was a fiery Free-Soil member of Congress who was active in both the abolition and temperance movements of the mid-19th century. In the quote, he is advocating for women's suffrage (his cousin was Elizabeth Cady Stanton). Those who opposed women's suffrage at this time justified their opinions by asserting that women need not vote since their husbands and other male relatives would make sure their interests were represented politically.

5. **A** Choice (A) is closest to the sentiment expressed in the quote. Although Smith was in favor of Prohibition, as in (C), this is not mentioned in the quote. Choice (D) may be true, but, again, it is not directly supported by the quote.

6. **C** Many supporters of women's suffrage were also abolitionists. In fact, Gerrit Smith was a big defender of John Brown.

7. **C** This question asks you to identify the source of the excerpt provided. Any time a question asks for a source, the excerpt is likely from a famous quote or speech. Upon reading the excerpt, there are several key clues provided. First, the provider alludes to the clanking of chains in Boston. Slavery and abolition had already occurred in Boston by the time of Dred Scott and John Brown, making (A) and (B) incorrect. Therefore, the excerpt must have come from a colonist. At the end of the excerpt, we see the famous line: "give me liberty, or give me death." This is an excerpt from Patrick Henry's passionate liberty speech, making (C) the correct answer.

8. **C** This question asks for the nature of the speech. Freedom and liberty in Boston were passionate cries for freedom and independence from British rule, making (C) correct. Although it is very tricky to fall into the trap of associating his pleas for freedom from chains with African American freedom, it is important to evaluate all of the answer choices.

9. **D** This question asks you to identify the group most likely to sympathize with the speech in the excerpt. The speech calls for Boston to stand up and fight for freedom and liberty. These are not (B), passionate cries of a Southerner, nor are they (C), the words of a loyalist to the British crown. Since the speech describes having "no election" and the clanking of chains in Boston, the nature of the speech is more revolutionary than of abolitionist nature, making (D) the better answer.

EXPLANATION FOR THE SHORT-ANSWER DRILL

1. The cartoon shows a black man poised to cast his ballot as flies hover around harassing him. He tells the flies to "Shoo!" with a smile on his face. The name of the cartoon is "XVth Amendment." Here are some facts relevant to this cartoon:

    - The Fifteenth Amendment guaranteed universal suffrage to blacks after the Civil War. Keep in mind, though, that some Freedmen in some states had voting rights even before the Civil War.

    - All amendments to the Constitution must be ratified by the states. Not all states ratified the Fifteenth Amendment immediately. In fact, the flies in this cartoon are labeled with the abbreviations of the Northern states that delayed ratification.

    - New York had the most restrictive laws against black suffrage. (This is why the biggest fly is labeled "NY," perhaps represented by Democrat governor John Hoffman.)

    - In some Southern states after the Civil War, black voters temporarily outnumbered disenfranchised Confederates.

    - The voter in this cartoon appears to be casting his ballot in public into a clear glass bowl, perhaps representing the lack of privacy afforded to voters at that time. Yet, he has a smile on his face, so he will not be dissuaded by either the "flies" or the public nature of his act.

2. Mary Rowlandson was a colonial woman who was captured and held hostage by Wampanoag Indians during the series of raids known as King Philip's War. After her ransom, she wrote a detailed narrative of her experiences, which became one of the most read books of the late 17th century. Her account is filled with atrocities committed by her captors and no doubt fueled suspicions in the colonists about the trustworthiness of local tribes. As you can see from this quote, she shared a view of Indians that many people had at the time: Indians were lawless savages, and God was on the side of the Protestant settlers. There are numerous examples of Indian aggression throughout the 17th and 18th centuries that could support this view.

    Henry Knox took the more modernist view that Indians could be "tamed" and taught to assimilate into American society and that warfare was not the answer. No doubt Knox's views were popular among some throughout the 19th century, eventually leading to the reservation system and the Dawes Act. Since we are sticking to events prior to 1800, it would be useful to discuss Indian cooperation with Europeans throughout the Seven Years' War.

EXPLANATION FOR THE DBQ DRILL

Document 1 is a good example of a document that starts out confusing but ends up being pretty straightforward. At first glance, this document makes very little sense; it is just a jumble of words and names. Do not panic; look for familiar elements. First, look at the source information. It is a telegram from a KGB agent. Therefore, it must have something to do with Soviet espionage. Now, look at the notes, and notice that they mention Julius Rosenberg and the Atomic Energy Project. Those references are probably all you need to know to understand why this document is included in the DBQ. It presents evidence that the Soviets were spying on the United States while it was developing the atomic bomb.

When you write your essay, do not fall into the trap of explaining every detail of this telegram. Your job is to analyze the importance of the document, not to describe exactly what it contains. This is true of every document in a DBQ, but it is particularly tempting here. You will be so proud that you have figured out what this document is all about that you might be tempted to spend a paragraph describing your achievement. Forget it. You have bigger fish to fry.

You probably asked yourself why this DBQ starts with a document from 1944, given that the question is about the period from 1945 through 1960. The document is here to demonstrate that there was some foundation for America's anticommunist fears after World War II. You can use this document as a springboard to discuss other reasons for that fear, such as the relative popularity of the American Communist Party (CPUSA) in the 1930s and the party's disproportionate representation in some labor unions. Mentioning unions then allows you to discuss labor problems in the postwar era. (Labor held more than 5,000 strikes in 1946 and 1947, which spurred the antiunion Taft-Hartley Act.)

This document can also be incorporated easily into an "America was too paranoid" essay because it raises the issue of the Rosenberg trial and the controversy over their sentence. Many people believe their execution resulted from anticommunist paranoia, not from reasoned consideration of their alleged crimes. (Albert Einstein testified that the Rosenbergs gave the Soviets nothing that they wouldn't have figured out on their own.) Of course, the Rosenberg trial generated a national debate, which illustrates the nation's preoccupation with communism during this period.

You may have thought of other issues that this document raises. That is good, and it highlights an important point: most DBQ documents will be adaptable to a discussion of many different events and ideas. Consequently, you have a lot of leeway in your essay. (Remember that there is no single correct answer to the DBQ.) It also means you cannot possibly discuss every event that relates to this question. There is simply too much to discuss. Believe it or not, that is good too. DBQ topics are so large that no one *expects* you to write the definitive essay on the subject. Hence, you will not be penalized for forgetting one or another event that illustrates your point as long as you back your points with other evidence.

Document 2 is taken from a speech in Congress by John F. Kennedy, and it raises several important issues. Primarily, it brings up the Chinese Revolution, which gives you an opportunity to discuss the expansion of communist power in other parts of the world. Using Document 2 as a starting point, you could discuss the Korean War, the crises in Eastern Europe in the 1950s (e.g., Hungary), and the fall of Cuba and other Latin American nations to communist insurgents. All of these events support the position that America's fear of communism was valid, especially if you choose to attribute these events to communist expansionism.

On the other hand, you might argue that this speech shows Kennedy demonstrating the same Cold War paranoia that later inspired the Bay of Pigs fiasco. You might attribute this speech to his political skills and argue that Kennedy is exploiting a sensitive issue for his own political gain. (Remember, many early "Cold Warriors" gained political support by accusing the government of "giving away" China to the Communists.) Interestingly, Kennedy felt it so important to keep China from communist control that he was willing to overlook the flagrant corruption of Chiang Kai-shek's government. If you think he was right, this document justifies American fears; if you argue that he was wrong, you can use it to illustrate how anticommunism distorted America's judgment.

Document 3 clearly supports the argument that Americans were paranoid about communism and that this paranoia was the result of propaganda. President Truman's reference to people "losing their jobs" opens the door for you to talk about blacklisting during the 1950s and, by extension, McCarthyism and other excesses of this anticommunist era. His description of those citizens who thought that the Declaration of Independence was a "subversive document" illustrates the conservatism of the era. However, Document 3 also gives you a chance to discuss Truman's anticommunism. Remember, he established loyalty boards with tremendous power to fire government employees merely on the suspicion of communist tendencies. Plus, his foreign policy initiatives, from containment to the Marshall Plan and the Truman Doctrine, might all be considered the ideas of an overzealous anticommunist. You certainly could argue that those policies antagonized communist countries and therefore exacerbated tensions. You could even say that the growing American-communist tension *resulted* from Truman's policies. As usual, nothing is cut-and-dried in the DBQ, which means that you have many options available to you.

Document 4 addresses two important issues, the hydrogen bomb and its chilling effect on America. The document is an advertisement that very clearly tries to exploit parents' fears as a means of selling them pictures of their children. While it is exploitative, it also indicates just how far fear of the H-bomb had infiltrated the American psyche. You can use this document as a starting point to discuss air-raid shelters, atomic bomb drills in school, the "Duck and Cover" propaganda campaign, and civil defense organizations. All of these events stem from American fear of the Communists. Most Americans were afraid of the USSR primarily because the USSR had the H-bomb. For many Americans, it was conceivable and even likely that the Soviets would use that bomb against the United States.

Document 5 is a cartoon depicting a European immigrant anarchist arriving in New York, poised to stab and bomb the Statue of Liberty. The cartoon satirizes the American pledge to welcome immigrants, some of whom are either a threat to American politics or perceived to be so by the public. The immigrant is sneaking up behind the Statue, so she is unaware of the threat. Most likely this cartoon was published in the early 1920s, when Italian anarchists were suspect, but the First Red Scare certainly influenced the sentiments of the Second Red Scare.

Document 6 is a quote from Senator Joseph McCarthy who claimed to have information regarding Communists who had infiltrated powerful positions in the military and government bureaucracies. McCarthy staged hearings to try to ferret out the Communists, but he was gradually discredited when proof of Communists could not be produced

Document 7 is an excerpt from a live broadcast by Edward R. Murrow. Murrow was a highly respected journalist with Democrat leanings who was at times vocal about his criticisms of society and the government. In this quote, he points out that McCarthy had gone too far in his accusations of Communist sympathizer, engaging in a witch hunt.

That's it for the documents. Now formulate a thesis. There are any number of positions you can argue on our sample question. The best route, as we just said, would be to attribute America's fear of the Communists to a combination of justifiable and exaggerated reasons. Furthermore, there are a number of ways you can choose to construct an essay that demonstrates this thesis. You might want to argue chronologically, indicating which events caused justifiable alarm and which were blown out of proportion by anticommunist propagandists. You might wish to divide the body of your essay into two large paragraphs, one dealing with the communist threat posed from abroad and the other dealing with the threat posed by American Communists.

Once you've figured out how and where to fit all your information into your argument, create an outline, and write your essay.

EXPLANATION FOR THE LONG ESSAY DRILL

As you begin to think about this prompt, you realize that the theme and therefore thesis of the essay should focus on the connection between slavery and the start of the war. You should begin by making notes or a set of columns of events related to slavery that occurred specifically during this period preceding the Civil War and how they may have contributed to the war. For instance, you could include some of the following key events in your essay:

- Compromise of 1850 (admission of California as a free state; popular sovereignty in territories; banning of slave trade in Washington D.C.; Fugitive Slave Law)

- *Uncle Tom's Cabin* by Harriet Beecher Stowe, 1852 (antislavery novel, fostered abolitionist sentiment)

- Election of 1852 (slavery was a key issue and caused intra- and interparty conflict)

- Kansas-Nebraska Act, 1854 (popular sovereignty in Kansas/Nebraska territories, negated the Missouri Compromise)

- Bleeding Kansas, 1855 (war between pro- and antislavery factions; Pottawatomie Creek Massacre)

- Election of 1856 (party lines are drawn on views of slavery)

- *Dred Scott v. Sanford*, 1857 (made the Missouri compromise unconstitutional)

- Lincoln-Douglas Debates, 1858 (Lincoln's house divided speech, open discussion on slavery in territories)

- Harper's Ferry Raid, 1859 (attempt to start an armed slave revolt)

- Election of 1860 (split of democratic party over views on slavery, election of pro-abolitionist Lincoln)

After you have assembled your list of events, you will need to evaluate which events share a common theme and can be written together to form paragraphs and the start of an outline. For the example above, you may have noticed that several of the events involve issues related to the stance of political parties. This could become the focus of one of your paragraphs. Two possible additional themes include pre-Civil War armed confrontations (such as Bleeding Kansas and the Harper's Ferry Raid) and the role of Popular Sovereignty in new states and territories. Remember, that as you write essays, you must structure your outline and arguments to a central theme, in this case, the connection between slavery and the start of the Civil War. Since you have only approximately 40 minutes to structure and write the long essay question, your sentences should be succinct, and your essay should have a clear thesis supported by your outside information. Be confident, pace yourself, and most importantly, stay on target.

REFLECT

Think about what you've learned in Part IV, and respond to the following questions:

- How long will you spend on multiple-choice questions?

- How will you change your approach to multiple-choice questions?

- What is your multiple-choice guessing strategy?

- How will you change your approach to the short-answer questions?

- How will you manage your time on the short-answer questions?

- How much time will you spend on the DBQ? The long essay question?

- Will you spend 15 minutes reading and planning? Or will you jump right into writing your essay?

- How will you change your approach to the essays?

- Will you seek further help, outside of this book (such as a teacher, tutor, or AP Students) on how to approach multiple-choice questions, the essays, or a pacing strategy?

Part V
Content Review for the AP U.S. History Exam

HOW TO USE THE CHAPTERS IN THIS PART

The history review is meant to serve as a supplement to the textbook you use in class. It is not a substitute for your textbook. However, it does cover all major subjects and terms that are likely to appear on the AP U.S. History Exam. If you are familiar with everything in this review, you should do very well on the AP Exam.

In the following content review chapters, you will find a summary of those events and actions that the writers of the AP Exam consider important. Because historical events often exemplify economic, social, and political trends, and because that's what makes those events important to historians (and to test writers), this review focuses on those connections. We have tried to make this section as interesting and as brief as possible while remaining thorough.

You may need to come back to these chapters more than once. Your goal is to obtain mastery of the content you are missing, and a single read of a chapter may not be sufficient. At the end of each chapter, you will have an opportunity to reflect on whether you truly have mastered the content of that chapter.

Additionally, we've provided review questions at the end of each chapter to quiz your retention of what you've read. Please note that these multiple-choice questions differ from the ones you'll see on the AP U.S. History Exam in that they refer to the content covered in the chapter and NOT to a specific source document. For source-based multiple-choice questions, see our Practice Tests as well as the drills in Chapter 5.

Chapter 6
Early Contact with the New World (1491–1607)

Colonization of North America (1607–1754)

True or False?

Q: Native American cultures tended to have limited or minimal impact on the environment.

NATIVE AMERICANS IN PRE-COLUMBIAN NORTH AMERICA

Historians refer to the period before **Christopher Columbus's** arrival in the "New World" as the **pre-Columbian** era. During this period, North America was populated by **Native Americans**—not to be confused with native-born Americans, a group that includes anyone born in the United States. Five percent of multiple-choice questions test you on this era, so it is important to understand the clash of cultures that occurred between the European settlers and the Native Americans, as well as their subsequent conflicts throughout American history.

Most historians believe that Native Americans are the descendants of migrants who traveled from Asia to North America. The migration likely occurred in multiple waves, from as early as 40,000 years ago to as recently as 15,000 years ago. During this period, the planet was significantly colder, and much of the world's water was locked up in vast polar ice sheets, causing sea levels to drop. The ancestors of the Native Americans could therefore simply walk across a **land bridge** from Siberia (in modern Russia) to Alaska. As the planet warmed, sea levels rose and this bridge was submerged, forming the **Bering Strait**. These people and their descendants eventually migrated south, either by boat along the Pacific coast or possibly along an ice-free corridor east of the Rocky Mountains, and went on to populate both North and South America.

At the time of Columbus's arrival, between 1 million and 5 million Native Americans lived in modern Canada and the United States; another 20 million populated Mexico. Native American societies in North America ran the gamut from small groups of nomadic hunter-gatherers to highly organized urban empires. In the year 1500, the Aztec capital of Tenochtitlan was more populous than any city in Europe, and both the Aztecs and the Maya are noted for their advances in astronomy, architecture, and art. While these civilizations were located in Mesoamerica, the territory that would become the United States was home to urban cultures as well, such as the **Pueblo people** of the desert southwest with their multistory stone houses consisting of hundreds of rooms and the **Chinook people of the Pacific Northwest who subsisted on hunting and foraging or the nomadic Plains Indians.** The first Native Americans to encounter Europeans were smaller tribes, such as the Iroquois and Algonquian, who had permanent agriculture and lived along the Atlantic Ocean; Columbus, mistakenly believing he had reached the East Indies, dubbed them "Indians," and the name stuck for centuries.

Maize

The domestication and cultivation of maize, or corn, began thousands of years ago in Mexico. The indigenous people of the region depended on this staple crop for much of their livelihood and the reliance on maize soon spread to much of North America. The transition from hunting and gathering to maize production enabled stable economies and organized societies to prosper throughout Mesoamerica and the Southwest region of the modern-day United States. Maize production also encouraged advancements in irrigation and other advanced agricultural practices.

EARLY COLONIALIZATION OF THE NEW WORLD (1491–1607)

The Early Colonial Era: Spain Colonizes the New World

Christopher Columbus arrived in the New World in 1492. He was not the first European to reach North America—the Norse had arrived in modern Canada around 1000—but his arrival marked the beginning of the Contact Period, during which Europe sustained contact with the Americas and introduced a widespread exchange of plants, animals, foods, communicable diseases, and ideas in the **Columbian Exchange**. Columbus arrived at a time when Europe had the resources and technology to establish **colonies** far from home. (A *colony* is a territory settled and controlled by a foreign power.) When Columbus returned to Spain and reported the existence of a rich new world with easy-to-subjugate natives, he opened the door to a long period of European expansion and colonialism.

During the next century, Spain was *the* colonial power in the Americas. The Spanish founded a number of coastal towns in Central and South America and in the West Indies, where the **conquistadors** collected and exported as much of the area's wealth as they could. Under Spain's **encomienda** system, the crown granted colonists authority over a specified number of natives; the colonist was obliged to protect those natives and convert them to Catholicism, and in exchange, the colonist was entitled to those natives' labor for such enterprises as sugar harvesting and silver mining. If this sounds like a form of slavery, that's because it was.

Spanish and Portuguese colonization of North America was also marked by liberal mixing of cultures, leading to a racial caste system, with Europeans at the top of the hierarchy, followed by **Mestizos** (those of mixed European and Native blood, **Zambos** (those of mixed African and Native American heritage) and full-blooded Africans at the bottom of the ladder. Meanwhile, the strength of Spain's navy, the **Spanish Armada**, kept other European powers from establishing much of a foothold in the New World. In 1588, the English navy defeated the Armada, and consequently, French and English colonization of North America became much easier.

> Much of early American history revolves around the conflict between Native Americans and European settlers. Europeans were generally victorious. Why? One seemingly obvious answer is that the Europeans had more advanced technology, but this wasn't actually a major factor. In fact, in many ways, the Native Americans' technology was superior: their canoes were far better at navigating North American rivers than any European ship, and their moccasins offered better footing than clumsy European boots. The most important factor, by a wide margin, was disease. Native Americans had never been exposed to European microbes and had never developed immunities to them. Epidemics, such as **smallpox**, devastated Native American settlements, sometimes killing 95% of the population.

True or False?

A: False! Even Native American societies that hadn't developed much in the way of agriculture often transformed the landscape through the strategic use of fire, which encouraged the growth of useful plants and attracted game animals. Many early European immigrants to North America remarked that the areas they were settling resembled parkland; this wasn't the natural condition of these regions, but it reflected the cultivation of the local environment by the Native Americans who had preceded them.

True or False?

Q: Pre-Columbian societies used horses and cows for transportation and agriculture.

Competition for Global Dominance

Once Spain had colonized much of modern-day South America and the southern tier of North America, other European nations were inspired to try their hands at New World exploration. They were motivated by a variety of factors: the desire for wealth and resources, clerical fervor to make new Christian converts, and the race to play a dominant role in geopolitics. The vast expanses of largely undeveloped North America and the fertile soils in many regions of this new land, opened up virtually endless potential for agricultural profits and mineral extraction. Concurrently, improvements in navigation, such as the invention of the **sextant** in the early 1700s, made sailing across the Atlantic Ocean safer and more efficient.

Intercontinental trade became more organized with the creation of **joint stock companies**, corporate businesses with shareholders whose mission was to settle and develop lands in North America. The most famous ones were the British East India Company, the Dutch East India Company, and later, the **Virginia Company,** which settled **Jamestown.**

Increased trade and development in the New World also led to increased conflict and prejudice. Europeans now debated how Native Americans should be treated. Spanish and Portuguese thinkers, such as **Juan de Sepúlveda** and **Bartolomé de Las Casas,** proposed wildly different approaches to the treatment of Native populations, ranging from peace and tolerance to dominance and enslavement. The belief in European superiority was nearly universal.

Some American Indians resisted European influence, while others accepted it. Intermarriage was common between Spanish and French settlers and the natives in their colonized territories (though rare among English and Dutch settlers). Many Indians converted to Christianity. Spain was particularly successful in converting much of Mesoamerica to Catholicism through the **Spanish mission system**. Explorers, such as **Juan de Oñate,** swept through the American Southwest, determined to create Christian converts by any means necessary—including violence.

As colonization spread, the use of African slaves purchased from African traders from their home continent became more common. Much of the Caribbean and Brazil became permanent settlements for plantations and their slaves. Africans adapted to their new environment by blending the language and religion of their masters with the preserved traditions of their ancestors. Religions such as **voodoo** are a blend of Christianity and tribal animism. Slaves sang African songs in the fields as they worked and created art reminiscent of their homeland. Some, such as the **Maroon** people, even managed to escape slavery and form cultural enclaves. Slave uprisings were not uncommon, most notably the Haitian Revolution.

The English Arrive

Unlike other European colonizers, the English sent large numbers of men and women to the agriculturally fertile areas of the East. Despite our vision of the perfect Thanksgiving table, relationships with local Indians were strained, at best. English intermarriage with Indians and Africans was rare, so no new ethnic groups emerged, and social classes remained rigid and hierarchical.

England's first attempt to settle North America came a year prior to its victory over Spain, in 1587, when **Sir Walter Raleigh** sponsored a settlement on Roanoke Island (now part of North Carolina). By 1590, the colony had disappeared, which is why it came to be known as the **Lost Colony**. The English did not try again until 1607, when they settled **Jamestown**. Jamestown was funded by a **joint-stock company**, a group of investors who bought the right to establish New World plantations from the king. (How the monarchy came to sell the rights to land that it clearly did not own is just the kind of interesting question that this review will not be covering. Sorry, but it is not on the AP Exam!) The company was called the **Virginia Company**—named for Elizabeth I, known as the Virgin Queen— from which the area around Jamestown took its name. The settlers, many of them English gentlemen, were ill-suited to the many adjustments life in the New World required of them, and they were much more interested in searching for gold than in planting crops. (The only "gold" to be found in Virginia was iron pyrite, aka "fool's gold," which the ignorant aristocrats blithely gathered up.) Within three months, more than half the original settlers were dead of starvation or disease, and Jamestown survived only because ships kept arriving from England with new colonists. **Captain John Smith** decreed that "he who will not work shall not eat," and things improved for a time, but after Smith was injured in a gunpowder explosion and sailed back to England, the Indians of the **Powhatan Confederacy** stopped supplying Jamestown with food. Things got so bad during the winter of 1609–1610 that it became known as "the **starving time**": nearly 90 percent of Jamestown's 500 residents perished, with some resorting to cannibalism. The survivors actually abandoned the colony, but before they could get more than a few miles downriver, they ran into an English ship containing supplies and new settlers.

One of the survivors, **John Rolfe,** was notable in two ways. First, he married Powhatan's daughter **Pocahontas**, briefly easing the tension between the natives and the English settlers. Second, he pioneered the practice of growing **tobacco**, which had long been cultivated by Native Americans, as a cash crop to be exported back to England. The English public was soon hooked, so to speak, and the success of tobacco considerably brightened the prospects for English settlement in Virginia.

Because the crop requires vast acreage and depletes the soil (and so requires farmers to constantly seek new fields), the prominent role of tobacco in Virginia's economy resulted in rapid expansion. The introduction of tobacco would also lead to the development of plantation slavery. As new settlements sprang up around Jamestown, the entire area came to be known as the **Chesapeake** (named after the bay). That area today comprises Virginia and Maryland.

Many who migrated to the Chesapeake did so for financial reasons. Overpopulation in England had led to widespread famine, disease, and poverty. Chances for improving one's lot during these years were minimal. Thus, many were attracted to the New World by the opportunity provided by **indentured servitude**. In return for free passage, indentured servants typically promised seven years' labor, after which they would receive their freedom. Throughout much of the 17th century, indentured servants also received a small piece of property with their freedom, thus enabling them (1) to survive and (2) to vote. As in Europe, the right to vote was tied to the ownership of property, and indentured servitude in America opened a path to land ownership that was not available to most working class men in populous Europe. However, indenture was extremely difficult, and nearly half of all indentured servants—most of whom were young, reasonably healthy men—did not survive their term of service. Still, indenture was common. More than 75 percent of the 130,000 Englishmen who migrated to the Chesapeake during the 17th century were indentured servants.

In 1618, the Virginia Company introduced the **headright system** as a means of attracting new settlers to the region and to address the labor shortage created by the emergence of tobacco farming, which required a large number of workers. A "head-right" was a tract of land, usually about 50 acres, that was granted to colonists and potential settlers.

In 1619, Virginia established the **House of Burgesses**, in which any property-holding, white male could vote. All decisions made by the House of Burgesses, however, had to be approved by the Virginia Company. That year also marks the introduction of **slavery** to the English colonies. (See the section later in this chapter, "Slavery in the Early Colonies.")

French Colonization of North America

At first glance, the French colonization of North America appears to have much in common with Spanish and English colonization. While the English had founded a permanent settlement at Jamestown in 1607, the French colonized what is today Quebec City in 1608. Like the Spanish missionaries, the French Jesuit priests were trying to convert native peoples to Roman Catholicism, but they were much more likely to spread diseases, such as smallpox, than to convert large numbers to Christianity. Like colonists from other European countries, the French were exploring as much land as they could, hoping to find natural resources, such as gold, as well as a shortcut to Asia.

Unlike the Spanish and English, however, the French colonists had a much lighter impact on the native peoples. Few French settlers came to North America, and those who did tended to be single men, some of whom intermarried with women native to the area. They also tended to stay on the move, especially if they were *coureurs du bois* ("runners in the woods") who helped trade for the furs that became the rage in Europe. True, the French ultimately did play a significant role in the French and Indian War (surprise!) from 1754–1763; however, their chances of shaping the region soon known as British North America were slim from the outset and faded dramatically with the **Edict of Nantes** in 1598.

The four main colonizing powers in North America interacted with the native inhabitants very differently:

- **Spain** tended to conquer and enslave the native inhabitants of the regions it colonized. The Spanish also made great efforts to convert Native Americans to Catholicism. Spanish colonists were overwhelmingly male, and many had children with native women, leading to settlements populated largely by mestizos, people of mixed Spanish and Native American ancestry.

- **France** had significantly friendlier relations with indigenous tribes, tending to ally with them and adopt native practices. The French had little choice in this: French settlements were so sparsely populated that taking on the natives head-on would have been very risky.

- **The Netherlands** attempted to build a great trading empire, and while it achieved great success elsewhere in the world, its settlements on the North American continent, which were essentially glorified trading posts, soon fell to the English. This doesn't mean they were unimportant. One of the Dutch settlements was New Amsterdam, later renamed New York City.

- **England** differed significantly from the three other powers in that the other three all depended on Native Americans in different ways: as slave labor, as allies, or as trading partners. English colonies, by contrast, attempted to exclude Native Americans as much as possible. The English flooded to the New World in great numbers, with entire families arriving in many of the colonies rather than just young men, and intermixing between settlers and natives was rare. Instead, when English colonies grew to the point that conflict with nearby tribes became inevitable, the English launched **wars of extermination**. For instance, the Powhatan Confederacy was destroyed by English "Indian fighters" in the 1640s.

The Métis

Métis (pronounced may-tee) is a term to describe people of Canada and parts of the northern United States who are of mixed Native American and European (usually French) descent.

The Métis are originally descended from 17th-century French trappers and traders who married Native, usually Algonquian, women. The Métis are a legally recognized indigenous people in modern-day Canada.

The Pilgrims and the Massachusetts Bay Company

During the 16th century, English Calvinists led a Protestant movement called **Puritanism** in England. Its name was derived from its adherents' desire to purify the Anglican church of Roman Catholic practices. English monarchs of the early 17th century persecuted the Puritans, and so the Puritans began to look for a new place to practice their faith.

One Puritan group, called **Separatists**—because they thought the Church of England was so incapable of being reformed that they had to abandon it—left England around this time. First, they went to the Netherlands but ultimately decided to start fresh in the New World. In 1620, they set sail for Virginia, but their ship, the *Mayflower*, went off course and they landed in modern-day Massachusetts. Because winter was approaching, they decided to settle where they had landed. This settlement was called **Plymouth**.

While on board, the travelers—called **Pilgrims** and led by William Bradford—signed an agreement establishing a "body politic" and a basic legal system for the colony. That agreement, **the Mayflower Compact**, is important not only because it created a legal authority and an assembly, but also because it asserted that the government's power derives from the consent of the governed and not from God, as some **monarchists** known as **Absolutists** believed.

Like the earlier settlers in Jamestown, the Pilgrims received life-saving assistance from local Native Americans. To the Pilgrims' great fortune, they had happened to land at the site of a Patuxet village that had been wiped out by disease; one inhabitant of that village, a man named Tisquantum, better known as **Squanto**, had been spared this fate because he had been captured years before and brought to Europe as a slave. He wound up in London, where he learned English and then returned to his homeland only to find it depopulated. Shortly thereafter, the Pilgrims arrived, and Squanto became their interpreter and taught them how best to plant in their new home.

In 1629, a larger and more powerful colony called **Massachusetts Bay** was established by Congregationalists (**Puritans** who wanted to reform the Anglican church from within). This began what is known as The Great Puritan Migration, which lasted from 1629 to 1642. Led by Governor **John Winthrop**, Massachusetts Bay developed along Puritan ideals. While onboard the ship *Arabella*, Winthrop delivered a now-famous sermon, "A Model of Christian Charity," urging the colonists to be a **city upon a hill**—a model for others to look up to. All Puritans believed they had a **covenant** with God, and the concept of covenants was central to their entire philosophy, in both political and religious terms. Government was to be a covenant among the people; work was to serve a communal ideal, and, of course, the Puritan church was always to be served. This is why both the Separatists and the Congregationalists did not tolerate religious freedom in their colonies, even though both had experienced and fled religious persecution.

The settlers of the Massachusetts Bay Colony were strict **Calvinists**, and Calvinist principles dictated their daily lives. For example, much has been written about the "Protestant work ethic" and its relationship to the eventual development of a market economy. In fact, some historians believe the roots of the Civil War can be traced back to the founding of the Chesapeake region and New England, as a plantation economy dependent on slave labor developed in the Chesapeake and subsequent southern colonies, while New England became the commercial center.

Two major incidents during the first half of the 17th century demonstrated Puritan religious intolerance. **Roger Williams**, a minister in the Salem Bay settlement, taught a number of controversial principles, among them that church and state should be separate. The Puritans banished Williams, who subsequently moved to modern-day Rhode Island and founded a new colony. Rhode Island's charter allowed for the free exercise of religion, and it did not require voters to be church members. **Anne Hutchinson** was a prominent proponent of *antinomianism*, the belief that faith and God's grace—as opposed to the observance of moral law and performance of good deeds—suffice to earn one a place among the "elect." Her teachings challenged Puritan beliefs and the authority of the Puritan clergy. The fact that she was an intelligent, well-educated, and powerful woman in a resolutely patriarchal society turned many against her. She was tried for heresy, convicted, and banished.

Puritan immigration to New England came to a near halt between 1649 and 1660, the years during which **Oliver Cromwell** ruled as Lord Protector of England. Cromwell's reign represented the culmination of the **English Civil Wars**, which the Puritans won. During the **Interregnum** (literally "between kings"), Puritans had little motive to move to the New World. Everything they wanted—freedom to practice their religion, as well as representation in the government—was available to them in England. With the restoration of the Stuarts, many English Puritans again immigrated to the New World. Not coincidentally, these immigrants brought with them some of the republican ideals of the revolution.

The lives of English settlers in New England and the Chesapeake differed considerably. Entire families tended to immigrate to New England; in the Chesapeake, immigrants were often single males. The climate in New England was more hospitable, and so New Englanders tended to live longer and have larger families than Chesapeake residents. A stronger sense of community, and the absence of tobacco as a cash crop, led New Englanders to settle in larger towns that were closer to one another; those in the Chesapeake lived in smaller, more spread-out farming communities. While both groups were religious, the New Englanders were definitely *more* religious, settling near meetinghouses. Another important difference between New England and the Chesapeake was in the use of slavery. New England farms were small and required less labor. Slavery was rare. Farms in middle and southern colonies were much larger, requiring large numbers of African slaves. In fact, at one time, South Carolina had a larger proportion of African slaves than European settlers.

Other Early Colonies

Several colonies were proprietorships; that is, they were owned by one person, who usually received the land as a gift from the king. **Connecticut** was one such colony, receiving its charter in 1635 and producing the **Fundamental Orders**, usually considered the first written constitution in British North America. **Maryland** was another, granted to Cecilius Calvert, Lord Baltimore. Calvert hoped to create a haven colony for Catholics, who faced religious persecution in Protestant England, but he also hoped to make a profit growing tobacco. In order to populate the colony's land more quickly, Calvert offered religious tolerance for all Christians, and Protestants soon outnumbered Catholics, recreating England's old tension between the faiths. After a Protestant uprising in England against a Catholic-sympathizing king, Maryland's government passed the **Act of Toleration** in 1649 to protect the religious freedom of most Christians, but the law was not enough to keep the situation in Maryland from devolving into bloody religious civil war for much of the rest of the century.

New York was also a royal gift, this time to James, the king's brother. The Dutch Republic was the largest commercial power during the 17th century and, as such, was an economic rival of the British. The Dutch had established an initial settlement in 1614 near present-day Albany, which they called New Netherland, and a fort at the mouth of the Hudson River in 1626. This fort would become New Amsterdam and is today New York City. In 1664, Charles II of England waged a war against the Dutch Republic and sent a naval force to capture New Netherland. Already weakened by previous clashes with local Native Americans, the Dutch governor, Peter Stuyvesant, along with 400 civilians, surrendered peacefully. Charles II's brother, James, became the Duke of York, and when James became king in 1685, he proclaimed New York a royal colony. The Dutch were allowed to remain in the colony on generous terms, and they made up a large segment of New York's population for many years. Charles II also gave **New Jersey** to a couple of friends, who in turn sold it off to investors, many of whom were Quakers.

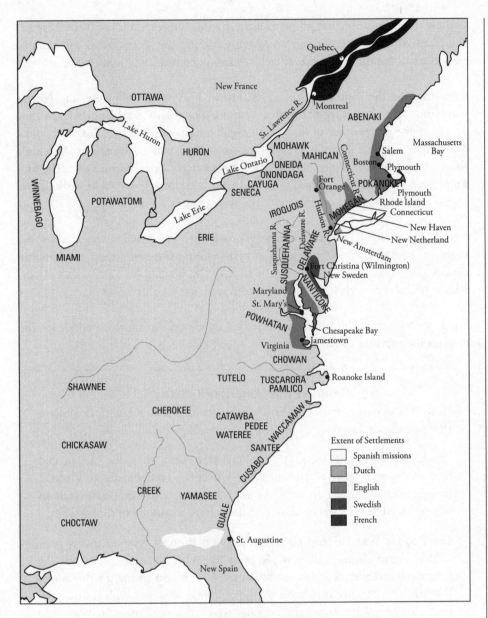

European Settlements in North America, 1650

Ultimately, the Quakers received their own colony. William Penn, a Quaker, was a close friend of King Charles II, and Charles granted Penn what became **Pennsylvania**. Charles, like most Anglicans, perceived the egalitarian Quakers as dangerous radicals, but the two men's friendship (and Charles's desire to export the Quakers to someplace far from England) prevailed. Penn established liberal policies toward religious freedom and civil liberties in his colony. That, the area's natural bounty, and Penn's recruitment of settlers through advertising, made Pennsylvania one of the fastest growing of the early colonies. He also attempted to treat Native Americans more fairly than did other colonies and had mixed results. His attitude attracted many tribes to the area but also attracted many European settlers who bullied tribes off of their land. An illustrative story: Penn made a treaty with the Delawares to take only as much land as could be walked by a man in three days. Penn then set off on a leisurely stroll, surveyed his land, and kept his end of the bargain. His son, however, renegotiating the treaty, hired three marathon runners for the same task, thereby claiming considerably more land.

Carolina was also a proprietary colony, but in 1729 it officially split into **North Carolina**, settled by Virginians as a Virginia-like colony, and **South Carolina**, settled by the descendants of Englishmen who had colonized Barbados. Barbados's primary export was sugar, and its plantations were worked by slaves. Although slavery had existed in Virginia since 1619, the settlers from Barbados were the first Englishmen in the New World who had seen widespread slavery at work. Their arrival truly marked the beginning of the slave era in the colonies.

Eventually, most of the **proprietary** colonies were converted to **royal** colonies; that is, their ownership was taken over by the king, who could then exert greater control over their governments. By the time of the Revolution, only Connecticut, Rhode Island, Pennsylvania, and Maryland were *not* royal colonies.

For an overview of which areas were settled by whom during this period, see the map on the previous page.

Geography = Destiny?
Here's a good general guide for remembering which colonies were established for what reasons: the northern colonies were mostly established for religious reasons, the southern for commercial gain.

Conflicts with American Indians

Here are some important conflicts between colonists and American Indians that you should know:

Powhatan Wars (1610–1677). The Powhatan Wars were the earliest conflicts between English settlers and the Powhatan confederacy in Virginia, mainly over territorial disputes. As a resolution to these conflicts, Indians were granted reservation land, one of the earliest examples of this practice.

The Pequot War (1636–1638). As the population of Massachusetts grew, settlers began looking for new places to live. One obvious choice was the Connecticut Valley, a fertile region with lots of access to the sea (for trade). The area was already inhabited by the Pequots, however, who resisted the English incursions. When the Pequots attacked a settlement in Wakefield and killed nine colonists, members of the Massachusetts Bay Colony retaliated by burning the main Pequot village, killing 400, many of them women and children. The result was the near-destruction of the Pequots in what came to be known as the Pequot War.

The Beaver Wars (1628–1701). The Iroquois Confederacy, spurred on by English allies, fought frequently with the French-backed Algonquian tribes of the Great Lakes region over fur and fishing rights. These conflicts were called the "Beaver" Wars because the beaver was an important fur animal hunted by Indians and European settlers throughout the region. When beaver numbers declined because of over-harvesting, territorial conflicts between trappers intensified. Though largely forgotten in popular history, the Beaver Wars were considered the bloodiest in North American history. (Hmm, where else did the French, English, and Indians fight over fur and fishing rights? Oh yeah, the Seven Years' War!)

Decline of the Huron Confederacy (1634–1649). At one time the Hurons numbered up to 40,000, living primarily near Lake Ontario and in parts of Quebec, with some groups as far south as West Virginia. During the 1630s, though, smallpox ravaged the tribes, and their numbers declined to around 12,000. Added to their woes were constant conflicts with other tribes for fur rights. The Huron were allies with the French and fought alongside them in the Seven Years' War.

King Philip's War (1675–1678). Metacomet, the leader of the Wampanoag tribe living near Narragansett Bay in Rhode Island, was neither a King nor named "Philip." The Wampanoags were surrounded by white settlements, and colonists were attempting to convert the Indians to English culture and religion. "Praying towns" were villages set up for the sole purpose of making converts to Christianity. Indians were also encouraged to give up their tribal clothing. Metacomet led attacks on several settlements in retaliation for this intrusion on Wampanoag territory. Soon after, he formed an alliance with two other local tribes. The alliance destroyed a number of English settlements but eventually ran out of food and ammunition. When Metacomet died, the alliance fell apart and the colonists devastated the tribes, selling many into slavery in the West Indies. King Philip's War marks the end of a formidable Native American presence among the New England colonists.

The Pueblo Revolt (1680). While the French and British played their political and economic chess games with Indian tribes in the East, the Spanish sought to maintain control of the Southwest. After years of domination by the fearsome Juan de Oñate, the Pueblo people of New Mexico led a successful revolt against the Spanish, killing hundreds and driving the remaining settlers out of the region. The Spanish returned in 1692, and though they regained control of the territory, they were more accommodating to the Pueblo, the fear of continued conflicts driving the need for compromise.

The Chickasaw Wars (1721–1763). The Chickasaw tribe (allied with the British) fought the Choctaw (allied with the French) for control of the land around the Mississippi River. The Chickasaw Wars were deadlier and more devastating than previous conflicts, since the Indians were supplied with guns from the Europeans. These prolonged wars halted only when the Treaty of Paris was signed at the end of the Seven Years' War.

Decline of the Catawba Nation (1700s). The Catawbas were at one time the most powerful and numerous tribe in the Carolina Piedmont. The Catawbas were allied with colonists and even fought alongside the Patriots during the Revolutionary War, but were engaged in constant warfare with other tribes, such as the Iroquois, the Algonquian, and the Cherokee. Catawba numbers were also weakened by smallpox epidemics. Eventually the Catawba were so decimated by war and disease that they temporarily ceded land and tribal status. Today, there are a few thousand Catawba still living in North Carolina.

Slavery in the Early Colonies

As mentioned above, the extensive use of African slaves in the American colonies began when colonists from the Caribbean settled the Carolinas. Until then, indentured servants and, in some situations, enslaved Native Americans had mostly satisfied labor requirements in the colonies. As tobacco-growing and, in South Carolina, rice-growing operations expanded, more laborers were needed than indenture could provide. Events such as Bacon's Rebellion (see Major Events of the Period for more on this) had also shown landowners that it was not in their best interest to have an abundance of landless, young, white males in their colonies either.

Enslaving Native Americans was difficult; they knew the land, so they could easily escape and subsequently were difficult to find. In some Native American tribes, cultivation was considered women's work, so gender was another obstacle to enslaving the natives. And as noted, Europeans brought diseases that often decimated the Native Americans, wiping out 85 to 95 percent of the native population. Southern landowners turned increasingly to African slaves for labor. Unlike Native Americans, African slaves did not know the land, so they were less likely to escape. Removed from their homelands and communities, and often unable to communicate with one another because they were from different regions of Africa, black slaves initially proved easier to control than Native Americans. The dark skin of the West Africans who made up the bulk of the enslaved population made it easier to identify slaves on sight, and the English colonists came to associate dark skin with inferiority, rationalizing Africans' enslavement.

The majority of the slave trade, right up to the Revolution, was directed toward the Caribbean and South America. Still, during that period more than 500,000 slaves were brought to the English colonies (of the over 10 million brought to the New World). By 1790, nearly 750,000 blacks were enslaved in England's North American colonies.

The shipping route that brought the slaves to the Americas was called the **Middle Passage** because it was the middle leg of the **triangular trade route** among the colonies, Europe, and Africa. Conditions for the Africans aboard were brutally inhumane, so intolerable that some committed suicide by throwing themselves overboard. Many died of sickness, and others died during insurrections. It was not unusual for one-fifth of the Africans to die on board. Most, however, reached the New World, where conditions were only slightly better. Mounting criticism (primarily in the North) of the horrors of the Middle Passage led Congress to end American participation in the Atlantic slave trade on January 1, 1808. Slavery itself would not end in the United States until 1865.

Slavery flourished in the South. Because of the nature of the land and the short growing season, the Chesapeake and the Carolinas farmed labor-intensive crops such as **tobacco**, **rice**, and **indigo**, and plantation owners there bought slaves for this arduous work. Slaves' treatment at the hands of their owners was often vicious and at times sadistic. While slavery never really took hold in the North the same way it did in the South, slaves were used on farms in New York, New Jersey, and Pennsylvania, in shipping operations in Massachusetts and Rhode Island, and as domestic servants in urban households, particularly in New York City. Although northern states would take steps to phase out slavery following the Revolution, there were still slaves in New Jersey at the outbreak of the Civil War. In both regions, only the very wealthy owned slaves. The vast majority of people remained at a subsistence level.

THE AGE OF SALUTARY NEGLECT (1650–1750)

British treatment of the colonies during the period preceding the **French and Indian War** (also called **the Seven Years' War**) is often described as **salutary neglect** or **benign neglect.** Although England regulated trade and government in its colonies, it interfered in colonial affairs as little as possible. Because of the distance, England set up absentee customs officials and the colonies were left to self-govern, for the most part. England occasionally turned its back to the colonies' violations of trade restrictions. Thus, the colonies developed a large degree of autonomy, which helped fuel revolutionary sentiments when the monarchy later attempted to gain greater control of the New World.

During this century, the colonies "grew up," developing fledgling economies. The beginnings of an American culture—as opposed to a transplanted English culture—took root.

English Regulation of Colonial Trade

Throughout the colonial period, most Europeans who thought about economics at all subscribed to a theory called **mercantilism**. Mercantilists believed that economic power was rooted in a favorable balance of trade (that is, exporting more than you import) and the control of **specie** (hard currency, such as gold coins). Colonies, they felt, were important mostly for economic reasons, which explains why the British considered their colonies in the West Indies that produced sugar and other valuable commodities to be more important than their colonies on the North American continent. The colonies on the North American continent were seen primarily as markets for British and West Indian goods, although they also were valued as sources of raw materials that would otherwise have to be bought from a foreign country.

In order to guarantee a favorable balance of trade, the British government encouraged manufacturing in England and placed **protective tariffs** on imports that might compete with English goods. A number of such tariffs, included in the **Navigation Acts**, were passed between 1651 and 1673. The Navigation Acts required the colonists to buy goods only from England, to sell certain of their products only to England, and to import any non-English goods via English ports and pay a duty on those imports. The Navigation Acts also prohibited the colonies from manufacturing a number of goods that England already produced. In short, the Navigation Acts sought to establish wide-ranging English control over colonial commerce. Also of note was the **Wool Act** of 1699, which forbade both the export of wool from the American colonies and the importation of wool from other British colonies. Some colonists protested this law by dealing only in flax and hemp. Likewise, the **Molasses Act** of 1733 imposed an exorbitant tax upon the importation of sugar from the French West Indies (thus protecting British merchants). New Englanders frequently refused to pay the tax, an early example of rebellion against the Crown.

The Navigation Acts were only somewhat successful in achieving their goal, as it was easy to smuggle goods into and out of the colonies. The colonists also did not protest aggressively against the Navigation Acts at the time, because they were entirely dependent on England for trade and for military protection.

Colonial Governments

Despite trade regulations, the colonists maintained a large degree of autonomy. Every colony had a **governor** who was appointed by either the king or the proprietor. Although the governor had powers similar to the king's in England, he was also dependent on colonial **legislatures** for money. Also, the governor, whatever his official powers, was essentially stranded in the New World. His power relied on the cooperation of the colonists, and most governors ruled accordingly, only infrequently overruling the legislatures.

Except for Pennsylvania (which had a unicameral legislature with just one house), all the colonies had **bicameral** legislatures modeled after the British Parliament. The lower house functioned in much the same way as does today's House of Representatives; its members were directly elected (by white, male property holders), and its powers included the "power of the purse" (control over government salaries and tax legislation). The upper house was made up of appointees, who served as advisors to the governor and had some legislative and judicial powers. Most of these men were chosen from the local population. Most were concerned primarily with protecting the interests of colonial landowners.

The British never tried to establish a powerful central government in the colonies. The autonomy that England allowed the colonies helped ease their transition to independence in the following century.

The colonists did make some small efforts toward centralized government. **The New England Confederation** was the most prominent of these attempts. Although it had no real power, it did offer advice to the northeastern colonies when disputes arose among them. It also provided colonists from different settlements the opportunity to meet and to discuss their mutual problems.

Major Events of the Period

Bacon's Rebellion took place on Virginia's western frontier in 1676. With virtually all coastal land having been claimed, newcomers who sought to start their own farms in the region were forced west into the back country. Encroaching on land inhabited by Native Americans made frontier farmers subject to raids. In response, the western settlers sought to band together and drive the native tribes out of the region. In this effort, they were stymied by the government in Jamestown, which did not want to risk a full-scale war. Class resentment grew as frontiersmen, many of whom had been indentured servants, began to suspect that eastern elites viewed them as expendable "human shields" serving as a buffer between them and the natives.

The farmers rallied behind **Nathaniel Bacon**, a recent immigrant who, despite his wealth, had arrived too late to settle on the coast. Bacon demanded that Governor **William Berkeley** grant him the authority to raise a militia and attack the nearby tribes. When Berkeley refused, Bacon and his men lashed out at the natives anyway, attacking not only the Susquehannock but also the Pamunkeys, who were actually allies of the English. The rebels then turned their attention to Jamestown, sacking and burning the city. The rebellion dissolved when Bacon suddenly died of dysentery, and the conflict between the colonists and Native Americans was averted with a new treaty, but Bacon's Rebellion is often cited as an early example of a populist uprising in America.

> Bacon's Rebellion is significant for other reasons not always discussed in most textbooks. Many disgruntled former indentured servants allied themselves with free blacks who were also disenfranchised—or unable to vote. This alliance along class lines, as opposed to racial lines, frightened many Southerners and led to the development of what would eventually become black codes following the Civil War. Bacon's Rebellion may also be seen as a precursor to the American Revolution. As colonists pushed westward, in search of land, but away from the commercial and political centers, they experienced a sense of alienation and desire for greater political autonomy. It is important to remember that Berkeley was the royal governor of Virginia, and the backcountry of Virginia was even farther from London.

Insurrections led by slaves did not begin until nearly 70 years later with the **Stono Uprising,** the first and one of the most successful slave rebellions. In September 1739, approximately 20 slaves met near the Stono River outside Charleston, South Carolina. They stole guns and ammunition, killed storekeepers and planters, and liberated a number of slaves. The rebels, now numbering about 100, fled to Florida, where they hoped the Spanish colonists would grant them their freedom. The colonial militia caught up with them and attacked, killing some and capturing most of the others. Those who were captured and returned were later executed. As a result of the Stono Uprising (sometimes called the **Cato Rebellion**), many colonies passed more restrictive laws to govern the behavior of slaves. Fear of slave rebellions increased, and New York experienced a "witch hunt" period, during which 31 blacks and 4 whites were executed for conspiracy to liberate slaves.

Speaking of witch hunts, the **Salem Witch Trials** took place in 1692. These were not the first witch trials in New England. During the first 70 years of English settlement in the region, 103 people (almost all women) had been tried on charges of witchcraft. Never before had so many been accused at once, however; during the summer of 1692, more than 130 "witches" were jailed or executed in Salem.

Historians have a number of explanations for why the mass hysteria started and ended so quickly. The region had recently endured the autocratic control of the **Dominion of New England**, an English government attempt to clamp down on illegal trade. In 1691, Massachusetts became a royal colony under the new monarchs, and suffrage was extended to all Protestants; previously only Puritans could vote, so this move weakened Puritan primacy. War against French and Native Americans on the Canadian border (called **King William's War** in the colonies and **the War of the League of Augsburg** in England) soon followed and further heightened regional anxieties.

To top it all off, the Puritans feared that their religion—which they fervently believed was the *only* true religion—was being undermined by the growing commercialism in cities like Boston. Many second- and third-generation Puritans lacked the fervor of the original Pilgrim and Congregationalist settlers, a situation that led to the **Halfway Covenant**, which changed the rules governing Puritan baptisms. (Prior to the passage of the Halfway Covenant in 1662, a Puritan had to experience the gift of God's grace in order for his or her children to be baptized by the church. With so many, particularly men, losing interest in the church, the Puritan clergy decided to baptize all children whose parents were baptized. However—here is the "halfway" part—those who had not experienced God's grace were not allowed to vote.) All of these factors—religious, economic, and gender— historians argue, combined to create **mass hysteria in Salem in 1692**. The hysteria ended when the accusers, most of them teenage girls, accused some of the colony's most prominent citizens of consorting with the Devil, thus turning town leaders against them. Some historians also feel that the hysteria had simply run its course.

As noted, the generations that followed the original settlers were generally less religious than those that preceded them. By 1700, women constituted the majority of active church members. However, between the 1730s and 1740s the colonies (and Europe) experienced a wave of religious revivalism known as the **First Great Awakening**. Two men, Congregationalist minister **Jonathan Edwards** and Methodist preacher **George Whitefield**, came to exemplify the period. Edwards preached the severe, predeterministic doctrines of Calvinism and became famous for his graphic depictions of Hell; you may have read his speech "Sinners in the Hands of an Angry God." Whitefield preached a Christianity based on emotionalism and spirituality, which today is most clearly manifested in Southern **evangelism**. The First Great Awakening is often described as the response of devout people to the **Enlightenment**, a European intellectual movement that borrowed heavily from ancient philosophy and emphasized rationalism over emotionalism or spirituality.

Whitefield was a native of England, where the Enlightenment was in full swing; its effects were also being felt in the colonies, especially in the cities. The colonist who came to typify Enlightenment ideals in America was the self-made and self-educated man, **Ben Franklin**. Franklin was a printer's apprentice who, through his own ingenuity and hard work, became a wealthy printer and a successful and respected intellectual. His ***Poor Richard's Almanack*** was extremely popular and remains influential to this day. (It is the source of such pithy aphorisms as "A stitch in time saves nine" and "A penny saved is a penny earned.") Franklin did pioneering work in the field of electricity. He invented bifocals, the lightning rod, and the Franklin stove, and he founded the colonies' first fire department, post office, and public library. Franklin espoused Enlightenment ideals about education, government, and religion and was, until Washington came along, the colonists' favorite son. Toward the end of his life, he served as an ambassador in Europe, where he negotiated a crucial alliance with the French and, later, the peace treaty that ended the Revolutionary War.

Life in the Colonies

Perhaps the most important development in the colonies during this period was the rate of growth. The population in 1700 was 250,000; by 1750, that number was 1,250,000. Throughout these years, the colonies began to develop substantial non-English European populations. Scotch-Irish, Scots, and Germans all started arriving in large numbers during the 18th century. English settlers, of course, continued to come to the New World as well. The black population in 1750 was more than 200,000, and in a few colonies (South Carolina, for example) they would outnumber whites by the time of the Revolution.

The vast majority of colonists—over 90 percent—lived in **rural areas**. Life for whites in the countryside was rugged but tolerable. Labor was divided along gender lines, with men doing the outdoor work such as farming, and women doing the indoor work of housekeeping and childrearing. Opportunities for social interaction outside the family were limited to shopping days and rare special community events. Both children and women were completely subordinate to men, particularly to the head of the household, in this patriarchal society. Children's education was secondary to their work schedules. Women were not allowed to vote, draft a will, or testify in court.

Blacks, most of whom were slaves, lived predominantly in the countryside and in the South. Their lives varied from region to region, with conditions being most difficult in the South, where the labor was difficult and the climate less hospitable to hard work. Those slaves who worked on large plantations and developed specialized skills, such as carpentry or cooking, fared better than did field hands. In all cases, though, the condition of servitude was demeaning. Slaves often developed extended kinship ties and strong communal bonds to cope with the misery of servitude and the possibility that their nuclear families might be separated by sale. In the North, where black populations were relatively small, blacks often had trouble maintaining a sense of community and history.

Conditions in the **cities** were often much worse than those in the country. Because work could often be found there, most immigrants settled in the cities. The work they found generally paid too little, and poverty was widespread. Sanitary conditions were primitive, and epidemics such as smallpox were common. On the positive side, cities offered residents much wider contact with other people and with the outside world. Cities served as centers for progress and education.

Citizens with anything above a rudimentary level of education were rare, and nearly all **colleges** established during this period served primarily to train ministers.

The lives of colonists in the various regions differed considerably. **New England** society centered on trade. Boston was the colonies' major port city. The population farmed for subsistence, not for trade, and mostly subscribed to rigid Puritanism. The **middle colonies**—New York, Pennsylvania, New Jersey—had more fertile land and so focused primarily on farming (they were also known as the "bread colonies" because of their heavy exports of grain). Philadelphia and New York City, like Boston, were major trade centers. The population of the region was more heterogeneous than was that of New England. The **lower South** (the Carolinas) concentrated on cash crops, such as tobacco and rice. Slavery played a major role on plantations, although the majority of Southerners were subsistence farmers who had no slaves. Blacks constituted up to half the population of some Southern colonies. The colonies on the **Chesapeake** (Maryland and Virginia) combined features of the middle colonies and the lower South. Slavery and tobacco played a larger role in the Chesapeake than in the middle colonies, but like the middle colonies, the Chesapeake residents also farmed grain and thus diversified their economies. The development of major cities in the Chesapeake region also distinguished it from the lower South, which was almost entirely rural.

Thus, the colonies were hardly a unified whole as they approached the events that led them to rebel. How then did they join together and defeat the most powerful nation in the world? The answer to this and other exciting questions awaits you in the next chapter.

Early colleges in the North include Harvard and Yale (established in 1636 and 1701, respectively). The College of William and Mary was chartered in the South in 1693.

Reasons for the Founding of Selected Colonies

Virginia (1607): Economic gain

Plymouth (1620): Religious freedom (Separatist Pilgrims)

Massachusetts (1629): Religious freedom (Nonseparatist Puritans); later merged with Plymouth

Maryland (1633): Religious freedom (Catholics)

Connecticut (1636): Religious differences with Puritans in Massachusetts

Rhode Island (1636): Religious freedom from Puritans in Massachusetts

New York (1664): Seized from Dutch

New Jersey (1664): Seized from Dutch

Delaware (1664): Seized from Dutch, who took it from Swedes

Pennsylvania (1682): Religious freedom (Quakers)

Georgia (1732): Buffer colony and alternative to debtors' prison

Summary

Here are the most important concepts to remember from the Early Contact period.

o   Native populations in North America were not monolithic; they were diverse. Tribal groups varied widely in their economies, level of civilization, and interaction with each other and Europeans.

o   The Columbian exchange revolutionized both European and Native cultures by expanding trade and technology and creating a racially mixed New World, stratified by wealth and status.

o   African slavery started in this period, gradually replacing Native slavery and European indentured servitude.

o   The belief in European superiority was a key rationale for the colonization of North America.

Here are the most important concepts to remember from the Colonization period.

o   Europeans and Native Americans vied for control of land, fur, and fishing rights.

o   The Spanish, French, Dutch, and British had different styles of interacting with Native populations.

Chapter 6 Review Questions

See Chapter 14 for answers and explanations.

1. Which of the following statements about indentured servitude is true?

    (A) Indentured servitude was the means by which most Africans came to the New World.
    (B) Indentured servitude never attracted many people because its terms were too harsh.
    (C) Approximately half of all indentured servants died before earning their freedom.
    (D) Indenture was one of several systems used to distinguish house slaves from field slaves.

2. The Mayflower Compact foreshadows the U.S. Constitution in which of the following ways?

    (A) It posits the source of government power in the people rather than in God.
    (B) It ensures both the right to free speech and the separation of church and state.
    (C) It limits the term of office for all government officials.
    (D) It establishes three branches of government in order to create a system of checks and balances.

3. The first important cash crop in the American colonies was

    (A) cotton
    (B) corn
    (C) tea
    (D) tobacco

4. The philosophy of mercantilism holds that economic power resides primarily in

    (A) surplus manpower and control over raw materials
    (B) control of hard currency and a positive trade balance
    (C) the ability to extend and receive credit at favorable interest rates
    (D) domination of the slave trade and control of the shipping lanes

5. Colonial vice-admiralty courts were created to enforce

    (A) Puritan religious edicts
    (B) prohibitions on antimonarchist speech
    (C) import and export restrictions
    (D) travel bans imposed on Native Americans

6. All of the following are examples of conflicts between colonists and Native American tribes EXCEPT

    (A) Bacon's Rebellion
    (B) the Pequot War
    (C) the Stono Uprising
    (D) King Philip's War

7. Which of the following statements about cities during the colonial era is NOT true?

    (A) Poor sanitation left colonial cities vulnerable to epidemics.
    (B) Religious and ethnic diversity was greater in colonial cities than in the colonial countryside.
    (C) Most large colonial cities grew around a port.
    (D) The majority of colonists lived in urban areas.

8. Colleges and universities during the colonial period were dedicated primarily to the training of

    (A) medical doctors
    (B) scientists
    (C) political leaders
    (D) the clergy

9. Which of the following is the best explanation for why the British did not establish a powerful central government in the American colonies?

    (A) The British cared little how the colonists lived so long as the colonies remained a productive economic asset.
    (B) Britain feared that the colonists would rebel against any substantial government force that it established.
    (C) Few members of the British elite were willing to travel to the colonies, even for the opportunity to govern.
    (D) Britain gave the colonies a large measure of autonomy as a first step in transitioning the region to independence.

REFLECT

Respond to the following questions:

- For which content topics discussed in this chapter do you feel you have achieved sufficient mastery to answer multiple-choice questions correctly?

- For which content topics discussed in this chapter do you feel you have achieved sufficient mastery to discuss effectively in a short-answer question or an essay?

- On which content topics discussed in this chapter do you feel you need more work before you can answer multiple-choice questions correctly?

- On which content topics discussed in this chapter do you feel you need more work before you can discuss them effectively in a short-answer question or an essay?

- What parts of this chapter are you going to review again?

- Will you seek further help, outside of this book (such as a teacher, tutor, or AP Students), on any of the content in this chapter—and, if so, on what content?

Chapter 7
Conflict and American Independence (1754–1800)

In 1754, the colonists still considered themselves English subjects. Very few could have imagined circumstances under which they would leave the British Empire. The events that led from almost universal loyalty to rebellion are frequently tested on the AP U.S. History Exam. Here is what you need to know:

Albany Plan of Union

In 1754, representatives from seven colonies met in Albany, New York, to consider the **Albany Plan of Union**, developed by Benjamin Franklin. The plan provided for an intercolonial government and a system for collecting taxes for the colonies' defense. At that meeting, Franklin also tried to negotiate a treaty with the Iroquois. Franklin's efforts to unite the colonies failed to gain the approval of a single colonial legislature. The plan was rejected because the colonists did not want to relinquish control of their right to tax themselves, nor were they prepared to unite under a single colonial legislature. Franklin's frustration was well publicized in one of the first American political cartoons—his drawing of a snake broken into pieces, under which lie the words "Join or Die."

The Seven Years' War (1754–1763)

Yes, the Seven Years' War lasted for nine years. It is also called the **French and Indian War**, which is almost equally confusing because the French and Indians fought on the same side, not against each other. The Seven Years' War was the British name for the war. The colonists called it the "French and Indian War" because that's who they were fighting. It was actually one of several "wars for empire" fought between the British and the French, and the Americans got stuck in the middle. This was arguably the first world war.

The war was the inevitable result of colonial expansion. (It was also caused by a number of inter-European power struggles, which is how Spain, Austria, Sweden, Prussia, and others got involved, but that is on the European history test, so you can worry about it some other time.) As English settlers moved into the Ohio Valley, the French tried to stop them by building fortified outposts at strategic entry spots. The French were trying to protect their profitable fur trade and their control of the region. A colonial contingent led by **George Washington** attacked a French outpost and lost badly. Washington surrendered and was allowed to return to Virginia, where he was welcomed as a hero. Other skirmishes and battles ensued, and in 1756, England officially declared war on France. Most Native Americans in the region, choosing the lesser of two evils, allied themselves with the French who had traditionally had the best relations with Native Americans of any of the European powers and whom, based on Washington's performance, they expected to win the war. The war dragged on for years before the English finally gained the upper hand. When the war was over, England was the undisputed colonial power of the continent. The treaty gave England control of Canada and almost everything east of the Mississippi Valley. The French kept only two sugar islands, underscoring the impact of mercantilism since the French prioritized two small but highly profitable islands over the large landmass of Canada.

William Pitt, the English Prime Minister during the war, was supportive of the colonists and encouraged them to join the war effort, promising them pay and some autonomy (this helped to create one of the first real senses of intercolonial unity). When the leadership in Britain changed after the war, that led to resentment by the colonists against the British rule.

The English victory spelled trouble for Native Americans, who had previously been able to use French and English disputes to their own advantage. They negotiated their allegiances in return for land, goods, and the right to be left alone. The Native Americans particularly disliked the English, however, because English expansionism was more disruptive to their way of life. The French had sent few colonists, and many of those colonists were fur trappers who did not settle anywhere permanently. In the aftermath of the war, the English raised the price of goods sold to the Native Americans (they now had a monopoly, after all) and ceased paying rent on their western forts. In response, Ottawa war chief **Pontiac** rallied a group of tribes in the Ohio Valley and attacked colonial outposts. The attacks and resultant wars are known as **Pontiac's Rebellion** (or **Pontiac's Uprising**). In response to Pontiac's Rebellion, the **Paxton Boys**, a group of Scots-Irish frontiersmen in Pennsylvania murdered several in the Susquehanook tribe.

In response to the initial attacks, the British government issued the **Proclamation of 1763**, forbidding settlement west of the rivers running through the Appalachians. The proclamation came too late. Settlers had already moved west of the line. The proclamation did have one effect, however. It agitated colonial settlers, who regarded it as unwarranted British interference in colonial affairs.

Pontiac's Rebellion was, in part, a response to the colonists expanding into the Ohio River Valley and encroaching on the Native Americans' lands. (Recall similar events such as the Pequot War and Bacon's Rebellion.) The British were forced to quell this rebellion at great cost in addition to the costs of fighting the French. They used germ warfare, in the form of smallpox-infected blankets, to help defeat the Ottawa. The resulting Proclamation of 1763 is significant for a number of reasons. The year 1763 is often viewed as a turning point in British-colonial relations in that it marks the end of salutary neglect. The Proclamation of 1763 may be viewed as the first in a new series of restrictions imposed on the colonists by the British Parliament, and in that way, it marks the first step on the "road to revolution." Furthermore, it established a pattern of demarcating "Indian Territory," a pattern that would be adopted and pursued by the United States government long after the colonists gained their independence. (See for example the **Indian Removal Act,** 1830.)

The Scots-Irish were a group of Protestant colonial settlers who emigrated from Ireland but were ethnically Scottish. They settled mainly in the Appalachians, from Pennsylvania to Georgia. As in the case of the Paxton Boys, the Scots-Irish were known for early conflicts with local Indian tribes. Their culture and folkways remain an integral part of modern Appalachian life.

The Sugar Act, the Currency Act, and the Stamp Act

One result of the Seven Years' War was that in financing the war the British government had run up a huge debt. The new king, **George III**, and his prime minister, **George Grenville**, felt that the colonists should help pay that debt. After all, they reasoned, the colonies had been beneficiaries of the war; furthermore, their tax burden was relatively light compared to that of taxpayers in England, even on the same goods. Meanwhile, the colonists felt that they had provided so many soldiers that they had fulfilled their obligation.

Accordingly, Parliament imposed new regulations and taxes on the colonists. The first was the **Sugar Act** of 1764, which established a number of new duties and which also contained provisions aimed at deterring molasses smugglers. Although Parliament had previously passed other acts aimed at controlling colonial trade and manufacturing, there was little colonial resistance prior to the decade leading up to the Revolutionary War. There were benefits to being part of the vast British Empire and most Americans accepted regulations of trade such as the **Navigation Acts** as part of **mercantilism**. Furthermore, although laws such as the Molasses Act of 1733 were on the books, smuggling was common practice and little revenue from taxes was actually collected. Some historians have gone so far as to suggest that Parliament never intended the Molasses Act to raise revenue but merely to function as a protective tariff aimed against French imports. Parliament was quite shrewd in passing the Sugar Act of 1764 in that this new act actually *lowered* the duty on molasses coming into the colonies from the West Indies. What angered the colonists the most was that this new regulation was to be more strictly enforced: duties were to be collected. It became more difficult for colonial shippers to avoid committing even minor violations of the Sugar Act. Furthermore, violators were to be arrested and tried in vice-admiralty courts, courts in which a single judge issued a verdict without the deliberation of a jury. It was this last provision of the Sugar Act that suggested to some colonists that Parliament was overstepping its authority and violating their rights as Englishmen.

Another Parliamentary act, the **Currency Act**, forbade the colonies to issue paper money. Collectively, the Sugar Act, Currency Act, and Proclamation of 1763 caused a great deal of discontent in the colonies, whose residents bristled at what they correctly viewed as British attempts to exert greater control. These acts signaled a clear end to Britain's long-standing policy of salutary neglect. That these acts came during a postwar economic depression further aggravated the situation. Colonial protest to these acts, however, was uncoordinated and ineffective.

That all changed when Parliament passed the **Stamp Act** the following year, 1765. The Stamp Act included a number of provocative elements. First, it was a tax specifically aimed at raising revenue, thus awakening the colonists to the likelihood that even more taxes could follow. The Stamp Act demonstrated that the colonies' tradition of self-taxation was surely being unjustly taken by Parliament, much to the dismay of many colonists. Second, it was a broad-based tax, covering all legal documents and licenses. Not only did it affect almost everyone, but it particularly affected a group that was literate, persuasive, and argumentative—namely, lawyers. Third, it was a tax on goods produced within the colonies.

Reaction to the Stamp Act built on previous grievances and, consequently, was more forceful than any protest preceding it. A pamphlet by James Otis, called *The Rights of the British Colonies Asserted and Proved*, laid out the colonists' argument against the taxes and became a bestseller of its day. Otis put forward the "No taxation without representation" argument that later became a rallying cry of the Revolution. Because the colonists did not elect members to Parliament, he argued, they were not obliged to pay taxes (following the accepted precept that no Englishman could be compelled to pay taxes without his consent). Otis did *not* advocate secession; rather, he argued for either representation in Parliament or a greater degree of self-government for the colonies. Neither the British nor the colonists had much interest in creating a colonial delegation to Parliament. The British scoffed at the notion, arguing that the colonists were already represented in Parliament. Their argument was rooted in the theory of **virtual representation**, which stated that members of Parliament represented all British subjects regardless of who elected them. The colonists, for their part, knew that their representation would be too small to protect their interests and so never pushed the issue. What they wanted, and what the British were refusing to give them, was the right to determine their own taxes.

Opponents of the Stamp Act united in the various colonies. In Virginia, Patrick Henry drafted the Virginia Stamp Act Resolves, protesting the tax and asserting the colonists' right to a large measure of self-government. (The Virginia legislature removed Henry's most radical propositions before passing the resolves.) In Boston, mobs burned the customs officers in effigy, tore down a customs house, and nearly destroyed the governor's mansion. Protest groups formed throughout the colonies, calling themselves **Sons of Liberty.** The opposition was so effective that, by the time the law was supposed to take effect, not one of the Crown's appointed duty collectors was willing to perform his job. In 1766, Parliament repealed the Stamp Act. Just as important, George III replaced Prime Minister Grenville, whom the colonists now loathed, with Lord Rockingham, who had opposed the Stamp Act. Rockingham oversaw the repeal but also linked it to the passage of the **Declaratory Act**, which asserted the British government's right to tax and legislate in all cases anywhere in the colonies. Thus, although the colonists had won the battle over the stamp tax, they had not yet gained any ground in the war of principles over Parliament's powers in the colonies.

The Townshend Acts

Rockingham remained prime minister for only two years. His replacement was William Pitt. Pitt, however, was ill, and the dominant figure in colonial affairs came to be the minister of the exchequer, Charles Townshend. Townshend drafted the eponymous **Townshend Acts**. The Townshend Acts, like the Stamp Act, contained several antagonistic measures. First, they taxed goods imported directly from Britain—the first such tax in the colonies. Mercantilism approved of duties on imports from other European nations but not on British imports. Second, some of the tax collected was set aside for the payment of tax collectors, meaning that colonial assemblies could no longer withhold government officials' wages in order to get their way. Third, the Townshend Acts created even more vice-admiralty courts and several new government offices to enforce the Crown's will in the colonies. Fourth, they suspended the New York legislature because it had refused to comply with a law requiring the colonists to supply British troops. Last, these acts instituted *writs of assistance*, licenses that gave the British the power to search any place they suspected of hiding smuggled goods.

The colonists got better at protesting with each new tax, and their reaction to the Townshend Acts was their strongest yet. The Massachusetts Assembly sent a letter (called the **Massachusetts Circular Letter**, written by Samuel Adams in 1768) to all other assemblies asking that they protest the new measures in unison. The British fanned the flames of protest by ordering the assemblies *not* to discuss the Massachusetts letter, virtually guaranteeing it to be all anyone *would* talk about. Governors of colonies where legislatures discussed the letter dissolved those legislatures, which, of course, further infuriated colonists. The colonists held numerous rallies and organized boycotts, and for the first time they sought the support of "commoners" (previously such protests were confined largely to the aristocratic classes), making their rallies larger and much more intimidating. The boycotts were most successful because they affected British merchants, who then joined the protest. Colonial women were essential in the effort to replace British imports with "American" (New England) products. After two years, Parliament repealed the Townshend duties, although not the other statutes of the Townshend Acts, and not the duty on tea.

Nonconsumption and Nonimportation

There were no police departments in colonial America. Communities were self-policing. If a man was beating his wife, groups of neighbors would gather and threaten him with dire consequences if he didn't stop. Patriot leaders leveraged this practice in organizing resistance to the Townshend and other duties. The colonists' only recourses were **nonconsumption** and **nonimportation**—in other words, to boycott British goods—but such a policy could be effective only if everyone participated. So it was that New England newspapers printed pleas to women in particular, who generally managed the family budget, not to buy British linen and tea, and exposed importers, such as one William Jackson who ran a shop called the Brazen Head. If these methods proved ineffective, then, yes, Patriot leaders would deploy thugs to get the point across. A few painful and humiliating tar-and-featherings went a long way, and imports from Britain dropped 40 percent by 1770.

The Quartering Act of 1765 stationed large numbers of troops in America and made the colonists responsible for the cost of feeding and housing them. Even after the Townshend duties were repealed, the soldiers remained—particularly in Boston. Officially sent to keep the peace, these soldiers in fact heightened tensions. For one thing, the detachment was huge—4,000 men in a city of only 16,000. To make matters worse, the soldiers sought off-hour employment and so competed with colonists for jobs. Numerous confrontations resulted, with the most famous on March 5, 1770, when a mob pelted a group of soldiers with rock-filled snowballs. The soldiers fired on the crowd, killing five—hence, the **Boston Massacre**. The propaganda campaign that followed suggested that the soldiers had shot into a crowd of innocent bystanders. Interestingly, John Adams defended the soldiers in court, helping to establish a tradition of giving a fair trial to all who are accused.

The Calm, and Then the Storm

Oddly enough, for the next two years, nothing major happened. The Boston Massacre shocked both sides into de-escalating their rhetoric, and an uneasy status quo fell into place during this period. Colonial newspapers discussed ways in which the relationship between the mother country and the colonies might be altered to satisfy both sides, but still, nobody except a very few radicals suggested independence.

Things picked up in 1772 when the British implemented the part of the Townshend Acts that provided for colonial administrators to be paid from customs revenues (and not by the colonial legislatures). The colonists responded cautiously, setting up groups called **Committees of Correspondence** throughout the colonies to trade ideas and inform one another of the political mood. The committees also worked to convince more citizens to take an active interest in the conflict. Writers such as **Mercy Otis Warren**, a friend of Abigail Adams and Martha Washington, published pamphlets calling for Revolution. *Letters From a Farmer in Pennsylvania* were a series of essays written by John Dickinson, uniting the colonists against the Townshend Acts.

Not long after, the British granted the foundering East India Tea Company a monopoly on the tea trade in the colonies as well as a portion of new duties to be collected on tea sales. The result was cheaper tea for the colonists, but the colonists saw a more important issue: Parliament was once again imposing new taxes on them. In Boston, the colonists refused to allow the ships to unload their cargo, and the governor refused to allow them to leave the harbor. On December 16, 1773, a group of Sons of Liberty, poorly disguised as Mohawks, boarded a ship and dumped its cargo into Boston Harbor. It took them three hours to jettison the approximately £10,000 worth of tea. The incident is known as the **Boston Tea Party.**

The English responded with a number of punitive measures, known collectively as the **Coercive Acts** (also called the **Intolerable Acts**). One measure closed Boston Harbor to all but essential trade (food and firewood) and declared that it would remain closed until the tea was paid for. Several measures tightened English control over the Massachusetts government and its courts, and a new, stricter Quartering Act put British soldiers in civilian homes. The Coercive Acts convinced many colonists that their days of semi-autonomy were over and that the future held even further encroachments on their liberties by the Crown. To make matters worse, at the same time Parliament passed the Coercive Acts, it also passed the **Quebec Act**, which, to the colonists' chagrin, (1) granted greater liberties to Catholics, whom the Protestant colonial majority distrusted, and (2) extended the boundaries of the Quebec Territory, thus further impeding westward expansion.

The colonists met to discuss their grievances. All colonies except Georgia sent delegates to the **First Continental Congress,** which convened in late 1774. All perspectives were represented—Pennsylvania's delegation included conservatives such as Joseph Galloway, while Virginia sent two radicals, Richard Henry Lee and **Patrick Henry.** The goals of the meeting were to enumerate American grievances, to develop a strategy for addressing those grievances, and to formulate a colonial position on the proper relationship between the royal government and the colonial governments.

The Congress came up with a list of those laws the colonists wanted repealed and agreed to impose a boycott on British goods until their grievances were redressed. The delegates also agreed to form a **Continental Association**, with towns setting up committees of observation to enforce the boycott; in time, these committees became their towns' de facto governments. Perhaps most important, the Congress formulated a limited set of parameters within which it considered Parliamentary interference in colonial affairs justified; all other spheres, the delegates agreed, should be left to the colonists themselves. This position represented a major break with British tradition and, accordingly, a major step toward independence.

Throughout the winter of 1774 and the spring of 1775, the committees of observation expanded their powers. In many colonies, they supplanted the British-sanctioned assemblies. They led acts of insubordination by collecting taxes, disrupting court sessions, and, most ominously, organizing militias and stockpiling weapons. As John Adams would later comment about the period, "The Revolution was effected before the war commenced. The Revolution was in the minds and hearts of the people…. This radical change in the principles, opinions, sentiments, and affections of the people was the real American Revolution."

The Shot Heard 'Round the World

The British underestimated the strength of the growing pro-revolutionary movement. Government officials mistakenly believed that if they arrested the ringleaders and confiscated their arsenals, violence could be averted. To that end, the English dispatched troops to confiscate weapons in Concord, Massachusetts, in April 1775. The troops had to first pass through Lexington, where they confronted a small colonial militia, called **minutemen** because they reputedly could be ready to fight on a minute's notice. Someone, probably one of the minutemen, fired a shot, which drew British return fire. When the **Battle of Lexington** was over, the minutemen had suffered 18 casualties, including 8 dead. The British proceeded to **Concord**, where a much larger contingent of minutemen awaited them. The Massachusetts militia inflicted numerous casualties on the British **redcoats** and forced them to retreat. That a contingent of colonial farmers could repel the army of the world's largest empire was monumental, which is why the **Battle of Concord** is sometimes referred to as "the shot heard 'round the world." The two opponents dug in around Boston, but during the next year only one major battle was fought. The two sides regrouped and planned their next moves.

For the colonists, the period provided time to rally citizens to the cause of independence. Not all were convinced. Among those remaining loyal to the Crown—such people were called **Loyalists**—were government officials, devout Anglicans (members of the Church of England), merchants dependent on trade with England, and many religious and ethnic minorities who feared persecution at the hands of the rebels. Many slaves believed their chances for liberty were better with the British than with the colonists, a belief strengthened when the royal governor of Virginia offered to free those slaves who escaped and joined the British army. The pre-Revolutionary War era saw an increase in the number of slave insurrections, dampening some Southerners' enthusiasm for revolution. The **patriots** were mostly white Protestant property holders and gentry, as well as urban artisans, especially

Big Man on Campus
Washington's future vice president, John Adams, once griped that "Washington was always selected by deliberative bodies to lead, whatever the cause, because he was always the tallest man in the room."

in New England, where Puritans had long shown antagonism toward Anglicans. Much of the rest of the population just hoped the whole thing would blow over. The Quakers of Pennsylvania, for example, were pacifists and so wanted to avoid war.

The **Second Continental Congress** convened during this period, just weeks after the battles of Lexington and Concord. Throughout the summer, the Congress prepared for war by establishing a **Continental Army**, printing money, and creating government offices to supervise policy. The Congress chose **George Washington** to lead the army because he was both well-liked and a Southerner (thus bolstering support in an area with many loyalists). There is a lot of interesting military history about Washington's command, but because the AP Exam ignores military history, so too does this review.

Not all delegates thought that war was inevitable, and many followed John Dickinson, who was pushing for reconciliation with Britain using the **Olive Branch Petition**. Adopted by the Continental Congress on July 5, 1775, following the skirmish at Breed's Hill, often known as Bunker Hill, the Olive Branch petition was a last-ditch attempt to avoid armed conflict. King George III, however, was hardly interested in the proposal since he considered the colonists to be in open rebellion given their boycotts, attacks on royal officials, and resistance at Lexington and Concord. Still, it is worth noting that just one year before the adoption of the Declaration of Independence, the colonial leaders were trying to reconcile with the mother country.

The Declaration of Independence

The rebels were still looking for the masterpiece of propaganda that would rally colonists to their cause. They got it in *Common Sense*, a pamphlet published in January of 1776 by an English printer named **Thomas Paine**. Paine not only advocated colonial independence, he also argued for the merits of republicanism over monarchy. The pamphlet was an even bigger success than James Otis's *The Rights of the British Colonies Asserted and Proved*. Though literacy rates in New England were somewhat higher, thanks to the Puritan legacy of teaching children to read the Bible, most of the nation's two million inhabitants could not read. Nevertheless, Paine's pamphlet sold more than 100,000 copies in its first three months alone, the proportional equivalent of selling 13 million downloads today. The secret to Paine's success was that *Common Sense* stated the argument for independence in plainspoken language accessible to colonists who couldn't always keep up with the lofty Enlightenment-speak of the Founding Fathers. It helped swing considerable support to the patriot cause among people who had worried about the wisdom of attacking the powerful mother country.

> The preamble of the Declaration of Independence begins with "We hold these truths to be self-evident, that all men are created equal, that they are endowed by their Creator with certain unalienable Rights, that among these are Life, Liberty and the pursuit of Happiness." This opening statement reflects the Enlightenment ideals that Thomas Jefferson strongly believed in, and outlines the philosophy of government that the American colonies believe in. The bulk of the Declaration is a list of grievances about George III and the British government, including taxation without representation, dissolving local representative government, keeping standing armies in the colonies during peacetime, cutting off trade with the rest of the world, and depriving American colonists of the right to trial by jury.

In June, the Congress was looking for a rousing statement of its ideals, and it commissioned **Thomas Jefferson** to write the **Declaration of Independence.** He did not let them down. The Declaration not only enumerated the colonies' grievances against the Crown, but it also articulated the principle of individual liberty and the government's fundamental responsibility to serve the people. Despite its obvious flaws—most especially that it pertained only to white, propertied men—it remains a work of enormous power. With the document's signing on July 4, 1776, the Revolutionary War became a war for independence.

Chronology of Events Leading to Revolutionary War	
1763	–French and Indian War ends –Pontiac's Rebellion –Proclamation of 1763
1764	–Sugar Act –Currency Act
1765	–Stamp Act –Stamp Act crisis –Sons of Liberty formed
1766	–Grenville replaced by Rockingham as prime minister –Stamp Act repealed –Declaratory Act
1767	–Townshend Acts
1770	–Townshend duties repealed (except tea tax) –Boston Massacre
1772	–parts of Townshend Acts implemented –Committees of Correspondence formed
1773	–British give the Dutch East India Tea Company monopoly on tea in colonies –Boston Tea Party
1774	–Coercive (Intolerable) Acts –Quebec Act –First Continental Congress meets –Continental Association forms
1775	–Battles of Lexington and Concord –Second Continental Congress meets
1776	–Declaration of Independence

The Battle of Saratoga (October 17, 1777) in upstate New York was a turning point in the American Revolution, as it was a decisive victory of American troops against British troops, ending the British prominence in upstate New York and serving as a recruitment tool for the Americans. With this victory, the French government agreed to a formal alliance with the Continental Congress, and began sending military advisers, weapons, and financial assistance.

The Battle of Yorktown (October 1781) was the symbolic end to the American Revolution, even though the British remained in New York City until 1783 and other British troops remained active in the South until 1782. The major British general, Cornwallis, was surrounded by the French navy on the York River and George Washington's troops via land, and surrendered after a lengthy siege. Cornwallis's surrender began a long period of negotiations between the American colonies and Great Britain, which would finally end the war in October of 1783.

After several years of fighting, the British surrendered at Yorktown in October of 1781. You should remember a few other facts about the war. The Continental Army (as opposed to local militias) had trouble recruiting good soldiers. Eventually, the Congress recruited blacks, and up to 5,000 fought on the side of the rebels (in return, most of those who had been slaves were granted their freedom). The **Franco-American Alliance**, negotiated by **Ben Franklin** in 1778, brought the French into the war on the side of the colonists, after the battle of Saratoga. This was hardly surprising given the lingering resentment of the French toward the English after the French and Indian War. It would be three years before French troops landed in America, but the alliance buoyed American morale, and with the help of militia units, especially in the South, the colonists kept up a war of attrition until support could arrive from France. By then, much like the United States in Vietnam almost two centuries later, the British found themselves outlasted and forced to abandon an unpopular war on foreign soil. The **Treaty of Paris**, signed at the end of 1783, granted the United States independence and generous territorial rights. (This Treaty of Paris is not to be confused with the Treaty of Paris that ended the French and Indian War or the Treaty of Paris that ended the Spanish-American War in 1898. Paris was all the rage as a treaty name, apparently.)

Neither the Declaration of Independence, with its bold statement that "all men are created equal," nor the revolution with its republican ideology, abolished slavery. These events also did not bring about a more egalitarian society. Like blacks, many women played a significant role in the Revolutionary War, either as "camp followers" or by maintaining households and businesses while the men were off fighting the Revolution. Many women also served as spies, while the British offered their slaves freedom if they fought for them. It would take another war to end slavery (the Civil War) and centuries of hard work toward progress to help bring about greater political and economic equality for women.

George Washington Versus Volunteer Militias

George Washington was one of the wealthiest men in America, and to a great extent his involvement with the independence movement grew out of his dissatisfaction with the mercantile system, which he felt was keeping him from expanding his fortune as much as he might have liked. The tobacco he sent to Britain never fetched the price he wanted, and the goods he received in return were too expensive and of shoddy quality. He wanted relief from British taxes and the freedom to sell to and buy from whomever he liked. The American Revolution was fueled in large part by libertarian sentiments such as these.

But after becoming commander of the Continental Army, Washington found that libertarian ideals sound terrific when you're a rich planter trying to fill your coffers, but don't work so well when you're trying to build a country or win a war. Washington pressed for a professional standing army, and demanded that the states raise money to pay the troops, but the libertarian-dominated Continental Congress replied that those ideas were precisely what they were fighting against and that Washington would have to make do with volunteers who paid their own way.

The Articles of Confederation

The colonies did not wait to win their independence from England before setting up their own governments. As soon as the Declaration of Independence was signed, states began writing their own constitutions. In 1777, the Continental Congress sent the **Articles of Confederation**, the first national constitution, to the colonies for ratification. The colonists intentionally created little to no central government since they were afraid of ridding themselves of Britain's imperial rule only to create their own tyrannical government. The articles contained several major limitations, as the country would soon learn. For one, the Articles gave the federal government no power to raise an army (which hurt the colonies during Shays's Rebellion). Some of the Articles' other major limitations on the federal government included the following:

- It could not enforce state or individual taxation, or a military draft.
- It could not regulate trade among the states or international trade.
- It had no executive or judicial branch.
- The legislative branch gave each state one vote, regardless of the state's population.
- In order to pass a law, 9/13 of the states had to agree.
- In order to amend or change the Articles, unanimous approval was needed.

After the Revolution, many new state constitutions made voting privileges, and even citizenship, contingent upon property ownership. This would not change entirely until the Andrew Jackson administration.

With the end of the war, the colonies had other issues to confront as well. The decrease in England's power in the region opened a new era of relations with Native Americans. This new era was even more contentious than the previous one because a number of tribes had allied themselves with the Crown. Second-class citizens and noncitizens—namely, women and blacks—had made sacrifices in the fight for liberation, and some expected at least a degree of compensation. **Abigail Adams** wrote a famous letter to her husband pleading the case for women's rights in the new government; she reminded John to "remember the ladies and be more generous and favorable to them than your ancestors." The number of free blacks in the colonies grew during and after the war, but their increased presence among free whites was also accompanied by a growth of racist publications and legislation. Such conditions led to the early "ghettoization" of blacks and, for similar reasons, other minorities.

The problems with the Articles of Confederation became apparent early on. The wartime government, unable to levy taxes, tried to finance the war by printing more money, which led, naturally, to wild inflation. After the war, the British pursued punitive trade policies against the colonies, denying them access to West Indian markets and dumping goods on American markets. The government, unable to impose tariffs, was helpless. A protective tariff would impose duties on imported goods; the additional cost would be added to the selling price, thereby raising the cost of foreign products. By making domestic products cheaper than imports, most tariffs protected American manufacturers. Having just fought a war in part caused by taxes imposed by a central authority, the newly independent Americans were reluctant to give this power to their new federal government. In fact, the first protective tariff in United States history wasn't passed until 1816. The issue of the tariff exposed another source of tension within the new country— economic sectionalism—a major conflict that eventually led the new nation to civil war and continues to play a role in partisan politics to this very day.

Translate the Answer Choice

(D) imposed high duties on foreign goods
Translation: *made it more expensive to buy stuff from other countries*

Furthermore, when state governments dragged their heels in compensating loyalists for lost property, the British refused to abandon military posts in the States, claiming that they were remaining to protect the loyalists' rights. The government, again, was powerless to expel them. Perhaps the rudest awakening came in the form of **Shays's Rebellion**. Daniel Shays was a Revolutionary War veteran who was not receiving his pay from the war. As the Massachusetts government was enforcing the ability of banks to repossess farms and foreclose on homes of people who could not pay, Shays was facing foreclosure. His plan was to take over the courthouses that were making these rulings. He and his men seized a weapons armory in Springfield and used those weapons to attack courthouses. The Massachusetts government couldn't mobilize any forces to stop Shays and his men, so private citizens organized to put the rebellion down. This was one of the leading reasons for the Constitutional Convention. As with the earlier **Bacon's Rebellion** and later **Whiskey Rebellion**, this rebellion revealed lingering resentment on the part of the backcountry farmers toward the coastal elite. One thing that especially worried the wealthy, though, was that the Articles of Confederation had created a national government that was essentially powerless to stop such rebellions.

The government under the Articles was not totally without its successes, though. Its greatest achievements were the adoption of ordinances governing the sale of government land to settlers. Best known is the **Northwest Ordinance of 1787**, which also contained a bill of rights guaranteeing trial by jury, freedom of religion, and freedom from excessive punishment. It abolished slavery in the Northwest territories (northwest of the Ohio River and east of the Mississippi River, up to the Canadian border), and it also set specific regulations concerning the conditions under which territories could apply for statehood. Thus, the ordinance is seen as a forerunner to the Bill of Rights and other progressive government policies. It was not so enlightened about Native Americans, however; in fact, it essentially claimed their land without their consent. War ensued, and peace did not come until 1795 when the United States gained a military advantage over the Miami Confederacy, its chief Native-American opponent in the area. The Northwest Ordinance remained important long after the Northwest territories were settled because of its pertinence to the statehood process and to the issue of slavery.

A New Constitution

By 1787, it was clear that the federal government lacked sufficient authority under the Articles of Confederation. **Alexander Hamilton** was especially concerned that there was no uniform commercial policy and feared for the survival of the new republic. Hamilton convened what came to be known as the **Annapolis Convention**, but only five delegates showed up! Subsequently, Congress consented to a "meeting in Philadelphia" the following May for the sole purpose of "revising the Articles of Confederation." This meeting would eventually become the now-famous Constitutional Convention, comprising delegates from all states except Rhode Island, which met throughout the long, hot summer of 1787.

Much has been written about the framers of the Constitution. There were 55 delegates: all men, all white, many of whom were wealthy lawyers or landowners, many of whom owned slaves. They came from many different ideological

A Controversial Interpretation

An Economic Interpretation of the Constitution of the United States by Charles Beard argues that the Constitution was written primarily to cater to the financial interests of the Founding Fathers. Beard's thesis has been important to constitutional scholars ever since its publication in 1913.

backgrounds, from those who felt the Articles needed only slight adjustments to those who wanted to tear them down and start from scratch. **The New Jersey Plan** called for modifications, and it also called for equal representation from each state. **The Virginia Plan**, largely the brainchild of James Madison, called for an entirely new government based on the principle of **checks and balances** and for the number of representatives for each state to be based upon the population of the state, giving some states an advantage.

The Virginia Plan called to create a three-tiered federal government with an executive branch led by a president, a legislative branch composed of a bicameral (two house) Congress, and a judicial branch composed of a Supreme Court. The legislature received the most attention from Madison. The new legislature would have expanded powers to enforce federal taxation, to regulate trade between the states, to regulate international trade, to coin and borrow money, to create a postal service, to authorize a military draft, and to declare war.

The president would be indirectly chosen by the Electoral College, a body of prominent political leaders that represented the popular vote of each state. In order to win a state's electoral votes, a presidential candidate must win a majority of the popular vote within that state. Each state's electoral count is the sum of their senators (two) and their representatives (determined by state population). The Electoral College gave states with larger populations more power in presidential elections.

The convention lasted for four months, over the course of which the delegates hammered out a bundle of compromises, including the **Great Compromise** (also known as the **Connecticut Compromise**), which blended the Virginia Plan and the New Jersey plan to have a bicameral legislature, and the **Constitution**. This bicameral legislature included a lower house (the House of Representatives) elected by the people and the upper house (the Senate) elected by the state legislatures. (Direct election of senators, believe it or not, is a 20th-century innovation.) The president and vice president were to be elected by the Electoral College, not the citizens themselves.

The delegates at the Constitutional Convention agreed that the international slave trade could not be ended until at least 1808. There was a debate about allowing Congress to place tariffs on exported goods, but the Southern states opposed this because they depended so much on foreign trade. A tax on imports was allowed to be passed (later will cause much controversy in the argument over states' rights).

The Constitution also laid out a method for counting slaves among the populations of Southern states for "proportional" representation in Congress, even though those slaves would not be citizens. This became known as the **Three-Fifths Compromise,** because each slave counted as three-fifths of a person. It also established three branches of government—the **executive**, **legislative**, and **judicial**—with the power of checks and balances on each other. Only three of the 42 delegates who remained in Philadelphia to the end refused to sign the finished document (two because it did not include a bill of rights).

Ratification of the Constitution was by no means guaranteed. Opposition forces portrayed the federal government under the Constitution as an all-powerful beast. These opponents, known as **Anti-Federalists**, tended to come from the backcountry and were particularly appalled by the absence of a bill of rights. Their position rang true in many of the state legislatures where the Constitution's fate lay, and some held out for the promise of the immediate addition of the **Bill of Rights** upon ratification. The **Federalist** position was forcefully and persuasively argued in the **Federalist Papers**, anonymously authored by **James Madison**, **Alexander Hamilton**, and **John Jay**. The Federalist Papers were published in a New York newspaper and were later widely circulated. They were critical in swaying opinion in New York, a large and therefore politically important state. (Virginia, Pennsylvania, and Massachusetts were the other powerhouses of the era.) The **Constitution** went into effect in 1789; the **Bill of Rights** was added in 1791.

The Washington Presidency

The Electoral College unanimously chose **George Washington** to be the first president. Washington had not sought the presidency, but as the most popular figure in the colonies, he was the clear choice, and he accepted the role out of a sense of obligation.

Knowing that his actions would set precedents for those who followed him in office, Washington exercised his authority with care and restraint. He determined early on to use his veto only if he was convinced that a bill was unconstitutional. He was comfortable delegating responsibility and so created a government made up of the best minds of his time. Although the Constitution does not specifically grant the president the duty or even the power to create a cabinet, every president since George Washington has had one. The cabinet is made up of the heads of the various executive departments, which have grown in number over the years, and it functions as the president's chief group of advisors.

Prominent among his cabinet selections were **Thomas Jefferson** as secretary of state and **Alexander Hamilton** as secretary of the treasury. These two men strongly disagreed about the proper relationship between the federal government and state governments. Hamilton favored a strong central government and weaker state governments. Jefferson, fearing the country would backslide into monarchy, or tyranny, favored a weaker federal government empowered mainly to defend the country and regulate international commerce. All other powers, he thought, should be reserved to the states.

Their argument was not a mere intellectual exercise. The new government was still defining itself, and each man had a vision of what this nation was to become. The debate came to the forefront when Hamilton proposed a **National Bank** to help

---

The Bill of Rights in a Nutshell

1. Freedom of religion, speech, press, assembly, and petition

2. Right to bear arms in order to maintain a well-regulated militia

3. No quartering of soldiers in private homes

4. Freedom from unreasonable search and seizure

5. Right to due process of law, freedom from self-incrimination, double jeopardy (being tried twice for the same crime)

6. Rights of accused persons; for example, the right to a speedy and public trial

7. Right of trial by jury in civil cases

8. Freedom from excessive bail and from cruel and unusual punishment

9. Rights not listed are kept by the people

10. Powers not listed are kept by the states or the people

regulate and strengthen the economy. Both houses of Congress approved Hamilton's plan, but Washington, uncertain of the bank's constitutionality, considered a veto. In the debate that followed, the two main schools of thought on constitutional law were established. On one side were the **strict constructionists**, led by Jefferson and **James Madison**. They argued that the Constitution allowed Congress only those powers specifically granted to it or those "necessary and proper" to the execution of its **enumerated powers**. While a bank might be "desirable" and perhaps beneficial, they argued, it was not "necessary," and thus its creation was beyond the powers of the national government. Hamilton took the opposing viewpoint, framing the **broad (loose) constructionist** position. He argued that the creation of a bank was an **implied power** of the government because the government already had explicit power to coin money, borrow money, and collect taxes. Hamilton put forward that the government could do anything in the execution of those enumerated powers— including create a bank—that was not explicitly forbidden it by the Constitution. Washington agreed with Hamilton and signed the bill.

Hamilton's tenure at treasury was a busy and successful one. Among his achievements was his successful handling of the **national debt** accrued during the war. Hamilton's financial plan called for the federal government to assume the states' debts (further increasing the federal government's power over them) and to repay those debts by giving the debt holders land on the western frontier. The plan clearly favored Northern banks, many of which had bought up debt certificates at a small portion of their worth. Northern states also had more remaining debt than Southern states, another reason why the plan drew accusations that Hamilton was helping the monied elite at the expense of the working classes. (Some issues are perennials of American politics; this is one of them. Opposition to tax increases is another.) Hamilton was able to strike a political deal to get most of his plan implemented. His concession was a Southern location for the nation's capital. In 1800, the capital was moved to **Washington, D.C.,** a city created to become the seat of government.

The **French Revolution** took place during the Washington administration, and it too caused considerable debate. Jefferson wanted to support the revolution and its republican ideals. Hamilton had aristocratic leanings and so disliked the revolutionaries, who had overthrown the French aristocracy. The issue came to the forefront when France and England resumed hostilities. The British continued to be America's primary trading partner after the war, a situation that nudged the United States toward neutrality in the French-English conflict. Even Jefferson agreed that neutrality was the correct course to follow. When French government representative **Citizen Edmond Genêt** visited America to seek its assistance, Washington declared the U.S. intention to remain "friendly and impartial toward belligerent powers." This was called the **Neutrality Proclamation**. Genêt's visit sparked large, enthusiastic rallies held by American supporters of the revolution.

Historians cite the differences between Hamilton and Jefferson as the origins of our two-party system. Those favoring a strong federal government came to be known as **Federalists** (not to be confused with the Federalists who supported ratification of the Constitution, even though they were often the same people), while the followers of Jefferson called themselves the Republicans, later known as

The Global Struggle for Independence

Historians often consider the American Revolution a primary inspiration for the French Revolution of the late 18th century. Likewise, the Haitian slave revolt and various uprisings in Latin America can be traced to the philosophies espoused by the early Patriots and Founding Fathers.

Democratic-Republicans to avoid confusion with members of the Republican Party created in the 1850s, a very different group which still survives today. The development of political parties troubled the framers of the Constitution, most of whom regarded parties as factions and dangerous to the survival of the Republic.

Our First Party System		
	Federalists	**Democratic-Republicans**
Leaders	Hamilton, Washington, Adams, Jay, Marshall	Jefferson, Madison
Vision	Economy based on commerce	Economy based on agriculture
Governmental Power	Strong federal government	Stronger state governments
Supporters	Wealthy, Northeast	Yeoman farmers, Southerners
Constitution	Loose construction	Strict construction
National Bank	Believed it was "necessary"	Believed it was merely "desirable"
Foreign Affairs	More sympathetic toward Great Britain	More sympathetic toward France

Note: The Federalist party would die out after the **Hartford Convention**, following the War of 1812. Hamilton's vision and programs would be carried out by the nationalist program and **Henry Clay's American System** during the **Era of Good Feelings**. The **Second Party System** would emerge during the presidency of **Andrew Jackson** and would consist of the **Whigs**, who embraced many Federalist principles and policies, and the **Jacksonian Democrats**, who saw themselves as the heirs of the Jeffersonian Republicans.

Hamilton's financial program not only stirred controversy in Congress and helped to create our two-party system but also instigated the **Whiskey Rebellion** in 1791, which began in western Pennsylvania when farmers resisted an excise tax on whiskey. As part of his financial program, Hamilton imposed the tax in an attempt to raise revenue to defray the debt incurred by the Revolution. Washington, determined not to let his new government tolerate armed disobedience, dispatched the militia to disperse the rebels. After the opposition was dispelled, the rebels went home, and although there were some arrests and two convictions, Washington eventually pardoned both men. The Whiskey Rebellion is significant because, like Bacon's Rebellion and Shays's Rebellion before it, the uprising demonstrated the lasting class tensions between inland farmers and the coastal elites who ran the new government. But while Shays's Rebellion demonstrated that the national government of the time had lacked the power to respond, Americans noted that the new government had power it wasn't afraid to use. Some saw fairness in Washington's actions; others saw the makings of tyranny. James Madison, among others, would retreat from his support of the Federalists to back Jefferson's camp of Democratic-Republicans.

After the **Battle of Fallen Timbers** in 1794, Washington sent John Jay to England to negotiate a treaty concerning the evacuation of the British from the Northwest Territory, as stipulated in the Treaty of Paris that concluded the Revolutionary War, as well as to discuss British violations of free trade. Although **Jay's Treaty** prevented war with Great Britain, opponents of the treaty believed Jay made too many concessions toward the British, who in essence were not respecting our rights as a sovereign nation (the treaty also involved paying some war debts). In 1796, Congress attempted to withhold funding to enforce the treaty. The House of Representatives asked Washington to submit all documents pertinent to the treaty for consideration. Washington refused, establishing the precedent of **executive privilege**, which is the right of the president to withhold information when doing so would protect national security (e.g., in the case of diplomatic files and military secrets). Jay's Treaty is often considered to be the low point of Washington's administration, and Jay himself was burned in effigy in the streets of New York.

At the same time, Washington sent Thomas Pinckney to Spain to negotiate use of the Mississippi River, duty-free access to world markets, and the removal of any remaining Spanish forts on American soil. During this mission, Pinckney was able to extract a promise from Spain to try to prevent attacks on Western settlers from Native Americans. The **Treaty of San Lorenzo**, also known as **Pinckney's Treaty**, was ratified by the U.S. Senate in 1796 and is often considered to be the high point of Washington's administration.

The end of Washington's presidency was as monumental as its beginning. Wishing to set a final precedent, Washington declined to run for a third term. In his famous **farewell address**, composed in part by Alexander Hamilton, he warned future presidents to "steer clear of permanent alliances with any portion of the foreign world." Washington's Farewell Address was published in newspapers around the United States in the fall of 1796. It warned Americans against sectional divisions, as well as political party conflict. The most prominent portion of the address focuses on international relations, or "foreign entanglements." Washington promoted the notion of having friendly relationships with all nations, but to avoid any permanent alliances. This warning remained a prominent part of American foreign policy through the mid-20th century, when the United States joined the North Atlantic Treaty Organization in 1949.

Republican Motherhood

During the 1790s, women's roles in courtship, marriage, and motherhood were all reevaluated in light of the new republic and its ideals. Although women were largely excluded from political activity, they had an important civil role and responsibility. They were to be the teachers and producers of virtuous male citizens.

While public virtue had been a strictly masculine quality in the past, *private* virtue emerged as a very important quality for women, who were given the task of inspiring and teaching men to be good citizens through romance and motherhood. The idea here is that a woman should entertain only suitors with good morals, providing more incentive for men to be more ethical. Women also held a tremendous influence on their sons, leading advocates for female education to speak out, arguing that educated women would be better mothers, who would produce better citizens. Even though the obligations of women had grown to include this new political meaning, traditional gender roles were largely unchanged as the education of women was meant only in service to husbands and family.

The idea of **Republican Motherhood** emerged in the early 1800s, as the importance of education emerged in American society. The role of the mother became more prominent in child-rearing, as mothers were now expected to raise educated children who would contribute positively to the United States.

The Adams Presidency

The Electoral College selected **John Adams**, a Federalist, as Washington's successor. Under the then-current rules, the second-place candidate became vice president, and so Adams's vice president was the Democratic-Republican Thomas Jefferson.

Following the Washington era, Adams's presidency was bound to be an anti-climax. Adams, argumentative and elitist, was a difficult man to like. He was also a hands-off administrator, often allowing Jefferson's political rival **Alexander Hamilton** to take charge. The animosity between Jefferson and Hamilton and the growing belligerence between the Federalists and Democratic-Republicans set the ugly, divisive tone for Adams's term.

Perhaps Adams's greatest achievement was avoiding all-out war with France. After the United States signed the Jay Treaty with Britain, France began seizing American ships on the open seas. Adams sent three diplomats to Paris, where French officials demanded a huge bribe before they would allow negotiations even to begin. The diplomats returned home, and Adams published their written report in the newspapers. Because he deleted the French officials' names and replaced them with the letters X, Y, and Z, the incident became known as the **XYZ Affair**. As a result, popular sentiment did a complete turnaround; formerly pro-French, the public became vehemently anti-French to the point that a declaration of war seemed possible. Aware of how small the American military was, Adams avoided the war (a war Hamilton wanted) and negotiated a settlement with a contrite France although he was not able to avoid the Naval skirmishes called the Quasi-War.

The Alien Act wanted to lengthen the amount of time it took for immigrants to become citizens (and thus eligible to vote) from 5 to 15 years. It also allowed the president to deport any "dangerous aliens."

The low point of Adams's tenure was the passage and enforcement of the **Alien and Sedition Acts**, which allowed the government to forcibly expel foreigners and to jail newspaper editors for "scandalous and malicious writing." The acts were purely political, aimed at destroying new immigrants'—especially French immigrants'—support for the Democratic-Republicans. Worst of all, the Sedition Act, which strictly regulated antigovernment speech, was a clear violation of the First Amendment. In a scenario almost unimaginable today, Vice President Jefferson led the opposition to the Alien and Sedition Acts. Together with Madison, he drafted the **Virginia and Kentucky Resolutions** (which were technically anonymous), which argued that the states had the right to judge the constitutionality of federal laws. The resolutions went on to exercise this authority they claimed, later referred to as **nullification**, by declaring the Alien and Sedition Acts void. Virginia and Kentucky, however, never prevented enforcement of the laws. Rather, Jefferson used the laws and the resolutions as key issues in his 1800 campaign for the presidency. Even today, states often pass resolutions similar to these to express their displeasure with the federal government.

Summary

Here are the most important concepts to remember from the American Independence period.

o   Britain's increased attempts to control the colonies and impose burdensome taxation led to the colonists' desire for revolution.

o   France, Britain, Spain, and the new United States vied for control of land; the borders of the new United States were constantly expanding.

o   The common people had changed their view of government. The belief in egalitarianism and democracy replaced trust in monarchy and aristocracy.

Chapter 7 Review Questions

See Chapter 14 for answers and explanations.

1. The Albany Plan of Union failed because

   (A) the plan required the Northeastern colonies to contribute a disproportionate share of the necessary troops and money
   (B) no political leader with national stature was willing to support the plan
   (C) there was no legitimate executive power to enforce it
   (D) none of the colonies was willing to share tax-collecting powers with a national entity

2. The American colonists objected to the policies imposed by Parliament after the French and Indian War for all of the following reasons EXCEPT

   (A) the new restrictions would hinder New England trade
   (B) their rights as Englishmen were being violated
   (C) they resented quartering British troops now that the French threat was removed
   (D) they believed they should be represented in Parliament if they were subjected to mercantilist restrictions

3. According to the theory of virtual representation,

   (A) colonists were represented in Parliament by virtue of their British citizenship
   (B) slaves were represented in Congress by virtue of the fact that their owners were voters
   (C) paper money has value by virtue of the fact that it is backed by the full faith and credit of the government
   (D) the best interests of criminal defendants are represented by their attorneys

4. The Stamp Act Congress of 1765 was historically significant in that it

   (A) represented a first step in colonial unity against Britain
   (B) demonstrated Parliament's determination to tax its American colonies
   (C) represented New England's determination to go to war against England
   (D) demonstrated the colonists' political and philosophical disagreement among themselves

5. Thomas Jefferson relied on the ideas of John Locke in writing the American Declaration of Independence in all of the following ways EXCEPT Locke's belief that

   (A) man is born free and equal
   (B) man must submit to the General Will to protect his natural rights
   (C) governments get their authority from the people, not God
   (D) the purpose of government is to protect man's natural rights

6. Historians often cite Shays's Rebellion (1786–1787) as a significant event in U.S. history because it

   (A) demonstrated the strength, yet fairness, of the newly created federal government
   (B) made many Americans realize that slavery could not last
   (C) made Americans realize that excessive taxation often leads to violence
   (D) demonstrated the weakness of the federal government under the Articles of Confederation

7. Under the Articles of Confederation, the national government had which of the following powers?

I. The power to collect taxes
II. The power to negotiate treaties
III. The power to supercede state law

(A) I only
(B) II only
(C) I and III only
(D) I, II, and III

8. George Washington established the principle of executive privilege in a dispute with Congress over the

(A) Alien and Sedition Acts
(B) legality of political parties
(C) Jay Treaty
(D) Whiskey Rebellion

9. The Age of Salutary Neglect drew to a close with

(A) the Boston Tea Party
(B) the formation of the Republic of Texas
(C) the Salem Witch Trials
(D) the end of the French and Indian War

10. Which of the following best summarizes the strict constructionist position on the establishment of the National Bank?

(A) All matters not clearly reconciled by the Constitution, such as the establishment of a national bank, must be arbitrated by the federal judiciary.
(B) The establishment of the National Bank is necessary to strengthen the United States economy and therefore must be allowed even if it is technically unconstitutional.
(C) The decision on whether to establish a National Bank, like all important governmental decisions, should be left in the hands of a powerful executive branch.
(D) The Constitution forbids the establishment of the bank because creating a bank is not among Congress's enumerated powers.

11. All of the following were immediate social or economic consequences of the American Revolution EXCEPT

(A) increased opportunities for land settlement in the West
(B) reform of primogeniture inheritance laws
(C) expanded rights for women to hold property
(D) the opening of many areas of trade and manufacture

REFLECT

Respond to the following questions:

- For which content topics discussed in this chapter do you feel you have achieved sufficient mastery to answer multiple-choice questions correctly?

- For which content topics discussed in this chapter do you feel you have achieved sufficient mastery to discuss effectively in a short-answer question or an essay?

- On which content topics discussed in this chapter do you feel you need more work before you can answer multiple-choice questions correctly?

- On which content topics discussed in this chapter do you feel you need more work before you can discuss them effectively in a short-answer question or an essay?

- What parts of this chapter are you going to review again?

- Will you seek further help, outside of this book (such as a teacher, tutor, or AP Students), on any of the content in this chapter—and, if so, on what content?

Chapter 8
Beginnings of
Modern American
Democracy
(1800–1848)

The "Revolution of 1800"

By 1800, the Federalist party was split, clearing the way to the presidency for the Democratic-Republicans. Two men ran for the party nomination: **Thomas Jefferson** and **Aaron Burr**. Each received an equal number of votes in the Electoral College, which meant that the Federalist-dominated House of Representatives was required to choose a president from between the two. It took 35 ballots, but Jefferson finally won. Alexander Hamilton swallowed hard and campaigned for Jefferson, with whom he disagreed on most issues and whom he personally disliked, because he believed Burr to be "a most unfit and dangerous man." Burr later proved Hamilton right by killing him.

The election was noteworthy for two reasons. For the second time in as many elections, a president was saddled with a vice president he did not want. That problem was remedied in 1804 with the **Twelfth Amendment** to the Constitution, which allowed electors to vote for a **party ticket**. The other, more important reason the election was significant is that in America's first transfer of power—from the Federalists to the Democratic-Republicans—no violence occurred, a feat practically unprecedented for the time. Jefferson referred to his victory and the subsequent change-over as "the bloodless revolution."

THE JEFFERSONIAN REPUBLIC (1800–1823)

Note: The next two sections primarily review political history. They are followed by a review of social and economic history between 1800 and 1860 because many of the important socioeconomic trends of the era developed over the course of several decades. The economic and social conditions of this period also played a major role in bringing about the Civil War, and the AP Exam often tests them in this context. That's why we'll review them as we get closer, chronologically, to the Civil War.

Jefferson's First Term

The transition of power from the Federalists to the Democratic-Republicans may have been a bloodless one, but it was not a friendly one. Adams was so upset about the election that he left the capital before Jefferson took office in order to avoid attending the inauguration ceremony. Before he left town, however, he made a number of **midnight appointments,** filling as many government positions with Federalists as he could. Jefferson's response was to refuse to recognize those appointments. He then set about replacing as many Federalist appointees as he could. He dismissed some, pressured others to retire, and waited out the rest. By his second term, the majority of public appointees were Democratic-Republicans.

Jefferson's refusal to accept Adams's midnight appointments resulted in a number of lawsuits against the government. One, the case of *Marbury v. Madison* reached the Supreme Court in 1803. William Marbury, one of Adams's last-minute appointees, had sued Secretary of State James Madison for refusing to certify his appointment to the federal bench. Chief Justice **John Marshall** was a Federalist, and his sympathies were with Marbury, but Marshall was not certain that the court could force Jefferson to accept Marbury's appointment. Marshall's decision in the case established one of the most important principles of the Supreme Court: **judicial review**. The court ruled that Marbury did indeed have a right to his judgeship but that the court could not enforce his right. Why? The Judiciary Act of 1789 gave the Supreme Court the authority to order federal appointees (such as Madison) to deliver appointments such as William Marbury's. Marshall believed that this act gave too much power to the Judicial Branch at the expense of Congress and the Presidency, and thus it was unconstitutional. In one fell swoop, Marshall had handed Jefferson the victory he wanted while simultaneously claiming a major role for the Supreme Court: the responsibility for reviewing the constitutionality of Congressional acts. Throughout the rest of his tenure, Marshall worked to strengthen that doctrine and, thus, the court.

The major accomplishment of Jefferson's first term was the **Louisiana Purchase**. When Spain gave New Orleans to the French in 1802, the government realized that a potentially troublesome situation was developing. The French, they knew, were more likely to take advantage of New Orleans' strategic location at the mouth of the Mississippi, almost certainly meaning that American trade along the river would be restricted. In hopes of averting that situation, Jefferson sent James Monroe to France. Monroe's mandate was to buy New Orleans for $2 million. Monroe arrived at just the right time. Napoleon was gearing up for war in Europe, and a violent slave revolt in Haiti against the French further convinced him to abandon French interests in the New World. The French offered to sell Monroe the whole Louisiana territory for $15 million.

Spain gave the United States the right to trade in New Orleans in the 1794 Pinckney Treaty. In exchange, the United States agreed to acknowledge the border between Georgia and Spanish Florida.

Thomas Jefferson was now faced with a dilemma. As secretary of state under Washington, he had argued for a strict interpretation of the Constitution, thus limiting the power of the federal government to those powers specifically stated in the Constitution. Nowhere did the Constitution authorize the president to purchase land, yet clearly Jefferson could not pass up this opportunity to double the size of the United States. Jefferson thought about trying to get a constitutional amendment added allowing him to buy land from other countries. Ultimately, Jefferson resolved the issue by claiming his presidential power to negotiate treaties with foreign nations. His decision to purchase Louisiana without Congressional approval was not unanimously applauded: New England Federalists opposed the Louisiana Purchase because they feared (correctly) that more Western states would be more Democratic states, and that they would lose political power. They formed a group called the **Essex Junto,** planning to secede from the United States (and asked Aaron Burr to be their leader), but the plan never fully materialized. Some Republicans, led by John Randolph of Virginia, criticized Jefferson for violating Republican principles. This group became known as the Quids.

Jefferson sent explorers, among them **Lewis and Clark**, to investigate the western territories, including much of what was included in the Louisiana territory. This trip included Sacajawea as the Shoshoni guide who helped Lewis and Clark negotiate with other Native American tribes on the way up the Missouri River. All returned with favorable reports, causing many pioneers to turn their attentions westward in search of land, riches, and economic opportunities. Those early explorers also reported back to Jefferson on the presence of British and French forts that still dotted the territory, garrisoned with foreign troops that had been (deliberately?) slow to withdraw after the regime changes of the previous half-century.

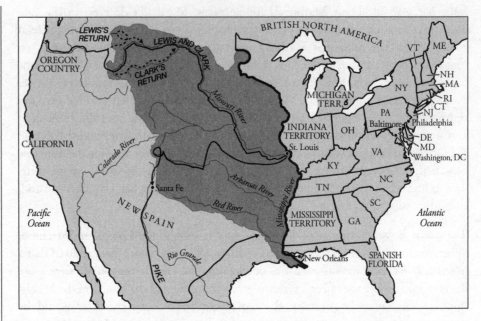

The Louisiana Purchase and the Lewis and Clark Expedition

In 1804, Jefferson won reelection in a landslide victory. During the 1804 elections, Aaron Burr ran for governor of New York. Again, Alexander Hamilton campaigned against Burr. When Burr lost, he accused Hamilton of sabotaging his political career and challenged him to a **duel** in which he killed Hamilton. Afterward, Burr fled to the Southwest, where he plotted to start his own nation in parts of the Louisiana Territory. He was later captured and tried for treason but was acquitted due to lack of evidence.

Jefferson's Second Term

Jefferson's second term did not go nearly as smoothly as his first. During these years, the United States got caught in the middle of yet another French-English dispute. The situation eventually led to the **War of 1812**.

In 1805, the British and French were at war and at a stalemate. In an effort to gain an advantage, each side began blockading the other's trade routes. The United States, dependent on both as trade partners, suffered greatly from the blockades. To add insult to injury, the British began stopping American ships and **impressing** sailors: that is, they declared, often with little or no proof, that those sailors had deserted from the British navy, and they forced them back into it. Unfortunately, the English were not as particular about whom they "reenlisted" as the Americans would have liked them to be. Tensions mounted and then boiled over when a British frigate attacked an American ship in American waters. Jefferson was at a loss. He couldn't go to war against the British because the U.S. Navy was no match for England's forces. So Jefferson responded with a boycott, biding his time while increasing military and naval appropriations.

Because both the British and the French continued to harass American ships, Jefferson lobbied for and won passage of the **Embargo Act of 1807**. The law basically shut down America's import and export business, with disastrous economic results. New England's economy collapsed, and smuggling became widespread. The New England states strongly opposed the Embargo Act, as they were the ones most impacted by an end of international trade. Many continued to trade with British Canada regardless. The Embargo Act also led to the Democratic Republicans losing many Congressional seats in the 1808 elections. The **Non-Intercourse Act of 1809** reopened trade with most nations, but it still officially banned trade with the two most significant trade partners, Britain and France. In the end, Jefferson decided, as had Washington before him, that two terms as president were enough. He endorsed his secretary of state, **James Madison**, who handily defeated the ever-weakening Federalists.

Madison's Presidency and the War of 1812

Madison sought a solution to America's trade problems, and Congress responded with **Macon's Bill No. 2**, a bill that reopened trade with both France and England. However, Madison promised that if either country renounced its interference with American trade, he would cut off trade with the other one. Napoleon made that promise, forcing the United States to cut off trade with England, but France then continued to harass American ships. The British, angry at the new embargo, stepped up their attacks on American ships, making a bad situation even worse. These developments helped build pro-war sentiments in the United States. Particularly anxious for a confrontation with the British were the Southern and Western **War Hawks**, who saw war as an opportunity to grab new territories to the west and southwest. There was also a strong desire among Western War Hawks to gain Canada from the British. Their leaders were **Henry Clay** and **John C. Calhoun**. Madison held out as long as he could but finally relented and asked Congress to declare war in 1812.

You should know several important points about the **War of 1812**. Once again, Native Americans aligned themselves with the British. The great chief **Tecumseh** unified area tribes in an effort to stop American expansion into Indiana and Illinois, both before and during the war. The British had been arming Native Americans in these Western territories against new American settlers. In an earlier battle against Tecumseh (the Battle of Tippecanoe), Gen. William Henry Harrison defeated Tecumseh's coalition of different tribes, and saw that they had British weapons. Meanwhile, his brother Tenskwatawa, also known as **the Prophet,** led an extensive revival of traditional Native American culture and religion. Tecumseh's coalition fell apart after he was killed in battle.

American forces were ill-prepared for the war, and much of the fighting went badly. The British captured Washington, D.C. in 1814 and set the White House on fire.

Effects of the War of 1812
- First and foremost, it represented the end of Native Americans' ability to stop American expansion.
- The American economy, by necessity, became less reliant on trade with Britain.
- It made Andrew Jackson into a celebrity and paved the way to his presidency.
- The victory in New Orleans led to national euphoria.
- The popularity of the war destroyed the Federalists, who had opposed it, and taught American politicians that objecting to going to war could be hazardous to their careers.

However, in most battles, America was able to fight to a stalemate. When English-French hostilities ended (with Napoleon's defeat), many of the issues that had caused the war evaporated, and the British soon negotiated peace. Unaware that the Treaty of Ghent had been signed in Belgium on December 24, 1814, and the war was over, General Andrew Jackson fought and won the Battle of New Orleans from January 8 until January 18, 1815, the only clear-cut U.S. victory of the war. The Federalists, opposed to the war because it disrupted trade and unaware that its end was coming, met in Hartford, Connecticut, to consider a massive overhaul of the Constitution or, failing that, secession. When the war ended soon after, most people considered the Federalists to be traitors, and their national party dissolved soon after the Hartford Convention (although the party continued to exert influence in some states through the next decade). The **Hartford Convention** itself brought many grievances, including the notion that two-thirds majority of Congress should be required to pass any laws dealing with trade, that a two-thirds majority be required to admit new states, and that no president can serve more than one four-year term and that two presidents in a row cannot come from the same state (all measures to retain some power for the Federalists).

The war had one clear positive result: it spurred **American manufacturing**. Cut off from trade with Europe, the states became more self-sufficient by necessity. New England became America's manufacturing center during the war, and after the war, the United States was less dependent on imports than it had been previously. (For more information on economic developments of the period, see pages 207–213.)

Throughout the rest of his tenure, Madison worked to promote national growth. At the same time, he remained true to his Democratic-Republican principles and so extended federal power only cautiously. Madison championed a combination of programs that included protective tariffs on imports, improvements to interstate roads (including expansion of the **National Road** from Maryland to Ohio), and the rechartering of the National Bank after the first National Bank's charter had expired. The National Bank was rechartered in 1816 and a new protective tariff was passed to protect the growing American industry. The programs were known collectively as the **American System**, sometimes referred to as the Nationalist Program. Speaker of the House **Henry Clay** lobbied for them so aggressively that many history books refer to "Henry Clay's American System."

Monroe's Presidency

The demise of the Federalists briefly left the United States with only one political party. This period of unity is referred to as the **Era of Good Feelings,** although the term belies the growing tension created by economic development and increased sectionalism. During this period, Chief Justice John Marshall's rulings continued to strengthen the federal government and its primacy. For example, *McCulloch v. Maryland* ruled that the states could not tax the National Bank, thus establishing the precedence of national law over state law. This case also reaffirmed the supremacy clause as the opposition was trying to challenge the constitutionality of the Bank of the United States.

The good feelings nearly came to an abrupt end in 1819 when a financial scare called the **Panic of 1819** threw the American economy into turmoil. The panic followed a period of economic growth, inflation, and land speculation, all of which had destabilized the economy. When the National Bank called in its loans, many borrowers couldn't repay them. The consequences included numerous mortgage foreclosures and business failures. Many people were thrown into poverty. Nonetheless, no nationally organized political opposition resulted from the panic, and Monroe easily won reelection in 1820.

The postwar period had also ushered in a new wave of westward expansion. As secretary of state under Monroe, **John Quincy Adams**, son of former president John Adams, deftly negotiated a number of treaties that fixed U.S. borders and opened new territories. The United States acquired Florida from the Spanish by the Adams-Onis Treaty in 1819. Adams also had to handle international tensions caused by a series of revolutions in Central America and South America, as the inhabitants of those regions won their independence from Spain. The U.S. was beginning to recognize the new South American nations largely to gain access to trade. Ultimately, events compelled Monroe and Adams to recognize the new nations. At the same time, they decided that America should assert its authority over the Western Hemisphere. The result was the **Monroe Doctrine**, a policy of mutual noninterference. You stay out of the Americas, Monroe told Europe, and we'll stay out of your squabbles. The Monroe Doctrine also claimed America's right to intervene anywhere in its own hemisphere, if it felt its security was threatened. No European country tried to intercede in the Americas following Monroe's declaration, and so the Monroe Doctrine *appeared* to work. Following the Napoleonic Wars, most European nations (particularly Spain) didn't have the military power to challenge the Monroe Doctrine or take back their colonies. No one, however, was afraid of the American military; Spain, France, and others stayed out of the Western Hemisphere because the powerful British navy made sure they did.

The Monroe Doctrine is the first of several "doctrines" you should know for the AP Exam. In general, these doctrines were presidential statements that became foreign policy. For example, in 1823, President Monroe warned European nations that the Western Hemisphere was closed to future colonization. This policy, together with the advice given in Washington's Farewell Address, secured American neutrality all the way until World War I. (The **Truman Doctrine**, issued at the end of World War II, is especially important, but you should also familiarize yourself with the Eisenhower Doctrine, the Nixon Doctrine, and most recently, the Bush Doctrine.)

The new period of expansion resulted in a national debate over slavery, as would every period of expansion to follow until the Civil War resolved the slavery question. In 1820, the Union consisted of 22 states. Eleven allowed slavery; 11 prohibited it. Missouri was the first state to be carved out of the Louisiana Purchase, and its application for statehood threatened the balance, particularly in the U.S. Senate. Henry Clay brokered the **Missouri Compromise**, which (1) admitted Missouri as a slave state, (2) carved a piece out of Massachusetts—Maine—and admitted Maine as a free state, (3) drew a line along the 36°30′ parallel across the Louisiana Territory, and (4) established the southern border of Missouri as the northernmost point at which slavery would then be allowed in the western territories of the United

The **Adams-Onis Treaty** promised that in exchange for Florida, the United States would never try to take actions to gain Spanish-held Mexico. This was later nullified when Mexico gained independence from Spain in the 1820s.

States, except of course for Missouri itself, which in a way violated the Missouri Compromise since it was north of the line. The compromise was the first in a series of measures forestalling the Civil War. It also split the powerful Democratic-Republican coalition, ending its 20-year control of national politics.

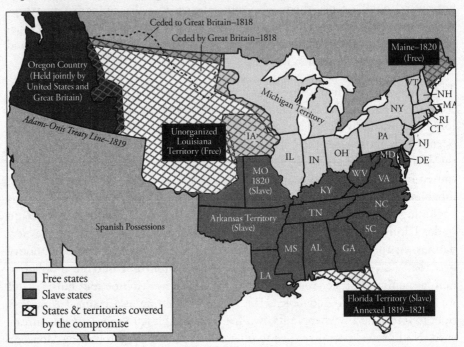

Missouri Compromise, 1820

POLITICAL EVENTS AND SOCIAL DEVELOPMENTS

The Election of 1824 and John Quincy Adams's Presidency

The **election of 1824** marked a major turning point in presidential elections. Prior to 1824, electors, who selected the president in the electoral college, had been chosen by a variety of methods. State legislatures chose many electors, although with each election the number of states using this method decreased. By 1824, a majority of states allowed voters to choose their presidential electors directly. In earlier elections, **congressional caucuses**, or groups of U.S. Congressmen, had chosen their parties' nominees, and electors, often chosen by those same congressmen or by their friends, had not challenged the choices. With more people voting directly for presidential electors, however, there was less and less voter support for the candidates nominated by party leaders in this era before primaries and caucuses. When the Democratic-Republican caucus chose William H. Crawford in 1824, others—among them John Quincy Adams, Henry Clay, and Andrew Jackson—decided to challenge the nomination. Their opposition, along with their accusations that the party caucuses were undemocratic, brought about the **demise of the caucus system**. Of the four, Andrew Jackson received the greatest number of popular votes and electoral votes; however, as none of the four had won a majority, the election was decided in the House of Representatives. There, Speaker of the House

Clay threw his support to Adams, thereby handing Adams the victory. Adams subsequently named Clay secretary of state, a position whose previous holders included Adams, Monroe, and Jefferson and that was therefore considered the gateway to the presidency. Jackson and other opponents of Clay's appointment alleged that Adams and Clay had struck a **corrupt bargain** and immediately vowed to see both removed in the election of 1828. One other thing to note about the 1824 election is that the Constitution states that in cases where there is no majority winner in the Electoral College, the three top electoral winners go on to House election (Henry Clay came in fourth, and thus was out of the running). William Crawford suffered a stroke after the inital election, and was never a real contender for the House vote.

Adams's presidency was impeded by a contrary Congress. (Remember, more congressmen had initially supported Jackson than Adams.) He had also been a Federalist congressman and was the son of a Federalist president, and every effort he made to strengthen the central government was thus viewed with deep suspicion. Jackson's supporters strongly favored **states' rights** and thwarted all of Adams's efforts to initiate improvements through the federal government. His proposals to impose new protective tariffs, build interstate highways, and establish federal schools and research centers were all met with steep opposition, though he did go on to found a naval college and become an influential congressman.

John Quincy Adams and Postmillennialism

Postmillennialism was a belief, widespread among 19th-century Christians, that Jesus would return only after a thousand-year golden age brought about by humankind. It was therefore a major progressive force in America, with adherents such as John Quincy Adams. Here is our sixth president calling for the United States to adopt the metric system—in the 1820s!

"But if man upon earth be an improvable being; if that universal peace, which was the object of a Saviour's mission, which is the desire of the philosopher, the longing of the philanthropist, the trembling hope of the Christian, is a blessing to which the futurity of mortal man has a claim of more than mortal promise; if the Spirit of Evil is, before the final consummation of things, to be cast down from his dominion over men, and bound in the chains of a thousand years, the foretaste here of man's eternal felicity, then this system of common instruments to accomplish all the changes of social and friendly commerce, will furnish the links of sympathy between the inhabitants of the most distant regions; the metre will surround the globe in use, as well as in multiplied extension; and one language of weights and measures will be spoken from the equator to the poles."

The Jackson Presidency and Jacksonian Democracy

Despite the political incorrectness of his policies by today's standards and reevaluation of Andrew Jackson by modern-day historians, the era of Jackson as president is an important period in American history. There are always more than a few multiple-choice questions on this material, and one of the essay questions often pertains to Jackson's administration or the concept of Jacksonian democracy.

Furious that he had been denied the presidency in 1824 despite winning a plurality of the vote (more votes than any other candidate, but short of a majority), Jackson put together a support network to assure wide popular support. A coalition of state political organizations, newspaper publishers, and other community leaders rallied around the campaign. That group became the present-day **Democratic** party. The campaign was vicious. While the candidates themselves stayed out of the fray—no presidential candidate would campaign on his own behalf until Stephen Douglas in 1860—their surrogates showed no restraint in slinging mud. Jackson's men accused Adams of being a corrupt career politician, while Adams's men accused Jackson of being a stupid and violent drunkard. Jackson was particularly infuriated by accusations that his wife was a bigamist—which was technically true, as she had married Jackson before her divorce was final. The **Coffin Handbill** accused Jackson of murdering his enlisted men during the Indian Wars. Those who consider today's smear campaigns unprecedented haven't studied much American history.

In 1828, Jackson won the election by a large margin; in so doing, he became the first president who wasn't either born in Virginia or named Adams. He was considered to have the interests of the West in mind, and he was seen as the epitome of a self-made man. Among his first acts, he dismissed numerous government officials and replaced them with political supporters. While almost every one of his predecessors had done exactly the same thing, because Jackson was the first true outsider-president, administration jobs that had previously circulated among a relatively insular circle of political supporters fell into new hands. Those who lost power criticized Jackson, but so too did the public, who noticed for the first time the cronyism already inherent in their government. Trading jobs for political favors came to be known as the **spoils system.** It was truly a case of "to the victor goes the spoils."

Jackson's popularity ushered in the age of **Jacksonian democracy**, which replaced Jeffersonian republicanism. Jefferson had conceived of a nation governed by middle- and upper-class educated property holders, in which the government would be only as large as necessary to provide an acceptable level of services. Jefferson also envisioned a nation of yeoman farmers—farmers who owned their land—whose liberty would be protected by limiting the power of the central government. Jacksonian democracy, on the other hand, benefited from **universal white manhood suffrage**, meaning the extension of voting rights to all white males, even those who did not own property. This, however, was the work of state legislatures; Jackson only benefited from it.

When "the West" Wasn't That West

In colonial times, any settlement that wasn't located right on the Atlantic Ocean was said to be located in "the west." By the early 19th century, definitions had changed—but not to their modern meanings. "The Northwest" consisted of northern states west of the Appalachians, such as Ohio, Indiana, and Illinois, which are now considered "the Midwest." (This is why Northwestern University is located not in, say, Seattle, but in Chicago.) "The Southwest" consisted of southern states west of the Appalachians, such as Alabama and Mississippi, which are now considered "the Deep South." Henry Clay and Andrew Jackson were considered the foremost Westerners of the period, and they were respectively from Kentucky and Tennessee.

A strong presidency also characterized Jacksonian democracy. Jackson parlayed his wide popularity into a mandate to challenge both Congress and the Supreme Court in a way that none of his predecessors had. You should note that, unlike Jeffersonian republicanism, Jacksonian democracy is *not* a coherent vision of how a government should function. Jacksonian Democrats saw themselves as champions of liberty, but they did not always act as such. Jackson was not as great a thinker as Jefferson, the Enlightenment scholar.

No policy of Jackson's has received more criticism by modern scholars than Jackson's treatment of the Cherokees with the **Indian Removal Act,** passed by Congress in 1830. In some ways, this represented a natural continuation of policy toward American Indians. Originally, it had been the British who established the concept that Native Americans were "foreign nations," and as such, the government could go to war and make treaties with them. These treaties often established what the British termed "Indian territory," as was the case with the **Proclamation of 1763** issued at the close of the **French and Indian War**.

When the Americans gained their independence, the U.S. government continued the treatment of Native Americans that had been established by the British. Some Americans, however, among them Thomas Jefferson, suggested assimilation into American culture as a solution to the "Indian Problem." Jefferson and others believed that if the Native Americans gave up their "hunting and gathering" lifestyle and adopted American farming techniques and culture—in essence, "learned to live on less land"—then the Americans and Native Americans might coexist peacefully.

By the time of Jackson's presidency, there were "Five Civilized Tribes" living in the South in the area east of the Mississippi River, among those the Cherokee nation. The Cherokees had developed a written language, converted to Christianity, and embraced agriculture as a way of life. Some Cherokees even owned slaves. (How much more "civilized" could these Native Americans become?!) The Cherokees had developed their own government and deemed themselves to be an independent republic within the state of Georgia. The problem arose when gold was discovered on Cherokee land and the citizens of Georgia demanded that the Cherokees comply with the provisions of the Indian Removal Act, a policy suggested by Monroe but enacted during Jackson's tenure in office. This act demanded that the Native Americans resettle in Oklahoma, which had been deemed Indian territory. Jackson, for his part, argued that moving away from white society was the best way to protect themselves from white encroachment and maintain their traditional customs. The Cherokees refused and brought their case to the Supreme Court. Although John Marshall, Chief Justice at the time, sided with the Cherokees in two cases, *Cherokee Nation v. Georgia* (1831) and *Worcester v. Georgia* (1832), Andrew Jackson refused to comply with the Court's decision and is reputed to have sneered, "John Marshall has made his decision, now let him enforce it." Between 1835 and 1838, thousands of Cherokees walked to Oklahoma under the supervision of the U.S. Army in what has come to be known as the **Trail of Tears.** Thousands died of sickness and starvation along the way. The other side of that is related to the Seminole in Florida. Refusing to leave their land, they initiated the Seminole War which lasted until the late 1830s. It was incredibly expensive and eventually the U.S. government gave up, allowing the Seminole to stay on their land.

One of the major issues of Jackson's presidency focused on **nullification**. The doctrine of nullification, first expressed by Jefferson and Madison in the Virginia and Kentucky Resolutions, holds that the individual states have the right to disobey federal laws if they find them unconstitutional. John Marshall had established that only the Supreme Court had the power of **judicial review,** in the landmark decision of *Marbury v. Madison* (1803). The **Tariff of 1828**, also known as the **Tariff of Abominations**, was passed during the Adams administration, but it almost turned into a national crisis during Jackson's administration. In 1828, **John C. Calhoun**, a South Carolinian who was Jackson's vice president, anonymously published "The South Carolina Exposition and Protest," arguing that states who felt the 50 percent

The Bank of the United States

In the 19th century, paper money was issued not by the government but by private banks. If you went to a bank for a $100 loan, the bank would print some money for you. It didn't necessarily have to have $100 worth of gold in its vaults to do this. If it had $10,000 worth of gold in its vaults, a bank might issue $100,000 in paper money—and as long as no more than 10 percent of that money was cashed in at the same time, the bank would be fine.

What kept such a bank from printing up a million dollars, or a trillion? The main answer was that people could pay their taxes with paper money and that paper collected at the Bank of the United States. Fear that the Bank would attempt to cash in a huge amount of paper at once kept smaller banks from overusing the printing presses. Once Andrew Jackson killed the Bank of the United States, however, **wildcat banks** did indeed spring up and issue paper money with abandon. Add the fact that the government stopped accepting paper money in payment for land, and people realized that all their paper money was now nearly worthless—a recipe for a major depression.

With only gold and silver now considered to have value, the stage was set for the late 19th century, when arguments over these metals would dominate the debate over economic policy.

tariff was unfairly high could nullify the law. By 1830, southern states were openly discussing nullification, as such protectionist tariffs cut into the trade with Britain on which the South relied to sell its cotton and buy British wools and certain other raw materials in return. Jackson, though a strong supporter of states' rights, thought nullification endangered the Union and was thus too extreme. After the **Tariff of 1832** failed to lower rates to an acceptable level, South Carolina nullified the tariff. Jackson had Congress authorize a **Force Bill**, threatening to call in troops to enforce the tariff, but Calhoun and Henry Clay (remember the Missouri Compromise?) brokered a behind-the-scenes compromise, lowering the tariff and diffusing tensions. After the compromise tariff was approved and accepted by South Carolina, the legislature nullified the Force Bill, for no purpose except to support the doctrine of nullification.

Jackson's economic policies demonstrated his distrust of both big government and Northeastern power brokers. He spent much of his two terms "downsizing" the federal government and strengthening the office of the presidency through his extensive use of the presidential veto. He fought against the **reform** movements of the time that called for increased government activism against social and economic problems. He saw to it that the **Second Bank of the United States (BUS)** failed by vetoing Congress's attempt to recharter the bank and by withdrawing federal funds and depositing them in state "**pet**" **banks**. He felt that the BUS protected Northeastern interests at the expense of the West. Jackson argued that the bank was an unconstitutional monopoly, but the Supreme Court ruled against him using a loose interpretation of the commerce clause (*McCulloch v. Maryland*, 1819). He was also suspicious of paper money, preferring "hard currency" such as gold or silver. His **Specie Circular**, which ended the policy of selling government land on credit (buyers now had to pay "hard cash"), caused a money shortage and a sharp decrease in the treasury, and it helped trigger the **Panic of 1837**. Congress overturned the circular in the last days of Jackson's final term.

Slavery grew to be an ever more controversial issue during the time of Jacksonian Democracy. As the Northern abolition movement grew stronger, the South experienced several slave revolts, which resulted in the use of more brutal disciplinary measures by slaveholders. The most famous of the insurrections was **Nat Turner's Rebellion**. Turner, a well-read preacher, had a vision, and he took this vision as a sign from God that a black liberation movement would succeed. As a result, he rallied a gang that proceeded to kill and then mutilate the corpses of 60 whites. In retaliation, 200 slaves were executed, some with no connection at all to the rebellion. Fearful that other slaves would hear of and emulate Turner's exploits, Southern states passed a series of restrictive laws, known as **slave codes**, prohibiting blacks from congregating and learning to read. Other state laws even prevented whites from questioning the legitimacy of slavery. After Turner's Rebellion, Virginia's House of Burgesses debated ending bondage but did not pass a law.

The Election of 1836 and the Rise of the Whigs

Jackson's Democratic party could not represent the interests of all its constituencies (Northern abolitionists, Southern plantation owners, Western pioneers), and inevitably, an opposition party, the **Whigs**, was formed. By 1834, almost as many congressmen supported the Whig Party as the Democratic Party. The Whigs were a loose coalition that shared one thing in common: opposition to one or more of the Democrats' policies. For example, while the Democrats favored limited federal government, many Whigs believed in government **activism,** especially in the case of social issues. Many Whigs were also deeply religious and supported the temperance movement and enforcement of the Sabbath. Still, the defining characteristic of the Whigs was their opposition to the Democrats.

In the election of 1836, Jackson supported his second vice president, Democrat **Martin Van Buren**. Van Buren had the misfortune to take over the presidency just as the country was entering a major economic crisis (the Panic of 1837). Van Buren made the situation worse by continuing Jackson's policy of favoring hard currency, thereby insuring that money would be hard to come by. The economic downturn lasted through Van Buren's term, practically guaranteeing that he would not be reelected.

In 1841, former military hero **William Henry Harrison** became the first Whig president. He died of pneumonia a month after taking office. His vice president, **John Tyler**, a former Democrat, assumed the presidency and began championing states' rights, much to his own party's chagrin. Tyler vetoed numerous Whig bills, which alienated Whig leadership; eventually his entire cabinet resigned in protest. Tyler is often referred to as the "president without a party," and his presidency lasted only one term.

> The Whigs had many of the same beliefs as the Federalists, especially support for manufacturing, opposition to new immigrants, and Westward Expansion.

ECONOMIC HISTORY (1800–1860)

This section discusses economic developments in the United States during the first part of the 19th century. These developments played an important role in the political events that led to the Civil War, and they helped to determine the different characteristics of the country's regions. Along with social developments (discussed in the next section), these economic factors laid the foundation for issues that would be important to American society for the following century (such as abolitionism, women's suffrage, and temperance).

Beginnings of a Market Economy

From the time they first arrived until the Revolutionary War era, most settlers in the United States raised crops for subsistence, rather than for sale at market. Most people made their own clothing and built their own furniture and homes, and they got by without many other conveniences. Cash transactions were relatively rare. Instead, people used ledgers to keep track of who owed what to whom and typically settled accounts when someone moved away or died.

Developments in manufacturing and transportation changed all that, however. By making it possible to mass produce goods and transport them across the country cheaply, a **market economy** began to develop. In a market economy, people trade their labor or goods for cash, which they then use to buy other people's labor or goods. Market economies favor those who specialize. For example, farmers who grow a single crop (monoculture) usually do better in a market economy than those who produce many different crops. One-crop farmers can offer buyers more of what they want. These farmers also do not have to look for different buyers for their many products. The trade-off, of course, is that these farmers are no longer self-sufficient. Instead, they become dependent on the market to provide some necessities. Furthermore, such farmers sometimes fall victim to overproduction, resulting in an unexpected, unwelcome drop in the price of their crop.

Market economies grow more quickly and provide more services than subsistence economies, and they also make people more interdependent. However, they are also much more prone to change. Any number of factors can halt a period of prosperity and throw the economy into a skid like the panics of 1819 and 1837. These changes are referred to as **boom-and-bust cycles.** During the first decades of the 19th century, the United States made a rapid transition from a subsistence economy to a market economy.

As stated earlier, the **War of 1812** and the events leading up to it forced the United States to become less dependent on imports and, consequently, to develop a stronger national economy. Two key advances, both developed by **Eli Whitney**, also played a major part in the process. The **cotton gin**, invented in 1793, revolutionized Southern agriculture by making it much easier to remove the seeds from cotton plants. (The machine was 5,000 percent more efficient than a human being.) The cotton gin made it easier and cheaper to use cotton for textiles, and as a result, the demand for cotton grew very rapidly into the early 1800s. As demand grew, so did cotton production in the South. Because cotton farming is labor intensive, the spread of cotton as the region's chief crop also intensified the South's dependence on slave labor. Other notable inventions that revolutionized agriculture include the steel plow and mechanical reaper.

Whitney's second innovation was the use of **interchangeable parts** in manufacturing. Whitney originally struck upon the idea while mass-producing rifles for the U.S. Army. Prior to Whitney's breakthrough, manufacturers had built weapons (and other machines) by hand, custom fitting parts so that each weapon was unique. The process was costly, time-consuming, and inconvenient, because replacing broken parts was extremely difficult. Whitney demonstrated the practicality of his invention to Thomas Jefferson and James Madison by disassembling a number of rifles, scrambling the parts, and then reassembling the rifles from whichever parts he picked out of the pile. Whitney's demonstration was a huge success, and soon his idea was being applied to all aspects of manufacturing.

Interchangeable parts gave birth to the **machine-tool industry**, which produced specialized machines for such growing industries as textiles and transportation. (Without interchangeable parts, such machines would have been impractical because they would have been too expensive to build and too difficult to fix.) Whitney's advances also helped promote the development of **assembly line production**. On an assembly line, products are constructed more efficiently by dividing the labor into a number of tasks and assigning each worker one task. Prior to assembly lines, each worker would create a product in its entirety. The result was a product that took longer to produce and was less uniform in quality.

The North and the Textile Industry

The above-mentioned developments first benefited the textile industry. Advances in machine technology, coupled with a U.S. embargo on British goods prior to and during the War of 1812—England was then America's chief source of textiles— spurred the development of textile mills in New England. During the first decade of the 19th century, mills produced thread and hired local women to weave the thread into cloth at home. The mills would then buy the finished cloth and sell it on the open market. The invention of the first **power loom**, in 1813, meant that textile manufacturers could produce both thread and finished fabric in their own factories quickly and efficiently. The resulting product was both of high quality and inexpensive—so much so that women who had previously woven their own fabrics at home started to buy cloth. **Samuel Slater**, the "Father of the American Industrial Revolution," designed the first American textile mills.

The rapid growth of the textile industry resulted in a shortage of labor in New England. Consequently, textile manufacturers had to "sweeten the pot" to entice laborers (almost all of whom were women from nearby farms) to their factories. The most famous worker-enticement program was called the **Lowell system** (or **Waltham system**), so named after the two Massachusetts towns in which many mills were located. The Lowell system guaranteed employees housing in respectable, chaperoned boardinghouses; cash wages; and participation in cultural and social events organized by the mill. The system, widely copied throughout New England, lasted until great waves of Irish immigration in the 1840s and 1850s made factory labor plentiful. Later, as working conditions started to deteriorate, workers began to organize **labor unions** to protect their interests. These early unions in the mid-1800s met with strong, frequently violent opposition from industry. Still, they ultimately succeeded. (We'll discuss labor unions in much more detail later, when we discuss the Gilded Age in the late 1800s and the Progressive era in the early 1900s.)

Other industries inevitably sprang up around the textile industry. **Clothing manufacturers**, also located primarily in the Northeast, transformed the textiles into finished products. **Retailers** sold the clothing and other manufactured products in their stores. **Brokers** acted as middlemen, buying and selling raw and finished products and trafficking them among manufacturers and retailers. **Commercial banks** lent money to everyone so that the wheels of commerce stayed well greased. Most significant, the **transportation industry** grew as a result of the need to ship these and other products across the country.

Transportation: Canals, Railroads, Highways, and Steamships

The Market Revolution

The changes caused by the development of better transportation and manufacturing had permanent altering effects on American society. Increasing numbers of Americans no longer relied solely on agriculture for their livelihoods; instead, they supported themselves by working in factories. Coal mining, too, became an important industry during this era.

Prior to the 1820s, travel and shipping along east-west routes was difficult, and most trade centered on the north-south routes along the Ohio and Mississippi Rivers. The construction of the **National Road** from Maryland to West Virginia (and ultimately to central Ohio) made east-west travel easier, but the big change came with the completion of the **Erie Canal** in 1825. Funded entirely by the state of New York, the Erie Canal linked the Great Lakes region to New York and thus to European shipping routes. Suddenly, it became lucrative for a Midwestern merchant or farmer to sell his products to Eastern buyers, and as a result, the Northeast soon established itself as the United States' center of commerce. The Erie Canal was so successful that, by 1835, its width and depth had to be nearly doubled to handle the traffic. Other regions tried to duplicate the Erie Canal's success, and during the 1830s, thousands of miles of canals were constructed throughout the Northeast and Midwest. None performed as well as the Erie Canal, and a number of those canals failed. Meanwhile, the railroads developed into a convenient means of transporting goods; by 1850, the **canal era** had ended.

The end of this era, however, did not mark the end of shipping as an important industry. The invention of the steam engine allowed for **steamships**, which traveled faster than sailing vessels. Steamships became important freight carriers and replaced sailing ships for long sea voyages. By 1850, passengers could travel by steamship from New York to England in 10 days; by sail, the same trip had taken more than a month. Steamships were not without their problems though; exploding boilers, burning ships, and other disasters accompanied the technological advances.

The Transportation Revolution

By 1855, the cost to send things across America had fallen to one-twentieth of what it had cost in 1825—and they arrived in one-fifth the time.

Similarly, **railroads** redefined land travel. America's first railroads were built during the 1830s, the first typically connecting only two cities. As the nation's rail network grew, a major problem arose. Different railroad lines could not be connected to one another because the width, or **gauge**, of their tracks was different. As a result, rail development proceeded slowly. When different railways converted to compatible systems, the government often paid the bill even though the railroads were privately owned. This hastened progress, and by 1853, New York and Chicago were linked by rail, as were Pittsburgh and Philadelphia. (Southern rail development was much slower, and superior rails gave the North a huge advantage during the Civil War.) We'll discuss the railroads further in the post–Civil War period, during which railroad construction really "picked up steam."

The increase in travel and shipping was helped considerably by the invention of the **telegraph**, which allowed immediate long-distance communication for the first time. The telegraph was like a primitive telephone, except that people communicated in **Morse code** rather than by speaking to one another. Americans quickly understood the benefits of telegraphic communications, and widespread use followed its invention almost immediately. Transatlantic telegraph cables, however, would not be successfully laid until 1866, after the Civil War.

Developments in transportation and communication during the first half of the 19th century revolutionized American commerce and culture but favored the Northeast and the West (today known as the Midwest). Products, people, and ideas traveled much faster in 1850 than they had in 1800.

Farming

Although American manufacturing grew at a rapid pace, agriculture remained by far the most common source of livelihood throughout the first half of the 19th century. Mechanization revolutionized farming during the period, as many machines came into common use during this time, including the mechanical plow, sower, reaper, thresher, baler, and cotton gin. The growth of the market economy also changed farming. In 1820, about one-third of all the food grown in the United States went to market. (The rest was kept for personal consumption.) By 1860, that fraction had doubled.

Farming continued in the Northeast, but not without difficulties. The region's rocky, hilly terrain was unsuitable to many of the machines that were making farming on the plains easier and cheaper. Furthermore, much of the farmland in the region had been over-farmed, and as a result, the quality of the soil had grown poor. Unable to compete with Midwestern grain farmers, some New England farmers quit cultivating grain and started raising livestock and growing fruits and vegetables. Others quit farming entirely and headed to the cities to take manufacturing jobs.

As mentioned above, the Midwest became America's chief source of grains, such as wheat and corn. Midwestern farms—much larger than New England farms—were also much more adaptable to the new technology that allowed farmers to nearly double production. Banks sprang up to lend farmers the capital necessary to buy modern equipment, and the trade routes created by rail and ship provided access to the markets these farmers needed to sell their crops in order to pay off their loans. The system worked well, except during the various financial crises of the first half of the century. The panics of 1819 and 1837 resulted in bank foreclosures on mortgages and other business loans, not just in the Midwest but all across the country. Not surprisingly, many people were thrown into poverty.

In the South, plantations focused primarily on cotton, especially in the Deep South; tobacco continued to be a major cash crop in the Upper South. The majority of Southerners owned small farms and did not own slaves. (In 1860, approximately one-quarter of white Southern families owned slaves.)

Westward Expansion

The Louisiana Purchase removed one major obstacle to U.S. western settlement, and the resolution of the War of 1812 removed another by depriving Native Americans of a powerful ally in Great Britain. By 1820, the United States had settled the region east of the Mississippi River and was quickly expanding west. Americans began to believe that they had a God-given right to the Western territories, an idea that came to be known as America's **Manifest Destiny**. Some took the idea of Manifest Destiny to its logical conclusion and argued that Canada, Mexico, and even all of the land in the Americas eventually would be annexed by the United States.

Western settlement was dangerous. The terrain and climate could be cold and unforgiving, and these settlers from the East were moving into areas that rightfully belonged to Native Americans and Mexicans, none of whom were about to cede their homes without a fight.

Texas presents a good case in point. When Mexico declared its independence from Spain in 1821, the new country included what is now Texas and much of the Southwest, including California. The Mexican government established liberal land policies to entice settlers, and tens of thousands of Americans (many of them cattle ranchers) flooded the region. In return for land, the settlers were supposed to become Mexican citizens, but they rarely did. Instead, they ignored Mexican law, including—and especially—the one prohibiting slavery. When Mexico attempted to regain control of the area, the settlers rebelled and declared independence from Mexico. It was during this period that the famous battle at the **Alamo** was fought (1836). For a while, Texas was an independent country, called the **Republic of Texas.** The existence of slavery in the area guaranteed a Congressional battle over statehood, and Texas was not admitted to the Union until 1845.

Farther west and north, settlers were also pouring into the **Oregon Territory**. During the early 1840s, thousands of settlers traveled to the Willamette Valley, braving a six-month journey on the Oregon Trail. Again, the Americans were not the first ones in; not only was there a large Native American population, but the British were also there, claiming the territory for Canada. The Russians also staked a claim, and both the British and the Americans saw them as a threat. The Polk administration eventually settled the territorial dispute by signing a treaty with England.

By the late 1840s, though, those heading along the Oregon Trail had a new destination—**California**. In 1848, the discovery of gold in the California mountains set off the **Gold Rush**, attracting more than 100,000 people to the Golden State in just two years. Most of these people did not strike it rich, but they settled the area after discovering that it was very hospitable to agriculture. Its access to the Pacific Ocean allowed major cities such as San Francisco to develop as important trade centers.

Economic Reasons for Regional Differences

Throughout the first half of the 19th century, three different sections of the country—North, South, and West, including what is today known as the Midwest —developed in very different directions. Accordingly, they did not see eye to eye on many issues; thus, historians often refer to **sectional strife** during this period.

The **North**, as mentioned earlier, was becoming industrialized. Technological advances in communications, transportation, industry, and banking were helping it become the nation's commercial center. Farming played less of a role in the Northeastern economy than it did elsewhere in the country, and legal slavery became increasingly uncommon in this region's states throughout the early 1800s.

The **South**, meanwhile, remained almost entirely agrarian. Its chief crops—tobacco and cotton—required vast acreage, and so Southerners were constantly looking west for more land. Anxious to protect slavery, which the large landholders depended on, Southerners also looked for new slave territories to include in the Union in order to strengthen their position in Congress and protect slavery from Northern legislators, who in ever-increasing numbers sought to make slavery illegal.

Western economic interests were varied but were largely rooted in commercial farming, fur trapping, and real-estate speculation. Westerners generally distrusted the North, which they regarded as the home of powerful banks that could take their land away. They had little more use for the South, whose rigidly hierarchical society was at odds with the egalitarianism of the West. Most Westerners wanted to avoid involvement in the slavery issue, which they regarded as irrelevant to their lives. Ironically, Western expansion was the core of the most important conflicts leading up to the Civil War.

Know Your Regional Trends

Remember these regional generalizations; by using them (and some common sense), you can often answer specific AP questions. Take, for example, a question dealing with a specific tariff. Even if you do not remember the details of the tariff—and chances are you will not—you should remember that the North, as a commercial and manufacturing center, would probably support it because a tariff makes imports more expensive and therefore reduces competition with American goods. Southerners would probably oppose it because a tariff reduces competition and therefore raises prices. (Also, tariffs helped the North, and Southerners did not like the North.) Likewise, as the 19th century turned to the 20th, Republicans tended to support a high tariff and the Democrats a lower one, so pay attention to who's in office, i.e., McKinley, Teddy Roosevelt, or Wilson. Note: The AP Exam asks about events that illustrate important general trends in American history. If there was a 19th-century tariff that the South supported and the North opposed, the test would not ask about it!

SOCIAL HISTORY, 1800–1860

The growth of the American economy in the early 19th century brought about numerous social changes. The invention of the cotton gin, coupled with the advent of the Industrial Revolution in England, altered Southern agriculture, resulting in the region's increased reliance on slave labor. The development of commerce led to a larger middle class, especially in the North but also in Southern and Midwestern cities. Industrialization resulted in bigger cities with large (and often impoverished) migrant and immigrant neighborhoods. Westward migration created a new frontier culture as pioneers dealt with the uniqueness of the West's landscape and climate. Each of these sets of circumstances influenced people's attitudes and ambitions and set the scene for the social and political events of the era.

The North and American Cities

As we discussed previously, the North became the nation's industrial and commercial center during the first half of the 19th century. Accordingly, it became home to many of the nation's major cities. In their early years, American cities faced numerous problems, chiefly the lack of powerful urban governments to oversee their rapid expansion. Modern waste disposal, plumbing, sewers, and incineration were still a long way off, and as a result, cities could be extremely toxic environments. The proximity in which people lived and worked, coupled with sanitation problems, made epidemics not only likely but inevitable.

City life was not, however, without its benefits. First, cities meant jobs. Many Northern farmers, unable to compete with cheaper produce carted in from the West and South by steamship and rail, moved to cities to work in the new factories. Craftsmen, such as tailors, cobblers, and blacksmiths, also found it easier to make a living in cities. Second, cities offered more opportunities for social advancement. In the 1830s and 1840s, as municipal governments grew, cities began to provide important services, such as public schooling. Labor unions began to form; although it would be many decades until they would come close to matching the power of business management, these unions still fought to bring about improvements in the lives of working people, even though they had quite limited success. Middle- and upper-class Americans in cities formed clubs and associations through which they could exert more influence on government and in society. Finally, cities provided a wide variety of leisure-time options, such as theater and sports.

Still, as in the South, there was a great disparity in the **distribution of wealth** in Northern cities. An elite few controlled most of the personal wealth and led lives of power and comfort. Beneath them was the **middle class**, made up of tradesmen, brokers, and other professionals. They worked to reach the plateau at which the women in their families could devote themselves to homemaking instead of wage earning. (Many middle-class women in their teens and early twenties worked—as salesclerks, teachers, and such—before settling down to marriage.) As wage-earning labor was more often performed away from the home, in factories and offices, the notion developed that men should work while women kept house and raised children. That notion, known as the **cult of domesticity**, was supported by popular magazines and novels that glorified home life. The middle classes also constituted much of the market for luxury goods such as housewares and fine furniture. Members of the middle class often rose from the **working class**. In working-class families, men often worked in factories or at low-paying crafts; women often worked at home, taking in sewing. Others worked as domestic servants, and most worked throughout their lives. Such families lived just above the poverty level, and any calamity—loss of a job, injury, sickness, or a death in the family—could plunge them irretrievably into debt. Those in **poverty** were most often recent immigrants. Their numbers swelled in the 1840s and 1850s when the great **immigration waves** from **Ireland** (to the cities in the North) and then **Germany** (to the West) reached

Lydia Maria Child
(1802–1880) was an author dedicated to the cult of domesticity. Her most famous book, *The American Frugal Housewife*, championed the achievement of well-planned housekeeping for even her poorest readers. Child was also an outspoken abolitionist and promoter of women's rights.

the United States. These immigration waves were met with hostility, especially from the working classes, who feared competition for low-paying jobs.

Occasionally tensions would boil over, and American cities were frequently the sites of riots. Particularly in the 1830s and 1840s, religious, ethnic, and/or class strife could escalate to violence and even result in fatalities. Such disturbances were largely responsible for the formation of municipal police departments, which replaced privately run security companies in enforcing the peace.

The South and Rural Life

There were few major urban centers in the South. The majority of Southerners lived instead in rural areas in near isolation. In 1860, the population density of Georgia was 18 people per square mile. Family, not surprisingly, played a dominant role in social life. After family came the church, and after the church, little else. There simply were not enough people around to support organized cultural and leisure events.

With almost no major cities, the South also had few centers of commerce, and while the North developed extensive networks of canals, railroads, and highways, the South's infrastructure remained fairly limited. The major city of the South, New Orleans, relied almost completely on waterways for its trade routes, and therefore grew much more slowly than did Northern cities such as New York and Boston. Consequently, the South did not develop a strong market economy, as did the North; many more Southerners made and grew most of their necessities for survival.

The wealthiest Southern citizens formed an aristocracy of plantation owners. As in the North, the wealthy made up a small minority, but in the South, this group dominated Southern society politically, socially, and economically. Less than one percent of the population owned more than 100 slaves. In fact, more than three-quarters of white Southerners owned no slaves. Of the rest, half owned five or fewer slaves. Only 10 percent of actual slaveholders—fewer than about 2 percent of the white population—held 20 or more slaves.

Plantation owners grew cotton throughout the Deep South and tobacco in the Middle Atlantic, alongside the crops they needed to support their families and slaves. Most convinced themselves that the slave system benefited all of its participants, *including* the slaves. This attitude, called **Southern paternalism**, relied on the perception of blacks as childlike and unable to take care of themselves. Many slaves discovered that life became easier for them when they reinforced such paternalistic instincts and adopted a submissive and grateful demeanor (which will be familiar to you if you've ever seen old Hollywood movies about this period). Slave owners almost always converted their slaves to Christianity, again convinced that they were serving the slaves' best interests. The slaves, in turn, adapted Christianity to their cultures and incorporated their own religions and traditions into their new faith.

Irish Immigration in the Early 19th century

In the early 19th century, Irish Catholic immigrants were primarily unskilled workers who settled in urban areas of the United States, getting jobs working on railroads and building canals. Many Irish also worked in the textile mills of the Northeast; some others worked as fishermen on the East Coast. The Know-Nothing party formed largely as a reaction to Catholic immigrants in the 1850s. Irish immigration continued to be prominent up until the turn of the century when numbers started to stabilize.

Slaves lived in a state of subsistence poverty. They were usually housed in one-room cabins with their families and often with another family. Conditions were overcrowded and unsanitary. Although work conditions varied from region to region and farm to farm, most worked extremely long hours at difficult and tedious labor, and conditions tended to be worse in the Deep South. (Any concern that slaveholders had for their slaves' welfare could arguably be attributed to the fact that importing African slaves was banned in 1808, making it essential to keep one's slaves alive and reproducing. In addition, the purchase price of a slave remained fairly high or even increased.) Moreover, most slaves lived in fear that their families would be broken up by the sale of one or more of them, or they would be sold "down river." Many were subjected to the abuses of vicious overseers.

Most slaves survived the physical and psychological degradation of slavery by developing a unique culture that tended to blend aspects of their African roots with elements of Christianity. Likewise, although slave revolts were rarely successful, many slaves developed subtle methods of resistance that enabled them to maintain an aspect of their dignity. This might include violating a local slave code and sneaking out at night to meet a loved one or managing to learn to read and write despite codes forbidding them to do so.

The majority of Southerners farmed smaller tracts of land. Planters (those with 20 or more slaves) were in the minority—the remaining landholders were **yeomen**, who sometimes had a few slaves but often none at all, working their small tracts of land with their families. Most were of Scottish and Irish descent and farmed in the hills, which were unsuitable for plantation farming. They grew subsistence crops, raised livestock, and sometimes produced a few cash crops, though limited access to Northern markets hindered profit making. Less fortunate were **landless whites**, who either farmed as tenants or hired themselves out as manual laborers. Elevation from this social stratum to the level of yeoman proved very difficult.

The South was also home to more than 250,000 **free blacks**, the descendants of slaves freed by their owners or freed for having fought in the Revolutionary War. Slave codes prevented them from owning guns, drinking liquor, and assembling in groups of more than three (except in church). Prejudice was a constant fact of life. Some owned land or worked at a trade, but most worked as tenant farmers or day laborers. Some were "mulattoes" (biracial individuals), some of whom led lives of relative luxury and refinement in the Deep South, particularly in and around New Orleans.

The West and Frontier Living

During this period, the frontier's boundaries constantly changed. In 1800, the frontier lay east of the Mississippi River. By 1820, nearly all of this eastern territory had attained statehood, and the frontier region consisted of much of the Louisiana Purchase. Settlers also moved to Texas and then to a part of Mexico, in the late 1820s and 1830s. By the early 1840s, the frontier had expanded to include the Pacific Northwest. In 1849, the Gold Rush drew numerous settlers, **Forty-Niners**, to California.

The United States government actively encouraged settlers to move west. It gave away, or sold at reduced rates, large tracts of land to war veterans. The government also loaned money at reduced rates to civilians so that they too could move west. Some settlers, called **squatters**, ignored the requirement to buy land and simply moved onto and appropriated an unoccupied tract as their own.

Settlers in the Ohio Valley and points west soon found that the area was hospitable to grain production and dairy farming. As previously discussed, much of the area was flat and could easily be farmed by new farm implements such as mechanical plows and reapers. Transportation advances made shipping produce easier and more profitable, and soon the Midwest came to be known as "the nation's breadbasket."

Fur trading was another common commercial enterprise on the frontiers. Fur traders were also called "over-mountain men." They were often the first pioneers in a region, and they constantly moved west, one step ahead of farming families. When they reached Oregon, they ran out of places to go. Furthermore, they had hunted beaver to near extinction. A group of former trappers formed the first American government in the Oregon Territory and began lobbying for statehood. The western frontier was also home to **cattle ranchers** and **miners**.

Frontier life was rugged, to say the least. To survive, settlers constantly struggled against the climate, elements, and Native Americans who were not anxious for the whites to settle, having heard about their treatment of Eastern tribes. Still, the frontier offered pioneers opportunities for wealth, freedom, and social advancement—opportunities that were less common in the heavily populated, competitive East and the aristocratic South. Those women who could handle the difficulties of frontier life found their services in great demand, and many made a good living at domestic work and, later, running boardinghouses and hotels. Because of the possibilities for advancement and for "getting a new start in life," the West came to symbolize freedom and equality to many Americans.

Religious and Social Movements

The 19th century saw the beginnings of true social reform in the United States, and much of the impulse to improve the lives of others came from citizens' religious convictions. In fact, early social reform movements grew out of the **Second Great Awakening**, which, like the first, was a period of religious revival, mainly among Methodists, Presbyterians, and Baptists. In the early 1800s, the expansion of the Enlightenment in the United States encouraged more education, which led to more secularism and a decline in church attendance. Preachers like Charles Finney toured the rural regions of western New York and the rural South, spreading evangelical religious beliefs. The Second Great Awakening peaked in the 1820s and 1830s, as church membership soared in the Baptist, Methodist and Presbyterian churches. New religions like the Mormons and Shakers were inspired by the Second Great Awakening, as were social reform movements like the temperance movement. Women were particularly inspired by the Second Great Awakening, and were encouraged to become active leaders in their new church communities.

The western and central regions of New York State were known as the **Burned-over District** for the spiritual fervor that figuratively set the area on fire.

Connections

The reform movements associated with The Second Great Awakening were a precursor to the later reform movements of the Progressive Era. Many of the issues debated in the early 19th century, such as women's suffrage and temperance, would not reach fruition until nearly one hundred years later.

Usually, the most active members of reform groups were women, particularly those of the middle and upper classes. **Temperance societies**, some of which tried to encourage people to sign the pledge not to drink and some of which sought outright prohibition of liquor, formed and remained powerful until the adoption of the Eighteenth Amendment in 1919 provided for nationwide prohibition. (Not coincidentally, prohibition finally succeeded at the same time it became evident to politicians that women would soon gain the right to vote.)

The temperance movement was largely promoted by Protestant churches and reformers, and tied to the rise in Irish and German immigrants who were mostly Catholic, representing the divide between the two branches of Christianity—this will later be expressed in the Nativist movement/Know-Nothing Party. These groups battled other vices as well, particularly **gambling**. By 1860, every state in the Union had outlawed **lotteries**, and many had prohibited other forms of gambling. Many Northern states also prohibited the manufacture or purchase of alcoholic beverages during this period. A group called "The Female Moral Reform Society" led the battle against **prostitution** in the cities, focusing not only on eliminating the profession but also on rehabilitating those women involved in it.

Reform societies also helped bring about **penitentiaries**, **asylums**, and **orphanages** by popularizing the notion that society is responsible for the welfare of its least fortunate. Asylums, orphanages, and houses of refuge for the poor were built to care for those who would previously have been imprisoned or run out of town. With leadership from Dorothea Dix, penitentiaries sought to rehabilitate criminals (rather than simply isolate them from society, as prisons do) by teaching them morality and a "work ethic."

Before we discuss the abolition movement, we need to mention a few other important movements of the period. **The Shakers**, a utopian group that splintered from the Quakers, believed that they and all other churches had grown too interested in this world and too neglectful of their afterlives. Shakers, followers of Mother Ann Lee, isolated themselves in communes where they shared work and its rewards; they also granted near-equal rights to women, even allowing them to attain priesthood. Believing the end of the world was at hand and that sex was an instrument of evil, the Shakers practiced celibacy; their numbers, not surprisingly, diminished. The Shaker revival ended during the 1840s and 1850s. Other Utopian groups included the Oneida community in New York and the New Harmony community in Indiana.

Perhaps the most well-known of these experimental communities was Brook Farm, established near Roxbury, Massachusetts, in 1841. Brook Farm was home to the Transcendentalists, a group of nonconformist Unitarian writers and philosophers who drew their inspiration from European romanticism. Transcendentalists believed that humans contained elements of the divine, and thus they had faith in man's, and ultimately society's, perfectibility. The most famous of these writers were Nathaniel Hawthorne, author of *The Scarlet Letter*; Ralph Waldo Emerson; and Henry David Thoreau. Thoreau is most noted for his publication of *Walden*, an account of the two years he spent living alone in a cabin on Walden Pond outside Concord, Massachusetts. Perhaps not as well-known, but equally significant, was Thoreau's demonstration of civil disobedience. Thoreau refused to pay taxes to a government that waged war against Mexico and subsequently enacted a Fugitive Slave Act as part of the **Compromise of 1850** (see the separate section on this in the next chapter).

Another important group involved in this American Renaissance was the **Hudson River School** painters, the first distinct school of American art. Their goal was to create a specific vision for American art, and they painted mostly landscapes that seemed to portray an awe for the wilderness and beauty of wild America. Like Thoreau and Emerson, the painters were influenced by European romanticism.

The **Mormons**, on the other hand, continue to thrive today. Joseph Smith formed the Church of Jesus Christ of Latter-Day Saints in 1830. Smith's preaching, particularly his acceptance of polygamy, drew strong opposition in the East and Midwest, culminating in his death by a mob while imprisoned in Illinois. The Mormons, realizing that they would never be allowed to practice their faith in the East, made the long, difficult trek to the Salt Lake Valley, led by Brigham Young. There, they settled and transformed the area from desert into farmland through extensive irrigation. The Mormons' success was largely attributable to the settlers' strong sense of community. Through their united efforts, they came to dominate the Utah territory.

The Second Great Awakening was only one source of the antebellum reform movements. By the 1820s and 1830s, most of the Founding Fathers were dead, but they left a legacy of freedom and equality, expressed in part in the Declaration of Independence as well as the Preamble to the Constitution. In the 1830s, "We, the People" still meant white males. Many women were active in the abolitionist movement, and it was their exclusion from participation at a worldwide antislavery convention held in London in 1840 that convinced women like Elizabeth Cady Stanton and Lucretia Mott to hold the first women's rights convention in 1848 in Seneca Falls in upstate New York (in the same Burned-over District from the Second Great Awakening). Stanton and Mott, along with other reformers, published the *Declaration of Rights and Sentiments of Women*, which they modeled after the American Declaration of Independence. The Declaration began, "We hold these truths to be self-evident, that all men *and women* are created equal...." Four years later, Stanton would team up with Susan B. Anthony, with whom she founded the **National Woman Suffrage Association** in 1869.

Finally, **Horace Mann** was instrumental in pushing for public education and education reform in general. He lengthened the school year, established the first "normal school" for teacher training, and used the first standardized books in education (*McGuffey's Reader* was used by 80 percent of public schools). Mann is noted for his belief that "Education is the great equalizer."

At about the same time that the members of the Hudson River School were busy capturing the transcendent elements of nature, **John James Audubon** was painting and cataloging birds for later publication in his seminal work on the subject, *The Birds of America*. Audubon discovered 25 new species of birds and was the inspiration for the Audubon Society, a nonprofit organization dedicated to the conservation of birds.

The Abolition Movement

Before the 1830s, few whites fought aggressively for the liberation of the slaves. The Quakers believed slavery to be morally wrong and argued for its end. Most other antislavery whites, though, sought gradual abolition, coupled with colonization, a movement to return blacks to Africa. For example, the **American Colonization Society**, established in 1816, sought to repatriate slaves to the newly formed country of Liberia in Africa. Many politicians supported the cause, including Henry Clay. The religious and moral fervor that accompanied the Second Great Awakening, however, persuaded more and more whites, particularly Northerners, that slavery was a great evil. As in other reform movements, women played a prominent role, such as the Grimke sisters from South Carolina, who were early abolitionists despite growing up in a slave-holding family..

White abolitionists divided into two groups. Moderates wanted emancipation to take place slowly and with the cooperation of slave owners. **Immediatists**, as their name implies, wanted emancipation at once. Most prominent among white immediatists was **William Lloyd Garrison,** who began publishing a popular abolitionist newspaper called the *Liberator* in 1831 and helped found the **American Antislavery Society** in 1833. His early subscribers were mostly free blacks, but as time passed, his paper caught on with white abolitionists as well.

Garrison fought against slavery and against moderates as well, decrying their plans for black resettlement in Africa as racist and immoral. Garrison's persistence and powerful writing style helped force the slavery issue to the forefront. His message, as you may imagine, did not go over well everywhere; some Southern states banned the newspaper, and others prohibited *anyone* from discussing emancipation. When congressional debate over slavery became too heated, Congress adopted a **gag rule** that automatically suppressed discussion of the issue. It also prevented Congress from enacting any new legislation pertaining to slavery. The rule, which lasted from 1836 to 1844, along with Southern restrictions on free speech, outraged many Northerners and convinced them to join the abolition movement.

The abolition movement existed prior to 1830, but it had been primarily supported by free blacks such as **David Walker**. A Bostonian, his Appeal to the Colored People of the World told all freed black people to work to end slavery. His work inspired William Lloyd Garrison. Abolition associations formed in every large black community to assist fugitive slaves and publicize the struggle against slavery; these groups met at a national convention every year after 1830 to coordinate strategies. In the 1840s, **Frederick Douglass** began publishing his influential newspaper *The North Star*. Douglass, an escaped slave, gained fame as a gifted writer and eloquent advocate of freedom and equality; his *Narrative of the Life of Frederick Douglass* is one of the great American autobiographies. Other prominent black abolitionists included **Harriet Tubman**, who escaped slavery and then returned south repeatedly to help more than 300 slaves escape via the **underground railroad** (a network of hiding places and "safe" trails); and **Sojourner Truth**, a charismatic speaker who campaigned for emancipation and women's rights.

Abolitionists' determination and the South's inflexibility pushed the issue of slavery into the political spotlight. Westward expansion, and the question of whether slavery would be allowed in the new territories, forced the issue further. Together, they set in motion the events that led up to the Civil War.

The AP and Retrospect

Abolitionism is an important topic on every AP U.S. History Exam. But it is worth noting that, right up to the Civil War, abolitionists were widely considered extremists. Far and away the leading reform movement of the time was the temperance movement. Nearly all abolitionists believed in temperance; few supporters of temperance were abolitionists. But as the abolition movement succeeded (slavery is now illegal), the success of the temperance movement was short-lived (Prohibition lasted only from 1920 to 1933), so you'll find a lot more questions about the former than about the latter.

Although slavery persisted in the United States, many European Enlightenment thinkers criticized slavery on human rights grounds. A member of the British Parliament, James Edward Oglethorpe, was among the first to argue against slavery. Granville Sharp, Hannah More, and William Wilberforce were also famous abolitionists.

Summary

Here are the most important concepts to remember from the American Democracy period.

o   The new United States struggled to define its ideals as boundaries changed and regional opinions clashed.

o   New developments in technology, agriculture, and commerce built wealth and infrastructure, transforming America from a wilderness to a developed society.

o   Relationships with Britain and France were problematic, each country playing one off the other. After the War of 1812, relationships stabilized.

o   Slavery became one of the most controversial issues in politics and the social sphere.

o   Abolitionists, feminists, and temperance activists organized, published, and lectured to promote their ideas.

Chapter 8 Review Questions

See Chapter 14 for answers and explanations.

1. Although the Supreme Court was the weakest of the three branches of government in the early days of the new republic, John Marshall strengthened the Court by

   (A) establishing the principle of federalism, giving federal courts the power to declare laws unconstitutional

   (B) declaring the Virginia and Kentucky Resolutions, which asserted the right of states to nullify federal laws, unconstitutional

   (C) establishing the principle of judicial review in the case of *McCulloch v. Maryland*

   (D) establishing the principle of judicial review in the case of *Marbury v. Madison*

2. The Louisiana Purchase was an important factor in the development of U.S. trade because it

   (A) opened new markets among the western Indian nations

   (B) gave the country complete control of the Mississippi River

   (C) added numerous French factories in the Louisiana Territory to the U.S. economy

   (D) facilitated the immediate completion of the transcontinental railroad

3. As a result of the Hartford Convention following the War of 1812,

   (A) the Federalist party lost credibility and eventually died out

   (B) the Constitution was amended to limit the president to two terms in office

   (C) the New England states threatened to secede

   (D) Congress passed the War Powers Act, limiting future presidents from gaining too much power during wartime, as Madison had

4. Andrew Jackson accused Henry Clay of using his influence to broker the "corrupt bargain" of 1824 (which cost Andrew Jackson the election) because Clay

   (A) was promised a cabinet position if John Quincy Adams was elected president

   (B) was promised the vice presidency if Jackson was defeated

   (C) knew Jackson did not support his "American System"

   (D) feared Jackson's pro-slavery stance on states' rights

5. The controversy over the tariff during the late 1820s and early 1830s demonstrated that

   (A) New Englanders were more radical than Southerners, as they had been since the days of the American Revolution

   (B) Andrew Jackson favored states' rights over federal supremacy

   (C) the system of checks and balances was flawed

   (D) economic sectionalism was a serious threat to national unity

6. Andrew Jackson's positions on the Second National Bank and the American System typified his

   (A) distrust of large national government programs

   (B) abhorrence of the spoils system

   (C) tendency to favor the interests of the Northeast

   (D) commitment to developing a national economy

7. The Cherokee of Georgia were forced off their land because

   (A) they refused to assimilate to the "American" way of life

   (B) gold was discovered in their territory and Georgians demanded that the Indian Removal Act be enforced

   (C) the Supreme Court refused to hear their cases

   (D) the Seminole tribe, their traditional enemy, conquered their territory

8. Brook Farm in Massachusetts, the Oneida Community in upstate New York, and New Harmony in Indiana were similar in that they

   (A) were religious communities inspired by the Second Great Awakening

   (B) demonstrated the attraction of communism to many Americans

   (C) failed because they practiced political and social equality within their own communities

   (D) were utopian communities designed to ameliorate the effects of a growing commercial society

REFLECT

Respond to the following questions:

- For which content topics discussed in this chapter do you feel you have achieved sufficient mastery to answer multiple-choice questions correctly?

- For which content topics discussed in this chapter do you feel you have achieved sufficient mastery to discuss effectively in a short-answer question or an essay?

- On which content topics discussed in this chapter do you feel you need more work before you can answer multiple-choice questions correctly?

- On which content topics discussed in this chapter do you feel you need more work before you can discuss them effectively in a short-answer question or an essay?

- What parts of this chapter are you going to review again?

- Will you seek further help, outside of this book (such as a teacher, tutor, or AP Students), on any of the content in this chapter—and, if so, on what content?

Chapter 9
Toward the
Civil War and
Reconstruction
(1844–1877)

POLITICAL AND JUDICIAL ACTIVITY BEFORE THE WAR

The election of 1844 pitted **James Polk** against Whig leader Henry Clay. Though the differences between the Whig and Democratic platforms may seem hazy by modern standards, and there was more than a little overlap, in one respect the two parties were sharply opposed. Above all else, the Whigs stood for a policy of **internal improvements**: building bridges, dredging harbors, digging canals, and in short civilizing the lands the United States already possessed. Democrats tended to be expansionists, set on pushing the nation's borders ever outward. They also felt that it was not the government's place to do anything with newly added land, and it should instead be kept in private hands, even if that meant living in a country of meandering dirt roads instead of railways. Compare Whig-dominated New England, dotted with bustling towns and busy factories, to the heavily Democratic South with its isolated plantations, and you have a sense of the two parties' disparate visions for America. The election was close, but Polk won.

The Polk Presidency

Polk took office with four goals, and having pledged to serve only one term, had only four years in which to accomplish them. The first goal was to restore the practice of keeping government funds in the Treasury; Andrew Jackson had kept them in so-called **pet banks**, and the results had been disastrous. The second was to reduce tariffs. Both of these were accomplished by the end of 1846.

In the last days of his administration, President Tyler had proposed the annexation of Texas. Northern congressmen were alarmed: Texas was huge and lay entirely south of the Missouri Compromise line, raising the prospect that it might end up being divided into as many as five slave states. They demanded that Polk maintain the balance by annexing the entirety of the Oregon Country, which stretched from the Mexican territory of Alta California at 42° north up to the Russian territory of Alaska at 54°40′ north. "54°40′ or Fight," they demanded—yes, this was *not* Polk's slogan, but one directed *at* him—but Polk recognized that the United States could hardly afford to fight two territorial wars at the same time, particularly if one was against Great Britain, the other claimant to the Oregon Country. Consequently, he conceded on demands for expansion deep into Canada and set about instead to negotiate a more reasonable American-Canadian border. The **Oregon Treaty**, signed with Great Britain in 1846, allowed the United States to acquire peacefully what is now Oregon, Washington, and parts of Idaho, Wyoming, and Montana. It also established the current northern border of the region.

Reasonably certain that war in the Northwest could be avoided, Polk concentrated on efforts to claim the Southwest from Mexico. He tried to buy the territory, and when that failed, he challenged Mexican authorities on the border of Texas, provoking a Mexican attack on American troops. Mexico was already agitated over the annexation of Texas, which had gained its independence from Mexico in 1836 (remember the Alamo?). Polk then used the border attack to argue for a declaration of war. Congress granted the declaration, and in 1846 the **Mexican-American War** began. Whigs, such as first-term member of the House of Representatives Abraham Lincoln, questioned Polk's claim that the Mexicans had fired first, but Congress declared war anyway.

The Mexican-American War did not have universal support from the American public. Northerners feared that new states in the West would become slave states, thus tipping the balance in Congress in favor of proslavery forces. Opponents argued that Polk had provoked Mexico into war at the request of powerful slaveholders, and the idea that a few slave owners had control over the government became popular. Those rich Southerners who allegedly were "pulling the strings" were referred to as the **Slave Power** by suspicious Northerners. The **gag rule** in 1836 raised suspicions of a Slave Power and the defeat of the **Wilmot Proviso**, a congressional bill prohibiting the extension of slavery into any territory gained from Mexico, reinforced those suspicions. The main thing to remember about the Wilmot Proviso is the outcome of the vote:

"Spot" Resolutions

Whigs were almost universally opposed to the Mexican-American War, as were abolitionists and anti-imperialists. When the young Whig Abraham Lincoln was a Representative in the U.S. Congress, he proposed a series of "spot" resolutions, demanding that Democrat President Polk reveal the exact "spot" where American blood had been spilled by Mexican soldiers, Polk's main argument when asking for the War. Lincoln was later criticized by some for this persistent approach and was nicknamed "spotty Lincoln."

Wilmot Proviso House vote	Whigs	Democrats
Northern	all in favor	all but four in favor
Southern	all but two opposed	all opposed

As you can see, the vote fell along not *party* lines but *sectional* ones, an ominous sign. Over the course of the next decade, the Democrats would become even more Southern-dominated than before, while the Whigs would split between the anti-slavery, Northern "Conscience Whigs" and the pro-slavery, Southern "Cotton Whigs," and would thus follow the Federalists into extinction. New parties would rise to take its place, the first of which was the **Free-Soil Party**, a regional, single-issue party devoted to the goals of the Wilmot Proviso. It should be noted that the Free-Soil Party was largely opposed to the expansion of slavery not because they were abolitionists but because they didn't want white settlers to have to compete with slave labor in new territories.

While debate raged on, so too did the Mexican War, which went very well for American forces. The United States prevailed so easily in Texas that Polk not only ordered troops south to Mexico but also across the Southwest and into California, hoping to grab the entire region by war's end. When the United States successfully invaded Mexico City, the war was over. In the **Treaty of Guadalupe Hidalgo** (1848), Mexico handed over almost all of the modern Southwest: Arizona, New Mexico, California, Nevada, and Utah. This is known as the **Mexican Cession**. The United States, in return, paid $15 million for the land.

The addition of this new territory greatly increased the nation's potential wealth, especially when gold was found at Sutter's Mill during the year that the treaty was signed. However, it also posed major problems regarding the status of slavery. The chief problem was this. By an accident of geography, it just so happened that, east of the Mississippi, the territory of the United States was divided evenly between lands suited for plantation agriculture, where slavery flourished, and those that were not, and where slavery died out shortly after independence. Now the country extended all the way to the Pacific—but even south of the Missouri Compromise line, lands west of the Mississippi were not suitable for growing cotton, or tobacco, or any of the traditional plantation crops. Southerners saw a future in which slavery was confined, not to the *southern half* of the country, but to the *southeastern quarter* of it, and where they would therefore be greatly outvoted should free-soil advocates decide to ban slavery everywhere. Southerners therefore decided that the time had come to rip up the Missouri Compromise and attempt to open up more areas to slavery. Their first step was to introduce the concept of **popular sovereignty**. Popular sovereignty meant that the territories themselves would decide, by vote, whether to allow slavery within their borders.

The Compromise of 1850: Major Players

Henry Clay

- Whig Senator from Kentucky
- Drafted and formally proposed the Compromise of 1850
- Helped to clarify the final boundaries of Texas
- Originally proposed banning slavery in the entire Mexican Cession
- Wanted a stringent Fugitive Slave Act

John Calhoun

- Democrat Senator from South Carolina
- Defender of slavery
- Opposed the Compromise of 1850
- Advocate for states' rights and secession
- Spurred notion of popular sovereignty for Mexican Cession territories

Daniel Webster

- Whig Senator from Massachusetts
- Supported the Compromise in order to preserve the Union and avert Civil War
- In the Seventh of March speech, characterized himself "not as a Massachusetts man, nor as a Northern man, but as an American..."
- Risked offending his abolitionist voter base by accepting the Compromise

The Compromise of 1850

Sectional strife over the new territories started as the ink was drying on the Treaty of Guadalupe Hidalgo. During the Gold Rush, settlers had flooded into California, and the populous territory wanted statehood. Californians had already drawn up a state constitution. That constitution prohibited slavery, and so, of course, the South opposed California's bid for statehood. At the very least, proslavery forces argued, southern California should be forced to accept slavery, in accordance with the boundary drawn by the Missouri Compromise of 1820. The debate grew so hostile that Southern legislators began to discuss openly the possibility of secession.

Democrat **Stephen Douglas** (not to be confused with black abolitionist Frederick Douglass) and Whig Henry Clay hammered out what they thought to be a workable solution, known as the **Compromise of 1850**. When presented as a complete package, the compromise was defeated in Congress. Douglas, however, realized that different groups supported different parts of the compromise, and so he broke the package down into separate bills. He managed to organize majorities to support each of the component bills, and thus ushered the entire compromise through Congress. Together, the bills admitted California as a free state, at the price of the enactment of a stronger **fugitive slave law**. They also created the territories of Utah and New Mexico, but they left the status of slavery up to each territory to decide only when it came time for each to write its constitution, thus reinforcing the concept of **popular sovereignty**. The Compromise of 1850 abolished the slave *trade*, not slavery itself, in Washington, D.C. Proponents of this provision argued that it was immoral to "buy and sell human flesh in the shadow of the nation's capitol."

Instituting popular sovereignty and a new fugitive slave law posed serious problems. The definition of popular sovereignty was so vague that Northerners and Southerners could interpret the law entirely differently to suit their own positions. The fugitive slave law, meanwhile, made it much easier to retrieve escaped slaves, but it required citizens of free states to cooperate in their retrieval. Abolitionists considered it coercive, immoral, and an affront to their liberty.

Antislavery sentiments in the North grew stronger in 1852 with the publication of *Uncle Tom's Cabin*, a sentimental novel written by Harriet Beecher Stowe, a then-obscure writer. Stowe, a Northerner, based her damning depictions of plantation life on information provided her by abolitionist friends. She wisely avoided political preaching, instead playing on people's sympathies. The book sold more than a million copies and was adapted into several popular plays that toured America and Europe. Like Thomas Paine's *Common Sense* during the Revolutionary War era, it was an extremely powerful piece of propaganda, awakening antislavery sentiment in millions who had never before given the issue much thought.

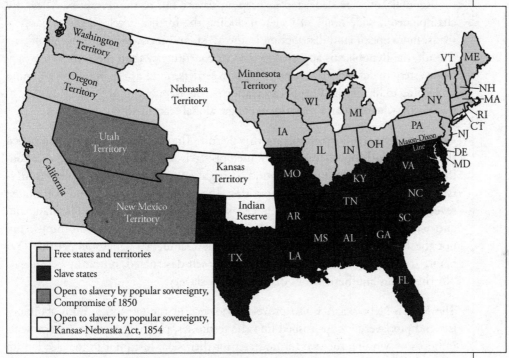

Kansas-Nebraska Act, 1854

The Kansas-Nebraska Act and "Bleeding Kansas"

After California, no new states would be admitted to the Union until 1858. However, the contentious status of the new territories proved increasingly problematic. Settlers entering the Kansas and Nebraska territories found no established civil authority. Congress also wanted to build railways through the territory, but they needed some form of government to impose order, secure land (a task that included driving out Native Americans), and supervise construction.

Illinois Senator Stephen Douglas promoted the Kansas-Nebraska Act because he wanted the transcontinental railroad to terminate in Illinois, which would bring money and jobs to his home state. Douglas worked to create a coalition of Southerners who would want to repeal the Missouri Compromise and Northerners who wanted the railroad to end in the Illinois region, getting the act passed through Congress over the strong objection of antislavery Whigs and antislavery Democrats. Northerners considered the new law a betrayal, regarding it as further evidence of the Slave Power's domination of government. In response, many Northern states passed laws weakening the fugitive slave act. These laws, called **personal liberty laws**, required a trial by jury for all alleged fugitives and guaranteed them the right to a lawyer. Southerners, who thought the fugitive slave law would be the final word on the issue, were furious.

The Kansas-Nebraska Act also drove the final stake into the heart of the Whig party. Antislavery Whigs, growing more impassioned about the issue and more convinced that the national party would never take a strong stand, joined Northern Democrats and former Free-Soilers (whose single issue was effectively defeated by Kansas-Nebraska) to form a new party, the **Republicans**. Though not abolitionist, the Republicans were dedicated to keeping slavery out of the territories. They also championed a wide range of issues, including the further development of national roads, more liberal land distribution in the West, and increased protective tariffs. As a result, the Republicans appealed to a wider constituency than the Free-Soilers had. Midwestern merchants and farmers, Western settlers, and Eastern importers all found something to like in the Republican platform. The Republican party grew quickly in the North, where it won a majority of congressional seats in 1854.

Another new party formed during this period. The **American** party, often called the **Know-Nothings** because they met privately and remained secretive about their political agenda, rallied around a single issue: hatred of foreigners (**nativism**), a perennial favorite in U.S. politics. The party grew quickly and dominated several state legislatures. It also spread some ugly anti-Irish, anti-German, and anti-Catholic propaganda. For a while it appeared that the Know-Nothings, and not the Republican party, would become the Democrats' chief competition. Yet before it could reach that pinnacle, the party self-destructed, primarily because its Northern and Southern wings disagreed over slavery.

The Kansas-Nebraska Act also provoked violence in the territories. Both abolitionists and proslavery groups rushed into the territories, planning to form governments in hopes of winning the two future states for their side. Just prior to the election for Kansas's legislature, thousands of proslavery Missourians (called **Border Ruffians**) temporarily relocated in Kansas, resulting in rival constitutions being sent to Washington: an antislavery one from Topeka and a proslavery one from Lecompton. President Franklin Pierce, a "doughface" (as Northerners who supported pro-Southern policies were called), recognized the Lecompton Constitution and promptly declared Kansas a slave territory. Proslavery forces took Pierce's recognition as a license to expel the free-soilers, and they demolished the free-soil city of Lawrence. In retaliation, radical abolitionist **John Brown** led a raid on a proslavery camp, murdering five. After that, the gloves *really* came off, as gangs from both sides roamed the territory and attacked the opposition. More than 200 people died in the conflict, which is how Kansas came to be known as **Bleeding Kansas**, or **Bloody Kansas**, during this period.

The events in Kansas further polarized the nation. The passions raised were even reflected in Congress when Preston Brooks, nephew of proslavery Senator **Andrew Butler**, savagely beat abolitionist Senator Charles Sumner on the head with a cane for a speech in which Sumner attacked both the South and Butler, using lewd metaphors about slavery. The crisis destroyed Pierce's political career, and the Democrats chose **James Buchanan** as their 1856 candidate. Buchanan's greatest political asset was that he had been out of the country for the previous four years and so could avoid blame for the disastrous results of the Kansas-Nebraska Act. In a sectional vote, Buchanan won the election, carrying the South, while the North split between Buchanan and Republican John Frémont. The Know-Nothings ran Millard Fillmore, who won 20 percent of the vote. It was the Know-Nothings' last hurrah.

Buchanan, Dred Scott, and the Election of 1860

As president, **James Buchanan** tried to maintain the status quo. He worked to enforce the fugitive slave act and opposed abolitionist activism in the South and West. Like many of the nation's leaders at the time, he was at a loss when it came to a permanent solution to the question of slavery. He hoped merely to maintain the Union until a solution presented itself.

Two days after Buchanan took office, the crisis over slavery escalated when the Supreme Court ruled in **Dred Scott v. Sandford**. Scott, a former slave whose master had taken him to territories where slavery was illegal, declared himself a free man and sued for his freedom. Scott won the case but lost the appeal, and the case finally wound up in the Supreme Court where Scott lost. At a time when many wanted to ignore the big questions surrounding slavery, Chief Justice Roger Taney (who wrote the majority decision) chose to attack them head-on. Taney's one-sided, proslavery decision declared that slaves were property, not citizens, and further, that no black person could ever be a citizen of the United States. Because blacks were not citizens, Taney argued, they could not sue in federal courts, as Scott had done. Moreover, he ruled that Congress could not regulate slavery in the territories, as it had done in passing the Northwest Ordinance in 1787 under the Articles of Confederation government and again in 1820 with the Missouri Compromise. This part of the decision not only nullified the now obsolete Missouri Compromise but also the Kansas-Nebraska Act, and it ruled out any hope of reviving the Wilmot Proviso, which was still championed by many Northerners and abolitionists.

In exercising judicial review and declaring the Missouri Compromise unconstitutional, Taney and the Court were in essence saying that slavery could go anywhere; the Republicans' goal of preventing the spread of slavery into the new territories was destroyed by the Court's ruling. The *Dred Scott* decision was thus a major victory for Southerners and a turning point in the "decade of crisis."

In the North, the Supreme Court decision was viciously denounced. Even those who lacked strong abolitionist sentiments feared that the decision tilted the balance of power too far in the South's favor. Many, including the press, regarded the decision as further proof of a Slave Power that, if left unchecked, would soon dominate the entire country, perhaps even forcing slavery on those states that did not want it. Meanwhile, the Democratic party was dividing along regional lines, raising the possibility that the Republicans might soon control the national government.

1858 was an off-year election, and it was in this politically charged atmosphere that the famous Lincoln-Douglas debates took place. Students often think the debates were for the presidential election, but they weren't. Douglas faced stiff competition for his Illinois Senate seat from **Abraham Lincoln**, a rising star in the newly formed Republican party. The race for Illinois's Senate seat gained national attention in part because of the railroad and telegraph. Stephen Douglas was viewed as the leading Democrat in the United States Senate, while Lincoln had gained his reputation as a Whig opposed to the Mexican War and Kansas-Nebraska Act.

In many ways, the Lincoln-Douglas debates gave voice to the issues and concerns that divided a nation heading for civil war. It was in this campaign that Lincoln delivered his famous "House Divided" speech ("this government cannot endure, permanently, half slave and half free"), while Douglas destroyed his political career in his attempt to defend popular sovereignty in what became known as the **Freeport Doctrine**. Douglas tried to depict Lincoln as an abolitionist, but Lincoln skillfully backed Douglas into a corner when he pushed him to reconcile popular sovereignty with the *Dred Scott* decision. Douglas suggested that slavery could not exist where local laws did not protect it. In essence, he contended, voters and residents of a territory could exclude slavery simply by not protecting a man's "property." Douglas alienated both Northern and Southern voters by his ambiguous stance on popular sovereignty and effectively destroyed any chance he might have had for winning the presidency in 1860.

Adding fuel to the secessionist fire was **John Brown**'s raid on **Harper's Ferry** in 1859. Brown hoped to spark a slave revolt but failed. After his execution, news spread that Brown had received financial backing from Northern abolitionist organizations. Brown became a martyr for the cause, celebrated throughout the North.

When it came time for the Democrats to choose their 1860 presidential candidate, their convention split. Northern Democrats backed Douglas; Southerners backed John Breckinridge. The election showed that the nation itself was on the brink of fracture. In the North, the contest was between Douglas and Republican nominee Abraham Lincoln. In the South, Breckinridge faced off against Constitutional Union Party nominee John Bell; Lincoln didn't even appear on Southern ballots. But the North held the majority of the electoral votes, so when Lincoln achieved a clean sweep there, he won the election. The response in Southern legislatures was to propose bills of secession.

Immediately after the election, Southern leaders who wanted to maintain the Union tried to negotiate and came up with the Crittendon Compromise. All hope of resolution died, however, when Lincoln refused to soften the Republican demand that slavery not be extended to the territories. Lincoln probably had no other political option, as to do otherwise would have been to abandon the principles of those who had supported his election. Lincoln and other Northern leaders were banking on the hope that the South was bluffing and would not secede.

In December 1860, three months before Lincoln's inauguration, South Carolina seceded from the Union. Within months, six other states had joined South Carolina to form the **Confederate States of America**; the states chose **Jefferson Davis** to lead the Confederacy. Cautiously, Lincoln decided to maintain control of federal forts in the South while waiting for the Confederacy to make a move. On April 12, 1861, it did, attacking and capturing **Fort Sumter**. No one died in this first battle of America's bloodiest war, the **Civil War**.

Fire-Eaters

The Fire-Eaters were a group of radical pro-slavery Southerners who wanted secession and the creation of the Confederacy. The most prominent leader of this group was Robert Barnwell Rhett of South Carolina, but John C. Calhoun was its most famous member. The Fire-Eaters also sought to reinstate the international slave trade, thus expanding slavery and making it more profitable.

THE CIVIL WAR AND RECONSTRUCTION (1860–1877)

For many people of the era, the Civil War was not solely (or even explicitly) about slavery. It is worth noting that Missouri, Kentucky, Maryland, and Delaware, the **Border States**, were slave states that fought for the Union. Except for active abolitionists, most Northerners believed they were fighting to preserve the Union. Most Southerners described their cause as fighting for their **states' rights** to govern themselves. But slavery was the issue that had caused the argument over states' rights to escalate to war. Lincoln's views on slavery evolved throughout the 1850s and the Civil War, but as late as 1862, Lincoln stated, "If I could save the Union without freeing any slaves I would do it, and if I could save the union by freeing all the slaves I would do it…. What I do about slavery, and the colored race, I do because I believe it helps to save the Union."

The Civil War took place not only on the battlefields but also in political, economic, and social realms. Although you do not need to know the military details of any specific battles for the AP Exam, you should know the political or diplomatic consequences of battles like Gettysburg or Antietam, and you do need to know how political, social, and economic conditions influenced the outcome of the war.

The Battle of Antietam, fought in September 1862, was the first battle fought in the East where the Union wasn't completely defeated. By forcing the Confederacy to retreat, the Union claimed the battle was a victory. This "victory" gave Lincoln the platform he needed to announce the Emancipation Proclamation. It was also important to show Britain and France that the Union wasn't a lost cause, and put off those countries possibly helping the Confederacy.

The Battle of Gettysburg was fought in southern Pennsylvania. It was the most northern point the Confederacy had reached at the time. Lee's troops suffered massive casualties and were forced to retreat. This served as a massive confidence boost for the Union.

Four months after the Battle of Gettysburg, President Lincoln delivered his most famous speech, the **Gettysburg Address**. In only two minutes, the Address helped to redefine the War as not only a struggle to preserve the Union, but also as a struggle for human equality.

The Civil War and the Confederacy

Ironically, as the Southern states fought to maintain the right to govern themselves locally, the Confederate government brought them under greater central control than they had ever experienced. Jefferson Davis understood the North's considerable advantages in population, transportation, and economics, and he knew that the weak, poorly organized state governments of the South could not mount an effective defense. Davis took control of the Southern economy, imposing taxes and using the revenues to spur industrial and urban growth; he took control of the railroads and commercial shipping; and he created a large government bureaucracy to oversee economic developments. Davis, in short, forced the South to compensate quickly for what it had lost when it cut itself off from Northern commerce. When Southerners opposed his moves, he declared martial law and suspended the writ of *habeas corpus*, a traditional protection against improper imprisonment, in order to maintain control. Lincoln was upsetting Northerners with some of the exact same steps, but the use of the presidential power chafed especially badly in the Confederacy, where many believed they had seceded precisely to avoid the federal government commanding too much power.

Davis had some success in modernizing the Southern economy, but the Confederacy lagged too far behind in industrialization to catch up to the Union. Rapid economic growth, furthermore, brought with it rapid **inflation**. Prices rose so quickly that paychecks and payments for crops became worthless almost as soon as they were made, plunging many Southerners into poverty. In 1862, the Confederacy imposed **conscription** (a military draft), requiring many small farmers to serve in the Confederate Army. This act caused even greater poverty in the country, as many families could not adequately tend their farms without their men.

Confederate conscription also created class conflict. The government allowed the wealthy to hire surrogates to perform military service in their place and exempted anyone who owned more than 20 slaves from military service (on the grounds that the large plantations these men ran fed the Confederacy and its army). In effect, the wealthy did not have to serve, while the poor had no choice. As a result, **class tensions** increased, leading ultimately to widespread desertions from the Confederate Army. Toward the end of the war, it also led many Southerners in small towns to ignore the government and try to carry on as if there was no war. Many resisted when asked to feed, clothe, or house passing troops.

The Civil War and the Union

The Northern economy received a boost from the war as the demand for war-related goods, such as uniforms and weapons, spurred manufacturing. The loss of Southern markets harmed the economy at first, but soon the war economy brought about a boom period. A number of entrepreneurs became extremely wealthy; many succumbed to the temptations of greed, overcharging the government for services and products (**war profiteering**). Some sold the Union government worthless, shoddy food and clothing, while government bureaucrats looked the other way for the price of a bribe. Corruption was fairly widespread, eventually prompting a yearlong congressional investigation.

Like the South, the North experienced a period of accelerated inflation, although Northern inflation was nowhere as extreme as its Southern counterpart. (In the North, prices rose between 10 and 20 percent annually; in the South, the inflation rate was well over 300 percent.) Workers, worried about job security in the face of mechanization and the decreasing value of their wages, formed **unions**. Businesses, in return, blacklisted union members, forced new employees to sign contracts in which they promised not to join unions, and used violence to break strikes. The Republican Party, then (as now) believing that government should help businesses but regulate them as little as possible, supported business in its opposition to unions.

Lincoln, like Davis, oversaw a tremendous increase in the power of the central government during the war. He implemented economic development programs without waiting for congressional approval, championed numerous government loans and grants to businesses, and raised tariffs to protect Union trade. He also suspended the writ of *habeas corpus* in the border states, to make it easier to arrest secessionists, especially in Maryland. During the war, Lincoln initiated the printing of a **national currency**. Lincoln's able treasury secretary, Salmon P. Chase, issued **greenbacks**, government-issued paper money that was a precursor to modern currency.

Emancipation of the Slaves

As previously stated, neither the Union nor the Confederacy initially declared the Civil War to be a war about slavery. The Constitution protected slavery where it already existed, so many opponents (including Republicans) were opposed to the *extension* of slavery into the new territories. As a presidential candidate, Lincoln had argued for gradual emancipation, compensation to slaveholders for liberated slaves, and the colonization of freed slaves somewhere outside the United States, perhaps in Africa. When the Union dissolved and the South left Congress, Lincoln was faced with a legislature much more progressive in its thoughts on slavery than he was. The **Radical Republican** wing of Congress wanted immediate emancipation. To that end, the radicals introduced the **confiscation acts** in Congress. The first (1861) gave the government the right to seize any slaves used for "insurrectionary purposes." The second (1862) was much wider in scope, allowing the government to liberate any slave owned by someone who supported the rebellion, even if that support was limited to paying taxes to the Confederate government. The second confiscation act, in effect, gave the Union the right to liberate all slaves. This act had little effect, however, because Lincoln refused to enforce it.

Soon after, however, Lincoln took his first cautious steps toward emancipation. The primary reason was pretty simple: slaves indirectly supported the Southern war effort. They grew the crops and cooked the meals that kept the rebel troops fed. Therefore, any strategy the Union army adopted had to include capturing slaves as a key element. But what to do with them once they were captured? Lock them up somewhere and return them to their owners after the war? They had to be freed, or the government of the United States would become the world's biggest slaveholder. And there were other advantages of making the freedom of the slaves one of the side effects of Union victory. One was that it kept Britain and France out of the war. Jefferson Davis had hoped that these countries would support the Confederacy in order to keep receiving shipments of Southern cotton, but once Lincoln made it explicit that Union victory would mean freedom for the slaves, European governments dared not attempt to come to the aid of the rebels for fear of being quickly toppled by an outraged public. Another advantage was that emancipation would provide a new source of troops for the Union side: "The bare sight of 50 thousand armed and drilled black soldiers on the banks of the Mississippi would end the rebellion at once," Lincoln mused. But he dared not make this move until after a Northern victory, lest it appear like a desperate response to the defeats skilled Southern generals were inflicting upon the Union. The moment came in September 1862, with the Union victory at Antietam.

In the aftermath of the battle, Lincoln issued the **Emancipation Proclamation**. Note that the Emancipation Proclamation, for all intents and purposes, actually freed no slaves. Instead, it stated that on January 1, 1863, the government would liberate all slaves residing in those states still "in rebellion." Throughout the war, Lincoln refused to acknowledge secession and insisted on referring to the Confederate states as "those states in rebellion." The Proclamation did not liberate the slaves in the border states such as Maryland, nor did it liberate slaves in Southern counties already under the control of the Union Army. Again, legally, Lincoln had no power to abolish slavery in areas governed by the U.S. Constitution. Abolitionists complained that the Proclamation liberated slaves only where the Union had

Gradual Emancipation
Lincoln's notion of "gradual emancipation" was inspired by a law in Pennsylvania passed in 1780 which guaranteed that all children born in Pennsylvania were free persons regardless of the condition or race of their parents. This model of freeing slaves in the North was common before the Civil War settled the question of slavery nationwide.

no power to enforce emancipation and maintained slavery precisely where it could liberate the slaves. The Proclamation also allowed Southern states to rejoin the Union *without* giving up slavery. On the positive side, the Emancipation Proclamation finally declared that the Civil War was, for the Union, a war against slavery, and thus changed the purpose of the war, much as the Declaration of Independence had changed the purpose of the Revolutionary War.

Not until two years later, while campaigning for reelection, did Lincoln give his support to complete emancipation. Just before the Republican convention, Lincoln lobbied for a party platform that called for a constitutional amendment prohibiting slavery; the result was the **Thirteenth Amendment**. After his reelection, Lincoln considered allowing defeated Southern states to reenter the Union and to vote on the Thirteenth Amendment. He tried to negotiate a settlement with Southern leaders along those lines at the **Hampton Roads Conference**. Lincoln also offered a five-year delay on implementing the amendment if it passed, as well as $400 million in compensation to slave owners. Jefferson Davis's commitment to complete Southern independence scuttled any chance of compromise.

The Election of 1864 and the End of the Civil War

As the 1864 presidential election approached, popular opinion in both the North and South favored an end to the war. In fact, Lincoln's Democrat opponent, George McClellan, most likely lost his bid for the presidency by defying the will of the majority of Democrats who favored a cessation of hostilities and negotiation with the North.

It should be reemphasized that less than one percent of the Southern population owned more than 100 slaves, and as the war dragged on, many small, non-slaveholding farmers resented the Confederacy and the war, which they now believed was being waged merely to protect the planter aristocracy's lifestyle. In the North, some "War Democrats" conceded that the war was necessary to preserve the Union. Others, called the **Copperheads**, accused Lincoln of instigating a national social revolution and criticized his administration's policies as a thinly disguised attempt to destroy the South. Nowhere, however, was opposition to the war more violent than in New York City, where racial, ethnic, and class antagonisms exploded into draft riots in July of 1863. Irish immigrants, mostly the poor working class who were already victims of **nativism**, resented being drafted into a war being fought to end slavery. Many immigrants feared that once freed, former slaves would migrate into Northern cities and compete with them for low-paying labor jobs. And yet, both sides fought on.

Just when a stalemate might have forced an end to the war, things began improving for the North. Victories throughout the summer of 1864 played a large part in helping Lincoln gain reelection. By the early spring of 1865, a Union victory was virtually assured, and the government established the **Freedman's Bureau** to help newly liberated blacks establish a place in postwar society. The Bureau helped with immediate problems of survival (food, housing) and developed social institutions, such as schools. Some historians see the Freedman's Bureau as the first federal, social welfare program in U.S. history. In April 1865, the Confederate leaders surrendered. John Wilkes Booth assassinated Lincoln just five days later, with devastating consequences for the reunited nation.

The Civil War was fought at enormous cost. More than 3 million men fought in the war, and of them, more than 500,000 died. At least as many were seriously wounded. Both governments ran up huge debts during the war, and much of the South was ravaged by Union soldiers. During **Sherman's March** from Atlanta to the sea in the fall of 1864, the Union Army burned everything in its wake (to destroy Confederate morale and deplete the South's material resources), foreshadowing the wide-scale warfare of the 20th century. From a political perspective, the war permanently expanded the role of government. On both sides, government grew rapidly to manage the economy and the war.

Reconstruction and Johnson's Impeachment

At war's end, three major questions faced the reunited nation. First, under what conditions would the Southern states be readmitted to the Union? Second, what would be the status of blacks in the postwar nation? Black leaders hoped that their service in the military would earn blacks equal rights. The newly liberated slaves, called freedmen, were primarily interested in the chance to earn wages and own property. And third, what should be done with the rebels?

Reconstruction may be seen as both a time period and a process. As a time period, Reconstruction usually refers to the years between 1865 and 1877, that is, from the end of the Civil War until the end of military reconstruction when the Union army withdrew from the South. The *process* of reconstruction, however, was complicated and complex, and some argue it continues to this day. Reconstruction involved readmitting the Southern states that had seceded from the Union; physically reconstructing and rebuilding Southern towns, cities, and property that had been destroyed during the war; and finally, integrating newly freed blacks into American society. It is this last process that has proven to be most difficult.

The process of reconstruction had begun even before the Civil War ended, although not without controversy. As president of the United States and commander-in-chief of the armed forces, Lincoln had claimed that he had the authority to determine the conditions under which the Southern states might be readmitted to the Union. Lincoln had no intention of punishing the South and wanted to end the war and reunite the nation quickly and painlessly, as his immortal words from his second inaugural address indicate: "With malice toward none, with charity for all, with firmness in the right as God gives us to see the right, let us strive on to finish the work we are in, to bind up the nation's wounds, to care for him who shall have borne the battle and for his widow and his orphan, to do all which may achieve and cherish a just and lasting peace among ourselves and with all nations."

Lincoln's plan is usually referred to as the **Ten-Percent Plan** and simply required that 10 percent of those voters who had voted in the 1860 election swear an oath of allegiance to the Union and accept emancipation through the Thirteenth Amendment. These men would then reorganize their state government and reapply for admission into the Union. Congress had another vision, however. It viewed the Southern states as "conquered territory" and as such, **Radical Republicans** in Congress argued, were under the jurisdiction of Congress, not the President. Most Republicans agreed that Lincoln's plan was too lenient and enacted the

Wade-Davis Bill in July of 1864. This act provided that former Confederate states be ruled by a military governor and required 50 percent of the electorate to swear an oath of allegiance to the United States. A state convention would then be organized to repeal their ordinance of secession and abolish slavery within their state.

It should be noted that neither Lincoln's Ten-Percent Plan nor the Wade-Davis Bill made any provisions for black suffrage. Lincoln pocket-vetoed the Wade-Davis Bill, effectively destroying it. (A pocket veto can occur only at the end of a congressional session. If the president does not sign a bill within 10 days and Congress adjourns within those 10 days, the bill dies and must be reintroduced when Congress reconvenes. Unlike a regular veto, which requires the president to explain his objections to a bill and can subsequently be overridden, a pocket veto does not need to be explained nor is it subject to another congressional vote. It cannot be overridden.) Lincoln was assassinated the following year.

With Lincoln's assassination, Vice President **Andrew Johnson** assumed the presidency. Johnson, a Southern Democrat, had opposed secession and strongly supported Lincoln during his first term. In return, Lincoln rewarded Johnson with the vice presidency. When the war ended, Congress was in recess and would not reconvene for eight months. That left the early stages of Reconstruction entirely in Johnson's hands.

Johnson had lifted himself from poverty and held no great love for the South's elite planters, and at first he seemed intent on taking power away from the old aristocracy and giving it to the yeomen. **Johnson's Reconstruction Plan**, which was based on a plan approved by Lincoln, called for the creation of provisional military governments to run the states until they were readmitted to the Union. It also required all Southern citizens to swear a **loyalty oath** before receiving amnesty for the rebellion. However, it barred many of the former Southern elite (including plantation owners, Confederate officers, and government officials) from taking that vow, thus prohibiting their participation in the new governments. According to this plan, the provisional governments would hold state constitutional conventions, at which time the states would have to write new constitutions eliminating slavery and renouncing secession. Johnson did not require the states to enfranchise blacks by giving them the vote.

The plan did not work, mostly because Johnson **pardoned** many of the Southern elite who were supposed to have been excluded from the reunification process. After the states drafted new constitutions and elected new governments, former Confederate officials were again in positions of great power. Furthermore, many of their new constitutions were only slight revisions of previous constitutions. Southern legislators also passed new **black codes** limiting freedman's rights to assemble and travel, instituting curfews, and requiring blacks to carry special passes. Many of them required blacks in the South to sign lengthy labor contracts. In the most egregious instances, state legislatures simply took their old slave codes and replaced the word *slaves* with *freedmen*. When Congress reconvened in December 1865, the new Southern senators included the vice president of the Confederacy and other Confederate officials. Northern congressmen were not pleased. Invoking its constitutional right to examine the credentials of new members, Congress voted not to seat the new Southern delegations. Next, it set about examining Johnson's Reconstruction plan.

Congress was divided among conservative Republicans, who generally agreed with Johnson's plan; moderates, who were a large enough contingent to swing a vote in one or the other direction; and Radical Republicans. The Radical Republicans wanted to extend democracy in the South. Following the Civil War, most important political positions were held by appointees; very few officials were directly elected. (Of course, women could not vote and black men could vote only in a few northern states at this time.) The most radical among the Radical Republicans advocated a reconstruction program that punished the South for seceding. Historians of the time suggested that revenge was the real motivation behind the passage of the Thirteenth Amendment, although contemporary historians have dismissed this idea. Under General Sherman's **Special Field Order No. 15**, land seized from the Confederates was to be redistributed among the new freedmen, but President Andrew Johnson rescinded Sherman's order, and the idea of giving freedmen **40 acres and a mule** never regained much ground.

All Republicans agreed that Johnson's Reconstruction needed some modification, but Johnson refused to compromise. Instead, he declared Reconstruction over and done with, vetoing a compromise package that would have extended the life of the Freedman's Bureau and enforced a uniform civil rights code on the South. Congress overrode Johnson's vetoes, which only increased tension between the two branches of the federal government.

In response, the radicals drew up the plan that came to be known as **Congressional Reconstruction**. Its first component was the **Fourteenth Amendment** to the Constitution. The amendment (1) stated that if you are born in the United States, you are a citizen of the United States and you are a citizen of the state where you reside; (2) prohibited states from depriving any citizen of "life, liberty, or property without due process of law"; (3) prevented states from denying any citizen "equal protection of the law"; (4) gave states the choice either to give freedmen the right to vote or to stop counting them among their voting population for the purpose of congressional apportionment; (5) barred prominent Confederates from holding political office; and (6) excused the Confederacy's war debt.

The first three points remain the most significant, to this very day, and are the basis for most lawsuits involving discrimination and civil rights. In fact, through a series of cases over the years, most of the first 10 amendments have been extended to the states through the due process clause of the Fourteenth Amendment. It is helpful to remember that the Bill of Rights protects the individual from the federal government, while the Fourteenth Amendment protects you from the state government. The Fourteenth Amendment was intended to clarify the status of newly freed slaves, address the issue of citizenship raised by the *Dred Scott* decision, and limit the effects of the black codes. The radicals hoped to force states to either extend suffrage to black men or lose power in Congress. In the **Swing Around the Circle** public speaking tour, Johnson campaigned against the amendment and lost. In the congressional election of 1866, the North voted for a Congress more heavily weighted toward the radical end of the political spectrum.

The new Congress quickly passed the **Military Reconstruction Act of 1867**. It imposed martial law on the South; it also called for new state constitutional conventions and forced the states to allow blacks to vote for convention delegates. The act also required each state to ratify the Fourteenth Amendment and to send its new constitution to Congress for approval. Aware that Johnson would oppose the new Reconstruction, Congress then passed a number of laws designed to limit the president's power. As expected, Johnson did everything in his power to counteract the congressional plan. The conflict reached its climax when the House Judiciary Committee initiated **impeachment proceedings** against Johnson, ostensibly for violating the Tenure of Office Act (which stated that the president had to secure the consent of the Senate before removing his appointees once they'd been approved by that body; Johnson had fired Secretary of War Edwin Stanton, a Radical Republican) but really because he was getting in the way of Reconstruction. Johnson was acquitted by one vote in the Senate, but the trial rendered Johnson politically impotent, and he served the last few months of his presidency with no hope of re-election.

With a new president, **Ulysses S. Grant**, in office, Congress forged ahead in its efforts to remake the South. The **Fifteenth Amendment**, proposed in 1869, finally required states to enfranchise black men. (Women's suffrage would have to wait another half-century.) In fact, Grant's win was mainly due to black votes. One of the reasons the Republicans created the Fifteenth Amendment was the hope that their party would continue to flourish with the addition of new black voters. Ironically, the Fifteenth Amendment passed only because Southern states were required to ratify it as a condition of reentry into the Union; a number of Northern states opposed the amendment.

The Failure of Reconstruction

Reconstruction had its share of successes while the North occupied the South. New state constitutions officially allowed all Southern men to vote (previous constitutions had required voters to own property) and replaced many appointed government positions with elected positions. New Southern governments, directed mostly by transplanted Northern Republicans, blacks, and Southern moderates, created public schools and those social institutions such as orphanages popularized in the North during the reform movement of the 1830s. The new governments also stimulated industrial and rail development in the South through loans, grants, and tax exemptions. The fact that blacks were serving in Southern governments represented a huge step forward, given the seemingly insurmountable restrictions placed on blacks only a few years earlier, though it would prove to be only a temporary victory.

However, ultimately, Reconstruction failed. Although government industrialization plans helped rebuild the Southern economy, these plans also cost a lot of money. High tax rates turned public opinion, already antagonistic to Reconstruction, even more hostile. Opponents waged a propaganda war against Reconstruction, calling Southerners who cooperated **scalawags** and Northerners who ran the programs **carpetbaggers**. (The name came from the suitcases they carried, implying they had come to the South merely to stuff their bags with ill-gotten wealth.) Many who participated in Reconstruction were indeed corrupt, selling their votes for money and favors.

It should be noted that Northerners were just as guilty as Southerners of corruption. The period following the Civil War is also known as the **Gilded Age** to suggest the tarnish that lay beneath the layer of gold. This is the era of political machines and "bosses," which will be discussed in a later chapter. Political scandal was not new at the time, and in fact, Grant's administration was wracked with political scandals and intrigue; Grant himself was supposedly innocent and oblivious to the goings on in his administration. Grant had no political experience when he became president; in fact, he was elected because he was a popular war hero, not an experienced political leader. Like Jackson, Grant appointed his friends and supporters to governmental positions, not necessarily those men most qualified, let alone those with the most integrity.

Unfortunately, although Grant was honest, his friends were not. A series of scandals broke out in the early 1870s, and while you don't need to know the details to do well on the AP Exam, the sheer length of the list should get the idea across:

> **Black Friday, 1869**
> **Credit Mobilier scandal, 1872**
> **New York Custom House ring, 1872**
> **Star Route frauds, 1872–1876**
> **Sanborn incident, 1874**
> **Pratt & Boyd scandal, 1875**
> **Whiskey Ring, 1875**
> **Delano affair, 1875**
> **Trading post scandal, 1876**
> **Alexander Cattell & Co. scandal, 1876**
> **Safe burglary, 1876**

These scandals diverted the public's attention away from the postwar conditions in the South.

Though the Civil War was officially over, a war of intimidation began, spear-headed by insurgent groups ranging from secretive terrorist groups, such as the **Ku Klux Klan**, who focused on murdering freedmen, to openly operating paramilitary forces, such as the **White League**, who focused on murdering Republicans. "These combinations amount to war," declared attorney general Amos Akerman, who had been posted to the Carolinas to try to speed trials of Klansmen along—a problem because local judges tended to be Klansmen as well. In some towns, the entire adult male population was engaged in battle against Reconstruction. Southern officials explained their failure to do anything to protect blacks and Republicans by complaining that if they obeyed their orders to round up insurgents, there would be mass starvation because nobody would be left to work. Grant and the Republicans in Congress got the Enforcement Acts passed, which allowed Grant to send in federal troops to oppose the Klan, and were successful in limiting that Klan's violence.

Also, because Reconstruction did nothing to redistribute the South's wealth or guarantee that the freedmen would own property, it did very little to alter the basic power structure of the region. Southerners knew that when the Northerners left, as they inevitably would, things would return to a condition much closer to the way they were before Reconstruction. As early as 1869, the federal government began sending signals that it would soon ease up restrictions. President Grant enforced the law loosely, hoping to lessen tensions and thereby hasten an

"A portion of our southern population hate the government of the United States, because they understand it emphatically to represent northern sentiment, and hate the negro because he has ceased to be a slave and has been promoted to be a citizen and a voter, and hate those of the southern whites who are looked upon as in political friendship with the north, with the United States Government and with the negro. These persons commit the violence that disturbs many parts of the south."
—Attorney General Amos Akerman

amicable reunion. Worse, throughout the 1860s and 1870s, the Supreme Court consistently restricted the scope of the Fourteenth and Fifteenth Amendments. In the *Slaughter-House* cases, the court ruled that the Fourteenth Amendment applied only to the federal government, not to state governments, an opinion the court strengthened in *United States v. Cruikshank*. In *United States v. Reese*, the court cleared the way for "grandfather clauses," poll taxes, literary tests, property requirements, and other restrictions on voting privileges. Soon, nearly all Southern states had restrictive laws that effectively prevented blacks from voting. Finally, because Grant's administration was so thoroughly corrupt, it tainted everything with which it was associated, including Reconstruction.

During the 1872 election, moderates calling themselves Liberal Republicans abandoned the coalition that supported Reconstruction. Angered by widespread corruption, this group hoped to end federal control of the South. Although their candidate, Horace Greeley, did not defeat Grant, they made gains in congressional and state elections. As a result, Grant moved further away from the radical position and closer to conciliation. Several congressional acts, among them the Amnesty Act of 1872, pardoned many of the rebels, thus allowing them to reenter public life. Other crises, such as the financial Panic of 1873, drew the nation's attention away from Reconstruction. By 1876, Southern Democrats had regained control of most of the region's state legislatures. These Democrats called themselves **Redeemers,** and their use of the word redemption suggested they intended to reverse Republican reconstruction policies as they returned to power.

The election of 1876 was one of the more infamously contested elections in American history, with both political parties accusing the other of fraud. Samuel J. Tilden, then governor of New York and a political reformer who had gone after **"Boss" Tweed**, the most notorious among the political bosses of the time, won the popular vote by a small margin but needed to win the electoral vote to gain the presidency. (Remember that according to the Constitution, if no one candidate receives a majority of electoral votes, the election is thrown into the House of Representatives. You should remember, for example, that Andrew Jackson lost the presidency to John Quincy Adams through a "corrupt bargain" in 1824.) Republicans challenged the election returns that favored Tilden in South Carolina, Louisiana, and Florida. Congress eventually stepped in to resolve the disputed election and created a special bipartisan electoral commission consisting of senators, representatives, and Supreme Court justices. Through a series of informal negotiations, a deal was struck that has come to be known as the **Compromise of 1877**. It was agreed that if Rutherford B. Hayes won the presidential election, he would end military reconstruction and pull federal troops out of South Carolina and Louisiana, thereby enabling Democrats to regain control of those states. Military reconstruction was thus ended, and it was business as usual in the South. Many historians feel that the federal government dropped the ball in 1877, for in many ways, life for blacks became worse, and it would take almost another 100 years for the federal government to live up to the ideal expressed in the Declaration of Independence: "that all men are created equal."

After the Compromise of 1877, many Southern leaders sought to emulate the industrialization of the North, coining the term "New South." Despite these aspirations, though, sharecropping and tenant farming would continue to dominate the region for many years.

Southern Blacks During and After Reconstruction

At the end of the Civil War, the former slaves were thrust into an ambiguous state of freedom. Most reacted cautiously, remaining on plantations as sharecroppers where they had been relatively well treated but fleeing from those with cruel overseers. Many set out in search of family members from whom they had been separated. The Freedman's Bureau helped them find new jobs and housing and provided money and food to those in need. The Freedman's Bureau also helped establish schools at all levels for blacks, among them Fisk University and Howard University. Unfortunately, the Freedman's Bureau was terribly underfunded and had little impact once military reconstruction came to an end.

When it became evident that the government would not redistribute land, blacks looked for other ways to work their own farms. The Freedman's Bureau attempted to establish a system in which blacks contracted their labor to whites, but the system failed. Instead, blacks preferred **sharecropping**, in which they traded a portion of their crop in return for the right to work someone else's land. The system worked at first, but unscrupulous landowners eventually used the system as a means of keeping poor farmers in a state of near slavery and debt. Abuses of the sharecropping system grew more widespread at the end of Reconstruction, at which point no court would fairly try the case of a sharecropper against a landowner. Sharecropping existed well into the middle of the 20th century and actually included more whites than blacks.

Not all blacks, however, suffered a dismal fate during Reconstruction. Mississippi, with its large black population, became the most progressive in its promotion of blacks to political office. **Hiram Revels** and **Blanche K. Bruce** of Mississippi became the first black senators in the U.S. Congress and were elected in 1870 and 1875, respectively, only a few short years after the end of the Civil War. **Robert Smalls** of South Carolina founded the Republican Party of that state and served in the U.S. House of Representatives in the 1880s.

Summary

Here are the most important concepts to remember from the Civil War/Reconstruction period.

o   Regional tensions over slavery and states' rights led to the Civil War, an event that radically changed American society and the role of the federal government in state affairs.

o   "Manifest Destiny" and a land acquisition from Mexico spurred America to fully settle the West.

o   Northern European immigrants continued to enter the country, motivated by industrial and agricultural opportunity.

o   It took many years for the South to fully recover from the economic and social upheaval of the Civil War.

Chapter 9 Review Questions

See Chapter 14 for answers and explanations.

1. As a result of the Mexican-American War, all of the following became part of the United States EXCEPT

    (A) California
    (B) Nevada
    (C) New Mexico
    (D) Texas

2. "Bleeding Kansas" was a direct result of the doctrine of

    (A) judicial review
    (B) imperialism
    (C) containment
    (D) popular sovereignty

3. As a result of the Emancipation Proclamation,

    (A) all slaves in the Union and the Confederacy were declared free
    (B) nearly 200,000 free blacks and escaped slaves joined the Union Army
    (C) Maryland seceded from the Union
    (D) African Americans in the United States received the right to vote

4. Andrew Johnson was impeached because

    (A) he refused to carry out Lincoln's plan for reconstruction
    (B) he vetoed the Wade-Davis Bill
    (C) Congress was controlled by Republicans and he was a Democrat
    (D) he violated the Tenure of Office Act by firing Secretary of War Stanton

5. The dispute over electoral votes in the election of 1876

    (A) was similar to the election of 2000 in that the Supreme Court ultimately had to step in and decide the election
    (B) was resolved by a special bipartisan commission and resulted in the end of military reconstruction
    (C) led many members of Congress to push for a Constitutional amendment to abolish the electoral college
    (D) was resolved when Samuel J. Tilden conceded the election to Rutherford B. Hayes

6. Following the Civil War, most freed slaves

    (A) stayed in the South and worked as sharecroppers
    (B) joined the pioneering movement as it headed West
    (C) moved to the North to work in factories
    (D) took work building the nation's growing railroad system

7. The Know-Nothing Party focused its efforts almost exclusively on the issue of

    (A) the right to bear arms
    (B) the prohibition of alcohol
    (C) women's rights
    (D) immigration

8. The Free-Soil party advocated which of the following?

   (A) The freedom of settlers within the territories to
       determine the slave status of their new state
   (B) Passage of the Homestead Act to give free land to
       all Western settlers
   (C) The exclusion of slavery from any of the new
       territories
   (D) The policy of giving newly freed slaves "40 acres
       and a mule" following the Civil War

9. The principle of popular sovereignty stated that

   (A) whenever a new area was settled, all United States
       citizens were required to vote on the slave status
       of that area
   (B) slavery would not be permitted in any area after
       1848
   (C) the president, after meeting with public interest
       groups, was to decide on whether slaves would
       be allowed in a given territory
   (D) settlers in the Western territories, not Congress,
       would decide whether to allow slavery in their
       territories

10. Which of the following is NOT a requirement set by the
    Reconstruction Act of 1867 for Southern states' readmis-
    sion to the Union?

    (A) Blacks had to be allowed to participate in state
        conventions and state elections.
    (B) The state had to ratify the Fourteenth Amendment
        to the Constitution.
    (C) The state had to pay reparations and provide land
        grants to all former slaves.
    (D) The state had to rewrite its constitution and ratify it.

REFLECT

Respond to the following questions:

- For which content topics discussed in this chapter do you feel you have achieved sufficient mastery to answer multiple-choice questions correctly?

- For which content topics discussed in this chapter do you feel you have achieved sufficient mastery to discuss effectively in a short-answer question or an essay?

- On which content topics discussed in this chapter do you feel you need more work before you can answer multiple-choice questions correctly?

- On which content topics discussed in this chapter do you feel you need more work before you can discuss them effectively in a short-answer question or an essay?

- What parts of this chapter are you going to review again?

- Will you seek further help, outside of this book (such as a teacher, tutor, or AP Students), on any of the content in this chapter—and, if so, on what content?

Chapter 10
The Industrial Revolution (1865–1898)

THE AGE OF INVENTION AND ECONOMIC GROWTH

In 1876, **Thomas A. Edison** built his workshop in Menlo Park, New Jersey, and proceeded to produce some of the most important inventions of the century. Edison's greatest invention was the **light bulb**. Edison's pioneering work in the development of **power plants** also proved immensely important. His advances allowed for the extension of the workday, which previously ended at sundown, and the wider availability of electricity. With that wider availability, Edison and other inventors began to create new uses for electricity, both for industry and the home. The last quarter of the 19th century is often called the **Age of Invention** because so many technological advances like Edison's were made. These advances, in turn, generated greater opportunities for **mass production**, which then caused the economy to grow at a tremendous rate. Not surprisingly, the people known as the "captains of industry" to their fans (and the "robber barons" to others), who owned and controlled the new manufacturing enterprises, became extremely rich and powerful during this period.

Industrialization, Corporate Consolidation, and the Gospel of Wealth

As more and faster machines became available to manufacturers, businessmen discovered that their cost per unit decreased as the number of units they produced increased. The more raw product they bought, the cheaper the suppliers' asking price. The closer to capacity they kept their new, faster machines running, the less the cost of labor and electricity per product. The lower their costs, the cheaper they could sell their products. The cheaper the product, the more they sold. That, simply put, is the concept of **economies of scale**.

The downside of this new business practice was that it required employees to work as efficiently, and repetitively, as machines. **Assembly line production** had begun to take hold when Eli Whitney developed interchangeable parts, but it reached a whole new level in Ford's plants in the early 20th century. This type of production required workers to perform a single task over and over, often (before labor reform) for 12 to 14 hours a day. Factories were dangerous; machine malfunctions and human error typically resulted in more than 500,000 injuries to workers per year.

The overriding concern for businessmen, however, was that profits continued to increase by huge margins. Although government made some efforts to regulate this rapid growth, these were tentative. Furthermore, the government remained uncertain as to how to enforce regulations, and widespread corruption existed among those bureaucrats charged with enforcing the regulations. Finally, the courts of the era (especially the Supreme Court) were extremely pro-business. With almost no restraint, businesses such as railroad companies followed the path that led to greater economies of scale, which meant larger and larger businesses. This was known as **corporate consolidation**.

One new form of business organization was called a **holding company**. A holding company owned enough stock in various companies to have a controlling interest in the production of raw material, the means of transporting that material to a factory, the factory itself, and the distribution network for selling the product. The logical conclusion is a **monopoly**, or complete control of an entire industry. One holding company, for example, gained control of 98 percent of the sugar refining plants in the United States. While the company did not control the entire sugar industry, it did control one very important aspect of it.

The most common forms of business consolidation at the end of the 19th century were **horizontal** and **vertical integration**. One is legal; one is not; both were practiced by "captains of industry" during the Gilded Age. For all intents and purposes, horizontal integration created monopolies within a particular industry, the best-known example being Standard Oil, created by John D. Rockefeller. In horizontal integration, several smaller companies within the same industry are combined to form one larger company, either by being bought out legally or by being destroyed through ruthless business practices such as cutthroat competition or pooling agreements. Many of these business practices are illegal today because of antitrust legislation passed at the turn of the 20th century. Vertical integration remains legal, however, provided the company does not become either a trust or a holding company, but rather allows other companies in the same industry to survive and compete in the marketplace. In vertical integration, one company buys out all the factors of production, from raw materials to finished product. For example, Swift Premium might control the stockyards, the slaughterhouse, and the processing and packaging plants but still compete with Oscar Mayer or Hebrew National.

Numerous problems arose because of this consolidation of power. First, rapid growth required lots of money. Businessmen borrowed huge sums, and when their businesses occasionally failed, bank failures could result. During the last quarter of the 19th century, the United States endured one major financial panic per decade. Although irresponsible investors caused the panics, the lower classes suffered the most, as jobs and money became scarce. Second, monopolies created a class of extremely powerful men whose interests clashed with those of the rest of society. As these businessmen grew more powerful, public resentment increased, and the government responded with laws to restrict monopolies (which the courts, in turn, weakened). The back-and-forth battle among the public, the government, and the courts is best exemplified by the **Sherman Antitrust Act of 1890**. Public pressure led to the passage of this law forbidding any "combination…or conspiracy in the restraint of trade."

Unfortunately, the wording of the Sherman Antitrust Act was ambiguous enough to allow the pro-business Supreme Court at the time to interpret the law as it saw fit. For example, in 1895, the Court ruled that E. C. Knight, the company that controlled 98 percent of the sugar refining plants in the United States, did not violate the Sherman Antitrust Act because local manufacturing was not subject to congressional regulation of interstate commerce. (*U.S. v. E. C. Knight Co.*, 1895.) On the other hand, labor unions were often found to be "in restraint of free trade" and declared illegal. This loophole was closed during Wilson's administration in 1914 with the passage of the Clayton Antitrust Act, which made allowances for collective bargaining.

Another "Gospel": The Social Gospel

Not to be confused with Carnegie's "Gospel of Wealth," the term "social gospel" was coined by Charles Oliver Brown in 1910. Some Protestants of the era articulated their social goals as the following:

"The great ends of the church are the proclamation of the gospel for the salvation of humankind; the shelter, nurture, and spiritual fellowship of the children of God; the maintenance of divine worship; the preservation of truth; the promotion of social righteousness; and the exhibition of the Kingdom of Heaven to the world."

Dismayed by poverty and urban slums, activists in the Social Gospel movement hoped that by promoting public health and education, the moral lives of the poor would begin to improve. Social Gospel activists also worked to abolish child labor and hoped to limit the number of hours employees could be required to work.

Another response to public pressure for reform came from industrialists themselves. Steel mogul **Andrew Carnegie** promoted a philosophy based on the work of Charles Darwin. Using Darwin's theory of evolution as an analogy, Carnegie argued that in business, as in nature, unrestricted competition allowed only the "fittest" to survive. This theory was called **Social Darwinism**. Aside from the fact that Carnegie's analogy to Darwin's theory was at best dubious, it also lacked consistency; while Carnegie argued against government regulation, he supported all types of government assistance to business (in the form of tax abatements, grants, tariffs, and so on). Carnegie further argued that the concentration of wealth among a few was the natural and most efficient result of capitalism. Carnegie also asserted that great wealth brought with it social responsibility. Dubbing his belief the **Gospel of Wealth**, he advocated philanthropy, as by building libraries and museums or funding medical research, but not charity. Some of his peers were as generous; others were not.

Factories and City Life

Manufacturers cut costs and maximized profits in every way they could imagine. They reduced labor costs by hiring **women** and **children**. In cities, where most factories were located, manufacturers hired the many newly arrived **immigrants** who were anxious for work. Because manufacturers paid as little as possible, the cities in which their employees lived suffered many of the problems associated with poverty, such as crime, disease, and the lack of livable housing for a rapidly expanding population. As mentioned before, factories were dangerous, and many families had at least one member who had been disabled at work. Insurance and workmen's compensation did not exist then, either.

The poverty level in cities also rose because those who could afford it moved away from the city center. As factories sprang up, cities became dirtier and generally less healthy environments. Advances in **mass transportation**, such as the expansion of railroad lines, streetcars, and the construction of subways, allowed the middle class to live in nicer neighborhoods, including bedroom communities in the suburbs, and commute to work. (The growing middle class was made up of managers, secretaries, bureaucrats, merchants, and the like.) As a result, immigrants and migrants made up the majority of city populations. Starting around 1880, the majority of immigrants arrived from Southern and Eastern Europe. (Prior to 1880, most immigrants to America came from northern and western Europe.) Prejudice against the new arrivals was widespread, and many immigrants settled in **ethnic neighborhoods** usually in **tenements**. Worse off still were **black** and **Latino** migrants. Many employers refused them any but the worst jobs.

Municipal governments of the era were not like those of today. In fact, such governments were practically nonexistent. Most Americans expected churches, private charities, and ethnic communities to provide services for the poor. However, many of those services were provided instead by a group of corrupt men called **political bosses**. Bosses helped the poor find homes and jobs; they also helped them apply for citizenship and voting rights. They built parks, funded auxiliary police and fire departments, and constructed roads and sewage lines. In return, they expected community members to vote as they were instructed. Occasionally, they also required "donations" to help fund community projects. Political bosses—whose organizations were called **political machines**—rendered services that communities would not otherwise have received. However, because the bosses resorted to criminal means to accomplish their goals, the cost of their services was high. The most notorious of these bosses was "Boss" Tweed of Tammany Hall in New York City.

William "Boss" Tweed became a New York City alderman in the 1850s. He expanded his influence by gaining a seat on New York's Board of Supervisors, which allowed him to embezzle millions of dollars through corruption in city construction projects. Tweed also became a prominent leader of Tammany Hall, the political machine of New York's Democratic Party. Tweed gave out jobs, homes, and protection to new immigrants in exchange for their votes in local elections. By the 1870s, Tweed's power became noticeable to leading journalists, including *The New York Times* and political cartoonist Thomas Nast. Nast drew images of Tweed's corrupt practices in *Harper's Weekly,* and *The New York Times* published ledgers proving that Tweed embezzled millions of dollars through extortion and fraudulent construction projects. One estimate claimed that Tweed charged the city of New York almost $180,000 ($2.5 million today) for 3 tables and 40 chairs, and that one worker earned over $130,000 ($1.8 million today) for two days' work. Tweed was eventually found guilty and died in prison in 1878, but not before escaping from prison and getting all the way to Spain, only to be recaptured because people recognized him from Nast's cartoons.

Widespread misery in cities led many to seek changes. Labor unions formed to try to counter the poor treatment of workers. Unions were considered radical organizations by many, and the government was wary of them; businesses and the courts were openly hostile to them. Hired goons and, in some cases, federal troops often broke strikes. Before the Civil War, the few unions that existed were small, regional, or local and represented workers within a specific craft or industry. One of the first national labor unions was the **Knights of Labor**, founded in 1869 by Uriah Stephens, a Philadelphia tailor.

The Knights organized skilled and unskilled workers from a variety of crafts into a single union. Their goals included (1) an eight-hour workday; (2) equal pay for equal work for men and women (this would not become a federal law until 1963); (3) child labor laws, including the prohibition of working under the age of 14; (4) safety and sanitary codes; (5) a federal income tax (not enacted until the ratification of the Sixteenth Amendment in 1913); and (6) government ownership of railroad and telegraph lines.

Identification

One important shift during the 19th century was that from vertical identification to horizontal identification. For example, in 1800, an apprentice shoemaker would likely to think of himself as belonging to a class with journeyman shoemakers and master shoemakers. By 1850, he would be much more likely to think of himself as belonging to a class with apprentice tailors and apprentice blacksmiths.

Although the Knights advocated arbitration over strikes, they became increasingly violent in efforts to achieve their goals. By the 1880s, after a series of unsuccessful strikes under the leadership of **Terrence Powderly**, the popularity of the Knights began to decline. The American public began to associate unions with violence and political radicalism. Propagandists claimed that unions were subversive forces— a position reinforced in public opinion by the **Haymarket Square Riot**. During an 1886 labor demonstration in Chicago's Haymarket Square, a bomb went off, killing police. Many blamed the incident on the influence of radicals within the union movement, although no one knew who set off the bomb.

In 1892, workers at Carnegie's Homestead Steel factory went on strike, protesting a wage cut and the refusal of factory manager Henry Clay Frick to allow them to form a union. Frick locked out the workers when their contract expired, hired replacement workers, and then called in the Pinkerton Detective force to prevent the steel workers from protesting. The ensuing clash between the Pinkertons and the strikers led to several deaths and the retreat of the Pinkertons. Eventually, the Pennsylvania state militia ended the strike, and Frick hired new workers to replace the striking workers.

In 1894, workers at the Pullman Palace Car Factory faced a wage cut and an increase in the cost of their housing. They organized a strike, and the American Railway Union (ARU) joined their strike in May, leading to over 250,000 railway workers walking off the job, shutting down rail travel in 27 states. ARU president Eugene Debs refused to end the strike, even after President Cleveland ordered the Army to stop the strike and Debs was ordered to stop the strike because it was disrupting delivery of federal mail. Debs was convicted and jailed for refusing to follow a court order. While in jail, Debs is said to have read Karl Marx's *Communist Manifesto*. When released from jail, he became active in the socialist movement, and eventually became the leader of the American Socialist party.

Many early unions did indeed subscribe to utopian and/or socialist philosophies. Later on, the **American Federation of Labor**, led by **Samuel Gompers**, avoided those larger political questions, concentrating instead on such "bread and butter" issues as higher wages and shorter workdays, an approach that proved successful. Gompers also realized that his union could gain more power if it excluded unskilled workers; the AFL was formed as a confederation of **trade unions** (i.e., unions made up exclusively of workers within a single trade). The history of early unions is marred by the fact that most refused to accept immigrants, blacks, and women among their memberships.

Charitable middle-class organizations, usually run by women, also made efforts at urban reform. These groups lobbied local governments for building-safety codes, better sanitation, and public schools. Frustrated by government's slow pace, their members also founded and lived in **settlement houses** in poor neighborhoods. These houses became community centers, providing schooling, childcare, and cultural activities. In Chicago, for example, **Jane Addams** founded Hull House to provide such services as English lessons for immigrants, day care for children of working mothers, childcare classes for parents, and playgrounds for children. Addams also campaigned for increased government services in the slums. She was awarded the Nobel Peace Prize for her life's work in 1931.

While the poor suffered, life improved for both the wealthy and the middle class. Increased production and wealth meant greater access to luxuries and more leisure time. Sports, high theater, vaudeville (variety acts), and, later, movies became popular diversions. It was also during this period that large segments of the public began to read **popular novels** and **newspapers**. The growth of the newspaper industry was largely the responsibility of **Joseph Pulitzer** and **William Randolph Hearst**, both of whom understood the commercial value of bold, screaming headlines and lurid tales of scandal. This new style of sensational reporting became known as **yellow journalism**.

Jim Crow Laws and Other Developments in the South

Most of the advances made during the machine age affected primarily Northern cities. In the South, agriculture continued as the main form of labor. The industrialization programs of Reconstruction did produce some results, however. Textile mills sprang up around the South, reducing cotton farmers' reliance on the North. Tobacco processing plants also employed some workers. Still, the vast majority of Southerners remained farmers.

Postwar economics forced many farmers to sell their land, which wealthy landowners bought and consolidated into larger farms. Landless farmers, both black and white, were forced into **sharecropping**. The method by which they rented land was called the **crop lien system**; it was designed to keep the poor in constant debt.

Because these farmers had no cash, they borrowed what they needed to buy seed and tools, promising a portion of their crop as collateral. Huge interest rates on their loans and unscrupulous landlords pretty much guaranteed that these farmers would never overcome their debt, forcing them to borrow further and promise their *next* crop as collateral. In this way, landlords kept the poor, both black and white, in a state of virtual slavery.

The advent of **Jim Crow laws** made matters worse for blacks. As the federal government exerted less influence over Southern states, towns and cities passed numerous discriminatory laws. The Supreme Court assisted the states by ruling that the Fourteenth Amendment did not protect blacks from discrimination by privately owned businesses and that blacks would have to seek equal protection from the states, not from the federal government. In 1883, the Court also reversed the Civil Rights Act of 1875 (which said that businesses and public facilities couldn't be segregated), thus opening the door to legal (*de jure*) segregation. In 1896, the Supreme Court ruled in *Plessy v. Ferguson* that the role of the federal government was not to maintain social equality. It went on to establish

Excerpt from Booker T. Washington's Atlanta Compromise speech.

"In conclusion, may I repeat that nothing in thirty years has given us more hope and encouragement, and drawn us so near to you of the white race, as this opportunity offered by the Exposition; and here bending, as it were, over the altar that represents the results of the struggles of your race and mine, both starting practically empty-handed three decades ago, I pledge that in your effort to work out the great and intricate problem which God has laid at the doors of the South, you shall have at all times the patient, sympathetic help of my race; only let this be constantly in mind, that, while from representations in these buildings of the product of field, of forest, of mine, of factory, letters, and art, much good will come, yet far above and beyond material benefits will be that higher good, that, let us pray God, will come, in a blotting out of sectional differences and racial animosities and suspicions, in a determination to administer absolute justice, in a willing obedience among all classes to the mandates of law. This, coupled with our material prosperity, will bring into our beloved South a new heaven and a new earth."

that "separate but equal" facilities for the different races were legal. In so doing, the Court set back the civil rights gains made during Reconstruction.

In this atmosphere, integration and equal rights for blacks seemed to most a far-off dream. **Booker T. Washington** certainly felt that way. A Southern black born into slavery, Washington harbored no illusions that white society was ready to accept blacks as equals. Instead, he promoted economic independence as the means by which blacks could improve their lot. To pursue that goal, he founded the Tuskegee Institute, a vocational and industrial training school for blacks. Some accused Washington of being an **accommodationist** because he refused to press for immediate equal rights. Others believed that Washington simply accepted the reality of his time when he set his goals. In his Atlanta Exposition, a famous speech delivered in Atlanta, Georgia, in 1895, Washington outlined his view of race relations. Washington's more aggressive rival W. E. B. Du Bois (see Chapter 11) referred to the speech, which he deemed submissive, as "The Atlanta Compromise."

The Railroads and Developments in the West

On the western frontier, **ranching** and **mining** were growing industries. Ranchers drove their herds across the western plains and deserts, ignoring property rights and Native American prerogatives to the land. Individual miners lacked the resources to mine and cart big loads, so mostly they prospected; when they found a rich mine, they staked a claim and sold their rights to a mining company.

In the second year of the Civil War, Lincoln issued a challenge to America not unlike Kennedy's 1961 pledge to reach the Moon—that before the decade was out, America would have a Transcontinental Railroad connecting one side of the country to the other. From 1863 to 1869, former farmers, immigrants, freed slaves, and Civil War veterans worked to make Lincoln's vision a reality. The railroad's arrival changed the West in many ways. The railroads, although owned privately, were built largely at the public's expense, through direct funding and substantial grants of land to the railroads. Both federal and local governments were anxious for rails to be completed and so provided substantial assistance. Although the public had paid for the rail system, rail proprietors strenuously objected to any government control of their industry, and it took years for railroad rates to come under regulation. Until they were regulated, the railroads would typically overcharge wherever they owned a monopoly and undercharge in competitive and heavily trafficked markets. This practice was particularly harmful to farmers in remote areas.

As railroad construction crawled across the nation, rail companies organized massive hunts for buffalo (considered a nuisance). Railroad bounty hunters hunted the herds to near extinction, destroying a resource upon which local Native Americans had depended. Some tribes, such as the Sioux, fought back, giving the government an excuse to send troops into the region. While Native Americans won some battles (notably at **Little Big Horn**, where George Custer met his death), the federal army ultimately overpowered them.

The railroads brought other changes as well. Rails quickly transformed depot towns into vital cities by connecting them to civilization. Easier, faster travel meant more contact with ideas and technological advances from the East. Developments in railroad technology had applications in other industries and so accelerated the Industrial Revolution. In addition, "railroad time," by which rail schedules were determined, gave the nation its first standardized method of time telling with the adoption of time zones.

As the rails pushed the country westward, settlers started filling in the territory. By 1889, North Dakota, South Dakota, Washington, and Montana were populous enough to achieve statehood; Wyoming and Idaho followed in 1890. The result of the 1890 census prompted the Progressive historian Frederick Jackson Turner to declare that the American frontier was gone, and with it the first period of American history. Turner argued that the frontier was significant in (1) shaping the American character, (2) defining the American spirit, (3) fostering democracy, and (4) providing a safety valve for economic distress in urban, industrial centers by providing a place to which people could flee. Historians refer to these ideas collectively as the **Turner** or **Frontier Thesis**.

In the Great Plains, farming and ranching constituted the main forms of employment. New farm machinery and access to mail (and mail-order retail) made life on the plains easier, but it was still lonely and difficult. The government, realizing the potential of the region as the nation's chief agricultural center, passed two significant pieces of legislation in 1862—the **Homestead Act** and the **Morrill Land-Grant Act**. Anxious to attract settlers to develop the West, the federal government offered 160 acres of land to anyone who would "homestead" it (cultivate the land,

> The **Nez Perce** were an Indian tribe in northeast Oregon. As it did with many tribes, the U.S. government forced them to migrate to a small reservation in Idaho. **Chief Joseph** led his people in resistance to this removal, but eventually surrendered to federal power. Along with Sitting Bull, Chief Joseph became one of the most well-known Indians of his time.

build a home, and live there) for five years. It was quickly discovered that 160 acres wasn't enough to productively farm on some of the very dry land in the West or to compete with some of the large-scale commercial agricultural farms, so subsequent acts had to give out more land if farmers agreed to irrigate the land or plant trees on the land. Of course, the government was giving away land that belonged to Native Americans. Furthermore, private speculators and railroad companies often exploited the law for their own personal economic gain. The Morrill Land-Grant Act set aside land and provided money for agricultural colleges. Eventually, agricultural science became a huge industry in the United States.

With many families and corporations heading West, both government and conservation groups sought for added protection of natural resources. The **U.S. Fish Commission** was created in 1871 to study, monitor, and preserve wild fisheries. Today the Fish Commission is part of the U.S. Fish and Wildlife Service, a division of the Department of the Interior. In 1892, naturalist **John Muir** created the **Sierra Club**, one of the first large organizations devoted to conservation in the United States. Later, President Theodore Roosevelt would be known as a president who furthered environmental preservation of the West through the National Parks system.

In this expansionist era, those who lost out the most were, of course, the Native Americans. At first, pioneers approached the tribes as sovereign nations. They made treaties with them, which the settlers or their immediate successors broke. The result was warfare, leading the government to try another approach. The new tack was to force Native Americans onto reservations, which typically were made up of the least desirable land in a tribe's traditional home region. The reservation system failed for a number of reasons, including the inferiority of the land, the grouping of incompatible tribes on the same reservation, and the lack of autonomy granted the tribes in managing their own affairs. Moreover, some Westerners simply ignored the arrangement and poached on reservation lands. Helen Hunt Jackson's book *A Century of Dishonor* detailed the injustices of the reservation system and inspired reformers to push for change, which came in 1887 in the form of the **Dawes Severalty Act**.

The Dawes Severalty Act broke up the reservations and distributed some of the land to the head of each Native American family. Similar to the Homestead Act, the allotment was 160 acres of land. This time, however, it was required that the family live on the land for 25 years, after which time the land was legally theirs. And the grand prize was American citizenship! The Dawes Act was intended as a humanitarian solution to the "Indian problem"; its main goal was to accelerate the assimilation of Native Americans into Western society by integrating them more closely with whites. Native Americans, naturally, resisted. Furthermore, poverty drove many to sell their land to speculators, leaving them literally homeless.

Some displaced Indians turned to religion for comfort. The **Ghost Dance Movement** started in 1889, inspired by the visions of the prophet Wovoka. In his prophecies, Wovoka promised followers that, through proper ceremony and supernatural magic, federal expansion in the West would end and Indians would live peacefully on their native lands. Many Lakota Sioux were active in the Ghost Dance Movement and later met their bloody fate at the hands of federal agents during the **Wounded Knee Massacre**, a dispute started by cavalry troops intent on disarming the members of the Pine Ridge Reservation. Hundreds of Lakota were killed or injured and the site of the battlefield is now a National Historic Landmark.

Civil Service Reform

The "spoils system" pioneered by Andrew Jackson meant that every time a new president took office, thousands of government jobs opened up, and it was the president's responsibility to fill them. This is what the presidents of the mid-19th century did with their days. For instance, even as the Civil War raged, Abraham Lincoln spent morning, afternoon, and evening dealing with the job applicants who lined up outside his office, the line winding through the White House and out the door onto Pennsylvania Avenue.

Within the Republican Party, who dominated control of the White House following the Civil War, a split developed between **Stalwarts**, who believed that all government jobs should go to loyal Republicans, and **Half-Breeds**, who thought that qualified Democrats should be able to keep their jobs even after a Republican was elected. When a frustrated job-seeker assassinated President Garfield, it became clear that something had to be done about the way government employment was handled. His successor, Chester Arthur, had been a Stalwart, but he signed the **Pendleton Civil Service Reform Act** that began the dismantling of the old spoils system.

National Politics

Mark Twain dubbed the era between Reconstruction and 1900 the **Gilded Age** of politics. Gilded metals have a shiny, gold-like surface, but beneath lies a cheap base. America looked to have entered a period of prosperity, with a handful of families having amassed unprecedented wealth, but the affluence of a few was built on the poverty of many. Similarly, American politics looked like a shining example of representative democracy, but just beneath the surface lay crass corruption and patronage. Political machines, not municipal governments, ran the cities.

Big business bought votes in Congress and then turned around and fleeced consumers. Workers had little protection from the greed of their employers because the courts turned a deaf ear to worker complaints. In other words, Twain was right on the money.

The presidents of this era were generally not corrupt. They were, however, relatively weak. (The president is only as powerful as his support allows him to be; thus popular presidents, such as Andrew Jackson and Franklin Roosevelt, were able to accomplish so much.) Don't expect too many questions about the presidents of this period, but for the record, **Rutherford B. Hayes, James Garfield**, and **Chester A. Arthur** concerned themselves primarily with civil service reform (see the accompanying box on the previous page), while **Grover Cleveland** believed that government governed best which governed least. **Benjamin Harrison** took the opposite tack, and he and his allies in the Capitol passed everything from the nation's first meat inspection act to the banning of lotteries to the purchase of several battleships. Much of the legislation we have discussed, from the Sherman Antitrust Act to the second Morrill Land-Grant Colleges Act, was passed under Harrison's watch. But the public's discomfort with the activism of Harrison and the **Billion-Dollar Congress** of 1890 led to Grover Cleveland's return to the White House.

In response to the outcry over widespread corruption, the government made its first stabs at regulating itself and business. Many states imposed **railroad regulations** because railroads were engaging in price gouging. In 1877, the Supreme Court upheld an Illinois state law regulating railroads and grain elevators in the case of *Munn v. Illinois*. This was a surprising decision, given that railroads crossed state lines and only Congress can regulate interstate commerce. The Court argued that states had the power to regulate private industry that served the "public interest." Although the Supreme Court would reaffirm Congress's authority nine years later in the *Wabash* case, when it ruled that states could *not* establish rates involving interstate commerce, an important precedent for regulating business in the public's interest had been established.

In 1887, just one year after the *Wabash* decision, Congress passed the first federal regulatory law in U.S. history. The **Interstate Commerce Act** set up the Interstate Commerce Commission (ICC) to supervise railroad activities and regulate unfair and unethical practices. (The ICC wasn't disbanded until the 1980s under the Reagan administration, when, in attempts to save money, the federal government deregulated many forms of transportation.)

It was also during this period that **women's suffrage** became an important political issue. **Susan B. Anthony** led the fight, convincing Congress to introduce a suffrage amendment to the Constitution. The bill was introduced every year and rarely got out of committee, but the fight had begun in earnest. Meanwhile, organizations such as the **American Suffrage Association** fought for women's suffrage amendments to state constitutions. By 1890, they had achieved some partial successes, gaining the vote on school issues. (Women finally gained the right to vote with the ratification of the Nineteenth Amendment in 1920—fifty years after male suffrage became universal.)

The Silver Issue and the Populist Movement

In the period after the Civil War, production on all fronts—industrial and agricultural—increased. Greater supply accordingly led to a drop in prices. For many farmers, lower prices meant trouble, as they were locked into long-term debts with fixed payments. Looking for a solution to their problem, farmers came to support a more generous money supply. An increase in available money, they correctly figured, would make payments easier. It would also cause inflation, which would make the farmers' debts (held by Northern banks) worth less. Not surprisingly, the banks opposed the plan, preferring for the country to use only gold to back its money supply.

The farmers' plan called for the liberal use of silver coins, and because silver was mined in the West, this plan had the added support of Western miners along with that of Midwestern and Southern farmers. Thus, the issue had a regional component. Because it pitted poor farmers against wealthy bankers, it also had elements of class strife. Although a complicated matter, the money issue was potentially explosive.

Although the Grangers were the most influential group of united farmers, with chapters from New England to the West, there were other groups started by minority farmers that are less well known but which made an impact in their local regions. **Las Gorras Blancas** was founded in 1889 by New Mexican farmers whose land was being taken by Anglo-American settlers. Though their tactics were at times violent, several of their leaders ran for political positions under the banner of the Populist Party. In Texas, the **Colored Farmers' Alliance**, formed in 1886, invited black farmers to organize for their collective interests. Like Las Gorras Blancas, the Colored Farmers were largely Populists.

The "silver versus gold" debate provided an issue around which farmers could organize. They did just that. First came the **Grange Movement**, which, founded in 1867, boasted more than a million members by 1875. The Grangers started out as cooperatives, with the purpose of allowing farmers to buy machinery and sell crops as a group and, therefore, reap the benefits of economies of scale. Soon, the Grangers endorsed political candidates and lobbied for legislation. The Grangers ultimately died out because of a lack of money, but they were replaced by **Farmers' Alliances**. The Alliances allowed women to be politically active (Mary Elizabeth Lease was a huge organizer for them), and they had branches all around the nation. The Farmers' Alliances were even more successful than the Grange movement, and they soon grew into a political party called the **People's Party**, the political arm of the **Populist** movement.

The Grangers were responsible for most of the laws regulating the railroads in the 1870s and 1880s. These are referred to as the Granger Laws.

The People's Party held a convention in 1892. (Their platform was called the Omaha Platform. It called for solidarity with industrial workers, opposition to immigration to help American workers, and trying to earn more support for Eastern laborers, among other things.) Aside from supporting the generous coinage of silver, the Populists called for government ownership of railroads and telegraphs, a graduated income tax, direct election of U.S. senators, and shorter workdays. Although their 1892 presidential candidate, James Weaver, came in third, he won more than 1 million votes, awakening Washington to the growing Populist movement.

As Cleveland took office in 1893, the country entered a four-year financial crisis. Hard economic times made Populist goals more popular, particularly the call for easy money. (Most people at the time, after all, had no money at all.) Times got so bad that even more progressive (some would say radical) movements gained popularity; in 1894, the **Socialists**, led by **Eugene V. Debs**, gained support. By 1896, the Populists were poised for power. They backed Democratic candidate **William Jennings Bryan** against Republican nominee **William McKinley**, and Bryan ran on a strictly Populist platform; he based his campaign on the call for **free silver**. He is probably best remembered for his "Cross of Gold" speech (a typical multiple-choice question). He argued that an easy money supply, though inflationary, would loosen the control that Northern banking interests held over the country. The Republicans, on the other hand, became solidly allied with big businesses, as McKinley received huge campaign contributions from large companies. Business leaders told their employees that they would lose their jobs if Bryan won the election. Bryan lost the campaign; this, coupled with an improved economy, ended the Populist movement.

Foreign Policy: The Tariff and Imperialism

Before the Civil War, most Americans earned their living by farming. By 1900, however, the United States had become the leading industrial power in the world. It is difficult for us to imagine the enormous controversy surrounding the issue of the tariff throughout U.S. history. Remember that there was no federal income tax until the Sixteenth Amendment was adopted in 1913. Clearly, the most infamous tariff was the **Tariff of Abominations** (1828). This ultimately triggered the nullification crisis during Jackson's first administration. Following the Civil War, the tariff came to dominate national politics, as industrialists competing in an international market demanded high tariffs to protect domestic industries. Farmers and laborers, on the other hand, were hurt by high tariffs. Generally, Democrats supported lower tariffs while Republicans advocated high, protective tariffs.

In 1890, Congress enacted the McKinley Tariff, which raised the level of duties on imported goods almost 50 percent. Certain products, however, such as unprocessed sugar, were put on a duty-free list. Then, in 1894, Congress passed the Wilson-Gorman Tariff, which essentially resembled the schedule established by the **McKinley Tariff**, despite heated debate between members of the House of Representatives and the Senate. The tariff issue not only dominated congressional debate, it also had a tremendous impact on foreign relations (see below). For example, the Wilson-Gorman Tariff is usually considered one of the causes of the **Spanish-American War**.

Throughout the machine age, American production capacity grew rapidly. As we have already discussed, not every American had enough money to buy the products he or she made at work. America began looking overseas to find **new markets**. Increased **nationalism** also led American business to look for new markets. America's centennial celebration in 1876 heightened national pride, as did awareness that the country was becoming a world economic power. As Americans became more certain that their way of life was best, they hoped to spread that around the globe. This philosophy led American influence to expand into a number of new arenas.

First, **William H. Seward**, secretary of state under Lincoln and Johnson, set the precedent for increased American participation in any and all doings in the Western Hemisphere. In particular, Seward engineered the purchase of Alaska and invoked the Monroe Doctrine to force France out of Mexico. In the following decade, American businesses began developing markets and production facilities in Latin America, and gradually they gained political power in the region.

An easy way to remember the Populists is through the book *The Wizard of Oz* by L. Frank Baum. The novel is reportedly a political allegory, with Dorothy representing the common man, her silver shoes (the movie changed them into ruby slippers) representing the silver standard, the scarecrow representing the farmer, and the Tin Man representing the industrial worker. William Jennings Bryan was said to be the model for the Cowardly Lion.

Theodore Roosevelt was assistant secretary of the Navy in 1898 during the Spanish-American War, and he ordered the U.S. Pacific Fleet to the Philippines. He then resigned from the Navy and led a volunteer regiment of cavalry troops in Cuba.

As long as America moved into regions to do business, it was practicing **expansionism**, which most Americans supported. When the United States took control of another country, however, it was exercising **imperialism**, a more controversial practice. A book by naval Captain Alfred T. Mahan, called *The Influence of Sea Power Upon History* (1890), piqued the government's interest in imperialism. Mahan argued that successful foreign trade relied on access to foreign ports, which in turn required overseas colonies, and colonies in turn required a strong navy. The book popularized the idea of the **New Navy**, and after the United States invested in upgrading its ships, it turned its attention to foreign acquisitions.

The search for a port along the trade route to Asia attracted the United States to **Hawaii**. Foreign missionaries had arrived in Hawaii in the early 1800s, but significant U.S. involvement there began in the 1870s, when American sugar producers started trading with the Hawaiians. Due in large part to American interference, the Hawaiian economy collapsed in the 1890s. The United States had allowed Hawaii tariff-free access to American markets. Then, when Hawaii became dependent on trade with the United States, the government imposed high tariffs (the McKinley Tariff mentioned above), thereby greatly diminishing Hawaiian exports. The white minority overthrew the native government, and, eventually, the United States annexed Hawaii. Japan was outraged; more than 40 percent of Hawaii's residents were of Japanese descent. That anger would resurface during World War II.

Another opportunity for American expansion arose when Cuban natives revolted against Spanish control. The revolution in **Cuba**, like the Hawaiian revolution, was instigated by U.S. tampering with the Cuban economy (by imposing high import tariffs, as discussed above). A violent Cuban civil war followed, reported in all its gory detail in the sensational Hearst newspaper (see "yellow journalism," earlier in this chapter). When an American warship, the *Maine*, exploded in the Havana harbor under circumstances that remain a mystery, the drumbeats for war grew deafening. In the ensuing war, the United States not only drove Spain out of Cuba, but also sent a fleet to the Spanish-controlled **Philippines** and drove the Spanish out of there too. In the **Treaty of Paris**, Spain granted Cuba independence and ceded the Philippines, Puerto Rico, and Guam to the United States. Remember that Hawaii was annexed the same year but not because of the Spanish-American War. Also, note that this was the third Treaty of Paris that matters in U.S. history. The first ended the French and Indian War in 1763, while the second ended the Revolutionary War in 1783.

Despite the Teller Amendment, in which the United States claimed it would not annex Cuba after Spain's departure from the island in 1898, U.S. troops remained in Cuba for another few years. Then, in 1901, Cuba was compelled to include a series of provisions in its new constitution. The United States made it quite clear that its troops would not leave unless Cuba agreed to these provisions, collectively known as the **Platt Amendment**. The United States was basically given control over Cuba's foreign affairs. Under the guise of protecting Cuba's political and social stability and thus its independence, the following terms were established: (1) Cuba was not permitted to sign any foreign treaty without the consent of the United States, (2) the United States could intervene in Cuban domestic and foreign affairs, and (3) the United States was granted land on which to build a naval base and coaling station. The Platt Amendment was ultimately repealed in 1934 during **FDR**'s administration as part of his **Good Neighbor Policy.** The United States continues to operate a naval station at Guantanamo Bay, however. (Yes, *that* Guantanamo Bay.)

Control of the Philippines raised a tricky question: "Should the United States annex the Philippines, or should it grant the country the independence its people sought?" Proponents of annexing the Philippines argued that if the United States granted Filipinos their independence, the archipelago would simply be conquered by another European nation, with the only result being that the United States would lose a valuable possession. Perhaps most compelling, and certainly the best-known rationale for U.S. annexation of the Philippine Islands, was the belief that the United States had a moral obligation to "Christianize and civilize" the Filipinos, who were already overwhelmingly Christian—albeit Catholic, which didn't count for some Protestant imperialists—and preferred to achieve "civilization" in their own way. The notion that people not of European extraction were unfit to rule themselves came to be known as the "white man's burden," from the title of a poem written by Rudyard Kipling in response to the United States' annexation of the Philippines. Opponents felt that the United States should promote independence and democracy, both noble national traditions. To control the Philippines, they argued, would make the United States no better than the British tyrants they overthrew in the Revolutionary War. In the end, the Senate voted to annex the Philippines. It was a very close margin. The Senate needed 56 votes to get the two-thirds majority needed to ratify a treaty, and got 57, meaning that there were 27 senators who opposed the treaty. Filipino nationalists responded by waging a guerrilla war against the United States. In response, the United States used incredibly brutal tactics to subdue the Filipino revolt and inflict huge casualties on the civilian population. Although the United States eventually gained control of the country, the Philippines remained a source of controversy for decades. The United States granted the Philippines independence in 1946.

As the United States acquired an overseas empire, a fundamental question arose as to the legal status of the native population living in these territories: "Does the Constitution follow the flag?" In other words, were colonial subjects entitled to the same protections and privileges granted to U.S. citizens by the Constitution? The Supreme Court settled this issue by a series of rulings known collectively as the **Insular Cases** (1901–1903). The Court ruled that the Constitution did *not* follow the flag; Congress was free to administer each overseas possession as it chose, depending on the particular situation in any given foreign territory.

Finally, America hoped to gain entry into Asian markets. To that end, McKinley sought an **Open Door Policy** for all Western nations hoping to trade with Asia. The European nations that had colonized China were not so keen on the idea; to their way of thinking, they fought for those markets and planned to keep them. When Chinese nationalists (known as the **Boxers**) rose against European imperialism and besieged the Beijing legation quarter, the United States sent troops to help suppress the rebels. In return, Germany, France, and England grew more receptive to America's foreign policy objectives.

American imperialism would continue through Theodore Roosevelt's administration. We'll discuss that period in the next chapter.

Summary

Here are the most important concepts to remember from the Industrial Revolution period.

o The Industrial Revolution changed not only industry, but also virtually every aspect of American daily life, ushering in urbanization and manufacturing, stimulating immigration and migration North.

o Large businesses stimulated economic growth and largely thrived on little to no governmental regulation.

o Work opportunities opened up for women and minorities—but also led to widespread child labor.

o Corruption in government and corporate abuses of power led to social reformers calling for change.

Chapter 10 Review Questions

See Chapter 14 for answers and explanations.

1. The scalawags were

   (A) another name for the Redeemers, who refused to accept the fact that the South had lost the Civil War
   (B) Northern politicians who traveled to the South after the Civil War to exploit the political and economic instability for their own personal gain
   (C) advocates of civil rights for the newly freed slaves
   (D) white Southerners who supported Republican policies during Reconstruction

2. Which of the following statements about Supreme Court decisions during the latter part of the nineteenth century is most accurate?

   (A) They reduced federal power over the states by narrowly defining the applicability of the Constitution to state law.
   (B) They cleared the way for the liberal reforms of the twentieth century by broadly interpreting constitutional guarantees of individual rights.
   (C) They had little practical effect because the executive branch consistently refused to enforce the Court's rulings.
   (D) They used the Fourteenth Amendment to create numerous environmental regulations and human rights, stifling American business growth.

3. The term *vertical integration* refers to

   (A) Reconstruction-era efforts to assimilate newly freed slaves into all social strata of American society
   (B) an architectural movement that sought to blend urban skyscrapers with the natural landscape surrounding them
   (C) the industrial practice of assigning workers a single, repetitive task in order to maximize productivity
   (D) control of all aspects of an industry, from production of raw materials to delivery of finished goods

4. The passage of the Pendleton Act was a direct result of the

   (A) assassination of Abraham Lincoln
   (B) failure of Reconstruction
   (C) assassination of James A. Garfield
   (D) Supreme Court decision in *Plessy v. Ferguson*

5. The Haymarket Affair represented a major setback for the

   (A) women's suffrage movement
   (B) civil rights movement for African Americans
   (C) Knights of Labor
   (D) Temperance movement

6. Japan was outraged by the American annexation of Hawaii in 1898 primarily because

   (A) Japan depended heavily on trade with Hawaii to support its economy
   (B) the United States had signed a treaty with Japan granting Japan rights to Hawaii
   (C) the Japanese were committed to the principle of self-rule throughout the Pacific
   (D) nearly half of Hawaii's residents were of Japanese descent

7. The "new immigrants" who arrived in the United States after the Civil War were different from the "old immigrants" in that they

   (A) came mostly from Latin American countries
   (B) settled in rural areas in the Midwest where land was plentiful
   (C) were better prepared than previous immigrants had been to face the challenges of urban life
   (D) spoke different languages and had different customs than most Americans and thus were not easily assimilated

8. The "Ghost Dance" movement among Western Native Americans stressed all of the following EXCEPT

(A) the belief that the world would soon come to an end
(B) rejection of alcohol and other trappings of white society
(C) unity among Native Americans of different tribes
(D) nonviolence

9. In the late nineteenth century, political machines such as Tammany Hall were successful primarily because

(A) they operated primarily in rural areas, where the government could not monitor their activities
(B) they focused on accomplishing only a narrow set of human rights objectives
(C) they championed the suffragettes and received their support in return
(D) machine politicians provided needed jobs and services to naturalized citizens in return for their votes

10. Which of the following was the intended result of the Dawes Severalty Act of 1887?

(A) Railroad companies would be persuaded to stop unfair pricing through a number of government incentives.
(B) Recently arrived European immigrants would be enticed into settling in the less populated West.
(C) Legislators would be less likely to accept bribes because of the severity of the penalty.
(D) Native Americans would be coaxed off reservations by land grants and would thus assimilate into Western culture.

REFLECT

Respond to the following questions:

- For which content topics discussed in this chapter do you feel you have achieved sufficient mastery to answer multiple-choice questions correctly?

- For which content topics discussed in this chapter do you feel you have achieved sufficient mastery to discuss effectively in a short-answer question or an essay?

- On which content topics discussed in this chapter do you feel you need more work before you can answer multiple-choice questions correctly?

- On which content topics discussed in this chapter do you feel you need more work before you can discuss them effectively in a short-answer question or an essay?

- What parts of this chapter are you going to review again?

- Will you seek further help, outside of this book (such as a teacher, tutor, or AP Students), on any of the content in this chapter—and, if so, on what content?

Chapter 11
The Early 20th
Century
(1890–1945)

THE PROGRESSIVE ERA AND WORLD WAR I (1900–1920)

The Populist movement dissipated, but not before raising the possibility of reform through government. The Populists' successes in both local and national elections encouraged others to seek change through political action. Building on Populism's achievements and adopting some of its goals (e.g., direct election of senators, opposition to monopolies), the **Progressives** came to dominate the first two decades of 20th-century American politics. While the Populists were mainly aggrieved farmers who advocated radical reforms, the Progressives were urban, middle-class reformers who wanted to increase the role of government in reform while maintaining a capitalist economy.

The Progressive Movement

One of the reasons Populism failed is that its constituents were mostly poor farmers whose daily struggle to make a living made political activity difficult. The **Progressives** achieved greater success in part because theirs was an urban, middle-class movement. Its proponents started with more economic and political clout than the Populists. Furthermore, Progressives could devote more time to the causes they championed. Also, because many Progressives were Northern and middle class, the Progressive movement did not intensify regional and class differences, as the Populist movement had.

The roots of Progressivism lay in the growing number of associations and organizations at the turn of the century. The National Woman Suffrage Association, the American Bar Association, and the National Municipal League are some of the many groups that rallied citizens around a cause or profession. Most of these groups' members were educated and middle class; the blatant corruption they saw in business and politics offended their senses of decency, as did the terrible plight of the urban poor.

Progressivism got a further boost from a group of journalists who wrote exposés of corporate greed and misconduct. These writers, dubbed **muckrakers** by Theodore Roosevelt, revealed widespread corruption in urban management (**Lincoln Steffens**'s *The Shame of the Cities*), oil companies (**Ida Tarbell's** *History of Standard Oil*), and the meatpacking industry (**Upton Sinclair's** *The Jungle*). Their books and news articles raised the moral stakes for Progressives.

Over the course of two decades, Progressives achieved great successes on both the local and national levels. They campaigned to change public attitudes toward education and government regulation in much the same way reformers of the previous century had campaigned for public enlightenment on the plight of orphans, prostitutes, and the mentally infirm.

New groups arose to lead the fight against discrimination but met with mixed success. **W. E. B. Du Bois** headed the **National Association for the Advancement of Colored People** (**NAACP**) in the quest for racial justice, an uphill battle so strenuous that, after a lifelong struggle, Du Bois abandoned the United States and moved to Africa. Meanwhile, women's groups continued to campaign for suffrage. The adamant, conservative opposition they faced gave birth to the **feminist** movement. One early advocate, **Margaret Sanger**, faced wide opposition for promoting the use of contraceptives (illegal in most places). The movement's greatest success was in winning women the right to vote, granted by the **Nineteenth Amendment** in 1920.

Wisconsin governor **Robert La Follette** led the way for many Progressive state leaders. Under his leadership, Wisconsin implemented plans for direct primary elections, progressive taxation, and rail regulation. Many states extended greater power to voters by adopting the **ballot initiative**, through which the voters could propose new laws; the **referendum**, which allowed the public to vote on new laws; and the **recall election**, which gave voters the power to remove officials from office before their terms expired. Working-class Progressives also won a number of victories on the state level, including limitations on the length of the work day, minimum-wage requirements, child labor laws, and urban housing codes. Many states adopted progressive income taxes (taxes that charge higher percentages for people with higher incomes), which served partially to redistribute the nation's wealth.

The most prominent Progressive leader was President **Theodore Roosevelt**. In the 1900 election, Republican party leaders chose Roosevelt to be McKinley's running mate because they feared McKinley might become too powerful. McKinley was a conservative president, and Roosevelt was expected to emulate his policies, though rumors had begun to circulate that Roosevelt harbored progressive sympathies. When McKinley was assassinated in 1901, Roosevelt succeeded him.

Roosevelt showed his more liberal tendencies early on. In 1902, he directed the Justice Department to investigate a major railroad company, and then broke it up following the Sherman Antitrust Act. That same year, he worked to negotiate a labor conflict between coal mine owners and coal workers, giving large concessions to the workers. After he convincingly won the 1904 election on the strength of his handling of Latin American affairs, Roosevelt began boldly enacting a progressive agenda. He was the first to successfully use the **Sherman Antitrust Act** against monopolies, and he did so repeatedly during his term, earning the nickname "the Trustbuster." As president, Roosevelt went beyond regulation corporations. Inspired by Upton Sinclair's groundbreaking book *The Jungle*, which described the dangerous conditions in America's meatpacking factories, Roosevelt encouraged Congress to pass the Meat Inspection Act, which created federal standards for meatpacking factories. Congress also passed the Pure Food and Drug Act, which required all processed food and drugs to include ingredient labels. Roosevelt's desire to conserve natural resources led him to preserve millions of acres of forested land and to encourage Congress to create the National Park Service and the National Forest Service. Presidents Taft and Wilson continued to promote Progressive ideals. **William Howard Taft**, who won the election of 1908, spearheaded the drive for two constitutional amendments, one that instituted a national income tax (the Sixteenth Amendment) and another that allowed for the direct election of senators (the Seventeenth Amendment). He pursued monopolies even more aggressively than Roosevelt. On the foreign policy front, Taft is best known for "**dollar diplomacy**," the attempt to secure favorable relationships with

Double Duty
William Howard Taft is the only former president to sit on the Supreme Court of the United States. He was the tenth Chief Justice, serving from 1921 to 1930.

Latin American and East Asian countries by providing monetary loans. Roosevelt wanted Taft to succeed him in the presidency, but when Taft took actions that Roosevelt opposed, Roosevelt challenged him for the 1912 Republican primary. Party bosses supported Taft's more conservative policies, leading Roosevelt to run for the presidency on the Progressive ticket. Roosevelt and Taft split the Republican vote.

The Progressive Era is a turning point in American history because it marks the ever-increasing involvement of the federal government in our daily lives. It's no coincidence that Prohibition took effect during this era. The third Progressive president was **Woodrow Wilson**, a Democrat who had to distinguish himself from Teddy Roosevelt, who ran for reelection (after Taft's one term) on the Bull Moose ticket in 1912. While Roosevelt's policies are often referred to as **New Nationalism**, Wilson referred to his ideas and policies as **New Freedom**. Thomas Jefferson had suggested limiting the power of the federal government in order to protect individual liberty, but Wilson now argued that the federal government had to assume greater control over business to protect man's freedom. For Roosevelt, there were "good trusts and bad trusts." For Wilson trusts were monopolies, which violated freedom for workers and consumers. Wilson was committed to restoring competition through greater government regulation of the economy and lowering the tariff.

Wilson created the **Federal Trade Commission**, lobbied for and enforced the **Clayton Antitrust Act of 1914**, and helped create the **Federal Reserve System**, which gave the government greater control over the nation's finances.

Progressivism lasted until the end of World War I, at which point the nation, weary from war and from the devastating **Spanish Flu** outbreak of 1918, stepped back from its moral crusade. The war had torn apart the Progressive coalition; pacifist Progressives opposed the war while others supported it. A **Red Scare**, heightened by the Russian Revolution, further split the Progressive coalition by dividing the leftists from the moderates. Moreover, the Progressive movement had achieved many of its goals, and as it did, it lost the support of those interest groups whose ends had been met. Some say that the Progressive movement was brought to an end, at least in part, by its own success.

Foreign Policy and U.S. Entry into World War I

Roosevelt differed from his predecessor on domestic policy, but he concurred with his foreign policy. Roosevelt was, if anything, an even more devout imperialist than McKinley had been. In 1903, the Roosevelt administration strong-armed Cuba into accepting the **Platt Amendment**, which essentially committed Cuba to American control. Under Platt's stipulations, Cuba could not make a treaty with another nation without U.S. approval, and the United States had the right to intervene in Cuba's affairs if domestic order dissolved. A number of invasions and occupations by the Marine Corps resulted. For 10 of the years between 1906 and 1922, the American military occupied Cuba, arousing anti-American sentiments on the island.

Roosevelt's actions were equally interventionist throughout Central America. During his administration, the country set its sights on building a canal through the Central American isthmus; a canal would greatly shorten the sea trip from the East Coast to California. Congress approved a plan for a canal through **Panama**, at the time a province of Colombia. Because Colombia asked for more than the government was willing to spend, the United States encouraged Panamanian rebels to revolt and then supported the revolution. Not surprisingly, the new Panamanian government gave the United States a *much* better deal. Because American commercial interests were so closely tied to the canal's successful operation, the United States military became a fixed presence throughout the region. During the next 20 years, troops intervened repeatedly, claiming that Latin American domestic instability constituted a threat to American security. This assertion came to be known as the **Roosevelt Corollary to the Monroe Doctrine** and is often referred to as the Big Stick Policy.

American foreign policy continued to adhere to the Monroe Doctrine, which asserted America's right to assume the role of an international police force and intervene anywhere in the Western Hemisphere where it felt its national security was at stake. It also stated that the United States wanted no part of Europe's internal disputes. American commitment to that aspect of the Monroe Doctrine would soon be tested, as Europe started down the path leading to **World War I**. Complicating matters was the fact that the United States and England were quickly forming a close alliance. To America's benefit, England had not opposed its many forays into Central American politics, although it could have. The British were not merely being friendly; they were trying to line up the United States as a potential ally in their ongoing rivalry with Germany, the other great European power of the era.

Fortunately, you do not need to know the tangled series of events that led Europe into war in 1914. You do, however, have to know about the United States' initial efforts to stay out of the war and the events that ultimately drew it into the conflict. Woodrow Wilson won the election of 1912, a three-way race in which the third-party candidate, Theodore Roosevelt, outpolled Taft, the Republican incumbent. Wilson entered office with less than a commanding mandate—only 40 percent of the electorate voted for him. However, with regard to the simmering European conflict, he and the electorate were of the same mind: the United States should stay out of it.

When war broke out in Europe in August 1914, Wilson immediately declared the U.S. policy of **neutrality**. Neutrality called for America to treat all the belligerents fairly and without favoritism. It was Wilson's hope that the United States would help settle the conflict and emerge as the world's arbiter. However, the neutrality policy posed several immediate problems, owing to America's close relationship with England and relatively distant relationship with Germany and Austria-Hungary. A number of Wilson's advisors openly favored the Allies (led by the British).

The situation quickly grew more complicated. England's strategic location and superior navy allowed it to impose an effective **blockade** on shipments headed for Germany, particularly those coming from the United States. Protests proved futile; the British government impounded and confiscated American ships. They then paid for the cargo, reducing the pressure that American merchants would otherwise have put on the U.S. government to take action against the blockade.

Germany attempted to counter the blockade with **submarines**, or **U-boats**. According to contemporaneous international law, an attacker had to warn civilian ships before attacking. Submarines could not do this because doing so would eliminate their main advantage. Furthermore, when the Germans attacked civilian ships, it was usually because those ships were carrying military supplies. The Germans announced that they would attack any such ship, but that did not satisfy Wilson, who believed that the Germans should adhere to the strict letter of international law. Thus, when the German submarines sank the passenger ship *Lusitania* in 1915 (killing 1,198 passengers, including 128 Americans), the action provoked the condemnation of both the government and much of the public. That the *Lusitania* was carrying tons of ammunition to the British was a fact that received much less public attention than did the loss of 1,198 innocent lives.

The sinking of the *Lusitania*, and the bad publicity it generated, led the Germans to cease submarine warfare for a while. Britain made steady gains, however, and as the U-boats were Germany's most effective weapon, the Germans resumed their use. In 1916, while Wilson was campaigning for reelection on the slogan "He kept us out of war," Germany sank another passenger liner, the *Arabic*. In response, Wilson, while still maintaining neutrality, asked Congress to put the military into a state of **preparedness** for war, just in case. While most Americans wanted to stay out of the war, popular support for entry was beginning to grow.

Then, in early 1917, the British intercepted a telegram from German Foreign Minister Zimmermann to the German ambassador to Mexico. The telegram, imaginatively called the **Zimmermann telegram**, outlined a German plan to keep the United States out of the European war. The telegram stated that *if* Mexico were to declare war on the United States, Germany would provide Mexico help in regaining the lands lost in the Mexican War. The telegram also suggested that Germany would help Japan if they, too, wanted to go to war against America. Published in newspapers around the country, the telegram convinced many Americans that Germany was trying to take over the world. Although the public was by no means universally behind the idea of war, the balance had shifted enough so that within a month, America would declare war on Germany.

World War I and Its Aftermath

As is often the case during wartime, the government's power expanded greatly during the three years America was involved in World War I. The government took control of the telephone, telegraph, and rail industries, and a massive bureaucracy arose to handle these new responsibilities. The **War Industry Board (WIB),** created to coordinate all facets of industrial and agricultural production, sought to guarantee that not only the United States but also the rest of the Allies would be well supplied. (European production had been drastically cut by the war.) The WIB had mixed success; like most large bureaucracies, it was slow and inefficient.

The government also curtailed individual civil liberties during the war. In response to the still-sizable opposition to U.S. involvement, Congress passed the **Espionage Act** in 1917 and the **Sedition Act** in 1918. The Espionage Act prohibited anyone from using the U.S. mail system to interfere with the war effort or with the draft that had been instituted under the **Selective Service Act of 1917** upon America's entry into the war. The Sedition Act made it illegal to try to prevent the sale of war bonds or to speak disparagingly of the government, the flag, the military, or the Constitution. Like the Alien and Sedition Acts in the late 1790s, both laws violated the spirit of the First Amendment but were worded vaguely, giving the courts great leeway in their interpretation.

In 1919, the Supreme Court upheld the Espionage Act in three separate cases, the most notable being *Schenck v. United States*. Schenck was a prominent socialist and ardent critic of American capitalism, who was arrested and convicted for violation of the Espionage Act when he printed and mailed leaflets urging men to resist the draft. Schenck argued that the draft was a blatant violation of the Thirteenth Amendment, whose ratification in 1865 had abolished slavery; the wording of the amendment, however, did not mention slavery but rather prohibited "involuntary servitude." Justice Oliver Wendell Holmes ruled that one's freedom of speech and other civil liberties, were not absolute and could in fact be curtailed if one's actions posed a "clear and present danger" to others or the nation. In essence, you cannot yell "FIRE!" in a crowded theater if there is no fire.

These laws soon became useful tools for the suppression of anyone who voiced unpopular ideas. A mood of increased paranoia pervaded the era, heightened by the **Russian Revolution** in 1917, which placed Russia under Bolshevik control. Suddenly, Americans began to fear a communist takeover. Radical labor unions, such as the International Workers of the World, were branded enemies of the state, and their leaders were incarcerated. Eugene Debs, the Socialist leader, was also imprisoned for criticizing the war. A new government agency, the **Federal Bureau of Investigation**, was created to prevent radicals from taking over; **J. Edgar Hoover** headed the nascent agency (and continued to run it until the 1970s). Business assumed greater power, while unions lost power. Under the pretext of stamping out radicalism, businesses increased their use of strikebreakers and other forceful tactics against unions. In April of 1919, a series of bombs exploded in several American cities, one damaging the home of Attorney General A. Mitchell Palmer. Ongoing fears of radicalism and the spread of communism following the Russian Revolution encouraged Palmer to organize a series of raids on suspected radical groups around the country. In the **Palmer Raids** in early 1920, the government abandoned all pretext of respecting civil liberties as its agents raided union halls, pool halls, social clubs, and residences. Over 10,000 were arrested in over 30 cities, but very few weapons or bombs were found. About 500 immigrants were eventually deported at the conclusion of the Palmer Raids.

The government helped create this frenzied atmosphere through its wartime propaganda arm, the **Committee on Public Information (CPI)**. As the war progressed, the CPI's messages grew more sensational. At lectures and movie theaters, in newspapers and magazines, the CPI created the image of the Germans as cold-blooded, baby-killing, power-hungry Huns. During this period, Americans rejected all things German; for example, they changed the name of sauerkraut to "liberty cabbage." More serious were the many acts of violence against German immigrants and Americans of German descent.

Wartime also presented new opportunities for women. Although the number of women in the workforce did not increase greatly during the war, their means of employment did change. Many women quit domestic work and started working in factories; at one point, 20 percent of factory-floor manufacturing jobs were held by women. (The symbol of Rosie the Riveter, however, belongs to World War II.) These workplace advances ended with the war, as veterans returned home and reclaimed their jobs.

Southern blacks, realizing that wartime manufacturing was creating jobs in the North, undertook a **Great Migration** to the big cities, like New York, Chicago, St. Louis, and Detroit. During the war, more than 500,000 blacks left the South in search of work. Many blacks joined the army; W. E. B. Du Bois encouraged blacks to enlist, hoping that military service would provide an inroad to social equality. Sadly, the army segregated blacks and assigned them mostly to menial labor. Fearful of the effects of integration, the army assigned black combat units to French command.

American participation in the war tipped the balance in the Allies' favor, and two years after America's entry, the Germans were ready to negotiate a peace treaty. Wilson wanted the war treaty to be guided by his **Fourteen Points**, his plan for world peace delivered to Congress in January of 1918, before the end of the war. The Fourteen Points called for free trade through lower tariffs and freedom of the seas; a reduction of arms supplies on all sides; and the promotion of self-determination, both in Europe and overseas—in other words, the end of colonialism. The plan also called for the creation of the League of Nations, a mechanism for international cooperation much like today's United Nations. Wilson's Fourteen Points served as a basis for initial negotiations, but the negotiations soon took a different direction.

The European Allies wanted a peace settlement that punished Germany, and ultimately they got it. Under the **Treaty of Versailles**, Germany was forced to cede German and colonial territories to the Allies, to disarm, to pay huge reparations, and to admit total fault for the war, despite other nations' roles in starting it. Most historians agree that by leaving Germany humiliated and in economic ruin, the Treaty of Versailles helped to set the stage for World War II. Although much of Wilson's plan was discarded, the Treaty of Versailles did create the League of Nations. Wilson hoped that the League would ultimately remedy the peace settlement's many flaws, but when he returned home, a rude surprise awaited him. According to the Constitution, the president has the power to negotiate treaties with foreign nations, but these treaties are subject to Senate ratification. This illustrates the principles of **separation of powers** and **checks and balances**.

At the center of the conflict was the debate over the League of Nations, particularly Article X of the League's covenant, which many people believed curtailed America's ability to act independently in foreign affairs, specifically Congress's power to declare war. The Senate split into three groups: Democrats, who sided with Wilson and were willing to accept America's entrance into the League of Nations; a group of Republicans who were totally opposed to the League and were known as the Irreconcilables; and the Reservationists, a group of Republicans led by **Henry Cabot Lodge**, Chairman of the Senate Foreign Relations Committee and Wilson's political nemesis and intellectual rival.

Much has been made of Wilson's stubbornness and inability to compromise, and in particular, his refusal to accept what were known as the Lodge Reservations.

Ultimately, the Democrats and Irreconcilables joined forces and defeated the treaty, which had been amended to include the changes suggested by Henry Cabot Lodge and the Reservationists. Thus, the United States was not a signatory of the Treaty of Versailles, nor did it ever join the League of Nations, an international organization envisioned by an American President to maintain world peace. Weary of war, America was receding into a period of isolationism. The public wanted less interaction with Europe, not more, as the League would have required. Wilson tried to muster popular support for the treaty. However, while campaigning, Wilson suffered a major stroke, thereby ending whatever chance the treaty may have had for ratification. Many people wonder whether the League of Nations would have been more successful in preventing World War II had the United States been a member.

THE JAZZ AGE AND THE GREAT DEPRESSION (1920–1933)

After World War I, the American economy went through a brief slump and then started to grow rapidly. By 1922, America was hitting new peaks of prosperity every day. The invention of a practical electric motor was largely responsible for the economic boom; like computers in the 1990s, electric motors became essential to work and home environments, driving industrial machines and household appliances. With the new prosperity, other industries arose to serve the growing middle class in its search for the trappings of affluence.

Pro-Business Republican Administrations

As the age of progressive reform ended, many Americans became more comfortable with the idea of large, successful businesses. Some of these businesses, such as department stores, offered both convenience and reasonable prices. Others, such as the automobile industry, offered products that made life more convenient and conferred status on their owners.

The government, which had worked closely with business leaders as part of the war effort, also grew to be more **pro-business** during the era. Government regulatory agencies (such as the Federal Trade Commission) more often assisted business than regulated it. Labor unions fell further out of public favor, particularly when they struck against industries necessary to keeping industrial America running smoothly. Unions striking for higher wages and safer work conditions in the steel, coal, and railroad industries were suppressed by federal troops. The Supreme Court overturned a minimum wage law for women and nullified child labor restrictions.

All three of the era's presidents—**Warren Harding**, **Calvin Coolidge**, and **Herbert Hoover**—pursued pro-business policies and surrounded themselves with like-minded advisors. Like Grant, Harding had the misfortune of surrounding himself with corrupt

Wilson and Race

For all his progressivism in other areas, Woodrow Wilson was an outspoken white supremacist. He issued executive orders to segregate the federal government, struck a clause on racial equality from the Covenant of the League of Nations, wrote admiringly of the Ku Klux Klan, and told racist jokes at Cabinet meetings.

advisors; several of his cabinet members wound up in prison. The most infamous incident of his administration was the **Teapot Dome Scandal**, in which oil companies bribed the secretary of the interior in order to drill on public lands. Conservative on economic issues, Harding proved more liberal than his predecessor Wilson on issues of civil liberty. He supported antilynching laws and tried to help farmers (who were benefiting less from the new economy than were middle-class city dwellers) by providing more money for farm loans. Harding died in office, and Coolidge, his vice president, assumed the presidency. When Coolidge ran for the presidency in 1924, he turned the election into a debate on the economy by running on the slogan "Coolidge prosperity." Coolidge won easily and, following his mandate, continued Harding's conservative economic policies. He also pushed for lower income-tax rates. We will discuss Hoover's presidency later, when we discuss the causes of the Great Depression.

The pro-business atmosphere of the era led to a temporary decline in the popularity of labor unions; membership levels dropped throughout the decade. Also contributing to this drop were the efforts of businesses to woo workers with pension plans, opportunities for profit sharing, and company parties and other events designed to foster a communal spirit at work. Businessmen hoped that, if they offered some such benefits, they could dissuade workers from organizing and demanding even more. Such practices were often referred to as **welfare capitalism**.

Modern Culture

No consumer product better typified the new spirit of the nation than the **automobile**. At first, automobiles were expensive conveniences, affordable only to the extremely wealthy; then, Henry Ford perfected the assembly line and mass production, which lowered the cost of automobiles. By the end of the decade, most middle-class families could afford a car. The automobile allowed those who worked in the cities to move farther away from city centers, thus giving birth to the **suburbs**, which, in turn, transformed the automobile from a convenience to a necessity. The impact of the automobile on the 1920s was tremendous, forcing areas to quickly develop roadways and the means of policing traffic. In 1929, with the population topping 100 million in the most recent census, more than 23 million automobiles were registered in the United States.

The **radio** followed automobiles in changing the nation's culture. Ten million families owned radios, and in cities it was not unusual for several families to gather at the home of a radio owner and settle in for the evening. As more houses gained access to electric power, household appliance sales boomed as well. The **advertising industry** grew up during the decade to hype all these new products. Although advertisements from that era look pretty goofy to us now, they were quite effective at convincing people to buy stuff they did not really need—not too different from today!

All this consumerism required money, and as single-earner households often couldn't afford to "keep up with the Joneses," more women entered the working world. While the vast majority of married women continued to stay at home, more than ever—about 15 percent—entered the work force. Women continued, as they had in the past, to work in predominantly female-dominated professions (often called "pink collar jobs"), such as school teaching or office-assistant work, and to earn much less than men.

Despite the persistence of traditional roles for women, a new image of American women emerged and became a symbol of the Roaring Twenties—the **flapper**. World War I, the allure of the "big city," the right to vote, and new attitudes brought about by the ideas of Sigmund Freud (whose ideas were just beginning to circulate in the United States during the 1920s) opened up a whole new world for this new generation of emancipated women. They discarded the corset, layers of petticoats and long, dark dresses worn by their Victorian grandmothers, in favor of waistless dresses worn above the knee (shocking!), flesh-colored silk stockings (brought back from Paris), cute little hats, strings of long beads, a wrist full of bracelets, and ruby-red lips. Many flappers risked ruining their reputation by smoking cigarettes; drinking in public (despite Prohibition); and dancing the tango, the lindy, and the shimmy.

The rapid modernization of American society was reflected in the way it entertained itself. **Movies** grew tremendously popular during the decade, reflecting back at the nation its idealized self-image; on movie screens, young, independent-minded, gorgeous heroes and heroines defied all odds to succeed in romance and—at the same time—strike it rich. Sports grew more popular as well, especially baseball, whose greatest player of the era, Babe Ruth, was idolized by millions. In literature, America gained international prominence through such world-class authors as **F. Scott Fitzgerald**, **Ernest Hemingway**, and playwright **Eugene O'Neill**. Ironically, many of these writers moved to Europe, where they chronicled their alienation from the modern era, which explains why they came to be known as the **lost generation**.

> F. Scott Fitzgerald's writings reflected disillusionment with the opulence and excess of the 1920s. *The Great Gatsby*, one of his most famous works, depicted an outsider's views of the lavish lifestyle of New York City's elite. Ernest Hemingway's experiences in World War I are reflected in many of his books, like *A Farewell to Arms* and *The Sun Also Rises*. Hemingway's realistic portrayal of war expressed his disillusionment with World War I, which is similar to many other Lost Generation writers.

In the largest black neighborhood of New York City, theaters, cultural clubs, and newspapers sprang up—a development called the **Harlem Renaissance**. W. E. B. Du Bois opened writers' centers, and his prominence helped draw attention to Harlem's cultural movement. Among the great figures of the Harlem Renaissance were the poets **Langston Hughes**, **Countee Cullen**, and **Zora Neale Hurston**. Another major black cultural development was the popularization of **jazz**. Because jazz featured improvisation and free-spiritedness, it came to be seen as emblematic of the era (which is how the decade came to be known as the **Jazz Age**). Probably the most popular and most gifted of the era's jazz musicians was trumpeter **Louis Armstrong**.

American Jewish culture also thrived in the early 20th century. There were a dozen Yiddish theaters in New York City alone, performing mostly satirical plays for Jewish audiences.

Backlash Against Modern Culture

Not all Americans were excited about the rapid transition into the modern age, and the 1920s were also a time of considerable reactionary backlash and renewed nativism. Most prominently, the **Ku Klux Klan** grew to more than 5 million members and widened its targets, attacking blacks, Jews, urbanites, and anyone whose behavior deviated from the Klan's narrowly defined code of acceptable Christian behavior. Anti-immigration groups grew in strength as well, targeting the growing number of southern and Eastern European immigrants. Accusations that America's newcomers were dangerous subversives intensified when two Italian immigrant anarchists, **Sacco and Vanzetti**, were arrested on charges of murder. (Their trial immediately became a cause célèbre for the political left, as the evidence against them was inconclusive. Nonetheless, they were convicted and executed.) At the start of the decade, the United States started setting limits and quotas to restrict immigration. The **Emergency Quota Act of 1924** set immigration quotas based on national origins and discriminated against the "new immigrants" who came from Southern and Eastern Europe. These limits were set to reduce "foreign influence" on the country.

Another famous trial also illustrated the societal tensions of the decade. In 1925, Tennessee passed a law forbidding teachers to teach the theory of evolution. **John Thomas Scopes** broke that law, and his trial (dubbed the **Scopes Monkey Trial**) drew national attention, due in part to the two prominent attorneys arguing the case—**Clarence Darrow** and **William Jennings Bryan**, who, you may recall, ran for president in 1896, 1900, and 1908. The case also captivated the nation because, for many, it encapsulated the debate over whether to stick with tradition or abandon it for progress's sake.

Nineteenth-century morals played a part in the institution of **Prohibition**, which banned the manufacture, sale, and transport of alcoholic beverages. The Prohibition movement had its roots in the reform campaigns of the 1830s and remained a mainstay of women's political agendas until, on the eve of women's enfranchisement (1917), the **Eighteenth Amendment** outlawed the American liquor industry. Many people soon came to resent the government's intrusion in what they considered a private matter. Prohibition was further weakened by the effectiveness of organized crime in producing and selling liquor, especially in the cities. Open warfare between competing gangs and between criminals and law enforcement earned this period the title of the **gangster era,** which inspired many movies and television series. Prohibition was repealed by the Twenty-first Amendment in 1933.

Herbert Hoover and the Beginning of the Great Depression

In 1928, the Republicans nominated **Herbert Hoover**. Like Coolidge, Hoover was able to parlay a strong economy into an easy victory. During his campaign, Hoover predicted that the day would soon come when no American would live in poverty. He turned out to be very wrong.

In October 1929, the bottom fell out of the stock market, and this was one of the reasons for the Great Depression, but not the main reason. Prices dropped, and no matter how far they dropped, nobody wanted to buy. Hoover and his advisers underestimated the damage that the stock market crash would eventually cause. Convinced that the economy was sound, Hoover reassured the public that only stock traders would be hurt because of their irresponsible speculation. (Traders had been allowed to buy on margin, which meant that they might have to put up only 10 or 20 percent of the cost of each stock, allowing them to borrow against future profits that might or might not materialize. Margin buying is a destabilizing practice that was made illegal soon after the crash.) Unfortunately, among those speculators were huge banks and corporations, which suddenly found themselves on the verge of bankruptcy and unable to pay employees or guarantee bank deposits.

Other factors contributed to plunging the nation into a deep depression. Immediately following World War I, the carnage of the conflict, along with Germany's disastrous attempts to satisfy its reparations obligations under the Treaty of Versailles, had put Europe's economy, and much of the rest of the world's, into a depression. Domestically, though, manufacturers and farmers had been overproducing for years, creating large inventories. This led factories to lay off workers and made the farmers' crops worth much less on the market. Furthermore, production of new consumer goods was outstripping the public's ability to buy them. Supply so exceeded demand for so many goods, that this might be the main underlying cause for the Great Depression, ultimately leading to deflation, unemployment, and business failures. Finally, government laxity in regulating large businesses had led to the concentration of wealth and power in the hands of a very few businessmen. When their businesses failed, many people were thrown out of work.

The Depression had a calamitous effect on tens of millions of Americans. People lost their jobs as their employers went bankrupt or, to avoid bankruptcy, laid off the majority of workers. People lost their life savings as thousands of banks failed, and many lost their homes when they could not keep up with mortgage payments. The homeless built shantytowns, sarcastically called **Hoovervilles.** In rural areas, farmers struggled to survive as produce prices dropped more than 50 percent. Furthermore, a prolonged drought afflicted the Great Plains area of the Midwest, turning the region into a giant **Dust Bowl**. The situation encouraged agrarian unrest; farmers fought evictions and foreclosures by attacking those who tried to enforce them. Farmers also conspired to keep prices at farm auctions low and then returned the auctioned property to its original owner. In addition, they formed the **Farmers' Holiday Association**, which organized demonstrations and threatened a nationwide walkout by farmers in order to raise prices.

At first, Hoover opposed any federal relief efforts because he believed they violated the American ideal of "rugged individualism," but as the Depression worsened, he initiated a few farm assistance programs and campaigned for federal works projects (such as the Hoover Dam and the Grand Coulee Dam) that would create jobs. He hoped that raising tariffs would help American business, but the **Hawley-Smoot Tariff** actually worsened the economy. The Hawley-Smoot Tariff was the highest protective tariff in U.S. history, and it was enacted during one of the worst economic depressions ever. After that, Hoover had Congress create the Federal Emergency Relief Administration. This provided government money to bail out large companies and banks, but only ones big enough to potentially pay the money back later on.

Hoover's most embarrassing moment came in 1932 when Congress considered early payment of benefits to World War I veterans. Tens of thousands of impoverished veterans and their families, calling themselves the **Bonus Expeditionary**

Force (BEF), came to Washington to lobby for the bill. When the bill was narrowly defeated, many refused to leave. They squatted in empty government offices or built shanties and stayed through the summer. In July, Hoover ordered the Army to expel them, which Douglas MacArthur chose to do with excessive force. Employing the cavalry and attacking with tear gas, Army forces drove the veterans from D.C. and then burned their makeshift homes. Two people died during the attack, and thousands were injured.

News of the Army attack on the BEF killed any chance Hoover had for reelection, partly because he had taken the heat for MacArthur's actions. Nonetheless, by the summer of 1932, he had already secured the Republican nomination. He ran a campaign stressing his traditional conservative values. (His main concession was to accept the repeal of Prohibition; Hoover had opposed repeal during his first term.) His opponent, New York Governor **Franklin D. Roosevelt**, argued for a more interventionist government. Roosevelt also promised relief payments to the unemployed, which Hoover had opposed throughout his term. Roosevelt won the election easily.

THE NEW DEAL AND WORLD WAR II (1934–1945)

In his inaugural address, Roosevelt declared war on the Depression, and he asked the country to grant him the same broad powers that presidents exercise during wars against foreign nations. He also tried to rally the public's confidence. In the most famous line of the speech, Roosevelt declared, "The only thing we have to fear is fear itself—nameless, unreasoning, unjustified fear." Both a powerful presidency and the people's confidence in Roosevelt played a large part in the implementation of his sweeping reforms, called the **New Deal**.

The First New Deal

Early in 1933, Roosevelt summoned an emergency session of Congress to work out the details of his recovery plan. The period that followed is often called the **First Hundred Days** because (1) that's how long it lasted, and (2) it was during this time that the government implemented most of the major programs associated with the **First New Deal**. (The **Second New Deal** began two years later.)

Roosevelt first sought to reestablish America's confidence in its banking system. The **Emergency Banking Relief Bill** put poorly managed banks under the control of the Treasury Department and granted government licenses (which functioned as seals of approval) to those that were solvent. In the first of many **fireside chats** broadcast over the radio, Roosevelt reassured the public that the banks were once again secure. More than 60 million Americans listened, and they obviously took Roosevelt at his word. The following week, millions redeposited the savings they had withdrawn during the bank failures of the previous years. American banks, once on the verge of ruin, were again healthy and could begin to contribute to the economic recovery. Later during the first hundred days, the government passed the **Banking Act of 1933**, which created the **Federal Deposit Insurance**

Corporation (**FDIC**) to guarantee bank deposits, which was a big deal since people used to lose all of the money in their accounts if a bank went bankrupt. Roosevelt also instituted a number of intentionally inflationary measures in order to artificially raise prices (to get more money flowing into the economy).

Roosevelt then set out to provide relief for the rural poor. At the time, farmers were overproducing. They hoped that by growing more they could make up for falling produce prices, but their efforts were futile; the more they produced, the further prices fell, just as they had in the 1800s during the time of the Populists. Roosevelt's solution was the **Agricultural Adjustment Act**, referred to as the **AAA**. (So many of Roosevelt's new agencies were referred to by their acronyms that the entire group became known as the **alphabet agencies.**) The AAA provided payments to farmers in return for their agreement to cut production by up to one-half; the money to cover this program came from increased taxes on meat packers, millers, and other food processors. A month later, Congress passed the **Farm Credit Act**, which provided loans to those farmers in danger of foreclosure.

Several other New Deal programs established government control over industry. The **National Industrial Recovery Act** (**NIRA**) consolidated businesses and coordinated their activities with the aim of eliminating overproduction and, by so doing, stabilizing prices. The NIRA also established the **Public Works Administration** (**PWA**), which set aside $3 billion to create jobs building roads, sewers, public housing units, and other civic necessities. At the same time, the **Civilian Conservation Corps** (**CCC**) provided grants to the states to manage their own PWA-like projects. In one of the New Deal's most daring moves, the government took over the **Tennessee Valley Authority** (**TVA**). Under government control the TVA (which provided energy to the Tennessee Valley region) expanded its operations greatly, which led to the economic recovery of the region.

In June 1933, Congress adjourned, ending the First Hundred Days. Most of the programs that made up the First New Deal were in place, although others, such as the creation of both the **National Labor Relations Board** (**NLRB**)—which mediated labor disputes—and the **Securities and Exchange Commission** (**SEC**)—which regulated the stock market—were not implemented until 1934. The First New Deal was an immediate success, both politically and economically; the unemployment rate fell and wages rose. In the midterm elections of 1934, the Democrats increased their majorities in both houses.

Keynesian Economics

Roosevelt's response to the Great Depression was guided by the work of the economist **John Maynard Keynes. Keynes** contended that depressions were the result of a vicious cycle in which people see that the economy is bad, so they fear that money will be hard to come by, so they don't spend the money they have, so businesses fail, so the economy worsens, so people fear that money will be hard to come by, and so on. The solution, Keynes argued, was for the government to step in and embark on a program of deliberate **deficit spending**, as the **multiplier effect** would ensure that every dollar spent would do several dollars' worth of good in reviving the economy. If the people who needed money the most received a little extra, they would spend it immediately on the things they needed; that money would go to businesses, who could afford to hire more people, who would start receiving paychecks and then spend that money, which would go to businesses, who could afford to hire more people, and so on. The success of Keynesian economics during the Roosevelt administration, especially as embodied in the United States' deficit spending during World War II, led to widespread acceptance of Keynes's theories, which resulted in nearly 30 years of economic expansion, from 1945 to 1973.

The Second New Deal

Not everyone, however, was enamored of the New Deal. In fact, both ends of the political spectrum criticized Roosevelt. **Conservatives** opposed the higher tax rates that the New Deal brought; they also disliked the increase in government power over business, and they complained that relief programs removed the incentive for the poor to lift themselves out of poverty. Additionally, the government had to borrow to finance all of its programs, and its **deficit spending** was also anathema to conservatives. **Leftists,** such as Huey Long, complained that the AAA policy of paying farmers *not* to grow was immoral, given that many Americans were still too poor to feed themselves. They also felt that government policy toward businesses was too favorable; they wanted more punitive measures, as many on the left blamed corporate greed for the Depression. The despair caused by the Depression provided fodder for a more radical left, and the **Socialists** (and, to a lesser extent, the **Communist Party of America**) were gaining popularity by calling for the nationalization (that is, a takeover by the government) of businesses.

Then, in 1935, the Supreme Court started to dismantle some of the programs of the First New Deal in a series of cases, one of which came to be known as the "sick chicken case." *Schechter Poultry Corp. v. United States* invalidated sections of the NIRA on the grounds that the codes created under this agency were unconstitutional. According to the Constitution, only Congress can make laws. However, the NIRA empowered an agency within the executive branch of government to set wage and price ceilings, maximum work hours, and regulations regarding labor unions. The court ruled that these codes were in effect "executive legislation" and beyond the limits of executive power.

Roosevelt had argued that like war, the Great Depression had created a national crisis that warranted the expansion of the executive branch of government. The following year, the Supreme Court struck down the AAA in *United States v. Butler*. In 1937, Roosevelt responded by attempting to "pack the court" with justices who supported his policies. The size of the Supreme Court had changed a few times since its creation, but Roosevelt's attempt to increase the size of the court from 9 justices to 15, giving him the power to pick justices whose views he liked, was too much for most Democrats, let alone Republicans. As a result, this **court-packing scheme** was rejected by Congress.

Roosevelt then continued with a package of legislation called the **Second New Deal**. First, he established the Emergency Relief Appropriation Act, which created the **Works Progress Administration** (**WPA**), whose name was later changed to the Works Project Administration. The WPA generated more than 8 million jobs, all paid for by the government. Along with public works projects, such as construction, the WPA also employed writers, photographers, and other artists to create travel guides and to record local and personal histories.

The summer of 1935 is often called Roosevelt's **Second Hundred Days** because the amount and importance of legislation passed then is comparable to that of the First Hundred Days. During this period, Congress passed legislation that broadened the powers of the **NLRB**, democratized unions, and punished businesses with anti-union policies. During this time, Congress also created the **Social Security Administration** to provide retirement benefits for many workers, including the

As a senator, and then governor, of Louisiana, Huey Long was a huge threat to FDR in 1934 and 1935 and strongly promoted a plan similar to Social Security, gaining him supporters around the country (and encouraging FDR to have Congress create the Social Security Act and increase income taxes). He was assassinated in the summer of 1935 by a man angry that Long had redistricted his father's judicial district.

disabled and families whose main breadwinner had died. Furthermore, the government increased taxes on wealthy individuals and top-end business profits. The cumulative effect of these programs led to the creation of the **New Deal coalition**, made up of union members, urbanites, the underclass, and blacks (who had previously voted Republican, out of loyalty to the party of Lincoln). This new Democratic coalition swept Roosevelt back into office with a landslide victory in 1936 and held together until the election of Reagan in 1980.

Roosevelt's Troubled Second Term

Several problems marred Franklin Roosevelt's second term. The first major failure of his presidency came as the term began. Angry that the Supreme Court had overturned much of the First New Deal and worried that the same fate awaited the Second New Deal, Roosevelt drafted a **Judicial Reorganization** bill. The bill proposed that Roosevelt be allowed to name a new federal judge for every sitting judge who had reached the age of 70 and had not retired; if passed, it would have allowed Roosevelt to add six new Supreme Court justices and more than 40 other federal judges. A not-so-subtle effort at **packing the courts** with judges more sympathetic to Roosevelt's policies, the bill was soundly defeated in the Democratic Congress, and Roosevelt came under intense criticism for trying to seize too much power. Ultimately, the court situation worked itself out to Roosevelt's benefit. A number of justices retired not long after the incident, and Roosevelt was able to replace them with more liberal judges.

In 1937, the economy went into a **recession**, a period of continually decreasing output. The cause was twofold: Roosevelt, satisfied that the New Deal was doing its job, cut back government programs in an effort to balance the budget. At the same time, the Federal Reserve Board tightened the credit supply in an effort to slow inflation. Both actions took money out of circulation, resulting in a slower economy. The recession lasted for almost three years and caused a substantial increase in the unemployment rate.

To top off Roosevelt's second term, by 1938, it was becoming evident that Europe might soon be at war again. This situation forced Roosevelt to withdraw some money from New Deal programs in order to fund a military buildup. The administration succeeded in passing a second Agricultural Adjustment Act that met the standards set by the Supreme Court's rejection of the first AAA; it also secured the **Fair Labor Standards Act**, which set a minimum wage and established the 40-hour workweek for a number of professions. Not long after, however, the New Deal came to an end.

Did the New Deal work? Historians like to debate this question. Those who argue "yes" point to the many people who escaped life-threatening poverty because of government assistance, and especially to the immediate relief provided by the First New Deal. They also point to the many reforms of banking, finance, and management/union relations. In these areas, the New Deal remade America in ways that are still recognizable today. Finally, proponents of the New Deal argue that Roosevelt should be praised for taking bold chances in a conservative political climate; he risked new initiatives when it was clear that old solutions were failing.

On the other hand, those who assert that the New Deal failed can point to the unemployment rate, which remained in double digits throughout the New Deal. Conservative historians argue that the New Deal thus did not solve the unemployment problem. Some on the left agree, contending that the New Deal was too small and too short-lived—look at how unemployment began to spike in 1937 when Roosevelt took his foot off the gas—and that it wasn't until the truly massive deficit spending program put in place in response to World War II that the economy began to recover in earnest. Furthermore, today's social welfare system stems from the New Deal; those who feel that the current American system has failed can point to Roosevelt as the man who started it all. Lastly, the New Deal did not benefit all equally. Minorities, in particular, reaped fewer (and sometimes no) benefits. The AAA actually hurt blacks and tenant farmers by putting them out of work; some of the public works projects underhired blacks, and almost all were segregated.

Foreign Policy Leading up to World War II

In the decade that followed World War I, American foreign policy objectives were aimed primarily at promoting and maintaining peace and have been described as "independent internationalism" rather than "isolationism." The **Washington Conference** (1921–1922) gathered eight of the world's great powers; the resulting treaty set limits on stockpiling armaments and reaffirmed the Open Door Policy toward China. In 1928, a total of 62 nations signed the **Kellogg-Briand Pact**, which condemned war as a means of foreign policy. Although it contained no enforcement clauses, the Kellogg-Briand Pact was widely considered a good first step toward a postwar age.

In Latin America, the United States tried to back away from its previous interventionist policy and replace it with the **Good Neighbor Policy** in 1934. The name, however, is misleading; the United States continued to actively promote its interests in Latin America, often to the detriment of those who lived there. However, the Platt Amendment was repealed at this time. The United States achieved its foreign policy objectives mainly through economic coercion and support of pro-American leaders (some of whom were corrupt and brutal). The United States also figured out how to maintain a strong but less threatening military presence in the area, both by paying for the privilege of maintaining military bases in the countries and by arranging to train the nations' National Guard units.

In Asia, the United States had less influence. Consequently, when Japan invaded Manchuria in 1931 (and in so doing violated the Kellogg-Briand Pact, which Japan had signed), the League of Nations was powerless, and the American government could do little. When Japan went to war against China in 1937, the United States sold arms to the Chinese and called for an embargo on arms sales to Japan. However, fearful of provoking a war with Japan, the government did not order an embargo on commercial shipments to Japan from the United States.

Throughout the Republican administrations of the 1920s, the U.S. government kept tariffs high; this policy is called **protectionism**. Early in Franklin Roosevelt's presidency, the government devised a method of using economic leverage as a foreign policy tool. The **Reciprocal Trade Agreements Act** allowed the president to reduce tariffs if he felt doing so would achieve foreign policy goals. Countries granted **most favored nation (MFN) trade status** were eligible for the lowest tariff rate set by the United States, if they played their cards right. MFN trade status remains a foreign policy tool today.

Disenchantment with the results of World War I fed isolationist sentiment, a stance amplified by the findings of the **Nye Commission**. Led by Senator Gerald Nye, the commission's report in 1936 revealed unwholesome activities by American arms manufacturers; many had lobbied intensely for entry into World War I, others had bribed foreign officials, and still others were currently supplying fascist governments with weapons. Congress responded by passing a series of **neutrality acts**. The first neutrality act (1935) prohibited the sale of arms to either belligerent in a war. (Roosevelt sidestepped this act in the 1937 sale of arms to China by simply refusing to acknowledge that China and Japan were at war.) The second neutrality act banned loans to belligerents.

All the while, Roosevelt poured money into the military—just in case. As it became more apparent that Europe was headed for war, Roosevelt lobbied for a repeal of the arms embargo stated in the first neutrality act so that America could help arm the Allies (primarily England, France, and, later, the Soviet Union). When war broke out, Congress relented with a third neutrality act, which allowed arms sales and was termed "cash and carry." It required the Allies to (1) pay cash for their weapons, and (2) come to the United States to pick up their purchases and carry them away on their own ships. From the outset of the war until America's entry in 1941, Roosevelt angled the country toward participation, particularly when Poland fell to German troops and other countries followed in rapid succession. In 1940, Hitler invaded France, and a German takeover of both France and England appeared a real possibility. The chance that America might soon enter the war convinced Roosevelt to run for an unprecedented third term. Again, he won convincingly.

Within the limits allowed by the neutrality acts, Roosevelt worked to assist the Allies. He found creative ways to supply them with extra weapons and ships; he appointed pro-Ally Republicans to head the Department of War and the Navy; and he instituted the nation's first peacetime military draft. It becomes increasingly difficult to describe U.S. foreign policy as isolationist by the 1940s. In 1941, Roosevelt forced the **Lend-Lease Act** through Congress, which permitted the United States to "lend" armaments to England, which no longer had money to buy the tools of war. Roosevelt sent American ships into the war zone to protect Lend-Lease shipments, an act which could easily have provoked a German attack. Later in the year, Roosevelt and British Prime Minister Winston Churchill met at the **Atlantic Charter Conference**. The Atlantic Charter declared the Allies' war aims, which included disarmament, self-determination, freedom of the seas, and guarantees of each nation's security.

Given all this activity in the European theater, it seems odd that America's entry to the war came not in Europe but in Asia. Japan entered into an alliance (called the **Tripartite Pact**) with Italy and Germany in 1940. By 1941, France had fallen to Germany, and the British were too busy fighting Hitler to block

Island-Hopping: Not Just a Vacation Strategy
"Island-hopping," also known as "leapfrogging," was a military strategy employed by the Allies in the Pacific War during World War II. Instead of attacking more obvious mainland targets first, this strategy sought to target Pacific islands that were not well defended but were later capable of providing access to the main islands of Japan. While General Douglas MacArthur took credit for inventing island-hopping, it was, in fact, a Naval innovation.

Japanese expansion, which had continued south into French Indochina (modern-day Vietnam, Cambodia, and Laos). The United States responded to Japanese aggression by cutting off trade to Japan, which was dependent on foreign imports. The embargo included oil, which Japan needed to fuel its war machine. Despite peace talks in November of 1941 between the United States and Japan to avoid war, the United States had broken Japan's secret communication codes and knew that Japan was planning an attack but did not know the location. Secretary of War **Henry Stimson** encouraged Roosevelt to wait for the Japanese attack in order to guarantee popular support for the war at home. He did not have to wait long. The Japanese attacked **Pearl Harbor**, Hawaii, on December 7, and U.S. participation in the war began.

World War II

Complicated military strategy and the outcome of key battles played a big part in World War II. Fortunately, you do not have to know much about them for the AP Exam; nor do you need to know about the many truly unspeakable horrors the Nazis perpetrated on Europe's Jews, gypsies, homosexuals, and dissidents. You should know about the various wartime conferences, however, when the Allies met to discuss military strategy and the eventual postwar situation. It was no secret that the Grand Alliance between the Soviet Union and the West was tenuous at best, held together by the thread of a common enemy but threatened by Stalin's impatience at the Allies' delay in opening a "second front" while the Soviets bore the brunt of the Nazi onslaught.

The Manhattan Project of 1942 was a concentrated research and development effort to develop the first atomic bombs. Based in Los Alamos, New Mexico, a team of more than 100,000 scientists and technicians created and tested nuclear bombs on the Pacific island of Bikini. Despite tight security measures, Soviet spies infiltrated the program, the most famous being **Ethel and Julius Rosenberg**.

The first meeting of the "big three" (Roosevelt, Churchill, and Stalin) took place in the Iranian capital of Tehran in November of 1943. It was here that they planned the Normandy invasion, **D-Day**, and agreed to divide a defeated Germany into occupation zones after the war. Stalin also agreed to enter the war against Japan once Hitler had been defeated. The Allies fought the Germans primarily in the Soviet Union and in the Mediterranean until early 1944, when Allied forces invaded occupied France (on D-Day). The Soviet Union paid a huge price in human and material loss for this strategy and after the war sought to recoup its losses by occupying Eastern Europe. In the Pacific, both sides incurred huge numbers of casualties. The Allies eventually won a war of attrition against the Germans, and the Americans accelerated victory in the East by dropping two atomic bombs on Japan.

D-Day occurred on June 6, 1944, and was the largest amphibious landing of all time.

As it had during the Civil War, World War I, and the New Deal, the government acquired more power than it previously had. The War Production Board allowed the government to oversee the mobilization of industry toward the war effort; in return, businesses were guaranteed generous profits. **Rationing** of almost all consumer goods was imposed. The government sponsored scientific research directed at improving weaponry, developing **radar**, sonar, and the atomic bomb during this period. The government also exerted greater control over labor. The **Labor**

Disputes Act of 1943 (passed in reaction to a disconcerting number of strikes in essential industries) allowed government takeover of businesses deemed necessary to national security, which gave the government authority to settle labor disputes. **Hollywood** was enlisted to create numerous propaganda films, both to encourage support on the home front and to boost morale of the troops overseas. Not surprisingly, the size of the government more than tripled during the war.

FDR signed the **Selective Training and Service Act of 1940**, which created the first peacetime draft in U.S. history and gave birth to the current incarnation of the Selective Service System, which ultimately provided about 10 million soldiers toward the war effort. (Although the draft was discontinued in 1973, after the United States' involvement in Vietnam, the Selective Service System remained in place and currently requires that all male citizens register for the draft within 30 days after turning 18.)

World War II affected almost every aspect of daily life at home and abroad. It created both new opportunities and new tensions within American society. More than a million African Americans served in the U.S. military during World War II, but they lived and worked in segregated units. The U.S. army was not desegregated until after the war, during the Truman administration in 1948. A popular image, familiar to most Americans, is that of Rosie the Riveter. Originally featured on a poster of the era, Rosie came to symbolize the millions of women who worked in war-related industrial jobs during World War II. Unfortunately for the cause of feminism, most women were expected to take off the coveralls and put the apron back on when the soldiers returned home.

Again, as during World War I, the government restricted civil liberties. Probably the most tragic instance was the **internment of Japanese Americans** from 1942 to the end of the war. Fearful that the Japanese might serve as enemy agents within U.S. borders, the government imprisoned more than 110,000 Asian Americans, over two-thirds of whom had been born in the United States and thus were U.S. citizens. Some were not even of Japanese descent. None of those interned was ever charged with a crime; imprisonment was based entirely on ethnic background. The government placed these Japanese Americans in desolate prison camps far from the West Coast, where they feared a Japanese invasion would take place. Most lost their homes and possessions as a result of the internment.

The Supreme Court upheld the constitutionality of both the evacuation and internment of Japanese Americans. As in the *Schenck* case of 1919, the Court ruled that a citizen's civil liberties can be curtailed and even violated in time of war. "Citizenship has its responsibilities as well as its privileges, and in time of war, the burden is always heavier. Compulsory exclusion of large groups of citizens from their homes, except under circumstances of direst emergency and peril, is inconsistent with our basic governmental institutions. But when under conditions of modern warfare our shores are threatened by hostile forces, the power to protect must be commensurate with the threatened danger..." wrote Justice Hugo Black in *Korematsu v. United States* (1944). It wasn't until 1988 that a government apology was made and reparations of about $1.6 million were disbursed to surviving internees and their heirs.

The End of the War

As the war neared its end in Europe, the apparent victors—the Allies—met to discuss the fate of postwar Europe. In February of 1945, the Allied leaders met at **Yalta** and in effect redrew the world map. By this time the Soviet army occupied parts of Eastern Europe, a result of the campaign to drive the German army out of the USSR.

Stalin wanted to create a "buffer zone" between the Soviet Union and Western Europe; he wanted to surround himself with nations that were "friendly" toward the government in Moscow. Because of the presence of the Red Army, Stalin was given a free hand in Eastern Europe, a decision the other Allies would later regret, with the promise to hold "free and unfettered elections" after the war. Despite this promise, Soviet tanks rolled into Romania three weeks after Yalta, thus beginning the establishment of Soviet **satellites** and the descent of the **Iron Curtain**. (The Iron Curtain was a metaphor coined by Winston Churchill in 1946 to describe the symbolic division of Eastern and Western Europe, thus the origins of the Cold War following World War II.)

The Allies agreed on a number of issues concerning borders and postwar settlements. They also agreed that once the war in Europe ended, the USSR would declare war on Japan. Toward the end of the war, the Allies agreed to help create the **United Nations** to mediate future international disputes. The Allies met again at **Potsdam** to decide how to implement the agreements of Yalta. This time, **Harry S. Truman** represented the United States, as Roosevelt had died in April. Things did not go as well at Potsdam; with the war's end closer and the Nazis no longer a threat, the differences between the United States and the Soviet Union were growing more pronounced.

While at the Potsdam Conference, the Allies created the Potsdam Declaration, which established the terms for the surrender of Japan, which included the removal of the emperor from power. Many historians believe this term kept the Japanese from agreeing to surrender, which then provoked the dropping of the atomic bombs.

Some argue that American-Soviet animosity prompted Truman's decision to use the **atomic bomb** against the Japanese. (By this argument, America feared Soviet entry into the Asian war where the Soviets might then attempt to expand their influence, as they were doing in Eastern Europe. Along the same line of reasoning, one could assert that the United States wanted to put on a massive display of power to intimidate the Soviets.) However, the manner in which the war in the Pacific had been fought to that point also supported Truman's decision. The Japanese had fought tenaciously and remained powerful despite the long war; casualty estimates of an American invasion of Japan ran upward of 500,000. Some military leaders estimated that such an invasion would not subdue Japan for years. In August, the United States dropped two atomic bombs, first on **Hiroshima** and then three days later on **Nagasaki**. The Japanese surrendered soon after.

Summary

Here are the most important concepts to remember from the early 20th-century period.

o   America transitioned from a largely rural and agricultural society to an urban industrialized society.

o   Land in the West was largely settled and the boundaries of the Continental United States became fixed.

o   America became embroiled in foreign conflicts.

o   Isolationism and anti-immigrant sentiment collided with globalism and social reform.

o   The Great Depression became the longest protracted economic challenge in American history.

o   American Indians settled on reservations as sovereign nations under the oversight of the Bureau of Indian Affairs.

o   Communications and transportation technologies revolutionized daily American life.

Chapter 11 Review Questions

See Chapter 14 for answers and explanations.

1. Muckrakers furthered the causes of the Progressive movement by

   (A) organizing grassroots campaigns for political reform at the state level
   (B) suing large companies and donating their court awards to Progressive campaigns
   (C) staging large, violent protests in support of Progressive goals
   (D) alerting the public to the social ills and corporate corruption targeted by Progressives

2. Prior to the administration of Theodore Roosevelt, the Sherman Antitrust Act had been used primarily to

   (A) dismantle corporate monopolies
   (B) suppress trade unions
   (C) impose import tariffs
   (D) enforce civil rights in the South

3. Following the Spanish-American War and the acquisition of territory overseas, in a series of cases known as the Insular Cases, the U.S. Supreme Court ruled that

   (A) natives living on American soil abroad were guaranteed the same rights and privileges as U.S. citizens living within the continental United States
   (B) colonial subjects within the American Empire were not entitled to the rights guaranteed by the U.S. Constitution
   (C) "the Constitution follows the flag"
   (D) Congress must relinquish control of these overseas possessions and honor their right of self-determination

4. Which of the following best summarizes the contents of the Zimmermann telegram, which was intercepted in 1917?

   (A) Germany offered Mexico a chance to regain the land it had lost in the Mexican Cession if Mexico attacked the United States and helped prevent the United States from assisting the Allies.
   (B) A British spy alerted the world to the existence of mass extermination camps in German-held territories.
   (C) The United States assured the British that it would join the war in Europe if the war were to continue for another year.
   (D) The owner of the Boston Red Sox revealed a plan to sell star player Babe Ruth to the New York Yankees for a large amount of cash.

5. Wilson's Fourteen Points plan for peace after World War I included all of the following EXCEPT

   (A) promotion of universal self-determination
   (B) lower tariffs to promote free trade
   (C) repayment of all Allied war expenses by Germany
   (D) across-the-board arms reductions

6. All of the following can be seen as clashes between traditional and modern culture during the post–World War I era EXCEPT

   (A) the rise of the Ku Klux Klan
   (B) the Teapot Dome Scandal
   (C) the Scopes Monkey Trial
   (D) the Emergency Quota Act of 1924

7. Buying "on margin" contributed to the stock market crash of 1929 because it

   (A) required investors to purchase only high-risk, volatile stocks
   (B) imposed high interest rates that discouraged trading
   (C) prevented traders from learning the true financial state of the companies in which they invested
   (D) allowed traders to pay for stock with projected future profits

8. Franklin Roosevelt invoked the Good Neighbor Policy in taking which of the following actions?

   (A) Providing England with munitions to defend itself against Germany
   (B) Creating the Tennessee Valley Authority to provide power in the poor rural South
   (C) Banning trade of war-related materials with Japan and freezing Japanese assets in the United States
   (D) Recalling U.S. troops from Nicaragua and Haiti

9. The Nye Commission report of 1936 reinforced American isolationism by

   (A) revealing unethical profiteering by American munitions companies during World War I
   (B) concluding that Germany had no interest in engaging the United States in war
   (C) listing the domestic programs that would have to be forfeited if the United States were to increase its overseas commitments
   (D) detailing deficiencies in all branches of the U.S. military

10. In its *Korematsu v. United States* decision, the Supreme Court ruled that

   (A) the wartime relocation of West Coast Japanese Americans was not unconstitutional
   (B) the Japanese government had no legitimate claim to reparations for the bombings of Hiroshima and Nagasaki
   (C) the U.S. government had violated the Constitution by entering the Korean War
   (D) immigration quotas based on race were unconstitutional

REFLECT

Respond to the following questions:

- For which content topics discussed in this chapter do you feel you have achieved sufficient mastery to answer multiple-choice questions correctly?

- For which content topics discussed in this chapter do you feel you have achieved sufficient mastery to discuss effectively in a short-answer question or an essay?

- On which content topics discussed in this chapter do you feel you need more work before you can answer multiple-choice questions correctly?

- On which content topics discussed in this chapter do you feel you need more work before you can discuss them effectively in a short-answer question or an essay?

- What parts of this chapter are you going to review again?

- Will you seek further help, outside of this book (such as a teacher, tutor, or AP Students), on any of the content in this chapter—and, if so, on what content?

Chapter 12
The Postwar Period and Cold War (1945–1980)

TRUMAN AND THE BEGINNING OF THE COLD WAR (1945–1953)

The end of World War II raised two major issues. The first concerned the survival of the combatants; with the exception of the United States, the nations involved in World War II had all seen fighting within their borders, and the destruction had been immense. The second issue involved the shape of the new world and what new political alliances would be formed. This question would become the major source of contention between the world's two leading political-economic systems, capitalism and communism.

The stakes in this power struggle, called the **Cold War** (because there was no actual combat as there is in a "hot war"), were high. Though the major powers (the United States and Soviet Union) didn't enter into combat in the Cold War, the United States did fight hot **proxy wars** in Korea and Vietnam during this time. The American economy was growing more dependent on exports; American industry also needed to import metals, a process requiring (1) open trade and (2) friendly relations with those nations that provided those metals. In addition, with many postwar economies in shambles, competition among the few reasonably healthy economies grew fiercer. Finally, those countries that were strongest before the war—Germany, Japan, and Great Britain—had either been defeated or seen their influence abroad greatly reduced. The United States and the Soviet Union emerged as the two new superpowers. Although they were allies during World War II, the war's end exposed the countries' many ideological differences, and they soon became enemies.

Truman and Foreign Policy

The differences between Soviet and American goals were apparent even before the war was over, but became even clearer when the Soviets refused to recognize Poland's conservative government-in-exile. (The Polish government had moved to England to escape the Nazis; this government was backed by the United States.) A communist government took over Poland. Within two years, pro-Soviet communist coups had also taken place in Hungary and Czechoslovakia. The propaganda in the United States and USSR during this period reached a fever pitch. In each country, the other was portrayed as trying to take over the world for its own sinister purposes.

Then, in 1947, communist insurgents threatened to take over both Greece and Turkey, but England could no longer prop up these nations. In a speech before Congress in which he asked for $400 million in aid to the two countries, Truman asserted, "I believe it must be the policy of the United States to support free peoples who are resisting attempted subjugation by armed minorities or outside pressures." This statement, called the **Truman Doctrine,** became the cornerstone of a larger policy, called **containment**, articulated by George Kennan. The idea of containment came from what is known as the **Long Telegram**, which Kennan sent to Washington from his duty station in Germany, in 1946. This policy said that the United States would not instigate a war with the Soviet Union, but it would come to the defense of countries in danger of Soviet takeover. The policy aimed to prevent the spread of communism and encourage the Soviets to abandon their aggressive strategies.

Meanwhile, the United States used a tried-and-true method to shore up its alliances—it gave away money. The **Marshall Plan**, named for Secretary of State

George Marshall, sent more than $12 billion to Europe to help rebuild its cities and economy. In return for that money, of course, countries were expected to become American allies. The countries were also required to work together to promote economic growth, and is the precursor to the European Union. Although the Marshall Plan was offered to Eastern Europe and the Soviet Union, no countries in the Soviet sphere participated in the program, as Stalin viewed the initiative as further evidence of U.S. imperialism. The United States also formed a mutual defense alliance with Canada and a number of countries in Western Europe called the **North Atlantic Treaty Organization** (**NATO**) in 1949. Truman did not have an easy time convincing Congress that NATO was necessary; remember, from the time of Washington's Farewell Address, American sentiment has strongly favored avoiding all foreign entanglements.

The crisis in **Berlin** the previous year, however, helped convince Congress to support NATO. The crisis represented a culmination of events after World War II. In 1945, Germany had been divided into four sectors, with England, France, the United States, and the USSR each controlling one. Berlin, though deep in Soviet territory, had been similarly divided. Upon learning that the three Western Allies planned to merge their sectors into one country and to bring that country into the Western economy, the Soviets responded by imposing a **blockade** on Berlin. Truman refused to surrender the city, however, and ordered airlifts to keep that portion under Western control supplied with food and fuel. The blockade continued for close to a year, by which point the blockade became such a political liability that the Soviets gave it up. Don't confuse the **Berlin Blockade** with the **Berlin Wall**. The Berlin Blockade occurred when the Soviets closed off access to the city during the Truman administration in 1948, while the Soviets erected the Berlin Wall in 1961 during the Kennedy administration to divide the city between the East and the West. Constructed of concrete and barbed wire, the wall separated the Soviet sector of Berlin from West Berlin and became a symbol of the Cold War. The wall was finally dismantled in 1989.

Not long after the United States joined NATO, the Soviets detonated their first atomic bomb. Fear of Soviet invasion or subterfuge also led to the creation of the **National Security Council** (a group of foreign affairs advisers who work for the president) and the **Central Intelligence Agency** (the United States' spy network).

> National Security Council 68 was a document that said the United States should invest much more money into military spending because they couldn't trust other countries to help protect them against communism.

As if Truman didn't have enough headaches in Europe, he also had to deal with Asia. Two issues dominated U.S. policy in the region: the **reconstruction of Japan** and the **Chinese Revolution**. After the war, the United States occupied Japan, and its colonial possessions were divided up. The United States took control of the Pacific Islands and the southern half of Korea, while the USSR took control of the northern half of Korea. Under the command of General Douglas MacArthur, Japan wrote a democratic constitution, demilitarized, and started a remarkable economic revival. The United States was not as successful in China, where it chose to side with Chiang Kai-shek's Nationalist government against **Mao Zedong**'s Communist insurgents, during China's 20-year civil war (Mao having taken control of China in 1949). Despite massive American military aid, the Communists overthrew the Nationalists, whose government was exiled to Taiwan. For decades, the United States refused to recognize the legitimacy of Mao's regime, creating another international "hot spot" for Americans. Truman also chose to aid the French during the Vietnamese war for independence in Indochina, although most Americans were not aware of this at the time.

McCarthyism

All this conflict with communists resurrected anticommunist paranoia at home, just as anticommunism had swept America during the Red Scare after World War I. In 1947, Truman ordered investigations of 3 million federal employees in a search for "security risks." Those found to have a potential Achilles' heel—either previous association with "known communists" or a "moral" weakness such as alcoholism or homosexuality (which, the government reasoned, made them easy targets for blackmail)—were dismissed without a hearing. In 1949, former State Department official **Alger Hiss** was found guilty of consorting with a communist spy (Richard Nixon was the congressman mostly responsible for Hiss's downfall). Americans began to passionately fear the "enemy within." Even the Screen Actors Guild, then headed by Ronald Reagan, attempted to discover and purge its own communists.

It was this atmosphere that allowed a demagogic senator named **Joseph McCarthy** to rise from near anonymity to national fame. In 1950, McCarthy claimed to have a list of more than 200 known communists working for the State Department. He subsequently changed that number several times, which should have clued people in to the fact that he was not entirely truthful. Unchallenged, McCarthy went on to lead a campaign of innuendo that ruined the lives of thousands of innocent people. Without ever uncovering a single communist, McCarthy held years of hearings with regard to subversion, not just in the government, but in education and the entertainment industry as well. Those subpoenaed were often forced to confess to previous associations with communists and name others with similar associations. Industries created lists of those tainted by these charges, called **blacklists**, which prevented the accused from working, just as blacklists had been used against union organizers at the turn of the last century. Eisenhower himself was worried about McCarthy and refused to speak against him, for fear that McCarthy would attack him. McCarthy's downfall came in 1954, during the Eisenhower administration, when he accused the Army of harboring communists. He had finally chosen too powerful a target. The Army fought back hard, and with help from **Edward R. Murrow**'s television show, in the **Army-McCarthy hearings**, McCarthy was made to look foolish. The public turned its back on him, and the era of **McCarthyism** ended, but public distrust and fear of communism remained.

"You've done enough. Have you no sense of decency, sir? At long last, have you left no sense of decency?"
—Army counsel Joseph Welch, speaking back to Joseph McCarthy at the hearings that would effectively end McCarthy's career.

Truman's Domestic Policy and the Election of 1948

The end of the war meant the end of wartime production. With fewer Jeeps, airplanes, guns, bombs, and uniforms to manufacture, American businesses started laying off employees. Returning war veterans further crowded the job market, and unemployment levels rose dramatically. At the same time, many people who had built up their savings during the war (since rationing had limited the availability of consumer goods) started to spend more liberally, causing prices to rise. In 1946, the inflation rate was nearly 20 percent. The poor and unemployed felt the effects the most. Truman offered some New Deal–style solutions to America's economic woes, but a new conservatism had taken over American politics. Most of his proposals were rejected, and the few that were implemented had little effect.

The new conservatism brought with it a new round of anti-unionism in the country. Americans were particularly upset when workers in essential industries went on strike, as when the coal miners' strike (by the **United Mine Workers**, or **UMW**) cut off the energy supply to other industries, shutting down steel foundries, auto plants, and more. Layoffs in the affected industries exacerbated tensions. Americans cared little that the miners were fighting for basic rights. Truman followed the national mood, ordering a government **seizure of the mines** when a settlement could not be reached. During a later railroad strike, Truman threatened to draft into the military those strikers who held out for more than he thought they deserved. Consequently, Truman alienated labor, one of the core constituencies of the new Democratic coalition. Labor and consumers, angry at skyrocketing prices, formed an alliance that helped the Republicans take control of the **Eightieth Congress** in the 1946 midterm elections.

Truman also alienated many voters (particularly in the South) by pursuing a civil rights agenda that, for its time, was progressive. He convened the **President's Committee on Civil Rights,** which in 1948 issued a report calling for an end to segregation and poll taxes, and for more aggressive enforcement of antilynching laws. Truman also issued an executive order forbidding racial discrimination in the hiring of federal employees and another executive order desegregating the Armed Forces. Blacks began to make other inroads. The NAACP won some initial, important lawsuits against segregated schools and buses; **Jackie Robinson** broke the color barrier in baseball; and black groups started to form coalitions with liberal white organizations, thereby gaining more political clout. These advances provoked an outbreak of flagrant racism in the South, and in 1948 segregationist Democrats, or **Dixiecrats,** abandoned the party to support Strom Thurmond for president.

With so many core Democratic constituencies—labor, consumers, Southerners—angry with the president, his defeat in 1948 seemed certain. Truman's popularity, however, received an unintentional boost from the Republican-dominated Congress. The staunchly conservative legislature passed several antilabor acts too strong even for Truman. The **Taft-Hartley Act**, passed over Truman's veto, prohibited "union only" work environments (called **closed shops**), restricted labor's right to strike, prohibited the use of union funds for political purposes, and gave

Let's Make A Deal

Both Theodore and Franklin Roosevelt, as well as FDR's successor Harry Truman, offered "deals" to the American public:

	President	What's the deal with this?
Square Deal	Theodore Roosevelt	Government promised to regulate business and restore competition
First New Deal	Franklin Roosevelt	Focused on immediate public relief and the recovery of banks
Second New Deal	Franklin Roosevelt	Addressed the shortcomings of the First New Deal and responded to a changing political climate
Fair Deal	Harry Truman	Extension of New Deal vision and provisions for reintegrating WWII veterans into society (e.g., the G.I. Bill)

the government broad power to intervene in strikes. The same Congress then rebuked Truman's efforts to pass health care reform; increase aid to schools, farmers, the elderly, and the disabled; and promote civil rights for blacks. The cumulative effect of all this acrimony made Truman look a lot better to those he had previously offended. Still, as election time neared, Truman trailed his chief opponent, Thomas Dewey. He then made one of the most brilliant political moves in American history. He recalled the Congress, whose majority members had just drafted an extremely conservative Republican platform at the party convention, and challenged them to enact that platform. Congress met for two weeks and did not pass one significant piece of legislation. Truman then went out on a grueling public appearance campaign, everywhere deriding the "do-nothing" Eightieth Congress. To almost everyone's surprise, Truman won re-election, and his coattails carried a Democratic majority into Congress.

The Korean War

The Korean War began in June of 1950, when communist North Korea invaded U.S.-backed South Korea. Believing the Soviet Union to have engineered the invasion, the United States took swift countermeasures. Originally intending only to repel the invasion, Truman decided to attempt a reunification of Korea after some early military successes. Under the umbrella of the United Nations, American troops attacked North Korea, provoking China, Korea's northern neighbor. (The Chinese were not too keen on the idea of hostile American troops on their border.) China ultimately entered the war, pushing American and South Korean troops back near the original border dividing North and South Korea. U.S. commander **Douglas MacArthur** recommended an all-out confrontation with China, with the objective of overthrowing the Communists and reinstating Chiang Kai-shek. Truman thought a war with the world's most populous country might be imprudent and so decided against MacArthur. When MacArthur started publicly criticizing the president, who was also the commander-in-chief, Truman fired him for insubordination. MacArthur was very popular at home, however, and firing him hurt Truman politically.

Although peace talks began soon after, the war dragged on another two years, into the Eisenhower administration. When the 1952 presidential election arrived, the Republicans took a page from the Whig playbook and chose **Dwight D. Eisenhower**, a war hero. By this point, the presidency had been held by the Democratic party for 20 years. Truman was unpopular; his bluntness is now seen as a sign of his integrity, but during his terms, it offended a lot of potential constituents. In short, America was ready for a change. Eisenhower beat Democratic challenger **Adlai Stevenson** easily.

Democrats also wanted Eisenhower for their presidential candidate. He had been the President of Columbia University and the Supreme Commander of NATO before winning the presidency.

THE EISENHOWER YEARS (1953–1961)

The 1950s are often depicted as a time of **conformity**. Across much of America, a **consensus of values** reigned. Americans believed that their country was the best in the world, that communism was evil and had to be stopped, and that a decent job, a home in the suburbs, and access to all the modern conveniences (aka **consumerism**) did indeed constitute "the good life." Congress had enacted the Serviceman's Readjustment Act, commonly known as the **G.I. Bill of Rights**, in June of 1944. It provided an allowance for educational and living expenses for returning soldiers and veterans who wished to earn their high school diploma or attend college. The G.I. Bill not only helped many Americans achieve the American dream but also helped stimulate postwar economic growth by providing low-cost loans to purchase homes or farms or to start small businesses. The 1950s also proved to be an era in which the civil rights movement built on the advances of the 1940s and met some violent resistance; an era plagued by frequent economic recessions; and an era of spiritual unrest that manifested itself in such emerging art forms as **Beat poetry and novels** ("Howl," *On the Road*), teen movies (*Blackboard Jungle*, *The Wild One*, *Rebel Without a Cause*), and **rock 'n' roll** (Elvis Presley, Little Richard, Jerry Lee Lewis, Chuck Berry).

> ## The Kitchen Debate
>
> Vice President Richard Nixon visited Moscow in 1959 for a cultural fair. While standing in a model American kitchen, Nixon ended up getting into an argument with Soviet leader Nikita Khrushchev that emblematized not only U.S.-Soviet relations but also common American attitudes toward gender in the 1950s. An excerpt:
>
> *Nixon*: I want to show you this kitchen. It is like those of our houses in California.
>
> *Khrushchev*: We have such things.
>
> *Nixon*: This is our newest model. This is the kind which is built in thousands of units for direct installations in the houses. In America, we like to make life easier for women.
>
> *Khrushchev*: Your capitalistic attitude toward women does not occur under communism.
>
> *Nixon*: I think that this attitude toward women is universal.

Domestic Politics in the 1950s

Eisenhower arrived at the White House prepared to impose conservative values on the federal government, which had mushroomed in size under Roosevelt and Truman. He sought to balance the budget, cut federal spending, and ease government regulation of business. In these goals he was, at best, only partly successful. The military buildup required by the continuing Cold War prevented Eisenhower from making the cuts to the military budget that he would have liked. He reduced military spending by reducing troops and buying powerful weapons systems (thus shaping the **New Look Army**), but not enough to eliminate deficit spending. The popularity of remaining New Deal programs made it difficult to eliminate them; furthermore, circumstances required Eisenhower to increase the number of Social Security recipients and the size of their benefits. Under Eisenhower, the government also began developing the **Interstate Highway System**, partly to make it easier to move soldiers and nuclear missiles around the country. The new roads not only sped up travel, but they also promoted tourism and the development of the suburbs. The initial cost, however, was extremely high. As a result, Eisenhower managed to balance the federal budget only three times in eight years.

Some of the most important domestic issues during the Eisenhower years involved minorities. In 1953, Eisenhower sought to change federal policy toward Native Americans. His new policy, called **termination**, would liquidate reservations, end federal support to Native Americans, and subject them to state law. However, in devising this policy, Eisenhower did not take Native American priorities into account. He aimed simply to reduce federal responsibilities and bolster the power of the states. Native Americans protested, convinced that termination was simply a means of stealing what little land the tribes had left. The plan failed and was ultimately stopped in the 1960s but not before causing the depletion and impoverishment of a number of tribes.

The civil rights movement experienced a number of its landmark events during Eisenhower's two terms. In 1954, the Supreme Court heard the case of **Brown v. Board of Education of Topeka**, a lawsuit brought on behalf of Linda Brown (a black school-age child) by the NAACP. Future Supreme Court Justice Thurgood Marshall argued the case for Brown. In its ruling, the Court overturned the "separate but equal" standard as it applied to education; "separate but equal" had been the law of the land since the Court had approved it in *Plessy v. Ferguson* (1896). In a 9 to 0 decision, the Court ruled that "separate educational facilities are inherently unequal" and that schools should desegregate with "all deliberate speed." Although a great victory for civil rights, *Brown v. Board of Education* did not immediately solve the school segregation problem. Some Southern states started to pay the tuition for white children to attend private schools in order to maintain segregation. Some states actually closed their public schools rather than integrate them. Although Eisenhower personally disapproved of segregation, he also opposed rapid change, and so did little. This inactivity encouraged further Southern resistance, and in 1957, the governor of Arkansas called in the state National Guard to prevent a group of black students, the **Little Rock Nine**, from enrolling in a Little Rock high school. Eisenhower did nothing until one month later, when the courts ordered him to enforce the law. Arkansas, in response, closed all public high schools in Little Rock for two years. Eisenhower supported the Civil Rights Acts of 1957 and 1960, which strengthened the voting rights protection of Southern blacks and the punishments for crimes against blacks, respectively.

Another key civil rights event, the **Montgomery bus boycott**, began in 1955 when **Rosa Parks** was arrested for refusing to give up her seat on a bus to a white man as was required by **Jim Crow** laws. Outrage over the arrest, coupled with long-term resentment over unfair treatment, spurred blacks to stay off Montgomery buses for more than a year. The boycott brought **Martin Luther King Jr.** to national prominence. Barely 27 years old at the time, King was pastor at Rosa Parks's church. Although King was clearly groomed for greatness—his grandfather had led the protests resulting in the creation of Atlanta's first black high school, his father was a minister and community leader, and King had already amassed impressive academic credentials (Morehouse College, Crozer Theological Seminary, University of Pennsylvania, and finally a Ph.D. from Boston University)—the year-long bus boycott gave him his first national podium. In the end, a ruling by the Supreme Court resulted in the integration of city buses in Montgomery and elsewhere.

King encouraged others to organize peaceful protests, a plan inspired by his studies of Henry David Thoreau and Mohandas Gandhi. In 1960, black college students in **Greensboro**, **North Carolina**, tried just that approach, organizing a sit-in at a local Woolworth's lunch counter designated "whites only." News reports of the sit-in, and the resultant harassment the students endured, inspired a sit-in movement that spread across the nation to combat segregation.

America Versus the Communists

There are a number of terms associated with the Cold War policy of Eisenhower and Secretary of State **John Foster Dulles** that you need to know. The administration continued to follow the policy of containment but called it **liberation** to make it sound more intimidating. It carried the threat that the United States would eventually free Eastern Europe from Soviet control. Dulles coined the phrase **massive retaliation** to describe the nuclear attack that the United States would launch if the Soviets tried anything too daring. **Deterrence** described how Soviet fear of massive retaliation would prevent their challenging the United States and led to an arms race. Deterrence suggested that the mere knowledge of **mutually assured destruction (MAD)** prevented both nations from deploying nuclear weapons. Dulles allowed confrontations with the Soviet Union to escalate toward war, an approach called **brinksmanship**. Finally, the Eisenhower administration argued that the spread of communism had to be checked in Southeast Asia. If South Vietnam fell to communism, the nations surrounding it would fall quickly like dominoes—hence, the **domino theory**.

Cold War tensions remained high throughout the decade. Eisenhower had hoped that the death of **Joseph Stalin** in 1953 might improve American-Soviet relations. Initially, the new Soviet leader **Nikita Khrushchev** offered hope. Khrushchev denounced Stalin's totalitarianism and called for "peaceful coexistence" among nations with different economic philosophies. Some Soviet client states took Khrushchev's pronouncements as a sign of weakness; rebellions occurred in Poland and Hungary. When the Soviets crushed the uprisings, U.S.-Soviet relations returned to where they were during the Stalin era. Soviet advances in nuclear arms development (the USSR exploded its first hydrogen bomb a year after the United States blew up its first H-bomb) and space flight (the USSR launched the first satellite, *Sputnik*, into space, motivating the United States to quickly create and fund the **National Aeronautics and Space Administration**, or **NASA**) further heightened anxieties.

Meanwhile, the United States narrowly averted war with the other communists, the Chinese. American-allied Taiwan occupied two islands close to mainland China, **Quemoy** and **Matsu**. The Taiwanese used the islands as bases for commando raids on the communists, which eventually irritated the Chinese enough that they bombed the two islands. In a classic example of brinksmanship, Eisenhower declared that the United States would defend the islands and strongly hinted that he was considering a nuclear attack on China. Tensions remained high for years, and Eisenhower's stance forced him to station American troops on the islands. During the 1960 presidential election, Kennedy used the incident as a campaign issue, arguing that the two small islands were not worth the cost of defending them.

The Arms Race

Size of bombs
- Atomic bomb dropped on Hiroshima, 1945: equal to 12,500 tons of TNT
- First hydrogen bomb test, 1952: equal to 10,400,000 tons of TNT
- Soviet Tsar Bomba test, 1961: equal to 57,000,000 tons of TNT

Number of warheads
- 1945: USA 6; USSR 0
- 1950: USA 369; USSR 5
- 1955: USA 3,057; USSR 200
- 1960: USA 20,434; USSR 1,605
- 1970: USA 26,119; USSR 11,643
- 1980: USA 23,764; USSR 30,062

Third World Politics

World War II resulted in the breakup of Europe's huge overseas empires. In the decades that followed the war's end, numerous countries in Africa, Asia, and South America broke free of European domination. These countries allied themselves with neither of the two major powers; for this reason they were deemed the **Third World**. Both America and the Soviets sought to bring Third World countries into their spheres of influence, as these nations represented potential markets as well as sources of raw materials. The two superpowers particularly prized strategically located Third World countries that were willing to host military bases.

Neither superpower, it turned out, was able to make major inroads in the Third World at first. **Nationalism** swept through most Third World nations, recently liberated from major world powers. Enjoying their newfound freedom, these countries were reluctant to foster a long-term alliance with a large, powerful nation. Furthermore, most Third World countries regarded both powers with suspicion. America's wealth fostered both distrust and resentment, prompting questions about U.S. motives. America's racist legacy also hurt it in the Third World, where most residents were nonwhite. Yet most Third World nations also saw how the Soviets dominated Eastern Europe and so had little interest in close relations with them. These new nations were not anxious to fall under the control of either superpower.

However, the United States tried to expand its influence in the Third World in other ways. For example, in 1956 in Egypt, the United States tried offering foreign aid, hoping to gain an ally by building the much-needed **Aswan Dam**. Egypt's nationalist leader Gamal Nasser suspected the Western powers of subterfuge; furthermore, he detested Israel, a Western ally. Eventually, he turned to the Soviet Union for that aid. Later that year, Israel invaded Egypt, followed by Britain and France, in an effort to gain control of the **Suez Canal**. President Eisenhower played the "good cop" and pressured Britain and France to withdraw. The American government also used **CIA covert operations** to provide a more forceful method of increasing its influence abroad. In various countries, the CIA coerced newspapers to report disinformation and slant the news in a way favorable to the United States, bribed local politicians, and tried by other means to influence local business and politics. The CIA even helped overthrow the governments of Iran and Guatemala in order to replace anti-American governments with pro-American governments. It also tried, unsuccessfully, to assassinate the communist leader of Cuba, **Fidel Castro**.

The 1960 Presidential Election

In 1960, Eisenhower's vice president, **Richard Nixon**, received the Republican nomination. The Democrats nominated Massachusetts senator **John F. Kennedy**. Similar in many ways, particularly in foreign policy, both candidates campaigned against the "communist menace" as well as against each other. Aided by his youthful good looks, Kennedy trounced an awkward Nixon in their first televised debate. Kennedy's choice of Texan **Lyndon Johnson** as a running mate helped shore up the Southern vote for the Northern candidate. Nixon, meanwhile, was hurt by his vice presidency, where he had often served the role of Eisenhower's "attack dog." The fact that Eisenhower did not wholeheartedly endorse Nixon also marred his campaign. Still, it turned out to be one of the closest elections in history, and some believe that voter fraud turned a few states Kennedy's way, without which Nixon would have won.

In his final days in office, Eisenhower warned the nation to beware of a new coalition that had grown up around the Cold War, which he called the military-industrial complex. The combination of military might and the highly profitable arms industries, he cautioned, created a powerful alliance whose interests did not correspond to those of the general public. In retrospect, many would later argue that in his final statement, Eisenhower had identified those who would later be responsible for the escalation of the **Vietnam War**.

THE TURBULENT SIXTIES

At the outset, the 1960s seemed the start of a new, hope-filled era. Many felt that Kennedy, his family, and his administration were ushering in an age of "Camelot" (the Broadway musical was very popular then). As Arthur had had his famous knights, Kennedy, too, surrounded himself with an entourage of young, ambitious intellectuals who served as his advisers. The press dubbed these men and one woman "the best and the brightest" America had to offer. Kennedy's youth, good looks, and wit earned him the adoration of millions. Even the name of his domestic program, the **New Frontier**, connoted hope. It promised that the fight to conquer poverty, racism, and other contemporary domestic woes would be as rewarding as the efforts of the pioneers who settled the West.

The decade did not end as it had begun. By 1969, America was bitterly divided. Many progressives regarded the government with suspicion and contempt, while many conservatives saw all dissidents as godless anarchists and subversives. Although other issues were important, much of the conflict centered on these two issues: the Vietnam War and blacks' struggle to gain civil rights. As you read through this summary of the decade, pay particular attention to the impact of both issues on domestic harmony.

Kennedy and Foreign Policy

Like Truman and Eisenhower, Kennedy perceived the Soviet Union and communism as the major threats to the security of the United States and its way of life. Every major foreign policy issue and event of his administration related primarily to these Cold War concerns.

Two major events during Kennedy's first year in office heightened American-Soviet tensions. The first involved **Cuba**, where a U.S.-friendly dictatorship had been overthrown by communist insurgents led by **Fidel Castro**. When Castro took control of the country in 1959, American businesses owned more than 3 million acres of prime Cuban farmland and also controlled the country's electricity and telephone service. Because so many Cubans lived in poverty, Cuban resentment of American wealth was strong, so little popular resistance occurred when Castro seized and nationalized some American property. The United States, however, was not pleased. When Castro signed a trade treaty with the Soviet Union later that year, Eisenhower imposed a partial trade embargo on Cuba. In the final days of his presidency, Eisenhower broke diplomatic relations with Cuba, and Cuba turned to the Soviet Union for financial and military aid.

Taking office in 1961, President Kennedy inherited the Cuban issue. Looking to solve the dilemma, the CIA presented the ill-fated plan for the **Bay of Pigs invasion** to the new president. The plan involved sending Cuban exiles, whom the CIA had been training since Castro's takeover, to invade Cuba. According to the strategy, the army of exiles would win a few battles, and then the Cuban people would rise up in support, overthrow Castro, and replace his government with one more acceptable to the United States. Kennedy approved the plan but did not provide adequate American military support, and the United States launched the invasion in April 1961. The invasion failed, the Cuban people did not rise up in support, and within two days Kennedy had a full-fledged disaster on his hands. Not only had he failed to achieve his goal, but he had also antagonized the Soviets and their allies in the process. His failure also diminished America's stature with its allies.

Later in the year, Kennedy dealt with a second foreign policy issue when the Soviets took aggressive anti-West action by erecting a wall to divide East and West Berlin. The **Berlin Wall**, built to prevent East Germans from leaving the country, had even greater symbolic significance to the democratic West. It came to represent the repressive nature of communism and was also a physical reminder of the impenetrable divide between the two sides of the Cold War.

In 1962, the United States and the Soviet Union came the closest they had yet to a military (and perhaps nuclear) confrontation. The focus of the conflict was once again Cuba. In October, American spy planes detected missile sites in Cuba. Kennedy immediately decided that those missiles had to be removed at any cost; he further decided on a policy of brinksmanship to confront the **Cuban missile crisis**. He imposed a naval quarantine on Cuba to prevent any further weapons shipments from reaching the island, and then went on national television and demanded that the Soviets withdraw their missiles.

By refusing to negotiate secretly, Kennedy backed the Soviets into a corner; if they removed the missiles, their international stature would be diminished, especially since the quarantine was effectively a blockade, which diplomats defined as an act of war on the part of the United States. Therefore, in return, the Soviets demanded that the United States promise never again to invade Cuba and that the United States remove its missiles from Turkey (which is as close to the USSR as Cuba is to the United States). When Kennedy rejected the second condition, he gambled that the Soviets would not attack in response. Fortunately, behind-the-scenes negotiations defused the crisis, and the Soviets agreed to accept America's promise not to invade Cuba as a pretext for withdrawing the missiles. In return, the United States secretly agreed to remove its missiles from Turkey a few months later, thus making it look like the United States had won. Recent scholarship suggests that it was the Soviet leader Khrushchev who prevented World War III and a nuclear holocaust.

The policy of containment even motivated such ostensibly philanthropic programs abroad as the **Peace Corps**. The Peace Corps' mission was to provide teachers and specialists in agriculture, health care, transportation, and communications to the

Kennedy Wasn't a Donut

A popular urban legend holds that when President Kennedy went to the Berlin Wall in 1963 and declared, *"Ich bin ein Berliner,"* he made a grammatical error and inadvertently called himself a jelly donut. Sadly for high school history teachers trying to get a laugh out of their classes, this isn't actually true. While the word *"ein"* is omitted when literally declaring one's residence, it is required for figurative statements such as Kennedy's. Kennedy made no error, and the donut legend didn't start circulating until a novelist joked about it 20 years later.

Third World, in the hopes of starting these fledgling communities down the road to American-style progress. The government called this process **nation building**. The Peace Corps had many successes, although the conflict between its humanitarian goals and the government's foreign policy goals often brought about failures as well. Furthermore, many countries did not want American-style progress and resented having it forced upon them.

The greatest theater for American Cold War policy during this era, however, was **Vietnam**, which will be discussed in greater detail shortly.

Kennedy and Domestic Policy

Kennedy began his presidency with the promise that America was about to conquer a **New Frontier**. He pushed through legislation that increased unemployment benefits, expanded Social Security, bumped up the minimum wage, and aided distressed farmers, among other measures.

Kennedy's civil rights agenda produced varied results. Kennedy supported **women's rights**, establishing a presidential commission that in 1963 recommended removing all obstacles to women's participation in all facets of society. Congress enacted the **Equal Pay Act** in 1963, which required that men and women receive equal pay for equal work. Unfortunately, employers continue to get around this federal law by simply changing job titles. However, it was only late in his presidency that Kennedy openly embraced the black civil rights movement. After almost two years of near inaction, in September 1962, Kennedy enforced desegregation at the University of Alabama and the University of Mississippi, where James Meredith was the first integrated student. In the summer of 1963, he asked Congress for legislation that would outlaw segregation in all public facilities. After Kennedy's assassination in November, Lyndon Johnson was able to push that legislation—the **Civil Rights Act of 1964**—through Congress on the strength of the late president's popularity and his own skills as a legislator.

John F. Kennedy also ordered his Attorney General, Robert F. Kennedy, to have the Justice Department order the Interstate Commerce Commission to make all public transportation integrated in response to the Freedom Riders.

Still, Kennedy's presidency proved an active period for the civil rights movement as a number of nongovernmental organizations mobilized to build on the gains of the previous decade. Martin Luther King Jr. led the **Southern Christian Leadership Conference (SCLC)**, which staged sit-ins, boycotts, and other peaceful demonstrations. The Congress of Racial Equality (CORE) organized the **Freedom Riders** movement; the Freedom Riders staged sit-ins on buses, sitting in sections prohibited to them by segregationist laws. They were initially an integrated group, as was the **Student Nonviolent Coordinating Committee (SNCC)**, which did grassroots work in the areas of voter registration and antisegregationist activism. Such groups met considerable resistance. In 1963, Mississippi's NAACP director, **Medgar Evers**, was shot to death by an anti-integrationist. Not long after, demonstrators in Montgomery, Alabama, were assaulted by the police and fire department who used attack dogs and fire hoses against the crowd. News reports of both events horrified millions of Americans and thus helped bolster the movement. So, too, for reasons mentioned above, did Kennedy's assassination.

Lyndon Johnson's Social Agenda

Like Kennedy, Lyndon Johnson made an early commitment to the civil rights movement, but unlike Kennedy, Johnson took immediate action to demonstrate that commitment. From the time he took office, Johnson started to lobby hard for the **Civil Rights Act of 1964**, which outlawed discrimination based on a person's race, color, religion, or gender. If you can remember only one federal law in U.S. history, this is it! The Civil Rights Act of 1964 is the most comprehensive piece of civil rights legislation enacted in U.S. history and the basis of all discrimination suits to this day. The law prohibited discrimination in employment as well as in public facilities (thus increasing the scope of Kennedy's proposed civil rights act).

Not long after, Johnson oversaw the establishment of the **Equal Employment Opportunity Commission (EEOC)** to enforce the employment clause of the Civil Rights Act. Johnson signed the **Voting Rights Act of 1965** after he was elected in his own right in 1964. This law cracked down on those states that denied blacks the right to vote despite the Fifteenth Amendment. He also signed another civil rights act banning discrimination in housing, and yet another that extended voting rights to Native Americans living under tribal governments.

Johnson had grown up poor and believed that social injustice stemmed from social inequality, and therefore, he advocated civil rights in employment. Toward the same end, he lobbied for and won the **Economic Opportunity Act**, which appropriated nearly $1 billion for poverty relief. After his landslide victory in the 1964 presidential election, Johnson greatly expanded his antipoverty program. A number of programs combined to form Johnson's **War on Poverty. Project Head Start** prepared underprivileged children for early schooling; **Upward Bound** did the same for high school students. **Job Corps** trained the unskilled so they could get better jobs, while **Volunteers in Service to America (VISTA)** acted as a domestic Peace Corps. In addition, **Legal Services for the Poor** guaranteed legal counsel to those who could not afford their own lawyers. To further assist the poor, Johnson founded the **Department of Housing and Urban Development (HUD)**, increased federal aid to low-income apartment renters, and built more federal housing projects, as well as establishing Medicare and Medicaid.

The legislation passed during 1965 and 1966 represented the most sweeping change to U.S. government since the New Deal. Johnson's social agenda was termed the **Great Society**. Best of all, taxpayers did not feel much pain. Increased tax revenues from a quickly expanding economy funded the whole package. Not everyone liked Johnson's agenda, however; many objected to any increase in government activity, and the extension of civil rights met with bigoted opposition, especially in the South. Thus, ironically, the huge coalition that had given Johnson his victory and his mandate for change started to fall apart because of his successes (and were hastened by a bitter national debate over American involvement in Vietnam).

The Civil Rights Movement

In the early 1960s, the civil rights movement made a number of substantial gains. Legislative successes such as those passed under Johnson's Great Society program provided government support. The movement also won a number of victories in the courts, particularly in the Supreme Court. Under Chief Justice **Earl Warren**, the Court, for a brief moment in history, was extremely liberal. The **Warren Court** worked to enforce voting rights for blacks and forced states to redraw congressional districts so that minorities would receive greater representation. The Warren Court expanded civil rights in other areas as well. Among its landmark rulings are those that prohibited school prayer and protected the right to privacy. The Warren Court also made several decisions concerning the rights of the accused. In *Gideon v. Wainwright,* the Court ruled that a defendant in a felony trial must be provided a lawyer for free if he or she cannot afford one. In ***Miranda v. Arizona***, the Court ruled that, upon arrest, a suspect must be advised of his or her right to remain silent and to consult with a lawyer.

Civil rights victories did not come easily. Resistance to change was strong, as evidenced by the opposition of state governments, police, and white citizens. In Selma, police prevented blacks from registering to vote; in Birmingham, police and firemen attacked civil rights protesters. All over the South, the **Ku Klux Klan** and other racists bombed black churches and the homes of civil rights activists with seeming impunity. In Mississippi, three civil rights workers were murdered by a group that included members of the local police department.

With news reports of each event, outrage in the black community grew. Some activists abandoned Martin Luther King's strategy of nonviolent protest. Among the leaders who advocated a more aggressive approach was **Malcolm X**, a minister of the **Nation of Islam**. Malcolm X urged blacks to claim their rights "by any means necessary." (His autobiography is an essential document of the history of racism in America.) Later, two groups that previously had preached integration—the **SNCC** and **CORE**—expelled their white members and advocated the more separatist, radical program of **Black Power**, with the Black Panthers being at the forefront of this movement. By 1968, when King was assassinated, the civil rights movement had fragmented, with some continuing to advocate integration and peaceful change, while others argued for empowerment through self-imposed segregation and aggression.

The New Left, Feminism, and the Counterculture

Black Americans were not the only ones challenging the status quo in the 1960s. Young whites, particularly those in college, also rebelled. For these young adults, the struggle was one against the hypocrisy, complacency, and conformity of middle-class life.

In 1962, the **Students for a Democratic Society** (SDS) formed. Its leftist political agenda, laid out in a platform called the **Port Huron Statement**, set the tone for other progressive groups on college campuses; these groups collectively became known as the **New Left**. New Left ideals included the elimination of poverty and racism and an end to Cold War politics. One particularly active branch of the New

On January 23, 1964, the Twenty-Fourth Amendment to the Constitution was ratified. This banned the use of the poll tax in all elections.

Beatniks

We usually associate cultural rebellion with the 1960s and early 1970s, but the **Beat Movement** got its start in the 1950s. Beat writers, such as Allen Ginsburg, William Burroughs, and Jack Kerouac, challenged the straight-laced conservatism of the Eisenhower era by publishing works championing bohemian lifestyles, drug use, and nontraditional styles of art. The Beatniks would later inspire the Hippies of the 1960s.

Left formed at the University of California at Berkeley. In 1964, students there protested when the university banned civil rights and antiwar demonstrations on campus. These protests grew into the **Free Speech movement**, which in turn fostered a number of leftist and radical political groups on the Berkeley campus.

Most New Left groups, however, were male-dominated and insensitive to the cause of women's rights. Women became frustrated with being treated as second-class citizens and started their own political groups. In 1963, Betty Friedan's book *The Feminine Mystique* openly challenged many people's assumptions about women's place in society. Friedan identified "the problem that has no name" and is credited with restarting the women's movement, a movement that had faded once women's suffrage was achieved with the Nineteenth Amendment in 1920. She was also one of the founders of **NOW**, the **National Organization for Women**, formed in 1966 to fight for legislative changes, including the ill-fated **Equal Rights Amendment (ERA)** to the Constitution. The modern movement for gay rights also began to solidify in the 1960s, with the first Gay Pride parades occurring on the anniversary of the **Stonewall riots,** an event at which gays fought back against the police in New York City.

Feminists fought against discrimination in hiring, pay, college admissions, and financial aid. They also fought for control of reproductive rights, a battle that reached the Supreme Court in the 1973 case *Roe v. Wade*, which enabled women to obtain abortions in all 50 states within the first trimester. Many states argued that they had an obligation to protect "life," as stipulated in the Fourteenth Amendment, and quickly passed state laws prohibiting a woman from having an abortion after the first three months of her pregnancy. Although there is no specific mention of a constitutional right to privacy, the Supreme Court had established this important precedent in 1965 in the case *Griswold v. Connecticut*. *Roe v. Wade* remains a controversial decision and continues to play a central role in American politics and society.

Rebellion against "the establishment" also took the form of nonconformity, a repudiation of the Eisenhower years. Hippies grew their hair long, wore tie-dyed shirts and ripped jeans, and advocated drug use, communal living, and "free love." Their way of life came to be known as the **counterculture** because of its unconventionality and its total contrast to the staid mainstream culture, which was typified by aging crooners and banal television variety shows. By the end of the 1960s, the counterculture became more widely accepted, and artists such as Andy Warhol, Bob Dylan, Jimi Hendrix, the Beatles, and the Rolling Stones were among the biggest moneymakers in the arts.

Concurrent with the rise in activism for civil rights and women's rights was the upsurge of interest in environmental issues. **Rachel Carson**, an American marine biologist wrote the seminal work of nonfiction, *Silent Spring*, a worldwide bestseller to this day. *Silent Spring* blew the whistle on the widespread use of

"There's a time when the operation of the machine becomes so odious, makes you so sick at heart, that you can't take part! You can't even passively take part! And you've got to put your bodies upon the gears and upon the wheels, upon the levers, upon all the apparatus, and you've got to make it stop! And you've got to indicate to the people who run it, to the people who own it, that unless you're free, the machine will be prevented from working at all!"

—Mario Savio, speaking from the steps of Sproul Hall at the University of California, Berkeley, on December 3, 1964 the chemical pesticide DDT, leading to its eventual ban. Meanwhile, legislators responding to industrial pollution passed the **Clean Air Act** of 1955, the first law to control the use of airborne contaminants.

The New Left, feminists, the counterculture, and others in the growing left wing of American politics almost uniformly opposed American participation in the Vietnam War. These groups' vocal protests against the war and the fierce opposition they provoked from the government and pro-war Americans created a huge divide in American society by 1968. Before we discuss that fateful year, it is important to understand how and why America became involved in Vietnam.

American Involvement in Vietnam, World War II–1963

From the Truman administration until the fall of Soviet Communism in 1991, U.S. foreign policy leaders asserted an American right to intervene anywhere in the world to stop the spread of communism and to protect American interests. Nowhere did that policy fail more miserably than in Vietnam, where the United States maintained an economic and military presence for almost 25 years. The Vietnam War divided America as no war before had.

The origins of America's involvement in Vietnam stretch back to World War II. From the late 19th century until World War II, Vietnam was a French colony. France exported the country's resources—rice, rubber, and metals—for French consumption. This foreign exploitation of Vietnam helped foster a nationalist Vietnamese resistance called the **Vietminh**, led by **Ho Chi Minh**. Ho had been schooled in France and had joined the French Communist Party before returning home. In fact, Ho Chi Minh was in Paris during the Versailles Peace Conference in 1919 and approached Woodrow Wilson at the time. Ho asked Wilson to honor his commitment to the right of nations to **self-determination**, as expressed in Wilson's **Fourteen Points**, and to help the Vietnamese expel the French from their country. Wilson ignored Ho Chi Minh's appeal.

Japan invaded Vietnam during World War II and ended French control of the country. Faced with a common enemy, the Vietnamese helped the Allies defeat Japan and probably expected to be granted their independence at the conclusion of the war, as India was in 1947. Shortly after the Japanese surrender in 1945, Ho drafted the Vietnamese Declaration of Independence modeled on the United States Declaration of Independence and the French Declaration of Rights of Man and Citizens.

The United States did not recognize Vietnamese independence nor the legitimacy of Ho's government, in part because of America's alliance with France (which wanted its colony back), and in part because Ho was a communist. Instead, the United States recognized the government of Bao Dai, the Vietnamese emperor whom the French had installed in the South, which France still controlled. Subsequently, Vietnam fought a war for independence against the French from 1946 until 1954, when the French were defeated at the Battle of Dien Bien Phu. Although Ho appealed to President Truman for assistance on several occasions, Truman never responded. Ho hoped the United States would honor its commitment to the principle of self-determination and empathize with the Vietnamese rather than support the colonial power. Truman continued to aid the French. The United States financed more than 80 percent of France's war effort in Indochina, a fact few Americans knew then or know now.

In 1954, all of the involved parties met in Geneva, Switzerland, and drew up the **Geneva Accords**, which divided Vietnam at the 17th parallel, with Communist forces controlling North Vietnam and (so-called) democratic forces controlling the South. It was agreed that this division was to be temporary and that elections would be held in two years to reunite the country and determine who would rule a unified Vietnam. The elections never took place, however. The United States, certain that Ho Chi Minh would win an election, sabotaged the peace agreement. First, the United States made an alliance with another South Vietnamese leader named **Ngo Dinh Diem** and helped him oust Bao Dai (whom the United States felt was too weak to control the country). Then, the CIA organized commando raids across the border in North Vietnam to provoke a Communist response (which the South Vietnamese could then denounce). Diem pronounced South Vietnam an autonomous country and refused to participate in the agreed-upon national election. The United States rallied Britain, France, Thailand, Pakistan, the Philippines, New Zealand, and Australia to form the NATO-like **Southeast Asia Treaty Organization** (SEATO) to provide for South Vietnam's defense against Communist takeover.

Unfortunately, the situation continued its downward spiral. Diem, it turned out, was a vicious leader. He took despotic control of South Vietnam, imprisoning political enemies, persecuting Buddhist monks, and closing newspapers that criticized his government. As a result, many South Vietnamese citizens joined the North Vietnamese side. These communist South Vietnamese insurgents were called the **Vietcong**. Rather than cut its losses, the United States continued to support Diem and the South Vietnamese economically. Committed to the policy of containment and intent on nation building, President Kennedy increased America's involvement in Vietnam by sending in military advisors known as the Green Berets. Finally, in 1963, the CIA helped the South Vietnamese military stage a coup to overthrow Diem's government. During the coup, Diem and his brother were killed and Kennedy was appalled by the outcome. A few weeks later, Kennedy was assassinated, and Johnson took control of America's war efforts.

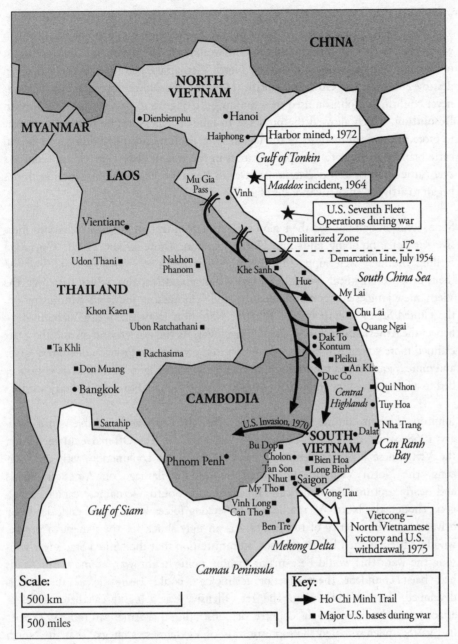

Southeast Asia During the Vietnam War

American Involvement in Vietnam, 1964–1968

Upon taking office, Johnson had the opportunity to withdraw American forces in a way that would not have embarrassed his administration. The United Nations, backed by France and the Vietcong, would have intervened and set up a coalition government to rule South Vietnam. Kennedy's advisers, however, convinced Johnson that U.S. forces could overwhelm any opposition in the region. He remained committed to using those forces to achieve "total victory."

In 1964, the United States supported a second coup in South Vietnam; apparently, the United States was not terribly selective as to who ran the country, so long as it was not the Communists. (The United States followed a similar pattern in Latin America.) The U.S. Army also started bombing the neighboring country of Laos, through which the North Vietnamese were shipping weapons to the Vietcong. Then, in August of the same year, reports stated that the North Vietnamese had fired on two American destroyer ships in the **Gulf of Tonkin**. (However, the North Vietnamese attack was never confirmed.) Johnson used the event to get Congress to pass the **Gulf of Tonkin Resolution**, which allowed the president to take any measures he deemed necessary to protect American interests in the region. The Tonkin Gulf resolution gave Johnson carte blanche to escalate U.S. participation in the war. It also is the closest Congress ever came to an official declaration of war in Vietnam. Thus, the first ground troops began to arrive in the early months of 1965.

Soon, Johnson had flooded the region with American troops. He also authorized massive Air Force bombing raids into North Vietnam. Those strikes, called "Operation Rolling Thunder," were supposed to last a few weeks, but continued for years. Many of them dropped chemical agents like Agent Orange and Napalm, which destroyed the Vietnamese jungles and contaminated the land. Throughout Johnson's administration, the United States essentially took over the war effort from the South Vietnamese—hence, the **Americanization** of the Vietnam War. As the war ground on and the draft claimed more young Americans, opposition to the war grew. Protest rallies grew larger and more frequent, and more and more young men either ignored their draft notices or fled to a foreign country (more than 30,000 went to Canada) to avoid military service.

Johnson's advisers continued to assure him that the war was "winnable" until January 1968, when the North Vietnamese launched the **Tet Offensive** (named after the Vietnamese holiday celebrating the New Year). In conjunction with the Vietcong, the North Vietnamese inflicted tremendous damage on American forces and nearly captured the American embassy in the South Vietnamese capital of Saigon. Though the North Vietnamese and Vietcong forces were, in the end, decisively driven back, the severity of the strikes was an ugly shock for the American people, who had been assured by the Johnson administration that the United States was winning the war. This would be a major turning point in the war, as most Americans had been confident their superior technology could easily defeat the underdeveloped Third World nation. The Tet Offensive was a highly calculated series of attacks carried out around the country, demonstrating that American military experts had vastly underestimated the sophistication of Vietnamese strategy. That the North Vietnamese and Vietcong could launch such a large-scale offensive and nearly succeed in taking the American embassy made the American public come to believe it was being lied to and that perhaps this war was not winnable.

The **My Lai Massacre** occurred the same year as the Tet Offensive. American soldiers were becoming more and more frustrated and began to act in unspeakable ways. The most publicized of these horrific events, although not an isolated occurrence, took place in a small village in South Vietnam, where U.S. soldiers abused, tortured, and murdered an estimated 347 to 504 innocent civilians, including women, children, and elderly Vietnamese too infirm to fight. When the story finally came to light in November 1969, the American public was outraged. Public opinion turned and protests against the war grew angrier and more frequent.

The Summer of 1968 and the 1968 Election

Johnson withdrew from the presidential race in large part because his association with the Vietnam War had turned many Americans against him, including many within his own party. Johnson's renomination would not have been easy; both **Eugene McCarthy** (no relation to Joseph McCarthy!) and **Robert Kennedy**, John F. Kennedy's brother and former attorney general, were poised to challenge him. Johnson's withdrawal opened the field to a third candidate, Vice President **Hubert Humphrey.**

Early in April 1968, a white assassin killed **Martin Luther King Jr.** His murder ignited a massive wave of civil unrest, including arson and looting of largely white-owned businesses, in more than 150 towns and cities. In Chicago, where the Democratic convention would later be held, the mayor ordered the police to shoot arsonists on sight. To say that King's assassination heightened the already considerable tension surrounding race relations would be a huge understatement. During this time, the Kerner Commission report on race relations came out, stating that "our nation is moving toward two societies, one white and one black—separate and unequal."

Then, in June, frontrunner for the Democratic nomination **Robert Kennedy** was assassinated. Kennedy had come to represent the last bastion of hope for many Americans. Young, handsome, and vital (like his adored older brother), Kennedy was also an aggressive advocate for the poor and a harsh critic of the war in Vietnam. Together, the two assassinations convinced many that peaceful change from within the political system was impossible.

Many disenchanted young Americans came to Chicago in August to demonstrate at the Democratic Convention against government policy. The police were ordered to break up the crowds of protesters, which they did with tear gas, billy clubs, and rifles. Images of American policemen in gas masks clubbing American citizens reached millions of living rooms across the country through television and the newspapers, presenting a picture eerily reminiscent of the police states *against* which America supposedly fought. When the convention chose pro-war Vice President Humphrey over the antiwar McCarthy *and* refused to condemn the war effort, the Democrats alienated many of their core constituency on the left.

Meanwhile, the Republicans handed their nomination to former vice president **Richard Nixon** at a rather peaceful convention. Then, a third candidate entered the national election, Alabama governor **George Wallace**, who ran a segregationist third-party campaign, much like Strom Thurmond had done in 1948 against Harry Truman. Wallace was popular in the South, which had traditionally voted Democratic. Thus, Humphrey was twice cursed: he had alienated his progressive urban base in the North and Wallace was siphoning his potential support in the South. Humphrey denounced the Vietnam War late in the campaign, but it was too little, too late. In one of the closest elections in history, Richard Nixon was elected president.

The *Counter* Counterculture

It would be easy to stereotype the 1960s and 1970s as a rollicking party filled with free love, new social ideas, and worthy political causes for which young people could devote their time. Not everyone in America embraced the changes of the 1960s, though. Dismayed with what they perceived to be the excesses of the civil rights movement, the counterculture movement, and feminism, some Americans were eager to bring the country back to traditional values based on religious principles. Other Americans were alarmed by the rising cost of social welfare programs created by the New Deal and Johnson's Great Society. The conservative resurgence began in the 1970s at the grassroots level with a variety of groups that focused on single issues such as ending abortion, criticizing affirmative action, or emphasizing traditional gender roles and the nuclear family. Many older people were suspicious of the largely young contingent who had come to question the values of their parents and grandparents. Religious people distrusted the rejection of traditional morals and spiritual beliefs. Southern segregationists resisted the Civil Rights movement. And some Americans who did not have strong political leanings simply tired of marches and protests and wanted to return to a more peaceful way of life.

One notable leader in the Conservative reaction to the changes of the 1960s was **Phyllis Schlafly.** She is most well known for lobbying against the **Equal Rights Amendment** (ERA) to the Constitution. The ERA passed Congress, but was never fully ratified by the states, in part due to efforts to quell it by Schlafly and her supporters. Opponents to the ERA claimed that it could lead to the conscription of women into war (the Vietnam draft was already highly controversial), negatively affect women in divorce cases, and even allow men entry to women's-only colleges and clubs. Whatever the effects of the ERA would have been, these warnings influenced the opinions of many Americans and thus the ERA was never fully ratified.

When Richard Nixon ran for office, he sought to appeal to Americans who did not fully embrace the cultural and political changes of the 1960s and 1970. Conservatives voted for Nixon in large numbers, hoping that he would reverse the trend of encroaching federal power, as did some Southern Democrats who distrusted the newer liberal social policies of their party.

Nixon, "Vietnamization," and Détente

Nixon entered office promising to end American involvement in Vietnam by turning the war over to the South Vietnamese, a process he called "Vietnamization." He soon began withdrawing troops; however, he also increased the number and intensity of air strikes. Like his predecessors, Nixon was a veteran cold warrior who believed that the United States could, and must, win in Vietnam. He ordered bombing raids and ground troops into Cambodia, in hopes of rooting out Vietcong strongholds and weapons supplies. American involvement in Vietnam dragged on until 1973, when Secretary of State **Henry Kissinger** completed negotiations for a peace treaty with the North Vietnamese.

There are a couple of postscripts to the Vietnam story. First, the negotiated peace crumbled almost as soon as American troops started to vacate the country. In 1975, Saigon fell to the North Vietnamese Army, and Vietnam was united under communist rule. Second, Congress passed the **War Powers Resolution** in 1973 in order to prevent any future president from involving the military in another undeclared war. The War Powers Resolution requires the president to obtain congressional approval for any troop commitment lasting longer than 60 days.

Nixon did have success, however, in his other foreign policy initiatives, especially those concerning the world's two other superpowers, the USSR and China. During Nixon's first term, the United States increased trade with the Soviets, and the administration negotiated the first of a number of arms treaties between the two countries. Results were even more dramatic with China. After a series of secret negotiations, Nixon traveled to communist China, whose government the United States had previously refused to acknowledge. Nixon's trip eased tensions, partly because at the time of the trip, Americans trusted the anticommunist Nixon to improve relations with China, and his trip opened trade relations between the two countries. It also allowed Nixon to use his friendship with the Chinese as leverage against the USSR, and vice versa. (The Chinese and the Soviets, despite both being communist, hated each other.)

The Nixon years added two new terms to the vocabulary of foreign policy. Together, Nixon and Kissinger formulated an approach called **détente**, a policy of "openness" that called for countries to respect each other's differences and cooperate more closely. Détente ushered in a brief period of relaxed tensions between the two superpowers but ended when the Soviet Union invaded Afghanistan in 1979. The **Nixon Doctrine** announced that the United States would withdraw from many of its overseas troop commitments, relying instead on alliances with local governments to check the spread of communism.

Nixon's Domestic Policy

Nixon could not match his successes overseas at home. During Nixon's presidency, the economy worsened, going through a period of combined recession-inflation that economists called stagflation. Nixon attempted to combat the nation's economic woes with a number of interventionist measures, including a price-and-wage freeze and increased federal spending. None of his efforts produced their intended results.

Politically, American society remained divided among the haves and have-nots, the conservatives and the progressives. Much of the political rhetoric on both sides painted the opposition as enemies of the "American way." Several confrontations on college campuses heightened political tensions, most notably when national guardsmen shot and killed four protesters at **Kent State University** in Ohio who were protesting the United States' decision to invade Vietcong camps in neutral Cambodia. This incident became synonymous with the division between the youth and middle America. A similar incident occurred at the historically black Jackson State University in Mississippi, but the media failed to report the incident—further evidence of continued racial conflict in American society. Meanwhile, urban crime levels rose, causing many to flee to the relative tranquility of the suburbs.

Still, in 1972, Nixon won re-election in one of the greatest landslide victories in American political history, defeating liberal Senator George McGovern. Although Nixon won the election easily, both houses of Congress remained under Democratic control, an indication of the mixed feelings many Americans felt toward their political leaders.

Watergate and Nixon's Resignation

In the summer of 1971, two major newspapers published the **Pentagon Papers**, a top-secret government study of the history of U.S. involvement in Vietnam. The study covered the period from World War II to 1968, and it was not complimentary. It documented numerous military miscalculations and flat-out lies the government had told the public. Even though the documents contained nothing about the Nixon administration, Nixon fought aggressively to prevent their publication. The United States was involved in secret diplomatic negotiations with North Vietnam, the USSR, and China at the time, and both Nixon and Henry Kissinger (Nixon's Secretary of State) believed that the revelation of secret government dealings in the past might destroy their credibility in the present.

Nixon lost his fight to suppress the Pentagon Papers, a loss that increased Nixon's already considerable paranoia. In an effort to prevent any further leaks of classified documents, Nixon put together a team of investigators called the **plumbers.** The plumbers undertook such disgraceful projects as burglarizing a psychiatrist's office in order to gather incriminating information on Daniel Ellsberg, the government official who had turned the Pentagon Papers over to the press. During the 1972 elections, the plumbers sabotaged the campaigns of several Democratic hopefuls and then botched a burglary of Democratic headquarters in the **Watergate** Hotel.

When the plumbers were arrested at the Watergate Hotel, the White House began an all-out effort to cover up the scandal. A Senate hearing into the matter began in early 1973 and dragged on, keeping the story alive in the news for the next year and a half. Information was slowly revealed that incriminated the president's closest advisers. They would resign, and then most would be tried and convicted of felonies. (Perjury and destruction of evidence were two popular and successful charges against them.) At last, it was discovered that Nixon had secretly taped all conversations in the White House, including many concerning Watergate. For the next year, a legal battle over the tapes raged; the Senate demanded them, and Nixon refused to turn them over, claiming executive privilege. All the while, more damning evidence came to light—much of it in the pages of *The Washington Post,* courtesy of investigative journalists **Bob Woodward** and **Carl Bernstein**—and more former Nixon associates were jailed. When the president lost the battle over the tapes—the Supreme Court ordered Nixon to turn them over to the Senate—he knew his days were numbered, as the tapes revealed a number of unsavory aspects of Nixon's character. Rather than face impeachment proceedings, Nixon resigned in August 1974. His vice president, **Gerald Ford**, took office and almost immediately granted Nixon a presidential **pardon**, thereby preventing a trial.

Gerald Ford

Gerald Ford became president when Nixon resigned. Ford had replaced Nixon's first vice president, **Spiro Agnew**, who had resigned in the face of impending criminal charges (relating to corruption during his tenure as governor of Maryland). When Ford selected Nelson Rockefeller as his vice president, it was the first time that neither the president nor the vice president had been elected by the public.

Ford's controversial **pardon** of Nixon brought the Watergate era to a close, but it also cost Ford politically, as it raised suspicions that Nixon and Ford had struck a deal. Ford's political fortunes were further undermined by the weak economy. People were encouraged to wear "WIN" buttons: Whip Inflation Now. An oil embargo organized by Arab nations (under the leadership of **OPEC**) against the United States increased fuel prices, which in turn caused the price of almost everything else to rise. Inflation, coupled with an increasing unemployment rate, and the damage done to his credibility by the media, especially parodies by the actor Chevy Chase on *Saturday Night Live,* sealed Ford's fate. In 1976, he was defeated by Democrat **Jimmy Carter.**

Jimmy Carter

Carter inherited a weakening economy. During his presidency, inflation exceeded 10 percent, and interest rates on loans approached 20 percent. Slow economic growth was coupled with inflation to worsen the stagflation that began in Nixon's term. Carter tried to balance the federal budget but failed (as had every president since Eisenhower).

Many of the nation's economic problems resulted from the increased cost of OPEC petroleum. In response, President Carter increased funding for research into alternative sources of power. Carter created a new, cabinet-level government agency, the **Department of Energy,** to oversee these efforts. Many Americans saw nuclear power as a solution to the nation's energy woes. Opponents argued that nuclear power plant failures were potentially catastrophic; their fears were reinforced when a Pennsylvania plant at **Three Mile Island** failed, releasing radioactive materials into the atmosphere.

The high point of the Carter administration came when President Carter personally brokered a **peace agreement between Israel and Egypt**. Israeli-Egyptian conflict dated to the moment of Israel's founding in 1948, when Israel was besieged by hostile Arab neighbors. Tensions between Israel and Egypt were heightened by the 1967 **Six Day War**, during which Israel took control of the Sinai Peninsula, a desert region belonging to Egypt. In 1978, however, the leaders of the two countries agreed to meet with each other, in each other's countries. It was a major breakthrough in Israeli-Arab relations; most Arab nations refused even to acknowledge Israel's existence. President Carter hoped to capitalize on this breakthrough. He invited the two leaders to **Camp David** and personally brokered an agreement between the two nations. Ever since, the United States has actively participated in peace negotiations in the region.

Carter enjoyed some foreign policy successes. Along with negotiating the peace treaty between Israel and Egypt, he also concluded an arms agreement with the Soviets. However, Carter also suffered some major setbacks. When the USSR invaded Afghanistan, Carter's efforts proved powerless in forcing a withdrawal. Carter also flip-flopped in Nicaragua, where first he befriended the revolutionary **Sandinista** government and then turned against them as they allied themselves more closely with the USSR and Cuba. Carter's worst crisis involved Iran, when American hostages were taken in retaliation for America's decades-long support of the repressive, deposed Shah. Held for more than a year, the hostages were released only after Ronald Reagan took office.

Carter made the promotion of human rights one of the cornerstones of his foreign policy—he also negotiated a treaty between the United States and Panama that gave control of the canal zone back to Panama and got the Senate to ratify it. He spent his retirement working ceaselessly with organizations like Habitat for Humanity.

Summary

Here are the most important concepts to remember from the Postwar Cold War period.

- After World War II, American life was economically prosperous—while fears of Communism dictated foreign policy.

- Left-wing liberalism promoted both a larger role for government in society and changing social norms.

- As industry and population grew, environmental concerns became more pressing.

Chapter 12 Review Questions

See Chapter 14 for answers and explanations.

1. All of the following threatened Harry Truman's chances for re-election in 1948 EXCEPT

   (A) Truman's positions on civil rights
   (B) rampant inflation
   (C) the Dixiecrat candidacy of Strom Thurmond
   (D) public dissatisfaction with the Korean War

2. Loyalty oaths, blacklists, and Alger Hiss are all associated with the

   (A) civil rights movement
   (B) New Deal
   (C) Red Scare
   (D) Great Society

3. John Foster Dulles, secretary of state under Eisenhower, intensified Cold War rhetoric with Washington's New Look defense program that emphasized

   (A) threatening Moscow with "massive retaliation"
   (B) containment
   (C) summit diplomacy
   (D) shuttle diplomacy

4. During the 1950s and early 1960s, the Warren Court was often criticized for

   (A) backing down from the Brown decision in its other civil rights rulings
   (B) exercising judicial restraint
   (C) protecting civil rights for African Americans while denying rights for political activists and communists
   (D) in effect, enacting "judicial legislation" through its rulings on individual rights

5. John F. Kennedy was unable to accomplish much of his stated civil rights agenda during his lifetime primarily because

   (A) the war in Vietnam demanded his full attention
   (B) African American leaders refused to work with him
   (C) his vice president, Lyndon Johnson, opposed any changes to civil rights law
   (D) Southern opposition to the civil rights movement made any association with it politically untenable

6. Which of the following does NOT accurately describe the presidential election of 1968?

   (A) The Democratic Party was fractured due to dissent over the Vietnam War.
   (B) A frontrunner for one of the major parties was assassinated during the primary season.
   (C) Both major-party candidates campaigned as Washington outsiders.
   (D) A third-party candidacy split the traditionally Democratic Southern vote.

7. Inflation throughout the 1970s was driven in large part by

   (A) the cost of funding the Vietnam War
   (B) rapidly increasing gasoline and oil prices
   (C) government investment in the space program
   (D) a dramatic reduction of income tax rates

8. The incident that began a chain of events that became one of the most infamous presidential scandals in American history and eventually led to the resignation of Richard Nixon was the

   (A) burglary of Daniel Ellsberg's psychiatrist's office
   (B) political sabotage of Nixon's opponent, George McGovern
   (C) illegal use of the CIA to hush up the FBI's investigation of the events surrounding the publication of the Pentagon Papers
   (D) break-in and attempted bugging of the Democratic party's national headquarters

REFLECT

Respond to the following questions:

- For which content topics discussed in this chapter do you feel you have achieved sufficient mastery to answer multiple-choice questions correctly?

- For which content topics discussed in this chapter do you feel you have achieved sufficient mastery to discuss effectively in a short-answer question or an essay?

- On which content topics discussed in this chapter do you feel you need more work before you can answer multiple-choice questions correctly?

- On which content topics discussed in this chapter do you feel you need more work before you can discuss them effectively in a short-answer question or an essay?

- What parts of this chapter are you going to review again?

- Will you seek further help, outside of this book (such as a teacher, tutor, or AP Students), on any of the content in this chapter—and, if so, on what content?

Chapter 13
Entering into
the 21st Century
(1980–Present)

REAGAN, H.W., CLINTON, AND W. (1980–2001)

The Reagan Candidacy

By the late 1970s, many Americans had grown tired of the conflicts of the previous decade. Many were uncomfortable with the growing cynicism toward political leaders. Jimmy Carter hit a raw nerve—and disturbed many Americans—when he complained in a speech that the people were letting themselves be overtaken by a "crisis of confidence." This came to be known as "the malaise speech," though Carter never used the word "malaise" in it.

Ronald Reagan saw that the nation was ready for a major change. In the 1980 presidential campaign, Reagan, a former actor and governor of California, presented himself as Carter's opposite and a Washington "outsider," not tainted by events of the previous two decades, much as Carter had portrayed himself as an outsider in 1976. While Carter blamed American self-indulgence and consumerism for the country's problems, Reagan stressed the positive aspects of America. Furthermore, many Americans who disagreed with Reagan's conservative politics nonetheless voted for him because they liked him and his "can-do" attitude. Further damaging Carter's chances was the third-party candidacy of liberal Republican John Anderson, who attracted a sizable "protest vote" from those who might otherwise have supported Carter. In the end, Reagan won the 1980 election by a landslide.

Supply-Side Economics

Ronald Reagan tried to revive the economy by applying the theory of **supply-side economics**. Reagan believed that if corporate taxes were reduced, those corporations would earn greater profits. They would then use those profits, he believed, to buy new equipment and hire more employees. As a result, wealth would **trickle down** by creating more jobs and reinvigorating the economy. (George H. W. Bush would refer to this policy as "voodoo economics.") Reagan coupled this with large-scale deregulation, particularly in the areas of banking, industry, and the environment. He also successfully lobbied Congress for an across-the-board tax cut for all Americans. This policy increased his popularity with most Americans, although many complained that tax cuts hurt the poor, who pay little in income tax but depend on federal enfranchisement programs (such as welfare, food stamps, and Medicaid) to survive.

At first, Reagan's economic policies had little effect. The country continued in a recession for almost two years before the economy revived. Even then, results were mixed. Although inflation subsided, there was continued criticism that, under Reagan, the rich were getting richer while the poor were getting poorer. Rather than reinvesting in the economy, as supply-side economics suggested, the rich used the money saved on taxes to buy luxury items.

Military Spending and Budget Deficits

Ronald Reagan frequently claimed that he sought to decrease the size of the federal government. He called his plan the **New Federalism**, but it was quite the opposite of federalism—its goal was to shift power from the national government to the states. Reagan suggested that the states take complete responsibility for welfare, food stamps, and other social welfare programs currently funded at the national level; in return, the national government would assume the entire cost of Medicaid. Reagan's goal was never accomplished, however. The states feared that the shift would greatly increase the cost of state government, which would require unpopular tax increases at the state level.

At the same time, Reagan convinced Congress to greatly increase military spending. He funded research into a space-based missile shield system called the **Strategic Defense Initiative**, or **SDI** (the program was dubbed "**Star Wars**" by both supporters and detractors). Arguing that America needed to more quickly develop superior arms, Reagan also escalated the arms race with the USSR. Some historians have argued that the arms race bankrupted the Soviet Union and helped bring about an end to the Cold War, while others mainly credit Soviet leader Mikhail Gorbachev for the Cold War's end.

Tax cuts, increased military spending, and the failure of Reagan's New Federalism plan combined to escalate the **federal budget deficit**. Government spending increased while government revenues shrank, forcing the government to borrow money. Congress blamed the deficit on Reagan's tax cuts and called for a tax increase. Reagan, on the other hand, argued that the fault was with Congress, which refused to decrease funding for social welfare programs at the rate the president requested. Neither side budged, and as a result, the federal deficit reached record heights during the Reagan administration.

Foreign Policy Under Reagan

In foreign policy, Reagan sought to end the Cold War by winning it on every front he could in any way he could. He supported repressive regimes and right-wing insurgents in El Salvador, Panama, the Philippines, and Mozambique, all because they opposed communism. During the Reagan administration, the U.S. military led an international invasion of **Grenada** to topple a new Communist government there.

One of Reagan's top foreign policy priorities was support for a group of Nicaraguan insurgents called the **Contras**. Reports that the Contras were torturing and murdering civilians led Congress to cut off aid to the group, but the Reagan administration was so fully committed to them and opposed to the Sandinistas, who were communists, that it devised a plan to fund them through other channels. The government secretly sold weapons to Iran and then used the income to buy guns for the Contras. The entire process was eventually discovered; it came to be known as the **Iran-Contra affair**. Critics argued that Iran-Contra represented a constitutional crisis, pointing out that the plan had denied Congress the "power of the purse" central to the system of checks and balances. Supporters claimed that the president had broken no laws and that his goals were good ones. Reagan himself claimed that he had no knowledge of the plan; Oliver North, a member of the Security Council, took full credit.

Another foreign policy setback came when the Reagan administration sent marines to **Lebanon** as part of a United Nations peacekeeping force. A suicide bomb killed 240 servicemen and led to an eventual pullout of troops.

Reagan's greatest successes in foreign policy came in U.S.-Soviet relations. At first, Reagan's hard-line anticommunism led to deterioration in relations. The rhetorical war between the two enemies was fierce, Reagan calling the Soviet Union "the evil empire," and hitting an all-time low when he jokingly declared that he had outlawed the USSR, and added "we begin bombing in five minutes." Although not meant to be heard by the public, the joke was picked up by a microphone and later broadcast repeatedly. The escalated arms race further destabilized relations by constantly altering the military balance of power. Ultimately, however, the arms race helped bring the adversaries to the bargaining table, as neither side could afford the high cost.

American-Soviet relations were further helped when reformer **Mikhail Gorbachev** rose to power in the Soviet Union. Gorbachev is best known for his economic policy of *perestroika*, or restructuring, and his social reforms collectively referred to as *glasnost*, or openness. Gorbachev loosened Soviet control of Eastern Europe, increased personal liberties in the Soviet Union, and eventually allowed some forms of free-market commerce in the Communist country. Reagan and Gorbachev met frequently and ultimately negotiated a withdrawal of nuclear warheads from Europe.

George H. W. Bush

The election of 1988 convinced many Americans that progressive liberalism was finally destroyed, as George Bush easily defeated the Democratic candidate, Michael Dukakis, who was then governor of Massachusetts. In accepting his party's nomination, George Bush called for "a kinder, gentler nation," and he is most remembered for declaring, "Read my lips: No new taxes." "Liberalism" had become the "L word," and feminism had become the new "F word." The conventional wisdom held that Americans had settled back into traditional American lifestyles that celebrated values such as family and abstinence from sex and drugs (Nancy Reagan had urged kids your age to "Just say NO!"). It appeared as if the **moral majority** had spoken.

The most significant events of the Bush presidency were the ending of the Cold War (symbolized by the dismantling of the Berlin Wall and breakup of the Soviet Union) and the **Persian Gulf War**. If containment had been the guiding policy during the Cold War, but the Soviet Union no longer posed a threat to the world order, it would be left to George Bush to set the course for U.S. foreign policy into the 21st century. The test came in August 1990, when Saddam Hussein, the leader of Iraq, invaded Iraq's tiny but oil-rich neighbor Kuwait. When Saddam seized Kuwait's oil fields and threatened the world's access to Middle East oil, Washington reacted immediately. Having learned from Vietnam, Bush built a consensus in Congress and assembled an international coalition against Iraq in the UN.

Operation Desert Storm consisted mostly of massive air strikes against strategic Iraqi targets, and most Americans watched the war from the safety of their homes on television as if it were a video game. The war ended quickly with few American casualties. Although Iraq was required to submit to UN inspectors to insure that there were no **weapons of mass destruction** or chemical warfare production facilities, Saddam Hussein remained in power, a decision many foreign policy experts later came to criticize. It appeared that U.S. foreign policy in the post–Cold War era would focus on political stability in the Middle East and defending human rights.

War	Afghanistan	Iraq
Years	2001 to Present	2003 to 2011
Presidents	George W. Bush, Barack Obama, Donald Trump	George W. Bush, Barack Obama
Conflict	After the terrorist attacks of September 11, 2001, the Bush administration vowed to rout terrorist group Al-Qaida from its strongholds in Afghanistan while also curbing the power of the Taliban, a militant Islamic political organization. Osama bin Laden, the leader of Al-Qaida, was finally captured and killed, but the Taliban still holds influence in rural regions of Afghanistan.	Dubious allegations that Saddam Hussein had helped to orchestrate 9/11, as well as his ongoing human rights violations against his own people and rumors of weapons of mass destruction (which were later found to be false), led the Bush administration to invade Iraq in March of 2003. United States armed forces remained in Iraq until 2011. Both the war in Iraq and the war in Afghanistan fell under the United States' larger foreign policy known as the **War on Terror**.
Outcome	The Afghanistan War has not officially ended. U.S. troops are still stationed in the region. The Afghanistan War is now the longest one in U.S. history.	Although Iraq is no longer run by the Hussein family, it struggles to rebuild politically and economically. Without a strong-arm dictator, various factions vie for power. The Iraq War continues to be controversial in American politics.

Post-1980 Society

Though the 1980s were before you were born and may even seem like ancient history to you, historians assert that it can take as many as 50 years or more before enough time has elapsed for people to evaluate the past objectively. Keeping that in mind, let's take a look at some of the major trends and developments that historians have begun to identify in the past 20 or 30 years.

Changing Demographics

As was the case a century ago, when predominantly Eastern European immigrants arrived by the millions onto America's shores, immigration in recent decades has significantly affected the shape and tenor of American society. In 1890, 86 percent of immigrants to the United States were from Europe. From the 1970s through today, however, the fastest-growing ethnic minorities in the United States have been **Hispanics** and **Asians**, and according to the 2000 census, Hispanics now outnumber African Americans as the largest minority in the United States. Much of this growth among Asians and Hispanics has been fueled by immigration.

Who?	Hispanic	Asian
How many?	Population increased from 6 million in 1960 to 50 million today.	Population increased by 70% in the 1980s (about 3 million in the decade). Today, there are about 12.8 million Asian immigrants.
From where?	Mexico, Puerto Rico, Cuba, El Salvador, Guatemala, Honduras, and Nicaragua	Philippines, China, South Korea, India
To where?	California, Texas, Florida, Southwest	Largely settled in California

The **Immigration Act of 1965** contributed significantly to the increase in immigration by members of these population groups. This legislation phased out all national quotas by 1968 and set annual limits on immigration from the Western Hemisphere and the rest of the world, essentially relaxing restrictions on non-European immigration. It gave priority to reuniting families and to certain skilled workers (particularly scientists) and **political refugees**. Though the vast majority of immigrants who entered under this legislation did so in order to join family members, searching for employment and escaping from persecution still ranked high among the most common reasons people came to the United States. Several groups admitted under these regulations included Cuban and Southeast Asian refugees created by **Fidel Castro's** revolution and the Vietnam War, respectively.

At the end of the 20th century, from 1970 to 2000, the number of foreign-born people living in the United States went from 10 million to 31 million, or 11 percent of the total population. Fifty-one percent of those foreign-born were from Latin America, while 27 percent were from Asia, the second-largest group. Not since the turn of the 20th century has the United States experienced a comparable surge in immigration. In 1915, immigrants made up 15 percent of the total population, the largest percentage in our history so far.

What will all these changes mean for American society? The increasing racial and ethnic diversity of our population has sparked heated debate not only on immigration policy but also on issues such as bilingual education and affirmative action. Discussions of immigration policy have generally centered on illegal immigration, the role and impact that immigrants have on the economy, and the extent to which an influx of new cultures, attitudes, and ideas will reshape society. Tensions created by this new wave of immigration have resulted in various measures to curb **illegal immigration**, abolish bilingual education in some states, and allow both low-skilled and high-skilled workers into the United States on a temporary basis to provide needed labor and services. In 1986, for instance, Congress passed the **Simpson-Mazzoli Act**, which outlawed the deliberate employment of illegal immigrants and granted legal status to some illegal aliens who entered the United States before 1982. However, problems persist.

Guest worker programs were an attempt to curb illegal immigration by offering temporary employment to workers. Workers would then return to their home countries once the period of employment ended. The **Bracero** program was one such guest worker agreement between the United States and Mexico, in which the U.S. hosted migrant farm workers. The program lasted from 1942 until 1964, when pressure to end the program was put on the government by organized labor who were frustrated at the decrease in wages that the spike in agricultural employment brought with it.

Diversity, Asset, or Liability?

Whether you believe that immigrants place a burden on social services or support and enrich the development of our economy and society, it is clear that the United States is in the midst of major demographic changes that are visible today. With each new wave of immigration, ethnic enclaves sprout in big cities and neighborhoods, contributing to America's unique mixture of peoples. A century ago, there were communities such as Little Italy in New York City or Chinatown in San Francisco. Today, reflecting more recent population trends, there are places like Little Havana in Miami, Florida, and Little Saigon in Orange County, California. Americans have also seen an increase in multilingual services and the media catering to Hispanics and Asians, in particular. Even political parties openly attempt to attract Hispanics in recognition of their potential political influence. The impact of these changing demographics will be felt for generations to come.

Arguments for diversity as an asset	Arguments for diversity as a liability
• Immigrants enrich the development of the economy and society.	• Immigration places a burden on social services.
• American identity has always evolved with new waves of immigration. The U.S. economy and culture both benefit from increasing access to economic opportunities for previously excluded groups.	• There exists an American identity that is threatened by the presence of cultures that are not presumed to fit into that identity. This attitude can be observed in the frustration expressed by some groups over the increase in multilingual services and media outlets targeting Hispanics and Asians.

The Clinton Presidency (1993–2001)

William Jefferson Clinton was the first Democrat to be elected president since Jimmy Carter. After more than a decade of Republican control of the White House, Clinton and **Al Gore** took control in January 1993. Although it is doubtful that you would be required to write an essay that went through the 1990s, you could see a few multiple-choice questions about the major events that occurred during Clinton's two terms as president. The following is a brief review of those issues and events.

The close of the 20th century brought with it radical changes in the way Americans do business. The idea of a local economy could no longer be considered without considerations of how the larger global community affects it. Further, the economy was jump-started by a revolution in digital technology that brought about new business opportunities as well as fast-paced breakthroughs that quickly made relatively new technology obsolete.

One significant change from the 1990s was the acceleration of **globalism**. As opposed to nationalism, in which a nation's affairs are focused inward, globalism promotes an interconnectivity of nations by way of economic agreements (typically promoting free trade reducing tariffs), immigration, and military intervention.

The first significant event of the Clinton presidency was the establishment of the **North American Free Trade Agreement (NAFTA)**. Although the treaty had been negotiated by the previous Republican administration, Clinton signed it into law in 1993. In a way, it was similar to the global treaty from 1947, the **General Agreement on Tariffs and Trade (GATT)**, which sought to reduce trade barriers such as tariffs and preferential treatment. In the case of NAFTA, it did exactly what it sounds like it did—eliminated trade barriers among the United States, Mexico, and Canada. While the treaty was severely criticized by American labor unions, who feared American companies would move their factories elsewhere in order to reduce costs with lower wages and operation costs, corporate interests supported it enthusiastically. Despite often speaking favorably about the concept of free trade, and gradually reducing tariff barriers over time, the United States has historically interfered with trade, usually in the form of high, protective tariffs, when it was beneficial to certain political and economic groups, but always under the guise of protecting the "national interest."

Also notable during Clinton's presidency was the **1994 Congressional Election**. Speaker of the House **Newt Gingrich**'s Contract with America outlined a specific series of laws the Republican Party wished to pass, designed to reduce taxes, consolidate government programs, and reform welfare entitlement programs. The Republicans won back control of Congress, but their power was limited by Clinton's moderating Democrat executive power. Clinton cooperated with the Republicans in Congress on some matters, especially reforming welfare and giving the states more control over administering benefits. This led to his winning the 1996 presidential election over Bob Dole.

No doubt, the most infamous event of Clinton's presidency was the Clinton-Lewinsky scandal that led to Clinton's impeachment during his second term in office. Some Clinton supporters believe that special prosecutor Kenneth Starr had it in for the Clintons, beginning with his accusations of their dubious real estate dealings in what came to be known as **Whitewater**. Regardless, the U.S. House of Representatives, which had a Republican majority at the time, impeached Clinton for perjury, obstruction of justice, and abuse of power. Remember that impeachment is the formal accusation of wrongdoing; it does not mean that the accused is thrown out of office. According to the Constitution, the House of Representatives has the "sole power of impeachment," and any federal official can be impeached for committing treason, bribery, or other "high crimes and misdemeanors." The United States Senate then has the "sole power to try all impeachments." Although Clinton was impeached, he was acquitted by the Senate and remained in office to finish his second term. Several federal judges have been impeached throughout American history, but Clinton was only the second president ever impeached. Lincoln's vice president, Andrew Johnson, was impeached, but he too was acquitted and was not thrown out of office. Students sometimes think that Nixon was impeached for his involvement in Watergate. Not quite. He resigned before the House of Representatives completed the process.

Clinton was really the first president to take office after the end of the Cold War, and he made it clear that one of his major foreign policy goals was the protection of human rights around the world, although some criticized his turning a blind eye to human rights violations in China, defending capitalism over democracy. In 1999, Clinton supported a bombing campaign in the former Yugoslavia under the auspices of NATO. Slobodan Milosevic, president of Serbia, was conducting a brutal policy of "ethnic cleansing" against Balkan Muslims. Milosevic was eventually tried and convicted for committing "crimes against humanity."

Other notable events that took place during the Clinton years include his "Don't ask, don't tell" policy pertaining to gays in the U.S. military and his appointments of Ruth Bader Ginsburg and Stephen Breyer to the Supreme Court. Two significant initiatives that failed were his proposal for a national health care program and campaign finance reform.

THE 2000 ELECTION

While it is incredibly unlikely that you will be asked to know anything specific about the George W. Bush administration, other than the obvious major events like 9/11 and the situation in Iraq (although certainly not in any detail), you may see a question about the 2000 election. According to the Constitution, a candidate must win a majority of electoral votes to win the presidential election. However, because of the "winner-take-all" system regarding the allotment of electoral votes in most states, it is possible for a candidate to win the majority of the popular vote nationwide but lose the presidency. Recall that this happened in 1824, when Jackson won a plurality of the popular vote, but John Quincy Adams became president, and again in 1876, when Samuel J. Tilden lost to Rutherford B. Hayes. On election night in November 2000, the major television networks erroneously reported that Al Gore had defeated George W. Bush. Through a convoluted series of mishaps with the voting procedure in Florida, Al Gore challenged the results of that election, but eventually the Supreme Court prevented a formal recount of the vote in Florida and George W. Bush, son of former president George H. W. Bush, was elected.

The George W. Bush presidency also marked the rise in **neoconservatism**, which literally means "new conservatism," a movement in sharp opposition to "paleo-conservatism" or the conservatism of prior Republican administrations. Neoconservatives, such as Vice-President Dick Cheney, Secretary of State Donald Rumsfeld, and advisor Paul Wolfowitz, promoted the idea of spreading democracy worldwide and putting American corporate interests first through the use of military actions abroad. Global trade and open immigration is a net positive for America in neoconservative thought.

Some former Democrats latched onto neoconservatism, while both staunch liberals and paleo-conservatives criticized the Bush Administration. For liberals, the Bush policies were symptomatic of excessive corporate power and global imperialism, while traditional conservatives such as Patrick J. Buchanan lamented the cost of military adventures overseas, the loss of domestic jobs incurred by global free-trade agreements, and the ravages of unrestricted immigration. Americans on both sides of the aisle, it seemed, had lost faith in the ability of the federal government to solve social and economic problems.

AFRICAN AMERICANS IN POLITICS

The first African American governor was P.B.S. Pinchback, who served as governor of Louisiana for 15 days, from December 29, 1872, to January 13, 1873.

Following the accomplishments of Freedom Summer in 1964, the **Voting Rights Act of 1965**, and the **Twenty-fourth Amendment** to the Constitution, measures such as literacy tests and poll taxes that had been used by many Southern states to deny African Americans the right to vote were summarily banned. The results in the South were dramatic: in 1960, only 20 percent of eligible African Americans had been registered to vote, but by 1971, that number had jumped to 62 percent. Cities such as Los Angeles, Chicago, Washington, D.C., Atlanta, and New Orleans elected their first African American mayors in the 1980s. The nation's first African American governor in recent memory was elected in 1990 in Virginia.

In 1968, **Shirley Chisholm** was the first African American woman elected to Congress; in 1972, she also became the first African American to run for president. **Reverend Jesse Jackson** also ran for the Democratic presidential nomination in 1984 and 1988, winning many of the primary elections. According to the U.S. Census Bureau in 2000, there were 1,540 African American legislators, representing 10 percent of the total number of legislators nationwide. **Colin Powell** and **Condoleezza Rice**, both Secretaries of State under **President George W. Bush,** occupied the most powerful political office that African Americans had held since Thurgood Marshall was appointed to the Supreme Court by Lyndon Johnson in the 1960s. Of course, those records were surpassed with the historic 2008 election of Barack Obama as president of the United States.

Urban Problems

As in the past, people in the 1950s and 1960s flocked to the cities for employment and cheaper housing. African Americans continued to move to Northern and Western cities as they had done during World Wars I and II, while other minorities, including immigrants from Latin America, were drawn to cities for similar reasons. By the 1970s and 1980s, however, mounting urban problems—overcrowding, increasing unemployment and crime rates, and decaying and inadequate housing and commercial areas—initiated a trend of mostly white, middle-class Americans leaving the cities for the suburbs (a phenomenon nicknamed "white flight"); the open spaces, shopping malls, and better-funded schools of the suburbs also enticed people to move. When middle-class families moved to the suburbs, businesses and industries that once provided vital jobs and tax revenue for cities followed. The result was that poor people and racial minorities remained in cities where there were insufficient funds for housing, sanitation, infrastructure, and schools.

Meanwhile, televised **urban riots** in the 1960s, such as those in Los Angeles, Chicago, and New York after the assassination of Martin Luther King Jr., only served to widen the gap between cities and suburbs and to heighten racial tensions. One of the worst urban riots occurred much later in 1992 in South Central Los Angeles, where many African Americans expressed outrage at the acquittal of four white police officers who were videotaped beating a black man, **Rodney King**.

Tensions between urban and suburban areas surfaced in ways that highlighted both racial and class animosity. In the period 1974–1975, the **forced busing** of students resulted in violence in South Boston when black students from a poorer section were bused into a predominantly white, working-class neighborhood school by court order. Buses were vandalized and attacked while riot police tried to quell the mob. White families moved from South Boston or sent their children to private schools, while even some black families opposed the forced busing, arguing instead that the schools in their black neighborhoods should receive better funding. Busing continued in many major cities through the late 1990s, and although many schools did achieve greater racial integration, the strategy was not without its critics. Indeed, the Supreme Court decision in *Milliken v. Bradley* (1974) held that an interdistrict remedy for unconstitutional segregation found in one district exceeded the scope of the violation.

But while the image of the scary inner city still has a hold on some imaginations, it is no longer supported by statistics. Both violent crime and property crime have plunged since the early 1990s, and crime in 2010 reached its lowest level in 40 years. In large urban areas, the drop in crime has been even more pronounced. Affluent young professionals have flocked back to city centers. There is an active debate over what has caused this encouraging trend—one theory credits falling levels of lead in the environment due to legislation in the early 1970s, as lead poisoning is linked to criminal activity. Whatever the reasons, the dramatic drop in crime has led to a revitalization of American cities over the course of the past 20 years.

AMERICA AND THE WAR ON TERROR

America entered a new phase of foreign policy when Osama bin Laden's Al Qaeda organization attacked the World Trade Center and the Pentagon on September 11, 2001. Two planes flew into the World Trade Center's Twin Towers, and one flew into the Pentagon. A fourth plane was allegedly planned to hit the White House, but passengers overcame the hijackers long enough to crash the plane into a field in Pennsylvania. In total, almost 3,000 civilians were killed on 9/11. The Bush Administration quickly got support from NATO (North Atlantic Treaty Organization) allies to launch an attack on the Taliban government in Afghanistan in October of 2001, where bin Laden and Al Qaeda were headquartered. The ensuing war led to the removal of the Taliban from power and a restoration of democracy in Afghanistan.

Allegations that Saddam Hussein helped to orchestrate 9/11, as well as his ongoing human rights violations against his own people and rumors of weapons of mass destruction, led the Bush administration to invade Iraq in March of 2003. American troops quickly seized Baghdad and Hussein went into hiding, leaving a power vacuum. American military leaders worked to establish a provisional government, but tensions between rival political and religious factions erupted, leading to a prolonged American occupation.

THE CONSERVATIVE RESURGENCE

Instrumental in energizing conservatives throughout the 1970s and 1980s were right-wing evangelical Christians, members of a branch of Protestantism that emphasized a "born-again" religious experience and adherence to strict standards of moral behavior taken from the Bible. **Evangelicalism**, particularly fundamentalist sects, became increasingly prominent in political life from the 1970s through the 1990s. Fundamentalists denounced the moral relativism of liberals and believed in a literal interpretation of the Bible. Evangelical groups also became increasingly political. Conservative evangelicals and fundamentalists such as **Billy Graham, Jerry Falwell,** and **Pat Robertson** helped to mobilize other like-minded citizens to support the Republican Party and bring together various conservative groups to form a movement known as the **New Right**. The growing strength of the New Right was evident in the key role it played in helping to elect **Ronald Reagan** in 1980, and in 1994 when the Republican Party under **Newt Gingrich** recaptured control of both houses of Congress under Democratic President **Bill Clinton**. Evangelical Christians continued to support Republicans with the election and re-election of George W. Bush.

DIGITAL REVOLUTION

Globalism's worldwide interconnectivity is both a cause and an effect of the **digital revolution**. As digital technology such as personal computers and cellular phones became easier to produce, they became cheaper to purchase. American turned to these new technologies for personal and business use as a result of the exponential increases in data storage offered by new devices. As you can probably guess, the 20 years between 1990 and 2010 saw significant changes in the ways Americans lived.

As access to the internet increased with the digital revolution, new business opportunities presented themselves. The **"dot-com bubble"** of the late 1990s involved widespread speculation on the value of internet-based companies before many of those sites were able to turn a profit. Predictably, the bubble burst by 2001, but not without creating its first wave of internet millionaires.

From 1990 until 2010, the number of manufacturing jobs in the United States decreased by a third. Around the turn of the century, these former manufacturing positions were replaced by retail jobs. However, the 2008—2009 recession reduced retail employment, and many Americans found new work in the booming healthcare industry.

DECLINE OF UNIONS

Throughout the second half of the 20th century, and in particular, its final three decades, union power and membership have declined. In addition to increased spending on the part of industry to advocate for anti-labor legislation, there are some other key factors at play.

The Taft Hartley Act of 1947—passed over Truman's veto—restricted the ability to strike as well as the preferential hiring of union members.

Union busting—President Reagan's 1981 mass firing of 3,000 striking air traffic controllers let industry know that union busting would be tolerated.

The generational divide has no doubt also played a role in the decline of unions—younger generations have not experienced the struggles that unions encountered to secure workers' rights and often fail to see the benefits that older workers see.

Wage Stagnation

Economists have noted that one of the most prominent effects of a decline in union membership is the growth in income inequality starting in the latter part of the 20th century. The inability to collectively bargain on the scale that unions could from World War II through the 1970s has led to a stagnation in wages. As union membership decreased—from 34 percent in 1979 to 10 percent in 2010—there has been a notable consolidation of wealth in the upper echelon of American earners.

REPEAL OF GLASS-STEAGALL

In 1933, President Roosevelt signed the **Glass-Steagall Act** (also known as the **Banking Act of 1933**). The act stemmed from the volatility of American banks leading up to the Great Depression. Banks were able to use their commercial deposits (from individuals and businesses) to speculate in the investment market. Since the investment market was not always predictable, banks that used commercial deposits for this purpose were often unstable. The Glass-Steagall Act forced banks to avoid a conflict of interest by deciding whether they would be commercial banks or investment banks and prohibited them from participating in more than one of these operations.

The **Gramm-Leach-Bliley Act** of 1999 effectively did away with this provision. Many economists, such as Joseph Stiglitz, argue that it is no surprise that within a decade of the repeal of Glass-Steagall, the American economy was brought to its knees by a recession stemming from banks offering home loans based on speculation of the value of those homes.

GENDER ROLES

Women have taken on larger roles in professional settings in the 21st century. However, many claim the glass ceiling (unfulfilled promises of advancement) still remains. The fact that the average age for first marriage has increased points to the fact that women are prioritizing their careers before settling down to have families. Further, the 2008 recession affected jobs traditionally held by men more than it affected jobs traditionally held by women. Therefore, women were increasingly a family's primary breadwinner at the start of the second decade of the 2000s.

Along with changing gender roles, the United States has seen an increase in women elected to political office. Besides Hillary Clinton's presidential campaign in 2016, Geraldine Ferraro and Sarah Palin each were nominated as running mates in the presidential campaigns of 1984 and 2008, respectively. Further, the number of women elected to Congress has reached historic levels.

In addition to changing demographics, analysts have also noticed new patterns in family structures over the latter half of the 20th century. While 87% of children lived in a two-parent household in 1960, only 73% did in 2000, and 69% do today. Consistent with this is the rise in one parent households: 9% of children lived in a one-parent household in 1960 compared with 26% today.

RECENT TRENDS

You are unlikely to see any questions on your test regarding the election of Barack Obama in 2008 or the election of President Donald Trump in 2016. In closing, however, it helps to know that the Bush and Obama administrations responded to the **financial crash of 2008** (exacerbated by the crisis in the mortgage industry) by providing financial assistance to major banks, popularly known as a "banker bailout." The most important piece of legislation passed under Obama's tenure was the **Affordable Care Act** or "Obamacare," a controversial set of laws that aimed to both regulate the medical industry and provide subsidies to uninsured Americans.

The **election of 2016** was a turbulent one, marked by ideological divisions within the Republican Party and a bitter rivalry between populist real estate mogul Donald Trump and Democrat insider Hillary Clinton. Clinton won the national popular vote, while Trump won the Electoral College. While political analysts still struggle to understand the dynamics that propelled Trump to victory, the consensus may conclude that a **new populism** has emerged in the United States—one of skepticism for established institutions and optimism regarding political "outsiders." If the trend continues, no doubt many changes will come to both domestic and foreign policy.

Another Course? Of Course!

If you can't get enough AP U.S. History and want to review this material with an expert, we also offer an online Cram Course that you can sign up for here: https://www.princetonreview.com/college/ap-test-prep.

Summary

Here are the most important concepts to remember from the pre-21st and early 21st-century period.

o   In response to a growing liberalization of government, Conservatives gained a new voice in public discourse.

o   After the collapse of the Soviet Union and the fall of the Berlin Wall, American fears shifted to the threat of Middle Eastern terrorism.

o   Immigration, both legal and illegal, grew exponentially, prompting internal debate.

o   The Internet revolution of the 1990s enhanced the economy and ushered in the Information Age, while domestic manufacturing jobs decreased. Many Americans were forced to seek alternative employment as large companies down-sized and outsourced jobs overseas.

o   The United States continued to pursue an interventionist foreign policy through the early 21st century.

o   Right-wing populism and left-wing socialism squared off before and during the Trump Administration.

Chapter 13 Review Questions

See Chapter 14 for answers and explanations.

1. The top goals of the Reagan presidency included

    (A) eliminating all social programs and balancing the federal budget
    (B) reducing the size of the federal government and increasing defense spending
    (C) using the federal government to enforce civil rights and reducing U.S. influence in Central America
    (D) increasing income tax rates and strengthening environmental regulations

2. Since the end of the Cold War, the continuing American impulse to intervene in the economic and political affairs of other nations around the world is motivated by all of the following EXCEPT

    (A) fears of renewed Soviet expansion
    (B) the protection of human rights
    (C) American economic interests
    (D) the desire to promote and develop democratic institutions in former communist and Third World nations

3. All of the following acts of President Ronald Reagan's administration are characterized as a return to conservative political values EXCEPT

    (A) cuts in the federal budget
    (B) the appointment of Sandra Day O'Connor to the Supreme Court
    (C) tax cuts for corporations
    (D) the loosening of government regulation

4. Which of the following did NOT contribute to the emergence of the New Right of the 1970s and 1980s?

    (A) The Moral Majority movement
    (B) The popularity of Ronald Reagan
    (C) The "stagflation" economic condition of the 1970s
    (D) A sudden drop in the stock market

5. In his 1985 State of the Union Address, Ronald Reagan articulated his foreign policy goals in what has come to be known as the Reagan Doctrine. Like Truman, Reagan pledged to

    (A) support anticommunist resistance movements, particularly in the Third World
    (B) sponsor covert military operations to overthrow communist regimes in Eastern Europe
    (C) ease tensions between the Soviet Union and the United States
    (D) broker a peace agreement between the Palestinians and the Israelis

6. During the 1990s, President George H. W. Bush

    (A) signed the welfare reform bill
    (B) persuaded Anwar Sadat and Menachem Begin to sign the Camp David Accords
    (C) sent troops to fight in the Persian Gulf War
    (D) cut taxes and social services

7. Which of the following actions by the Clinton administration was most harmonious with Liberal Democrat values?

    (A) Military peacekeeping interventions in the Balkans and Somalia
    (B) Welfare benefit reform to encourage young mothers to reenter the work force
    (C) Free trade agreements such as NAFTA and GATT
    (D) The effort to pass a universal health care legislation in the Congress

8. Which one of these presidents was best known for the campaign promise "Read my lips: No new taxes!"?

    (A) Jimmy Carter
    (B) Ronald Reagan
    (C) George H. W. Bush
    (D) Bill Clinton

REFLECT

Respond to the following questions:

- For which content topics discussed in this chapter do you feel you have achieved sufficient mastery to answer multiple-choice questions correctly?

- For which content topics discussed in this chapter do you feel you have achieved sufficient mastery to discuss effectively in a short-answer question or an essay?

- On which content topics discussed in this chapter do you feel you need more work before you can answer multiple-choice questions correctly?

- On which content topics discussed in this chapter do you feel you need more work before you can discuss them effectively in a short-answer question or an essay?

- What parts of this chapter are you going to review again?

- Will you seek further help, outside of this book (such as a teacher, tutor, or AP Students), on any of the content in this chapter—and, if so, on what content?

Chapter 14
Chapter Review
Questions:
Answers and
Explanations

CHAPTER 6 REVIEW QUESTIONS

1. **C** Indentured servitude promised freedom and a parcel of land to those who survived its seven-year term of service. Fewer than half did; most indentured servants worked in the fields performing grueling labor, and many died as a result. Indentured servitude was available only to the English, and nearly 100,000 took advantage of it.

2. **A** The Mayflower Compact states that government derives its power from the consent of the governed, not from divine mandate. This distinguishes government under the Mayflower Compact from the monarchial government the Pilgrims left behind in England.

3. **D** Virginia, one of the earliest colonies, developed around the tobacco trade; tobacco was the colonies' first important cash crop. Choice (A), cotton, did not become a major export until the early 19th century, when the invention of the cotton gin made large-scale cotton farming practical.

4. **B** During the colonial era, the British subscribed to the economic theory of mercantilism, which held that a favorable balance of trade and control of hard currency were the keys to economic power. Ultimately, the theory of capitalism, famously championed by Adam Smith, supplanted mercantilism as the predominant economic theory of the West.

5. **C** During the Age of Salutary Neglect, Britain regarded the colonies primarily as a market for exports and a resource of raw materials. England imposed numerous import and export restrictions on the colonies in an effort to maintain its monopoly on colonial markets. Naturally, the colonists tried to smuggle cheaper goods into the country and smuggled products out of the country in order to sell them. The British established their own military-style courts—called vice-admiralty courts—to enforce trade laws because they knew the colonists themselves would not.

6. **C** The Stono Uprising was an early slave rebellion (1739) in which African slaves rose against their oppressors. The Stono Uprising is sometimes referred to as the Cato Rebellion.

7. **D** The vast majority of colonists lived in rural areas. By 1750, roughly 5 percent of the colonial population resided in cities. Philadelphia, Boston, Williamsburg, Baltimore, and Boston were the most important cities of the era; all were built around ports.

8. **D** The purpose of America's first colleges was to train homegrown clergy so that the colonies would no longer have to import its clergy from England. The four oldest extant colonial universities—Harvard, William & Mary, Yale, and Princeton—were all originally affiliated with specific Protestant faiths.

9. **A** Provided the colonies continued to buy British goods and to supply the British with raw materials, England did not care how the colonies governed themselves. England did impose its will (through the vice-admiralty courts) when the colonies attempted to shirk their economic responsibilities but otherwise took a laissez-faire approach. As a result, the colonies developed a tradition of independence that contributed to their eventual rebellion against the Crown.

CHAPTER 7 REVIEW QUESTIONS

1. **D** Benjamin Franklin developed the Albany Plan, a first stab at a united colonial government empowered to collect taxes and raise a military. Although the delegations to Albany signed off on the plan, none of the colonial legislatures would have anything to do with it; they were uninterested in ceding any powers, even in the interest of strengthening the colonies as a whole. Franklin responded with his famous "Join or Die" cartoon, which showed the colonies as a snake cut into segments, each representing a colony.

2. **D** 1763, the year the Treaty of Paris ended the French and Indian War, is often considered to be a major turning point in British-colonial relations, as it marked the end of Britain's policy of salutary neglect. Beginning with the Proclamation of 1763, the colonists began to feel England tightening the screws. The passage of the Sugar and Stamp Acts set off a chain of new restrictions that set the colonists on the road to revolution. Although you no doubt know the phrase "No taxation without representation!" the colonists did not actually want to send colonial representatives to sit in the British Parliament in London. Rather, as the resolutions of the Stamp Act Congress make clear, they believed that only their own colonial legislatures had the power to tax them. They initially understood that they were British subjects and that Parliament had the right to enact mercantilist restrictions to regulate trade. However, they soon voiced their concern that there was a significant difference between taxation and legislation.

3. **A** In the run-up to the Revolutionary War, colonists complained that Parliament had no business taxing them because the colonists lacked representation in the legislature. Their slogan, "No taxation without representation!" neatly summed up their argument (and it was catchy too!). The British responded with the theory of virtual representation, which stated that the colonists were represented in Parliament because members of Parliament represent all British citizens, not just the voters who elected them. Like most political debates, this one reeked of disingenuousness on both sides. The colonists knew that any delegation they sent to Parliament would be essentially powerless; what they really wanted was the right to set their own taxes, not to have them be set by a representative in the legislature. The British knew full well that their members of Parliament (MPs) did not give a tinker's damn about the colonists or their interests; what they wanted was for the colonists to shut up and pay their taxes.

4. **A** A recent DBQ on the AP Exam asked to what extent the colonists had developed a sense of unity by the eve of the Revolution. One could certainly argue that most colonists considered themselves to be loyal British subjects even after fighting had begun in Lexington and Concord in April 1775. Many historians view the Declaration of Independence, written in July 1776, as propaganda to convince those still loyal to England to fight for their independence. At the start of the French and Indian War, Benjamin Franklin had proposed the Albany Plan of Union, which was rejected by the colonists in favor of maintaining individual colonial sovereignty. The Stamp Act Congress of 1765 is historically significant because it marks the beginning of colonial unity and resistance against the British.

5. **B** Much of the American Declaration of Independence is derived from the writings of John Locke, particularly his *Two Treatises of Government,* published in 1690, in which he challenged the theory of divine right of kings and put forth what is known as social contract theory. Both Locke and Rousseau believed that man was born free, but it was Rousseau who argued that "Man must be forced to be free" and submit to the "General Will."

6. **D** The Articles of Confederation had intentionally created a weak central government, granting Congress few regulatory powers so as to avoid recreating an American Parliament. Shays's Rebellion threatened the survival of the newly established republic because the farmers in western Massachusetts were rebelling against their state government for the very same reason the colonists had rebelled against England—taxes. Under the Articles of Confederation, Congress could neither raise nor support a federal militia, so when Massachusetts requested federal assistance in squelching Daniel Shays and his farmer friends, no help was available. Had this question been about the Whiskey Rebellion during George Washington's administration, (A) would have been the correct answer. Choice (A) also demonstrates the difference between the limited power of the federal government under the Articles of Confederation and the stronger federal government established by the Constitution. Choice (C) is not correct, although excessive taxation was certainly one of the major causes of the American Revolution and subsequent rebellions. It is interesting to note that we did not have a federal income tax until the Sixteenth Amendment was ratified in the early 20th century.

7. **B** The Articles of Confederation were established to provide a limited framework to organize the states under a single banner. However, they had very little power (purposefully) so that each state could decide its own legislation and government. States were expected to establish taxation, and Congress under the Articles of Confederation was not allowed to set up taxes (eliminating I). Furthermore, the whole purpose of the Articles of Confederation was to provide a legal document to enforce states' rights, not undermine them (eliminating III). The Articles of Confederation did, however, provide a framework for how the United States government would represent the states in foreign diplomatic matters such as treaties (making II correct).

8. **C** Washington's presidency was all about establishing precedents. He was extremely conscious of this fact and proceeded cautiously throughout his two terms, aware that future presidents would follow his example. Thus, he rarely used his presidential veto, hoping to encourage future executives to accommodate the legislature on most matters. He didn't want the Congress to have complete control over the executive branch, though; he believed in the system of checks and balances. Thus, when the House of Representatives demanded all of Washington's papers regarding negotiations for the unpopular Jay Treaty, Washington refused. He reasoned that the papers were none of the House's business because only the Senate—with whom Washington did share the papers—is required to ratify treaties. His action established the precedent of executive privilege, a nebulous executive right to protect sensitive information and executive privacy. The right is occasionally invoked by the executive and almost as frequently challenged by the legislature, with the two typically working out a solution of compromise before the matter can reach the courts.

9. **D** The French and Indian War gave the British unchecked control over North America and a huge war debt. Searching for ways to repay the debt, the British sought greater contributions from, and subsequently greater control over, its American colonies. The Age of Salutary Neglect, an era during which the British basically allowed the colonies to govern themselves, was over.

10. **D** The strict constructionist interpretation of the Constitution is that Congress may use only those powers specifically enumerated in the Constitution. Other powers, regardless of how necessary they may be to national interests, are prohibited. The broad constructionist interpretation, in contrast, holds that Congress has numerous implied powers. For example, Congress has the power to print money, borrow money, and collect taxes; thus, the Constitution implies that Congress has the power to create a bank, the proper instrument for exercising these powers.

11. **C** First, cross out the "EXCEPT" and think "Yes" or "No" for each answer choice. The era is the American Revolution: think late 1700s, the colonies break from Great Britain, main disputes are taxing and trading laws, most people live on the Atlantic coast. Choices (A) and (D) are firmly within the era, and a "Yes" means to eliminate the choice. Maybe (B) leaves you a little clueless, but if you had to choose between (B) and (C), which one of these things is least like the others? Which answer choice stretches the era's boundaries? Obviously, (C) is the "No," the anti-era exception and the right answer. Women's rights did not become an issue until more than a century later, in the late 1800s, during the first women's movement.

CHAPTER 8 REVIEW QUESTIONS

1. **D** John Marshall was not the first Chief Justice of the Supreme Court, but he certainly was the man most responsible for giving the Court its teeth and much of the power it wields today. *Marbury v. Madison* was Marshall's first significant decision and established the principle of judicial review, which enables the Court to declare a federal or state law unconstitutional. Choice (C), *McCulloch v. Maryland,* was another landmark decision of the Marshall Court; this case dealt with the Second Bank of the United States and established the principle of federal supremacy. And it is important to note that while Marshall was an important federalist, he did not establish the principle.

2. **B** The Louisiana Purchase grew out of the government's efforts to purchase New Orleans from the French; President Jefferson wanted control of the city because it sits at the mouth of the Mississippi River, an essential trade route. Jefferson sent James Monroe to France to negotiate the sale. The French, desperate for cash and nearly as desperate to divest themselves of New World holdings, offered to sell the entire massive Louisiana Territory, giving the United States control of both banks of the Mississippi River (as well as a tremendous amount of western land). As a result, American traders could travel the length of the river unimpeded, and trade subsequently boomed. Many of the incorrect answers to this question are anachronistic; the date of the purchase was too early for there to be "numerous French factories" in the territory, as in (C), or to allow for "the immediate completion of the transcontinental railroad," as in (D).

3.   **A**   The War of 1812 was very unpopular with New England Federalists who called the war "Mr. Madison's War." The economic policies of Jefferson and Madison disrupted trade, and as a result, were detrimental to New England merchants and shippers. Consequently, a group of New England Federalists met in Hartford, Connecticut, in 1814 to articulate a list of grievances against the Democratic-Republicans and their policies. While some men suggested secession, others suggested amending the Constitution to protect New England's commercial interests against what they perceived to be a dangerous, growing threat from the agrarian, Republican South. Because we "defeated" the British in what is often termed the Second War for Independence, the Federalists were seen as big babies and ultimately discredited. With the election of James Monroe in 1816, the United States had entered the Era of Good Feelings, a relatively brief period when there was only one political party—the Republicans. Although the War of 1812 damaged New England commerce initially, in the long run, the Embargo Act of 1807 and the War of 1812 forced Americans to be less dependent on British goods and indirectly stimulated the growth of industry in antebellum New England.

4.   **A**   The election of 1824 is one of the more infamous elections in American political history and exposes one of the unanticipated flaws in the Electoral College system. Because of the winner-take-all system of awarding electoral votes in most states, it is possible for a candidate to actually win the popular vote nationwide but lose the election. According to the Constitution, a candidate must win a majority, not a plurality, of electoral votes to win the presidential election. If no one candidate receives the requisite majority, the election is "thrown into the House," and the House of Representatives chooses the president from among the top three candidates. In the event this occurs, each state casts only one vote. Because there were five candidates running for president in 1824, it was almost impossible for anyone to receive a majority. Realizing that he did not have enough support to win the presidency, Henry Clay threw his support to John Quincy Adams in exchange for Adams's promise to make Clay his secretary of state. Jackson believed he lost the election because of this "corrupt bargain."

5.   **D**   The tariff in question here is the infamous Tariff of Abominations, so named by the Southern states that protested that this protective tariff benefited the New England manufacturers at the expense of cotton exporters in the South. The enactment of the Tariff of 1828 led to the nullification crisis a few years later when South Carolina declared the tariff null and void. (A similar situation had occurred in 1798 when Jefferson and Madison penned the Virginia and Kentucky resolutions in protest against the Alien and Sedition Acts.) In the case of *Marbury v. Madison*, Marshall had argued that only the Supreme Court, not individual states, could rule a law to be unconstitutional. Eventually, a compromise tariff was brokered, and the crisis was resolved. Nevertheless, the nullification crisis during Andrew Jackson's administration exposed the increasing tension of economic sectionalism that would propel the nation to civil war 30 years later.

6.   **A**   Andrew Jackson generally sided with the states on the issue of states' rights, preferring to limit the powers of the federal government to only those he perceived to be essential. He also favored his Western constituency to the power elite of the Northeast, whom he regarded with suspicion. Thus,

Jackson scuttled the Second National Bank, a large federal program championed by Northeastern bankers, and the American System, a large public works program.

7. **B** The Cherokee were considered part of the "Five Civilized Tribes" living in the South, having established a republic in the state of Georgia. Unfortunately the discovery of gold within the Cherokee nation's borders was the catalyst for the tribe's forced relocation. Georgian citizens wanted to enforce the Indian Removal Act in order to have access to the territory. Although the Supreme Court ruled in favor of the Cherokees, President Andrew Jackson did not comply with the decision. States' rights were an important issue during Jackson's presidency, and he did not want to intervene on behalf of the Cherokee nation.

8. **D** Brook Farm, the Oneida Community, and New Harmony were all utopian communities that arose during the antebellum period in response to what some people perceived to be the ill effects of a growing commercial society.

CHAPTER 9 REVIEW QUESTIONS

1. **D** This is a trick question. Texas was annexed by the United States in 1845, prior to the start of the Mexican-American War. All the other territories mentioned in the answer choices came to the United States as a result of the Treaty of Guadalupe Hidalgo, which ended the war.

2. **D** The term "Bleeding Kansas" refers to the battle in Kansas between pro-slavery and abolitionist forces. The doctrine of popular sovereignty had created the circumstances that led to the gruesome conflict; it left the slave status of each territory up to its residents, to be decided at the time when the territory was ready to write a constitution and apply for statehood. Both sides wanted Kansas badly, and both sent representatives into the territory to form governments. President Pierce recognized the pro-slavery government, but abolitionist forces cried "foul" and continued their fight to establish Kansas as a free state. More than 200 people died in the resulting skirmishes.

3. **B** The Emancipation Proclamation did not free all the slaves. Instead, it freed only those slaves in rebel territories not controlled by the Union. In other words, it was completely unenforceable; it immediately took effect only in those places where Union forces had no power to act, but it ultimately had a significant impact as Union troops took over Confederate territory. The Emancipation Proclamation had a huge symbolic effect, though, as it clearly cast the Civil War as a war against slavery. Free blacks and escaped slaves rushed to join the cause; nearly 200,000 joined the Union army as a consequence of the Emancipation Proclamation.

4. **D** Many historians argue that Andrew Johnson was neither the man nor the politician that Lincoln was. Johnson locked horns with the Radical Republicans in Congress over several issues pertaining to Reconstruction. Johnson had vetoed the Tenure of Office Act, which required a president to obtain Senate approval before firing an appointed official. The Senate argued that if it had the power to confirm nominations, it should also be allowed to have a say in the event a president

wanted to fire someone. Congress overrode Johnson's veto; Johnson fired his secretary of war, the Radical Republican Henry Stanton; and the House of Representatives impeached the President of the United States for the first time in American history. Johnson was acquitted, however, by one vote in the Senate and thus remained in office to finish his term.

5. **B** The election of 1876 is another one of the disputed elections in American political history. Although Samuel J. Tilden, then Governor of New York, won the popular vote nationwide, there were several states that contested the results of the election. Consequently, a special bipartisan commission was set up to determine the outcome of the election. In what became known as the "Compromise of 1877," Rutherford B. Hayes won the presidential election by a margin of one single electoral vote. Hayes had promised to remove federal troops still stationed in the South after the Civil War, thus ending military reconstruction.

6. **A** Remember that most slaves had no job skills and could neither read nor write. They had no money and nowhere to go when slavery was abolished. Some slaves took off in search of their scattered families, but most stayed exactly where they were and worked as tenant farmers or sharecroppers.

    Under the new wage-labor system, plantations were subdivided into smaller farms of 30 to 50 acres, which were then leased to freedmen under a one-year contract. Tenants would work a piece of land and turn over 50 percent of their crops to the landlord. Often, other expenses, such as rent for a run-down shack or over-priced groceries, available only through the landowner, would be deducted from whatever was produced. One of the services initially provided by the Freedmen's Bureau was to help freed slaves who could neither read nor write understand the contracts they were about to sign. The system of sharecropping persisted well into the 20th century, keeping many blacks in positions of poverty and degradation.

    Choice (C) is incorrect for reasons stated above. The Great Migration of Southern blacks into Northern cities did not take place until World War I, long after Reconstruction. Choice (D) is incorrect because Chinese immigrants were used to construct our nation's railroad system, much of which had been completed by the end of the Civil War.

7. **D** The Know-Nothings were a nativist group formed in response to the growing concentration of immigrants—particularly Italian and Irish Catholics—in Eastern cities. The party grew out of a number of secret societies whose members were instructed to tell outsiders nothing, hence the party's name. When asked anything about their groups, Know-Nothings would respond, "I know nothing." Their program included a 25-year residency requirement for citizenship; they also wanted to restrict all public offices to only those who were native-born Americans. By 1855, they had changed their name to the American Party, and in 1856, they fielded a presidential candidate (former president Millard Fillmore). Within a few years, the party had disbanded, destroyed by their disagreements over slavery. Most Northern Know-Nothings joined the Republican party.

8. **C** The Free-Soil Party was created in the mid-1840s and was more like a faction or interest group than a political party. However, unlike a faction, it developed a political platform and nominated a candidate (Martin Van Buren) for the presidential election of 1844. The Free-Soil party attracted antislavery "Conscience" Whigs, former members of the Liberty party, and pro-Wilmot Proviso Democrats. The Wilmot Proviso was rejected by Congress but suggested that there be no slavery in

any territory acquired from Mexico. Free-Soilers were opposed to the extension of slavery into the new territories. Remember: The Constitution protected slavery where it already existed, but many people believed Congress could prevent the further spread of slavery as the United States acquired new land. Although the Free-Soil party did not exist for long, its major principles were adopted by the new Republican party, which was formed in 1854 and was opposed to the extension of slavery into the new territories.

9. **D** In the election of 1848, the Democrats realized that their party was crumbling because its members could not agree on whether to allow slavery in the Western territories. They sought a policy to appease both abolitionists and slaveholders; the result of that search was the concept of popular sovereignty. By allowing the settlers to decide the slave status of an area, popular sovereignty took some pressure off Congress, which was growing increasingly divided over the issue. It also took pressure off the political parties, which were coming apart due to the irreconcilable regional differences of their members. Henry Clay invoked the notion of popular sovereignty in the Compromise of 1850, but the compromise contained a purposefully ambiguous interpretation of what popular sovereignty meant. While the ambiguous wording was necessary to make the Compromise of 1850 possible, it also made future disagreements over the issue inevitable.

10. **C** The Reconstruction Act of 1867, Congress's plan for the rehabilitation of the South, was much harsher than President Johnson's plan. Johnson, like Lincoln (who began planning the method for readmitting Southern states before his assassination), wanted a reconciliatory plan that punished only the most prominent leaders of the secession. Radical Republicans in Congress wanted something much tougher, and Johnson's plan was so lenient (in the first postwar Congress, Johnson's plan would have allowed the former president of the Confederacy to take a seat in the Senate) that it drove many moderates into the radicals' camp. The result was the Reconstruction Act, a punitive measure that imposed a number of strict requirements on Southern states as preconditions for their readmission to the Union. Choices (A), (B), and (D) list all of those preconditions; the fact that Congress did not impose any requirements such as the one described in (C) pretty much doomed postwar Southern blacks to poverty.

CHAPTER 10 REVIEW QUESTIONS

1. **D** The scalawags were white Southerners who supported Republican policies during Reconstruction. Carpetbaggers were Northerners who traveled south to exploit the turmoil following the Civil War for their own political gain. The Redeemers were white Democrats who were determined to get revenge on the Republicans for imposing their radical policies of Reconstruction on Southern states and thus hoped to "redeem" the South.

2. **A** If you remember that the Supreme Court of the late 19th century was extremely conservative and extremely pro-business—and you should remember that, because it's important—you should have been able to eliminate (B) and (D) immediately. If you remember the profound impact of such decisions as *Plessy v. Ferguson*—and you should also remember that—you could have eliminated (C).

3. **D** "Vertical integration" is another name for monopoly. Monopolies ran rampant in the late 1800s; the government did little to prevent them, and the courts actively encouraged them. Of the incorrect answers, (C) refers to assembly line production, and (A) and (B) are just made up.

4. **C** James A. Garfield's presidency is remembered for one thing: Garfield's assassination at the hands of a disgruntled office seeker. His assassin, Charles Guiteau, was actually a mentally disturbed individual who imagined himself an important player in Garfield's electoral success. Guiteau convinced himself that he deserved a big fat government job as a reward for his efforts, and when he received none he retaliated by shooting Garfield. Garfield's successor, Chester Arthur, signed the Pendleton Act, which replaced the spoils system Guiteau had hoped to exploit with a merit-based system for selecting civil servants.

5. **C** Although one might certainly make a valid claim that labor unions were necessary during the late 19th century when working conditions were dangerous, unsanitary, and exploitative, unions were very unpopular because they were associated with political radicalism and violence. The Haymarket incident began as a mass meeting organized by anarchists, held in Haymarket Square in Chicago in 1886 in sympathy and protest of events related to striking workers at the McCormick Harvester Company plant nearby. When police tried to break up the meeting, someone threw a bomb into the crowd, leaving seven policemen dead and several wounded. This incident convinced the American public that unions were dangerous and ultimately led to the decline of the Knights of Labor.

6. **D** If you can't immediately identify the correct answer to this one, use common sense to eliminate incorrect answers. Japan is a huge nation relative to Hawaii; its economy couldn't realistically depend on trade with the island, so eliminate (A). Choice (B) contradicts one of the main themes of the period—the Age of Imperialism, when every Western power, including the United States, was gathering colonies in the East. Would the United States have ceded Hawaii to Japan during that period? Unlikely, and much less likely still that the AP Exam would ask about an anomalous agreement. Choice (C) suggests Japan was a bastion of democracy in the late 19th century; in fact, it was ruled by an emperor.

7. **D** Historians describe the immigrants who came to the United States before the Civil War as "old immigrants." These men and women came predominantly from countries in northwestern Europe. For the most part, they were Protestants and spoke English and easily became part of the melting pot we call America. Following the Civil War, however, the "new immigrants" came predominantly from nations in southeastern Europe, including Russians, Italians, and Poles. Many of these people were Catholics and Jews and were culturally very different from most Americans by that point. These new immigrants were not easily assimilated. They tended to settle among themselves

in ethnic neighborhoods in major cities like New York and Chicago where there was a demand for unskilled labor in the numerous factories of these big cities.

8. **D** The Ghost Dancers arose in the late 1800s when the sad fate awaiting the great Native American tribes of the era was becoming all too apparent. Wovoka, a Paiute Indian, started the Ghost Dance movement, which resembled a religious revival. It centered on a dance ritual that enabled participants to envision a brighter future, one in which whites no longer dominated North America. Wovoka preached unity among Native Americans and the rejection of white culture and its trappings, especially alcohol. He also preached the imminent end of the world, at which point the Indian dead would rise to reclaim the land that was rightfully theirs. Sioux Ghost Dancers believed in the power of "ghost shirts," garments blessed by medicine men that were capable of stopping bullets. This belief led to a rise in Sioux militancy and ultimately contributed to their massacre at Wounded Knee in 1890.

9. **D** Waves of European immigration throughout the 19th century swelled cities' populations. Governments of the time were nowhere near as activist as they are today, and only a very few provided even minimal services to immigrants as they accommodated themselves to their new homeland; ethnic communities and churches were expected to provide such services. A number of enterprising, unscrupulous men recognized in these immigrants the opportunity for great political power. Such men, known as political bosses, helped immigrants find homes and jobs and acquire citizenship and voting rights. In essence, these bosses created entire communities and then provided them with all sorts of services: food and loans for the poor, parks and protection for the community. In return, the communities were expected to provide loyal political support, which they did, originally out of loyalty, and later, as the machines became extremely powerful, out of both loyalty and fear. The bosses could then hand an election to a politician of their choice, in return for favors. Political machines filled a need, albeit in an expensive and unethical way. They fell from power when governments started to provide many of the services machines had provided.

10. **D** In the 1860s, the government initiated its reservation policy by which Native Americans were granted (usually less desirable) portions of the lands they inhabited. The policy failed on many fronts, and by the 1880s the government was searching for a different tack. Congress struck on the Dawes Severalty Act, which offered individual Native Americans 160-acre plots in return for leaving their reservations; through this program, Congress hoped to hasten the assimilation of Native Americans, whose cultures most congressmen held in contempt. The results were not good. Most American Indians preferred to remain among their tribes and did not accept the offer. Those who did accept usually ended up selling their land to whites, who often placed considerable pressure on them to do so.

CHAPTER 11 REVIEW QUESTIONS

1. **D** "Muckrakers" is a term Theodore Roosevelt coined to describe the investigative journalists of his day. They included Ida Tarbell, whose book on Standard Oil revealed corruption in the oil industry and big business in general; Upton Sinclair, whose stomach-turning account of the meatpacking industry drove public outcry for government regulation of food production (the Food and Drug Administration was created as a result of Sinclair's book *The Jungle*); and Lincoln Steffens, whose *The Shame of the Cities* exposed many Americans to the extent of urban poverty and corruption in urban government. Muckrakers helped fuel the public outcry for government reform, the main goal of the Progressive movement.

2. **B** Conservative courts and pro-business administrations allowed the Sherman Antitrust Act to be used to restrain labor but rarely to restrain business. Theodore Roosevelt changed all that. With public support Roosevelt transformed the Sherman Antitrust Act into a tool with which to break up monopolies. He focused his attention on corrupt monopolies whose activities countered the public interest, leaving alone trusts that operated more or less honestly. His approach garnered broad public acclaim, earning him the nickname "the Trustbuster."

3. **B** As a result of winning the Spanish-American War in 1898, the United States acquired Guam, Puerto Rico, the Philippines, and for all intents and purposes, Cuba. (Although we had claimed we had no interest in acquiring Cuba and could empathize with its colonial status, having once been a colony ourselves, the Platt Amendment rendered the island a virtual colony of the United States.) The situation in the Philippines created intense debate between business interests that saw the enormous economic benefits to acquiring "stepping stones" to profitable Chinese trade, and those Americans who believed having colonies contradicted our fundamental democratic principles. Once we acquired overseas possessions, a question arose as to the rights and privileges of the native peoples living within the American Empire. In a series of Supreme Court cases known as the Insular Cases, the Court ruled that the "Constitution did not follow the flag," and thus, colonial subjects were not entitled to the same rights as U.S. citizens living at home or abroad.

4. **A** This is a straight recall question. You either know what the Zimmermann telegram is or you don't. If you know it, you're going to get this question right. If you don't, use Process of Elimination to get rid of anachronistic answers, as in (B), or answers that seem un-AP-like because they don't reinforce important themes of U.S. history, as in (D). You should know, however, that the Zimmermann telegram was one of the reasons the United States entered World War I.

5. **C** In the aftermath of World War I, President Wilson favored a peace that would promote openness in international affairs, free trade, and diplomacy. He also sought universal arms reductions and a mechanism for enforcing world peace, which was to be achieved through the League of Nations. He did not seek a punitive treaty that forced Germany to pay heavy reparations; the European allies, however, insisted. Wilson was able to negotiate very little of his Fourteen Points plan, but he remained optimistic that the League of Nations would eventually broker a fairer postwar peace. Unfortunately, Wilson's hopes were never realized.

6. **B** The Ku Klux Klan evoked the execrable Southern traditions of racism and physical intimidation against the modern drive for expanded civil rights. The Scopes Monkey Trial pitted religion against the modern notion of evolution. The Emergency Quota Act of 1924 was passed to check immigration from non-western European countries; its champions felt the nation's western European traditions were threatened by immigrants from Southern Europe, Eastern Europe, South America, and Asia. Prohibition pitted religion against modern licentiousness. The Teapot Dome Scandal, on the other hand, was just an example of good old-fashioned political corruption.

7. **D** Buying "on margin" allowed investors to buy stock with only a small amount of cash; the rest was borrowed from stockbrokers and banks against the presumed profits from subsequent stock sales. The system worked only as long as stock prices kept rising; once they started to fall, all hell broke loose. In response to market weakness in the fall of 1929, investors who had long believed the market was overvalued started to sell off their stocks, causing prices to drop. Noting the market downturn, stockbrokers demanded that clients repay margin loans and, when their clients couldn't repay, dumped the stocks on the market in order to recoup some of their losses. The law of supply and demand sent stock prices spiraling uncontrollably downward. Over a period of two months, the market lost nearly half its value and many, many investors—including some of the nation's biggest banks—were ruined.

8. **D** Roosevelt coined the phrase "Good Neighbor Policy" to reflect a shift in American attitudes toward Latin America. In the past, American intervention in the region had incited great resentment of the United States. Roosevelt announced a new U.S. commitment to autonomy throughout the hemisphere and showed his intentions by withdrawing U.S. troops from Nicaragua and Haiti. He later resisted sending troops to Cuba to quell a revolution.

9. **A** Americans were already predisposed to isolationism by nature before they heard the results of the Nye Commission's investigations. They had been promised that World War I was "the war to end all wars." Less than 20 years later, Europe was apparently on the verge of another big confrontation. The sentiment in the United States was, "Let them sort this out themselves." Those feelings were strengthened when the Nye Commission revealed that many American munitions companies had violated an arms embargo in order to arm the nation's enemies. It further revealed that U.S. banks had lobbied for entry into the war in order to protect more than $2 billion in loans to Britain and its allies. The report left Americans more cynical about the motives of its leaders and less susceptible to calls for intervention overseas.

10. **A** Fred Korematsu was among the more than 110,000 Japanese Americans ordered to relocate from the West Coast to internment camps during World War II. Korematsu refused, was arrested, and took his case all the way to the Supreme Court. The Court ruled that the government had not exceeded its power, noting that extraordinary times sometimes call for extraordinary measures; three of the nine justices dissented. History has not judged Roosevelt's internment policy kindly. In 1998, Fred Korematsu was awarded the Presidential Medal of Honor.

CHAPTER 12 REVIEW QUESTIONS

1. **D** The Korean War didn't begin until 1950.

2. **C** Fear of communist infiltration and subversion reached hysterical proportions in the post–World War II era, making all sorts of excessive responses to the communist threat not only possible but likely. Loyalty oaths were instituted by private companies, state governments, and even the federal government, based on the apparent belief that communist spies are capable of espionage but not of lying under oath. Blacklists banned suspected subversives from work in many industries, destroying the lives of many innocent people. Alger Hiss was accused of passing government secrets to the Soviet Union. He professed his innocence to his dying day, although Soviet files released in the post-Soviet era suggest his guilt. The Hiss case was front-page news. Richard Nixon played a prominent role in Hiss's prosecution, thereby earning Nixon the national spotlight for the first time.

3. **A** The key to this question is the phrase "intensified Cold War rhetoric." Words like "massive retaliation" didn't exactly improve relations with the Soviet Union. While (B), containment, was the guiding principle of U.S. foreign policy throughout the Cold War, this question is asking something more specific. And although Dulles did forge many alliances with smaller nations (collective security), (A) is a better answer. Choice (C), summit diplomacy, was practiced by Reagan and Gorbachev, while the term "shuttle diplomacy," (D), was applied to Henry Kissinger under Nixon.

4. **D** You should be familiar with the important decisions of the Marshall Court (1801–1835) and the Warren Court (1953–1969). Marshall is remembered as a Federalist who strengthened the new federal government and encouraged economic development of the new nation. The Warren Court was an activist court, best remembered for increasing the rights of individuals, specifically the rights of the accused. (For example, the *Gideon* and *Miranda* cases were decided by the Warren Court.) According to the Constitution, only Congress can make laws, but in effect, many of the Warren decisions established social policy, which many conservative critics saw as "judicial legislation."

5. **D** Kennedy's victory in 1960 was by the tiniest of margins. He could not have won, or governed, without the support of Democrats in the South, many of whom opposed any federal strengthening of civil rights law. As a result, Kennedy had to tread carefully on the issue of African American civil rights, a cause he had supported forcefully during his campaign. He used the attorney general's office to bring suits to force desegregation of Southern universities and appointed African Americans to prominent positions in his administration but made no effort at civil rights legislation until his final year in office. After Kennedy's assassination, new President Lyndon Johnson invoked Kennedy's memory and commitment to civil rights to force the Civil Rights Act of 1964 through Congress.

6. **C** The Republican candidate, Richard Nixon, was a former vice president. The Democratic candidate, Hubert Humphrey, was the current vice president and, before that, a longtime senator. Neither could have campaigned as a Washington outsider, and neither did. The Democrats were fractured over the war; the party was home to both aggressive cold warriors and the antiwar movement. Robert Kennedy was assassinated in June; many believe he would have won the nomination had he not been killed. George Wallace formed a third party and campaigned on states' rights and segregation, siphoning off key votes in the South, where the Democrats had traditionally done well. Nixon's only opposition in the Republican primaries came from Nelson D. Rockefeller, who campaigned halfheartedly, and Ronald Reagan, who, at the time, was seen as too extreme to ever win the presidency. Reagan never changed, but the country did.

7. **B** Gasoline and oil prices shot through the roof in the 1970s, affecting a wide range of industries that relied on the fuels to run. The result was widespread inflation throughout the decade.

8. **D** This is the event that started it all—the break-in to the Watergate complex in Washington, D.C., where the Democratic party had its national headquarters. All of the other choices became part of the cover-up and are known collectively as "Watergate," which ultimately forced the resignation of Richard Nixon, the only president to resign in American history. Nixon resigned before he was impeached and was subsequently pardoned by Gerald Ford.

CHAPTER 13 REVIEW QUESTIONS

1. **B** Reagan believed in limited federal government. Part of his goal in lowering tax rates was to reduce the federal budget (thus federal programs). But Reagan was also a stalwart cold warrior who believed that military strength was the best check against the Soviet Union and communism in general. He campaigned vigorously for new weapons systems, including the Strategic Defense Initiative, a space-based, antimissile system dubbed "Star Wars."

2. **A** Though American relations with Russia remain uneasy, fears of Soviet expansion are a thing of the past; the Soviet Union ceased to exist in 1991, ending the Cold War.

3. **B** In 1981, Ronald Reagan, in a move supported by various groups across the political spectrum, made Sandra Day O'Connor the first woman to serve on the Supreme Court. All the other choices represent typically conservative policy decisions by Reagan.

4. **D** Although there was a brief drop in the stock market in 1987 (known as Black Friday), this was not a contributing factor to the emergence of the New Right. All of the other factors did lead to this renewal of conservatism.

5. **A** There are several presidential doctrines you should know for this exam—for example, the Monroe Doctrine and the Truman Doctrine. In most cases these "doctrines" were delivered as speeches to Congress but became statements of U.S. foreign policy. Alarmed by the establishment of Soviet satellites in Eastern Europe and the potential Soviet threat to Greece and Turkey following World War II, Truman pledged his support to prevent the spread of communism in Europe (although he did not use those exact words). As a cold warrior, Ronald Reagan was committed to providing covert and overt assistance to anticommunist resistance movements, particularly in nations like Afghanistan and Nicaragua.

6. **C** This is a factoid question. President George H. W. Bush led the brief Persian Gulf War in 1990. Choice (B) is Carter and (D) is Reagan. Choice (A) is President Clinton.

7. **D** Liberal Democrats would have mixed feelings about war and free trade, so rule out (A). Welfare benefit reform was in fact designed to get young mothers off welfare, so this was not necessarily a boon to the Democrats. The most ambitious effort by the Clinton administration was to pass a universal health care bill, but this ultimately did not pass Congress.

8. **C** This is another factoid question. This was President George H. W. Bush's campaign promise (though the promise was not kept).

Chapter 15
Key Terms and Concepts

A NOTE ON THE KEY TERMS

The list of key terms that follows provides a comprehensive review of U.S. history. We've separated the terms into categories: concepts, events, people, and policies (which includes major Supreme Court decisions and important federal legislation). Write a brief explanation or identification of each term in the space provided. Some students even find making flash cards helpful.

Keep the following suggestions in mind as you go through these terms. If it is a concept, do not simply write a definition; try to think of a historical example that illustrates the concept. For example, you might define *evangelicalism* and then cite the Great Awakening as an example. Be certain you can explain the causes and effects of each major event. This will help you with the essay questions for which you are required to showcase an analytical understanding of issues. The Supreme Court cases and major laws should be placed within their historical context. It is always useful to ask yourself the question "Why at this time?" Again, you should not merely state what the Court decided or law required but also understand the case's or law's impact on American society at the time.

Most of these terms are printed in **bold**, *italic*, or ***bold italic*** type throughout the history review of the book (Chapters 6 through 13). If you cannot find a particular term in this book, use your textbook or the Internet.

Chapter 6: Early Contact with the New World and Colonization of North America

Concepts

Slave codes _____

City upon a hill _____

Encomiendas _____

Evangelicalism _____

Headright system _____

Indentured servitude _____

Joint-stock company _____

Mercantilism _____

Middle Passage _____

Praying towns _____

Proprietary colony _____

Puritanism _____

Royal colony _____

Salutary neglect _____

Slavery _____

Tariffs _____

Events

Bacon's Rebellion _____

Glorious Revolution in England _____

The Great Awakening _____

Huron Confederacy _____

King Philip's War _____

Pequot War _____

Pueblo Revolt _____

Salem witch trials _____

Spanish mission system _____

The "starving time" _____

Stono Uprising _____

People (Individuals and Groups)

Anne Hutchinson _____

Bartolomé de las Casas _____

Benjamin Franklin _____

Calvinists _____

Congregationalists _____

George Whitefield _____

Huguenots _____

John Rolfe _____

John Smith _____

Jonathan Edwards _____

Juan de Oñate _____

Maroons _____

Metacomet _____

Pilgrims _____

Pocahontas _____

Powhatan Confederacy _____

Puritans _____

Roger Williams _____

Separatists _____

Sir Walter Raleigh _____

Virginia Company _____

Wampanoags _____

Places

Cahokia _____

The Chesapeake _____

Jamestown _____

The Lower South _____

Massachusetts Bay colony _____

Middle colonies _____

New England _____

Policies, Agreements, Court Rulings, Etc.

Act of Toleration _____

Dominion of New England _____

Fundamental Orders of Connecticut _____

Halfway Covenant _____

Maryland Toleration Act _____

Mayflower Compact _____

Navigation Acts _____

Chapter 7: Conflict and American Independence

Concepts

Checks and balances _____

Common Sense _____

Hamilton's Financial Plan _____

Kentucky and Virginia Resolutions _____

Loose constructionism _____

Mercantilism _____

Nullification_____

Republican Motherhood _____

Strict constructionism _____

Tariffs_____

Virtual representation _____

Washington's Farewell Address_____

Events

Battle of Concord _____

Battle of Fallen Timbers_____

Battle of Saratoga_____

Battle of Lexington _____

Boston Massacre _____

Boston Tea Party _____

French Revolution _____

Haitian Revolution _____

Pontiac's Rebellion _____

Seven Years' War (French and Indian War) _____

Shays's Rebellion _____

Whiskey Rebellion _____

XYZ Affair _____

People (Individuals and Groups)

Abigail Adams _____

Adam Smith _____

Alexander Hamilton _____

Anti-Federalists _____

Benjamin Franklin _____

Chief Little Turtle _____

Committees of Correspondence _____

Democratic-Republican Party _____

East India Tea Company _____

Federalists _____

George III _____

George Grenville _____

George Washington _____

Iroquois _____

James Madison _____

John Adams _____

John Jay _____

Loyalists _____

Mercy Otis Warren _____

Minutemen _____

Patrick Henry _____

Patriots _____

Paxton Boys _____

Redcoats_____

Sons of Liberty_____

Thomas Jefferson _____

Thomas Paine_____

Places

Concord and Lexington, Massachusetts_____

Washington, D.C. _____

Policies, Agreements, Court Rulings, Etc.

Three-Fifths Compromise _____

Albany Plan of Union _____

Alien and Sedition Acts _____

Annapolis Convention_____

Articles of Confederation_____

Bill of Rights _____

Constitution _____

Continental Army _____

Currency Act _____

Declaration of Independence_____

Declaratory Act _____

First Bank of the United States _____

First Continental Congress _____

Franco-American Alliance _____

Great Compromise (Connecticut Compromise) _____

Intolerable Acts _____

Jay's Treaty _____

National Bank _____

Navigation Acts _____

New Jersey Plan_____

Northwest Ordinance _____

Olive Branch Petition _____

Pinckney's Treaty _____

Proclamation of 1763 _____

Proclamation of Neutrality _____

Quebec Act _____

Second Continental Congress _____

Stamp Act _____

Sugar Act _____

Townshend Acts _____

Treaty of Paris _____

Virginia Plan _____

Chapter 8: Beginnings of Modern American Democracy

Concepts

"54°40' or Fight!" _____

American System _____

"Boom and bust" _____

Caucus system _____

"Corrupt bargain" _____

Cult of domesticity _____

Era of Good Feelings _____

Gag rule _____

Impressment _____

Jacksonian Democracy _____

Judicial review _____

Labor unions _____

Manifest Destiny _____

Monroe Doctrine _____

"Pet" banks _____

Revivalism _____

Second Great Awakening _____

Spoils system _____

States' rights _____

Temperance _____

Transcendentalism _____

Underground Railroad _____

Universal manhood suffrage _____

Utopian communities _____

Events

Battle of the Alamo _____

Election of 1824 _____

Lewis and Clark Expedition _____

Nat Turner's Rebellion _____

Nullification crisis _____

Panic of 1819 _____

Panic of 1837 _____

Seneca Falls Convention _____

Seminole Wars _____

Trail of Tears _____

War of 1812 _____

People (Individuals and Groups)

Aaron Burr _____

American Antislavery Society _____

American Colonization Society _____

Andrew Jackson _____

Charles G. Finney _____

David Walker _____

Democrat Party _____

Democratic-Republican Party _____

Dorothea Dix _____

Eli Whitney _____

Federalist Party _____

Frederick Douglass _____

Freedmen _____

Harriet Tubman _____

Henry Clay _____

Henry David Thoreau _____

Horace Mann _____

Hudson River School _____

James K. Polk _____

John C. Calhoun _____

John Marshall _____

John Quincy Adams _____

John Tyler _____

Lydia Maria Child _____

Martin Van Buren _____

Mormons _____

Mulattoes _____

Ralph Waldo Emerson _____

Samuel Slater _____

Shakers _____

Sojourner Truth _____

Tecumseh _____

War Hawks _____

Whig Party _____

William Henry Harrison _____

William Lloyd Garrison _____

Places

Brook Farm _____

Erie Canal _____

Lowell, Massachusetts _____

National Road _____

Oregon Territory _____

Republic of Texas _____

Policies, Agreements, Court Rulings, Etc.

Cherokee Nation v. Georgia _____

Embargo Act _____

Force Bill _____

Hartford Convention _____

Indian Removal Act _____

Louisiana Purchase _____

Marbury v. Madison _____

McCulloch v. Maryland _____

Missouri Compromise _____

Non-Intercourse Act _____

Oregon Treaty _____

Second Bank of the United States _____

Specie Circular _____

Tariff of 1828 (Tariff of Abominations) _____

Worcester v. Georgia _____

Chapter 9: Toward the Civil War and Reconstruction

Concepts

"40 acres and a mule" _____

Black codes _____

Conscription _____

Habeas corpus _____

Inflation _____

Loyalty oath _____

Nativism _____

Popular sovereignty _____

Segregation _____

Sharecropping _____

Uncle Tom's Cabin _____

Events

Battle of Fort Sumter _____

Battle of Gettysburg_____

Battle of Little Big Horn _____

Compromise of 1850_____

Election of 1860 _____

Emancipation Proclamation_____

Bleeding Kansas _____

Gold Rush _____

Great Migration _____

Impeachment of Andrew Johnson _____

Mexican-American War _____

Minstrel shows_____

Sand Creek Massacre _____

Sherman's March to the Sea _____

People (Individuals and Groups)

Abraham Lincoln_____

Andrew Johnson _____

Carpetbaggers _____

Civil War _____

Copperheads _____

Dred Scott_____

Exodusters _____

Forty-Niners _____

Freedman's Bureau _____

Free-Soil Party _____

Harriet Beecher Stowe _____

Hiram Revels_____

James Buchanan_____

James K. Polk_____

Jefferson Davis_____

John Breckenridge _____

John Brown _____

John C. Calhoun _____

Know-Nothing Party _____

Ku Klux Klan_____

Matthew Perry _____

Millard Fillmore_____

Radical Republicans_____

Republican Party _____

Robert Smalls_____

Scalawags _____

Stephen Douglas _____

Ulysses S. Grant_____

Places

36°30' _____

54°40' _____

Confederate States _____

Fort Sumter _____

Harper's Ferry, West Virginia _____

Policies, Agreements, Court Rulings, Etc.

10% Plan_____

Thirteenth Amendment _____

Fourteenth Amendment_____

Fifteenth Amendment _____

Compromise of 1850_____

Compromise of 1877_____

Dred Scott v. Sandford _____

Hampton Roads Conference _____

Homestead Act _____

Fugitive Slave Act_____

Kansas-Nebraska Act _____

Personal liberty laws_____

Reconstruction Act _____

Treaty of Guadalupe Hidalgo_____

Wade-Davis Bill _____

Wilmot Proviso _____

Chapter 10: The Industrial Revolution

Concepts

Assembly line manufacturing_____

"Cross of Gold" speech _____

Economies of scale_____

Ghost Dance _____

The Gilded Age _____

The gold standard _____

Gospel of Wealth _____

Laissez-faire economics _____

Monopolies _____

The New South _____

Political bosses _____

Referendum _____

The silver standard _____

Social Darwinism_____

Social Gospel _____

Socialism _____

Temperance _____

Tenement housing _____

Trusts_____

Women's suffrage _____

Events

Haymarket Square Riot _____

Homestead Strike_____

Pullman Strike _____

Wounded Knee Massacre_____

People (Individuals and Groups)

American Federation of Labor (AFL)_____

American Socialist Party_____

American Suffrage Association _____

Andrew Carnegie _____

Benjamin Harrison _____

Booker T. Washington _____

"Boss" Tweed _____

Chester A. Arthur _____

Chief Joseph _____

Colored Farmers' Alliance _____

Cornelius Vanderbilt _____

Elizabeth Cady Stanton _____

Eugene V. Debs _____

Farmers' Alliances _____

Frederick Jackson Turner _____

The Grange _____

Grover Cleveland_____

Ida Wells-Barnett_____

James Garfield_____

John D. Rockefeller_____

John Muir _____

J.P. Morgan _____

Las Gorras Blancas_____

Mother Jones _____

Knights of Labor _____

Populist Party_____

Rutherford B. Hayes _____

Samuel Gompers _____

The Sierra Club _____

"Stalwarts and half-breeds" _____

Standard Oil _____

Susan B. Anthony _____

Tammany Hall _____

Thomas Edison _____

U.S. Steel _____

William H. Seward _____

William Jennings Bryan _____

William McKinley _____

Places

Alaska _____

Hawaii _____

Indian reservations _____

Land-grant colleges _____

Philippines _____

Settlement houses _____

Policies, Agreements, Court Rulings, Etc.

Civil Rights cases _____

Chinese Exclusion Act _____

Dawes Act _____

Interstate Commerce Act _____

Jim Crow laws _____

McKinley Tariff _____

Open Door Policy _____

Pendleton Civil Service Reform Act _____

Plessy v. Ferguson _____

Sherman Antitrust Act _____

Chapter 11: The Early 20th Century

Concepts

Christian Fundamentalism_____

Conservatism _____

Court-packing _____

Dollar Diplomacy _____

Fireside chats _____

Interventionism _____

Isolationism _____

Jazz _____

Labor strikes _____

Liberalism _____

New Deal_____

New Nationalism_____

Protectionism_____

Rationing_____

Roosevelt Corollary to the Monroe Doctrine_____

Sonar _____

Square Deal _____

Suburbs _____

Xenophobia _____

Yellow journalism_____

Events

Bombing of Hiroshima and Nagasaki _____

D-Day _____

Dust Bowl _____

First Red Scare_____

The Great Depression _____

Harlem Renaissance_____

Manhattan Project_____

Palmer Raids _____

Potsdam Conference _____

Russian Revolution _____

Sacco and Vanzetti Trial _____

Scopes "Monkey" Trial_____

Sinking of the *Lusitania*_____

Spanish-American War_____

Spanish Flu _____

Teapot Dome Scandal _____

World War I_____

Yalta Conference _____

Zimmermann telegram _____

People (Individuals and Groups)

Allied Powers _____

American Expeditionary Force_____

Axis Powers _____

Bonus Expeditionary Force _____

Calvin Coolidge_____

Communist Party of America _____

Countee Cullen _____

Ernest Hemingway_____

Eugene O'Neill _____

Flappers _____

Florence Kelley _____

Franklin D. Roosevelt _____

F. Scott Fitzgerald _____

Gangsters_____

Harry S. Truman _____

Henry Cabot Lodge_____

Herbert Hoover _____

Huey Long_____

Ida Tarbell _____

J. Edgar Hoover _____

Jane Addams _____

John Maynard Keynes _____

Joseph Pulitzer _____

Langston Hughes _____

Lost Generation _____

Louis Armstrong _____

Margaret Sanger _____

Muckrakers _____

National Association for the Advancement of Colored People (NAACP) _____

Progressive Party _____

Robert LaFollette _____

Theodore Roosevelt _____

Tripartite Pact _____

Upton Sinclair _____

Warren G Harding _____

W.E.B. Du Bois _____

William Howard Taft _____

William Randolph Hearst _____

Woodrow Wilson _____

Zora Neale Hurston _____

Places

"Hoovervilles" _____

Hull House _____

Japanese Internment Camps _____

Panama Canal _____

Pearl Harbor, Hawaii _____

Policies, Agreements, Court Rulings, Etc.

14 Points _____

Eighteenth Amendment (Prohibition) _____

Nineteenth Amendment _____

Agricultural Adjustment Act (AAA) _____

Atlantic Charter _____

Civilian Conservation Corps (CCC) _____

Clayton Antitrust Act _____

Emergency Banking Relief Bill_____

Emergency Quota Act _____

Fair Labor Standards Act _____

Federal Bureau of Investigation (FBI) _____

Federal Deposit Insurance Corporation (FDIC) _____

Federal Reserve Act _____

Federal Trade Commission (FTC) _____

Good Neighbor Policy _____

Hawley-Smoot Tariff _____

Immigration Act of 1924_____

Labor Disputes Act _____

League of Nations _____

Lend-Lease Act _____

Most favored nation (MFN) trade status _____

National Industrial Recovery Act (NIRA) _____

Neutrality Acts_____

North Atlantic Treaty Organization (NATO) _____

Platt Amendment_____

Public Works Administration (PWA)_____

Schenck v. United States _____

Securities and Exchange Commission (SEC) _____

Selective Service Act_____

Sherman Antitrust Act _____

Social Security Act_____

Tennessee Valley Authority (TVA) _____

Treaty of Versailles _____

United Nations _____

Washington Naval Conference_____

Works Progress Administration (WPA) _____

Chapter 12: The Postwar Period and Cold War

Concepts

Baby boom _____

Blacklisting _____

Black Power _____

Cold War _____

Communism _____

Containment _____

Decolonization_____

Détente _____

Domino theory _____

Environmentalism _____

Fair Deal _____

Feminism_____

The Great Society_____

Hydrogen bomb_____

Military-industrial complex _____

Mutually assured destruction (MAD) _____

Nation-building_____

New Frontier _____

Proxy wars _____

Rock and roll_____

Sexual revolution _____

The Silent Majority _____

Space race _____

Truman Doctrine_____

Events

Bay of Pigs Invasion_____

Berlin Blockade/Airlift _____

Chinese Revolution _____

Civil Rights movement _____

Cuban Missile Crisis _____

Kent State Massacre _____

Korean War _____

Middle East oil crisis _____

Montgomery bus boycott_____

My Lai Massacre _____

Suez Crisis _____

Tet Offensive _____

Vietnam War _____

Watergate scandal_____

World War II _____

People (Individuals and Groups)

Adlai Stevenson _____

Alger Hiss _____

Beatniks _____

Black Panthers _____

Dixiecrats_____

Douglas MacArthur _____

Dwight D. Eisenhower _____

Earl Warren _____

Eugene McCarthy _____

Fannie Lou Hamer_____

Fidel Castro _____

Freedom Riders _____

George Wallace _____

Gerald Ford _____

Gloria Steinem_____

Henry Kissinger _____

Ho Chi Minh _____

Hubert Humphrey_____

Jackie Robinson _____

Jimmy Carter _____

John F. Kennedy _____

John Foster Dulles _____

John Lewis _____

Joseph McCarthy _____

Joseph Stalin _____

Lyndon Johnson _____

Malcolm X _____

Martin Luther King, Jr. _____

Mao Zedong _____

Medgar Evers _____

National Organization for Women (NOW) _____

Nikita Khrushchev _____

Phyllis Schlafly _____

Rachel Carson _____

Richard Nixon _____

Robert Kennedy _____

Rosa Parks _____

Southern Christian Leadership Conference (SCLC) _____

Students for a Democratic Society _____

Thurgood Marshall _____

Vietcong _____

Woodward and Bernstein _____

Places

Aswan Dam _____

Berlin Wall _____

Gulf of Tonkin _____

Suez Canal _____

Sun Belt _____

Policies, Agreements, Court Rulings, Etc.

Bakke v. University of California _____

Brown v. Board of Education _____

Camp David accords _____

Central Intelligence Agency (CIA) _____

Civil Rights Act _____

Clean Air Act _____

Department of Housing and Urban Development (HUD) _____

Equal Rights Amendment _____

Geneva Accords _____

Gideon v. Wainwright _____

Griswold v. Connecticut _____

Head Start _____

Interstate Highway Act _____

Marshall Plan _____

Miranda v. Arizona _____

National Aeronautics Space Administration (NASA) _____

National Security Council _____

Organization of the Petroleum Exporting Countries (OPEC) _____

Peace Corps _____

Roe v. Wade _____

Southeast Asia Treaty Organization (SEATO) _____

Taft-Hartley Act _____

Voting Rights Act _____

War Powers Resolution _____

Chapter 13: Entering into the 21st Century

Concepts

Amnesty (immigration) _____

Christian evangelical movement _____

Contract with America _____

"Don't Ask, Don't Tell" _____

Glasnost _____

Illegal immigration _____

Libertarianism _____

Militia movement _____

Moral majority _____

Neo-conservatism _____

Perestroika _____

"Read my lips: No new taxes!" _____

Stagflation _____

Star Wars missile defense system _____

Supply-side economics _____

Trickle-down economics _____

"War on Terror" _____

Events

9/11 _____

Afghanistan War _____

Bosnia conflict _____

Congressional Election of 1994 _____

Iraq War _____

Iran-Contra Affair _____

Iran Hostage Crisis _____

Los Angeles riots (Rodney King) _____

Monica Lewinsky scandal _____

Oklahoma City bombing _____

OPEC oil embargo _____

Persian Gulf War _____

Somalia conflict _____

Whitewater scandal _____

People (Individuals and Groups)

Al Gore _____

Bill Clinton _____

Colin Powell _____

Condoleezza Rice_____

Dick Cheney _____

Donald Rumsfeld_____

George H.W. Bush_____

George W. Bush_____

Janet Reno _____

Jesse Jackson _____

Mikhail Gorbachev _____

Newt Gingrich_____

Planned Parenthood_____

Ronald Reagan_____

Timothy McVeigh _____

Places

Grenada _____

Nicaragua_____

Policies, Agreements, Court Rulings, Etc.

Citizens United v. Federal Election Commission _____

General Agreement on Tariffs and Trade (GATT) _____

North American Free Trade Agreement (NAFTA) _____

Simpson-Mazzoli Act_____

Part VI
Practice Test 2

Practice Test 2

AP® United States History Exam

SECTION I, PART A: Multiple Choice

DO NOT OPEN THIS BOOKLET UNTIL YOU ARE TOLD TO DO SO.

At a Glance

Time
55 minutes
Number of Questions
55
Percent of Total Score
40%
Writing Instrument
Pencil required

Instructions

Section I, Part A, of this exam contains 55 multiple-choice questions. Fill in only the ovals for numbers 1 through 55 on your answer sheet. Because this section offers only four answer options for each question, do not mark the (E) answer circle for any question.

Indicate all of your answers to the multiple-choice questions on the answer sheet. No credit will be given for anything written in this exam booklet, but you may use the booklet for notes or scratch work. After you have decided which of the suggested answers is best, completely fill in the corresponding oval on the answer sheet. Give only one answer to each question. If you change an answer, be sure that the previous mark is erased completely. Here is a sample question and answer.

Sample Question

The first president of the United States was
(A) Millard Fillmore
(B) George Washington
(C) Benjamin Franklin
(D) Andrew Jackson

Sample Answer

Ⓐ ● Ⓒ Ⓓ

Use your time effectively, working as rapidly as you can without losing accuracy. Do not spend too much time on any one question. Go on to other questions and come back to the ones you have not answered if you have time. It is not expected that everyone will know the answers to all of the multiple-choice questions.

Your total score on the multiple-choice section is based only on the number of questions answered correctly. Points are not deducted for incorrect answers or unanswered questions.

SECTION I, PART B: Short Answer

At a Glance

Time
40 minutes
Number of Questions
3
Percent of Total Score
20%
Writing Instrument
Pen with black or dark blue ink
Questions 1 and 2
Mandatory
Question 3 or 4
Choose One Question

Instructions

For Section I, Part B of this exam, answer Question 1 and Question 2 and **either** Question 3 **or** Question 4. Write your responses in the Section I, Part B: Short-Answer Response booklet. You must write your response to each question on the lined page designated for that response. Each response is expected to fit within its designated page. Fill in the circle on the Section I, Part B: Short-Answer Response booklet indicating whether you answered Question 3 or Question 4. Failure to do so may delay your score.

GO ON TO THE NEXT PAGE.

UNITED STATES HISTORY
SECTION I, Part A
Time—55 minutes
55 Questions

Directions: Each of the questions or incomplete statements below is followed by four suggested answers or completions. Select the one that is best in each case and then blacken the corresponding space on the answer sheet.

Questions 1 - 3 refer to the illustration and excerpt below.

THE BURNING OF JAMESTOWN, 1676

"Whereas complaint has been made to this Board by Capt. William Pierce, Esq., that six of his servants and a negro of Mr. Reginald's has plotted to run away unto the Dutch plantation from their said masters,...the court taking the same into consideration as a dangerous precedent for the future time (if left unpunished), did order that Christopher Miller, a Dutchman (a prime agent in the business), should receive the punishment of whipping,...the said Peter Milcocke to receive thirty stripes and to be Burnt in the cheek with the letter R,...the said Richard Cockson, after his full time Expired with his master, to serve the colony for two years and a half, and the said Richard Hill to remain upon his good behavior until the next offense, and the said Andrew Noxe to receive thirty stripes, and the said John Williams, a Dutchman and a [surgeon] after his full time of service is Expired with his master, to serve the colony for seven years, and Emanuel, the Negro, to receive thirty stripes and to be burnt in the cheek with the letter R and to work in shackles one year or more as his master shall see cause."

Decisions of the General Court, 1640

GO ON TO THE NEXT PAGE.

1. The excerpt best supports which one of the following conclusions?

    (A) English colonists sought to control the native populations through missions and religious conversions.

    (B) Trade alliances with American Indians promoted the economic health of early Chesapeake settlements.

    (C) A shortage of indentured servants led to the emergence of the African slave trade.

    (D) The Chesapeake colonies relied on labor-intensive agriculture, a system that utilized both white and African indentured servants.

2. Why were confrontations such as those in the excerpt rare in the New England colonies?

    (A) New England populations were largely homogenous with economies based on subsistence farming, rather than cash crops.

    (B) Puritan law forbade the sale or ownership of slaves.

    (C) Indentured servants in New England were largely treated fairly, serving for short terms before gaining freedom.

    (D) Negotiations after King Philip's War had ensured the return of indentured servants back to Europe.

3. Which of the following protests is most similar to the burning of Jamestown shown in the picture?

    (A) The Whiskey Rebellion

    (B) The Montgomery Bus Boycott

    (C) Nat Turner's Rebellion

    (D) The Bonus Expeditionary Force march on Washington

GO ON TO THE NEXT PAGE.

Questions 4 - 6 refer to the illustration below.

Recommended to Congress by Lord S____e.

I have them all in a String.

I'll tomahawk the dog.

I'll scalp him.

O Cruel Fate! Is this the return for our loyalty?

Is this a Peace, when Loyalists must bleed?

It is a Bloody Piece of work indeed.

The Savages let loose, OR the Cruel Fate of the Loyalists

4. The cartoon above supports which one of the following conclusions?

   (A) After the British victory in the Seven Years' War, many Indians sought revenge on British aristocrats.
   (B) The French withdrawal from North America after the Seven Years' War led to various conflicts between Indians and colonial settlers.
   (C) During and after the Revolutionary War, American sentiment toward those loyal to Britain became increasingly hostile.
   (D) Indian warriors were eager to fight alongside American patriots during the American Revolution.

5. The Seven Years' War is also popularly labeled the "French and Indian War." Why?

   (A) The French fought various Indian tribes throughout the Northeast for control of trapping rights and major waterways.
   (B) The French were aided throughout the war by various Indian tribes fighting in alliance with them.
   (C) Most Indian tribes sided with the British, defending their lands against French invaders from the North.
   (D) Many French settlers, particularly in the Maritime provinces of Canada, intermarried with native peoples, and thus were allied against the British in subsequent territorial conflicts.

6. Which of the following best describes the causal link between the Seven Years' War and the Revolutionary War?

   (A) Britain's defeat after the Seven Years' War led to massive debt for the crown, prompting an effort to collect taxes from the Thirteen Colonies.
   (B) Emboldened by their victories during the Seven Years' War, colonial elites challenged the crown, pushing for independence before the working-class populace was ready to accept it.
   (C) Britain's massive debt after the Seven Years' War resulted in a push for greater control over the Thirteen Colonies, sparking debate among colonists over the pursuit of independence.
   (D) Disillusioned by their experiences in the Seven Years' War, colonial militia members formed the Sons of Liberty, a radical group calling for independence from the crown.

GO ON TO THE NEXT PAGE.

Questions 7 - 9 refer to the excerpt below.

"...Let me now take a more comprehensive view, and warn you in the most solemn manner against the baneful effects of the spirit of party generally.

"There is an opinion that parties in free countries are useful checks upon the administration of government, and serve to keep alive the spirit of liberty. This within certain limits is probably true; and in governments of a monarchical cast patriotism may look with indulgence, if not with favor, upon the spirit of party. But in those of the popular character, in governments purely elective, it is a spirit not to be encouraged. From their natural tendency it is certain there will always be enough of that spirit for every salutary purpose; and there being constant danger of excess, the effort ought to be by force of public opinion to mitigate and assuage it. A fire not to be quenched, it demands a uniform vigilance to prevent its bursting into a flame, lest, instead of warming, it should consume."

President George Washington, Farewell Address, 1796

7. The sentiments expressed by Washington in his Farewell Address most warn against partisan divisions that occurred before which of the following conflicts?

(A) The War of 1812
(B) The Civil War
(C) The Nullification Crisis of 1832
(D) The Korean War

8. Washington's Farewell Address best exemplifies which of the following political philosophies?

(A) Federalism
(B) Anti-Federalism
(C) Republicanism
(D) Sectionalism

9. Elsewhere in the Address, Washington promotes which of the following approaches to foreign policy?

(A) Neutrality
(B) Imperialism
(C) Isolationism
(D) Dollar Diplomacy

GO ON TO THE NEXT PAGE.

Questions 10 - 12 refer to the excerpt below.

"Some men look at constitutions with sanctimonious reverence, and deem them like the ark of the covenant, too sacred to be touched. They ascribe to the men of the preceding age a wisdom more than human, and suppose what they did to be beyond amendment….But I know also, that laws and institutions must go hand in hand with the progress of the human mind. As that becomes more developed, more enlightened, as new discoveries are made, new truths disclosed, and manners and opinions change with the change of circumstances, institutions must advance also, and keep pace with the times."

Thomas Jefferson, 1816

10. Which of following Amendments to the Constitution is most directly an example of the sentiments expressed above?

(A) The First Amendment, which guaranteed the right to free speech

(B) The Tenth Amendment, which allows powers not granted to the federal government be granted to the states

(C) The Nineteenth Amendment, which guaranteed all women the right to vote

(D) The Twenty-first Amendment, which repealed the prohibition of alcohol

11. Which of the following best describes a contributing factor in the crafting of the United States Constitution?

(A) Individual state constitutions written at the time of the Revolution tended to cede too much power to the federal government, leading to a call for reform on the part of Anti-Federalists.

(B) The weaknesses of the Articles of Confederation led James Madison to question their efficacy and prompted a formation of the Constitutional Congress in 1787.

(C) Difficulties over trade and foreign relations led to a repeal of overly restrictive tariffs required by the Articles of Confederation.

(D) Washington's embarrassing failure at the Whiskey Rebellion led to Federalist demands for a new framework for federal power.

12. Which of the following statements is most accurate regarding the existence of political parties in the early United States?

(A) After the drafting of the Constitution, continued debates about states' rights and competing economic interests led to the formation of political parties, such as the Federalists and the Democratic-Republicans.

(B) Although Washington warned against the influence of political parties, he reluctantly accepted the endorsement of the Federalist party.

(C) Political parties did not exist until the War of 1812, when Federalists asserted control over foreign policies with France and Britain.

(D) Two major political parties dominated early presidential elections until John Quincy Adams founded the Whig party in 1824.

GO ON TO THE NEXT PAGE.

Questions 13 - 17 refer to the excerpt below.

"Is there no danger to our liberty and independence in a bank that in its nature has so little to bind it to our country? The president of the bank has told us that most of the State banks exist by its forbearance. Should its influence become concentrated, as it may under the operation of such an act as this, in the hands of a self-elected directory whose interests are identified with those of the foreign stockholders, will there not be cause to tremble for the purity of our elections in peace and for the independence of our country in war? Their power would be great whenever they might choose to exert it; but if this monopoly were regularly renewed every fifteen or twenty years on terms proposed by themselves, they might seldom in peace put forth their strength to influence elections or control the affairs of the nation. But if any private citizen or public functionary should interpose to curtail its powers or prevent a renewal of its privileges, it cannot be doubted that he would be made to feel its influence."

President Andrew Jackson, Veto of the Bank of the United States, 1832

13. In the excerpt above, which quote best explains why Jackson chose to veto the recharter of the Second Bank?

    (A) "but if any private citizen"
    (B) "the president of the bank"
    (C) "this monopoly"
    (D) "interests are identified with those of foreign stockholders"

14. Which of the following events most directly caused the formation of the Second Bank of the United States?

    (A) The failure of the Specie Circular
    (B) Unregulated currency and federal debts after the War of 1812
    (C) Efforts by Alexander Hamilton to stabilize the national economy
    (D) Federalist counter-reaction to the extreme budget-cutting under Jefferson

15. The debate over the First Bank of the United States was significant because it raised the issue of

    (A) whether the new government should issue paper currency
    (B) how strictly the Constitution should be interpreted
    (C) whether the United States should pay back its war debt to France
    (D) whether the president had the power to act unilaterally on important economic issues

16. The election of 1824 marked a turning point in presidential politics because, for the first time,

    (A) the presidency was won by someone who was not a member of the Federalist Party
    (B) a presidential and vice-presidential candidate ran together on one ticket
    (C) all the candidates campaigned widely throughout the states
    (D) the system of choosing nominees by congressional caucus failed

17. John Taylor of Caroline was a Virginia senator who served in office from 1792 to 1824. He distrusted large banking institutions and generally defended the institution of slavery. He was once quoted as saying that "...if Congress could incorporate a bank, it might emancipate a slave." Taylor is best categorized as

    (A) a Jeffersonian Democrat
    (B) a Jacksonian Democrat
    (C) a Republican
    (D) a Whig

GO ON TO THE NEXT PAGE.

Questions 18 - 21 refer to the map below.

Southeastern Indian Lands, 1830

← Indian Removal Routes

18. Supreme Court decisions concerning American Indian tribes in 1831 and 1832

   (A) reinforced the rights of states to remove Indians from disputed lands

   (B) denied them the right to sue in federal court but affirmed their rights to land that was traditionally theirs

   (C) voided previous treaties between Indian tribes and the United States on the grounds that the treaties were unfair

   (D) ruled that the federal government had a unilateral right to relocate Indians to lands west of the Mississippi

19. Which of the following factors are most likely to have caused the migration shown in the map above?

   (A) Federal Executive branch mandates

   (B) Supreme Court judicial decisions

   (C) Legislative incentives for homesteading in the West

   (D) State legislative mandates for Indian removal

20. Which event in Native American history is LEAST similar to the migration depicted in the map above?

   (A) The Trail of Tears

   (B) King Philip's War

   (C) The Pequot War

   (D) The Battle of Little Big Horn

21. Which of the following is true of the Dawes Severalty Act of 1887?

   (A) In honoring communal landholdings, it reflected an appreciation of Indian culture.

   (B) It was an attempt to assimilate the Indians into American society through individual land grants.

   (C) It compensated Indians for the land they had lost at the Battle of Wounded Knee.

   (D) It outlawed individual land ownership by Indian leaders.

GO ON TO THE NEXT PAGE.

Questions 22 - 25 refer to the excerpt below.

"On the 4th day of March next, this party will take possession of the Government. It has announced that...a war must be waged against slavery until it shall cease throughout the United States.

The guaranties of the Constitution will then no longer exist; the equal rights of the States will be lost. The slave-holding States will no longer have the power of self-government, or self-protection, and the Federal Government will have become their enemy.

Sectional interest and animosity will deepen the irritation, and all hope of remedy is rendered vain, by the fact that public opinion at the North has invested a great political error with the sanction of more erroneous religious belief.

We, therefore, the People of South Carolina...have solemnly declared that the Union heretofore existing between this State and the other States of North America, is dissolved, and that the State of South Carolina has resumed her position among the nations of the world, as a separate and independent State."

"Declaration of the Immediate Causes Which Induce and Justify the Secession of South Carolina from the Federal Union," 1860

22. Which of the following was an immediate consequence of the secession of South Carolina?

   (A) Southern Democrats appealed to the powers of Congress to stop military action against South Carolina.
   (B) Abraham Lincoln signed the Emancipation Proclamation.
   (C) Other Southern states seceded from the Union, forming the Confederacy.
   (D) Jefferson Davis drafted Confederate soldiers into war, defending the siege on Fort Sumter.

23. The sentiments above are most consistent with which of the following ideologies?

   (A) States' Rights
   (B) Nullification
   (C) Neutrality
   (D) Civil disobedience

24. In the excerpt above, the reference to "the sanctions of a more erroneous religious belief" most probably refers to

   (A) Southern Baptist justification of slavery on the grounds of white racial superiority
   (B) the Puritan abolition of slavery in New England states
   (C) Jewish acceptance of slavery in the Torah
   (D) Christian abolitionist rejection of slavery on moral grounds

25. Which of the following best explains why South Carolina chose to secede from the Union in 1860?

   (A) The failures of the Compromise of 1850 hindered South Carolina's trade relationships with Western states, leading to severe economic recession.
   (B) The Battle of Fort Sumter occurred in Charleston, prompting public outrage over Union aggression.
   (C) President Lincoln signed the Emancipation Proclamation, thus undermining slavery in the South.
   (D) Lincoln's election on a Free-Soil platform led Southern politicians to conclude that secession was necessary.

GO ON TO THE NEXT PAGE.

Questions 26 - 28 refer to the excerpt below.

"The Opposition tells us that we ought not to govern a people without their consent. I answer, the rule of liberty that all just government derives its authority from the consent of the governed, applies only to those who are capable of self-government. We govern the Indians without their consent, we govern our territories without their consent, we govern our children without their consent. How do they know that our government would be without their consent? Would not the people of the Philippines prefer the just, human, civilizing government of this Republic to the savage, bloody rule of pillage and extortion from which we have rescued them? And, regardless of this formula of words made only for enlightened, self-governing people, do we owe no duty to the world? Shall we turn these peoples back to the reeking hands from which we have taken them? Shall we abandon them, with Germany, England, Japan, hungering for them? Shall we save them from those nations, to give them a self-rule of tragedy?...Then, like men and not like children, let us on to our tasks, our mission, and our destiny."

Albert J. Beveridge, "The March of the Flag," 1898

26. The sentiment expressed by Beveridge best exemplifies which of the following?

    (A) Imperialism
    (B) Anti-imperialism
    (C) Isolationism
    (D) Manifest Destiny

27. The United States became politically engaged with the Philippines after what military conflict?

    (A) Mexican-American War
    (B) World War II
    (C) Spanish-American War
    (D) The Boxer Rebellion

28. Which of the following rationales does Beveridge employ in his argument?

    (A) The closing of the western frontier impels the United States to expand its territory overseas.
    (B) Governing territories confers economic benefits to both European and nonwhite nations.
    (C) Powerful nations have a moral duty to govern less developed nations.
    (D) Racial superiority confers responsibility to the United States and Europe over the affairs of developing nations.

GO ON TO THE NEXT PAGE.

Questions 29 - 33 refer to the excerpt below.

"Whereas the laws and treaties of the United States, without interfering with the free expression of opinion and sympathy, or with the commercial manufacture or sale of arms or munitions of war, nevertheless impose upon all persons who may be within their territory and jurisdiction the duty of an impartial neutrality during the existence of the contest; And Whereas it is the duty of a neutral government not to permit or suffer the making of its waters subservient to the purposes of war;

"Now, Therefore, I, Woodrow Wilson, President of the United States of America, in order to preserve the neutrality of the United States…do hereby declare and proclaim….

"That the statutes and the treaties of the United States and the law of nations alike require that no person, within the territory and jurisdiction of the United States, shall take part, directly or indirectly, in the said wars, but shall remain at peace with all of the said belligerents, and shall maintain a strict and impartial neutrality…."

Woodrow Wilson, 1914

29. The statement above was most likely prompted by which of the following world events?

(A) Cuban revolt against Spanish control
(B) Adolph Hitler's invasion of Poland
(C) Austria-Hungary's declaration of war against Serbia
(D) Mussolini's invasion of Ethiopia

30. The statement above is most in harmony with the sentiments in which of the following speeches?

(A) Washington's Farewell Address
(B) George H. W. Bush's "A Thousand Points of Light"
(C) Lincoln's Gettysburg Address
(D) Franklin D. Roosevelt's "Day of Infamy"

31. All of the following increased federal government power during World War I EXCEPT the

(A) War Industries Board
(B) Food Administration
(C) Espionage Act
(D) Dawes Plan

32. Which of the following statements about the Treaty of Versailles is true?

(A) The United States Senate rejected it because it treated Germany too leniently.
(B) The United States Senate rejected it because it required increased American involvement in European affairs.
(C) The United States Senate approved it, with reservations concerning the division of Eastern Europe.
(D) It was never voted on by the United States Senate.

33. Which of the following statements is most accurate?

(A) After World War I, debates intensified over American involvement overseas.
(B) After World War I, Americans generally favored the new era of American involvement overseas.
(C) American involvement in World War I was an extension of a long tradition of involvement overseas.
(D) American involvement in World War I was a direct result of "dollar diplomacy."

GO ON TO THE NEXT PAGE.

Questions 34 - 36 refer to the excerpt below.

"Since the foundations of the American commonwealth were laid in colonial times over 300 years ago, vigorous complaint and more or less bitter persecution have been aimed at newcomers to our shores. Also the congressional reports of about 1840 are full of abuse of English, Scotch, Welsh immigrants as paupers, criminals, and so forth. Old citizens in Detroit of Irish and German descent have told me of the fierce tirades and propaganda directed against the great waves of Irish and Germans who came over from 1840 on for a few decades to escape civil, racial, and religious persecution in their native lands. The "Know-Nothings," lineal ancestors of the Ku-Klux Klan, bitterly denounced the Irish and Germans as mongrels, scum, foreigners, and a menace to our institutions, much as other great branches of the Caucasian race of glorious history and antecedents are berated to-day....But to-day it is the Italians, Spanish, Poles, Jews, Greeks, Russians, Balkanians, and so forth, who are the racial lepers....In this bill we find racial discrimination at its worst—a deliberate attempt to go back 84 years in our census taken every 10 years so that a blow may be aimed at peoples of eastern and southern Europe, particularly at our recent allies in the Great War—Poland and Italy."

Robert H. Clancy, *Congressional Record*, 68th Congress, 1st Session, 1924

34. The excerpt above is most likely a response to

    (A) World War I patriotism
    (B) immigration quotas
    (C) labor strikes
    (D) the Red Scare

35. What best accounts for the sharp increase of immigrants during the period 1880–1910?

    (A) Many Southern and Eastern Europeans turned to America for financial gain and political freedom.
    (B) Irish farmers were forced to leave their homes due to agricultural disasters.
    (C) Germans were seeking ways to avoid military conscription.
    (D) The United States welcomed immigrants by providing housing and employment.

36. Which one of the following legislative acts is most closely an example of nativism?

    (A) The Wagner Act of 1935
    (B) The Alien and Sedition Acts of 1798
    (C) The Espionage Act of 1917
    (D) The Immigration and Nationality Act of 1965

GO ON TO THE NEXT PAGE.

Questions 37 - 41 refer to the graph below.

U.S. Unemployment Rate, 1930–1945

37. The graph above is consistent with which of the following statements about the era portrayed?

(A) Unemployment rates began to drop with the election of Herbert Hoover in 1933.

(B) Franklin D. Roosevelt's New Deal produced a constant decrease in U.S. unemployment rates.

(C) A full economic recovery did not occur until the U.S. involvement in World War II.

(D) A brief economic recovery in 1937 sparked a sudden increase in U.S. employment.

38. Which of the following was NOT a major contributing factor to the onset of the Great Depression?

(A) Technological advances had allowed farmers and manufacturers to overproduce, creating large inventories.

(B) The federal government interfered too frequently with the economy, causing investors to lose confidence.

(C) Stock investors had been allowed to speculate wildly, creating an unstable and volatile stock market.

(D) Major businesses were controlled by so few producers that the failure of any one had a considerable effect on the national economy.

39. The Agricultural Adjustment Act of 1933 sought to lessen the effects of the Depression by

(A) paying farmers to cut production and, in some cases, destroy crops

(B) purchasing farms and turning them into government collectives

(C) instituting an early retirement program for farmers over the age of 50

(D) encouraging farmers to increase production

40. The dismal plight of the "Dust Bowl" refugees was captured in

(A) Harriet Beecher Stowes' *Uncle Tom's Cabin*
(B) F. Scott Fitzgerald's *The Great Gatsby*
(C) Theodore Dreiser's *An American Tragedy*
(D) John Steinbeck's *The Grapes of Wrath*

41. In response to several unfavorable Supreme Court rulings concerning New Deal programs, Franklin Roosevelt

(A) urged the voting public to write letters of protest to Supreme Court justices

(B) submitted four separate Constitutional amendments broadening the powers of the presidency

(C) abandoned the New Deal and replaced it with a laissez-faire policy

(D) proposed legislation that would allow him to appoint new federal and Supreme Court judges

GO ON TO THE NEXT PAGE.

Questions 42 - 46 refer to the excerpt below.

"We found that not only was it a civil war, an effort by a people who had for years been seeking their liberation from any colonial influence whatsoever, but also we found that the Vietnamese whom we had enthusiastically molded after our own image were hard put to take up the fight against the threat we were supposedly saving them from.

"We found most people didn't even know the difference between communism and democracy. They only wanted to work in rice paddies without helicopters strafing them and bombs with napalm burning their villages and tearing their country apart. They wanted everything to do with the war, particularly with this foreign presence of the United States of America, to leave them alone in peace, and they practiced the art of survival by siding with whichever military force was present at a particular time, be it Viet Cong, North Vietnamese or American."

John Kerry, 1971

42. The conflict described above is most likely a result of which of the following doctrines?

   (A) Imperialism
   (B) Containment
   (C) "Big-stick" diplomacy
   (D) Isolationism

43. The most important factor in the defeat of Democratic presidential candidates in the elections of 1952 and 1968 was

   (A) the American public's desire to avoid conflict and return to a more conservative political and social life
   (B) the Democratic Party platform pledge to increase taxes in order to pay off the national debt
   (C) the Democratic candidates' controversial positions on civil rights legislation
   (D) the Democratic Party's unequivocal support of the Equal Rights Amendment

44. The two political issues that most concerned the counterculture movement of the 1960s were

   (A) U.S. involvement in Vietnam and flag burning
   (B) the civil rights movement and censorship
   (C) U.S. involvement in Vietnam and the civil rights movement
   (D) censorship and the draft

45. Which of the following best characterizes the policy of *détente*?

   (A) Direct confrontation
   (B) Covert sabotage
   (C) Decolonization
   (D) Mutual coexistence

46. From the quote above, it is reasonable to infer that

   (A) many Vietnamese viewed the United States as a colonial influence
   (B) most Vietnamese were opposed to Communism
   (C) most Vietnamese favored Communism
   (D) some Viet Cong fought alongside American troops in opposition to North Vietnam

GO ON TO THE NEXT PAGE.

Questions 47 - 50 refer to the excerpt below.

"Yesterday, December 7, 1941—a date which will live in infamy—the United States of America was suddenly and deliberately attacked by naval and air forces of the Empire of Japan. The United States was at peace with that nation and, at the solicitation of Japan, was still in conversation with its Government and its Emperor looking toward the maintenance of peace in the Pacific. Indeed, one hour after Japanese air squadrons had commenced bombing…the Japanese Ambassador to the United States and his colleague delivered to the Secretary of State a formal reply to a recent American message. While this reply stated that it seemed useless to continue the existing diplomatic negotiations, it contained no threat or hint of war or armed attack….The attack yesterday…has caused severe damage to American naval and military forces. Very many American lives have been lost. In addition American ships have been reported torpedoed on the high seas….As Commander-in-Chief of the Army and Navy, I have directed that all measures be taken for our defense."

President Franklin D. Roosevelt, radio address, December 8, 1941

47. Which of the following best describes the relationship between the United States and the Empire of Japan in the years leading up to this speech?

(A) Japan and the United States maintained an alliance against Nazi Germany.

(B) The United States and Japan developed tensions over which country rightfully controlled Hawaii.

(C) The United States depended on loans from Japan to stay afloat during the Great Depression.

(D) Japan resented the economic embargoes placed against it by the United States.

48. The above statements were most likely made after which major event?

(A) The bombing of Pearl Harbor

(B) The sinking of the *U.S.S Maine*

(C) The bombing of the *U.S.S. Liberty*

(D) The Boxer Rebellion

49. Which of the following was the most immediate consequence of the events described in the excerpt above?

(A) Trade embargoes with Japan extending up through the 1980s

(B) The Battle of Normandy

(C) The internment of Japanese-Americans

(D) The bombing of Nagasaki

50. Which of the following statements best characterizes the economic consequences of the declaration of war described above?

(A) Decreased trade with Asian nations precipitated economic recession in both the United States and Europe.

(B) The war-ravaged condition of Asia and Europe allowed the United States to emerge as one of the most prosperous nations on Earth.

(C) Cold War tensions isolated the economies of both the Soviet Union and the United States, leading to economic struggle for both nations.

(D) Japan was subsequently required to pay reparations to the United States, forcing it into a prolonged depression.

GO ON TO THE NEXT PAGE.

Questions 51 - 53 refer to the excerpts below.

"In the new Code of Laws which I suppose it will be necessary for you to make I desire you would Remember the Ladies, and be more generous and favorable to them than your ancestors. Do not put such unlimited power into the hands of the Husbands. Remember all Men would be tyrants if they could. If particular care and attention is not paid to the Ladies we are determined to foment a Rebellion, and will not hold ourselves bound by any Laws in which we have no voice, or Representation."

Abigail Adams, in a letter to John Adams, 1776

"Special legislation for woman has placed us in a most anomalous position. Women invested with the rights of citizens in one section—voters, jurors, office-holders—crossing an imaginary line, are subjects in the next. In some States, a married woman may hold property and transact business in her own name; in others, her earnings belong to her husband. In some States, a woman may testify against her husband, sue and be sued in the courts; in others, she has no redress in case of damage to person, property, or character. In case of divorce on account of adultery in the husband, the innocent wife is held to possess no right to children or property, unless by special decree of the court. But in no State of the Union has the wife the right to her own person, or to any part of the joint earnings of the co-partnership during the life of her husband. In some States women may enter the law schools and practice in the courts; in others they are forbidden. In some universities girls enjoy equal educational advantages with boys, while many of the proudest institutions in the land deny them admittance, though the sons of China, Japan and Africa are welcomed there. But the privileges already granted in the several States are by no means secure."

Susan B. Anthony, "Declaration of Rights for Women," July 4, 1876

51. The sentiments expressed in the first excerpt by Abigail Adams best exemplify which of the following ideologies?

(A) Second-wave feminism
(B) Jeffersonian democracy
(C) Republican motherhood
(D) Libertarianism

52. The sentiments expressed in the second excerpt by Susan B. Anthony are most likely in support of

(A) the Equal Rights Amendment
(B) universal suffrage
(C) states' rights
(D) prohibition

53. The excerpts above best support which of the following conclusions?

(A) The Second Great Awakening, along with various social reform movements, secured full rights for women by the turn of the nineteenth century.
(B) Before 1876, American women had no right to own property or vote in national elections.
(C) Women's rights movements flourished in response to inconsistent legislation and unequal distributions of power throughout the nation.
(D) American feminists in the nineteenth century largely focused on suffrage, shunning other social issues such as abolition and prison reform.

GO ON TO THE NEXT PAGE.

Questions 54 and 55 refer to the excerpt below.

"The violent tendencies of dangerous cults can be classified into two general categories—defensive violence and offensive violence. Defensive violence is utilized by cults to defend a compound or enclave that was created specifically to eliminate most contact with the dominant culture. The 1993 clash in Waco, Texas at the Branch Davidian complex is an illustration of such defensive violence. History has shown that groups that seek to withdraw from the dominant culture seldom act on their beliefs that the endtime has come unless provoked."

"Project Megiddo," U.S. Department of Justice, 2000

"Madam Attorney General, I am extremely disappointed in the decisions that have been made out of the Department of Justice, the Federal Bureau of Investigation, and the Bureau of Alcohol, Tobacco and Firearms. In Philadelphia, we had a mayor that bombed people out of an eviction. In Jonestown, we lost the life of my colleague, Congressman Ryan,...because of a miscalculation about cult people. We had Patty Hearst and the Symbionese Liberation Army. We had Wounded Knee with the Indians. Now, when in God's name is the law enforcement at the Federal level going to understand that these are very sensitive events that you cannot put barbed wire, guns, FBI, Secret Service around them, send in sound 24 hours a day and night and then wonder why they do something unstable? The root cause of this problem was that it was considered a military operation, and it wasn't. This is a profound disgrace to law enforcement in the United States of America, and you did the right thing by offering to resign...."

U.S. Representative John Conyers, Events Surrounding the Branch Davidian Cult Standoff in Waco, Texas: Hearing Before the Committee on the Judiciary, House of Representatives, 1993

54. The above excerpts most closely support which of the following inferences?

(A) In the 1990s, antigovernment sentiment, in response to excessive uses of federal power to resolve domestic conflicts, inspired dangerous cults such as the Branch Davidians.

(B) In 1993 Attorney General Janet Reno launched an offensive against the Branch Davidian cult, later drawing criticism from Congress for her heavy-handed approach.

(C) Fearing the offensive violence perpetrated by the Branch Davidian cult, Attorney General Janet Reno sent troops to quell the subsequent standoff and later faced congressional criticism.

(D) Attorney General Janet Reno resigned from office in part due to Congressional pressure put on President Clinton by Representative John Conyers.

55. In the second excerpt, Representative Conyers refers to "Wounded Knee" as an example of

(A) a violent cult
(B) a federal misuse of power
(C) the site of a bombing
(D) a recent conflict between federal agents and Lakota Indians

GO ON TO THE NEXT PAGE.

UNITED STATES HISTORY
SECTION I, Part B
Time—40 minutes

Directions: Answer Question 1 **and** Question 2. Answer **either** Question 3 **or** Question 4.

Write your responses in the Section I, Part B: Short-Answer Response booklet. You must write your response to each question on the lined page designated for that response. Each response is expected to fit within the space provided.

In your responses, be sure to address all parts of the questions you answer. Use complete sentences; an outline or bulleted list alone is not acceptable. You may plan your answers in this exam booklet, but no credit will be given for notes written in this booklet.

Question 1 is based on the excerpts below.

"The Democrats represented a wide range of views but shared a fundamental commitment to the Jeffersonian concept of an agrarian society. They viewed the central government as the enemy of individual liberty….They believed that government intervention in the economy benefited special-interest groups and created corporate monopolies that favored the rich. They sought to restore the independence of the individual—the artisan and the ordinary farmer—by ending federal support of banks and corporations and restricting the use of paper currency, which they distrusted. Their definition of the proper role of government tended to be negative….Reformers eager to turn their programs into legislation called for a more active government. But Democrats tended to oppose programs like educational reform mid the establishment of a public education system. They believed, for instance, that public schools restricted individual liberty by interfering with parental responsibility and undermined freedom of religion by replacing church schools.

Mary Beth Norton, historian, *A People and a Nation, Volume I: to 1877* (2007)

"FREE-SOIL PARTY—a political party in the United States, which was organized in 1847-1848 to oppose the extension of slavery into the Territories. It was a combination of the political abolitionists many of whom had formerly been identified with the...Whigs, and the faction of the Democratic party...who favoured the prohibition of slavery,...in the territory acquired from Mexico. The party was prominent in the presidential campaigns of 1848 and 1852.

Encyclopedia Britannica, 1911

1. Using the excerpts above, answer parts (a), (b), and (c).

   a) Briefly explain ONE additional characteristic of the Democratic Party not explicitly mentioned in the excerpts above.

   b) Briefly explain one historical event from the time period in question that could support Norton's interpretation.

   c) Briefly explain ONE piece of evidence regarding the Free-Soil Party not directly mentioned in the excerpt.

GO ON TO THE NEXT PAGE.

Question 2 is based on the following image.

2. Use the image above and your knowledge of history to answer parts (a), (b), and (c).

    a) Explain the point of view in the image regarding ONE of the following:
        * Family life
        * The role of women
        * Social class

    b) Explain how ONE element of the image expresses the point of view you identified in part a.

    c) Explain how the point of view you identified in part a helped to shape ONE significant historical event prior to 1800.

GO ON TO THE NEXT PAGE.

Question 3 or 4

Directions: Answer **either** Question 3 **or** Question 4.

3. United States historians have debated the role of Jeffersonian democracy during the period 1800–1824.

    Answer parts (a), (b), and (c).

    a) Briefly explain the basic principles of Jeffersonian democracy.

    b) Choose ONE of the events listed below and explain why your choice represents a shift in the ideals of Jeffersonian democracy during the period 1800–1824. Provide at least ONE piece of evidence to support your explanation.
    - The Louisiana Purchase
    - Marbury v. Madison
    - The War of 1812
    - The Monroe Doctrine

    c) Briefly explain why ONE of the other options is not as persuasive as the one you chose.

4. Answer parts (a), (b), and (c).

    a) Briefly explain ONE reason for the popularity of the Progressive movement during the first two decades of the twentieth century.

    b) Briefly explain a SECOND reason for the popularity of the Progressive movement during the same period.

    c) Briefly explain ONE example of how the American people resisted changes brought about by the Progressive movement during the same period.

END OF SECTION I

GO ON TO THE NEXT PAGE.

AP® United States History Exam

SECTION II: Free Response

DO NOT OPEN THIS BOOKLET UNTIL YOU ARE TOLD TO DO SO.

At a Glance

Total Time
1 hour, 40 minutes
Number of Questions
2
Percent of Total Score
40%
Writing Instrument
Pen with black or dark blue ink

Question 1 (DBQ): Mandatory

Suggested Reading and Writing Time
60 minutes

Reading Period
15 minutes. Use this time to read Question 1 and plan your answer. You may begin writing your response before the reading period is over.
Suggested Writing Time
45 minutes
Percent of Total Score
25%

Question 2, 3, or 4: Choose One Question

Answer Question 2, Question 3, or Question 4
Suggested Writing Time
40 minutes
Percent of Total Score
15%

Instructions

The questions for Section II are printed in the orange Questions and Documents booklet. You may use that booklet to organize your answers and for scratch work, but you must write your answers in this Section II: Free Response booklet. No credit will be given for any work written in the Questions and Documents booklet.

The proctor will announce the beginning and end of the reading period. You are advised to spend the 15-minute period reading the question and planning your answer to Question 1, the document-based question. If you have time, you may also read Questions 2, 3, and 4. Do not begin writing in this booklet until the proctor tells you to do so.

Section II of this exam requires answers in essay form. Write clearly and legibly. Circle the number of the question you are answering at the top of each page in this booklet. Begin each answer on a new page. Do not skip lines. Cross out any errors you make; crossed-out work will not be scored.

Manage your time carefully. The proctor will announce the suggested time for each part, but you may proceed freely from one part to the next. Go on to Question 2, 3, or 4 if you finish Question 1 early. You may review your responses if you finish before the end of the exam is announced.

After the exam, you must apply the label that corresponds to the long-essay question you answered—Question 2, 3, or 4. For example, if you answered Question 2, apply the label ②. Failure to do so may delay your score.

GO ON TO THE NEXT PAGE.

UNITED STATES HISTORY
SECTION II
Total Time—1 hour, 40 minutes

Question 1 (Document-Based Question)
Suggested reading and writing time: 1 hour

It is suggested that you spend 15 minutes reading the documents and 45 minutes writing your response.

Note: You may begin writing your response before the reading period is over.

Directions: Question 1 is based on the accompanying documents. The documents have been edited for the purpose of this exercise.

In your response you should do the following.

- Respond to the prompt with a historically defensible thesis or claim that establishes a line of reasoning.
- Describe a broader historical context relevant to the prompt.
- Support an argument in response to the prompt using at least six documents.
- Use at least one additional piece of specific historical evidence (beyond that found in the documents) relevant to an argument about the prompt.
- For at least three documents, explain how or why the document's point of view, purpose, historical situation, and/or audience is relevant to an argument.
- Use evidence to corroborate, qualify, or modify an argument that addresses the prompt.

GO ON TO THE NEXT PAGE.

1. To what extent was the breakup of the Union in 1861 a result of the conflict over slavery and to what extent was it due to other factors? Using your knowledge of the antebellum period, construct an essay that explains the reasons the nation went to war and what circumstances led to this point of national crisis.

   Use the documents and your knowledge of the time period 1844–1861 to construct your answer.

Document 1

Source: "Annexation," by John L. O'Sullivan, *United States Magazine and Democratic Review*, July 1845

Why, were other reasoning wanting, in favor of now elevating this question of the reception of Texas into the Union, out of the lower region of our past party dissension, up to its proper level of a high and broad nationality, it surely is to be found, found abundantly, in the manner in which other nations have undertaken to intrude themselves into it, between us and the proper parties to the case, in a spirit of hostile interference against us, for the avowed object of thwarting our policy and hampering our power, limiting our greatness and checking the fulfillment of our manifest destiny to overspread the continent allotted by Providence for the free development of our yearly multiplying millions.

Document 2

Source: President James K. Polk's War Message to Congress, May 11, 1846

As war exists, and notwithstanding all our efforts to avoid it, exists by the act of Mexico herself, we are called upon by every consideration of duty and patriotism to vindicate with decision the honor, rights and dignity of this country.

GO ON TO THE NEXT PAGE.

Document 3

Source: Representative David Wilmot, from the Congressional Globe, 29th Congress, 2nd session, Appendix, February 8, 1847

But, sir, the issue now presented is not whether slavery shall exist unmolested where it now is, but whether it shall be carried to new and distant regions, now free, where the footprint of a slave cannot be found. This, sir, is the issue. Upon it I take my stand, and from it I cannot be frightened or driven by idle charges of abolitionism.

I ask not that slavery be abolished, I demand that this government preserve the integrity of free territory against the aggressions of slavery—against its wrongful usurpations.

Sir, I was in favor of the annexation of Texas….Yes, sir, here was an empire larger than France given up to slavery. Shall further concessions be made by the North? Shall we give up free territory, the inheritance of free labor? Must we yield this also?

…But, sir, we are told that the joint blood and treasure of the whole country being expended in this acquisition, therefore it should be divided, and slavery should be allowed to take its share. Sir, the South has her share already.

…Now, sir, we are told that California is ours, that New Mexico is ours—won by the valor of our arms. They are free. Shall they remain free? Shall these fair provinces be the inheritance and homes of the white labor of freemen or the black labor of slaves? This, sir, is the issue.

GO ON TO THE NEXT PAGE.

Document 4

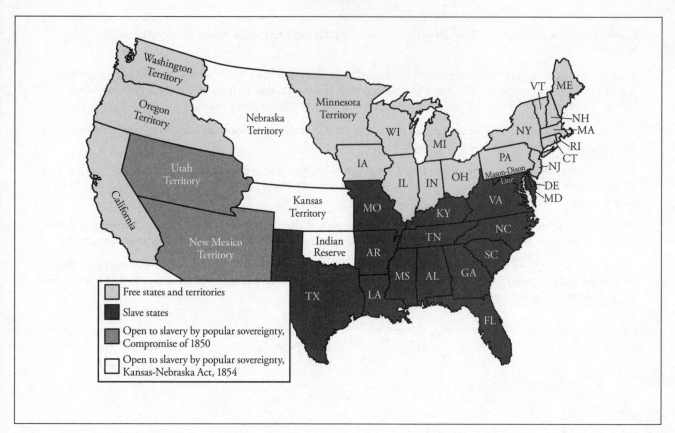

Legend:
- Free states and territories
- Slave states
- Open to slavery by popular sovereignty, Compromise of 1850
- Open to slavery by popular sovereignty, Kansas-Nebraska Act, 1854

Map labels: Washington Territory, Oregon Territory, California, Utah Territory, New Mexico Territory, Nebraska Territory, Minnesota Territory, Kansas Territory, Indian Reserve, WI, IA, IL, MI, IN, OH, MO, KY, AR, TN, MS, AL, GA, TX, LA, FL, VA, NC, SC, NY, VT, ME, NH, MA, RI, CT, PA, NJ, DE, MD, Mason-Dixon Line

GO ON TO THE NEXT PAGE.

Document 5

Source: Roger Taney, in the Supreme Court opinion in *Dred Scott v. Sandford*, 1857

The right of property in a slave is distinctly and expressly affirmed in the Constitution…. No word can be found in the Constitution which gives Congress a greater power over the slave property or which entitles property of that kind to less protection than property of any other description.

Document 6

Railroad Routes, 1850

Railroad Routes, 1860

GO ON TO THE NEXT PAGE.

Document 7

PROGRESSIVE DEMOCRACY—PROSPECT OF A SMASH UP.

END OF DOCUMENTS FOR QUESTION 1

GO ON TO THE NEXT PAGE.

Question 2, 3, or 4 (Long Essay)

Suggested writing time: 40 minutes

Directions: Answer Question 2 **or** Question 3 **or** Question 4.

In your response you should do the following.

- Respond to the prompt with a historically defensible thesis or claim that establishes a line of reasoning.
- Describe a broader historical context relevant to the prompt.
- Support an argument in response to the prompt using specific and relevant examples of evidence.
- Use historical reasoning (e.g., comparison, causation, continuity or change over time) to frame or structure an argument that addresses the prompt.
- Use evidence to corroborate, qualify, or modify an argument that addresses the prompt.

2. Evaluate the extent to which the first Great Awakening marked a turning point in the development of an American identity.

   In the development of your argument, explain what changed and what stayed the same from the period immediately before the Great Awakening (early 1700s) to the period immediately after the Great Awakening (1750s).

3. Evaluate the extent to which farmers and factory workers did not easily adapt to changes stemming from industrialization in the years 1865–1900.

4. Evaluate the extent to which it was social and economic issues within the United States that influenced U.S. foreign policy in the 1920s.

WHEN YOU FINISH WRITING, CHECK YOUR WORK ON SECTION II IF TIME PERMITS.

STOP

END OF EXAM

_____

Practice Test 2:
Answers and
Explanations

ANSWER KEY

Section I, Part A: Multiple-Choice Questions

1. D	20. B	39. A
2. A	21. B	40. D
3. C	22. C	41. D
4. C	23. A	42. B
5. B	24. D	43. A
6. C	25. D	44. C
7. A	26. A	45. D
8. C	27. C	46. A
9. A	28. C	47. D
10. D	29. C	48. A
11. B	30. A	49. C
12. B	31. D	50. B
13. D	32. B	51. C
14. B	33. A	52. B
15. B	34. B	53. C
16. D	35. A	54. B
17. A	36. B	55. B
18. B	37. C	
19. A	38. B	

SECTION I, PART A: MULTIPLE-CHOICE QUESTIONS

Questions 1–3

The introduction of tobacco would lead to the development of plantation slavery. As new settlements sprang up around Jamestown, the entire area came to be known as the Chesapeake (named after the bay). That area today is comprised mostly of Virginia and Maryland. Many who migrated to the Chesapeake did so for financial reasons. Overpopulation in England had led to widespread famine, disease, and poverty. Chances for improving one's lot were minimal. Thus, many were attracted to the New World by the opportunity provided by indentured servitude. In return for free passage, indentured servants promised seven years' labor, after which they received their freedom.

1. **D** The excerpt mentions only one of the servants as Negro (Emanuel), so we can logically infer that both whites and blacks served in this capacity. Choices (A), (B), and (C) are all unsupported by the excerpt.

2. **A** The lives of English settlers in New England and the Chesapeake differed considerably. Entire families tended to emigrate to New England; in the Chesapeake, immigrants were often single males. The climate in New England was more hospitable, and so New Englanders tended to live longer and have larger families than Chesapeake residents. A stronger sense of community, and the absence of tobacco as a cash crop, led New Englanders to settle in larger towns that were closer to one another; those in the Chesapeake lived in smaller, more spread-out farming communities.

3. **C** The South experienced several slave revolts, which resulted in the use of more brutal disciplinary measures by slaveholders. The most famous of the insurrections was Nat Turner's Rebellion. Turner, a well-read preacher, had a vision, and he took this vision as a sign from God that a black liberation movement would succeed. As a result, he rallied a gang that proceeded to kill and then mutilate the corpses of 60 whites. In retaliation, 200 slaves were executed, some with no connection at all to the rebellion. Choice (A), the Whiskey Rebellion, was a dispute over taxes, not labor. Choice (B), Montgomery Bus Boycott, was not related to disgruntled laborers, either. And (D), the Bonus Expeditionary March, was about unpaid compensation for veterans.

Questions 4–6

Loyalists were American colonists who remained loyal to the British Empire and the British monarchy during the Revolutionary War. They were opposed by the Patriots, those who supported the revolution. When their cause was defeated, about 15 percent of the Loyalists fled to other parts of the British Empire.

4. **C** The key to understanding this cartoon is in recognizing the reference to "Loyalists." Loyalists had no relevance during the Seven Years' War, so rule out (A) and (B). As for the Indians, they are not meant to be taken too literally, so rule out (D). The Indians represent the "savage" new country, which will not tolerate loyalty to the British crown.

5. **B** In fact, the Seven Years' War lasted for 10 years. It is also called the French and Indian War, which is almost equally confusing because the French and Indians fought on the same side, not against each other (for the most part). The Seven Years' War was the British name for the war. The colonists called it the "French and Indian War" because that's who they were fighting. It was actually one of several "wars for empire."

6. **C** Great Britain's massive debt from the Seven Years' War resulted in renewed efforts to consolidate imperial control over North American markets, taxes, and political institutions—actions that were supported by some colonists but resisted by others. Be careful—Britain was not defeated in this war, so rule out (A). Choice (B) is incorrect because many working-class people favored revolution. Choice (D) is unsupportable.

Questions 7–9

The end of Washington's presidency was as monumental as its beginning. Wishing to set a final precedent, Washington declined to run for a third term. In his famous farewell address, composed in part by Alexander Hamilton, he warned future presidents to "steer clear of permanent alliances with any portion of the foreign world." Washington's call for neutrality defined American foreign policy from 1800 until the late 1890s (during which the United States pursued a policy of imperialism) and then again from the end of World War I until 1941.

7. **A** In the excerpt, Washington warns against the "baneful effects" of political parties. During the War of 1812, the War Hawks, largely Anti-Federalists, saw war as an opportunity to grab new territories to the west and southwest. Their leaders were Henry Clay and John C. Calhoun. Federalists, on the other hand, opposed to the war because it disrupted trade and unaware that its end was coming, met in Hartford, Connecticut, to consider a massive overhaul of the Constitution or, failing that, secession. When the war ended soon after, most people considered the Federalists to be traitors, and their national party dissolved soon after the Hartford Convention. If you chose (B), you were close, but the Civil War involved more than just partisan divisions; it was fueled by geographical, economic, and ideological differences too. Choices (C), the Nullification Crisis of 1832, and (D), the Korean War, were not primarily partisan conflicts.

8. **C** Washington was not explicitly a Federalist, so rule out (A), and he was certainly not an Anti-Federalist, so rule out (B). He preaches *against* sectionalism, so rule out (D). Washington's political views most embody Republicanism—which stresses liberty and "unalienable" rights as central values, makes the people as a whole sovereign, rejects aristocracy, expects citizens to be independent in their performance of civic duties, and vilifies corruption.

9. **A** A key message in the address is the necessity of neutrality regarding foreign affairs. Choice (C), isolationism, is close but too extreme. Choice (A) is the best answer.

Questions 10–12

Although Jefferson was a strict constructionist, he did favor providing a means for the American people to amend their Constitution, as shown in this excerpt: "As new discoveries are made, new truths disclosed, and manners and opinions change with the change of circumstances, institutions must advance also, and keep pace with the times."

10. **D** Although all of the Constitutional Amendments represent changes to the original document, the Twenty-first Amendment best exemplifies the sentiment in Jefferson's quote. After only 15 years of banning alcohol, the Eighteenth Amendment (Prohibition) was repealed by the Twenty-first.

11. **B** James Madison led the charge to form a Constitutional Congress and draft the Constitution. It was primarily the weaknesses of the Articles of Confederation that led to their rejection. They did not impose tariffs, so rule out (C). Choice (A) is incorrect because the federal government was weak in 1787. Choice (D) is wrong because Washington responded to the Whiskey Rebellion with much force. (If you picked (D), you are confusing Shays's Rebellion with the Whiskey Rebellion.)

12. **B** In Washington's Farewell address, he denounces political parties. So Washington was the one president who was not officially affiliated with any party, although he was endorsed by the Federalists. Choice (A) is a tempting answer, but political parties existed *before* the drafting of the Constitution. That also rules out (C). Choice (D) is incorrect because the Whig Party formed in reaction to Jackson's policies, well after John Quincy Adams left office.

Questions 13–17

Jackson's economic policies demonstrated his distrust of both big government and Northeastern power brokers. He fought the Second Bank of the United States because he felt it protected Northeastern interests at the expense of the West. He was wary of creating an unconstitutional monopoly and of dealing with the mostly British investors. He was also suspicious of paper money, preferring "hard currency" such as gold or silver. His Specie Circular, which ended the policy of selling government land on credit (buyers now had to pay "hard cash"), caused a money shortage, a sharp decrease in the treasury, and overall economic hardship. Congress overturned the circular in the final days of Jackson's final term.

13. **D** Jackson was not opposed to a bank run by private citizens per se, as in (A), but he was wary of allowing foreign shareholders to control American economic interests.

14. **B** In the aftermath of the War of 1812, the federal government suffered from the disarray of an unregulated currency and a lack of fiscal order; business interests sought security for their government bonds. A national alliance arose to create a central bank to address these needs. Choice (C) is tempting, but it refers to the First Bank, not the Second.

15. **B** As the United States' first secretary of the treasury, Alexander Hamilton had to handle the nation's considerable war debt. His solution included the formation of a national bank, modeled on the Bank of England. Through the bank, Hamilton hoped to consolidate and manage the nation's debt and provide an agency through which a national currency could be circulated. He also wished to broaden the powers of the federal government (Hamilton, a Federalist, favored a strong central government). Both houses of Congress approved Hamilton's plan, but Washington (then president) was reluctant to sign the bill because he was uncertain of its constitutionality. (Note: Washington performed very conservatively as president, aware that any action he took would set a precedent for his followers. Accordingly, he used his veto only when he was certain that a bill was unconstitutional.) The debate that followed defined the two main schools of thought on constitutional law. On one side were the strict constructionists, led

by Jefferson and Madison. Both were wary of a strong central government and interpreted the Constitution accordingly. The strict constructionists argued that the Constitution allowed Congress only those powers specifically granted it or those "necessary and proper" to the execution of its enumerated powers. While a bank might be convenient and perhaps beneficial, they argued, it was not necessary, and thus its creation was beyond the powers of the national government. Hamilton, not surprisingly, disagreed. In his "Defense of the Constitutionality of the Bank," he proposed what has come to be known as the broad-constructionist view. He argued that the creation of a bank was an implied power of the government, because it already had explicit power to coin money, borrow money, and collect taxes. Hamilton argued that the government could do anything in the execution of those enumerated powers—including creating a bank—that was not explicitly forbidden by the Constitution. Washington agreed with Hamilton and signed the bill.

16. **D** Between 1800 and 1820, party nominees to the presidency were chosen by congressional caucus and then approved by state electors (delegates to a state nominating convention). Before 1824, electors were chosen by a variety of methods. Many electors were chosen by state legislatures, which chose electors who agreed with the choices of the caucus (often they were the same men who had participated in the caucus). By 1824, however, a majority of states allowed voters to choose their presidential electors directly. When the Republican caucus chose William H. Crawford in 1824, others, among them John Quincy Adams, Henry Clay, and Andrew Jackson, decided to challenge the nomination. Their opposition, along with their accusations that the caucuses were undemocratic, brought about the demise of the caucus system.

17. **A** Jeffersonian Democrats believed in a republican government and equality of political opportunity, with a priority for the "yeoman farmer," "planters," and the "plain folk." They were antagonistic to the aristocratic elitism of merchants and bankers and generally favored, or tolerated, slavery. Choice (B) is incorrect because there were some Free-Soil Jacksonians.

Questions 18–21

When the state of Georgia tried to relocate the Cherokee tribe, Chief Justice John Marshall ruled that only the federal government, not the states, had authority over Native Americans within the boundaries of the United States. President Jackson didn't like Marshall's rulings and simply ignored them, pursuing an aggressive policy aimed at pushing tribes farther and farther west. The result was the Trail of Tears, the involuntary westward migration of the Cherokees. Over one-quarter died of disease and exhaustion during the three- to four-month forced march (supervised by the U.S. Army).

18. **B** In the 1831 case *Cherokee Nation v. Georgia,* Chief Justice John Marshall ruled that American Indian tribes were neither foreign nations nor states, and as such had no standing in federal court. In short, he ruled they had no right to sue. He argued further, however, that the tribes had a right to their lands and could not be forced to give them up by anyone, including the federal government. The 1832 case *Worcester v. Georgia* reaffirmed that position.

19. **A** As noted above, it was President Jackson who was largely responsible for relocating the Cherokees, not the Supreme Court or the Legislature.

20. **B** King Philip's War was an armed conflict between Indian inhabitants of present-day New England and English colonists. The war is named after the Indian chief, Metacomet, known to the English as "King Philip." This war is least like the migration depicted in the map—the Cherokee Trail of Tears, as in (A)—because it did not lead to a forced migration. King Phillip's warriors prevailed over the short term. Choice (D), the Battle of Little Big Horn, is a tempting answer, but ultimately the Lakota Sioux were forced to leave their territories and migrate to reservations.

21. **B** In the 1860s, the government initiated its "reservation policy," by which Native Americans were granted (usually less desirable) portions of the lands they inhabited. The policy failed on many fronts, and by the 1880s, the government was searching for a different tack. Congress struck on the Dawes Severalty Act, which offered individual Native Americans 160-acre plots in return for leaving their reservations; through this program, Congress hoped to hasten the assimilation of Native Americans, whose cultures most congressmen held in contempt. The results were not good. Most American Indians preferred to remain among their tribes and did not accept the offer. Those who did accept usually ended up selling their land to whites, who often placed considerable pressure on them to do so.

Questions 22–25

After the election of Lincoln was announced, South Carolina seceded from the Union and was soon joined by Alabama, Mississippi, Florida, Georgia, Louisiana, and Texas. Several months later the other four states—Virginia, North Carolina, Arkansas, and Tennessee—joined the secession, and the Confederacy was formed.

22. **C** This is a question of chronology. There was no Confederacy until South Carolina seceded first, so rule out (D). By the time the Civil War started, Southern Democrats appealed more to Jefferson Davis than to Washington, D.C., so rule out (A). Lincoln did not sign the Emancipation Proclamation until much later in the War, so rule out (B).

23. **A** In the excerpt, South Carolina is protesting the violation of "the equal rights of the states." Choice (B), nullification, is a good trap answer because South Carolina did attempt to nullify the Whiskey Tariff under President Jackson. Choice (D), civil disobedience, cannot be right because that sort of protest is nonviolent in nature.

24. **D** The Quakers believed slavery to be morally wrong and argued for its end. More generally, the religious and moral fervor that accompanied the Second Great Awakening persuaded many Northern whites that slavery was a great evil. Southern Baptists, (A), were not strongly abolitionist or supporters of slavery. Puritans disapproved of slavery, as in (B), but they did not successfully ban it from the Massachusetts Bay colony. Choice (C), Jews, is irrelevant to this question.

25. **D** Again, an issue of chronology. Choices (B) and (C) occurred after South Carolina's secession. Trade issues, as in (A), were not a primary reason for South Carolina's exit.

Questions 26–28

Albert Beveridge was a U.S. Senator from 1899 to 1911 and was an intellectual leader of the Progressive movement. Beveridge is known as one of the great American imperialists. He supported the annexation of the Philippines.

26. **A**   In the excerpt, Beveridge is arguing that America is justified in ruling over less developed nations with or without their consent, but that those nations would surely appreciate the "just, human, civilizing" influence of the West. These sentiments are the hallmark of Imperialism. Choice (D), Manifest Destiny, pertains more to domestic expansion, rather than international affairs.

27. **C**   During the Spanish-American War, the United States not only drove Spain out of Cuba, but also sent a fleet to the Spanish-controlled Philippines and drove the Spanish out of there too. In the Treaty of Paris, Spain granted Cuba independence and ceded the Philippines, Puerto Rico, and Guam to the United States.

28. **C**   Beveridge uses largely moral arguments, stating that less developed nations must be "rescued" from "the savage, bloody rule of pillage and extortion." There is no mention of economic benefits, or racial superiority, so rule out (B) and (D), respectively. Choice (A) is describing Manifest Destiny, not Progressive Imperialism.

Questions 29–33

When war broke out in Europe in August 1914, Wilson immediately declared the U.S. policy of neutrality. Neutrality called for America to treat all the belligerents fairly and without favoritism. It was Wilson's hope that the United States would help settle the conflict and emerge as the world's arbiter. However, the neutrality policy posed several immediate problems, owing to America's close relationship with England and relatively distant relationship with Germany and Austria-Hungary. A number of Wilson's advisors openly favored the Allies (led by the British).

29. **C**   Since 1914 was the beginning of World War I, only (C) is relevant. All the other answers represent conflicts in a different era.

30. **A**   Washington's Farewell Address advocated neutrality in foreign affairs. Choice (D), Roosevelt's speech, is a declaration of war against Japan. Choice (B) is largely unrelated to war. The Gettysburg Address (C) was a speech given during the Civil War, so is unrelated to issues of neutrality.

31. **D**   The Dawes Plan (1924) attempted to facilitate German reparation payments. By loaning $200 million in gold bullion to Germany, the United States hoped to stabilize the German economy and enable Germany to pay off its debts.

32. **B**   Many Americans supported the U.S. war effort only grudgingly, and then only after German (and, to a lesser extent, British) interference with American shipping had provoked the United States to take action. Many argued that America should stick to the foreign policy suggested in both George Washington's farewell address and the Monroe Doctrine, and therefore (1) avoid political alliances with other countries and (2) remain neutral regarding European conflicts. Wilson negotiated the Treaty of Versailles (the peace treaty following World War I) for the United States. He

was unable to get a treaty that reflected his conciliatory Fourteen Points, as the Allies demanded a treaty that punished Germany harshly. Nonetheless, Wilson did the best he could and returned with a document he was ready to present to the Senate. The treaty included provisions for the League of Nations (which Wilson had fought hard for) and contained a clause that could have been interpreted as committing the American military to the defense of European borders. Wilson, a Democrat, tried to sell this treaty to the Republican Senate, but he could not muster the two-thirds majority required for ratification, and so the treaty was never approved by the United States.

33.   **A**   The global ramifications of World War I and wartime patriotism and xenophobia, combined with social tensions created by increased international migration, resulted in a general sentiment of isolationism in America.

Questions 34–36

The Emergency Quota Act of 1921 restricted immigration into the United States. The Immigration Act of 1924 was a United States federal law that limited the annual number of immigrants who could be admitted from any country to 2% of the number of people from that country who were already living in the United States in 1890, down from the 3% cap set by the Immigration Restriction Act of 1921, according to the Census of 1890. The law was aimed at further restricting immigration of Southern Europeans, Eastern Europeans, and Jews, in addition to prohibiting the immigration of Arabs, East Asians, and Indians. According to the U.S. Department of State Office of the Historian, the purpose of the act was "to preserve the ideal of American homogeneity." Congressional opposition was minimal.

34.   **B**   Clancy is denouncing immigration quotas as "racial discrimination at its worst." Choice (A) is far too positive for the tone of this excerpt. Choice (C), labor strikes, are not mentioned. Choice (D), the Red Scare, is a tempting choice, but the excerpt does not mention Communism specifically. Many of the ethnic groups mentioned are wholly unconnected to Communism.

35.   **A**   The largest wave of immigration to this country occurred during this period and was a result of political and economic upheaval. This so-called "new immigration" brought immigrants from Southern and Eastern Europe as well as Asia. Between 1880 and 1910, approximately 12 million people came to the United States, many to escape poverty or political persecution.

36.   **B**   The Alien and Sedition Acts were four bills that were passed by the Federalists and signed into law by President John Adams in 1798 in the aftermath of the French Revolution and during an undeclared naval war with France. The Naturalization Act increased the residency requirement for American citizenship from 5 to 14 years, and it allowed the president to imprison or deport aliens who were considered "dangerous to the peace and safety of the United States." This act was repealed in 1802 by the Naturalization Law of 1802. Choice (D) is a good trap answer, but the Immigration and Nationality Act actually encouraged immigration, rather than discouraged it.

Questions 37–41

The New Deal was a series of domestic programs enacted in the United States between 1933 and 1936 and a few that came later. The programs were in response to the Great Depression, and they focused on what historians call the "3 Rs": Relief, Recovery, and Reform. That is, Relief for the unemployed and poor; Recovery of the economy to normal levels; and Reform of the financial system to prevent a repeat depression.

37. **C** According to the graph, unemployment generally decreased from 1933 onward, but it did not decrease in 1937, so rule out (B). Hoover was not elected in 1933, nor did his administration successfully decrease unemployment, so rule out (A). Careful with (D)—unemployment increased in 1937; therefore, employment *decreased*. Since the United States entered World War II in the early 1940s, (C) is a reasonable inference.

38. **B** In fact, the federal government did almost nothing to regulate the economy even though many within the government foresaw the potential for economic disaster. Many possible remedies—an income tax to redistribute wealth, a tighter money supply to discourage speculation, aggressive enforcement of antitrust regulations—were rejected. Meanwhile, manufacturers were overproducing, causing them to stockpile large inventories and lay off workers; consumers weren't making enough money to buy what, in some cases, they built at work; and the wealth of the nation was concentrated in a very few, often irresponsible, hands. The system was too fragile, and when it started to tumble, it fell entirely to pieces very quickly.

39. **A** As he began his first term, Roosevelt was faced with an agricultural market in which the bottom had dropped out; farmers had so overproduced that their crops were worth virtually nothing. Roosevelt's solution, the Agricultural Adjustment Act (AAA), provided payments to farmers in return for their agreement to cut production by up to one-half. The money to cover this program came from increased taxes on meat packers, millers, and other food processors. The program stabilized agricultural prices and increased American income from imports, but it came to an end when the Supreme Court declared it unconstitutional in 1936. A second AAA in 1938 served much the same purpose while avoiding those aspects that voided the first AAA.

40. **D** John Steinbeck's 1939 best-selling novel, *The Grapes of Wrath*, depicts the lives of farmers forced to flee the drought-ridden Midwest during the Depression years. About 350,000 Oklahomans and Arkansans trekked to southern California in search of work.

41. **D** The question refers to Roosevelt's notorious "court packing" plan. Unhappy with the Supreme Court and the federal judiciary, whose conservatism frequently resulted in the nullification of New Deal programs, Roosevelt proposed that he be allowed to name a new federal judge for every sitting judge who had reached the age of 70 and not retired. The plan would have allowed Roosevelt to add six new Supreme Court justices and more than 40 other federal judges. The proposal was not at all popular and was roundly defeated in the Senate. It also helped fuel the arguments of those who contended that FDR had grown too powerful. Not long after the "court packing" incident, several conservative justices retired and FDR replaced them with liberals, so he achieved his goal despite the failure of his plan.

Questions 42–46

The United States sought to "contain" Soviet-dominated communism through a variety of measures, including military engagements in Korea and Vietnam. The Vietnam War, in particular, saw the rise of sizable, passionate, and sometimes violent antiwar protests that became more numerous as the war escalated. Young Americans debated the merits of a large nuclear arsenal, the "military industrial complex," and the appropriate power of the executive branch in conducting foreign and military policy. The antiwar movement reached its apex in the mid-1960s and generated a variety of political and cultural responses.

42. **B** The conflict in Vietnam was an attempt to contain the spread of Communism in Southeast Asia. It was not an attempt to control the Vietnamese government over the long-term, so rule out (A). Choice (C), "Big-stick" diplomacy, may involve the threat of force, but it does not necessarily lead to war. Choice (D), isolationism, would have prevented American involvement in Vietnam.

43. **A** The election of Eisenhower in 1952 reflected the desire of many Americans to disentangle the country from the Korean War and to return to a more conservative economic policy, which they hoped would lead to an economic boom that could keep pace with the baby boom. The election of Nixon in 1968 also reflected a desire for a return to a more conservative social and political approach. George Wallace, running as a third-party candidate, received almost 10 million votes in this election by appealing to those who believed in segregation, states' rights, and "law and order." Democratic candidate Hubert Humphrey suffered from his close ties to President Lyndon Johnson, who had escalated the Vietnam War. It also didn't help that the Democratic National Convention of 1968 was the scene of bitter riots and violence in the streets of Chicago, whereas the Republican convention that year ran without a hitch. In both the elections of 1952 and 1968, Americans were tired of conflict and wanted to return to good times. The more conservative Republican Party was the answer to their wishes.

44. **C** The two largest issues that concerned the counterculture movement were the civil rights of minorities and the war in Vietnam. The many demonstrations that took place during this period (such as the civil rights march on Washington in 1963 and the antiwar "moratoriums" in Washington during 1968 and 1969) had these two issues as their primary focus. Choice (A), flag-burning, was practiced, but was not a major political issue. Censorship, as mentioned in (B) and (D), was not a major issue either.

45. **D** President Nixon and Henry Kissinger formulated an approach called *détente*, which called for countries to respect each other's differences and cooperate more closely. *Détente* ushered in a brief period of relaxed tensions between the two superpowers but ended when the Soviet Union invaded Afghanistan in 1979. The Nixon Doctrine announced that the United States would withdraw from many of its overseas troop commitments, relying instead on alliances with local governments to check the spread of communism.

46. **A** In the excerpt, Kerry states that the Vietnamese were "a people who had for years been seeking their liberation from *any colonial influence whatsoever*," but they were also "hard put to take up the fight against the threat we were supposedly saving them from." Thus, it is fair to infer that the Vietnamese did not welcome U.S. involvement in their affairs. Since "most people didn't even know the difference between communism and democracy," rule out (B) and (C). Choice (D) is false and unsupported by the excerpt.

Questions 47–50

The "Day of Infamy" Speech was a speech delivered by President Franklin D. Roosevelt one day after the Empire of Japan's attack on Pearl Harbor Naval Base, Hawaii. Within an hour of the speech, Congress passed a formal declaration of war against Japan and officially brought the United States into World War II. The address is regarded as one of the most famous American political speeches of the 20th century.

47. **D** Japan's invasion of China led the United States to place economic sanctions on Japan. Despite negotiations between the two countries to end the embargoes, no satisfactory progress was made and Japan decided to attack the naval base in Hawaii. Choice (D) is correct. Japan held an alliance with Germany, but neither held one with the United States. Eliminate (A). Hawaii was unquestionably United States territory, so (B) is incorrect. While the United States was in a deep recession during the years leading up to the attack on Pearl Harbor, it received no financial aid from Japan. Eliminate (C).

48. **A** The date, 1941, places this speech at the beginning of World War II, so only (A) is in the right era.

49. **C** Normandy is irrelevant to Japan, so rule out (B). Choice (A) might sound tempting, but it is false; trade relationships with Japan were healthy after World War II. Choice (D) is likewise tempting, but it occurred at the end of World War II. President Truman dropped the bombs, not FDR.

50. **B** There are many red herrings here. You can rule out (A), (C), and (D) by simply remembering that the American economy was very strong after World War II and that Japan was not punished for its actions in the War. In fact, General Douglas MacArthur aided in the rebuilding of Japan, and Japan developed a very strong economy, particularly throughout the 1970s and 1980s.

Questions 51–53

The history of the modern western feminist movements is divided into three "waves." Each wave dealt with different aspects of the same feminist issues. The first wave comprised women's suffrage movements of the 19th and early 20th centuries, promoting women's right to vote. The second wave was associated with the ideas and actions of the women's liberation movement beginning in the 1960s. The second wave campaigned for legal and social equality for women. The third wave is a continuation of, and a reaction to, the perceived failures of second-wave feminism, beginning in the 1990s.

51. **C** Abigail Adams, the wife of John Adams, was not a feminist in the strictest sense, but the sentiments in this excerpt do embody the precepts of Republican Motherhood, which called on white women to maintain and teach republican values within the family and granted women a new importance in American political culture. The Adamses were not Jeffersonian Democrats or libertarians, in the modern sense, so rule out (B) and (D), respectively.

52. **B** 1876 puts this excerpt squarely in the realm of first-wave feminism, which largely campaigned for universal suffrage for all, including women. Choice (A), the Equal Rights Amendment, is a good trap answer, but it was not proposed (and it never passed!) until the 20th century.

53. **C** Susan B. Anthony's quote clearly shows that women's rights varied wildly by state of residence. Choice (B) is too extreme. Choice (A) is likewise too extreme because women did not have "full rights" until the 1970s. Choice (D) is untrue because many first-wave feminists did champion other causes, such as abolition and prohibition.

Questions 54–55

The 1993 Waco Incident was a violent siege launched by American federal agents against a civilian religious group. The Branch Davidians were led by David Koresh and lived in a commune near Waco, Texas. After suspecting Koresh of child molestation and weapons violations, Attorney General Janet Reno organized a full-scale military assault on the compound. Seventy-six people died in the siege, mostly women and children. Public opinion turned sour on Reno after this heavy-handed use of federal power. This incident, along with the Ruby Ridge incident in 1992, fueled antigovernment sentiment in radical conservative militia circles.

54. **B** A careful reading of the excerpts can help you to use POE. We have no evidence that the Branch Davidians were "antigovernment," (A). According to the first excerpt, they were employing "defensive" measures in response to perceived threats by the federal government, not "offensive" tactics. This likewise rules out (C). Choice (D) is tempting, but notice that Conyers says the Attorney General "offered" to resign. It does not say that she did. (In fact, she did not.)

55. **B** It helps if you remember that the Wounded Knee incident occurred in 1890, a heavy-handed assault by the U.S. Army against the Lakota Indians. Choice (A) is a good trap, but an Indian tribe is not a cult. There was no bombing, so rule out (C), and Wounded Knee was not a recent conflict, so rule out (D).

SECTION I, PART B: SHORT-ANSWER QUESTIONS

Question 1

a) The easiest way to answer this question is to focus on the broad acceptance of slavery within most of the Democratic Party before the Civil War. You may have mentioned some of the following facts:

- The Democrats held the presidency during Polk's administration from 1844 to 1848, and then again during Pierce's and Buchanan's administrations from 1852 to 1860. As a national party, the Democrats tried their hardest to straddle both sides of the slavery issue. Polk's acquisition of new territory, however, heightened tensions on the slavery issue.
- The Democrats considered Pierce a "safe" nominee for president in 1852 because nobody knew who he was. Also, the Democrats hoped that the Compromise of 1850 had laid the slavery issue to rest for a while. In 1856, they chose Buchanan because he had been out of the country on diplomatic service and therefore had not been muddied by the slavery debate.
- By 1860, the party had split, literally. It held two conventions and nominated two candidates, one a Southerner (John C. Breckinridge), the other a Midwesterner (Stephen Douglas). Slavery had torn the party apart, into regional divisions.
- The Wilmot Proviso, authored by Democrat David Wilmot, would have banned slavery in the southwestern territories annexed from Mexico. John C. Calhoun, also a Democrat, fought the Wilmot Proviso strenuously. He argued that the federal government had no right to regulate slavery in the territories; most other Southern politicians soon picked up his argument.
- Antislavery Democrats called pro-slavery Democrats "hunkers," implying that they were so hungry for political power that they would court slave owners. Pro-slavery Democrats called antislavery Democrats "barn burners" because, they said, such folks would burn down the barn in order to kill the rats.

b) This question is asking you to provide a historical event to support Norton's interpretation. You can use one of the points outlined in part (a) as long as you link it to a statement made in Norton's quote. For instance, you can establish that Democrats saw the right to own slaves as a matter of "personal liberty" for those in an "agrarian society." Aside from the issue of slavery, you may also have used one of the following:

- The "Corrupt Bargain" of the Election of 1824 had convinced Jacksonian Democrats that the established government was run by elites who could not be trusted to adhere to the will of the people.
- Jackson, the first Democrat President, exercised the veto more often than all other presidents combined.
- Jackson opposed Reformers on other issues, too, such as the rights of the Cherokee Indians during the Trail of Tears.

c) For this question, you may have used some of the following:

- The Free-Soil Party formed around a single issue—preventing slavery in the territories annexed from Mexico.
- The Compromise of 1850, and particularly its stricter fugitive slave law, helped the party gain support in the North. It attracted antislavery Democrats and "Conscience Whigs."
- The Republican Party eventually absorbed much of the Free-Soil Party. The two parties had virtually identical policies on slavery. Because the Republicans appealed to a wider range of voters, many Free-Soilers felt they could better accomplish their objectives in the larger Republican Party.

Give yourself extra points if you mentioned the following:

- The Free-Soil Party elected nine congressmen in 1848.
- The *Dred Scott* decision killed the Free-Soil Party once and for all by taking away its one issue. Free-Soilers wanted the federal government to regulate slavery; *Dred Scott* ruled that it could not.

Question 2

This is a painting called *The Copley Family* from 1776. The Revolutionary Era was interesting not only because it changed the nation's form of government but also because America was forming its own distinctive style in architecture, clothing styles, and the family.

a) For this question, you may have mentioned some of the following:

- Family life is joyful and idealized in this picture.
- "Republican Motherhood" describes women's roles present in the emerging United States before, during, and after the American Revolution. The belief was that women should uphold the ideals of republicanism, in order to pass on republican values to their children. The "Republican Mother" was considered responsible for upholding the morality of her husband and children.
- The family in this photo is part of the upper class and is surrounded by lavish furnishings.

b) For this question, you may have mentioned some of the following:

- The overall scene is one which depicts family harmony. Three generations sit in close proximity. The younger children climb joyfully over their mother and grandfather. One daughter stares in a serious manner at the viewer, suggesting that she is reserved in the presence of an "outsider."
- In the background is a scene depicting perfect natural beauty, suggesting that the harmony of the family is part of the harmony of the natural world.

- The male members of the family look much like the Founding Fathers, reminding the viewer that the ideals of family life echo the ideals of the new Republic.
- The wealth of the family reminds the viewer of the prosperity of the new American nation.
- The mother in the photo is serene and immersed in the needs of her children, thus embodying the spirit of Republican Motherhood.
- The children are the center of attention in the picture, while the male members of the family are more reserved and take the back chairs. The children are the future of the new Republic.
- The oldest man looks to the side, perhaps representing the past, while the younger father looks at the viewer, perhaps representing the present. The mother looks at her children, representing the future.

c) The most obvious events to focus on here would be either the Revolution or the founding of the new Republic.

- As noted above, the ideal of Republican Motherhood was meant to create children with a strong foundation in the morals and ideals of America. This would be instrumental in the crafting of the Constitution and the unity of the states.
- As for social class, the Revolution was organized by members of the upper class after their bold signing of the Declaration of Independence. The picture reinforces the idea of their nobility.
- It required strong families to settle in the New World, creating communities and state governments from an uncharted wilderness. Fathers and sons fought together in the Revolution, while mothers sacrificed their sons to the cause.

Question 3

Note the dates. The years given are 1800–1824. You know that Jefferson served two terms as president, from 1800–1808, and that he was succeeded by James Madison (1809–1816) and then James Monroe (1817–1824). These three were known as the "Virginia Dynasty," and it was only with the 1824 election of former Federalist John Quincy Adams of Massachusetts that the "Dynasty" ended. So remember that you are not limiting yourself to Jefferson in this essay. You are being asked to address all three presidencies.

a) Your answer to this question may have included some of the following:

- Jeffersonian Democracy stood for a limited central government, states' rights rather than federal rights, strict construction of the Constitution, a devotion to agricultural interests, a restricted military, and support of the Bill of Rights.
- Jefferson was followed by Madison and then Monroe, and they were all Virginian Republicans who shared the same basic ideals.
- During this period, Republicans started to act like Federalists.

Give yourself extra credit for mentioning the following:

- It was common practice for the secretary of state to become president after serving in the previous cabinet. Madison was Jefferson's secretary of state before assuming the presidency, and Monroe was Madison's secretary of state before he became president.
- The election of 1800 was viewed as "The Revolution of 1800" because (a) the Republicans replaced the Federalists in the executive branch, and (b) no blood was shed in this transfer of power from one political party to the other.
- Jefferson stated in his inaugural address: "We are all Republicans, we are all Federalists."

b) Your answer to this question may have included some of the following:

The Louisiana Purchase

- There was no provision in the Constitution for the purchase of the Louisiana Territory, and Jefferson was acting like a "loose constructionist" when he purchased it.
- The Louisiana Purchase doubled the size of this country and was sold to us by France for $15 million.
- Although Jefferson had doubts about whether the United States had the authority to accept the offer, he agreed to it by reasoning that it would benefit the entire country, and it had the support of Congress.
- The Louisiana Purchase provided the country with national unity and boosted the popularity of the Republicans.

Give yourself extra credit for mentioning the following:

- The decline of the Federalists as a result of the Louisiana Purchase

Marbury v. Madison

- The court case of 1803 established the power of Judicial Review.
- John Marshall was the Supreme Court Justice who ruled on this case.
- This case, like the Louisiana Purchase, extended the power of the judiciary, and thus the federal government.

Give yourself extra credit for mentioning the following:

- While the case itself was over a minor issue (the power of the court to force the delivery of a commission), it actually gave the Supreme Court the enormous power of being able to nullify an act of Congress.
- This case was over the "midnight appointments" of John Adams, which the newly elected Jefferson was trying to block.
- Jefferson also tried to block other Federalist judicial measures by supporting the impeachment of Federalist Justice Samuel Chase.

The War of 1812

- The Jeffersonians were acting like Federalists in the expansionist and militaristic venture known as the War of 1812.
- The war called into question the classic Republican commitments to limited federal power and peace.
- The war was conducted during the presidency of James Madison.

Give yourself extra credit for mentioning the following:

- The United States started the fight because it felt the British were violating American neutrality rights at sea and also stirring up trouble on the western frontier.
- The "War Hawks" in Congress were led by Henry Clay of Kentucky and John C. Calhoun of South Carolina, representing the support of the West and South.
- The country was divided on this war, both by region and by political alliances.
- Jefferson's Embargo Act of 1807, which prohibited our trade with foreign nations, harmed the nation's economy and plunged us into a depression.

- The Embargo Act was followed by the Non-Intercourse Act of 1809 and then Macon's Bill No. 2, in 1810. All three acts aimed at settling the violation of neutral shipping rights peacefully.
- Madison, like Jefferson, attempted a combination of economic pressure and diplomacy to deal with Britain, but ultimately brought us into war.
- The New England Federalists were so opposed to "Mr. Madison's War" that they came close to secession at the Hartford Convention of 1814. (You would really make a reader's day if you included this one!)
- Tecumseh, and his brother "The Prophet," of the Shawnee tribe attempted to unite all Indians east of the Mississippi River but were destroyed by General William Henry Harrison at the Battle of Tippecanoe. (What does this say about the Jeffersonian ideal of all men being endowed by their creator with inalienable rights to life, liberty, and the pursuit of happiness?)

The Monroe Doctrine

- The Monroe Doctrine warned European nations not to interfere in the affairs of the Western Hemisphere and also claimed for us the right to intervene anywhere in our own hemisphere if we felt our security was threatened.
- The Monroe Doctrine represented bold nationalism and was applauded by the American public, though its full impact wasn't felt for quite some time, when it was later viewed as the cornerstone of our foreign policy. Nationalism signified quite a shift in Jeffersonian ideals and later took the form of economic growth and expansionism.
- The Monroe Doctrine, although issued under President James Monroe, was written by his secretary of state, John Quincy Adams. During Monroe's presidency, Adams helped to usher in a new wave of westward expansion, which was followed by our recognition of new nations in Central and South America.

Give yourself extra credit for mentioning the following:

- At the time of the Monroe Doctrine, the Republican Party was the only organized force in American politics because the Federalists had ceased running candidates after 1816.
- Even though we proclaimed neutrality in the wars between Spain and its rebellious colonies, we were selling ships and supplies to the insurgents, and when Monroe established diplomatic relations with Latin American countries, we became the first nation to do so.
- The Monroe Doctrine gave us the appearance of isolationism because we had "warned" European nations to stay out of our affairs, but in reality we had merely stated our nationalistic and patriotic fervor of the time.

c) For this question, you may have used some of the points listed under part (b), while focusing on the lack of "seismic shift" inherent in each event.

Here are some examples:

- The Louisiana Purchase was largely noncontroversial and a bargain piece of territory for the amount of land acquired. The territories acquired were not developed until after the age of Jeffersonian democracy had expired.
- *Marbury v. Madison* would not have cumulative effect until well after the time period in question. It set a precedent for greater consolidation of power at the federal level, but did not represent a shift within this time period.
- Since Anti-Federalist Democratic-Republicans prevailed in the War of 1812, it affected Federalists and not the Jeffersonian democrats themselves. It was the outgrowth of their influence, not its instigator.
- The Monroe Doctrine pertained to strictly foreign policy, so would not have represented a strong shift within the party ideals, which were largely concerned with domestic issues.

Question 4

a) and b) This essay gives you an opportunity to discuss the causes of the Progressive movement and its achievements. The following is a list of facts and concepts you might have included in your essay.

- Public disenchantment with business practices—By 1900, many major businesses were controlled by virtual monopolies. Those who controlled the businesses were fabulously wealthy; those who worked for them were impoverished. Businesses had little regard for the welfare of their workers or their customers. The government and judiciary proved to be shamelessly pro-business in their policies and rulings.

- Public horror at city conditions—Business's abuses adversely influenced the state of the cities. Urban dwellers lived under cramped, unsanitary conditions. Often entire families, including children, worked in factories for sub-living wages. City governments were controlled by political machines, who helped their impoverished patrons survive but did nothing for their long-term welfare.

- Growth of the middle class—During this time, the U.S. middle class was growing. With their new-found comfort and respectability, many middle-class Americans wanted to increase their political power. They formed associations such as the lawyers' American Bar Association and the women's National Woman Suffrage Association. The groups served as interest groups that lobbied for progressive reform. Many in the middle class, outraged by the excesses of business and the corruption of government, fought to correct them.

- Progressivism built on the foundation laid by the Populist movement of the 1890s—Populism had fought for moral causes, sought to counter the trend toward monopoly, and worked to widen access to the democratic process. Progressivism picked up these traditions, and so inherited the farmers and clergy who had made up the Populist coalition.

- Journalists helped the spread of Progressivism—With magazine articles and books like Upton Sinclair's *The Jungle*, American "muckrakers" broadened public awareness of corporate excesses.

- Teddy Roosevelt's presidency—Roosevelt used the office of the presidency as a "bully pulpit" to popularize Progressive ideals. During his tenure, he filed numerous antitrust suits against large corporations, tightened food and drug regulations, created national parks, and broadened the government's power to protect land from overdevelopment. Roosevelt took many of the cues from the book *The Promise of American Life* by Herbert Croly. The book argues forcefully for using the power of the central government to effect progressive reform.

Give yourself extra points if you mentioned the following:

- Other Progressive successes broadened the movement's appeal. On the state and local level, many new regulations were enacted, including child labor laws, limits on the lengths of the work day, minimum wage requirements, corrupt-practices acts, and housing codes. Many states adopted the initiative, referendum, and recall, thus empowering voters. Cities improved public transportation, adopted stricter health codes, and converted to a city-manager system. States introduced income taxes to redistribute wealth and provide public services.

- Wisconsin governor Robert La Follette led the way for many Progressive state leaders. He initiated such reforms as direct primaries, equitable tax structures, and the regulation of railways, all later adopted by many other states.

- Taft and Wilson continued the Progressive tradition in the White House. Taft strengthened antitrust law and expanded conservation efforts. During his term, two Progressive amendments, the national income tax and the direct election of senators, were added to the Constitution. Wilson created the Federal Trade Commission, lobbied for and enforced the Clayton Antitrust Act, and helped create the Federal Reserve, which gave the government greater control over the nation's finances. During his term, the Nineteenth Amendment gave women the right to vote.

c) For this question you may have mentioned some of the following:

- The many successes of Progressivism actually helped bring about its downfall. Each success satisfied a portion of the Progressive coalition, and once satisfied, these people tended not to work as hard for Progressive goals.
- World War I also split the Progressive coalition. Some supported the war while others opposed it, but the feelings on both sides of the issue were strong. When the war ended, with Americans tired of crusading for justice, the Progressive movement petered out.
- Businesses or those who objected to bigger government involvement in the lives of its citizens would have worked to stop or dismantle the goals of Progressives.
- Republican Presidents of the 1920s, such as Harding and Coolidge, deliberately failed to enforce some of the laws and initiatives passed by Progressives, thus undermining their agenda.

SECTION II, QUESTION 1: THE DOCUMENT-BASED QUESTION

The document-based question begins with a mandatory 15-minute reading period. During these 15 minutes, you should (1) come up with some information not included in the given documents (your outside knowledge) to include in your essay, (2) get an overview of what each document means, (3) decide what opinion you are going to argue, and (4) write an outline of your essay.

The first thing you will be inclined to do, after reading the question, is to look at the documents. Resist temptation. Instead, the first thing you should do is brainstorm for several minutes about what the question is asking of you. Try to list everything you remember about the causes of the Civil War. This list will serve as your reference to the outside information you must provide in order to earn a top grade.

Then, and only then, read over the documents. As you read them, take notes in the margins and underline those passages that you are certain you are going to refer to in your essay. If a document helps you remember a piece of outside information, add that information to your brainstorming list. If you cannot make sense of a document, don't worry. You may omit mention of <u>one</u> of the documents and still score well on the DBQ.

Here is what you need to look for in each document to get the most out of it:

- The author
- The date
- The audience (for whom was the document intended?)
- The significance

Remember: You are being asked to write 50 percent document interpretation and 50 percent outside information. Don't get so lost in the documents that you forget to bring in outside information. Readers will not be able to give you a high score unless you have both! What readers really don't like is a laundry list of documents: that is, a paper in which the student merely goes through the documents, explaining each one. Those students are often the ones who forget to bring in outside information, because they are so focused on going through the documents.

So, what is this DBQ all about?

This DBQ asks you two things: (1) to what extent was the Civil War caused by slavery and to what extent was it caused by other factors, and (2) what circumstances led to the breakup of the Union? In the first part, you are actually being asked to identify factors *other than slavery* that caused the breakup of the Union, although you aren't being asked to rule out slavery as a cause. Your job is to decide how much of the Civil War was caused by slavery and how much was caused by other factors. In those other factors, you might find ideas that will help you answer the second part.

Note that the question asks, "to what extent." That means you are being asked to rank the causes of the Civil War. You might state that slavery was the leading cause, but there were other causes. You might state that slavery was only one of several equally important causes leading up to the war. You might state that all the other causes had slavery at the root, or you might state that too much weight has been given to slavery as the single cause of the war. There is no right answer. You could earn a top score by writing about how slavery was only a fraction of the issue, and the student sitting across the room from you could also earn a top score by stating that slavery was the only issue!

The Documents

Document 1 is the article from which the famous phrase "Manifest Destiny" was taken. O'Sullivan states that it is the American destiny, ordained by God, to populate the country from coast to coast, in order to provide "for the free development of our yearly multiplying millions." The use of the word "free" should not be over-looked, and the idea that we should challenge any foreign power who attempts to "thwart our policy," "hamper our power," or "limit our greatness" also needs to be addressed. As stated earlier, the Mexican War and cession, which rested upon Manifest Destiny, should not be overlooked in any discussion about the Civil War.

Document 2: This declaration of war against Mexico links that war with the war that followed (like we saw in Document 1). Note the use of the words "honor, rights and dignity of this country." Clearly, in Polk's opinion, it was our right and responsibility to thwart Mexico in territorial expansion, but these words also sound like abolitionist words, so the issue of slavery also fits in well here. An astute student might also relate this document to the "spot" resolutions, in which Congressman Abraham Lincoln asked President James K. Polk to identify the exact "spot" where "American blood had been shed on American soil."

Document 3 is taken from Pennsylvania Representative David Wilmot's proposal before Congress. The Wilmot Proviso proposed that Congress award President Polk the $2 million he asked for while the United States was fighting the Mexican War, and in return that any land we wrested from Mexico remain free from slavery. If you were going to argue that U.S. territorial expansion, or the Mexican War, was a major factor in the breakup of the Union, you would certainly want to use this document to support your thesis. The Wilmot Proviso passed the House twice but was defeated in the Senate. Clearly, the argument over the acquisition of vast western lands added to the sectional debate over the extension of slavery. If you were going to argue that slavery was the most significant reason for the breakup of the Union, you could still use this document in that context. If it weren't for the issue of slavery, the issue of what to do with the Mexican cession wouldn't have been so heated.

Document 4, which shows the territorial changes of the Compromise of 1850, can be used in a multitude of ways. First, it speaks to the issue of what efforts were made to keep the Union together. Second, it displays the precarious state of the Union, with free and slave states vying for power. Third, it covers the issue of popular sovereignty in the Utah and New Mexico territories. Lastly, it shows California entering the Union as a free state. An astute student would also want to point out the aspects of the compromise that the map does not show: namely, that it was crafted by Mr. Compromise himself, Henry Clay, and that, in addition to territorial matters, it endorsed a tougher Fugitive Slave Law to pacify the South. It should be pointed out that the compromise bought time for the nation, and that while it was far from perfect, it held up the Union for another 11 shaky years. Another way this document could be used would be if your thesis includes the failure of the era's compromises, and/or ineffectual or misguided politicians.

Document 5: This well-known, unfortunate Supreme Court case turned a man into property. Dred Scott, a slave in Missouri, was taken to the free state of Illinois and then to the free territory of Wisconsin, where he lived for several years before returning to Missouri. Once he returned to Missouri, he sued for his freedom, arguing that his period of residence on free soil made him a free citizen. After he lost in the Missouri Court, he appealed to the Supreme Court, where Southern Democrat Chief Justice Roger Taney ruled against Scott. Abolitionists felt that he should be free under the Missouri Compromise, because Scott had lived in free land, above the 36°30′ line. If he lost his freedom once he returned, then didn't that nullify the Missouri Compromise? This document is filled with goodies. The slavery issue is front and center, as is the issue of political endeavor, whether successful or not. If you are arguing that slavery was at the center of our disunion, clearly the Supreme Court decision illustrates that fact. If you are arguing that the political climate, leaders, laws, court cases, and resolutions were behind the breakup of the union, this document serves you well, too.

Document 6 illustrates the differences between the North and South in terms of industrial development. In the 1850s, there was an explosion of new railroad construction, most of which was concentrated in the North. The many miles of track that existed in the North highlight the economic struggle that took place between the agricultural South and the industrial North. In Charles and Mary Beard's interpretation of what caused the Civil War, they argue that the war was not fought over slavery per se, but that it represented a deeply rooted economic struggle, akin to the American Revolution, that brought about major changes in class relations and power. The North wielded its industrial might over the less-advanced agrarian South, with the effect of destroying the cotton economy and plantation system.

Document 7: This cartoon shows the Democratic Party headed for disaster in the election of 1860. The party is not only split internally, represented by the politicians in the cart headed in different directions, but also about to be rammed by the oncoming train of the Republican Party (note that a train is a much more modern form of transportation!). The Democrats, splintered into two, offered the presidential candidacies of both Stephen Douglas, who had the support of the North, and John Breckinridge (President James Buchanan's vice president) of Kentucky, who had the support of the South. The Republicans ran Abraham Lincoln, and the Constitutional Union Party ran John Bell of Tennessee. The election of Lincoln sealed the fate of the Union. Because he would not compromise on the issue of slavery in the territories, and perhaps because he underestimated the secession movement of the South, the Union fell apart. This document can be used to illustrate the political breakdown leading to the war, and it could also be used to demonstrate the power of the slavery issue.

Outside Information

We have already discussed much more than you could possibly include in a 45-minute essay. Do not worry. You will not be expected to mention everything or even most of what we have covered in the section above. You will, however, be expected to include some outside information—that is, information not mentioned directly in the documents.

Here is some outside information you might have used in your essay. The information is divided into two groups: general concepts and specific events.

General Concepts
- One thing to keep in mind when looking toward the catalyst that began the Civil War is the settling of new territory. Think about the conflicts caused by whether or not new territory is to become free land or allow slavery.

- With old parties fracturing, new parties began to emerge. The redrawing of the political lines created a new way of looking at the parties' electoral strongholds.
- An age-old argument over the causes of the Civil War involves the claim of "states rights." This claim views slavery as a symptom of a larger critique of federal overreach, if not an outright rejection of federalism. It should be noted that this idea was popularized in the 20th century during the emergence of the "Lost Cause" defense of the Confederacy.
- The economic disparity between the rapidly industrializing North and the agrarian South was the source of consternation. In the early years of the republic, both sides had a dependence on one another. With the emergence of new technologies, the North was able to thrive with less dependence on the South.
- On a related note, cultural differences between the two sides, no doubt related to economics, but also religion and social norms, created in many ways, created two de facto separate nations.

Specific Events

- The acquisition of new territory following the Mexican-American War led to consternation over which states would be free and which would allow slavery. The Compromise of 1850 was put forth by Henry Clay and Stephen Douglas to try to appease both sides: the Fugitive Slave Act would be strengthened, but California would enter the union as a free state and Utah would be a free territory. Further, the slave trade in Washington, D.C. (though not slavery) was banned. The Compromise of 1850, passed as smaller bills, shows us that the slavery issue was not close to being resolved by the middle of the 19th century.
- The Whigs split into two parties over the slavery issue, the Democrats became even more dominant in the South, and the new Free-Soil Party emerged to stop the spread of slavery—though the aims of this latter group were selfish, as white settlers did not want to compete with slave labor.
- The Kansas-Nebraska Act, which repealed the Missouri Compromise, allowing slavery to be left up to the residents of the two territories erupted into violence in a series of events that led the territory to be known as Bleeding Kansas.
- John Brown's raids in both Kansas and Harper's Ferry led him to be seen as a martyr to the cause of abolition.
- The Election of 1860 saw the Democrats split along geographical lines, as well as southern states begin a process of secession with the election of Republican Abraham Lincoln.
- Fort Sumter
- During the war, border states (Delaware, Maryland, Kentucky Missouri) were slave states that nonetheless fought for the Union. This is the kind of thing that makes you wonder whether the war went deeper than the slavery issue.

Choosing a Side

The first thing you want to do is to decide what kind of a statement you are going to make. You have already brainstormed all your outside information, made some notes or a quick outline, and decided where to plug in the documents. Because there is no right way to answer this, and many ways to make your argument, here are some positions you might want to argue.

- Slavery was an issue in the breakup of the Union, but it wasn't the only one. There were other equally important factors, such as

    1) the differences in regional lifestyles, with the North being more industrial and the South being more agricultural
    2) the erosion of the traditional party system, including the splintering of the Democratic and Whig parties, which paved the way for the Republican Party

3) a generation of blundering political leaders, from Polk to Buchanan

4) the passions of a few zealous reformers

5) the effect of the Mexican War and the popular sovereignty crisis that ensued over the territories

- Slavery was the underlying issue from which all other issues flowed. If it hadn't been for slavery, the issue of territorial expansion, political alignments, and differences in economies wouldn't have been enough to rip the Union apart.

- Politics tore the country apart. The laws and compromises made by a well-intentioned government backfired on the nation. If it hadn't been for the Missouri Compromise, the Compromise of 1850, and the Kansas-Nebraska Act, the North and South may have stayed united, accepting their differences.

- The Civil War was caused by the idea of Manifest Destiny, the belief that it was the nation's God-given right to expand across the continent, gobbling up all available land. If Americans hadn't held these beliefs, the issue of slavery may not have extended to such a widespread area.

Planning Your Essay

Unless you read extremely quickly, you probably won't have time to write a detailed outline for your essay during the 15-minute reading period. However, it is worth taking several minutes to jot down a loose structure of your essay, because it will actually save you time when you write. First, decide on your thesis and write it down in the test booklet. Then take a few minutes to brainstorm all the points you might put in your essay. Choose the strongest points and number them in the order you plan to present them. Lastly, note which documents and outside information you plan to use in conjunction with each point. If you organize before you write, the actual writing process will go much more smoothly. More important, you will not write yourself into a corner, and suddenly find yourself making a point you cannot support or heading toward a weak conclusion (or worse still, no conclusion at all).

What You Should Have Discussed

Regardless of which thesis you choose, your essay should discuss all of the following:

- the issue of slavery
- the Mexican War and cession
- the *Dred Scott* decision
- the Northern industrial economy versus the Southern agricultural one
- the issue of popular sovereignty in the territories
- the Compromises of 1820 and 1850
- abolitionists
- the Kansas-Nebraska Act

Give yourself very high marks for outside knowledge if you mention any five of the following:

- the Lincoln-Douglas debates
- the Freeport Doctrine
- John Brown
- "Bleeding Kansas"
- the Fugitive Slave Act
- personal liberty laws
- Harriet Beecher Stowe's *Uncle Tom's Cabin*

- the Republican Party
- Whigs
- Free-Soilers
- spot resolution
- the Tallmadge Amendment
- William Lloyd Garrison's *The Liberator*
- the Brooks-Sumner affair
- the Gadsden Purchase

Give yourself a pat on the back if you mention any of the following:

- the Ostend Manifesto
- Hinton Helper's *Impending Crisis of the South*
- the Know-Nothing Party
- the Lecompton Constitution
- the Crittenden Compromise
- Conscience Whigs
- Cotton Whigs
- "Barnburners"
- Henry Clay
- Franklin Pierce
- James K. Polk
- James Buchanan
- Millard Fillmore
- Lewis Cass
- Roger Taney
- John C. Calhoun

SECTION II: THE LONG ESSAY QUESTION

Question 2

The first Great Awakening lasted for only a couple decades, but went on to influence the way many Americans, both the faithful and the skeptical, see religion. The period of the 1730s and 1740s saw a religious revival that was influenced by a variety of factors, but perhaps most strikingly, the Enlightenment. European ideals of rationalism and scientific inquiry had begun to take hold in the colonies to the chagrin of those who saw the world through a more spiritual lens. After a period of waning religiosity in much of the colonies, the Great Awakening was spurred by those turning toward an emotional religious experience, in sharp contrast to the Enlightenment thinkers of the day. It is no accident that a similar movement took place concurrently in Europe.

The part of the prompt that asks about an American identity can seem somewhat vague—use this to your advantage. How do you see the American relationship with religion? Tie this inseparable part of the American identity to that brief period in the 18th century.

Important facts to mention about the Great Awakening:

- While some of the earliest settlers of the American colonies were quite religious (the Puritans come to mind), subsequent generations were less so. In this regard, the Great Awakening was seen as necessary by many religious leaders.
- The gatherings, or revivals, had their earliest occurrences in New England in the 1710s.
- Jonathan Edwards's harsh brand of Calvinism ("Sinners in the Hands of an Angry God," anyone?) gained traction during this period.
- George Whitefield, rejecting the Enlightenment trends of his native England, popularized the connection between Christianity and emotionalism in the American colonies.
- While the Great Awakening radically transformed Christianity in the United States, denominations such as Catholics, Quakers, and Lutherans were largely unaffected.

Give yourself extra points for mentioning the following:

- The Great Awakening was transdenominational: it crossed over the various Protestant denominations to create an evangelical Christianity.
- John Wesley helped create Methodism and gained traction with his charismatic, outdoor preaching. His insistence on repentance was in stark contrast to the predestination theology of Edwards.
- Many of the framers of the United States (Thomas Jefferson, John Quincy Adams, Benjamin Franklin, Thomas Paine) held a religious belief—deism—that was in stark contrast to the emotional fervor of evangelism.

Ways the Great Awakening impacted the American identity:

- Subsequent awakenings followed throughout the 19th and 20th centuries, evidence of a consistent presence of this brand of Christianity in American culture.
- The Evangelical movement grew and remained a permanent part of American identity, impacting voting blocs up to the present day.
- The Great Awakening created a common identity for Christians in the United States.
- Culture wars that have recurred throughout United States history (slavery, Scopes trial, Civil Rights, abortion, and same-sex marriage, to name a few) are underpinned by evangelical thought.

Give yourself extra points for mentioning the following:

- The appeal to the law of God, rather than on political authority, inspired radical uprisings, including the American Revolution. Jefferson, though a deist, nonetheless referenced the colonists' authority to rebel as given by the "Supreme Judge of the World."
- Many evangelicals (particularly Methodists) held abolitionist views informed by their religious convictions. Conversely, many evangelicals also used their faith to justify the institution of slavery. This same dichotomy existed during the Civil Rights movement of the 20th century.

About the Structure of Your Essay

Begin the essay with some background information to introduce the Great Awakening. Make sure you mention your definition of "American identity" for the purposes of this essay, and include a claim that clearly articulates the impact that this time period had on the American identity. To fully develop your analysis, you want to make sure your body paragraphs connect the people and events from the Great Awakening to a more long-term legacy. You want to show your grader that you understand events from this early period of American history and can see how they affect the country for years to come.

Question 3

This is a nice prompt to work with because you can easily support or refute the prompt by using many of the same examples. Either you can argue that farmers and factory workers DID adapt by pushing for certain changes OR you can simply argue that the solutions farmers and factory workers sought did not come easily; therefore, they did not adapt effectively. Many of these key points can be used for either side of the issue, therefore a good candidate for the "modify" approach. The "modify" approach will allow you to adjust the prompt in your own words to argue a third possible stance, which can pull evidence from both sides of the issue and offer a more nuanced argument.

Farmers

- Thanks to the Homestead Act and the Transcontinental Railroad, Eastern farmers were able to move their cash-crop farming westward. On the flip-side, the Homestead Act attracted so many new farmers that there was a gradual loss of land available for homesteading.
- Farmers started to view agriculture more as a business than as a way of life. Transportation and marketing made farming more lucrative.
- Many farmers readily adopted mechanization to improve overall productivity. On the downside, much of this machinery was bought on credit. (Cue the Grangers and the Populists.)
- Founded in 1867 as a social organization, the Grange established cooperatively owned stores, grain elevators, and warehouses for farming members. Grangers also experimented with cooperative marketing of farm products and cooperative purchasing of seed, fertilizer, machinery, and other commodities.
- Farmers generally supported the Interstate Commerce Act of 1887, which cleaned up some of the corruption in the railroad industry.
- *Munn v. Illinois* likewise regulated railroads as utilities.
- Populists demanded a silver-standard currency in order to increase the amount of money in circulation and prevent deflation. Later, Populists appealed to urban factory workers. Populists "spoke truth to power" by challenging the established two-party system.

Industrial Workers

- The big point here would be labor unions: National Labor Union (1866), Knights of Labor (1869), American Federation of Labor (1886)
- Famous strikes: Molly McGuires (1876), Great Railroad Strike (1877), Haymarket Riot (1886), Homestead (1892), Pullman Strike (1894)
- Children were sent to work in mills and factories to increase family income (an adaptation, though an unfortunate one).
- In the later years of this period, single women entered the paid labor force in increasing numbers, also an adaptation.
- Pullman Strike—a nationwide railroad strike in the United States in the summer of 1894

About the Structure of Your Essay

Whether you decide to support, refute, or modify, start with a broad overview of the Industrial Revolution. Then choose three examples to focus on in more depth. It's okay—in fact, very good— to make brief references to lots of names, dates, and events, but be sure to provide analysis, not just factual data.

Question 4

This essay asks you to delve into U.S. foreign policy in the post–World War I period. You will need to be clear on what our foreign policy was, and then select two or three main examples to explain what influenced our policy. The first thing you need to do in this essay is explain our foreign policy during the 1920s. Contrary to common belief, the United States was not entirely isolationist at that time, although we did refuse to join the League of Nations. Yes, we were fearful of being pulled into another world war, but we did make arrangements with other nations that would advance our interests while also aiming for peace.

Social Issues

- The Red Scare. This was the time of the Palmer raids, rising nativism, a resurgence of the Klan, anti-unionism, and restrictive immigration laws.
- Fundamentalism. You should include the Scopes Monkey Trial and the Prohibition movement, and, of course, Harding's "return to normalcy" pledge, which kicked off the decade.
- Cultural modernism, including women getting the right to vote, a loosening of morals, and the Lindbergh flight
- In terms of the economy, you would have to mention the boom years (1922–1928), which were followed by the stock market crash and the Depression. You should also mention the concepts of consumerism and materialism.
- Because this essay asks you to concentrate on U.S. foreign policy, you need to be sure to connect all these aspects of the social climate with the views toward international involvement. The prevalence of xenophobia during this time obviously influenced the will to involve the United States in the affairs of other countries. The United States was, however, willing to deal with other countries for economic gain, rather than for political or social reasons.

Give yourself extra points for mentioning the following:

- Attorney General A. Mitchell Palmer's raids on suspected radicals, his assistant J. Edgar Hoover, the bombs that went off in the spring of 1919, and the anti-union and antistrike activities of the U.S. government during Palmer's tenure
- The attack on IWW members, the attack on "radical" newspapers and literature, the "100 Percent Americanism" movement, the rise in Klan membership and lynching, the stand taken against feminist demands, and the general xenophobia that gripped the nation
- The trial and execution of two radical immigrants, Sacco and Vanzetti; the Emergency Quota Act of 1921; and the Johnson-Reed Immigration Act of 1924
- Henry Ford and the automobile, leisure-time activities, sports, movies, the "Jazz Age," and any other subjects

Economic Issues

- Before World War I, the United States had been a debtor nation, and after the war it emerged as a creditor nation, having lent over $10 billion to the Allies.
- Under the Treaty of Versailles, Germany was required to pay $30 billion in reparations to the Allies, but was bankrupt and couldn't pay.
- The Dawes Plan of 1924 established a flow of payments from the United States to Germany and from Germany to the Allies.
- Tariff walls resulted in international and domestic economic distress.

Give yourself extra points for mentioning the following:

- The Fordney-McCumber Tariff of 1922 created a high tariff barrier around the United States and resulted in economic dislocation here and abroad.
- Charles Dawes, an American banker, became Coolidge's vice president and was the mastermind behind the Dawes plan. He also won the Nobel Peace Prize for his efforts, even though the plan didn't solve the international economic crisis.
- The United States was not only lending money overseas, but also investing in European industry and in Latin American ventures as well.

Political Ideology

- The three Republican presidents of the 1920s—Harding (1921–1923), Coolidge (1923–1929), and Hoover (1929–1933)—all had pro-business views.
- The Washington Conference of 1921 aimed to promote peace, cut military spending, and endorse world disarmament.
- The Kellogg-Briand Pact renounced war as an instrument of national policy.
- The Republican Congress refused to permit the United States to join the League of Nations and sign the Treaty of Versailles.

Give yourself extra points for mentioning the following:

- The Nine-Power Treaty, the Five-Power Treaty, and the Four-Power Treaty resulted from the Washington Conference and dealt with issues of territorial integrity and disarmament.
- The Harding scandals and his unexpected death in 1923
- Harding's appointments of Hoover as secretary of commerce and Mellon as secretary of the treasury
- Coolidge's attitude toward the economy ("The business of America is business") and his belief in limited government
- Coolidge's refusal to pay World War I veterans their bonuses early
- Coolidge's veto of the McNary-Haugen Bill of 1928 to help farmers
- Hoover's work during World War I as head of the Food Administration and his campaign against Al Smith of New York in 1928
- Hoover's suggestion that poverty was eliminated and his belief in self-help
- The influence of Henry Cabot Lodge, chairman of the Senate Foreign Relations Committee, on U.S. foreign policy

About the Structure of Your Essay

You would have to begin with an explanation of U.S. foreign policy during the 1920s and follow with a discussion of what influenced this policy. Your essay would then include an analysis of the social, economic, and political pressures of the postwar period, focusing on the two or three main points about which you know the most. In sum, your essay would outline the varying forces that defined our international relations in the 1920s.

Practice Test 3

AP® United States History Exam

SECTION I, PART A: Multiple Choice

DO NOT OPEN THIS BOOKLET UNTIL YOU ARE TOLD TO DO SO.

At a Glance

Time
55 minutes
Number of Questions
55
Percent of Total Score
40%
Writing Instrument
Pencil required

Instructions

Section I, Part A, of this exam contains 55 multiple-choice questions. Fill in only the ovals for numbers 1 through 55 on your answer sheet. Because this section offers only four answer options for each question, do not mark the (E) answer circle for any question.

Indicate all of your answers to the multiple-choice questions on the answer sheet. No credit will be given for anything written in this exam booklet, but you may use the booklet for notes or scratch work. After you have decided which of the suggested answers is best, completely fill in the corresponding oval on the answer sheet. Give only one answer to each question. If you change an answer, be sure that the previous mark is erased completely. Here is a sample question and answer.

Sample Question

The first president of the United States was
(A) Millard Fillmore
(B) George Washington
(C) Benjamin Franklin
(D) Andrew Jackson

Sample Answer

Use your time effectively, working as rapidly as you can without losing accuracy. Do not spend too much time on any one question. Go on to other questions and come back to the ones you have not answered if you have time. It is not expected that everyone will know the answers to all of the multiple-choice questions.

Your total score on the multiple-choice section is based only on the number of questions answered correctly. Points are not deducted for incorrect answers or unanswered questions.

SECTION I, PART B: Short Answer

At a Glance

Time
40 minutes
Number of Questions
3
Percent of Total Score
20%
Writing Instrument
Pen with black or dark blue ink
Questions 1 and 2
Mandatory
Question 3 or 4
Choose One Question

Instructions

For Section I, Part B of this exam, answer Question 1 and Question 2 and **either** Question 3 **or** Question 4. Write your responses in the Section I, Part B: Short-Answer Response booklet. You must write your response to each question on the lined page designated for that response. Each response is expected to fit within its designated page. Fill in the circle on the Section I, Part B: Short-Answer Response booklet indicating whether you answered Question 3 or Question 4. Failure to do so may delay your score.

GO ON TO THE NEXT PAGE.

UNITED STATES HISTORY
SECTION I, Part A
Time—55 minutes
55 Questions

Directions: Each of the questions or incomplete statements below is followed by four suggested answers or completions. Select the one that is best in each case and then blacken the corresponding space on the answer sheet.

Questions 1 - 3 refer to the excerpt below.

"From the large body of poor drifters, many of them diseased, feckless, or given to crime, came a great part of the labor supply of the rich sugar islands and the American mainland. From the London of Pepys and then of Hogarth, as well as from many lesser ports and inland towns, the English poor, lured, seduced, or forced into the emigrant stream, kept coming to America for the better part of two centuries. It is safe to guess that few of them, and indeed few persons from the other sources of emigration, knew very much about what they were doing when they committed themselves to life in America."

Richard Hofstadter, historian, *America at 1750: A Social Portrait,* 1971

1. The people described in the above quote were most likely

(A) slaves
(B) indentured servants
(C) inmates in a penal colony
(D) fugitives seeking religious freedom

2. The need for labor on the American mainland in 1750 was most directly the result of

(A) the cultivation of tobacco
(B) expansion of Northern manufacturing
(C) the invention of the cotton gin
(D) the decline of slavery after Bacon's Rebellion

3. The people described in the quote above most likely emigrated to

(A) Northern New England
(B) New Amsterdam
(C) The Chesapeake
(D) St. Augustine

GO ON TO THE NEXT PAGE.

Questions 4 - 6 refer to the excerpt below.

"I think the authors of that notable instrument intended to include all men, but they did not mean to declare all men equal in all respects. They did not mean to say all men were equal in color, size, intellect, moral development, or social capacity. They defined with tolerable distinctness in what they did consider all men created equal—equal in 'certain inalienable rights, among which are life, liberty, and the pursuit of happiness.' This they said, and this they meant. They did not mean to assert the obvious untruth that all were then actually enjoying that equality, or yet that they were about to confer it immediately upon them. In fact, they had no power to confer such a boon. They meant simply to declare the right, so that the enforcement of it might follow as fast as circumstances should permit."

Abraham Lincoln, October 15, 1858

4. The excerpt directly quotes which of the following historical documents?

(A) The Magna Carta
(B) The Declaration of the Rights of Man
(C) The Declaration of Independence
(D) The U.S. Constitution

5. At that time of Lincoln's speech, the ideas expressed in the excerpt would have been directly opposed by

(A) Daniel Webster
(B) Stephen Douglas
(C) William Lloyd Garrison
(D) Andrew Johnson

6. The excerpt best reflects which of the following?

(A) Disagreement over the application of the phrase "all men are created equal" to people of certain racial groups
(B) Fear that the United States would be split by a civil war
(C) Conflicts over how slavery could be contained to the Southern states
(D) Beliefs that the secession of South Carolina was imminent

GO ON TO THE NEXT PAGE.

Questions 7 - 10 refer to the excerpts below.

"The United States hereby agrees and stipulates that the country north of the North Platte river and east of the summits of the Big Horn mountains [in South Dakota] shall be held and considered to be un-ceded Indian territory, and also stipulates and agrees that no white person or persons shall be permitted to settle upon or occupy any portion of the same; or without the consent of the Indians, first had and obtained, to pass through the same."

Treaty of Fort Laramie Article XVI, 1868

"[General George A.] Custer's journey began at Fort Abraham Lincoln on the Missouri River on July 2, 1874. By the end of that month they had reached the Black Hills [of South Dakota], and by mid-August had confirmed the presence of gold fields in that region. The discovery of gold was widely reported in newspapers across the country. Custer's florid descriptions of the mineral and timber resources of the Black Hills, and the land's suitability for grazing and cultivation…received wide circulation, and had the effect of creating an intense popular demand for the 'opening' of the Hills for settlement."

United States v. Sioux Nation of Indians, 1980

7. Based on the wording of the Treaty of Fort Laramie, white settlement of the Black Hills in the 1870s

   (A) was a violation of the terms of the treaty
   (B) was justified, since gold prospecting was not mentioned in the treaty
   (C) was a threat to Indian interests in the region, though not illegal
   (D) was beneficial to the economic interests of both Indian tribes and white settlers in the region

8. Which of the following generalizations can be correctly inferred from the above excerpts?

   (A) Treaties such as Fort Laramie successfully controlled the incursion of white settlers into Sioux Indian territories in the years following the Civil War.
   (B) Treaties between the U.S. government and American Indians after the Civil War generally encouraged the formation of strong, independent tribes.
   (C) Treaties such as Fort Laramie were often short-lived, leading to future conflict between the U.S. government and the affected Indian tribes.
   (D) The Treaty of Fort Laramie was in place for over one hundred years until the U.S. Supreme Court finally ruled it unconstitutional.

9. Article 16 of the treaty most likely reflected which of the following sentiments?

   (A) A desire by many American Indians to peacefully share land with white settlers
   (B) A desire by many in the U.S. government to peacefully share land with native Indian tribes
   (C) A desire by many American Indians to legally establish claim to their native lands
   (D) A desire by many American Indians to forever ban white trespass onto their native lands

10. The 1980 decision in *United States v. Sioux Nation of Indians* most likely stated that

   (A) the seizure of land for gold prospecting in the 1870s was a violation of the Treaty of Fort Laramie
   (B) Custer's seizure of land for gold prospecting was justified under the Fourth Amendment to the U.S. Constitution
   (C) the Sioux Nation had failed to establish its claim to the Black Hills region and had thus no rights to compensation for any prior seizures of land
   (D) the 1868 Treaty of Fort Laramie made no provision for the undisturbed use of land by the Sioux Nation

GO ON TO THE NEXT PAGE.

Questions 11 - 14 refer to the table below.

Foreign-Born Population and Percentage of Total Population
for the United States: 1850 to 2010
(Numbers in millions)

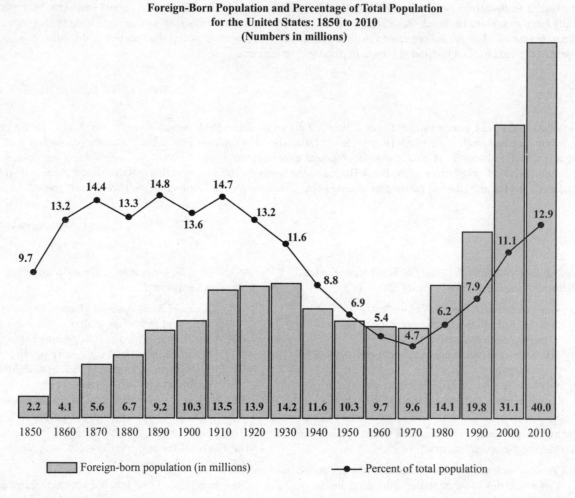

Source: U.S. Census Bureau

11. Which of the following most directly contributed to the overall trend depicted in the table?

(A) Worldwide economic and banking crises
(B) The progressive industrialization of the United States after the Civil War
(C) The rise of the Populist Party
(D) A rise in refugees following major wars in Europe and Asia

12. According to the table, the total foreign-born population was dramatically lower in 1970. This is most likely due in part to

(A) a decline in the need for agricultural labor
(B) the internment of Japanese Americans during World War II
(C) immigration acts passed in the 1920s which limited the number of immigrants from certain countries
(D) the Chinese Exclusion Act of 1882

GO ON TO THE NEXT PAGE.

13. Nativist sentiment in the time periods depicted in the table manifested in all of the following ways EXCEPT

    (A) establishment of settlement houses
    (B) mandatory literacy tests
    (C) the rise of the eugenics movement
    (D) increased membership in the Ku Klux Klan

14. The majority of immigrants who arrived in the United States between 1960 and 1990 settled in the

    (A) Northwest
    (B) Midwest
    (C) South
    (D) Southwest

GO ON TO THE NEXT PAGE.

Questions 15 - 17 refer to the excerpt below.

"Under free trade the trader is the master and the producer the slave. Protection is but the law of nature, the law of self-preservation, of self-development, of securing the highest and best destiny of the race of man. [It is said] that protection is immoral….Why, if protection builds up and elevates 63,000,000 [the U.S. population] of people, the influence of those 63,000,000 of people elevates the rest of the world. We cannot take a step in the pathway of progress without benefitting mankind everywhere. Well, they say, 'Buy where you can buy the cheapest'….Of course, that applies to labor as to everything else. Let me give you a maxim that is a thousand times better than that, and it is the protection maxim: 'Buy where you can pay the easiest.' And that spot of earth is where labor wins its highest rewards."

President William McKinley, 1892

15. Protectionism, as defined by McKinley's quote, is

    (A) opposed to free trade
    (B) supportive of free trade
    (C) designed to lower prices on consumer goods
    (D) harmful to organized labor unions

16. Which political party would have opposed McKinley's argument in this excerpt?

    (A) Republicans
    (B) Democrats
    (C) Know-Nothings
    (D) Whigs

17. In order to achieve his goals, President McKinley would be most likely to support

    (A) raising tariffs on imported goods
    (B) raising taxes on American corporations
    (C) raising prices on retail goods
    (D) lowering tariffs on imported goods

GO ON TO THE NEXT PAGE.

Questions 18 - 20 refer to the excerpt below.

"At the end of its war for independence, the United States comprised thirteen separate provinces on the coast of North America. Nearly all of 3.9 million people made their living through agriculture while a small merchant class traded tobacco, timber, and foodstuffs for tropical goods, useful manufactures, and luxuries in the Atlantic community. By the time of the civil war, eight decades later, the United States sprawled across the North American continent. Nearly 32 million people labored not just on farms, but in shops and factories making iron and steel products, boots and shoes, textiles, paper, packaged foodstuffs, firearms, farm machinery, furniture, tools, and all sorts of housewares. Civil War–era Americans borrowed money from banks; bought insurance against fire, theft, shipwreck, commercial losses, and even premature death; traveled on steamboats and in railway carriages; and produced 2 to 3 billion of goods and services, including exports of 400 million. This dramatic transformation is what some historians of the U.S. call the market revolution."

John Lauritz Larson, historian, *The Market Revolution in America,* 2009

18. Before the Civil War, which of the following resulted most directly from the trends described in the excerpt?

(A) A decline in sectional tensions between the North and South

(B) A strengthening of traditional gender roles

(C) Greater equality among wealthy and poorer classes

(D) An increased need for slavery in the South

19. In what other time period did the United States see similar economic growth?

(A) The Revolutionary War era

(B) The Gilded Age

(C) The Progressive Era

(D) The Great Depression

20. Which of the following contributed most directly to the Market Revolution?

(A) Improvements in transportation

(B) Increased immigration

(C) The rise of the abolition movement

(D) An increase in federal tariffs on imported goods

GO ON TO THE NEXT PAGE.

Questions 21 - 23 refer to the excerpt below.

"Real obstructions of the law, giving real aid and comfort to the enemy, I should have been glad to see punished more summarily and severely than they sometimes were. But I think that our intention to put out all our powers in aid of success in war should not hurry us into intolerance of opinions and speech that could not be imagined to do harm, although opposed to our own. It is better for those who have unquestioned and almost unlimited power in their hands to err on the side of freedom."

Supreme Court Justice Oliver Wendell Holmes, dissenting opinion in *Baltzer v. United States,* 1919

21. Ideas which correlate with the sentiments of Justice Holmes in the excerpt quoted above are mostly found in

   (A) the Declaration of Independence
   (B) the First Amendment to the U.S. Constitution
   (C) the Federalist Papers
   (D) the Civil Rights Act of 1964

22. Justice Holmes's statement in the excerpt was most likely a reaction to

   (A) the Wilson Administration's prosecution of antiwar protestors during World War I
   (B) the Great Migration of African Americans from the South to the North
   (C) the successes of the woman's suffrage movement
   (D) nativism after World War I

23. Which of the following actions is most directly opposed to the values expressed in the excerpt?

   (A) Efforts to detect communists in the federal government during the 1950s
   (B) Antiwar protests during the early 1970s
   (C) Nuclear disarmament treaties during the 1980s
   (D) Military interventions in the Middle East after September 2001

GO ON TO THE NEXT PAGE.

Questions 24 and 25 refer to the excerpt below.

"Actual or potential resistance was a main factor in the development of Britain's southern strategy. Influenced in part by slaves' combative and aggressive behavior, British military leaders and Crown officials seized upon the idea of intimidating independence-minded white southerners with the threat of a slave rising without, however, actually inciting one. In the end the British strategy of manipulating conflict between the races became a rallying cry for white southern unity and impelled the South toward independence. The need to weaken slaves' zeal for service with the British, which threatened to expose the moral absurdity of a society of slaveholders proclaiming the concepts of natural rights, equality, and liberty, formed part of the complex interaction of events that constituted the revolutionary war in the South. To that extent, the American Revolution in the South was a war about slavery, if not a war over slavery."

Sylvia R. Frey, historian, *Water from the Rock: Black Resistance in a Revolutionary Age,* 1991

24. Which of the following primary sources would most likely support Frey's argument in the excerpt?

(A) Statistics measuring the growth of the slave population in the South throughout the eighteenth century

(B) The number of slave uprisings in the late eighteenth century

(C) Eighteenth-century purchase and sales records of slaves by the largest plantations in the South

(D) An eighteenth-century slaveholder's diary documenting daily life on a plantation

25. Which of the following contributed most to the increased use of slave labor in the South during the eighteenth century?

(A) The Spanish Mission system's promotion of Catholicism

(B) Sustained cultivation and demand for tobacco and cotton

(C) The spread of ideas associated with European Enlightenment

(D) The policy of "salutary neglect" practiced by British monarchs

GO ON TO THE NEXT PAGE.

Questions 26 - 28 refer to the excerpt below.

"Even after Emancipation, courts and legislatures struggled to determine what the end of slavery meant. Clearly African-Americans could no longer be treated as property, to be bought and sold. But, in 1865, it was not clear what rights ex-slaves would have….Sadly, within half a century of the end of the Civil War most blacks in the United States, ninety percent of whom still lived in the former slave states, had been segregated, reduced to dire poverty, and denied access to the nation's political institutions. It would take [time] to fulfill some of these promises laid out in the Thirteenth Amendment of the United States Constitution."

Paul Finkelman, historian, "Slavery in the United States: Persons or Property?" from
The Legal Understanding of Slavery: From the Historical to the Contemporary, 2012

26. The excerpt most strongly supports which of the following statements?

(A) The Thirteenth Amendment guaranteed full human rights to emancipated slaves.
(B) After the Civil War, African Americans continued to be treated as property.
(C) The Thirteenth Amendment abolished the institution of slavery.
(D) Most African Americans in the United States continue to live in dire poverty.

27. Which of the following factors most directly fulfilled "some of the promises laid out in the Thirteenth Amendment" as mentioned in the excerpt?

(A) The success of the Populist Party in the late 19th century
(B) A rise in Progressive reform movements in the early twentieth century
(C) The resurgence of the Ku Klux Klan in the early 20th century
(D) The Civil Rights Movement of the mid-20th century

28. Which of the following statements best explains the uncertainty regarding the legal status of former slaves after the Civil War?

(A) The American Constitution did not mention slavery until the adoption of the Thirteenth Amendment.
(B) Widespread racism prevented the Supreme Court from ruling favorably on the issue of African American civil rights.
(C) The Three-Fifths Compromise had previously established the idea that slaves possess only a fraction of the rights of non-slaves.
(D) The Emancipation Proclamation merely freed slaves but did not bestow upon them any specific rights or freedoms.

GO ON TO THE NEXT PAGE.

Questions 29 – 32 refer to the image below.

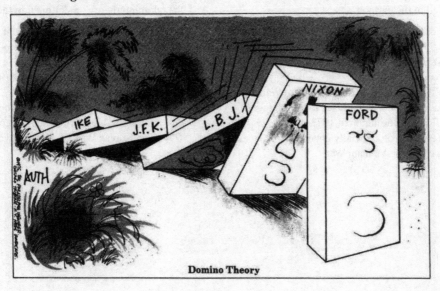

Domino Theory

Source: Tony Auth, "Domino Theory," *The Philadelphia Inquirer*, ©1976.

29. The image most closely reflects the political results of which of the following opinion trends in U.S. political and foreign policy in the 20th Century?

(A) A decline in public support for the Korean War

(B) An increase in public support for the Vietnam War

(C) The inability to achieve a clear victory during World War II

(D) The desire to contain communism in developing parts of the world

30. The image most directly supports the idea that U.S. foreign policy during the 20th century emphasized

(A) stopping the spread of communism in Asia

(B) a Cold War arms race with the Soviet Union

(C) the desire to defend human rights in developing nations

(D) supporting the Non-Aligned Movement in Asia

GO ON TO THE NEXT PAGE.

31. Which of the following is the most direct result of the situation portrayed in the cartoon?

   (A) President Ford pursued nuclear disarmament treaties with the Soviet Union in the mid-1970s.
   (B) U.S. involvement in World War II brought an end to military conflict in Europe.
   (C) Because of the unpopularity of the Vietnam War, there was widespread public resistance to the passage of the War Powers Resolution of 1973.
   (D) In 1975, President Ford officially ended U.S. involvement in the Vietnam War.

32. Which of the following conflicts was most influenced by the "domino theory" mentioned in the cartoon?

   (A) The Revolutionary War, since it motivated other countries to push for independence and political reform
   (B) The Civil War, since the Confederate states left the Union in quick succession
   (C) World War II, since multiple countries around the world ultimately joined the conflict
   (D) The Korean War, since it involved the attempt to contain communism

GO ON TO THE NEXT PAGE.

Questions 33 - 36 refer to the excerpts below.

"The wisest among my race understand that the agitation of questions of social equality is the extremest folly, and that progress in the enjoyment of all the privileges that will come to us must be the result of severe and constant struggle rather than of artificial forcing. No race that has anything to contribute to the markets of the world is long in any degree ostracized. It is important and right that all privileges of the law be ours, but it is vastly more important that we be prepared for the exercise of these privileges. The opportunity to earn a dollar in a factory just now is worth infinitely more than the opportunity to spend a dollar in an opera-house."

Booker T. Washington, "Atlanta Compromise" speech, 1895

"This group of men honor Mr. Washington for his attitude of conciliation toward the white South; they accept the "Atlanta Compromise" in its broadest interpretation....But, nevertheless, they insist that the way to truth and right lies in straightforward honesty, not in indiscriminate flattery; in praising those of the South who do well and criticizing uncompromisingly those who do ill; in taking advantage of the opportunities at hand and urging their fellows to do the same, but at the same time in remembering that only a firm adherence to their higher ideals and aspirations will ever keep those ideals within the realm of possibility."

W.E.B. Dubois, "Of Mr. Booker T. Washington and Others," 1903

33. Which of the following actions by people living in the late nineteenth century would be an example of "artificial forcing" as mentioned in the Booker T. Washington excerpt?

   (A) An African American buys property from a white landowner and starts a successful business.
   (B) An African American runs for state elected office.
   (C) A group of African Americans organize politically to challenge Jim Crow laws.
   (D) African Americans in the South start a school for poor children in their community.

34. Booker T. Washington and W.E.B. Dubois most disagreed on whether

   (A) confrontation of the white majority was the most effective means of creating social change
   (B) the most desirable goal was equal rights for African Americans
   (C) inequalities in wealth had their roots in slavery
   (D) African Americans had opportunities for bettering their social standing

35. It can be demonstrated from the excerpts that Booker T. Washington and W.E.B. Dubois shared the view that

   (A) the movement for advancement of African Americans was part of a broader effort for social change in other segments of society
   (B) desegregation of schools was a desirable goal
   (C) violence was a necessary part of any movement for social change
   (D) African Americans should enjoy greater rights and social privileges than they had previously been given

36. W.E.B. Dubois's statements suggest that he most disagreed with

   (A) the sentiments expressed in the Atlanta Compromise
   (B) the notion that expanded rights and privileges for African Americans would happen slowly over time
   (C) the idea that expanded rights and privileges for African Americans would happen naturally without direct political action
   (D) the folly of agitation regarding questions of social equality

GO ON TO THE NEXT PAGE.

Questions 37 - 39 refer to the map below.

37. The territorial acquisitions shown in the southwestern region of the map most directly resulted from

   (A) treaties made with Indian tribes
   (B) the Louisiana Purchase
   (C) the Mexican-American War
   (D) the Spanish-American War

38. Which of the following provided the philosophical basis for the acquisition of land in the West during the time periods reflected on the map?

   (A) The abolition movement
   (B) The belief in Manifest Destiny
   (C) Popular Sovereignty implemented under the Kansas-Nebraska Act
   (D) The policy of Containment

39. The acquisition of territory in the time periods shown in the map exacerbated debates regarding

   (A) the Homestead Act
   (B) the sharing of mineral rights with native Indian tribes
   (C) the extension of citizenship rights to Indians
   (D) the expansion of slavery in newly acquired territories

GO ON TO THE NEXT PAGE.

Questions 40 and 41 refer to the excerpts below.

"Under a government which imprisons any unjustly, the true place for a just man is also a prison….Cast your whole vote, not a strip of paper merely, but your whole influence. A minority is powerless while it conforms to the majority; it is not even a minority then; but it is irresistible when it clogs by its whole weight. If the alternative is to keep all just men in prison, or give up war and slavery, the State will not hesitate which to choose. If a thousand men were not to pay their tax bills this year, that would…be…the definition of a peaceable revolution, if any such is possible."

Henry David Thoreau, "Resistance to Civil Government," 1849

" [I]heard Thoreau's lecture before the Lyceum on the relation of the individual to the State—an admirable statement of the rights of the individual to self-government, and an attentive audience. His allusions to the Mexican War, to Mr. Hoar's expulsion from Carolina, his own imprisonment in Concord Jail for refusal to pay his tax, Mr. Hoar's payment of mine when taken to prison for a similar refusal, were all pertinent, well considered, and reasoned. I took great pleasure in this deed of Thoreau's."

Bronson Alcott, *Journals,* 1848

40. Thoreau's remarks in the excerpt most clearly demonstrate his support of which of the following ideas or events?

(A) The Revolutionary War
(B) The Second Great Awakening
(C) Civil disobedience
(D) Transcendentalism

41. Henry David Thoreau's actions later influence which of the following leaders

(A) Theodore Roosevelt
(B) Martin Luther King Jr.
(C) Huey Long
(D) Gloria Steinem

GO ON TO THE NEXT PAGE.

Questions 42 and 43 refer to the excerpt below.

"The only proper basis for the protection of…all animals is an economic one, and must be based upon carefully constructed and properly enforced laws for the conservation of all species for the benefit of future generations of our citizens, rather than based on local opinion….This expenditure for the protection of fish and game is clearly a wise economy, tending to prevent the annihilation of birds and other animals valuable to mankind which might otherwise become extinct."

Massachusetts Commission on Economy and Efficiency, 1912

42. Which of the following developments may have contributed most directly to the opinions reflected in the excerpt?

(A) A decrease in numbers of commercial fish in coastal and inland waters of the United States

(B) The erosion of agricultural soil during the Dust Bowl

(C) The growth of suburban housing in land previously held as wilderness

(D) The near extinction of the buffalo

43. What president encouraged the ideas of conservation and preservation during the early twentieth century?

(A) Theodore Roosevelt
(B) William McKinley
(C) Woodrow Wilson
(D) Warren G. Harding

GO ON TO THE NEXT PAGE.

Questions 44 - 46 refer to the excerpt below.

"Unlike its apparent strength in current times, conservatism not so long ago was a decidedly unpopular and much-derided philosophy. As recently as the late 1970s, conservatism was seen as a permanent minority philosophy in America; in fact, it was so much in the minority that there was a question as to whether the conservative cause would even survive. Within mainstream political culture, conservative ideals had been marginalized for half a century, since the late 1920s. Thus, for conservatives, the story of that long hiatus from popular embrace, which reached its peak in the 1960s, is a story of dogged perseverance—a story of unrelenting commitment to a set of ideals rooted in three centuries of American history."

Patrick M. Garry, historian, "A Turning Point for Modern Conservatism," 2007

44. All of the following could support Garry's assertions about conservatism EXCEPT

(A) the defeat of Barry Goldwater in the Election of 1964
(B) the continued expansion of Great Society programs from the 1960s onward
(C) the election of Ronald Reagan in 1980
(D) the fall of the Berlin Wall in 1989

45. One way in which conservatism stands in opposition to liberal principles is by claiming that

(A) liberalism threatens traditional family values
(B) liberals tend to engage in futile military interventions abroad
(C) liberals ignore the concerns of minority racial groups
(D) liberals devote too little money to social programs for the poor

46. Christian evangelicals in the late twentieth century would be most likely to oppose

(A) spending on social welfare programs
(B) federal tax cuts
(C) the Persian Gulf War
(D) national abortion rights

GO ON TO THE NEXT PAGE.

Questions 47 - 49 refer to the excerpts below.

"I have at length the pleasure to enclose you the favorable result of the Convention at Boston. The amendments are a blemish, but are in the least Offensive form….The Convention of New Hampshire is now sitting. There seems to be no question that the issue there will add a seventh pillar, as the phrase now is, to the Federal Temple."

James Madison, letter to George Washington, 1788

"The adjournment of New Hampshire, the small majority of Massachusetts, a certainty of rejection in Rhode Island, the formidable opposition in the state of New York, the convulsions and committee meetings in Pennsylvania, and above all the antipathy of Virginia to the system, operating together, I am apprehensive will prevent the noble fabric from being enacted."

Cyrus Griffin, letter to James Madison, 1788

47. The "pillar," "temple," and "noble fabric" mentioned in the excerpts above most closely refer to

   (A) the rise of sectionalism in the early Republic
   (B) unity of the states in the ratification of the U.S. Constitution
   (C) the proliferation of political parties in the early Republic
   (D) the victory of George Washington in early presidential elections

48. In 1788, political disagreements typically centered on

   (A) balance of power between the states and federal government
   (B) abolition of slavery
   (C) westward expansion
   (D) the election of George Washington

49. Which of the following political parties expressed the most opposition to the excessive use of federal power?

   (A) Federalists
   (B) Democratic-Republicans
   (C) Whigs
   (D) Populists

GO ON TO THE NEXT PAGE.

Questions 50 - 52 refer to the excerpt below.

"Whereas it is expedient that new provisions and regulations should be established for improving the revenue of this kingdom, and for extending and securing the navigation and commerce between Great Britain and your Majesty's dominions in America, which, by the peace, have been so happily enlarged: and whereas it is just and necessary, that a revenue be raised, in your Majesty's said dominions in America, for defraying the expenses of defending, protecting, and securing the same; we, your Majesty's most dutiful and loyal subjects, the commons of Great Britain, in parliament assembled, being desirous to make some provision, in this present session of parliament, towards raising the said revenue in America, have resolved to give and grant unto your Majesty the several rates and duties herein after-mentioned…"

English Parliament, Sugar Act, 1764

50. According to the excerpt, the Sugar Act was passed for which of the following reasons?

(A) To promote the interests of colonial manufacturers
(B) To raise money for the kingdom of Great Britain
(C) To establish an economic system based on mercantilism
(D) To promote peace with neighboring European colonies

51. One eventual effect of the Sugar Act was that it

(A) was never enforced due to widespread colonial smuggling
(B) contributed to colonial unrest, thus fostering a move toward independence
(C) created tensions with France
(D) led to the Boston Tea Party

52. Which historical event prompted the need for the Sugar Act?

(A) The Seven Years' War (French and Indian War)
(B) The Boston Tea Party
(C) The Boston Massacre
(D) The Proclamation of 1763

GO ON TO THE NEXT PAGE.

Questions 53 - 55 refer to the excerpt below.

"Income inequality, moreover, had declined since the 1930s and was historically modest as of 1965 for a variety of reasons. Corporate salaries, while enabling a very comfortable lifestyle for those near the top, were far less remunerative than in later years....To be sure, the United States was by no means an egalitarian society: in 1964, 34.6 million people (more than 17 percent of the population) lived below the government's official poverty lines. For a family of four, this was $3,130 a year. America's social safety net, having expanded only slowly since World War II, remained more porous than those in northern European nations. Labor unions, which had grown substantially since the 1930s, were starting to weaken. Still, income inequality was as low in early 1965 as it ever had been in the modern history of the country."

James T. Patterson, historian, *The Eve of Destruction: How 1965 Transformed America*, 2012

53. All of the following actions by the federal government could have served to lessen income inequality EXCEPT

   (A) the creation of a national minimum wage
   (B) the desegregation of the military
   (C) the creation of the Securities and Exchange Commission
   (D) the creation of the Federal Housing Authority

54. One significant result of the economic trend described in the excerpt was the

   (A) weakening of the Civil Rights movement
   (B) decrease in the number of immigrants seeking entry to the United States
   (C) increase in the number of Americans living in suburban areas
   (D) decrease in the number of women in the workforce

55. President Lyndon Johnson's Great Society initiatives passed in the 1960s were designed to address which of the following issues mentioned in the excerpt?

   (A) Growing affluence had exaggerated the effects of racial discrimination.
   (B) Pockets of poverty persisted despite overall affluence.
   (C) A rising standard of living encouraged increased union membership among the working class.
   (D) Private industry boomed in spite of a corporate tax rate.

GO ON TO THE NEXT PAGE.

UNITED STATES HISTORY
SECTION I, Part B
Time—40 minutes

Directions: Answer Question 1 **and** Question 2. Answer **either** Question 3 **or** Question 4.

Write your responses in the Section I, Part B: Short-Answer Response booklet. You must write your response to each question on the lined page designated for that response. Each response is expected to fit within the space provided.

In your responses, be sure to address all parts of the questions you answer. Use complete sentences; an outline or bulleted list alone is not acceptable. You may plan your answers in this exam booklet, but no credit will be given for notes written in this booklet.

Question 1 is based on the excerpts below.

"John Brown's effort was peculiar. It was not a slave insurrection. It was an attempt by white men to get up a revolt among slaves, in which the slaves refused to participate. In fact, it was so absurd that the slaves, with all their ignorance, saw plainly enough it could not succeed. That affair, in its philosophy, corresponds with the many attempts, related in history, at the assassination of kings and emperors. An enthusiast broods over the oppression of a people till he fancies himself commissioned by Heaven to liberate them. He ventures the attempt, which ends in little else than his own execution."

Abraham Lincoln, speech given in 1860

"I said John Brown was an idealist. He believed in his ideas to that extent that he existed to put them all into action; he said 'he did not believe in moral suasion, he believed in putting the thing through.' He saw how deceptive the forms are. We fancy, in Massachusetts, that we are free; yet it seems the government is quite unreliable. Great wealth, great population, men of talent in the executive, on the bench—all the forms right,—and yet, life and freedom are not safe. Why? Because the judges rely on the forms, and do not, like John Brown, use their eyes to see the fact behind the forms."

Ralph Waldo Emerson, "Remarks At a Meeting for the Relief of the Family of John Brown, at Tremont Temple, Boston," 1859

1. Using the excerpts above, answer parts (a), (b), and (c).

   a) Briefly explain ONE major historical difference between Lincoln's and Emerson's interpretations of the actions of John Brown.

   b) Briefly explain ONE other specific historical event or development that is not explicitly mentioned in the excerpts that could be used to support Lincoln's interpretation.

   c) Briefly explain ONE other specific historical event or development that is not explicitly mentioned in the excerpts that could be used to support Emerson's interpretation.

GO ON TO THE NEXT PAGE.

Question 2 is based on the following images.

Image 1: "Family in room in tenement house," Jessie Tarbox Beals, 1910

Image 2: "Cornelia Stewart's Bedroom," late 1800s.
Cornelia Stewart was the wife of A.T. Stewart of Stewart's Department Store.

GO ON TO THE NEXT PAGE.

2. Using the images above, answer parts (a), (b), and (c).

   a) Briefly explain the social and economic conditions of the people who lived in conditions similar to those in image 1.

   b) Briefly explain the social and economic conditions of the people who lived in conditions similar to those in image 2.

   c) Briefly explain ONE development in the period 1865 to 1940 that could be interpreted as a reaction to the discrepancies in the two lifestyles pictured in each photograph.

GO ON TO THE NEXT PAGE.

Question 3 or 4

Directions: Answer **either** Question 3 **or** Question 4.

3. Answer parts (a), (b), and (c).

   a) Briefly explain ONE of the historical developments that led to the creation of the Compromise of 1850.

   b) Briefly explain ONE of the components of the Compromise of 1850.

   c) Briefly explain ONE outcome of the Compromise of 1850.

GO ON TO THE NEXT PAGE.

4. Answer parts (a), (b), and (c).

   a) Briefly explain ONE important way in which the Vietnam War (1955–1975) marked a change in the relationship between the United States and the rest of the world.

   b) Briefly explain ONE important way in which the Vietnam War transformed United States society.

   c) Briefly explain ANOTHER important way in which the Vietnam War transformed United States society.

END OF SECTION I

AP® United States History Exam

SECTION II: Free Response

DO NOT OPEN THIS BOOKLET UNTIL YOU ARE TOLD TO DO SO.

At a Glance

Total Time
1 hour, 40 minutes
Number of Questions
2
Percent of Total Score
40%
Writing Instrument
Pen with black or dark blue ink

Question 1 (DBQ): Mandatory

Suggested Reading and Writing Time
60 minutes

Reading Period
15 minutes. Use this time to read Question 1 and plan your answer. You may begin writing your response before the reading period is over.
Suggested Writing Time
45 minutes
Percent of Total Score
25%

Question 2, 3, or 4: Choose One Question

Answer Question 2, Question 3, or Question 4
Suggested Writing Time
40 minutes
Percent of Total Score
15%

Instructions

The questions for Section II are printed in the orange Questions and Documents booklet. You may use that booklet to organize your answers and for scratch work, but you must write your answers in this Section II: Free Response booklet. No credit will be given for any work written in the Questions and Documents booklet.

The proctor will announce the beginning and end of the reading period. You are advised to spend the 15-minute period reading the question and planning your answer to Question 1, the document-based question. If you have time, you may also read Questions 2, 3, and 4. Do not begin writing in this booklet until the proctor tells you to do so.

Section II of this exam requires answers in essay form. Write clearly and legibly. Circle the number of the question you are answering at the top of each page in this booklet. Begin each answer on a new page. Do not skip lines. Cross out any errors you make; crossed-out work will not be scored.

Manage your time carefully. The proctor will announce the suggested time for each part, but you may proceed freely from one part to the next. Go on to Question 2, 3, or 4 if you finish Question 1 early. You may review your responses if you finish before the end of the exam is announced.

After the exam, you must apply the label that corresponds to the long-essay question you answered—Question 2, 3, or 4. For example, if you answered Question 2, apply the label ②. Failure to do so may delay your score.

GO ON TO THE NEXT PAGE.

UNITED STATES HISTORY
SECTION II
Total Time—1 hour, 40 minutes

Question 1 (Document-Based Question)

Suggested reading and writing time: 1 hour

It is suggested that you spend 15 minutes reading the documents and 45 minutes writing your response.

Note: You may begin writing your response before the reading period is over.

Directions: Question 1 is based on the accompanying documents. The documents have been edited for the purpose of this exercise.

In your response you should do the following.

- Respond to the prompt with a historically defensible thesis or claim that establishes a line of reasoning.
- Describe a broader historical context relevant to the prompt.
- Support an argument in response to the prompt using at least six documents.
- Use at least one additional piece of specific historical evidence (beyond that found in the documents) relevant to an argument about the prompt.
- For at least three documents, explain how or why the document's point of view, purpose, historical situation, and/or audience is relevant to an argument.
- Use evidence to corroborate, qualify, or modify an argument that addresses the prompt.

GO ON TO THE NEXT PAGE.

1. Analyze the extent to which the social and economic experiences of African Americans who migrated within the United States represented both change and continuity in the twentieth century.

Document 1

Source: *The Promised Land: The Great Black Migration and How it Changed America,* by Nicholas Lemann, 1991

[The Great Migration] was one of the largest and most rapid mass internal movements in history—perhaps the greatest not caused by the immediate threat of execution or starvation. In sheer numbers it outranks the migration of any other ethnic group—Italians or Irish or Jews or Poles—to [the United States]. For blacks, the migration meant leaving what had always been their economic and social base in America, and finding a new one.

Document 2

Source: U.S. Census

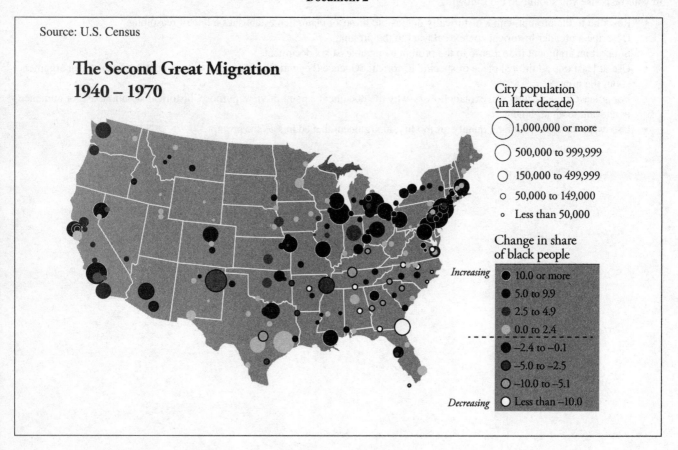

The Second Great Migration 1940 – 1970

City population (in later decade)
- 1,000,000 or more
- 500,000 to 999,999
- 150,000 to 499,999
- 50,000 to 149,000
- Less than 50,000

Change in share of black people

Increasing
- 10.0 or more
- 5.0 to 9.9
- 2.5 to 4.9
- 0.0 to 2.4

- −2.4 to −0.1
- −5.0 to −2.5
- −10.0 to −5.1

Decreasing
- Less than −10.0

GO ON TO THE NEXT PAGE.

Document 3

Source: A sign outside the Sojourner Truth housing project in Detroit, 1942

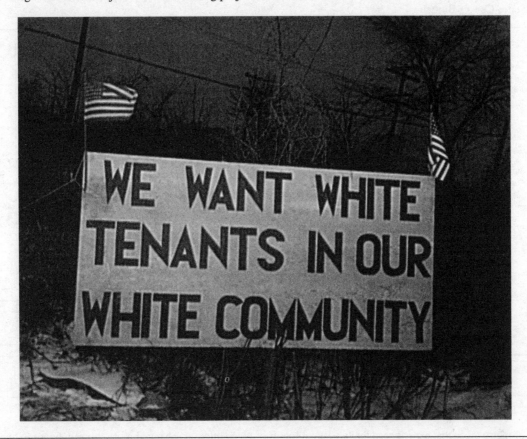

GO ON TO THE NEXT PAGE.

Document 4

Source: Table 14. Illinois—Race and Hispanic Origin for Selected Large Cities and Other Places: Earliest Census to 1990, United States Census Bureau

Census year (national rank through 100, state rank through 3)[1]	Total population		Race								White	Black
			White		Black		American Indian, Eskimo, and Aleut		Asian and Pacific Islander		Other race		Hispanic origin (of any race)		White, not of Hispanic origin	
	Number	Percent	Number	Percent	Number	Percent	Number	Percent	Number	Percent	Number	Percent	Number	Percent	Number	Percent
Chicago																
1980 (2, 1)	3 005 072	100.0	1 490 216	49.6	1 197 000	39.8	6 072	0.2	69 191	2.3	242 593	8.1	422 063	14.0	1 299 557	43.2
Sample	3 005 078	100.0	1 512 411	50.3	1 197 174	39.8	6 804	0.2	73 745	2.5	214 944	7.2	423 357	14.1	1 311 808	43.7
1970 (2, 1)	3 366 957	100.0	2 207 767	65.6	1 102 620	32.7	6 575	0.2	29 687	0.9	20 308	0.6	(NA)	(NA)	(NA)	(NA)
15% sample	3 362 947	100.0	2 219 145	66.0	1 098 824	32.7	44 978	1.3					247 343	7.4	1 985 295	59.0
5% sample	3 366 805	100.0	2 217 712	65.9	1 102 457	32.7	46 636	1.4					247 857	7.4	1 992 024	59.2
1960 (2, 1)	3 550 404	100.0	2 712 748	76.4	812 637	22.9	3 394	0.1	19 182	0.5	2 443	0.1	(NA)	(NA)	(NA)	(NA)
1950 (2, 1)	3 620 962	100.0	3 111 525	85.9	492 265	13.6	775	-	14 163	0.4	2 234	0.1	(NA)	(NA)	(NA)	(NA)
1940 (2, 1)	3 396 808	100.0	3 114 564	91.7	277 731	8.2	274	-	4 239	0.1	(X)	(X)	16 438	0.5	3 098 126	91.2
5% sample	(NA)	100.0	3 118 680	91.8	(NA)	(NA)	(NA)	(NA)	(NA)	(NA)	(X)	(X)	16 460	0.5	3 102 220	91.3
1930	3 376 438	100.0	3 137 093	92.9	233 903	6.9	246	-	5 196	0.2	(X)	(X)	(NA)	(NA)	(NA)	(NA)
"Mexican" in Other race	3 376 438	100.0	3 117 731	92.3	233 903	6.9	246	-	5 196	0.2	19 362	0.6	(NA)	(NA)	(NA)	(NA)
1920 (2, 1)	2 701 705	100.0	2 589 169	95.8	109 458	4.1	94	-	2 984	0.1	(X)	(X)	(NA)	(NA)	(NA)	(NA)
1910 (2, 1)	2 185 283	100.0	2 139 057	97.9	44 103	2.0	108	-	2 015	0.1	(X)	(X)	(NA)	(NA)	(NA)	(NA)
1900 (2, 1)	1 698 575	100.0	1 667 140	98.1	30 150	1.8	8	-	1 277	0.1	(X)	(X)	(NA)	(NA)	(NA)	(NA)
1890 (2, 1)	1 099 850	100.0	1 084 998	98.6	14 271	1.3	14	-	567	0.1	(X)	(X)	(NA)	(NA)	(NA)	(NA)

Lower portion (right columns show **Black**: Total, Free, Slave):

Census year	Total population		White		Black		American Indian, Eskimo, and Aleut		Asian and Pacific Islander		Other race		Black — Total		Black — Free		Black — Slave	
1880 (4, 1)	503 185	100.0	496 495	98.7	6 480	1.3	37	-			173	-						
1870 (5, 1)	298 977	100.0	295 281	98.8	3 691	1.2	5	-			-							
1860 (9, 1)	112 172	100.0	111 214	99.1	958	0.9	-		-				955	100.0	955	100.0	-	-
1850 (24, 1)	29 963	100.0	29 640	98.9	323	1.1	(NA)	(NA)	(NA)	(NA)			323	100.0	323	100.0	-	-
1840 (92, 1)	4 470	100.0	4 417	98.8	53	1.2	(NA)	(NA)	(NA)	(NA)			53	100.0	53	100.0	-	-

Document 5

Source: "The New Great Migration: Black Americans' Return to the South, 1965–2000," by William H. Frey

The list of metro areas that experienced the largest net losses of black migrants changed most abruptly between the late 1960s and late 1970s…with the exception of Pittsburgh, the 10 largest net losses at the metropolitan level between 1965 and 1970 occurred in the South, and mostly in Deep South areas, including three each in Alabama (Birmingham, Mobile, and Montgomery) and Louisiana (New Orleans, Lafayette, and Shreveport). But in the late 1970s, industrial shake-outs in the Northeast and Midwest fueled a new migration of blacks out of several metropolitan areas that were their major destinations in earlier decades…. In fact, only New Orleans—a metro that continues to lose black migrants today-represents the South on the "bottom 10" list in the late 1970s….

Now, more educated blacks are migrating to Southern destinations at higher rates than those with lower educational levels … [this] pattern is mirrored in white migration to the South during the same period. As with the black population, the South gained whites at all education levels, though net gains were larger for higher-educated whites.

GO ON TO THE NEXT PAGE.

Document 6

Source: "The New Great Migration: Black Americans' Return to the South, 1965–2000" by William H. Frey

Top 10 States for Black Net Migration Gains, 1965–1970 and 1995–2000

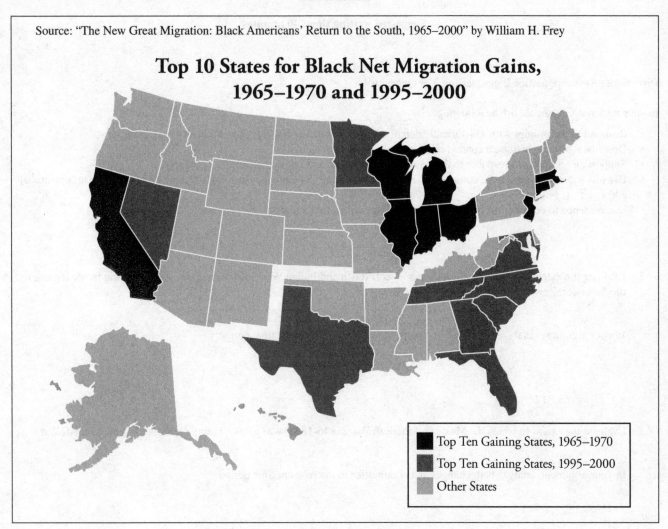

Top Ten Gaining States, 1965–1970
Top Ten Gaining States, 1995–2000
Other States

END OF DOCUMENTS FOR QUESTION 1

GO ON TO THE NEXT PAGE.

Question 2, 3, or 4 (Long Essay)

Suggested writing time: 40 minutes

Directions: Answer Question 2 **or** Question 3 **or** Question 4.

In your response you should do the following.

- Respond to the prompt with a historically defensible thesis or claim that establishes a line of reasoning.
- Describe a broader historical context relevant to the prompt.
- Support an argument in response to the prompt using specific and relevant examples of evidence.
- Use historical reasoning (e.g., comparison, causation, continuity or change over time) to frame or structure an argument that addresses the prompt.
- Use evidence to corroborate, qualify, or modify an argument that addresses the prompt.

2. Evaluate the extent to which the Seven Years' War (French and Indian War, 1754–1763) was a contributing factor leading to the American Revolution.

   In your argument, analyze both changes and continuities in the relevant time period.

3. Evaluate the extent to which the Mexican-American War (1846-1848) was a contributing factor leading to the Civil War.

   In your argument, analyze both changes and continuities in the relevant time period.

4. Evaluate the extent to which World War I was a contributing factor leading to the first Red Scare.

   In your argument, analyze both changes and continuities in the relevant time period.

WHEN YOU FINISH WRITING, CHECK YOUR WORK ON SECTION II IF TIME PERMITS.

STOP

END OF EXAM

Practice Test 3:
Answers and
Explanations

ANSWER KEY

Section I, Part A: Multiple-Choice Questions

1. B	20. A	39. D
2. A	21. B	40. C
3. C	22. A	41. B
4. C	23. A	42. A
5. B	24. B	43. A
6. A	25. B	44. D
7. A	26. C	45. A
8. C	27. D	46. D
9. C	28. A	47. B
10. A	29. D	48. A
11. B	30. A	49. B
12. C	31. D	50. B
13. A	32. D	51. B
14. D	33. C	52. A
15. A	34. A	53. B
16. B	35. D	54. C
17. A	36. C	55. B
18. D	37. C	
19. B	38. B	

SECTION I, PART A: MULTIPLE-CHOICE QUESTIONS

Questions 1–3

Beginning in the 17th century, early British colonies, such as in the Chesapeake and North Carolina, became wealthy through the cultivation of tobacco, a lucrative export business targeted to European merchants. Although slavery would later become the preferred mode of labor, early workers were indentured servants. Indentured servants were largely poor people from England, Ireland, and France who were lured across the Atlantic by the promise of a new life, freedom, adventure, and job security. Most indentured servants were young males, some were children, and some who were not persuaded to go willingly would be kidnapped and taken to America. Once on American soil, they signed 5- to 10-year contracts, committing to a term of labor. The lives of indentured servants were often harsh and dangerous; some died before their contracts expired.

1. **B** We can find clues within Hofstadter's quote: the "labor supply" is from England (not Africa) and they "committed themselves," so they cannot be slaves (A). Although some of them may have been "given to crime," there is no evidence that they were convicted inmates (C). There is no mention of religious freedom, so rule out (D).

2. **A** Using the clues described above, we know that these workers are indentured servants. Indentured servants were hired to work in agriculture. "Manufacturing" as we now know it would not have existed in 1750, so rule out (B). Choice (D) is testing your knowledge of Bacon's Rebellion, an uprising by indentured servants in Virginia in 1676. It did not lead to a decline in slavery; in fact, many slaves were brought in to replace the indentured servants after 1676. So, we are left with (A) and (C). As you may know, the cotton gin was not invented until 1793. Cotton production is linked to slavery. The indentured servants of the 17th and 18th centuries were more likely hired to work in Southern tobacco plantations.

3. **C** We know that the people described in the quote are indentured servants, since they came from England and "committed themselves" to labor in America and the West Indies. So where was labor most needed in 1750? Not in Northern New England (A), since the harsh climate and rocky soil allowed for only small subsistence farms. New Amsterdam (B) was a small Dutch settlement created to protect Dutch interest in the fur trade. St. Augustine in 1750 was controlled by Spain (D). That leaves us with (C). The Chesapeake region was known for its cultivation of tobacco and import of indentured servants.

Questions 4–6

During the Lincoln-Douglas debates of 1858, Abraham Lincoln appeared on the national scene as an antislavery Republican. He ran against the incumbent Senator Stephen Douglas in the U.S. Senate race in Illinois. Lincoln challenged Douglas to a series of debates in which he deftly explained his belief that the nation's opposition to slavery could not be grounds for compromise, and challenged the fundamental morality of Douglas's support of the Dred Scott decision and the Kansas-Nebraska Act.

4. **C** The phrase "life, liberty, and the pursuit of happiness" occurs in the Preamble to the Declaration of Independence. The meaning of the Declaration was a heated topic in the Lincoln-Douglas debates. Lincoln thought that the language of the Declaration was universal. In the excerpt, Lincoln clarifies this perspective by noting that "all men are created equal" although they do not all currently enjoy equal rights.

5. **B** Douglas argued that the phrase "all men are created equal" in the Declaration referred to white men only.

6. **A** Toward the end of the excerpt, Lincoln mentions "all people, of all colors, everywhere," so he is explicitly talking about race. He does not explicitly mention slavery (C), and South Carolina's secession (D) does not occur until 1860. Choice (B) may seem close, but the excerpt is about human rights, not the threat of war.

Questions 7–10

The Treaty of Fort Laramie was an agreement between the United States and the Sioux Nation signed in 1868, which purported to grant ownership of the Black Hills, South Dakota area to the Sioux, thus denying the possibility of white settlement in the area. As with other treaties of its kind, the Treaty of Fort Laramie was broken, in part due to the discovery of gold in the Black Hills. The excerpt from the ruling in *United States v. Sioux Nation of Indians* documents the fact that General George A. Custer was instrumental in luring whites to the Black Hills region and thus violating the terms of the treaty.

7. **A** The Treaty states that "no white person or persons shall be permitted to settle upon or occupy any portion of" the land in question, so white settlement of this area in the 1870s was a clear violation of the treaty. After whites began to prospect for gold in the Black Hills, General Custer was defeated by the Sioux at the Battle of Little Bighorn, one in a series of battles instigated by the violation of the treaty.

8. **C** The Treaty of Fort Laramie was signed in 1868, while Custer's journey from Fort Abraham Lincoln commenced in 1874. We can infer from these dates that it was only a few short years from the signing of the treaty before whites began to enter the Black Hills region. This directly contradicts answer (A). Choice (B) is unlikely, since the violations of treaties led to more uncertainty for Indians. Choice (D) is unsupported by the information given, and is incorrect. In fact, *United States v. Sioux Nation of Indians* ruled that the Sioux nation had incurred damages from the violation of the treaty and awarded it several million dollars in compensation.

9. **C** The Treaty states that "no white person or persons shall be permitted to settle upon or occupy any portion of" the land in question, so rule out (A) and (B). Choice (D) is too extreme, since there is a provision in Article XVI for whites to travel through the region "with consent."

10. **A** The wording of Article XVI is unambiguous and clearly contradicts (D). The Sioux *could establish a claim under Article XVI,* so rule out (C). Choice (B) is incorrect, since the Fourth Amendment prohibits the search and seizure of private property without just cause.

Questions 11–14

The table measures the foreign-born population of the United States every 10 years (census years) from 1850 to 1910. The trend is toward a general increase in foreign-born residents, but with a sharp decline from 1930 to 1970. Thus, we see a clear indication that immigration trends must have changed in the years previous to 1970. We can infer that the children of foreign-born people were then citizens, thus not accounted for in this table, but we can also infer that there must have been a decrease in immigration, thus no displacement of the foreign-born numbers. Then we see a spike in foreign-born residents from 1980 onward.

11. **B**   The *overall* trend is toward greater immigration from all areas of the world. The one constant in the United States since 1870 has been progressive industrialization.

12. **C**   The question is asking about the *total* foreign-born population, so (B) is too narrow. Choice (D) is also too narrow and occurred too early to affect the population in 1960. Choice (A) is incorrect. The need for agricultural labor likely increased in the 20th century and would not have affected all ethnic groups.

13. **A**   Nativism is a term that refers to a native population's desire to limit foreign immigration and promote the interests of the native-born. Literacy tests (B) were used by labor unions throughout the 1890s to 1920s to exclude non-English-speaking immigrants from the labor pool. Eugenics (C) was popular following World War I. Eugenicists sought to maintain the genetic purity of the United States; thus they would have been skeptical of immigration. The Ku Klux Klan (D) was a white nationalist group based largely in the South. Although it started as a reaction to the emancipation of the slaves after the Civil War, the KKK quickly expanded as a reaction to foreign immigration, including anti-Semitism and anti-Catholicism within its milieu. That leaves us with settlement houses (A). Settlement houses, such as Hull House started by Jane Addams, sought to help immigrants in major cities by providing them with financial assistance, education, and healthcare.

14. **D**   According to the table, immigration from Latin America exploded during the latter half of the 20th century. Most of these immigrants settled in California and other areas of the Southwest. Numbers of immigrants have always been high in New York City, but California has experienced a higher number of newcomers than even this melting pot.

Questions 15–17

President William McKinley was a powerful, pro-business Republican. He sponsored the legislation that created the eponymous McKinley Tariff, which raised taxes on many goods by about 50 percent. The primary purpose of tariffs was not to raise revenue, but to boost American businesses by giving them a price advantage over foreign competitors.

15. **A**   According to McKinley's quote, "Under free trade the trader is the master and the producer the slave…" and "protection…is where labor wins its highest rewards." So, in McKinley's view, free trade is disadvantageous to both American businesses and their employees. Protectionism does not lower prices on goods (C), since McKinley believes there is a "maxim…a thousand times better" than "Buy where you can buy the cheapest."

16. **B**   Since McKinley was a Republican, rule out (A). Know-Nothings (C) were concerned with immigration issues. Whigs (D) disbanded before the Civil War.

17. **A**   McKinley does not mention tariffs in the excerpt, but he is well known for the protective McKinley tariff, along with some minor tariffs designed to give American businesses a boost over foreign competition. Choice (B) would not be helpful to American businesses. While (C) may be a by-product of tariffs, this answer is too broad and does not differentiate between American and foreign goods.

Questions 18–20

Larson's quote explains in detail what comprised the Market Revolution: a transition throughout the 19th century from an agricultural economy to an industrial one. The North was developed first, where new factories sprang up, using new methods of production such as interchangeable parts (parts made to a standard so that they can be easily replaced). Urban centers grew as people migrated from the farmlands to the cities. Improvements in transportation and communication systems were in demand to keep pace with industrial expansion. Railroad networks were built throughout the North, and the use of the telegraph aided in running this sprawling network. In time, the South caught up to these changes, and today the United States is a largely industrial nation.

18. **D** Use Process of Elimination. Sectional tensions (A) would have been high before the Civil War, due to divisions over slavery. Choices (B) and (C) were not natural outgrowths of the Market Revolution, since many young women worked in factories and industrialization created deeper divisions between the wealthy factory owners and poorer factory workers. Choice (D) is correct, since the invention of the cotton gin by Eli Whitney allowed for the efficient removal of seeds from cotton tufts. Coupled with enormous English demand for huge quantities of cotton, this encouraged the South to continue to focus on cotton production, which in turn fueled increased demand for slave labor.

19. **B** Following the Civil War, many factors contributed to the rapid rise of industrialization and manufacturing. Remember these important ones: abundant natural resources, a large and available pool of labor (ex-soldiers, freed slaves, immigrants, women, and children), improved transportation (railroads), and other new technologies (such as the telegraph).

20. **A** Improvements in transportation, such as the building of railroads, invention of the steamship for river trade, and improvements to roads and canals, all allowed for more efficient trade. Choice (B) occurred during the same time, but was not a direct cause of industrialization. If anything, it may have been a result, since many immigrants came to America to take the jobs that had already become available in city factories. Abolition (C) is unrelated to the Market Revolution, and (D) is in the wrong time period: tariffs came in *after* American industry had already established itself.

Questions 21–23

Baltzer v. United States (1919) and *Schenck v. United States* (1919) were landmark Supreme Court cases which ruled that speech which is intended to result in a crime and that poses a "clear and present" danger in its expression is not protected speech under the First Amendment. Justice Oliver Wendell Holmes was one of the dissenters in the Baltzer case, and the excerpt here expresses his opinion that there is danger in the impulse to suppress unpopular speech and that "it is better for those who have unquestioned and almost unlimited power in their hands to err on the side of freedom."

21. **B** Since Holmes's quote is concerned with the tendency toward "intolerance of opinions and speech" and "freedom," the First Amendment is most relevant to these sentiments. The First Amendment guarantees freedom of speech.

22. **A** Holmes is addressing the need to tolerate opinions and speech that might be "opposed to our own." Choice (B) does not involve speech, so eliminate it. Although the speech of activists associated with women's suffrage (C) or nativism (D) may have been unpopular with some, these people were never

arrested by the government for their divergent views. President Wilson did, however, authorize the arrest of many antiwar protestors under the Espionage Act of 1917. The protestors distributed literature encouraging draft dodging, thus leading to the *Baltzer v. United States* and *Schenck v. United States* decisions, which ruled that speech encouraging illegal activity was not protected under the First Amendment.

23.   **A**   Since Holmes's quote addresses the issue of freedom of speech, an action which seeks to limit speech or beliefs would be the most directly opposed to his sentiments. In the vanguard of the deep anti-communist sentiment in the 1950s was Senator Joseph R. McCarthy, who led a crusade to rid the government of supposed communists, and their "fellow travelers," or "sympathizers." McCarthy's tactics, which became known as McCarthyism, were ruthless, and his claims were often unsubstantiated. Choice (B) is the opposite of what we are looking for, since antiwar protestors are employing freedom of speech, not denouncing it. Choices (C) and (D) are unrelated to freedom of speech.

Questions 24–25

This may initially sound like a description of the Civil War, but a careful reading of the excerpt reveals that it is actually describing the British strategy of attempting to manipulate the Southern colonies before the American Revolution. According to Frey, "the British strategy of manipulating conflict between the races became a rallying cry for white southern unity and impelled the South toward independence."

24.   **B**   According to Frey, "British military leaders and Crown officials seized upon the idea of intimidating independence-minded white southerners with the threat of a slave rising," so knowing the prevalence (or lack thereof) of slave uprisings would help to evaluate the relevance of this statement. Choices (A) and (C) may help to establish raw numbers of slaves, but do not give us any insight into their proclivity to rebel, or white plantation owners' fears of such rebellions. Choice (D) is vague and irrelevant to Frey's argument.

25.   **B**   Plantation systems developed to produce single crops, such as tobacco, rice, indigo, and, later, cotton—also known as cash crops, because they were sold as well as consumed by the growers. This type of farming was labor-intensive and opened the door for the slave trade, which had been carried on by English merchants since at least the 16th century, and which increased steadily throughout the 17th, 18th, and the first half of the 19th centuries.

Questions 26–28

For newly emancipated slaves, Reconstruction brought good news and bad. The good news was that the Thirteenth Amendment, which prohibited slavery, was passed. The bad news was that Southerners passed the Black Codes, rules that restricted African Americans from many rights of citizenship.

26.   **C**   There are several tempting answers here, but we must pick the choice that is most *definitely* true based on Finkelman's statements. The Thirteenth Amendment did abolish slavery, though it did not guarantee full human rights for the emancipated slaves (A), as supported by Finkelman's quote. Choice (B) is directly contradicted by the quote. Choice (D) is a good trap answer, but this statement is worded in the present tense and is unsupported by the excerpt.

27. **D** The Populist Party (A) did not work explicitly toward expanded rights for African Americans. Since Finkelman's quote includes fulfilling "some of these promises laid out in the Thirteenth Amendment," (C) cannot be correct. Choice (B) is close, but Progressive reformers were more focused on securing rights for workers, women, and the poor. Only the Civil Rights Movement (D) would fully ensure equal legal protections for African Americans.

28. **A** Use Process of Elimination. The Emancipation Proclamation (D) was not a legal document per se. The Thirteenth Amendment was the formal legal measure imposed by Congress to free the slaves. Choice (B) is not supported by any specific facts; the Supreme Court would not have been necessary to secure rights for African Americans had Congress and the States done that job. Choices (A) and (C) are very close choices, but (A) is better. The Three-Fifths Compromise was used to apportion Congressional representation at the founding of the Republic, but it did not, strictly speaking, limit the rights of African Americans. The uncertainty regarding their rights is more clearly due to the lack of explicit mention of slavery in the Constitution.

Questions 29–32

This set of questions is asking you to interpret a cartoon which depicts five presidents (Eisenhower "Ike," Kennedy "JFK," Johnson "LBJ," Nixon, and Ford) lined up like dominoes toppling each other. The caption reads "The Domino Theory." To understand this cartoon, you need to know that all five of these presidents involved U.S. troops in the Vietnam War, spanning from the 1950s to 1975. The term "domino theory" typically refers to the fear that once a certain country adopts a communist form of government, that other countries around it will "fall like dominoes" and become communist, too. Here, the cartoonist is parodying this notion by showing that the presidents "fell like dominoes," too, probably because the conflict was transferred from one administration to the next, with increasing public dissatisfaction with the results of the war.

The nation's approach to Vietnam was the ultimate Cold War policy gone awry. Although the Vietnam War is at its core a story of anticommunists versus communists, the full narrative is much more complicated. The war was waged between the communist North Vietnamese, with support from their Chinese, Soviet, and Viet Cong allies, and the government of South Vietnam, supported by its primary ally, the United States. Following the military defeat and subsequent withdrawal of the French from Indochina, Vietnam was partitioned into Northern and Southern states. The government of North Vietnam and their Viet Kong allies in the South sought to reunify Vietnam under a single communist government. The United States justified its involvement in Vietnam as part of a larger containment strategy, the crux of which was to stop the expansion of communism on a state-by-state basis, wherever revolutionary elements pursued the establishment of communist rule. This containment doctrine had at its intellectual heart domino theory, which held that if one country in a region fell to communism, all of the nations in that region were then put at risk of falling.

29. **D** The cartoon portrays the five U.S. presidents who were directly involved in executing military decisions for the Vietnam War. The cartoon is unrelated to the Korean War (A) or World War II (C). Choice (B) is incorrect, since public sentiment toward the Vietnam War tended to turn more negative, not toward greater support. Choice (D) is the best choice.

30. **A** The Vietnam War was an attempt to contain the spread of communism in Asia. It was not rooted in a desire to defend human rights, per se (C). Choice (B) is irrelevant to the cartoon. The Non-Aligned Movement (D) pertains to a group of smaller countries who have attempted to maintain

independence from major countries, so the United States would not have supported this effort, nor was Vietnam a member of this group until 1976, after the war ended.

31. **D** The Tet Offensive failed in its goal of overthrowing the South Vietnamese government, but it turned the tide of the war nonetheless, as it persuaded many American voters that despite extra-ordinary effort and enormous sacrifice, the United States was no closer to victory than when the war began. A significant antiwar movement grew throughout the 1960s, which was both a reflection of and a stimulus for the larger countercultural movement of the decade. A growing sense that the United States was mired in a quagmire in Southeast Asia, along with increasingly vocal public opposition to the war, led to a slow, but steady reduction in American force levels until President Ford officially ended the war in 1975 (D). Choice (C) may look tempting, but the War Powers Resolution was, in fact, an attempt to curb the executive power to commit troops to war without the consent of Congress. Antiwar activists would not have opposed this idea.

32. **D** The Korean War, which occurred under Truman, became a stage on which Cold War hostilities were played out. After World War II, Korea had been divided into North Korea, under Soviet control, and South Korea, under American occupation. Following the withdrawal of both Soviet and U.S. troops at the end of World War II, North Korea, led by Soviet-trained military leaders and equipped with Soviet arms, attacked South Korea without provocation, with the declared intention of unifying the Korean peninsula. The initial North Korean invasion across the 38th parallel into South Korea pushed overwhelmed South Korean defenders back to the so-called Pusan Perimeter. Led by America, the United Nations Security Council declared North Korea an aggressor and sent a force led by General MacArthur to the region under orders to defend South Korea.

Questions 33–36

Many strong African American leaders emerged during the Progressive Era. The National Association for the Advancement of Colored People (NAACP) and the National Urban League were multiracial groups founded to combat racial discrimination and pursue political, educational, social, and economic equality for all people. While most African Americans were in favor of racial equality, they were split as to how this could best be achieved. Booker T. Washington, an educator who founded the Tuskegee Institute, an all-black vocational school (and later, a university), advocated that, rather than fight for political rights, African Americans should strive for economic equality through job training and hard work. Washington presented these views at the Atlanta Exposition in 1895 in a speech known as the Atlanta Compromise. Whites welcomed Washington's views as they advised African Americans to work quietly rather than to agitate openly for equality. In sharp contrast to Washington, W. E. B. Du Bois, who helped found the NAACP, argued that African Americans should aggressively pursue political, social, and economic rights. Du Bois believed that a "Talented Tenth" of the African American population should assume roles of academic and community leadership, advancing the race through intellect and skill.

33. **C** According to Washington's statements, "artificial forcing" is political action that leads to "agitation of questions of social equality." Choice (C) involves the most direct political action. All of the other answers involve more indirect or individual actions that Washington would support as beneficial to the African American community.

34. **A** Washington and Dubois did not disagree upon the roots of African American suffering (C) or the worthiness of equal rights for all (B). They did, however, disagree upon the means by which to achieve these goals (A). Choice (D) is incorrect, since Dubois does mention that there is a "way for a people to gain their reasonable rights."

35. **D** Neither speaker mentions desegregation (B) or violence (C). They also do not mention other types of social change (A). Choice (D) is the most reasonable answer and would be a sentiment shared by every civil rights activist of the era.

36. **C** According to Dubois's statements, he does "accept the Atlanta Compromise" in its broadest interpretation" (A) and does "not expect that the free right to vote, to enjoy civic rights, and to be educated, will come in a moment" (B). Choice (D) is something with which Washington would disagree, not Dubois.

Questions 37–39

The map portrays a number of territorial acquisitions, including the Louisiana Purchase, Florida, Oregon Territory, and the lands ceded by Mexico after the Mexican-American War.

37. **C** The Mexican-American War officially began after Mexican troops crossed the Rio Grande into disputed territory, and President James K. Polk secured a declaration of war. While the progression of the war was neither as easy nor as swift (the war dragged on for more than a year and a half) as Polk had hoped, its outcome was everything that he had desired. With the Treaty of Guadalupe-Hidalgo (1848), Mexico acknowledged the Rio Grande as the southern border of Texas and ceded the territories of California and New Mexico to the United States.

38. **B** Generally, Westerners supported territorial expansion and subscribed to the notion of Manifest Destiny, which held that it was America's destiny to expand beyond its current boundaries across the North American continent.

39. **D** These new territories increased the tension between free and slave states in the populace and in Congress. Even as the Mexican-American War was being fought, representatives from the North and the South began disputing how this new territory would be organized, slave or free. The Homestead Act (A) did not occur until after the Civil War and was not broadly controversial. Choices (B) and (C) were not concerns during the time periods depicted on the map.

Questions 40–41

In this excerpt, Thoreau explicitly advocates the nonpayment of taxes. Specifically, Thoreau protested the Mexican-American War by failing to pay a small poll tax and was subsequently jailed for his actions. The excerpt from Bronson Alcott's *Journals* demonstrates that Thoreau's actions were inspiring to other intellectuals of his time.

40. **C** Henry David Thoreau pioneered the practice of civil disobedience—that is, nonviolent resistance of authorities who enforce unjust laws. Although he was a transcendentalist (D), a movement associated with The Second Great Awakening (B), this excerpt is focused on political action, not spirituality.

41. **B** Thoreau advocated nonviolent resistance of authorities who enforce unjust laws (civil disobedience). This philosophy inspired activists like Martin Luther King, Jr. and formed the basis for many of the tactics of the Civil Rights movement.

Questions 42–43

The conservation movement came to prominence during the Progressive Era. While some conservationists, such as John Muir, sought to preserve nature on idealistic grounds, believing that a minimum of human interference with natural resources was always preferable, some conservationists took a more pragmatic approach, believing that conservation of resources was necessary in order to ensure the continued use of those resources by humans.

42. **A** Choosing the best answer is a matter of recognizing that the excerpt was written in 1912 (well before the growth of suburban developments (C)) and is by a commission in Massachusetts, far from the Dust Bowl (B) or buffalo (D).

43. **A** President Theodore Roosevelt was an environmentalist. He was instrumental in the establishment of the National Park system and he advocated for federal management of natural resources through the National Conservation Commission.

Questions 44–46

In Garry's view, conservatism was "marginalized" from the Great Depression to the 1970s, overshadowed by the New Deal, Great Society, and 1960s countercultural revolution. Conservative ideas survived through "dogged perseverance—a story of unrelenting commitment to a set of ideals rooted in three centuries of American history."

44. **D** Barry Goldwater (A) was a conservative presidential candidate in 1964. His loss to Lyndon Johnson (Democrat) could certainly support Garry's argument that conservatives were the underdogs for 50 years. Conservatives would have opposed Great Society programs (B) designed to raise taxes and spend money on poverty programs. Choice (C) is a tricky answer, but notice that Garry acknowledges the "strength" of conservatism in "current times." He mentions that "conservatism was seen as a permanent minority philosophy in America" "as recently as the late 1970s," implying that the 1980s may have reversed the trend. Choice (D) is the best answer, since the fall of the Berlin Wall is less relevant to American conservatism than the election of a president.

45. **A** Social conservatives care deeply about traditional family values. They do not usually blame liberals for needless wars (B) or promote government programs targeted to racial or social groups (C), (D).

46. **D** Christian evangelicals are often conservatives who focus their political energies on social issues regarding traditional family values. Possibly the most divisive issue since the 1970s has been the national legalization of abortion in all 50 states following the *Roe v. Wade* Supreme Court decision. Christian evangelicals are less focused on spending issues (A) than are secular conservatives and they have not been vocally opposed to most wars (C). Tax cuts (B) would not be opposed by most Christian evangelicals.

Questions 47–49

In 1787, our newly independent nation convened a Constitutional Convention during which the U.S. Constitution, the foundation for the government of the United States, was written. The Constitution was ratified and passed in 1788, the date in which both of the excerpts were written. Griffin's letter helps to establish that there was some wrangling and uncertainty regarding the various states and whether they would ratify.

47. **B**   The letter from Griffin lists the states that had yet to ratify the Constitution. Madison's letter confirms that the "Convention" had convened and that there were "amendments" to the document. Both speakers are referring to the states about to ratify.

48. **A**   Eliminate (B) and (C), since they occur in the wrong time period. George Washington's presidency (D) was not controversial. The degree to which states and the federal government would share power is known as federalism (A) and was the most controversial issue of this time period.

49. **B**   Federalists supported a strong central government, while Jeffersonian anti-Federalists were suspicious of such a government. Jefferson's party was known as the Democratic-Republicans.

Questions 50–52

Directly following the French and Indian War, George Grenville was appointed Prime Minister of the colonies. He sought tighter control over the American Colonies in order to raise revenues for Great Britain. In addition to stricter enforcement of existing trade laws, Grenville passed other unpopular laws. The Sugar Act (also known as the Revenue Act), which placed new duties on certain foreign goods (not just sugar), basically forced the colonies to conduct all trade through England. Although the Sugar Act resembled the Navigation Acts, by which the colonists had long abided, the fact that it was explicitly designed to raise revenue upset the colonists, who felt as if the mother country was trying to take advantage of them. Colonial legislatures sent petitions to Parliament, arguing that the act would hurt trade for Britain as well as the colonies and that the colonists had not consented to the act's passage. Grenville ignored the colonists' pleas as he proceeded with his plans to increase Britain's revenue.

50. **B**   The excerpt mentions "improving the revenue of this kingdom," "that a revenue be raised…for defraying…expenses." So, raising money was the primary purpose of the Sugar Act.

51. **B**   Laws such as the Sugar Act contributed to colonial unrest, since it reinforced the notion that the colonists were victims of "taxation without representation." Choice (A) may have looked tempting, but this was actually true of the Molasses Act. The Sugar Act was indeed enforced. France (C) would not have been affected by the Sugar Act, and (D) was true of the Tea Act, not the Sugar Act.

52. **A**   The French and Indian war had been enormously expensive for the British, and they felt that the American colonists did not share equally the burden of the war costs. This led to a cascade of Acts, such as the Sugar Act, designed to raise revenue for the Mother Country.

Questions 53–55

The decade following World War II brought general affluence and an improved standard of living for most Americans. The excerpt by James Patterson points out that there was a relatively low level of income inequality in America in the 1950s and 1960s compared to the soaring wealth of the rich in the 1920s and the booming economy of the 1980s and 1990s.

53. **B** A national minimum wage (A) would ensure that even the lowest-paid workers in America earn an income beyond a set threshold. The creation of the Securities and Exchange Commission (C) helped to regulate Wall Street, thus reining in potential corruption at the top. The creation of the Federal Housing Authority (FHA) (D) helped low- and middle-income Americans to more easily purchase a home. The desegregation of the military (B) would have virtually no impact on income inequality.

54. **C** This is entirely a test of your knowledge of the era. After World War II, the Civil Rights Movement (A) experienced some notable victories (*Brown vs. Board of Education,* the Civil Rights Act, etc.). Immigration (B) began to increase and more women joined the workforce (D). Choice (C) is the best answer, since the proliferation of the automobile and reliable jobs encouraged many Americans to live in the suburbs.

55. **B** When Lyndon B. Johnson assumed the presidency, he outlined ambitious goals for the nation, arguing that government should play a greater role in people's lives. He called his vision the Great Society, promising a country in which poverty, disease, and lack of education, could and should be eliminated. His most important legislation was the Economic Opportunity Act (1964), which was billed as "The War on Poverty."

SECTION I, PART B: SHORT-ANSWER QUESTIONS

Question 1

The Kansas-Nebraska Act helped set the stage for one of the first violent confrontations stemming from the slavery issue. Because the fate of each locality in the Kansas-Nebraska Act hinged on a popular vote, hundreds of pro-slavery and antislavery activists poured into the territories in hopes of swaying the outcome of the referendum. Often armed and ready to fight, Kansas became a literal battleground between pro-slavery and antislavery factions. "Bleeding Kansas," as the region came to be known, was the site of several prominent attacks on opposing groups' settlements. The most famous incident was John Brown's raid, where Brown, a radical slavery opponent, led a group that murdered pro-slavery settlers. Later John Brown led a separate raid on the U.S. arsenal at Harper's Ferry (then in the state of Virginia) hoping to seize a cache of weapons with which to arm a slave uprising. Brown's raid failed and Brown himself was captured by a detachment of Marines under the command of then Col. Robert E. Lee, tried for treason, and hanged.

Many Republicans, such as Abraham Lincoln, sought to distance themselves from the actions of John Brown. In the excerpt cited, Lincoln denies that Brown's efforts were successful or supported by the slaves themselves. He calls his actions "absurd" and merely leading to Brown's own demise.

Many committed abolitionists, on the other hand, maintained that Brown's actions were the natural result of the moral desperation brought on by the continuation of slavery, and praised Brown as a kind of martyr for the cause of abolition. In Emerson's speech, he labels Brown an "idealist" who saw the necessity of action. Emerson refers to the "forms" or social and political institutions which perpetuated slavery, contrasted with the "facts" of moral reality.

a) An effective answer to part (a) will highlight differences between Lincoln's and Emerson's positions on John Brown including

- Whether he was misguided or heroic
- Whether or not he accomplished anything useful
- Whether or not his actions were destined for failure
- Whether Brown was egocentric or self-sacrificing
- Whether or not violence is effective in promoting a just cause

b) Lincoln's view is that John Brown was misguided and ineffective and an example of a revolutionary who thought too highly of his own place in history, thus leading to his own demise. This question is asking for an event or development to support his view. You could have used one of the following, being sure to highlight the unsuccessful aspects of these events:

- Bacon's Rebellion
- Stono Rebellion
- Nat Turner's Rebellion
- The seizure of *La Amistad*
- Bleeding Kansas

c) Emerson's view is that John Brown was an idealist whose actions were noble and motivated by the knowledge of truth. This question is asking for an event or development to support his view. You could have used one of the following, or even events from the part (b) list, being sure to highlight the successful or idealistic aspects of these events:

- 1733 slave insurrection on St. John, Virgin Islands
- Haitian Revolution
- Civil War

Question 2

In Image 1, we see a family of seven living in a very small room that contains one bed, a crib, and shabby furnishings. The family is dressed in such a manner that we would assume they are low-paid workers, perhaps in a factory. "Tenements" were city apartments for the poor, and in 1910 there would have been little to no government assistance for the poor. Child labor was common in such communities and this family might be recent immigrants.

In Image 2, we see a lavishly appointed bedroom, typical of that of a wealthy family in the Gilded Age. According to the caption, this is the bedroom of the wife of A.T. Stewart, owner of a successful department store in New York City in the late 1800s. Notice that her bedroom is larger than the tenement family's one room, so we can infer that her house is massive in comparison to their dwelling. The two pictures illustrate the great disparities in wealth between the rich and the poor during the height of the Industrial Revolution.

a) Your answer to this question should mention several of the following:

- A move away from agricultural work and rural living to urban factory work
- A large increase in unskilled and semi-literate workers, largely immigrants
- Child labor
- A large number of female workers, especially in textile mills
- Laissez-faire economics
- Social Darwinism
- Virtually no government safety net for the poor (welfare benefits, food stamps, subsidized housing, Medicaid, etc.)
- Little workplace safety regulations
- The rise of labor unions

b) Your answer to this question should mention several of the following:

- The flowering of industry after the Civil War
- "Robber barons"/captains of industry: Carnegie, Rockefeller, Vanderbilt, etc.
- Increased mechanization of industry and assembly-line production leading to the need for large numbers of factory workers
- Low federal income tax rates, encouraging the accumulation of wealth at the top of society
- Laissez-faire economics
- Social Darwinism
- The Gospel of Wealth
- Intermarriage within wealthy families, encouraging a consolidation of wealth
- Inexpensive labor, which allowed for lavish home building among the wealthy

c) Your answer to this question may have focused on one of the following:

- Rise of the Progressive Party
- Muckraking journalism: McClure's magazine, Ida M. Tarbell's *The History of the Standard Oil Company*, Upton Sinclair's *The Jungle*, Jacob Riis's *How the Other Half Lives*
- The Sherman Antitrust Act of 1890 and Clayton Antitrust Act
- Settlement houses (Jane Addams's Hull House in Chicago)
- Interstate Commerce Act of 1887
- The growth of labor unions: Knights of Labor; the American Federation of Labor (AFL), led by Samuel Gompers; and the Industrial Workers of the World (IWW), referred to as "Wobblies," a militant anti-capitalist group
- Union strikes
- State Workmen's Compensation laws
- Child labor laws
- New Deal reforms: regulation of banks, Social Security, government work programs

Question 3

a) Territorial expansion increased the tension between free and slave states in Congress. Even as the Mexican-American War was being fought, representatives from the North and the South began disputing how this new territory would be organized, slave or free. The Gold Rush forced the decision; in 1849, California petitioned Congress for admittance into the Union as a free state. President Zachary Taylor, a Whig, supported admittance. Serious talk of secession circulated among Southerners.

b) and c) Henry Clay, by then an elder statesman, proposed a series of resolutions in hopes of preserving the free/slave state balance and avert the impending threat of Southern secession. Congressional squabbling followed, but included a number of notable Senate floor speeches, The Great Debate, by Clay, Daniel Webster, and John C. Calhoun. With the help of Stephen Douglas, a senator from Illinois, a deal that became known as the Compromise of 1850 was struck. The compromise admitted California as a free state and maintained Texas as a slave state. The rest of the territory in question was divided at the 37th parallel into New Mexico and Utah. These two territories would be "unrestricted"—each locality would decide its own status. The compromise also abolished the slave trade in the District of Columbia.

Henry Clay

- Whig Senator from Kentucky
- Drafted and formally proposed the Compromise of 1850
- Helped to clarify the final boundaries of Texas
- Originally proposed banning slavery in the entire Mexican Cession
- Wanted a stringent Fugitive Slave Act

John Calhoun

- Democrat Senator from South Carolina
- Defender of slavery
- Opposed the Compromise of 1850
- Advocate for states' rights and secession
- Spurred notion of popular sovereignty for Mexican Cession territories

Daniel Webster

- Whig Senator from Massachusetts
- Supported the Compromise in order to preserve the Union and avert Civil War
- In the *Seventh of March* speech, characterized himself "not as a Massachusetts man, nor as a Northern man, but as an American…."
- Risked offending his abolitionist voter base by accepting the Compromise

Question 4

This question calls for a brief overview of the history of the Vietnam War, along with a discussion of some of its impacts on American society.

a) Although the Vietnam War is at its core a story of anticommunists versus communists—not an especially unique one in the annals of Cold War geopolitics—the full narrative is much more complicated. The war was waged between the communist North Vietnamese, with support from their Chinese, Soviet, and Viet Cong (a South Vietnamese communist guerilla group) allies, and the government of South Vietnam, supported by its primary ally, the United States. The United States justified its involvement in Vietnam as part of a larger containment strategy, the crux of which was to stop the expansion of communism on a state-by-state basis, wherever revolutionary elements pursued the establishment of communist rule. This containment doctrine had at its intellectual heart domino theory, which held that if one country in a region fell to communism, all of the nations in that region were then put at risk of falling. The U.S. military presence in Vietnam increased dramatically following the 1964 Gulf of Tonkin incident. Be sure to mention that:

- Unlike the Korean War, U.S. casualty rates were much higher.
- Depending on your point of view, you could argue that the failures of the Vietnam War created more caution in American interventionism (it was not as smooth-sailing as the Korean War) OR that it ended interventionism on grounds of containment (no major conflicts over communism after 1975).

b) and c) Effective answers to parts (b) and (c) should mention some of the following:

- Protest of the draft, draft-dodging, emigrations to Canada
- Military draft not used since the Vietnam War
- Intense war protests (i.e., Kent State Massacre)
- The Pentagon Papers
- First war to be televised
- Nixon's policy of détente

SECTION II, QUESTION 1: THE DOCUMENT-BASED QUESTION

The document-based question begins with a mandatory 15-minute reading period. During these 15 minutes, you should (1) come up with some information not included in the given documents (your outside knowledge) to include in your essay, (2) get an overview of what each document means, (3) decide what opinion you are going to argue, and (4) write an outline of your essay.

The first thing you will be inclined to do, after reading the question, is to look at the documents. Resist that temptation. Instead, the first thing you should do is brainstorm for several minutes about what the question is asking of you. Try to list everything you remember about the Great Migrations. This list will serve as your reference to the outside information you must provide in order to earn a top grade.

Then, and only then, read over the documents. As you read them, take notes in the margins and underline those passages that you are certain you are going to refer to in your essay. If a document helps you remember a piece of outside information, add that information to your brainstorming list. If you cannot make sense of a document, don't worry. You may omit mention of <u>one</u> of the documents and still score well on the DBQ.

Here is what you need to look for in each document to get the most out of it:

- The author
- The date
- The audience (for whom was the document intended?)
- The significance

Remember: You are being asked to write 50 percent document interpretation and 50 percent outside information. Don't get so lost in the documents that you forget to bring in outside information. Readers will not be able to give you a high score unless you have both! What readers really don't like is a laundry list of documents: that is, a paper in which the student merely goes through the documents, explaining each one. Those students are often the ones who forget to bring in outside information, because they are so focused on going through the documents.

So, what is this DBQ all about?

This DBQ can be seen in three parts: (1) What motivated the Great Migrations? (2) What were the outcomes of the Great Migrations? And (3) How have the reasons for African American migration changed over time? For the first part, discuss slavery in the South, the end of the Civil War, Jim Crow laws, industrialization in the North, and urbanization. For the second part, discuss economic growth, the establishment of large African American communities in Northern cities, and subsequent discrimination in housing ordinances, hiring practices, etc.

In the final part of the essay, use Documents 5 and 6 to demonstrate that the migration patterns of African Americans have recently shifted from "South to North" to "North to South." Some African Americans are seeking to return to the home of their ancestors and are responding, in part, to the recent manufacturing boom and growth of suburbs in Southern cities. This net southern migration is, in large part, supported by increased opportunities for those with higher education and continued systemic racism presenting difficulties for African Americans in the workplace in both the North and South.

The Documents

In **Document 1,** Lemann establishes that the Great Migration of African Americans was significant on a scale that shadows immigration to the United States during this same period. Historians often distinguish between two periods of the Great Migration: the First Great Migration from the end of World War I up to the Great Depression, which involved African Americans moving from Southern rural areas to northern industrial cities, and a Second Great Migration after World War II, which brought African Americans not only to the north, but also to the West. The motivations for migration were largely economic, but also social: the attitudes of those in the North were thought to be less racist than those in the South.

Document 2 shows that the Second Great Migration led to decreasing numbers of African Americans in Southern cities such as Jacksonville, Nashville, and Birmingham, while many Northern and Western cities experienced a sharp increase in African Americans. It is important to consider the social and economic issues faced by the United States during these decades in order to find underlying causes of the Second Great Migration. For one, the 1940s saw an increase in manufacturing due to the American entrance into World War II. The postwar economic boon came with an increase in manufacturing jobs, offering further economic incentives for migration. Also consider the persistence of Jim Crow Era discrimination in the South, particularly before the 1954 *Brown v. Board of Education* case and the 1964 Civil Rights Act.

Document 3 establishes that not all Northern cities, in this case Detroit, welcomed African Americans with open arms. Two pieces of Lyndon Johnson's Great Society legislation connect to this image: the development of the department of Housing and Urban Development and the Housing Rights Act. The department of Housing and Urban Development provided safe, decent housing for low-income Americans. Further, the Housing Rights Act prohibited discrimination in home sales and rentals—the kind of discrimination seen in the image. Some low-income African American migrants moved into government-sponsored housing projects, while others were free to purchase or rent housing anywhere they could afford. This migration led some whites to fear the demographic changes in their city and brought up decidedly ugly intimidation techniques.

Document 4 shows the increase in population in Chicago over a 150-year time period. A careful study of the racial numbers demonstrates that the numbers of African Americans increased by over 300% after World War II with a slight decrease or stabilization during the 1980s. Note the dramatic jumps. By 1950, following World War II's industrial boon, the African American population in Chicago increased by over 5%. Over the next decade, that percentage increased by another 10% as the U.S. manufacturing continued to grow following the war. Numbers of whites in Chicago declined noticeably during this same time period, likely due to "white flight."

Document 5 discussed the change in migration patterns in metro areas from a northward trend during and shortly after the Civil Rights Movement of the 1960s to a more recent southward trend due to systemic racism and changes in job opportunities in the North during the late 1970s. This document is helpful in understanding the motivation for the shift in migration towards the southward trend we see today.

Document 6 confirms that the Second Great Migration meant significant increases in the population of African Americans in Northern and Western states, while the trend in the 1990s was toward increases in Southern states. There are many factors at play, including manufacturing jobs disappearing, business moving to the "Sun Belt," deterioration of urban neighborhoods, and greater opportunities in the workplace for those with higher education in the South.

Outside Information

We have already discussed much more than you could possibly include in a 45-minute essay. Do not worry. You will not be expected to mention everything or even most of what we have covered in the section above. You will, however, be expected to include some outside information—that is, information not mentioned directly in the documents.

Here is some outside information you might have used in your essay. The information is divided into two groups: general concepts and specific events.

General Concepts

- In American history, the movement of African Americans has been both about survival and opportunity. The Great Migration of the early 20th century saw an escape from a violent South, as well as the search for decent industrial jobs in the North. What we want to consider in this essay is the extent to which African Americans found either the security or economic opportunity promised in the North.
- The migration of African Americans brought with it competition for jobs. Working-class whites, including immigrants, often showed intolerance toward African Americans due to this competition. The dream of a more tolerant North with economic opportunities did not necessarily pan out for all African American migrants.
- One constant from life in the South for African Americans was religious instructions. In the South, Christian churches provided a social infrastructure and organizing vehicle in African American communities. Those institutions were retained following the move to northern cities, often in ad hoc "store-front" churches. Other African Americans found social and economic support in a renewed interest in Islam. The Nation of Islam, for instance, maintained a focus on personal decorum and responsibility in the black community.
- As occurred in the early days of Reconstruction, African American political representation once again became a reality. In cities that became increasingly African American, some of the first black mayors were elected. The phenomenon of "white flight" left a primarily black voting bloc in many regions. Nonetheless, the black franchise was still not absolute, particularly before the 24th Amendment and the 1965 Voting Rights Act.
- The hope that African American migrants would escape the discrimination and bigotry of the South by moving to the North was dashed by housing discrimination, voter intimidation, job discrimination, and random acts of violence.

Specific Events

- You should be familiar with the Great Migration. Beginning at the start of the First World War, the Great Migration saw a swell of African American migrants moving to northern cities until the Great Depression, though some historians document the event as lasting through the 1960s (in reality, the migration appears to have occurred in a couple waves). While less than 10% of African Americans lived in the North in the first decade of the 20th century, the onset of World War I saw migrants moving to northern cities for manufacturing job opportunities created by the war effort.
- The Harlem Renaissance was a flowering of black culture and art. Located in New York City, writers and artists such as Langston Hughes, Zora Neale Hurston, and Louis Armstrong created an artistic "rebirth" that coincided with the Great Migration. The hope was that this movement would create social and economic opportunities for northern blacks. The reality was more complex—Duke Ellington, star musician on the stage of the Cotton Club, was not allowed to sit in the audience due to the club's policy of racial discrimination.

- The landmark case *Brown v. Board of Education* prohibited discrimination in school, presumably creating equal opportunities for children of all races. The implementation of this ruling caused much difficulty, with some schools openly defying the Court ruling in the South. In the North, school integration was promoted through a process known as "bussing," allowing students in the inner city to attend schools in white neighborhoods. This program was met with resistance in white communities, including a riot in Boston in the 1970s.

- The Civil Rights Acts (1964, 1965, and 1968) created a *de jure* equality for African Americans. No longer would Jim Crow laws stand in the way of a person's access to public accommodations. More significant to northern blacks, who were less likely to face Jim Crow laws, was the 1968 legislation that prohibited housing discrimination.

- In response to integrated schools and the new housing equality, whites left cities for the suburbs in a phenomenon sociologists call white flight. This created a de facto segregation in schools and neighborhoods and also affected property values.

- By the 1960s, African Americans continued to face poverty at disproportional rates. The plans of Lyndon Johnson's Great Society attempted to combat poverty and create opportunity. Some of these programs included the Economic Opportunity Act, Head Start, Upward Bound, Job Corps, VISTA, and the Department of Housing and Urban Development.

- Black nationalism and black pride movements saw urban African Americans look to provide for their community through education, food programs, healthcare, and dozens of initiatives carried out by the Black Panthers.

Choosing a Side

The first thing you want to do is to decide what kind of a statement you are going to make. You have already brainstormed all your outside information, made some notes or a quick outline, and decided where to plug in the documents. Because there is no right way to answer this, and many ways to make your argument, here are some positions you might want to argue.

- Since the end of the Civil War, African Americans have always been more mobile than whites, tending to follow economic opportunities and seeking homes with others like them.

- African American migration in the past 20 years represents a radical departure from the migrations of the 20th century, since African Americans are moving from North to South. According to Document 5, they tend to be better educated than their migrant predecessors. We can infer that this shift may represent a different perception regarding racism and geography.

- Northern economies have become hostile to the needs of African Americans (high levels of unemployment, high cost of living, urban racial tensions), while the South is now more embracing (a growth in manufacturing, historically black communities and colleges, less disparity in the quality of public schools).

Planning Your Essay

Unless you read extremely quickly, you probably won't have time to write a detailed outline for your essay during the 15-minute reading period. However, it is worth taking several minutes to jot down a loose structure of your essay, because it will actually save you time when you write. First, decide on your thesis and write it down in the test booklet. Then, take a few minutes to brainstorm all the points you might put in your essay. Choose the strongest points and number them in the order you plan to present them. Lastly, note which documents and outside information you plan to use in conjunction with each point. If you organize before you write, the actual writing process will go much more smoothly. More important, you will not write yourself into a corner, and suddenly find yourself making a point you cannot support or heading toward a weak conclusion (or worse still, no conclusion at all).

What You Should Have Discussed

Regardless of which thesis you choose, your essay should discuss all of the following:

- Since the prompt asks you to analyze "change and continuity," you should note that the regions of the country affected by the Great Migration have remained fairly constant: the urban Northeast, Great Lakes region, and California.
- The reasons for migration have always revolved around economic and social concerns.
- The "change" has been in the direction of migration: only recently have African Americans been moving South instead of North.
- Document 5 suggests that the new migrants are better educated and placed within the economy compared with their sharecropping ancestors.
- Regardless of time period or motivation, African Americans have tended to migrate to certain areas rather than disbursing evenly throughout the country (no major changes in parts of the rural Midwest, Plains, Rocky Mountains, Northern New England, Alaska).
- Racial tensions are highest in areas affected by migration.
- Migration slowed after the 1960s.

SECTION II: THE LONG ESSAY QUESTION

Your task here is to choose ONE of the prompts and present a historically defensible thesis backed up with relevant evidence. For each of the prompts, your thesis is likely to either make the case that the Seven Years' War did or did not contribute to the Revolution, that the Mexican-American War did or did not contribute to the Civil War, OR that World War I did or did not contribute to the Red Scare. Saying that these events *did* contribute to their respective wars is likely to be the easier position for most students taking this test, although it would be possible to qualify this position with relevant exceptions.

Question 2

If your thesis maintains that the Seven Years' War *did* largely contribute to the Revolution, you may have mentioned some of the following:

- British debt following the Seven Years' War directly led to heavier taxation of the colonies (e.g., Sugar Act, Stamp Act).
- The heavier taxation that followed the Seven Years' War affected the wealthy, elite colonists who later provided the structure and organization to launch the Revolution. The Founding Fathers were plantation owners and merchants whose interests were directly tied to the changes wrought by the Seven Years' War.
- The Albany Plan of Union proved to colonists that they were capable of organizing for a common cause.
- The Proclamation of 1763 was issued after Britain's victory at the Seven Years' War. It forbade all settlement west of the Appalachian Mountains. Any previously issued land grants were now worthless, thus angering American colonists and leading to a spirit of revolution.

- Before the Seven Years' War, colonists were largely self-sufficient, running their own affairs through local governments and militias. After the War, the British took a more active role in governing and policing the colonies, leading to such incidents as the Boston Massacre, the revocation of the charter of Massachusetts, and quartering of soldiers. This led to colonial discontent and eventual revolution.
- France may have been more inclined to help the colonists during the Revolution as revenge for its prior losses during the Seven Years' War.
- Despite its victory, Britain was weakened financially by the War, possibly leading to an increased boldness on the part of colonists who saw Britain as vulnerable.

If your thesis maintains that the Seven Years' War *did not* contribute much to the start of the Revolution, you may have mentioned some of the following:

- Life did not change significantly for the masses of poor and middle-class colonists who later went on to form the backbone of the Continental Army. Especially those living in Southern colonies would have been indifferent to the effects of the Seven Years' War.
- Taxation and regulation of trade existed before the Seven Years' War.
- It was really the shift from Salutary Neglect to tighter control that prompted independence, not the Seven Years' War itself.
- The true impetus for revolution was philosophical: republicanism, natural rights, the Enlightenment, Hobbes, Locke, perhaps even the First Great Awakening.
- Mercantilism had become unduly burdensome and had existed long before the Seven Years' War.
- Colonists *were* largely British, thus culturally tied to the Motherland, and saw themselves as dependent on Britain economically.
- The Seven Years' War demonstrated to colonists that they needed the protection of a strong military power.
- There were always Loyalists who resisted the notion of pursuing independence from the Crown. The Seven Years' War had no effect on the sentiments of those disinclined to the Revolution.

Question 3

If your thesis maintains that the Mexican-American War *did* do much to launch the Civil War, you may have mentioned some of the following:

- The lands acquired under the Mexican Cession were fertile and viable for cotton production, thus leading to the possible need for slave labor.
- The Civil War was inextricably linked to debates about slavery. The Mexican-American War gave the United States access and control to new territories that would later seek statehood. Whether these territories and states would have legal slavery became the most hotly debated issue in Congress at this time.
- "Popular sovereignty" was cited by many as the easiest way to settle the free-state/slave-state conundrum. Most dramatically in the case of the Kansas-Nebraska Act, popular sovereignty tacitly assumed the rights of particular localities to determine their own destinies, thus contributing to notions of secession on the part of disgruntled Southern states.
- Southern Democrats had explicitly supported the War for the express purpose of expanding slavery (a jab in the eye to Northern Whigs).

If your thesis maintains that the Mexican-American War *did not* contribute significantly to the Civil War, you may have mentioned some of the following:

- The slave-state/free-state debate existed long before the Mexican-American War, at least as far back as the Missouri Compromise.
- The Compromise of 1850 was, in fact, "the straw that broke the [Southern] camel's back," not the Mexican-American War. In other words, it was the way the Mexican Cession was handled that enhanced tensions between North and South, not the War itself.
- Slavery was already a highly controversial issue well before the Mexican-American War. William Lloyd Garrison published the "The Liberator" as early as 1831.
- The Gag Rule prevented Congress from settling the issue of slavery by legislative (peaceful) means.
- Fugitive slave laws and *Dred Scott v. Sandford* did more to heighten tensions over slavery than merely the acquisition of new territories.
- The Civil War also revolved around issues of states' rights and the uses of nullification, issues that reared their heads under President Andrew Jackson and were unconnected to slavery per se.

About the Structure of Your Essay

As you compose your essay, you want to stay focused on cause and effect. Therefore, the analysis of the earlier event has to come back to your claim about whether or not that event was a factor leading to the latter event. An effective way to do this would be to include a component from each event in a particular body paragraph and flesh out the link (or lack thereof) between the two. Remember you are not just listing facts but also directly addressing the cause-and-effect question.

Question 4

Your task in this essay is an analysis of both World War I and the Red Scare, a frenzied time in which government officials searched for Communists within the United States, in order to establish the connection between the two. Due to the contemporaneous nature of the time period (U.S. involvement in World War I lasted from 1917 until 1918 and the first Red Scare lasted from 1917 until 1920), the connections may seem obvious. However, you need to be careful to not just list events that may have happened concurrently. Rather, you should establish a link between the two to best highlight the cause-and-effect relationship. World War I, which the United States entered reluctantly several years after Europe commenced fighting, not only created a wave of anti-German hysteria in the United States, but also fears of Communism. Russia, after all, had withdrawn from the war due to the chaotic communist revolution happening on its home front.

Begin your essay with a short overview of the two events mentioned in the prompt. Make sure that you quickly move the discussion into a clear claim about the relationship between the First World War and the first Red Scare. You can, of course, claim that the wheels of the Red Scare were set in motion before World War I began, but you will find rich opportunities for connections between the two events, as well.

Things you may want to mention about World War I:

- Isolationist foreign policy characterized the Wilson Administration.
- German submarine attacks killed American citizens, fomenting an anti-German sentiment in the United States.
- Eugene Debs was imprisoned for his opposition to the war. His arrest highlights the connection between Socialist political activity and opposition to the war.
- The Espionage Act prevented anyone from using the U.S. mail system to interfere with the war

effort or with the draft. The act helped stoke a suspicion that would become a normal part of American life during the Red Scare.

- The Sedition Act furthered that suspicion by making it illegal to try to prevent the sale of war bonds or to speak disparagingly of the government, the flag, the military, or the Constitution.
- *Schenck v. United States* was a Supreme Court case that challenged the constitutionality of the Espionage Act. Schenck was a prominent socialist and ardent critic of American capitalism, who was arrested and convicted when he printed and mailed leaflets urging men to resist the draft. The Court upheld the Espionage Act.

Give yourself extra points for mentioning the following:

- The government helped create this frenzied atmosphere through its wartime propaganda arm, the Committee on Public Information. Germans were portrayed as bloodthirsty and decidedly anti-American.
- Anti-German sentiment progressed during the war. Violence persisted against German immigrants. Schools largely stopped teaching the German language, while streets with German names changed their signs. Even innocuous references to German culture were rejected: sauerkraut became "liberty cabbage."

Things you might want to mention about the Red Scare:

- One fear of communism in the United States was how it would impact the war effort: the Russian Revolution forced the nation's withdrawal from World War I in order to deal with matters on the home front.
- The Bolshevik control of Russia created tensions among U.S. government officials about what would happen in the United States if a popular Communist movement gained steam.
- Federal and local governments held deep suspicions against union activities. Closely associated with Marxist ideas, organizations of laborers also fell victim due to xenophobia: many members were German and Russian. This period saw business assume greater power, while unions lost power.
- The Federal Bureau of Investigation, headed by J. Edgar Hoover, was created to keep radicals at bay.
- The Palmer Raids saw the government and its agents raid union halls, pool halls, social clubs, and residences. Over 10,000 union members were arrested in over 30 cities, but very few weapons or bombs were found. About 500 immigrants were eventually deported at the conclusion of the Palmer Raids.

Give yourself extra points for mentioning the following:

- The Progressive Party, a one-time advocate for unions, had begun to split between left wing and moderates over the war and the Red Scare.
- Sacco and Vanzetti's sham trial stands as an illustration of the anti-immigrant and anti-union sentiment of the late 1910s and early 1920s. The Red Scare, like the anti-German sentiment during World War I, was kept alive through widespread xenophobia.
- The Emergency Quota Act of 1924 also shows the influence of xenophobia on federal policy. The quotas discriminated against the "new immigrants" who came from Southern and Eastern Europe—hotbeds for socialist activity.

About the Structure of Your Essay

The task on this question is to find a cause and effect between two events that happened nearly simultaneously. For your claim, make it clear in your introductory paragraph whether the feelings of World War I led to the Red Scare or the two events happened concurrently due to common factors in each. No matter what you argue, to tackle the body paragraphs, look for undercurrents that were common to both events. There seems to be plenty of opportunity to discuss how xenophobia played into both events. Further, a distrust of Socialists could be the topic of another body paragraph. Be consistently deliberate with your analysis as you explain whether the relationships between the events are parallel occurrences or cause and effect.

Practice Test 4

AP® United States History Exam

SECTION I, PART A: Multiple Choice

DO NOT OPEN THIS BOOKLET UNTIL YOU ARE TOLD TO DO SO.

At a Glance
Time 55 minutes **Number of Questions** 55 **Percent of Total Score** 40% **Writing Instrument** Pencil required

Instructions

Section I, Part A, of this exam contains 55 multiple-choice questions. Fill in only the ovals for numbers 1 through 55 on your answer sheet. Because this section offers only four answer options for each question, do not mark the (E) answer circle for any question.

Indicate all of your answers to the multiple-choice questions on the answer sheet. No credit will be given for anything written in this exam booklet, but you may use the booklet for notes or scratch work. After you have decided which of the suggested answers is best, completely fill in the corresponding oval on the answer sheet. Give only one answer to each question. If you change an answer, be sure that the previous mark is erased completely. Here is a sample question and answer.

Sample Question   Sample Answer

The first president of the United States was   Ⓐ ● Ⓒ Ⓓ
(A) Millard Fillmore
(B) George Washington
(C) Benjamin Franklin
(D) Andrew Jackson

Use your time effectively, working as rapidly as you can without losing accuracy. Do not spend too much time on any one question. Go on to other questions and come back to the ones you have not answered if you have time. It is not expected that everyone will know the answers to all of the multiple-choice questions.

Your total score on the multiple-choice section is based only on the number of questions answered correctly. Points are not deducted for incorrect answers or unanswered questions.

SECTION I, PART B: Short Answer

At a Glance
Time 40 minutes **Number of Questions** 3 **Percent of Total Score** 20% **Writing Instrument** Pen with black or dark blue ink **Questions 1 and 2** Mandatory **Question 3 or 4** Choose One Question

Instructions

For Section I, Part B of this exam, answer Question 1 and Question 2 and **either** Question 3 **or** Question 4. Write your responses in the Section I, Part B: Short-Answer Response booklet. You must write your response to each question on the lined page designated for that response. Each response is expected to fit within its designated page. Fill in the circle on the Section I, Part B: Short-Answer Response booklet indicating whether you answered Question 3 or Question 4. Failure to do so may delay your score.

GO ON TO THE NEXT PAGE.

UNITED STATES HISTORY
SECTION I, Part A
Time—55 minutes
55 Questions

Directions: Each of the questions or incomplete statements below is followed by four suggested answers or completions. Select the one that is best in each case and then blacken the corresponding space on the answer sheet.

Questions 1 - 3 refer to the excerpt below.

"I long to hear that you have declared an independency—and by the way in the new Code of Laws which I suppose it will be necessary for you to make I desire you would Remember the Ladies, and be more generous and favorable to them than your ancestors. Do not put such unlimited power into the hands of the Husbands. Remember all Men would be tyrants if they could. If particular care and attention is not paid to the Ladies we are determined to foment a Rebellion, and will not hold ourselves bound by any Laws in which we have no voice, or Representation."

Abigail Adams, Letter to John Adams, 1776

1. This passage best reflects which of the following issues?

   (A) The pursuit of an Equal Rights Amendment
   (B) Women's access to education
   (C) The American Women's Suffrage Movement
   (D) The disparity of rights afforded to the different genders during the Colonial period

2. According to the excerpt, which event was Abigail Adams most concerned with?

   (A) The Declaratory Act
   (B) The Boston Tea Party
   (C) The creation of a post-Revolution government
   (D) The ratification of the Code of Laws

3. When Abigail Adams notes that she hopes her husband would "be more generous and favorable to them than your ancestors," she is most directly referring to

   (A) the historical subjugation of women
   (B) the loss of rights that women in the colonies experienced
   (C) the high regard her husband's ancestors placed upon women
   (D) the hope that the revolution will include women in the militias

GO ON TO THE NEXT PAGE.

Questions 4 – 6 refer to the illustration below.

Puck Magazine, 1872

4. The cartoon above supports which of the following points of view?

   (A) President Grant plans to lead an armed invasion of the South.
   (B) The southern states must carry the full weight of the Civil War costs.
   (C) The United States government played a role in carpetbagging.
   (D) The Grant Administration plans to confiscate weapons from Southerners.

5. Which of the following legislative acts paved the way for the event depicted in the illustration?

   (A) The Freedmen's Bureau Bill, giving assistance to freed slaves in the Reconstruction South.
   (B) The Morrill Act, offering land grants for the establishment of agricultural colleges.
   (C) The Reconstruction Act, dividing the South into military districts.
   (D) The Enforcement Act, protecting the rights of African Americans to vote and receive equal protection.

6. Supporters of President Grant would respond to the artist of this cartoon by noting which of the following?

   (A) The protection of the rights of freedmen is necessary for a successful Reconstruction.
   (B) Southern Democrats should share equally in the process of Reconstruction.
   (C) The former Confederate states are responsible for their own rebuilding.
   (D) Military Reconstruction is unconstitutional.

GO ON TO THE NEXT PAGE.

Questions 7 – 10 refer to the graph below.

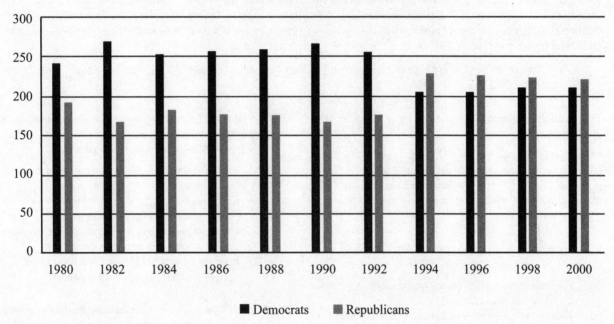

Number of Seats in Congress Won by Each Party
from the 1980 Election to the 2000 Election

■ Democrats   ■ Republicans

7. Which of the following conclusions is most directly supported by the overall trend depicted in the graph?

(A) For the most part, the party of the presidential election winner gained a majority of the seats in Congress.

(B) In Congressional elections, the American electorate tended to favor the party that opposed the president.

(C) Republican congressional dominance continued through much of the late 20th century.

(D) The Contract with America allowed the Democrats to maintain power.

8. The trend in the graph most directly contributed to which of the following developments after 2000?

(A) A sustained budgetary surplus

(B) A powerful check on the power of the executive

(C) Congressional support for neoconservative legislation

(D) A wave of bipartisan cooperation in Congress

9. The pattern depicted in the first half of this graph (pre-1990) was characterized by

(A) dominance of the GOP in federal politics

(B) the need for bipartisanship to pass legislation

(C) close congressional votes due to an evenly split legislature

(D) unchecked Democratic power in the U.S. government

10. Which of the following events highlighted the most dramatic change featured in the graph?

(A) The midterm elections brought about a Republican Congress to balance out the federal government during the presidency of Bill Clinton.

(B) The year of George H.W. Bush's election changed the balance of Congress.

(C) Ronald Reagan enjoyed a long period of his party's electoral success in Congress.

(D) Bill Clinton's reelection coincided with the loss of his party's control over Congress.

GO ON TO THE NEXT PAGE.

Questions 11 - 14 refer to the excerpt below.

"As to conditions in South Carolina, Mr. Hine states his opinion thus: 'In general, I found these were considerably worse than conditions in North Carolina, both as to the age and number of small children employed, though several of the mill towns in North Carolina approached the worst ones in South Carolina….In Chester, South Carolina, an overseer told me frankly that manufacturers all over the South evaded the child labor law by letting youngsters who are under age help older brothers and sisters. The names of the younger ones do not appear on the company books and the pay goes to the older child who is above twelve.'"

Rev. A. E. Seddon, et.al., "Account of Investigations Made in the Cotton Mills of North and South Carolina," 1909

11. The situation presented in the passage above was primarily driven by

(A) strict labor laws
(B) the demands of an agricultural economy
(C) loose enforcement of the Supreme Court's ruling
(D) the increased work opportunities presented by the Industrial Revolution

12. Which of the following trends was typical of labor situations like that in South Carolina?

(A) There were strict limits placed on the number of hours children may work.
(B) Women and children provided cheap labor sources for companies trying to save money.
(C) Employers preferred to hire men.
(D) A dearth of laborers drove up wages.

13. Mr. Hine's reference to "letting youngsters who are under age help older brothers and sisters" most likely reflected which of the following sentiments of the era?

(A) The most productive labor force is often the youngest.
(B) Child labor was a positive social force with measurable benefits for children.
(C) Congress had no power to regulate business that did not participate in interstate commerce.
(D) It was more preferable for children to engage in rigorous labor than it was for women.

14. Which of the following actions contributed the most to reducing the circumstances faced by the children described in this excerpt?

(A) Widespread campaigns spearheaded by the captains of industry
(B) Executive orders from the McKinley administration
(C) Supreme Court decisions of the 1880s and 1890s
(D) Legislative successes at the state and local level during the Progressive movement

GO ON TO THE NEXT PAGE.

Questions 15 - 17 refer to the excerpts below.

"The People of the State of Illinois to all Constables, Sheriffs and Coroners of State, Greeting:

Whereas complaint hath been made before me, one of the justices of the peace within and for the county of Hancock aforesaid, upon the oath of Francis M. Higbee of said county, that Joseph Smith, [et. al.], of said county did on the 10th day of June instant commit a riot at and within the county aforesaid, wherein they, with force and violence broke into the office of the Nauvoo Expositor, and unlawfully and with force burned and destroyed the printing press, type and fixtures of the same, being the property of William Law."

Warrant for the Arrest of Joseph Smith, 1844

"But perhaps the greatest attraction of Mormonism was the promise that each follower would be granted an extraordinarily intimate relationship with God. Joseph [Smith] taught and encouraged his adherents to receive personal communiqués straight from the Lord. Divine revelation formed the bedrock of the religion."

Jon Krakauer, *Under the Banner of Heaven: A Story of Violent Faith,*
(c) 2004, Anchor Books, a Division of Penguin Random House

15. Religious movements such as Mormonism were facilitated by which of the following factors?

    A)   A rejection of individualism
    B)   A resistance to social reforms
    C)   Greater social and geographical mobility
    D)   An embracing of rationalism

16. Joseph Smith's converts would most likely have been drawn from which of the following groups?

    A)   lapsed Catholics from large Eastern cities
    B)   Protestants from Western New York, Pennsylvania, and Ohio
    C)   well-educated atheists from academia
    D)   Massachusetts Puritans seeking freedom from a tyrannical church

17. The events surrounding the issuance of this warrant can best be understood in the context of which larger American trend?

    (A)   Populism
    (B)   Abolition
    (C)   The Second Great Awakening
    (D)   Manifest Destiny

GO ON TO THE NEXT PAGE.

Questions 18 and 19 refer to the image below.

Westward the Course of Empire Takes Its Way, Emanuel Leutze, 1861

18. Which of the following concepts is depicted in the painting?

    (A) Impressment
    (B) Revivalism
    (C) Manifest Destiny
    (D) Transcendentalism

19. Which of the following events had the most significant impact on the image depicted above?

    (A) The Second Great Awakening
    (B) The Underground Railroad
    (C) The Hartford Convention
    (D) The Louisiana Purchase

GO ON TO THE NEXT PAGE.

Questions 20 - 23 refer to the excerpts below.

"The American people can not use a dishonest medium of exchange; it is ours to set the world its example of right and honor. We can not fly from our world duties; it is ours to execute the purpose of a fate that has driven us to be greater than our small intentions. We can not retreat from any soil where Providence has unfurled our banner; it is ours to save that soil for liberty and civilization."

Senator Albert Beveridge, "The March of the Flag," 1898

"We hold that the policy known as imperialism is hostile to liberty and tends toward militarism, an evil from which it has been our glory to be free. We regret that it has become necessary in the land of Washington and Lincoln to reaffirm that all men, of whatever race or color, are entitled to life, liberty, and the pursuit of happiness. We maintain that governments derive their just powers from the consent of the governed. We insist that the subjugation of any people is 'criminal aggression' and open disloyalty to the distinctive principles of our Government."

American Anti-Imperialist League Platform, 1899

20. Which of the following would supporters of Beveridge's assert about the United States as an "example of right and honor"?

(A) Intervention in the Spanish colony of Cuba
(B) Exploitation of the sugar crop in Hawaii
(C) The purchase of Alaska
(D) The Open Door Policy in China

21. In the second excerpt, the American Anti-Imperialist League most consistently criticized imperialism by claiming that it

(A) is unconstitutional
(B) is a waste of military spending
(C) is unjust to make profit from the land resources of a foreign people
(D) denies people in colonized lands access to core American values

22. These arguments from the late 1800s mirror arguments about what other foreign policy issue in American history?

(A) The Vietnam War
(B) World War I
(C) The Monroe Doctrine
(D) The Persian Gulf War

23. In asserting that "we can not retreat from any soil where Providence has unfurled our banner," Albert Beveridge argues that

(A) the United States has a moral obligation to take care of the people in its colonies
(B) American expansion must increase at any cost
(C) military commitments have become so entrenched in the colonies that the United States cannot leave
(D) anti-imperialist groups lack patriotism

GO ON TO THE NEXT PAGE.

Questions 24 - 26 refer to the 1856 illustration below.

FORCING SLAVERY DOWN THE THROAT OF A FREESOILER

24. What event most directly contributed to the issues presented in this image?

(A) The Mexican-American war
(B) The Compromise of 1850
(C) The Kansas-Nebraska Act
(D) The Dred Scott Supreme Court case

25. What were the goals of the Free Soil Party?

(A) To abolish slavery nationwide
(B) To prohibit the spread of slavery in new territories
(C) To provide free homesteads for farmers in the Midwest
(D) To allow voters to determine if slavery would spread to new territories

26. In the decade following the publication of the image, which of the following parties emerged as a viable opposition to the expansion of slavery?

(A) The American Party
(B) The Republican Party
(C) The Populist Party
(D) The Socialist Party

GO ON TO THE NEXT PAGE.

Questions 27 and 28 refer to the excerpt below.

"We meet in the midst of a nation brought to the verge of moral, political, and material ruin. Corruption dominates the ballot-box, the Legislatures, the Congress…. The people are demoralized; The newspapers are largely subsidized or muzzled, public opinion silenced, business prostrated, homes covered with mortgages, labor impoverished…. The fruits of the toil of millions are badly stolen to build up colossal fortunes for a few, unprecedented in the history of mankind; and the possessors of these, in turn, despise the Republic and endanger liberty. From the same prolific womb of governmental injustice we breed the two great classes—tramps and millionaires."

Ignatius Donnelly, Farmer's Alliance Convention, February 1892

27. Donnelly's Farmer's Alliance was most closely aligned with which of the following political parties?

   A) Republican
   B) Populist
   C) Green
   D) Free Soil

28. Those aligned with Donnelly's political views would have been most organized to promote legislation to stop which of the following practices?

   (A) Price gouging in the railroad industry
   (B) The Black Codes of the Reconstruction Era
   (C) Radical demonstrations by labor unions
   (D) The trustbusting of the Progressive Movement

GO ON TO THE NEXT PAGE.

Questions 29 - 31 refer to the map below.

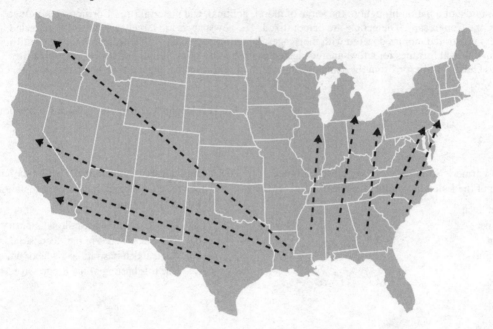

Twentieth Century African American Migration Patterns

29. Which of the following trends contributed most directly to the migrations depicted in the map?

   (A) Deregulation in the manufacturing industry
   (B) The proliferation of Jim Crow Laws
   (C) Supreme Court decisions striking down Civil Rights legislation
   (D) Increased agricultural production in the North

30. The initial stages of the migrations shown in the map were accelerated by

   (A) a drought in the American South
   (B) young men avoiding conscription into World War I
   (C) openings in manufacturing jobs caused by World War I
   (D) educational opportunities in the northern and western states

31. Which of the following situations resulted from the migrations depicted in the map?

   (A) Widespread acceptance of the migrants in their new cities
   (B) Congressional legislation prohibiting such migrations
   (C) Increased racial tensions in northern cities
   (D) Desegregation in the South

GO ON TO THE NEXT PAGE.

Questions 32 and 33 refer to the excerpts below.

Article II

In the cession made by the preceeding article are included the adjacent Islands belonging to Louisiana all public lots and Squares, vacant lands and all public buildings, fortifications, barracks and other edifices which are not private property.—The Archives, papers & documents relative to the domain and Sovereignty of Louisiana and its dependances will be left in the possession of the Commissaries of the United States, and copies will be afterwards given in due form to the Magistrates and Municipal officers of such of the said papers and documents as may be necessary to them.

Article III

The inhabitants of the ceded territory shall be incorporated in the Union of the United States and admitted as soon as possible according to the principles of the federal Constitution to the enjoyment of all these rights, advantages and immunities of citizens of the United States, and in the mean time they shall be maintained and protected in the free enjoyment of their liberty, property and the Religion which they profess.

Treaty between the United States of America and the French Republic, 1802

32. The treaty between the United States and France was primarily driven by

(A) Napoleon's sudden need to divest from the New World
(B) Jefferson's aggressive approach to increasing the land mass of the United States
(C) the threat of war between the two nations
(D) pressure from New England Federalists

33. The document reflects an early incarnation of which concept?

(A) Non-Intercourse
(B) Embargos
(C) Manifest Destiny
(D) The Monroe Doctrine

GO ON TO THE NEXT PAGE.

Questions 34 - 37 refer to the excerpt below.

"...Russian rulers have invariably sensed that their rule was relatively archaic in form, fragile and artificial in its psychological foundation, unable to stand comparison or contact with political systems of Western countries. For this reason they have always feared foreign penetration, feared direct contact between Western world and their own, feared what would happen if Russians learned truth about world without or if foreigners learned truth about world within. And they have learned to seek security only in patient but deadly struggle for total destruction of rival power, never in compacts and compromises with it."

George Kennan, Telegram to the State Department, 1946

34. Kennan's message in the excerpt most directly reflected which of the following developments of the mid-twentieth century?

   (A) A prolonged period of recession
   (B) The United States' participation in proxy wars around the world
   (C) The baby boom
   (D) A Truman-endorsed doctrine of neutrality

35. Which of the following developments best represents a logical extension of the ideas expressed in the excerpt?

   (A) The United States joins the United Nations.
   (B) The United States Congress passes the GI Bill.
   (C) President Eisenhower presents Congress with the Federal Aid Highway Act.
   (D) Foreign aid is given to Greece and Turkey to help rebuild after World War II.

36. The telegram most directly advocates a United States foreign policy that emphasizes

   (A) continued peace talks with the Soviet Union
   (B) preventing the spread of Communism beyond where it already was practiced
   (C) increased trade partnerships with Soviet nations
   (D) aggressive military action taken against the Soviet Union

37. What was one domestic outcome of this increased tension between the United States and the Soviet Union?

   (A) The Second Red Scare
   (B) The creation of the Interstate Highway System
   (C) The de-segregation of the U.S. military
   (D) The rise of a new consumer culture in the United States

GO ON TO THE NEXT PAGE.

Questions 38 - 40 refer to the excerpt below.

"Both of these men, Mr. Hoover and Mr. Roosevelt, came out and said there had to be a decentralization of wealth, but neither one of them did anything about it. But, nevertheless, they recognized the principle. The fact that neither one of them ever did anything about it is their own problem that I am not undertaking to criticize; but had Mr. Hoover carried out what he says ought to be done, he would be retiring from the President's office, very probably, 3 years from now, instead of 1 year ago; and had Mr. Roosevelt proceeded along the lines that he stated were necessary for the decentralization of wealth, he would have gone, my friends, a long way already, and within a few months he would have probably reached a solution of all of the problems that afflict this country."

Senator Huey Long, radio address, 1934

38. Which of the following issues of the period was Long most likely concerned with in the excerpt?

(A) The challenges President Roosevelt will face in his reelection campaign
(B) The economic downturn experienced by business leaders
(C) The disparity between the wealthy and the poor
(D) The legacy of President Hoover

39. When Long says "had Mr. Hoover carried out what he says ought to be done," Long is referring most directly to

(A) saving the banks from collapse
(B) ending Prohibition
(C) incentivizing businesses to hire more workers
(D) policies that impose higher taxes on wealthier Americans to benefit programs which aid the working class

40. The ideas of Huey Long, as expressed in the excerpt, had the most in common with the ideas of the

(A) Federalists of the 1790s
(B) Whigs of the 1840s
(C) Know-Nothings of the 1850s
(D) Populists of the 1890s

GO ON TO THE NEXT PAGE.

Questions 41 - 44 refer to the table below.

1824 Presidential Election Results

Presidential Nominee	State	Political Party	Electoral College Votes	Popular Vote
John Quincy Adams	MA	Democratic-Republican	84	113,122
Andrew Jackson	TN	Democratic-Republican	99	151,271
William H. Crawford	GA	Democratic-Republican	41	40,856
Henry Clay	KY	Democratic-Republican	37	47,531

41. The table supports which of the following conclusions about the 1824 presidential election?

(A) Not a single candidate earned a plurality of votes.
(B) Henry Clay was the least popular of the candidates.
(C) None of the candidates secured the necessary majority of electoral votes to claim victory.
(D) Andrew Jackson won the presidency.

42. Which of the following factors most directly contributed to the closeness of this election?

(A) Because all candidates were from the same party and considered "political insiders," they were viewed by much of the public as too similar to one another.
(B) The support given the party caucus's preferred candidate was balanced out by the popular support for alternate candidates.
(C) The similar geographic origins of the candidates created an even split among the electorate.
(D) The candidates were supported by roughly the same number of voters around the country.

43. Which of the following developments emerged due to the outcome of this election?

(A) A "corrupt bargain" in which Henry Clay convinced Congress to elect Adams to the presidency
(B) A cooperative relationship between the incoming president and his Congress
(C) A renewed support for the caucus system
(D) A political alliance created between Henry Clay and Andrew Jackson

44. Which of the following was a key difference between the top two vote earners?

(A) Adams represented an agricultural region of the United States while Jackson campaigned on urban interests.
(B) Adams advocated low tariffs while Jackson was interested in expanding the use of tariffs.
(C) Adams supported a stronger federal government while Jackson advocated for more states' rights.
(D) Adams pushed for a "hard money" policy while Jackson ensured that the Second National Bank would continue.

GO ON TO THE NEXT PAGE.

Questions 45 - 47 refer to the excerpt below.

"And certainly, certainly, this is the glory of America, with all of its faults. This is the glory of our democracy. If we were incarcerated behind the iron curtains of a Communistic nation we couldn't do this. If we were dropped in the dungeon of a totalitarian regime we couldn't do this. But the great glory of American democracy is the right to protest for right. My friends, don't let anybody make us feel that we are to be compared in our actions with the Ku Klux Klan or with the White Citizens Council. There will be no crosses burned at any bus stops in Montgomery."

Rev. Martin Luther King, Jr., The Montgomery Bus Boycott Speech, 1955

45. Martin Luther King references "the iron curtains of a Communistic nation" in order to

(A) highlight the importance of the fight against Communism

(B) reference a nation that models the ideals King espouses

(C) draw a contrast between how the United States and the Soviet Union afford civil liberties

(D) point out the flaws of American democracy

46. This speech was most directly influenced by which event?

(A) The passage of the Voting Rights Act

(B) The arrest of a civil rights activist in Montgomery, Alabama

(C) The backlash experienced by the Little Rock Nine

(D) The Greensboro Sit-ins

47. The reference to "no crosses burned at any bus stops" underscores which ideal?

(A) To fight injustice by any means necessary

(B) The pursuit of black nationalism

(C) To remain neutral

(D) A commitment to nonviolence

GO ON TO THE NEXT PAGE.

Questions 48 and 49 refer to the excerpt below.

"If I am right, the problem that has no name stirring in the minds of so many American women today is not a matter of loss of femininity or too much education, or the demands of domesticity. It is far more important than anyone recognizes. It is the key to these other new and old problems which have been torturing women and their husbands and children, and puzzling their doctors and educators for years. It may well be the key to our future as a nation and a culture. We can no longer ignore that voice within women that says: 'I want something more than my husband and my children and my home.'"

Betty Friedan, *The Feminine Mystique*, 1963

48. Which of the following primary sources would most likely support Friedan's argument in the passage?

   (A) Marriage records from the middle of the twentieth century

   (B) Diary entries of housewives with references to their ambitions

   (C) Data showing the true costs of the demands of domesticity

   (D) Speeches by early twentieth-century suffragettes

49. Friedan's argument in the excerpt most strongly influenced the

   (A) women's liberation movement

   (B) lowering of the median age of first marriage

   (C) ratification of the Nineteenth Amendment

   (D) passage of new laws to guarantee equal wages among the sexes

GO ON TO THE NEXT PAGE.

Questions 50 and 51 refer to the excerpt below.

"The right of citizens of the United States to vote in any primary or other election for President or Vice President, for electors for President or Vice President, or for Senator or Representative in Congress, shall not be denied or abridged by the United States or any State by reason of failure to pay any poll tax or other tax."

Twenty-fourth Amendment to the Constitution, 1964

50. Which form of voter suppression remained legal following the passage of this amendment?

   (A) Literacy tests
   (B) Property taxes
   (C) Grandfather clauses
   (D) Sex discrimination

51. Poll taxes in Southern states were originally created in reaction to which of the following?

   (A) Women's suffrage
   (B) The end of slavery
   (C) The direct election of senators
   (D) Lowering of the voting age

GO ON TO THE NEXT PAGE.

Questions 52 - 55 refer to the excerpt below.

"The economic ills we suffer have come upon us over several decades. They will not go away in days, weeks, or months, but they will go away. They will go away because we as Americans have the capacity now, as we've had in the past, to do whatever needs to be done to preserve this last and greatest bastion of freedom.

"In this present crisis, government is not the solution to our problem; government is the problem. From time to time we've been tempted to believe that society has become too complex to be managed by self-rule, that government by an elite group is superior to government for, by, and of the people. Well, if no one among us is capable of governing himself, then who among us has the capacity to govern someone else? All of us together, in and out of government, must bear the burden. The solutions we seek must be equitable, with no one group singled out to pay a higher price."

President Ronald Reagan, First Inaugural Address, 1981

52. Which of the following proved to be an asset to Ronald Reagan's 1980 campaign?

(A) His candid arguments that Americans were largely responsible for the economic crisis
(B) His status as an outsider
(C) Popular support of the Republican Party in the late 1970s
(D) His considerable experience in national politics

53. Which of the following is an example of the "economic ills" Reagan refers to in the speech?

(A) Irresponsibly low tax rates
(B) An excessive military budget
(C) The burst of the dot-com bubble
(D) The energy crisis

54. President Reagan supported which of the following economic policies?

(A) Keynesian economics
(B) Trickle-down economics
(C) Welfare state
(D) Deficit spending

55. When President Reagan insists that the "solutions we seek must be equitable, with no one group singled out to pay a higher price," the group he refers to is most likely which of the following?

(A) Immigrant communities
(B) Wealthy Americans and business interests
(C) African Americans
(D) The middle class

GO ON TO THE NEXT PAGE.

UNITED STATES HISTORY
SECTION I, Part B
Time—40 minutes

Directions: Answer Question 1 **and** 2. Answer **either** Question 3 **or** Question 4.

Write your responses in the Section I, Part B: Short-Answer Response booklet. You must write your response to each question on the lined page designated for that response. Each response is expected to fit within the space provided.

In your responses, be sure to address all parts of the questions you answer. Use complete sentences; an outline or bulleted list alone is not acceptable. You may plan your answers in this exam booklet, but no credit will be given for notes written in this booklet.

Question 1 is based on the chart below.

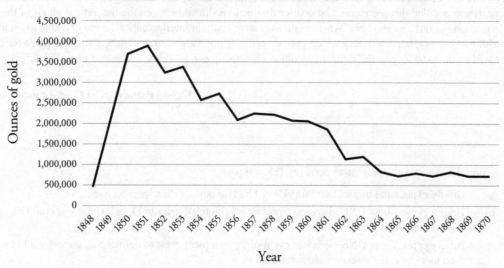

Production from the California Gold Rush

1. Using the chart above, answer parts (a), (b), and (c).

   a) Briefly explain ONE way in which the Gold Rush transformed the West.

   b) Briefly explain one way in which the Gold Rush impacted the development of the United States.

   c) Briefly explain a SECOND economic boom in American history and how it impacted a particular region of the United States.

GO ON TO THE NEXT PAGE.

Question 2 is based on the excerpts below.

"I believe, Your Honor, in common with all Socialists, that this nation ought to own and control its own industries. I believe, as all Socialists do, that all things that are jointly needed and used ought to be jointly owned that industry, the basis of our social life, instead of being the private property of a few and operated for their enrichment, ought to be the common property of all, democratically administered in the interest of all.

"I am opposing a social order in which it is possible for one man who does absolutely nothing that is useful to amass a fortune of hundreds of millions of dollars, while millions of men and women who work all the days of their lives secure barely enough for a wretched existence."

Eugene Debs, Statement to the Court, 1918

"Upon these two basic certainties, first that the "Reds" were criminal aliens and secondly that the American Government must prevent crime, it was decided that there could be no nice distinctions drawn between the theoretical ideals of the radicals and their actual violations of our national laws. An assassin may have brilliant intellectuality, he may be able to excuse his murder or robbery with fine oratory, but any theory which excuses crime is not wanted in America. This is no place for the criminal to flourish, nor will he do so so long as the rights of common citizenship can be exerted to prevent him."

A. Mitchell Palmer, "The Case Against the 'Reds,'" 1920

2.   Using the excerpts above, answer parts (a), (b), and (c).

a)   Briefly explain the impact that World War I had on both of these perspectives.

b)   Briefly explain how ONE historical event or development prior to Debs's statement could be used to support his assertion about industry.

c)   Briefly explain how ONE historical event or development prior to Palmer's statement could be used to support his assertion about radicals.

GO ON TO THE NEXT PAGE.

Question 3 or Question 4

Directions: Answer **either** Question 3 **or** Question 4.

3. With regard to William Lloyd Garrison, Frederick Douglass, and Harriet Beecher Stowe, answer parts (a), (b), and (c).

   a) Briefly explain which of the three people had the largest impact on the abolition of slavery.

   b) Briefly explain why the other two people did not play as large of a role in abolishing slavery, making sure to explain their roles in the abolition movement.

   c) Briefly explain how one other person or group helped to abolish slavery.

4. Answer parts (a), (b), and (c).

   a) Briefly explain ONE reason for the emergence of the Populist movement during the final decades of the nineteenth century.

   b) Briefly explain one example of how the goals of the Populist movement were challenged during the same time period.

   c) Briefly explain one way that the Populist movement impacted the United States in the years following its prominence.

END OF SECTION I

AP® United States History Exam

SECTION II: Free Response

DO NOT OPEN THIS BOOKLET UNTIL YOU ARE TOLD TO DO SO.

At a Glance

Total Time
1 hour, 40 minutes
Number of Questions
2
Percent of Total Score
40%
Writing Instrument
Pen with black or dark blue ink

Question 1 (DBQ): Mandatory

Suggested Reading and Writing Time
60 minutes

Reading Period
15 minutes. Use this time to read Question 1 and plan your answer. You may begin writing your response before the reading period is over.
Suggested Writing Time
45 minutes
Percent of Total Score
25%

Question 2, 3, or 4: Choose One Question

Answer Question 2, Question 3, or Question 4
Suggested Writing Time
40 minutes
Percent of Total Score
15%

Instructions

The questions for Section II are printed in the orange Questions and Documents booklet. You may use that booklet to organize your answers and for scratch work, but you must write your answers in this Section II: Free Response booklet. No credit will be given for any work written in the Questions and Documents booklet.

The proctor will announce the beginning and end of the reading period. You are advised to spend the 15-minute period reading the question and planning your answer to Question 1, the document-based question. If you have time, you may also read Questions 2, 3, and 4: Do not begin writing in this booklet until the proctor tells you to do so.

Section II of this exam requires answers in essay form. Write clearly and legibly. Circle the number of the question you are answering at the top of each page in this booklet. Begin each answer on a new page. Do not skip lines. Cross out any errors you make; crossed-out work will not be scored.

Manage your time carefully. The proctor will announce the suggested time for each part, but you may proceed freely from one part to the next. Go on to Question 2, 3, or 4 if you finish Question 1 early. You may review your responses if you finish before the end of the exam is announced.

After the exam, you must apply the label that corresponds to the long-essay question you answered—Question 2, 3, or 4. For example, if you answered Question 2, apply the label ②. Failure to do so may delay your score.

GO ON TO THE NEXT PAGE.

UNITED STATES HISTORY
SECTION II
Total Time—1 hour, 40 minutes

Question 1 (Document-Based Question)
Suggested reading and writing time: 1 hour

It is suggested that you spend 15 minutes reading the documents and 45 minutes writing your response.

Note: You may begin writing your response before the reading period is over.

Directions: Question 1 is based on the accompanying documents. The documents have been edited for the purpose of this exercise.

In your response you should do the following.

- Respond to the prompt with a historically defensible thesis or claim that establishes a line of reasoning.
- Describe a broader historical context relevant to the prompt.
- Support an argument in response to the prompt using at least six documents.
- Use at least one additional piece of specific historical evidence (beyond that found in the documents) relevant to an argument about the prompt.
- For at least three documents, explain how or why the document's point of view, purpose, historical situation, and/or audience is relevant to an argument.
- Use evidence to corroborate, qualify, or modify an argument that addresses the prompt.

GO ON TO THE NEXT PAGE.

1. To what extent does the outcome of the Constitutional Convention represent change and/or continuity in respect to the ideals set out in the Declaration of Independence?

Document 1

Source: The Declaration of Independence, Thomas Jefferson, et. al., 1776

We hold these truths to be self-evident, that all men are created equal, that they are endowed by their Creator with certain unalienable Rights, that among these are Life, Liberty and the pursuit of Happiness.

Document 2

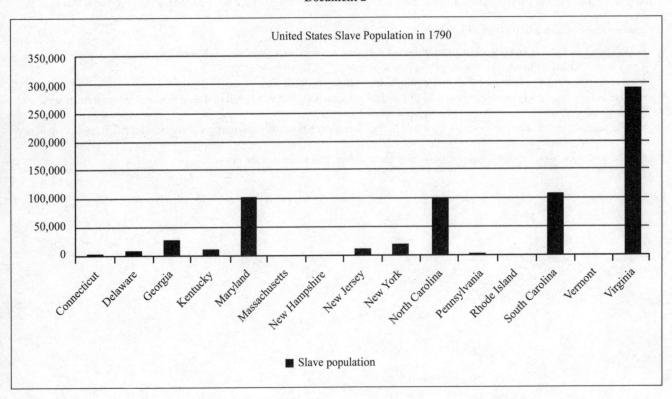

United States Slave Population in 1790

■ Slave population

GO ON TO THE NEXT PAGE.

Document 3

Source: James Madison, Federalist #63, 1788

Thus far I have considered the circumstances which point out the necessity of a well-constructed Senate only as they relate to the representatives of the people. To a people as little blinded by prejudice or corrupted by flattery as those whom I address, I shall not scruple to add, that such an institution may be sometimes necessary as a defense to the people against their own temporary errors and delusions.

Document 4

United States Population in 1790

Northern States		Southern States	
Connecticut	237,255	Delaware	59,096
Massachusetts	378,566	Georgia	82,548
New Hampshire	141,889	Kentucky	73,667
New Jersey	184,139	Maryland	319,728
New York	340,241	North Carolina	395,005
Pennsylvania	443,611	South Carolina	249,073
Rhode Island	69,112	Virginia	747,550

Document 5

Source: George Mason, *Virginia Journal,* September, 1787

In the House of Representatives there is not the substance but the shadow only of representation; which can never produce proper information in the legislature, or inspire confidence in the people; the laws will therefore be generally made by men little concerned in, and unacquainted with their effects and consequences.

GO ON TO THE NEXT PAGE.

Document 6

Source: Alexander Hamilton, Speech at the Philadelphia Convention, 1787

All communities divide themselves into the few and the many. The first are the rich and wellborn, the other the mass of the people....The people are turbulent and changing; they seldom judge or determine right. Give therefore to the first class a distinct, permanent share in the government. They will check the unsteadiness of the second, and as they cannot receive any advantage by change, they therefore will ever maintain good government.

Document 7

Source: Thomas Jefferson, Letter to Francis Hopkinson, 1789

What I disapproved from the first moment, also, was the want of a bill of rights to guard liberty against the legislative as well as the executive branches of the government; that is to say, to secure freedom in religion, freedom of the press, freedom from monopolies, freedom from unlawful imprisonment, freedom from a permanent military, and a trial by jury, in all cases determinable by the laws of the land. I disapproved, also, the perpetual reeligibility of the President. To these points of disapprobation I adhere.

END OF DOCUMENTS FOR QUESTION 1

GO ON TO THE NEXT PAGE.

Question 2, 3, or 4 (Long Essay)

Suggested writing time: 40 minutes

Directions: Answer Question 2 **or** Question 3 **or** Question 4.

In your response you should do the following.

- Respond to the prompt with a historically defensible thesis or claim that establishes a line of reasoning.
- Describe a broader historical context relevant to the prompt.
- Support an argument in response to the prompt using specific and relevant examples of evidence.
- Use historical reasoning (e.g., comparison, causation, continuity or change over time) to frame or structure an argument that addresses the prompt.
- Use evidence to corroborate, qualify, or modify an argument that addresses the prompt.

2. Evaluate the extent to which the Townshend Acts were a contributing factor leading to the Revolutionary War.

   In your argument, analyze both changes and continuities in the relevant time period.

3. To what extent did the impact of immigration on the United States reflect both continuity and change in the mid-19th century (1820–1870) and in the industrial period (1880–1920)?

   In the development of your argument, explain the reasons for the similarities and differences.

4. To what extent did the successes of two postwar periods in the United States, post–Civil War (1865–1876) and post–World War II (1945–1961), represent both continuity and change?

   In the development of your argument, explain the reasons for the similarities and differences.

WHEN YOU FINISH WRITING, CHECK YOUR WORK ON SECTION II IF TIME PERMITS.

STOP

END OF EXAM

Practice Test 4:
Answers and
Explanations

ANSWER KEY

Section I, Part A: Multiple-Choice Questions

1. D	20. A	39. D
2. C	21. D	40. D
3. A	22. A	41. C
4. C	23. B	42. B
5. A	24. C	43. A
6. A	25. B	44. C
7. B	26. B	45. C
8. C	27. B	46. B
9. B	28. A	47. D
10. A	29. B	48. B
11. D	30. C	49. A
12. B	31. C	50. A
13. C	32. A	51. B
14. D	33. C	52. B
15. C	34. B	53. D
16. B	35. D	54. B
17. C	36. B	55. B
18. C	37. A	
19. D	38. C	

SECTION I, PART A: MULTIPLE-CHOICE QUESTIONS

Questions 1–3

One of Abigail Adams's letters to her husband became well known for its advocacy of women. The "Remember the Ladies" letter used revolutionary language (tyrants, rebellion) to urge John Adams to treat women well under the new government.

1. **D** Adams is hopeful that her husband and his colleagues will "remember the ladies" due to the disparity of rights available to the sexes. According to the text, Adams feared that women would have no voice, as would be expected during the Colonial period, so (D) is the correct answer. The fight for an Equal Rights Amendment and the suffrage movement did not take hold until much later in American history, so cross off (A) and (C). Women of privilege already had access to education at this point, albeit training for domesticity. Eliminate (B).

2. **C** This letter was written in March, 1776, at the time Thomas Jefferson was composing the Declaration of Independence. Since the United States was about to declare its independence, it was also planning to create a new government. Choice (C) is correct. Be careful not to confuse the Declaration of Independence with the Declaratory Act—the latter is a British Act that asserts the Empire's ability to levy taxes in America.

3. **A** The reference to her husband's ancestors reflects a tone that reaches far back into history—a history that has largely excluded women from decision-making positions. Therefore, the answer is (A), which refers to the treatment of women throughout history. This contradicts (C). Choice (B) is incorrect because women did not hold any rights during the colonial period that were unique for the time. There is no reference to women in the military, so (D) is not supported by the text.

Questions 4–6

Following the Civil War, many Northerners sought economic opportunities in the war-damaged South. These Northerners were known as "carpetbaggers," so called due to the types of bags into which these folks packed their belongings when they relocated to the South. Southerners resented the fact that outsiders would come to their hometowns to make money when the economy was so tight following the war, so "carpetbagger" became a derisive term. Adding to the resentment was the fact that the federal government created avenues for carpetbaggers to find employment.

4. **C** The enormous bag on the back of the woman coupled with the date under the photo indicates that this image depicts a carpetbagger during the time of Reconstruction. She is accompanied by military personnel and carrying President Grant on her bag, conveying the idea that the federal government is using carpetbaggers to influence the South. Be careful—(A) may bring the Reconstruction Act to mind. While the Reconstruction Act represented the presence of the United States military in the South, it was not an invasion, per se, and the image of the woman and her bag would not be consistent with this interpretation. Choice (A) is incorrect.

5. **A** The Freedmen's Bureau established schools and provided opportunities for carpetbaggers to become teachers. Choice (B) is incorrect because while the Morrill Act led to the establishment of schools, those schools were institutions of higher learning and were not associated with carpetbaggers. Choice (C) is incorrect because the Reconstruction Act established a military presence in the South, but was not a program that attracted carpetbaggers. Choice (D) is also incorrect, as the Enforcement Act protected African Americans from intimidation at voting booths and therefore is not related to this image.

6. **A** The position of the cartoonist is that the northern Republicans are using the carpetbaggers to profit from rebuilding of the South. In response, supporters of President Grant would defend the policy of Reconstruction. In order to defend the federal presence in the South, Republicans would have claimed that it is necessary for the government to take an active role, including protecting the rights of former slaves. This is consistent with (A).

Questions 7–10

This chart shows how Congress moved from Democratic dominance to Republican dominance over the course of 20 years. It is important to note how this data compares with the party that controlled the White House at various points—Ronald Reagan and George H.W. Bush, Republicans, were in office from 1981 to 1993, and Bill Clinton, a Democrat, held the Oval Office from 1993 through the end of the decade.

7. **B** The incumbent president from 1982 until 1992 was Republican. From 1994 to 2000, it was a Democrat. It would appear that voters were trying to balance the ticket by voting the opposition party into more and more congressional seats. This fits with (B) and is the opposite of the claim made by (A). The Republican congressional majority was new in 1994, so (C) is incorrect. Choice (D) is incorrect because the Contract with America was a plan offered by the Republicans.

8. **C** The trend in the graph shows the success of the GOP in Congress in the late 1990s. This trend continued for much of the first decade of the new century. Under President Bush, the Republican-led Congress ushered in a wave of neoconservatism, promoting the idea of spreading democracy worldwide and putting American corporate interests first through the use of military actions abroad. Since Congress was the same party as the president, they mostly cooperated with him and did not act as a check on his power. Eliminate (B). Choice (A) is incorrect because the U.S. budget surplus at the end of the 1990s went away after 2000 amidst tax cuts and wars. With few exceptions, Congress remained largely partisan after 2000, so (D) is incorrect.

9. **B** Since a Republican held the Oval Office, there was not unchecked Democratic power in the government. Choice (D) is incorrect. Likewise, (A) is incorrect because of the split power in government. However, this split would necessitate bipartisanship for laws to get passed. Choice (B) is correct. There is no data present on this chart about how close congressional votes were, so eliminate (C).

10. **A** Congressional power shifted from the Democrats to the Republicans in 1994, so focus on that year for the dramatic change. 1994 was a midterm election (congressional races occurred, but there was no presidential election). Choice (A) is correct. Choice (B) is incorrect because George H.W. Bush was elected in 1988, a year that Democrats retained control of Congress. Ronald Reagan had a Democratic-controlled Congress throughout his presidency, so (C) is incorrect. Choice (D) is also incorrect because Bill Clinton was reelected in 1996, two years *after* his party, the Democrats, lost control in Congress.

Questions 11–14

This document discusses the prevalence of child labor in South Carolina. The document is from 1909, which is the reform-oriented Progressive Era, but a federal ban on the practice of child labor did not actually occur until the late 1930s with the Fair Labor Standards Act. This document discusses how child labor, despite being illegal at the local level, could still be practiced by evading the law.

11. **D** With an increasing amount of productivity during the Industrial Revolution, new jobs opened up around the country. Industrialists turned to women and children as a low-cost way to fill these new positions, so (D) is correct. Since this productivity was the result of manufacturing and not agriculture, (B) is incorrect. Choice (A) is incorrect because strict labor laws would have prevented this kind of child labor. Choice (C) is incorrect because in 1909, there was not yet a Supreme Court ruling on child labor. Further, the courts favored business and not the working class during this period.

12. **B** Women and children, who were, for the most part, powerless in society could easily be exploited for cheap labor, so (B) is the strongest. This would also eliminate (C). There were plenty of manufacturing jobs for workers in the late 19th and early 20th century, so eliminate (D). The text provides evidence that child labor persisted, so the limits placed on the amount of hours worked was likely not strictly enforced. Eliminate (A).

13. **C** The reference to "letting youngsters who are under age help older brothers and sisters" occurs in the context of a discussion about evading child labor laws. Such laws were feckless and Congress could not interfere with the practices of private businesses at the time. The Commerce Clause was Congress's tool for regulating business, and the courts of the day did not see child labor that does not cross state lines to be an example of interstate commerce. Therefore, (C) is correct.

14. **D** Captains of industry looked to maximize profit and child labor was cheap, which helped to increase corporate profits. Eliminate (A). Both the McKinley administration and the Supreme Court of the Gilded Age were pro-business, so neither prioritized ending child labor. Both (B) and (C) are wrong. The reforms of the Progressive Movement often focused on labor practices. Even though there was not a lasting federal law that combated child labor until 1938, the Progressives had enough success at the local level to begin to put an end to the practice of child labor. Choice (D) is correct.

Questions 15–17

Joseph Smith founded the Church of Latter Day Saints in western New York in 1830. After encountering difficulty establishing themselves in Ohio and Missouri, Smith and his followers, known as Mormons, moved to Illinois. Smith was killed by a mob in Illinois and Brigham Young eventually led the Mormons to Utah, where they experienced considerably less resistance. This warrant for Joseph Smith's arrest describes Smith breaking into a newspaper office to destroy its printing press. One can imagine why Smith, an outsider who came to Illinois to find converts, would not see the local press as an ally.

15.   **C**   The rise of democratic and individualistic beliefs (A), a reaction against pure rationalism (D), and economic changes in society, along with greater social and geographical mobility (C), all contributed to a Second Great Awakening among Protestants that influenced moral and social reforms (B) and inspired religious movements such as Mormonism.

16.   **B**   The date of 1844 should remind you that we are in the midst of the Second Great Awakening. This was a Protestant religious movement whose adherents were over-represented in rural parts of the East such as Pennsylvania, New York, and Ohio. Not many Catholics (A) would likely be drawn to Mormonism, nor would atheists (C). Answer (D) is outside the era, since Puritans were active in the 17th and 18th centuries.

17.   **C**   The Populist movement occurred in the late 19th century as a reaction to abusive business practices, not as a religious movement. Choice (A) is incorrect. The Church was not founded for the purpose of ending slavery, so eliminate (B). Choice (D) is incorrect because even though the Mormons moved West, religious persecution, not Manifest Destiny, was their motivation. The Second Great Awakening, a period of religious revival, provides a fitting backdrop for the development of this new religion. Choice (C) is the correct answer.

Questions 18–19

This painting, *Westward the Course of Empire Takes Its Way,* by Emanuel Leutze, was painted in 1861, just a year before the Homestead Act. The painting depicts settlers looking out over unsettled land. This painting captures the ideal of mid-19th-century politicians and pioneers alike—the West was America's to discover and settle. This concept is known as Manifest Destiny.

18.   **C**   The image shows a group of people discovering a new land. The rugged landscape and the painting's title indicate that this event takes place in the West. Westward expansion was part of Manifest Destiny, the idea that Americans had a right to settle the West. Choice (A) is incorrect because impressment refers to forcing people to join a military against their will. Choice (C) is correct. Revivalism describes a movement to revive religious zeal, which is not evidenced in this painting. Eliminate (B). Transcendentalism was practiced mostly in New England, not in the West, so (D) is incorrect.

19.   **D**   Thomas Jefferson's Louisiana Purchase of 1803 doubled the size of the United States and created opportunities for pioneers to explore and settle the West. Americans spent the next several decades doing just that. Choice (D) is correct.

Questions 20–23

These two documents highlight a debate of the late 19th and early 20th centuries—imperialism. In this text, Senator Beveridge of Indiana advocates the expansion of the United States to new territories in order to spread American ideals. Of course, the natural resources and military advantages are also beneficial, albeit less moral, reasons for expansion. The American Anti-Imperialist League, on the other hand, uses the American ideals of self-governance and liberty to argue the immorality of imperialism.

20. **A** Beveridge notes that "it is ours to save that soil for liberty and civilization"; therefore, the correct answer should focus not on the exploitation of natural resources, but on noble pursuits, such as enhancing freedom in other parts of the world. Choices (B), (C), and (D) all focus on economic exploitation and the control of resources. Choice (A) is correct because imperialists claimed that the Spanish mistreated Cuban colonists.

21. **D** The American Anti-Imperialist League claimed that "governments derive their just powers from the consent of the governed." Consent of the governed is a core American right that was denied to colonized people, specifically in the *Insular Cases,* which ruled that Constitutional protections and privileges are not extended to noncitizen residents of American colonies. Choice (D) is correct.

22. **A** The argument highlighted in these two texts revolves around the ability of the United States to interfere with and influence foreign nations. The answer choice that comes closest to this situation is the Vietnam War, (A). The Monroe Doctrine focused on the United States keeping foreign powers out of the Western Hemisphere, so eliminate (C). The United States engaged in World War I due to attacks on its merchant ships and the Zimmerman Telegram. Eliminate (B). Choice (D) is also incorrect because the Persian Gulf War likewise was not an attempt to spread the ideals of "liberty" in the way that the Spanish American War (how the United States acquired Cuba) and Vietnam were.

23. **B** Use Process of Elimination. Imperialists such as Beveridge were often interested in spreading American influence throughout the world, but not always with a focus on the well-being of the colonized people. Eliminate (A). Beveridge does not discuss military commitments in this passage, so (C) is incorrect. Beveridge also did not attack the patriotism of his opponents, so eliminate (D). Choice (B) is the only answer remaining and is therefore correct.

Questions 24–26

As the Whigs split over the slavery issue, new parties arose to oppose the expansion of slavery—including the Free-Soil Party, a regional, single-issue party. The Free-Soil Party was largely opposed to the expansion of slavery not because they were abolitionists but because they didn't want white settlers to have to compete with slave labor in new territories. The men on the right are standing on planks labeled "Democratic Platform," conveying the idea that slavery is being forced upon the new territories by the Democrats.

24. **C** The Kansas-Nebraska Act effectively allowed slavery in the new territories of Kansas and Nebraska. Since this was the single issue the Free-Soil Party promoted, Free-Soilers were politically at the mercy of the pro-slavery Democrats. Choose (C).

25. **B** Don't be taken in by (A). The Free-Soil Party did not take on the overly ambitious task of advocating for abolition nationwide. The purpose of the Free-Soil Party—as implied by its name—was to prevent slavery from expanding into the new territories, a necessary task after the end of the Whig Party. Choice (B) is correct.

26. **B** The Socialist Party and the Populist Party arose in America during the Gilded Age, decades after the end of slavery. Eliminate (C) and (D). The American Party was also known as the Know-Nothing Party and opposed immigration. They did not stand for the end of slavery expansion. Eliminate (A). The Republican Party came to national prominence in the 1850s due to its opposition to the expansion of slavery. Choose (B).

Questions 27–28

Ignatius Donnelly delivered his speech in 1892 to the Farmer's Alliance. In this era, the Grangers, a farmer's organization, had organized politically to form the Populist Party, a movement dedicated to righting some of the wrongs Donnelly highlights: corruption, overindebtedness to banks, poverty, and economic imbalances between the rich and poor.

27. **B** In the 1890s, the Populist Party sought to curb the power of banks and the railroad industry, hoping to further the interests of farmers and other working-class people. Republicans (A) of this era would have been more closely aligned with business and banking interests. The Green Party (C) did not exist at this time, and the Free Soil Party (D) had disbanded after the Civil War, since it was dedicated to abolitionism. Choice (B) is the correct answer.

28. **A** Even though the federal government helped to create necessary infrastructure such as railroad, private companies ended up running them, often engaging in price gouging, which created a difficult situation for farmers who depended on railroads. The case *Munn v. Illinois* specifically dealt with grain elevators that were overcharging customers for storage. The state of Illinois imposed a maximum price that a business may charge for grain storage, which was challenged in court. The Supreme Court decided in favor of Illinois, affirming that state governments may regulate private businesses. Choice (A) is correct.

Questions 29–31

This map shows the paths taken by African Americans who left the South during the 20th century. Depending on where the migrants lived, they would typically end up in cities such as New York, Philadelphia, Cleveland, Chicago, and Detroit, or move westward toward Washington and California. Much of the migration occurred during the early part of the century. The injustices inherent in the post-*Plessy v. Ferguson* era, as well as the expansion of northern manufacturing jobs, were primary motivators for migrants of the early 1900s.

29. **B** The 1896 Supreme Court case *Plessy v. Ferguson* created the doctrine of "separate but equal." This was used to expand discriminatory Jim Crow laws throughout the South. The hostilities and frustrations that came with "separate but equal" motivated many African Americans to move north and west for better opportunities and less discrimination. Choice (B) is the correct answer.

30. **C** Since this map focuses on the 20th century, World War I would be a notable event from its initial stages. The war had two major effects on manufacturing: men left jobs to go fight, and the need for industrial production increased with the demands of the war. Both of these issues led to employment opportunities in the North, which coincided with the destinations of the migrants, making (C) the correct answer.

31. **C** As African Americans sought employment in the North, they began competing with whites for jobs. This spurred resentment from the white community as well as periodic acts of violence against blacks in cities such as Chicago. Therefore, (C) is correct. The resistance African Americans encountered contradicts (A). Choice (B) is not supported by any actual legislation. Desegregation did not occur until the latter half of of the 20th century. Eliminate (D).

Questions 32–33

This treaty is better known as the Louisiana Purchase. Napoleon wanted to get out of the Western Hemisphere following the Haitian slave revolt. Even though Jefferson wanted to purchase only New Orleans, which would provide the United States with a strategic trade port, he was enticed by the low price to purchase the entire Louisiana Territory from the French.

32. **A** Thomas Jefferson had no intention to increase the size of the United States. He wanted to purchase only the city of New Orleans for economic and military strategy. However, the opportunity for the entire Louisiana Purchase was presented to Jefferson for an exceptionally low price. Choice (B) is incorrect. Jefferson saw France as an ally, so there was no threat of war between the two nations, making (C) incorrect. New Englanders opposed the purchase.

33. **C** Manifest Destiny, the idea that Americans had a right to settle the West, was accelerated by the Louisiana Purchase, making (C) correct. The Non-Intercourse Act and Embargo Act came a few years after the Louisiana Purchase and were created to keep the United States from trading with France and Great Britain while the two were at war. Eliminate (A) and (B). The Monroe Doctrine was not established until a few years later and asserted the necessity of keeping foreign powers out of the Western Hemisphere, which is not relevant to the Louisiana Purchase. Choice (D) is incorrect.

Questions 34–37

George Kennan wrote this document, the Long Telegram, to recommend a strategic foreign policy to the Truman Administration. In this passage, Kennan describes the zero-sum approach of the Soviets—they never make compacts or compromises, only to destroy rival power. Kennan's recommendation becomes known as containment policy—the United States will not seek war with the Soviets, but will also limit the spread of Soviet influence.

34. **B** The Long Telegram informed Truman's containment policy, which, while not directly fighting the Soviet Union, brought the United States to intervene in other parts of the world where Communism was spreading. Choice (B) is correct. Eliminate (D) since this policy is certainly not one of neutrality. The end of World War II brought about a healthy economy, so (A) is incorrect. While there was a baby boom following the Second World War, it is irrelevant to Truman's containment policy. Eliminate (C).

35. **D** An effective way to prevent the spread of Communism was to help the countries most at risk repair following the war. This was done through financial aid (the Marshall Plan) to two countries right in the USSR's backyard—Greece and Turkey. Choice (D) is the correct answer. While (A), (B), and (C) are all events that occurred in the years following the Second World War, they did not directly hold off the spread of Communism, which was the central tenet of containment policy.

36. **B** Containment policy was intended to stop the spread of Communism, though not to directly fight the Soviet Union, so eliminate (D). For a long time in the early part of the Cold War, there was little in terms of peace talks and the United States created an embargo on trade with the Eastern Bloc and the Soviet Union. Eliminate (A) and (C). Choice (B) is correct because it describes the strategy behind containment policy.

37. **A** The fear of Communism's spread was alive and well on the American home front. Senator McCarthy took advantage of this situation, creating a witch hunt for Communists in the United States government. Similar fears existed in the business world and in the entertainment industry. The fear of Communism in America was reminiscent of the Red Scare of 1919 and 1920 and was seen as a Second Red Scare. Choice (A) is correct.

Questions 38–40

Huey Long was initially a supporter of Franklin Roosevelt, but felt that Roosevelt had abandoned his more Progressive ideals. Senator Long strongly believed in a decentralization of wealth—allowing wealth to spread among the social classes. Long represented a vociferous voice of opposition from the American Left, an ironic stance according to the businesses and millionaires who saw FDR's policies as too left-wing to begin with.

38. **C** Senator Long states that both President Hoover and President Roosevelt claimed "there had to be a decentralization of wealth, but neither one of them did anything about it." Long implies that decentralizing wealth was the right thing to do and would lead to electoral success for candidates who campaign on it. Decentralization of wealth refers to spreading wealth from the few to the many. This is consistent with (C).

39. **D** Senator Long advocates decentralizing wealth in America, so "doing what ought to be done" refers to policies that would decentralize wealth. Choice (D) is correct because it describes policies that fund public programs with higher taxes on the wealthiest Americans.

40. **D** Senator Long's message is critical of the wealthiest class of Americans. This skeptical view of the upper class and business was shared by the frustrated farmers and union workers in the Gilded Age who created the Populist Party. Choice (D) is correct.

Questions 41–44

This chart shows the electoral vote and popular vote totals from the 1824 election. This was one of the more noteworthy elections in American history due to the fact that there was no winner in the electoral college. Andrew Jackson was the largest vote getter by a long shot, but according to the Constitution, this election had to be decided by Congress. Henry Clay was the Speaker of the House and was able to convince the legislative body to vote for the most realistic candidate who was not Andrew Jackson.

41. **C**   This election was decided by the House of Representatives because not a single candidate received a majority of votes—one more than half of all electoral votes. Choice (C) is the correct answer. Choice (B) is incorrect because Henry Clay was not the least popular candidate: Clay had nearly 7,000 more popular votes than Crawford. Choice (D) is incorrect because the House chose Adams in this election, not Jackson. Be careful not to choose (A). It is incorrect because a plurality of votes means the most votes when no candidate receives a majority. Andrew Jackson received a plurality of both the popular votes and the electoral votes.

42. **B**   Choice (A) is incorrect because, although the candidates were all from the same party, Andrew Jackson was certainly not considered an "insider" in Washington politics. Eliminate (C) because the table shows that the candidates represented distinct geographic regions in the United States. Choice (D) is incorrect because the table shows that there were strong disparities in votes received among the field of candidates. Choice (B) is correct because while some states used a caucus system to allow Congressional representatives to nominate the party favorite, such as Adams, Jackson's success came from states that allowed direct election of presidential electors.

43. **A**   Since the House of Representatives was tasked with choosing the president, Speaker of the House Henry Clay held considerable power. He supported John Quincy Adams, effectively handing him the election. In return, Clay became the secretary of state. Andrew Jackson criticized this political move as "a corrupt bargain." Choice (A) is correct.

44. **C**   Choice (A) is incorrect because Jackson, a Tennessean, represented a more rural base, while Adams, from New England, had more urban connections. Adams supported tariffs, which were opposed by Jackson's supporters, so eliminate (B). Choice (D) is incorrect because Jackson vetoed the recharter of the Second National Bank, leading to its closure. Choice (C) is correct because it properly designates Adams as a supporter of expanding federal power and Jackson as an advocate of states' rights.

Questions 45–47

This speech by Dr. Martin Luther King Jr. in Montgomery, Alabama came on the heels of the arrest of Rosa Parks. By championing the Montgomery Bus Boycott, King was introduced to the United States as an advocate of nonviolent resistance. This speech celebrates the ability to protest in the United States, a freedom not guaranteed in the Soviet Union.

45. **C**   Dr. King precedes the reference to the "iron curtains" by mentioning the "glory of our democracy." That is, he celebrates the freedom to be able to speak out against the injustices of the government, a core civil liberty. Choice (C) is the correct answer.

46. **B** The date (1955) and the references to bus stops in Montgomery bring to mind the civil disobedience of Rosa Parks, an event that set off the Montgomery Bus Boycott, a pivotal moment in the Civil Rights Movement. Choice (B) is the correct answer since it mentions the arrest of a civil rights activist (Parks).

47. **D** One of the key components of Dr. King's philosophy is nonviolence. He believed in confronting hatred and bigotry with direct action motivated by love. While the Ku Klux Klan was known for burning crosses, Dr. King explained to his followers that returning that kind of violence is not acceptable. Therefore, (D) is correct.

Questions 48–49

Betty Friedan's book *The Feminine Mystique* openly challenged many people's assumptions about women's place in society. Frustrated with being treated as second-class citizens, women became more politically active during the 1960s. Friedan's book, and work as a founder of NOW (the National Organization of Women), reawakened the women's movement, which had faded since the passage of the Nineteenth Amendment in 1920.

48. **B** Friedan writes about "the problem that has no name stirring in the minds of so many American women today." The issue she describes is not quantifiable—it is the feeling women have about wanting more out of life than domesticity. Choices (A) and (C) would not work because they are both empirical data. Eliminate (D) because it is too early for the time period referenced in this passage. Choice (B) is correct because it is a source that can illuminate the inner feelings of women in the 1960s.

49. **A** The Nineteenth Amendment had been ratified long before Friedan wrote *The Feminine Mystique*, so eliminate (C). There is no evidence that the median age of first marriage was lowered—in fact, the movement that Friedan championed saw a rise in the age of first marriage due to women being able to prioritize their education and career. Eliminate (B). Choice (D) is incorrect as no such law was passed. The late 1960s saw a women's liberation movement that can be traced back to the ideas outlined in Friedan's book. Choice (A) is correct.

Questions 50–51

The Twenty-fourth Amendment to the Constitution was ratified in 1964. The Amendment calls for an end to the poll tax, one of several practices used since Reconstruction to prevent African Americans from voting. It is important to note the historical context of this Amendment. It was the second of four amendments passed over a 10-year period, making the 1960s an unusually active time for amending the Constitution. It also came during a time of significant civil rights legislation including the 1964 Civil Rights Act, the 1965 Voting Rights Act, and the 1968 Housing Rights Act.

50. **A** The 1965 Voting Rights Act was necessary due to local election boards in the South giving unfair (and impossibly difficult) literacy tests to African American voters. Since the right to vote, per the Fifteenth Amendment, was not denied to African Americans, this was not considered unconstitutional. The Twenty-fourth Amendment may have eliminated the unfair poll tax, but did not fix all discrimination at the polls. Choice (A) is correct.

51. **B** Following the passage of the Fifteenth Amendment, Southern Democrats were afraid of the newly freed population of African Americans controlling elections due to their numbers. In response to this fear, many states passed discriminatory legislation to make voting difficult, if not impossible. These methods included poll taxes, literacy tests, and grandfather clauses. Therefore, (B) is the correct answer.

Questions 52–55

Ronald Reagan was the beneficiary of a number of factors that led to his election in 1980. In this document, he discusses a couple of them: the ongoing economic crisis and a general growing mistrust of government. Reagan's position as a political outsider permitted him to be seen as a credible personality when speaking on the concerns of Americans.

52. **B** Ronald Reagan was elected in 1980 despite the bad taste left in Americans' mouths after the Watergate scandal of the 1970s, so (C) is incorrect. Choice (A) is also incorrect because it attributes a speech made by President Carter ("the malaise speech") to Reagan. Although Reagan was governor of California, he did not yet have much experience in national politics, so eliminate (D). Instead, Reagan's appeal largely came from his status as a plain-spoken outsider. Choice (B) is correct.

53. **D** Ronald Reagan was elected on the heels of an economic crisis that frustrated many Americans, who viewed then-president Jimmy Carter's handling of it unfavorably. The economic crisis stemmed from the increased cost of OPEC petroleum, leading to long lines at gas pumps and increased prices elsewhere. This was indeed an energy crisis, so (D) is correct.

54. **B** Since Ronald Reagan favored tax cuts and fewer regulations on business, he favored a system that would create a larger supply of goods and services in America. This is known as trickle-down (or supply-side) economics, so the correct answer is (B).

55. **B** President Reagan is responding to calls for greater responsibility to be placed on wealthier Americans through taxation. Like many fiscal Conservatives, Reagan wanted the rates between the different social classes to be equal. Therefore, the single group he does not want singled out is the wealthier Americans. The correct answer is (B).

SECTION I, PART B: SHORT-ANSWER QUESTIONS

Question 1

a) and b) Some ways the discovery of gold in California impacted the United States:

- With 100,000 people moving West to seek riches, the population of this region exploded, leading to statehood for a number of new viable territories.
- The development of San Francisco, located on the Pacific Ocean, created new trade options for the United States.
- The settlement of a city on the Pacific Ocean gave access to a new wave of immigrants.
- The Gold Rush gave impetus for the construction of a transcontinental railroad.

c) An economic boom is a short period of economic expansion. Along with the benefits of an expanding economy are some drawbacks, namely inflation. Some later examples of economic booms include the following:

- Industrialization (Northern manufacturing cities). Per capita incomes doubled in the late 19th century as industries were able to operate as economies of scale bringing about widespread employment and production.
- Mid-1920s boom (urban and suburban regions). A real estate bubble (more houses were built than there were people interested in buying them) and a debt bubble (fueled by a new era of advertising, people outspent their means by purchasing on margin) led to an unsustainable boom characterized by low interest rates and an unprecedented availability of credit.
- Post–World War II boom (nationwide). With the return of workers following the war, American production and consumerism picked up, coinciding with another boom—the Baby Boom.
- The dot-com boom (Silicon Valley, Northern California). The dot-com bubble expanded rapidly in the late 1990s due to speculation on the worth of Internet holdings. This bubble burst in 2000 when prices came back down to earth.

Question 2

a) Think about the opposite sides of the political spectrum each man represents—and how those opposite sides both converge in the World War I home front. Both the radical, Eugene Debs, and the attorney general, A. Mitchell Palmer, had their careers impacted by World War I, though for different reasons. Debs, a Socialist, saw World War I as a war that served only to further the interests of industrialists. In fact, Debs was imprisoned due to his outspokenness against the war and Woodrow Wilson. He even ran for president in 1920 from the comfort of his jail cell. Mitchell, by contrast, was a supporter of the war effort and was suspicious of German and Russian immigrants. As both groups were often associated with union activity (they were after all, largely working class), Palmer saw them as potential threats for staging attempts at a socialist overthrow, as was seen in Russia.

b) Some important facts about Eugene Debs's views on American industry:

- Debs was president of the American Railway Union in the 1890s.
- Debs was imprisoned for his role in the Pullman Strike. While in prison, he read Karl Marx's *Communist Manifesto* and became a socialist.
- Debs was an early leader of the Socialist Party of America, running for president on the party's ticket numerous times.

World War I and Eugene Debs:

- Debs denounced World War I, urging folks to avoid the draft. This violated the Sedition Act, leading to his trial and conviction.
- Socialism, with roots in Germany, was seen as a foreign threat.
- The development of the Russian Revolution, which ultimately pulled Russia out of World War I to deal with its internal rebellion, raised suspicions in the United States. Government officials feared that the presence of socialists in the United States could lead to a similar rebellion, and the defeat of the United States in World War I.

Give yourself extra points for mentioning either of these facts:

- Socialists viewed World War I as a capitalist conspiracy theory that pitted workers from different countries against one another for the benefit of industrialists. The Eugene Debs–led Socialist Party of America fractured over support for the war. Debs, running on an antiwar platform from his prison cell, won 3.4 percent of the popular vote as the Socialist Party of America's candidate in 1920.
- The Supreme Court upheld the Sedition Act (and Debs's conviction) in his appeal, *Debs v. United States*. A similar upholding of the Sedition Act occurred in the more familiar *Schenk v. United States*.

c) Some important facts related to A. Mitchell Palmer's experiences with radicals.

- Palmer was Woodrow Wilson's Attorney General.
- His house was damaged in 1919, when a series of bombs exploded in several American cities.
- Following the Russian Revolution, fears of Communism spreading throughout the United States led to a series of raids, the Palmer Raids, on suspected radical groups. The Palmer Raids violated civil liberties by raiding union halls, social clubs, and private homes and ultimately deporting about 500 immigrants.

World War I and Government Agencies:

- As attorney general, Mitchell oversaw the implementation of the Sedition Act, overseeing the deportation of hundreds of foreign-born residents.
- The Palmer Raids did not come out of nowhere—the Committee on Public Information created the paranoia upon which the Red Scare developed.

Question 3

It is up to you to do the analysis that will determine which of the three had the largest impact on the abolition of slavery. But here are some key points that your answer should include about each person:

a) Choose one of the three abolitionists, being specific about their impact on ending slavery. Don't get too hung up on which is the "best" answer. As long as you clearly explain their impact on the abolition movement with clear facts, you should be okay on this question.

b) Bolstered by facts about each abolitionist, create analysis by explaining the difficulties the two remaining abolitionists faced, as well as the barriers that existed to keep their mission from being completed as quickly as they may have wished.

Some facts you might be interested in using for both parts (a) and (b) are below:

William Lloyd Garrison

- Garrison was inspired by the abolitionist work of freed slave David Walker.
- A white immediatist, Garrison published an abolitionist newspaper known as *The Liberator*.
- Key to Garrison's messaging was his ability to convey the abolitionist message to white audiences.
- Garrison assisted in founding the American Antislavery Society.
- Garrison believed in pacifist methods and only reluctantly supported the Civil War.
- Garrison opposed plans by moderate abolitionists to resettle blacks in Africa.
- *The Liberator* was banned in some Southern states.
- Garrison saw the need to overthrow the current American regime since it was based on a Constitution that allowed slavery.

Frederick Douglass

- Douglass was an escaped slave who wrote about and spoke on freedom for African Americans.
- Douglass advocated for the education of African Americans.
- Douglass, inspired by *The Liberator,* published an abolitionist newspaper called *The North Star.*
- Against the wishes of the American Antislavery Society, which wanted Douglass to simply tell the story of an escaped slave, Douglass spoke out against the racism evident in the North.
- In contrast to Garrison, Douglass was supportive of violent rebellions against slavery, such as the one at Harper's Ferry.
- Douglass, unlike Garrison, believed that the Constitution's references to slavery were mere compromises that saw slavery as a temporary institution and that, at its core, the Constitution was an abolitionist document.

Harriet Beecher Stowe

- Stowe was a northern novelist who wrote *Uncle Tom's Cabin*.
- Her book used stories that Stowe had heard about plantation life from her abolitionist friends to demonstrate the evils of slavery to a wide audience.
- Stowe's approach was largely an emotional, rather than political, appeal.
- With a million copies sold, *Uncle Tom's Cabin* placed the slavery issue on the forefront of American society, forcing people to take a side on the issue.

c) Oh, there are plenty. Take your pick: Lyman Beecher, Nathaniel Taylor, Charles G. Finney, Theodore D. Weld, Arthur and Lewis Tappan, Elizur Wright, Jr., Wendell Phillips, Gerrit Smith, Edmund Quincy, Lucy Stone, William and Ellen Craft, Solomon Northrup, and of course, John Brown.

Question 4

a) Factors leading to the Populist Movement

- Farmers had created an alliance through the Grange and, later, the Farmer's Alliance in order to operate as an economy of scale. These alliances gave farmers political power, allowing them to organize and support candidates.
- Farmers experienced significant debt due to a series of recessions following the Civil War, among other factors, notably the Panic of 1873 and the Panic of 1893.
- Inflation due to increased prices. With production increasing in the years after the Civil War, prices dropped and farmers could make less money with their crops. Increasing production only made the situation worse, so farmers advocated for use of silver-backed currency to bring down the value of the dollar, and thus, their debt.
- High interest rates.
- Farmers were being taken advantage of through price gouging on the railroads.
- Other groups who felt pinched by big business found an attractive alliance with one another, including unions, socialists, and anarchists.
- The Panic of 1893 led to increased membership of the Populist Party and the Democrats to nominate a Populist Movement candidate, William Jennings Bryan, in 1896.

b) Challenges faced by the Populist Movement

The Populist Movement, made up of farmers and factory workers, did not have the financial backing that the major parties, particularly the business-friendly Republican Party, had. An effective answer to this question should mention the 1896 election—the Democratic Party, riding the wave of the Populist fervor, nominated the Populists' proffered candidate, William Jennings Bryan. Following Bryan's loss in 1896, and the recovery from the Panic of 1893, the Populist Party dwindled out of significance.

In summary, it was the lack of establishment roots that caused the party its most pressing problems in terms of both funding and sustainability.

c) Future impact of the Populist Movement

The goals of the Populist Movement were not realized with the 1896 election. Bryan lost the election to William McKinley and the movement died off shortly thereafter due to improvements in the economy. However, the goals of the Populists were revived a decade later by the Progressive Movement. With more backing from urban elites, the Progressive Movement was able to accomplish many of the goals of the Populist Movement:

- Shorter work days
- Federal income tax (Sixteenth Amendment)
- Direct election of senators (Seventeenth Amendment)
- Government regulation of railroads and other public goods
- Referendums and recall elections

The Progressives, however, did not end the gold standard. That came in 1933 in reaction to the Great Depression.

SECTION II, QUESTION 1: THE DOCUMENT-BASED QUESTION

The document-based question begins with a mandatory 15-minute reading period. During these 15 minutes, you should (1) come up with some information not included in the given documents (your outside knowledge) to include in your essay, (2) get an overview of what each document means, (3) decide what opinion you are going to argue, and (4) write an outline of your essay.

The first thing you will be inclined to do, after reading the question, is to look at the documents. Resist that temptation. Instead, the first thing you should do is brainstorm for several minutes about what the question is asking of you. Try to list everything you remember about the Constitutional Convention. This list will serve as your reference to the outside information you must provide in order to earn a top grade.

Then, and only then, read over the documents. As you read them, take notes in the margins and underline those passages that you are certain you are going to refer to in your essay. If a document helps you remember a piece of outside information, add that information to your brainstorming list. If you cannot make sense of a document, don't worry. You may omit mention of <u>one</u> of the documents and still score well on the DBQ.

Here is what you need to look for in each document to get the most out of it:

- The author
- The date
- The audience (for whom was the document intended?)
- The significance

Remember: You are being asked to write 50 percent document interpretation and 50 percent outside information. Don't get so lost in the documents that you forget to bring in outside information. Readers will not be able to give you a high score unless you have both! What readers really don't like is a laundry list of documents: that is, a paper in which the student merely goes through the documents, explaining each one. Those students are often the ones who forget to bring in outside information, because they are so focused on going through the documents.

So, what is this DBQ all about?

This DBQ can be seen in three parts: (1) What were the ideals of the Declaration of Independence? (2) What were the outcomes of the Constitutional Convention? And (3) to what extent did these ideas differ from one another? For the first part, recall the major components of Jefferson's document (part of which is one of the documents included in this section). The themes of universal equality as well as life, liberty, and the pursuit of happiness provided the young nation with lofty goals. When the time came to turn these founding principles into an actual functioning government, the Founders had to make many compromises. For the second part, discuss those compromises (e.g. Great Compromise, Three-Fifths Compromise). How did they come about? What did they look like in practice?

In the final part of the essay, evaluate the extent to which the compromises at the Constitutional Convention upheld the original ideals that Jefferson espoused. Was the Constitution, in its original form, a document that upheld equality for all? Did it have mechanisms to guarantee life, liberty, and the pursuit of happiness?

The Documents

Document 1: This is the most famous line from the Declaration of Independence. Authored by Thomas Jefferson, the entire document reflects the attitude of the Enlightenment philosophy. This document is key to your essay because it outlines the key values that you will be analyzing. Take the ideas presented here and hold them up to the Constitutional Convention. Were they reflected in the document that came out of the Convention?

Document 2 shows us the slave populations in the various states in 1790. Virginia is clearly the largest stake holder in the slave system. It is no coincidence that many of the Founders (Jefferson included) were Virginian slaveholders. Think about how that may have impacted the proceedings at the Constitutional Convention. One of the toughest defenses of the Constitution is to explain why there is permissive language about slavery when the Declaration of Independence stated that "all men are created equal."

Document 3: In Federalist 63, James Madison does not convey a high opinion of the American citizenry. In this document, he argues for the necessity of the Senate to protect Americans from themselves (Americans evidently didn't know what was best for them). Keep in mind that the Senate, as described in the Constitution, was unelected, while the House of Representatives was chosen by the people. The thinking here is that the Senate would be dignified and educated, while the House may fall prey to people's short-term decision-making. The Declaration was written because the colonists had no say in the decisions of the British government. Think about whether this squares with the unelected lawmakers prescribed by Madison in Federalist 63.

Document 4: Virginia had the largest population of all the states in 1790. It is not even close. Under a purely representational system, Virginia would get the most representatives in Congress. Other states, particularly New Jersey, found that unfair and the Great Compromise at the Constitutional Convention led to a bicameral house—one proportional and one with each state getting equal representation. Considering each of Virginia's two senators represented an average of 375,000 people and each of Delaware's two senators represents 30,000 people, it would seem that smaller states had more representation per capita in the Senate than did the large states. You should assess how this lines up with the value of equality from the Declaration of Independence.

Document 5: George Mason refused to sign the Constitution, and he aired his complaints about the document in a letter (of which this passage is only a small part). The reasons for his refusal to sign are many, but in this passage, you should focus on the contrast of "shadow" and "substance." It appears that Mason does not regard the House of Representatives to be a true representation of the people due to their position as elected officials. You need to evaluate whether the House was successful in bringing about a representative system longed for in the Declaration of Independence.

Document 6: Like his *Federalist Papers* coauthor, James Madison, Alexander Hamilton does not have high regard for the masses. In this speech, he pretty openly claims that the government is to be maintained by the elite and be a check on the masses. The masses presumably would be happy with the idea of representative government and will prevent the elite from any radical changes due to their irascibility. Seems stable enough. Again, evaluate whether this is the representative government Jefferson held in esteem as he railed in the Declaration of Independence against the excesses of the British Crown.

Document 7: Following the ratification of the Constitution, Jefferson was still not happy with the new government. As author of the Declaration, perhaps Jefferson was dissatisfied with how far from his initial vision for an independent United States this new government had strayed. His specific complaints, as mentioned in this document, are the lack of a bill of rights and the lack of term limits for the president. Think about how these complaints compare with the values set out in the Declaration of Independence.

Outside Information

We have already discussed much more than you could possibly include in a 45-minute essay. Do not worry. You will not be expected to mention everything or even most of what we have covered in the section above. You will, however, be expected to include some outside information—that is, information not mentioned directly in the documents.

Here is some outside information you might have used in your essay. The information is divided into two groups: general concepts and specific events.

General Concepts

- The ideals that informed the Declaration of Independence were the Enlightenment philosophies of Europe. Jefferson incorporated much of John Locke's ideas about natural rights, while also including the social contract philosophy of Jean-Jacques Rousseau.
- The Declaration of Independence, by word count, was primarily focused on grievances against the British Crown. The resentment toward a distant monarch was a key component of the Declaration of Independence. It also gave the Framers some idea of what to avoid when developing their own constitution. There was much thought during the Constitutional Convention about whether the executive office would too closely resemble a throne.
- Nowhere did the final draft of the Constitution stand in more contrast to the claim that "all men are created equal" than with the slavery issue. The question of slavery was left to compromise, rather than aligned with Jefferson's lasting words. It should be noted that Jefferson, along with other Framers, owned slaves. Viewing slaves as property, some Framers may not have actually seen the contradictory nature between the two documents.
- One common theme that seems to arise in the Declaration as well as the Constitution (at least in the Bill of Rights), is the concept of freedom. Drawing from Jefferson's understanding of Locke, the Declaration sees freedom and self-determination as a fundamental human right. These same ideals are on display in most of the amendments in the Bill of Rights.
- Ask whether the new constitution had created a republic or a monarchy, Benjamin Franklin is said to have remarked, "a republic, if you can keep it." The precariousness of the new republic did not necessarily lend itself to the quixotic ideals of Jefferson's document. Rather, the Framers needed to create a system that would last. While freedom and liberty were key themes in the Constitutional Convention, the need to create a stable republic may have been the primary goal for many of the Framers.

Specific Events

- The Philadelphia Convention is important to investigate, since it gives us insight into what ideas were bandied about. The Framers came with a variety of perspectives, many of which were limited by compromise. In this regard, the Philadelphia Convention may have seen very little of any specific ideal from the Declaration of Independence carried out to its pure iteration.
- For an even closer analysis of the ideas debated at the Constitutional Convention, look no further than the *Federalist Papers*. Hamilton, Madison, and Jay argued in favor of the Federalist perspective and were often critical of unbridled liberty. Some of the values articulated by Jefferson in the Declaration of Independence were tempered by appeals to stability in the *Federalist Papers*.
- The *Federalist Papers* were written to convince the New York delegation to ratify the Constitution. The wavering opinion on the Constitution stemmed largely from an opposition to federalism. There was concern that the Constitution would not guarantee the freedoms fought for in the Revolutionary War (and promised in the Declaration of Independence)—that states would have self-determination free from an outside government.

Choosing a Side

The first thing you want to do is to decide what kind of a statement you are going to make. You have already brainstormed all your outside information, made some notes or a quick outline, and decided where to plug in the documents. Because there is no right way to answer this, and many ways to make your argument, here are some positions you might want to argue.

- By including slavery and an unequal representation of people around the nation, the Constitutional Convention provided a clear shift away from the ideals presented in the Declaration of Independence.
- Through the protections offered by the Bill of Rights and limitations placed on the power of the government, the Constitution is a true manifestation of the values articulated by Thomas Jefferson in the Declaration of Independence.
- Although the Founders aimed to carry the lofty goals of the Declaration of Independence into the Philadelphia Convention, the compromises that were necessary to create a Constitution limited the document to a point at which it only partially conveyed the ideals of the Declaration.

Planning Your Essay

Unless you read extremely quickly, you probably won't have time to write a detailed outline for your essay during the 15-minute reading period. However, it is worth taking several minutes to jot down a loose structure of your essay, because it will actually save you time when you write. First, decide on your thesis and write it down in the test booklet. Then, take a few minutes to brainstorm all the points you might put in your essay. Choose the strongest points and number them in the order you plan to present them. Lastly, note which documents and outside information you plan to use in conjunction with each point. If you organize before you write, the actual writing process will go much more smoothly. More importantly, you will not write yourself into a corner, and suddenly find yourself making a point you cannot support or heading toward a weak conclusion (or worse still, no conclusion at all).

What You Should Have Discussed

Regardless of which thesis you choose, your essay should discuss all of the following:

- The Constitutional Convention
- The Declaration of Independence
- The Great Compromise
- The Three-Fifths Compromise
- The contrasts between large states and small states
- The contrasts between northern states and southern states
- Thomas Jefferson
- Checks and balances
- *Federalist Papers,* Alexander Hamilton, James Madison, and John Jay

Give yourself very high marks for outside knowledge if you mention any five of the following:

- George Washington
- Articles of Confederation
- New Jersey Plan
- Virginia Plan
- Bicameral legislature

- Benjamin Franklin
- George Mason
- George III
- Electoral College
- Bill of Rights
- Committee of Eleven

Give yourself a pat on the back if you mention any of the following:

- Virtual representation
- Roger Sherman
- The presence of slave owners at the Convention
- John Locke
- Gouverneur Morris
- Caucus system
- Elbridge Gerry
- Edmund Randolph

SECTION II: THE LONG ESSAY QUESTION

Question 2

This essay asks you to evaluate a series of laws passed by the British government that were intended to exert control over the colonists. We all know that taxation without representation was a key argument of the Declaration of Independence, but the 1767 Townshend Acts went beyond taxation. They created new courts to serve the monarchy's interest, while also disabling colonial self-rule. In this essay, consider how colonists reacted to the acts. Those reactions were the seeds for the revolutionary actions that would follow at Lexington and Concord in Massachusetts, in Independence Hall in Philadelphia, and on battlefields throughout the colonies.

You should start the essay with an explanation of the Townshend Acts—they were implanted by Charles Townshend, the minister of the exchequer under prime minister William Pitt. The acts were varied, but served to simultaneously strong-arm and fundraise off the colonists. The Townshend Acts came in the wake of colonists withholding the salaries of government officials in a negotiating ploy.

What to mention about the Townshend Acts:

- The law provided colonists with a tax on goods imported from Britain. This was a departure from earlier practices that saw taxes on European goods, though not on British ones.
- The Townshend Acts used revenue collected from duties to pay government officials stationed in the colonies.
- New courts and government offices were established in the colonies in order to more efficiently execute royal orders.
- The New York legislature was temporarily shut down as punishment for refusing to supply British troops.
- The Townshend Acts also permitted British officials unfettered access to private residences if they suspected smuggled goods.

Give yourself extra points for mentioning the following:

- The Townshend Acts had precedent. The Declaratory Act from the previous year established the crown's authority to tax and legislate throughout the colonies.
- The British power to search private residences was known as a *writ of assistance*.

Colonial reaction to the Townshend Acts:

- The Massachusetts Circular Letter called for protest against the law. What is important is that this was one of the first ways the various colonies cooperated to plan resistance.
- Boycotts against the acts led British merchants, who were fast losing money, to join the colonists' cause.
- Colonists bought American goods as a form of protest, boosting the New England economy.
- Parliament's eventual repeal of most of the Townshend duties reinforced the power of the colonists' organizing power.
- When the British began paying their officials with revenue from the new duties, colonists formed Committees of Correspondence, cementing the union of colonial resistors to the British crown.
- Mary Otis Warren wrote pamphlets in favor of a revolution against the British.

Give yourself extra points for mentioning the following:

- The colonists had a road map for resisting the Townshend Acts: Patrick Henry and the Sons of Liberty effectively put pressure on Parliament to repeal the Stamp Act in 1766.
- British quartering, made worse by the Townshend Acts, ultimately led to the Boston Massacre.
- John Dickinson's *Letters from a Farmer in Pennsylvania* was a unifying force for colonists resisting the Townshend Acts.
- The First Continental Congress was established in order to discuss colonial grievances about British taxation.
- The colonies united with a Continental Association, which was intended to enforce boycotts.

About the Structure of your Essay

You need to explain why each component of the Townshend Acts inspired anger and resistance in the colonies. Then, explore how each of the colonial reactions to the Townshend Acts brought the colonies closer together and another step toward revolting against the Crown. All of the facts you can include are great—just make sure to use analysis to make it clear how the events surrounding the Townshend Acts brought both parties toward the Revolutionary War.

Question 3

This essay asks you to investigate two periods of immigration. Be specific about who immigrated to the United States during each period, giving a couple examples of immigrant experiences from each wave. Pay close attention to which experiences are similar (continuities) and which were unique to each wave of immigration (changes).

Mid-19th Century

- Irish immigration
  - Many left Ireland due to famine (potato famine)
  - Moved to northern cities
  - Competed with laborers for jobs
  - Experienced hostility due to anti-Catholic bias

- German immigration
  - Many left to escape civil unrest (1848 revolution in Germany)
  - Moved to the West and Midwest
  - Competed with laborers for jobs
  - Tended to be higher educated than Irish immigrants
  - Many Germans were Catholic and experienced hostility due to their religion

Give yourself extra points if you mention the following:

- Both groups allied with Democrats due to the party's working class outreach.
- "No Irish Need Apply" signs
- Anti-Catholic riots in northern cities (there was a famous one in Philadelphia in 1844)
- Nativist parties such as the Know-Nothings
- The temperance movement targeted Irish and German immigrants and promoters of social ills such as drinking alcohol.
- Unions prohibited immigrants from joining their ranks
- Transcontinental railroad construction

Industrial period

- Immigrants and migrants made up the majority of city populations.
- Immigrants typically settled into ethnic neighborhoods (Little Italy, Chinatown, etc.) in tenements.
- Anti-immigrant bias waged against non-Protestant groups and those not considered white
- Knights of Labor and other unions petitioned the government to restrict immigration.
- Haymarket Riot
- Birds of Passage—immigrants who came to the United States to work and then return to their former countries
- Rise of eugenics
- Southern European immigration
  - Largely Italian and Greek
  - Roman Catholic and Eastern Orthodox
- Eastern European immigration
  - Largely Polish, Russian, Serb, Slovak, and Croat
  - Roman Catholic (Polish), Eastern Orthodox, and Jewish

- Asian immigration
  - Largely Chinese and Japanese
  - Primary workers on Central Pacific Railroad were Chinese.
  - Chinese Exclusion Act passed in 1882
  - Gentleman's Agreement of 1907 between the United States and Japan limited the number of immigrants from Japan to America.

Give yourself extra points if you mention the following:

- The role of immigrants in machine politics
- George Washington Plunkitt
- Settlement houses
- Immigration Act of 1882
- Alien Contract Labor Law of 1885
- Ford Committee
- Dillingham Commission
- Immigration Restriction League
- Josiah Strong's "Our Country" expressed concerns about the new immigrants bringing papism (loyalty to the pope) and alcoholism to the United States with the 1906 Naturalization Act.
- Anarchist Exclusion Act of 1901 following the assassination of President McKinley
- Congress required a literacy test as part of the immigration process in 1917.

About the Structure of Your Essay

You would begin by explaining the two periods of immigration. A strong essay would follow up the introductory paragraph with body paragraphs that juxtapose the eras based on themes. In other words, it's preferable to have a paragraph that evaluates the causes of each wave of immigration and another paragraph that analyzes the challenges experienced by immigrants from each period than it is to just write a body paragraph on the first era and then a body paragraph on the second era.

Question 4

This essay asks you to delve into two postwar periods to evaluate the relative successes of each. You want to think about a definition of "success" on this question. Does success mean a return to prewar norms? Does it mean to thrive economically? Does it require preventing such a conflict from happening again? Is it a little bit of all of these issues? Those questions are up to you to answer depending on the pieces of information you choose to include in your essay.

Post–Civil War United States

Concepts you may want to mention:

- Ironclad oath
- Union League
- Exodusters
- Benjamin "Pap" Singleton
- Homestead Act
- Reconstruction Act
- Ten Percent Plan
- Wade-Davis Bill

- Thirteenth, Fourteenth, and Fifteenth Amendments
- Hiram Revels
- Radical Republicans
- Impeachment of Andrew Johnson
- Carpetbaggers
- Ulysses Grant
- Transcontinental Railroad
- Freedman's Bureau
- Black Codes
- Segregation
- Civil Rights Act of 1875
- Compromise of 1877

Post–World War II United States

Concepts you may want to mention:

- Loyalty oath
- Blacklisting
- Eugene McCarthy
- Baby boom
- Sun belt
- Cold War
- Truman Doctrine/Containment
- Joseph Stalin
- Korean War
- Berlin Blockade and Airlift
- Decolonization
- Interstate Highway Act
- Dwight Eisenhower
- John Kennedy
- New Frontier
- Hydrogen Bomb
- Military Industrial Complex
- Nation-building
- Dixiecrats
- Civil Rights Movement

About the Structure of Your Essay

You should begin the essay with brief overviews of the two postwar periods. A strong essay would follow up the introductory paragraph with body paragraphs that juxtapose the eras based on themes. In other words, it's preferable to have a paragraph that evaluates what is similar (continuities) and different (changes) between the two eras in terms of economic recovery followed by a paragraph comparing them on a different theme than it is to just write a body paragraph on the post–Civil War era and then a body paragraph on the post–World War II era. Try to compare these two periods with an in-depth discussion of 2–3 themes (presented in 2–3 body paragraphs).

1. YOUR NAME:
(Print)
Last   First   M.I.

SIGNATURE: _____ DATE: ___ / ___ / ___

HOME ADDRESS: _____
(Print)   Number and Street

_____
City   State   Zip Code

PHONE NO. : _____
(Print)

5. YOUR NAME

First 4 letters of last name				FIRST INIT	MID INIT

A A A A   A A
B B B B   B B
C C C C   C C
D D D D   D D
E E E E   E E
F F F F   F F
G G G G   G G
H H H H   H H
I I I I   I I
J J J J   J J
K K K K   K K
L L L L   L L
M M M M   M M
N N N N   N N
O O O O   O O
P P P P   P P
Q Q Q Q   Q Q
R R R R   R R
S S S S   S S
T T T T   T T
U U U U   U U
V V V V   V V
W W W W   W W
X X X X   X X
Y Y Y Y   Y Y
Z Z Z Z   Z Z

IMPORTANT: Please fill in these boxes exactly as shown on the back cover of your test book.

2. TEST FORM

3. TEST CODE   **4. REGISTRATION NUMBER**

0 A 0 0 0 0 0 0 0 0 0 0
1 B 1 1 1 1 1 1 1 1 1 1
2 C 2 2 2 2 2 2 2 2 2 2
3 D 3 3 3 3 3 3 3 3 3 3
4 E 4 4 4 4 4 4 4 4 4 4
5 F 5 5 5 5 5 5 5 5 5 5
6 G 6 6 6 6 6 6 6 6 6 6
7 7 7 7 7 7 7 7 7 7
8 8 8 8 8 8 8 8 8 8
9 9 9 9 9 9 9 9 9 9

6. DATE OF BIRTH

Month	Day	Year
JAN		
FEB		
MAR	0 0	0 0
APR	1 1	1 1
MAY	2 2	2 2
JUN	3 3	3 3
JUL	4	4 4
AUG	5	5 5
SEP	6	6 6
OCT	7	7 7
NOV	8	8 8
DEC	9	9 9

7. SEX
MALE
FEMALE

The Princeton Review®

Section I   Start with number 1 for each new section.
If a section has fewer questions than answer spaces, leave the extra answer spaces blank.

1. A B C D   31. A B C D   61. A B C D   91. A B C D
2. A B C D   32. A B C D   62. A B C D   92. A B C D
3. A B C D   33. A B C D   63. A B C D   93. A B C D
4. A B C D   34. A B C D   64. A B C D   94. A B C D
5. A B C D   35. A B C D   65. A B C D   95. A B C D
6. A B C D   36. A B C D   66. A B C D   96. A B C D
7. A B C D   37. A B C D   67. A B C D   97. A B C D
8. A B C D   38. A B C D   68. A B C D   98. A B C D
9. A B C D   39. A B C D   69. A B C D   99. A B C D
10. A B C D   40. A B C D   70. A B C D   100. A B C D
11. A B C D   41. A B C D   71. A B C D   101. A B C D
12. A B C D   42. A B C D   72. A B C D   102. A B C D
13. A B C D   43. A B C D   73. A B C D   103. A B C D
14. A B C D   44. A B C D   74. A B C D   104. A B C D
15. A B C D   45. A B C D   75. A B C D   105. A B C D
16. A B C D   46. A B C D   76. A B C D   106. A B C D
17. A B C D   47. A B C D   77. A B C D   107. A B C D
18. A B C D   48. A B C D   78. A B C D   108. A B C D
19. A B C D   49. A B C D   79. A B C D   109. A B C D
20. A B C D   50. A B C D   80. A B C D   110. A B C D
21. A B C D   51. A B C D   81. A B C D   111. A B C D
22. A B C D   52. A B C D   82. A B C D   112. A B C D
23. A B C D   53. A B C D   83. A B C D   113. A B C D
24. A B C D   54. A B C D   84. A B C D   114. A B C D
25. A B C D   55. A B C D   85. A B C D   115. A B C D
26. A B C D   56. A B C D   86. A B C D   116. A B C D
27. A B C D   57. A B C D   87. A B C D   117. A B C D
28. A B C D   58. A B C D   88. A B C D   118. A B C D
29. A B C D   59. A B C D   89. A B C D   119. A B C D
30. A B C D   60. A B C D   90. A B C D   120. A B C D

The Princeton Review®

Completely darken bubbles with a No. 2 pencil. If you make a mistake, be sure to erase mark completely. Erase all stray marks.

1. YOUR NAME:
(Print)
Last   First   M.I.

SIGNATURE: _____ DATE: ___ / ___ / ___

HOME ADDRESS: _____
(Print)
Number and Street

_____
City   State   Zip Code

PHONE NO. : _____
(Print)

5. YOUR NAME

First 4 letters of last name				FIRST INIT	MID INIT

A B C D E F G H I J K L M N O P Q R S T U V W X Y Z (columns repeated)

IMPORTANT: Please fill in these boxes exactly as shown on the back cover of your test book.

2. TEST FORM

3. TEST CODE

0 A 0 0 0 ...
1 B 1 1 1 ...
2 C 2 2 2 ...
3 D 3 3 3 ...
4 E 4 4 4 ...
5 F 5 5 5 ...
6 G 6 6 6 ...
7 7 7 7 ...
8 8 8 8 ...
9 9 9 9 ...

4. REGISTRATION NUMBER

0 1 2 3 4 5 6 7 8 9

6. DATE OF BIRTH

Month	Day		Year	
JAN				
FEB				
MAR	0	0	0	0
APR	1	1	1	1
MAY	2	2	2	2
JUN	3	3	3	3
JUL		4	4	4
AUG		5	5	5
SEP		6	6	6
OCT		7	7	7
NOV		8	8	8
DEC		9	9	9

7. SEX
MALE
FEMALE

The Princeton Review®

Section I   Start with number 1 for each new section.
If a section has fewer questions than answer spaces, leave the extra answer spaces blank.

1. A B C D
2. A B C D
3. A B C D
4. A B C D
5. A B C D
6. A B C D
7. A B C D
8. A B C D
9. A B C D
10. A B C D
11. A B C D
12. A B C D
13. A B C D
14. A B C D
15. A B C D
16. A B C D
17. A B C D
18. A B C D
19. A B C D
20. A B C D
21. A B C D
22. A B C D
23. A B C D
24. A B C D
25. A B C D
26. A B C D
27. A B C D
28. A B C D
29. A B C D
30. A B C D

31. A B C D
32. A B C D
33. A B C D
34. A B C D
35. A B C D
36. A B C D
37. A B C D
38. A B C D
39. A B C D
40. A B C D
41. A B C D
42. A B C D
43. A B C D
44. A B C D
45. A B C D
46. A B C D
47. A B C D
48. A B C D
49. A B C D
50. A B C D
51. A B C D
52. A B C D
53. A B C D
54. A B C D
55. A B C D
56. A B C D
57. A B C D
58. A B C D
59. A B C D
60. A B C D

61. A B C D
62. A B C D
63. A B C D
64. A B C D
65. A B C D
66. A B C D
67. A B C D
68. A B C D
69. A B C D
70. A B C D
71. A B C D
72. A B C D
73. A B C D
74. A B C D
75. A B C D
76. A B C D
77. A B C D
78. A B C D
79. A B C D
80. A B C D
81. A B C D
82. A B C D
83. A B C D
84. A B C D
85. A B C D
86. A B C D
87. A B C D
88. A B C D
89. A B C D
90. A B C D

91. A B C D
92. A B C D
93. A B C D
94. A B C D
95. A B C D
96. A B C D
97. A B C D
98. A B C D
99. A B C D
100. A B C D
101. A B C D
102. A B C D
103. A B C D
104. A B C D
105. A B C D
106. A B C D
107. A B C D
108. A B C D
109. A B C D
110. A B C D
111. A B C D
112. A B C D
113. A B C D
114. A B C D
115. A B C D
116. A B C D
117. A B C D
118. A B C D
119. A B C D
120. A B C D

The Princeton Review

Completely darken bubbles with a No. 2 pencil. If you make a mistake, be sure to erase mark completely. Erase all stray marks.

1. YOUR NAME:
(Print)   Last   First   M.I.

SIGNATURE: _____   DATE: ___ / ___ / ___

HOME ADDRESS: _____
(Print)   Number and Street

City   State   Zip Code

PHONE NO. : _____
(Print)

IMPORTANT: Please fill in these boxes exactly as shown on the back cover of your test book.

2. TEST FORM

3. TEST CODE

4. REGISTRATION NUMBER

5. YOUR NAME

First 4 letters of last name | FIRST INIT | MID INIT

6. DATE OF BIRTH

Month	Day	Year
JAN		
FEB		
MAR	0 0	0 0
APR	1 1	1 1
MAY	2 2	2 2
JUN	3 3	3 3
JUL	4	4 4
AUG	5	5 5
SEP	6	6 6
OCT	7	7 7
NOV	8	8 8
DEC	9	9 9

7. SEX
MALE
FEMALE

The Princeton Review

Section I

Start with number 1 for each new section.
If a section has fewer questions than answer spaces, leave the extra answer spaces blank.

1. A B C D
2. A B C D
3. A B C D
4. A B C D
5. A B C D
6. A B C D
7. A B C D
8. A B C D
9. A B C D
10. A B C D
11. A B C D
12. A B C D
13. A B C D
14. A B C D
15. A B C D
16. A B C D
17. A B C D
18. A B C D
19. A B C D
20. A B C D
21. A B C D
22. A B C D
23. A B C D
24. A B C D
25. A B C D
26. A B C D
27. A B C D
28. A B C D
29. A B C D
30. A B C D

31. A B C D
32. A B C D
33. A B C D
34. A B C D
35. A B C D
36. A B C D
37. A B C D
38. A B C D
39. A B C D
40. A B C D
41. A B C D
42. A B C D
43. A B C D
44. A B C D
45. A B C D
46. A B C D
47. A B C D
48. A B C D
49. A B C D
50. A B C D
51. A B C D
52. A B C D
53. A B C D
54. A B C D
55. A B C D
56. A B C D
57. A B C D
58. A B C D
59. A B C D
60. A B C D

61. A B C D
62. A B C D
63. A B C D
64. A B C D
65. A B C D
66. A B C D
67. A B C D
68. A B C D
69. A B C D
70. A B C D
71. A B C D
72. A B C D
73. A B C D
74. A B C D
75. A B C D
76. A B C D
77. A B C D
78. A B C D
79. A B C D
80. A B C D
81. A B C D
82. A B C D
83. A B C D
84. A B C D
85. A B C D
86. A B C D
87. A B C D
88. A B C D
89. A B C D
90. A B C D

91. A B C D
92. A B C D
93. A B C D
94. A B C D
95. A B C D
96. A B C D
97. A B C D
98. A B C D
99. A B C D
100. A B C D
101. A B C D
102. A B C D
103. A B C D
104. A B C D
105. A B C D
106. A B C D
107. A B C D
108. A B C D
109. A B C D
110. A B C D
111. A B C D
112. A B C D
113. A B C D
114. A B C D
115. A B C D
116. A B C D
117. A B C D
118. A B C D
119. A B C D
120. A B C D

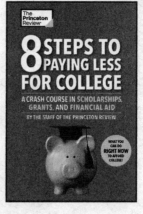